VAN MORRISON

Johnny Rogan has written many books, including
highly acclaimed music biographies and studies of
the Byrds, Neil Young, the Kinks, John Lennon,
Roxy Music, Crosby, Stills, Nash & Young and
the Smiths. His controversial *Morrissey & Marr:
The Severed Alliance* became a best-seller, and
Starmakers & Svengalis, a history of British Pop
management, was adapted by the BBC.

ALSO BY JOHNNY ROGAN

Timeless Flight: The Definitive Biography Of The Byrds

Neil Young: Here We Are In The Years

Roxy Music: Style With Substance

Van Morrison: A Portrait Of The Artist

The Kinks: The Sound And The Fury

Wham! (Confidential): The Death Of A Supergroup

Starmakers & Svengalis: The History Of British Pop Management

The Football Managers

The Guinness Encyclopaedia Of Popular Music (co-ed.)

Morrissey & Marr: The Severed Alliance

The Smiths: The Visual Documentary

The Complete Guide To The Music Of The Smiths & Morrissey/Marr

The Complete Guide To The Music Of Neil Young

Crosby, Stills, Nash & Young: The Visual Documentary

The Complete Guide To The Music Of John Lennon

The Byrds: Timeless Flight Revisited – The Sequel

The Complete Guide To The Music Of The Kinks

Neil Young: Zero To Sixty: A Critical Biography

Anthology Contributions

The Bowie Companion

The Encyclopedia Of Popular Music

The Mojo Collection

Oxford Originals: An Anthology Of Writing From Lady Margaret Hall, 1879—2001

JOHNNY ROGAN

Van Morrison

No Surrender

VINTAGE BOOKS
London

Published by Vintage 2006

2 4 6 8 10 9 7 5 3 1

First published in Great Britain in 2005 by Secker & Warburg

Vintage
Random House, 20 Vauxhall Bridge Road,
London SW1V 2SA

Random House Australia (Pty) Limited
20 Alfred Street, Milsons Point, Sydney,
New South Wales 2061, Australia

Random House New Zealand Limited
18 Poland Road, Glenfield,
Auckland 10, New Zealand

Random House (Pty) Limited
Isle of Houghton, Corner of Boundary Road & Carse O'Gowrie,
Houghton, 2198, South Africa

The Random House Group Limited Reg. No. 954009
www.randomhouse.co.uk/vintage

A CIP catalogue record for this book
is available from the British Library

ISBN 9780099431831 (from Jan 2007)
ISBN 0099431831

Papers used by Random House are natural,
recyclable products made from wood grown in
sustainable forests. The manufacturing processes
conform to the environmental regulations of the
country of origin

Printed and bound in Great Britain by
Cox & Wyman Ltd, Reading, Berkshire

"Rogan's got something to hide. What's he hiding? I'd like to do a book on him" Van Morrison

CONTENTS

ACKNOWLEDGEMENTS

This book has probably had the longest gestation of any I have written. Research on the project started at the dawn of the Eighties and I continued to interview people sporadically over the next 20 years. There were, of course, key periods when I devoted months or even years of full-time work to this enterprise. Looking back at the chronology, I was struck by some odd coincidences in the timing of my research. When I first started on the Morrison story, the 1981 Hunger Strike had just ended and the name Bobby Sands was still on everyone's lips. It was a sad and volatile time in Belfast. At that point, most of my research was done in London and Dublin where I interviewed various musicians, producers and former associates of Morrison. Apart from prying open the Monarchs' story for the first time ever, I tended to downplay the significance of the city of Morrison's birth. I was not there when – according to a major feature in the *New Musical Express* – he flew in specifically to complain to the local media that I had supposedly slammed down the phone on him. The first stage of this project concluded at that moment.

Flash forward a decade and the next important phase of this book began with the announcement of the Peace Treaty in 1994. Within days, I was on the streets of Belfast, visiting the Falls and the Shankill and conducting countless interviews with local musicians and former Morrison acolytes, most of whom had never spoken publicly about the man. Many Protestants were sceptical about the treaty, but there was still a detectable optimism in a city that had seen so many false dawns. It was while analysing Belfast before the Troubles that I began to appreciate the extent to which Morrison's life had been determined by the events of his childhood and adolescence. In the meantime, I had travelled to the East and West of America to conduct other interviews but prevarication followed. Those very few people who knew anything about my work expressed amazement that my mountain of notes and interviews remained sealed in a box.

It was not a lack of interviewees or writing time that continued to delay this project but the vast amount of background reading required, particularly on the cultural and political history of Ulster. As a result, the bulk of the writing finally occurred through 1999–2002. Even then, I preferred to avoid completion, feeling that it would be far better to re-read the entire text from a fresh perspective and arrange publication to coincide with the year of Morrison's sixtieth birthday. By then, I was well into my third decade of interviewing people and simultaneously reviewing an ever-evolving history of the Troubles, which looked like reaching an awkward denouement. Whether it was purely coincidence that events in Ulster seemed to kick-start or forestall the book at various times, I will leave the reader to decide.

Thanks to David Milner at Secker & Warburg who agreed to commission this book unseen and, more importantly, accepted my unusual terms, which included a clause allowing me the best part of six years to complete the work. By delivery time, the editorial task was firmly in the hands of Geoff Mulligan and Stuart Williams to whom I am also grateful.

Many biographies are conceived and written over a relatively short time-span, but the beauty of this project has been the gradual accumulation of research material and the conducting of exclusive interviews over a period in excess of 23 years.

The extensive footnotes at the rear of the book provide detailed information about primary and secondary sources, including specific dates for all the interviews conducted herein.

I would like to thank the following people (in alphabetical order) whom I interviewed: Keith Altham, Don Arden, Herbie Armstrong, Jim Armstrong, Harry Baird, Ruby Bard, Eric Bell, Seán Boyne, Éamon Carr, Roy Carr, Gwen Carson (McIlroy), Don Charles, Tadgh Coughlan, Phil Coulter, Clive Culbertson, Terry Davis, Rod Demick, Ann Denvir, John Etherington, Bill Flanagan, Harvey Goldsmith, Ursula Graham-White, Tony Hall, Bobby Hamilton, David Hammond, Katie Hannon, Billy Harrison, Peter Hayden, Alan Henderson, Billy Hollywood, Nicky Horne, Gil Irvine, George Jones, Roy Kane, Billy Kennedy, Eddie Kennedy, Tom Kielbania, Terry King, Linda Gail Lewis, Kenny Lynch, Michael Maggid, Sam Mahood, Dino Martin, Gavin Martin, Janet Martin, Mary Martin, Phil May, Billy McAllen, Jackie McAuley, Éamonn McCann, Nancy McCarter, Cecil (Cezil) McCartney, Colin McClelland, Joan McClelland, Cynthia MacHenry (Russell), Marion McKeone, Billy Moore, Gerry

O'Hare, Andrew Oldham, Larry Page, David Parkinson, Larry Parnes, John Payne, Stephen Pillster, Kenneth Pitt, John Platania, Dick Rowe, Brian Russell, Rusty, Tommy Scott, Joel Selvin, Sam Smyth, Mervyn Solomon, Philip Solomon, Geordie (G.D.) Sproule, Screaming Lord Sutch, Bobby Tench, Deborah Thompson, John Tobler, Steve Turner and Eric Wrixon. I would also like to credit and thank the late Timothy White for kindly interviewing Joe Smith, whose comments proved enlightening; Reiseal Ní Cheilleachair for interviewing the talkative Michelle Rocca, and then providing some key names from the Dublin set; special thanks from way back to my still anonymous mystery kinsman who taped Violet Morrison during the Troubles; plus, Joel Selvin for direction on legal documentation and access to his revealing interview with Janet 'Planet' Morrison. Finally, a special tribute to the late Donall Corvin for extracts from his Van Morrison interview and unrealized book project.

There were also a number of people who provided passing assistance or offered nuggets of additional information: David Arden, Trevor Badger, Stuart Bailie, Eddie Braddock, Reiseal Ní Cheilleachair, Ulf Cronquist, Jackie Cuddihy, Peter Doggett, Roy Esmonde, Pete Frame, David French, Simon Gee, Stephen Gordon, Doug Hinman, Chris Hodgkin, David Kenyon, George Kenyon, Andy Kershaw, Bunny Lewis, Martin Lynch, Éamonn McCann, Stephen McGinn, Shane MacGowan, Harry (Mack) Megahey, Danny Morrison, Kate Murphy, Nora Nolan, Chris O'Donnell, Mal Peachey, John Quinlan, Alan Robinson, Kevin Rowland, Cathy Shea, Pete Short, Shel Talmy, Chip Taylor, Twinkle (Lynn Ripley), Teresa Walsh, Jean Webster, Robin Williamson and John Wilson.

Introduction

Van Morrison has always been a well-travelled man whose life has included long stints in Belfast, London, New York, Boston, the West Coast of America and Dublin. Inevitably, each new sojourn has subtly altered his musical palette, critical standing and public image. In Belfast, he was the rough-hewed blues singer; in London, the R&B shouter with pop chart potential; in New York and Boston, the FM/AM radio crossover stylist of 'Brown Eyed Girl' fame; in San Francisco, he was transformed into the pastoral, quasi-mystical singer-songwriter; in Bath and back in London, he was known as the spiritual seeker whose New Age music was said to promote meditation and much else; in Dublin, he re-emerged as the unlikely socialite whose 'Irishness' intersected with such disparate homegrown talents as the Chieftains, Sinéad O'Connor and Brendan Bowyer.

Notwithstanding all these changes, Morrison has been extraordinarily consistent in both his attitude and world view. Early experiences in Belfast had a profound effect on not only his music and lyrics but also his personality. So many of his songs conjure fractured memories of his childhood and adolescence. His work is littered with Belfast place names: Cyprus Avenue, Fitzroy Avenue, Sandy Row and, of course, his birthplace – Hyndford Street.

The employment of Belfast as a symbolic backdrop for his work was unusual enough but there was more. Over the years his personality has taken on a peculiarly Ulster-like intransigence, strangely in keeping with the political ethos of East Belfast. The dogmatic stubbornness, suspicion and fear of betrayal historically associated with Ulster Unionism has become for Morrison an enduring character trait. In one sense, his whole life can be seen as an extended metaphor of the psychological and political 'No Surrender' siege mentality of Unionist Ulster. His history represents both a flight from and a reconciliation with a Belfast long lost in time. Morrison's work still seems haunted by mythic memories of an idealized, peaceful Northern Ireland before the Troubles. This is his personal lost Eden.

Morrison documented aspects of his Belfast upbringing on the celebrated *Astral Weeks* which was recorded and released in late 1968, the very moment when the civil rights marches were starting in Northern Ireland. For political writer and socialist Éamonn McCann this was not mere coincidence, but synchronicity. He saw the album as akin to a revolution in the head and a cultural corollary to his own political awakening. "*Astral Weeks* is a bit like the 1916 Easter Rising . . . We were ready for revolution, we were calling for revolution and there was this revolution in the mind of this tight little prod from Belfast, from all the way across the Atlantic . . . That's perhaps a fanciful thought, but it seemed that it was there in terms of popular culture . . . The shape of the politics we have now in Northern Ireland was really determined back then. That period is absolutely crucial. Everything changed in a tumult." The cultural and political implications of those changes throughout the entire island of Ireland form the backbone of this book

The common view of Morrison's career trajectory is that he left the North and reinvented himself in America, but this is only partly true. Belfast always remained a ghost in the background. Over and over again, Morrison would return to his homeland and transmute its geography and character into his personal landscape. Even his oft-noted spiritual odyssey and involvement in a variety of New Age pursuits reflected the pick 'n' mix mentality of Protestant Ulster with its constantly evolving, breakaway groups and kaleidoscopic sects. As time passed, his personality and public persona more and more resembled the 'No Surrender' mindset. By the end of the Seventies, Morrison was conducting a rather odd relationship with the media, agreeing to be interviewed, yet hating and sometimes sabotaging that process. This was very different from Bob Dylan, whose spiky press conferences were frequently hilarious and showed none of the bitterness of Morrison's pained encounters. Later, Morrison learned to conduct his media relations with better planning, limiting access and often choosing interviewers with care. Yet there remained a fascinating disparity between the music he was making and the words emanating from him into print. Matters regarded as irrelevant or beneath contempt by his contemporaries became major issues for Morrison. Biographies, interviews, articles or even fanzine pieces written about him could easily produce vicious diatribes in response. If a broadsheet innocently referred to him as a rock star, he would take great exception and perhaps even write a note of complaint. When the Belfast Blues Society tried to honour the man with a plaque, a retaliatory solicitor's letter was despatched immediately. Those who knew Morrison mainly through his music recognized his sensitivity, but many were still puzzled by his lack of grace. Although Morrison would not have it so, music and image are inextricably linked, even in the rarefied world he chooses to inhabit. Frequently, his self-righteousness and vehemence have made him resemble nothing less than a craggy, rock 'n' roll parody of Ian Paisley.

Indeed, the 'No Surrender' siege mentality has been the one great constant throughout his career and can be traced back to his earliest days. Although a self-professed free thinker and outsider, Morrison's psychology was nevertheless stamped by his environment. The lexicon of Unionist Ulster – 'No Surrender', 'Whatever You Say, Say Nothing', 'Ulster Will Fight – And Ulster Will Be Right' – appears to have permeated the core of his essence and fashioned his personality. As his contemporary Sam Smyth says, "East Belfast runs through him like Blackpool rock."

'No Surrender' is a state of mind as much as it is a state of action. Its provenance is Ulster and its history is long. Nearly a hundred years ago, the writer J.B. Woodburn attempted to define the qualities of an Ulsterman, observing: "He is determined to the verge of stubbornness and will accept no compromise; stern, dogged, and strong of purpose; independent, self-contained, and self-reliant, able to stand on his own feet, and intensely proud of the fact. He has the passion, alertness and quickness of the Celt in addition to the adventurous spirit of the Norseman. He is steadfast and industrious beyond most races. In his uncultivated state he is blunt of speech and intolerant of shams, and lacks the attractiveness of manner of the Southerner."

Reading this, Morrison's character comes immediately to mind. Moreover, the sense of place, so palpable in his work, may well have exacerbated these traits. Beyond the pop star trappings, the troubled time in New York, the failed marriage, fatherhood, affluence, the idyllic retreat in rural California, rehabilitation in London and the hobnobbing with Dublin society, the spectral vision of golden age Belfast remains. It is an obsessive remembrance that has constantly invaded Morrison's art and imagination, fuelling his suspicion and shaping his character. Ultimately, Morrison has become an imperfect mirror of his environment and upbringing. His heritage – political, religious and cultural – has stalked and defeated, through the sheer weight of recollection and ancestry, all his attempts at escape or reinvention. He remains the living embodiment of 'No Surrender'.

ONE

Ulster Says No!

Within the Irish literary and musical tradition, Belfast has often been overshadowed by the cultural richness of Dublin. While almost every street in the Republic's capital has been immortalized by novelists and enshrined within the work of James Joyce, Belfast has, until relatively recently, seemed undervalued as a cultural centre. In popular music, Van Morrison would make Belfast the ongoing subject of his personal odyssey. Often, the presence of the city in his songs has proven so palpable that it has almost become a character telling its own story. Over the years he has embraced, championed, abandoned and rediscovered Belfast as the fount of his inspiration. Even during his self-imposed exile from the city, amid the commercial and artistic peak years in America, it remained a shadowy presence, a shrouded subtext in his work. At times, its very absence spoke volumes about his state of mind. Any commentator attempting to understand the complex psychology of Morrison is inexorably drawn back to Belfast. Morrison's sense of place, his spiritual unrest, his granite obduracy, his Presbyterian-like pragmatism and that peculiarly insular 'No Surrender' Ulster mentality that dominates his every public utterance and action all testify to the profound influence that Belfast has had in shaping his psyche and determining his world view. Understanding Morrison's Belfast – its traditions, its fears, its prejudices and its characters – not only enriches any appreciation of his music but provides invaluable insight into the many contradictions of the man.

There is considerable drama in the history of Belfast. Its rise from a small market town to a prominent city was one of the great success stories of the Industrial Revolution. Belfast's cultural history on the traced back at least as far as 1737 when Francis Joy – a metaphorical ancestor of Morrison's own mysterious Madame Joy – established the *Belfast Newsletter*. A desire for autonomy in religious and political life was strengthened by the presence of Presbyterian settlers transplanted from Scotland. They erected countless churches and encouraged philosophical study and education with the grandly named Belfast Society For Promoting Knowledge.

By the mid-nineteenth century, Belfast had its own university and was developing as an industrial heartland. When Edward Harland and Gustav W. Wolff took over the shipping firm of Robert Hickson in 1858, they transformed the industry and founded arguably the greatest shipyard in the world. The triumph of Harland & Wolff was even more remarkable considering that Belfast lacked such key resources as coal and iron. A reliance on imported material meant that the city's development as a port was crucial. The local linen industry flourished following mechanization and a large tobacco factory and rope works boosted commerce. Canny mercantile minds blessed with a twin love of Mammon and God were welcomed.

By 1901, within the space of a century, Belfast's population had risen from 20,000 to a staggering 350,000. This industrial utopia came at a heavy price tag. A mid-century census confirmed that 50 per cent of the population was under 20 and the average age of death was a barely believable nine years. The chief reason why most people failed to reach their tenth birthday was the frightening number of children forced to work in factories under appalling conditions, made worse by the constant threat of disease. Tuberculosis was the killer. When walking through the crowded rows of Belfast tenements you could almost taste the saturated TB sheets.

The turn of the century brought new hope to the city, mainly thanks to a regular water supply and a proper sewage system. Improvements in sanitation saved countless lives and the prospect of full employment brought a sense of renewed confidence to the city. Labourer John Stitt was courting a girl named Alice McIver at this time and on 1 April 1907, they were married at the Albertbridge Congregational Church. Van Morrison's maternal lineage was forged at a crucial moment in Belfast's history. Harland & Wolff was prospering and made world headlines with the construction and launch of the *Titanic* in 1911–12.

As the War years beckoned more vessels were needed and the shipyards responded. The workforce was proud and loyal. Harland & Wolff rightly boasted that they made boys into men and men into giants.

Even in the best of times, Belfast was driven by religious and political issues. Ireland was still part of the United Kingdom with a population of 4.25 million of which less than 25 per cent was Protestant. Many of these, including Van Morrison's ancestors, were descended from Scottish settlers and concentrated in the North East in a Machiavellian attempt to colonize the island. During the late nineteenth century, there had been campaigns for a Dublin-based, all-Ireland Parliament with limited powers, which would take responsibility for Irish domestic affairs under the aegis of the British Crown. In 1886, the Liberal Party under William Gladstone had proposed a modest Home Rule Bill which was scuppered by the Conservative Party, whose chief agitator Randolph Churchill famously declared, "The Orange card would be the one to play". He subsequently went to Belfast and stirred up sectarian passions. In galvanizing support from the Protestant lodges in the North and fomenting their fears of the overwhelming Catholic majority, the Tories were able to kill the bill. Six years later, a second Home Rule Bill was passed by the House of Commons but vetoed by the House of Lords.

The long fight for independence by Irish nationalists was rekindled in 1910 when the Liberal Party, led by Herbert Asquith, urgently needed support from Irish Members of Parliament in order to retain office. A deal was struck and matters reached a critical stage in 1912 when the House of Commons passed the third Home Rule Bill. Its implementation seemed unstoppable but it was bitterly opposed by key members of the British establishment, most notably the Conservative leader Andrew Bonar Law – the son of an Ulster Presbyterian minister – whose policy echoed Randolph Churchill's ominous warning: "Ulster Will Fight – And Ulster Will Be Right".

Militant Ulster Unionists required no prompting. Fears of crippling economic problems resulting from a break with the British market alarmed and united the predominantly Protestant Northern population, particularly in Belfast, then one of the richest cities in the British Empire. If the Union could not be saved by constitutional means, then its supporters were ready to take up arms in defiance. Under the leadership of Sir Edward Carson, a provisional government of Ulster was formed and a volunteer army pledged to defend loyalist rights. Some 471,414 citizens signed the Ulster Solemn League & Covenant, unveiled at Belfast's City Hall on 28 September 1912. Anti-papal cries of "Home Rule Is Rome Rule" echoed the unremitting beat of the loyalist lambeg drum. Amid the unrest over 2,000 Catholics were forcibly expelled from the Belfast shipyards. As the Catholic workers staggered out, they were showered with "Belfast confetti" – a combination of rivets and iron nuts.

In January 1913, the newly named Ulster Volunteer Force announced that it was ready to take on the British Army, if necessary, in order to stay part of Britain. Even the Tory leader Bonar Law advocated this civil disobedience and law-breaking, telling Unionists, "There are things stronger than parliamentary majorities. I can imagine no length of resistance to which Ulster will go in which I shall not support them." His protestations were supported by British officers at the Curragh camp who mutinied rather than opposing Carson's private army.

By inflaming religious prejudices, the Tories manoeuvred their political opponents towards a policy of withdrawing all or part of Ulster from Home Rule. It was the Liberal Party member, T.G. Agar-Robartes who had first suggested removing the four Protestant counties: Antrim, Armagh, Down and Londonderry/Derry. Carson concluded that this was not enough and suggested that the nine-county province of Ulster should be excluded from Home Rule. Ironically, in light of subsequent events, this proposal – which would have provided an overall Catholic majority in Ulster – might ultimately have led to a democratically elected united Ireland. But that point was lost on most nationalists, whose chief concern was securing Home Rule for the entire island.

It was now clear that an Amendment Bill dealing with the 'Ulster question' would have to be introduced despite objections from the nationalist Irish Parliamentary Party whose leader John Redmond had implored: "the two nation theory is to us an abomination and a blasphemy". Political journalist Arthur Griffith, who had founded the radical militant party Sinn Féin in 1905, also spoke of Partition in religious terms: "Ireland cannot shift her frontiers; the Almighty traced them beyond the currency of men to modify." These views were reiterated more prosaically by the Republican socialist James Connolly who feared for an Ireland politically divided by religion in which the Orange Order would hold sway in the North. "Belfast is bad enough as it is," he warned. "What it would be like under such rule the wildest imagination cannot conceive. Filled with the belief that they were defeating the Imperial Government and the nationalists combined, the Orangemen would have scant regard for the rights of the minority left at their mercy."

By early 1914, the increasingly beleaguered John Redmond had agreed to some accommodation by accepting British Prime Minister David Lloyd George's County Option Scheme which offered individual counties the chance to opt out of Home Rule for a maximum of six years. Carson recoiled in indignation at this proposal and refused to accept "a sentence of death with a stay of execution for six years". His rhetoric was well-founded for it was obvious that five of Ulster's nine counties, with their Catholic majorities, would elect for Home Rule. Even if the six-year ruling was removed from the equation, it was unlikely that a four-county exclusion zone could survive, politically or economically. Knowing that some form of Home Rule was inevitable Carson was reluctantly forced to change tack and, in July 1914, elected to push for a six-county bloc – an extremely worrying tactic from the nationalist viewpoint since it guaranteed a Unionist majority in the North under a guise of reasonableness in surrendering Donegal, Monaghan and Cavan. Summarily repudiated by nationalists, it gradually won support among pragmatic Protestants as their likeliest hope of maintaining the Union.

The Home Rule Bill entered the Statute Book on 15 September 1914, but its implementation, along with the Amendment Bill, was delayed until the end of the Great War. With the vexed question of Partition still unresolved, there was always the likelihood of some militant response in the South from the radical IRB (Irish Republican Brotherhood) or disenchanted Irish Volunteers. But when insurrection finally came, the circumstances would take the world by surprise.

Back in East Belfast, Van Morrison's paternal grandparents, George Albert Morrison and Margaret Young, were a courting couple heading for the altar. They had decided to marry at the end of the long holiday weekend and chose Easter Monday, 24 April 1916. It was a crisp, fine morning as they independently set out for the noon service at the Westbourne Presbyterian Church. The twelve bells chimed as they prepared to exchange vows. At that identical moment, less than a hundred miles south, the Angelus bells were ringing across Dublin as people flocked to midday mass. None were aware that they were about to witness one of the most important and momentous events in the history of Ireland. A doomed procession of hard-line patriots marched down Middle Abbey Street, then descended upon the General Post Office in Sackville Street. At 12.45pm, their spiritual leader Pádraig Pearse walked out of the building and declared the birth of the Irish Republic as an independent state. News of what was happening in Dublin did not reach the Morrisons until hours later. "Sinn Féiners have seized the Post Office in Dublin," they were told. In the House of Commons, Edward Carson, who had recently advised Unionists to resist officers of the Crown with arms, told his fellow MPs: "Gentlemen, we should be ready to put down these rebels now and ever more." The story of the insurgence was relayed internationally, and what sounded like a minor rebellion rapidly took on immense significance. The Easter Rising was successfully transformed into a propagandist blood sacrifice after the British executed 15 of the insurgents, including the signatories of the Republican proclamation. Public opinion in Ireland changed utterly and support switched from the nationalist constitutionalists to the Republican revolutionaries. On the eve of his execution, Pádraig Pearse, the chief doctrinaire of blood sacrifice, had written an elegy *The Wayfarer*, in which he acknowledged: "The beauty of the world hath made me sad/This beauty that will pass". W.B. Yeats recognized a more complex aesthetic at the heart of the Rising, rightly observing in his poem *Easter 1916* that "a terrible beauty" had been born.

By 1918, the ailing John Redmond's Irish Parliamentary Party had been replaced as the main political force by Sinn Féin whose ascendancy was confirmed after the British War Cabinet enforced conscription on Ireland. Three years of guerrilla warfare in Ireland followed before the nationalists and the British were forced to the negotiating table in search of a settlement.

On 23 June 1921, King George V opened the Parliament of Northern Ireland at Stormont, Belfast. Partition of a six-county Ulster was now a political reality. Lloyd George had craftily offered the Irish Treaty delegation the compromise of a vaguely concocted Boundary Commission whose findings it was hoped would remove Fermanagh and Tyrone from the province, thereby possibly rendering Northern Ireland unworkable. Under immense pressure from Lloyd George, and with a settlement in jeopardy, the delegation from Dublin accepted Dominion status (similar to that in Canada, South Africa, Australia and New Zealand) for 26 of the 32 counties, complete with an Oath of Fidelity to the Crown and Partition subject to a Boundary Commission. Chairman and guerrilla warfare strategist Michael Collins understood the fearful implications of these concessions all too well and privately declared with prophetic accuracy: "I may have signed my actual death-warrant."

On 7 February 1922, Dáil Éireann ratified the Treaty by a small majority and, five months later, the people of the new Irish Free State (Saorstát Éireann) supported that decision in their first General Election. Anti-Treatyites, led by Éamon de Valera, refused to recognize the Free State and the South was plunged into civil war, which effectively left the newly established Northern Ireland in an even more powerful position. By the time the conflict was over, Ireland had lost most of its most influential nationalist figures. The demoralized new Irish government half-heartedly pursued the Boundary Commission, whose findings ended in stalemate. A six-county Northern Ireland – Antrim, Armagh, Derry/Londonderry, Down, Fermanagh, Tyrone – was now firmly established. Unionist politicians, ever cautious, preached the doctrine of eternal vigilance against the threat of a united Ireland. The cries of 'No Surrender' would echo down through the generations for the remainder of the century.

This was the new statelet that Van Morrison's parents were born into during the early Twenties. It was, in many respects, a place apart – partitionist and isolationist in character and philosophy. Ulster Unionists inculcated a loyalist mindset which influenced every aspect of Northern life. Whereas the populace had once seen themselves as 'imperialist Irish', recent events ensured that it was now their exclusively 'Ulster identity' that prevailed. Political historian Alvin Jackson observed perceptively; "For loyalists 'Ulster' became the geographical corollary of being 'Unionist' . . . 'Irishness' was an unavoidable but uncomfortable element of the Unionist heritage and was consigned after 1920 to a mental and constitutional quagmire."

The Morrison dynasty was forged in the smithy of this isolated Ulster. Violet Stitt entered the world on 24 September 1921 in her family home at 47 Connswater Street. Eight months later on 21 May 1922, George Morrison was born at 142 Lord Street. Both of their fathers (John Stitt and George Morrison Snr, respectively) were toiling as labourers in the shipyards then but these were troubled times in Ulster. Partition may have saved the Union but it did little to assist community relations. Anti-Catholic pogroms in Belfast ended in riots and death. In the year of George Morrison's birth there were 97 reported cases of murder in Belfast alone, and 59 of attempted murder. More than a quarter of the city's Catholic population, totalling 23,000, were evicted or burnt out of their homes. The shipyards were again depopulated of 'Fenians' by their fellow workers. In a familiar pattern, sectarianism was closely linked with fears of unemployment and economic decline. A post-war slump had plunged Belfast into an unprecedented recession. Reduced demand for raw materials and a lack of income to purchase goods created a frightening downward spiral. The shipyards were badly hit resulting in mounting unemployment and in 1927 the linen mills began their inexorable decline.

By the autumn of 1932, over 48,000 people in Belfast were unemployed and half that number were ineligible for government benefits. Many were forced into the workhouse. In October that year there was a civil demonstration in Belfast which was brutally suppressed by the police. Political observers, seeking solace in the chaos, detected the spark of socialist revolution. Journalist J.J. Kelly, who witnessed the gathering, wrote vividly of this people's rising:

When Orangemen and Catholics, the lines of starvation already etched in their hollow cheeks, gripped hands and declared emotionally, "Never again will *they* divide us", there was consternation in the ranks of the professional politicians. Trouble was brewing in the city. But on that wintry day in October one felt that a climax had been reached. A big unemployment demonstration had been banned. On the Shankill Road crowds of growling men lounged about – waiting. The police stood around too. It was early in the afternoon. Suddenly a big red-faced woman with a black shawl thrown over her shoulders, wisps of hair hanging over her eyes, appeared almost, it seemed, from nowhere. Wild-eyed and panting from exertion, she ran to the crowds of men and in quick, terse language told them that the unemployed and the police were in conflict on the Falls Road – one man was killed and others were wounded – and the fighting was still going on.

"Are youse goin' to let them down?" she almost shrieked . . . A cheer went up.

"No, by heavens, we are not", they roared back, and in a twinkling a veritable orgy of destruction had begun. Windows were smashed in, shops looted, bread tossed out from them to women, hams and beef thrown out from others. Flames appeared. "Here are the peelers", shouted some as an armoured car appeared. There was a rattle of gunfire. Pandemonium broke loose, when the police and rioters got to grips. The whole of the Shankill was aflame. From other parts of the city there were similar reports.

The socialist *Daily Worker* similarly wrote of "Catholic and Orangemen united against the common imperialist enemy." This was a happy delusion which fatally underestimated the power of the Orange card in Northern politics. Hard-line Unionists were deeply suspicious of socialism which they invariably equated with Irish nationalist interests. The newly-formed Ulster Protestant League quickly issued a statement insisting that the demonstration had been "used as a cloak by the communist Sinn Féin element to start a revolution in our province. We also greatly deplore that some of our loyal Protestant unemployed were misled to such an extent that they associated themselves with the enemies of their faith and principles."

Violet Stitt's elder sister Sarah started dating a shipyard labourer, Victor Wardlow, around this time and before long the pair married and settled at 53 Trillick Street in the close-knit East Belfast community. It was in that home that their daughter, Gloria Wardlow, was born on 2 November 1932. Later eulogized in song, Gloria had a tough childhood, with food shortages and unemployment rife, in one of the worst periods in Belfast's history.

In 1933, Harland & Wolff failed to launch a single vessel and the smaller Workman & Clark shipyard went out of business the following year. Inflammatory speeches hardened prejudices, convincing many moderates that Catholics should be barred from employment. Northern Ireland Prime Minister Lord Craigavon echoed the sepulchral beat of the lambeg drum by reassuring Unionist militants: "I am an Orangeman first and a politician and a member of parliament afterwards . . . all I boast is that we are a Protestant parliament and a Protestant state." Prime Minister elect, Basil Brooke, was even less subtle, urging, "I recommend those people who are loyalists not to employ Roman Catholics, 99 per cent of whom are disloyal". As the provocative political writer Paul Foot later observed: "Even in racialist South Africa, it was considered reasonable for white people to employ black people in their houses. Nowhere in the world was bigotry taken quite to such extravagant lengths as it was in Northern Ireland."

The bitter fruits of Orange sectarianism were harvested in the terrible ugliness of the 1935 riots. Mobs brandishing iron bars turned up outside factories and mills beating workers into unconsciousness. During the summer, 430 Catholic homes were razed and 2,241 residents were evacuated from Protestant areas.

The sectarian blood-letting caused a momentary hiatus and, as before, it was events outside the province that saved Belfast from self-immolation. A rearmament programme leading up to the Second World War brought new employment to the shipyards. Full bellies and the focus on an outside enemy deflected the cries of 'No Surrender' towards Germany.

Seeking employment in the shipyards at this time almost invariably required membership of an Orange order or recommendation from a family member. George Morrison was well placed enough to join Harland & Wolff as an electrician, just as the firm was emerging from the economic doldrums; his girlfriend Violet Stitt was also working long hours at one of the linen mills among a workforce that was predominantly female.

Wartime Belfast was not a happy courting ground. The city's air-raid precautions were pitiful and there was a worrying lack of bomb shelters. East Belfast, home of Harland & Wolff, was targeted by the German Luftwaffe and large areas of the district were destroyed. On one night alone (15–16 April 1941) 11 churches were destroyed along with several schools, hospitals and the central library. The situation was so dire that Éire, a neutral country during the War, despatched fire engines to assist their neighbours. The night ended with 745 fatalities and hundreds more injured. Emergency facilities were required to feed over 70,000 homeless and an estimated 100,000 were evacuated from Belfast the following day. Having survived this terrible year, George and Violet were married at St Donard's Church, Bloomfield Road, on Christmas Day. The picturesque church with its pretty, manicured lawn was still undergoing renovation following the German onslaught. When required to sign their marriage certificate the groom lied about his age, claiming he was 21 instead of 19. The deception was a chivalrous act intended to spare Violet the indignity of having married a younger man, even though there was less than a year between them. Witnessing the ceremony were Violet's brother John and sister Sarah.

A few months before the marriage, Violet's mother, the recently widowed Alice Stitt, had moved into 125 Hyndford Street, East Belfast. The terraced house had previously been the home of Robert Cairns, a shipyard riveter who lived there till 1936 after which it was occupied for five years by a certain M.E. Martin. It was not until 1944 that George and Violet were registered as the main occupants. The following year, on 31 August, George Ivan Morrison was born in the house. Although they were still in their early twenties, the Morrisons – for reasons that were never publicly revealed – did not have another child.

Four months after the baby's birth, the 'Big Man' arrived in East Belfast. Nineteen-year-old Ian Paisley had been invited to preach at the Ravenhill Evangelical Church on Glentoran Street. He made such an impression on the congregation that the church invited him to become their pastor. On 1 August 1946, the noted evangelist and 'tornado of the pulpit' W.P. Nicolson laid hands on Paisley and proclaimed: "I have one prayer for this young man, that God will give him a tongue like an old cow. Young man, go into a butcher's shop and try and run your hand along a cow's tongue, it's as sharp as a file."

The prayer proved prophetic and Paisley's serrated tongue became a potent weapon of papal abuse and evangelical fervour. Before long, Paisley founded the Free Presbyterian Church, dedicated to rooting out Protestant apostasy, exposing the Pope as the Anti-Christ and advancing its fundamentalist belief in the true word. His influence on religious and political matters in the North was to prove incalculable.

After marrying Eileen Cassells, the daughter of an East Belfast shop-keeper, Paisley set up home in Beersbridge Road, which was connected to the bottom of Hyndford Street. He later moved up the road to the plusher environs of Cyprus Avenue. Paisley's firebrand evangelism was intoxicating and once directed towards political ends engulfed the lives of the local community, including those unconnected with the Free Presbyterian Church. Part of the appeal was a righteous holier-than-thou parochialism which advocated loyalty to the Crown and the triumph of a Protestant ascendancy as fulfilling God's ineffable plan. "God has a people in this province," he pronounced. "There are more born-again people in Ulster to the square mile than anywhere else in the world. God has a purpose for this province and this plant of Protestantism sown here in the north eastern part of this island." The purpose, as preached by Paisley, was all too often articulated in a stream of negatives that betrayed the community's age-old fears: 'No Surrender', 'Ulster Says No', 'No Popery Here'.

Morrison started school in 1950 at Elmgrove Primary, Beersbridge Road, near to Paisley's home. For the first couple of years there, the child was known as George Morrison before adopting his middle name Ivan, which appeared on later school reports. In this, he followed his grandfather George who was always known by his middle name, Albert. Young Morrison was a preternaturally quiet boy whose lack of siblings meant that he had no immediate role models on whom to practise his social skills. Introspection was an easier option. One person who was capable of bringing him out of himself was his first cousin, Gloria Wardlow. Thirteen years his senior, she was something of an elder sister figure during his childhood and a welcome link between the adolescent and the adult world. Her own father, Victor Wardlow, who ended his working life as a packer, had died some time before and she was now working in a linen factory and living nearby in Dunraven Park. It was during Morrison's first year at school, a few months before his sixth birthday, that the 18-year-old Gloria married a boilermaker, Thomas Harrison Gordon, in the spring of 1951. The service took place at St Donard's, the same church where Morrison's parents were married. The couple subsequently moved to the Straight in Cregagh on the Castlereagh Road. Along with the Stitts, the Gordon family would remain close to the Morrison clan throughout the Fifties.

As an only child, Morrison's isolation was heightened when his father left the family to find work in America. Distant relatives had previously settled in Detroit and Toronto, and Morrison senior was keen to follow their lead. Although emigration was discussed on several occasions, the moment of departure passed and the family remained behind in East Belfast. After a lengthy period employed as a railroad electrician in Motor City, the wandering father returned home armed with a collection of records and presents for the family. Young Ivan, who already owned a shelf full of Wild West stories, was delighted to receive a cowboy outfit with the name Tex Ritter emblazoned on the chaps. Gil Irvine, a childhood friend who lived a few doors away on Hyndford Street, also received an unexpected gift. "It was a real leather holster with a cowboy gun," he enthuses. "Not like the little silver painted ones that we usually had. It was a prized possession of mine for a long, long time, so it was." The boys drifted through hours and days playing Cowboys and Indians in fields that became prairie plains or in demolished buildings that resembled the aftermath of a US cavalry bombardment. Morrison adored Hopalong Cassidy and told his parents that he wanted to be a cowboy when he grew up. They even took a photo of him in the front room looking resplendent in his fancy Western regalia. He had an uncharacteristially broad smile on his face.

There were a large number of families in Hyndford Street who, unlike the Morrisons, were busily replenishing Belfast's population after the War. Kids of various ages would mix together and make up their own games with a bat, ball or skipping rope borrowed from the washing line. Street games were extremely popular and brightly-coloured marbles and cigarette cards were not merely collected or bartered but won and lost in long, intense games of skill. Back indoors, Morrison contented himself with the less frantic hobby of stamp collecting. He also had a fine collection of toy soldiers specially made by his father during breaks at the Short & Harland aircraft munitions factory where he now worked.

Away from the street, the boys would swim in the nearby Beechie River or cycle to Rockport, just outside Holywood. "We'd get up to all sorts of adventures," Gil Irvine remembers. "There were the

Sandhills, which was open ground where you'd find all kind of things to do. We dug large holes, made huts under the ground and covered the top with corrugated iron." During one game, Irvine chased Morrison on to the top of a scaffolding and watched with shocked amazement as his pal fell and broke his arm. A period of convalescence followed.

Saturday afternoons were usually spent at the cinema's minor matinees, one of the most popular children's entertainments of the era. There were six cinemas to choose from in Morrison's vicinity, including the Ambassador, the Castle Picture House, and the Astoria. Their favourite was the Strand on Holywood Road where they cheered the black and white celluloid cowboy as he escaped cliff-hanging catastrophes, outgunned sadistic, black-hearted, black-hatted outlaws, saved helpless families from marauding injuns and rode off triumphantly into the sunset only to return next week for a new adventure.

Late afternoon would usually conclude with a game of soccer at which the yet-to-be-podgy Morrison revealed an unexpected proficiency. Some felt that with enough practise and dedication, he might even have rivalled his ace football playing cousin, Jackie Stitt. "Van could have been a good sportsman," Irvine contends, "but he had no interest in it at all. He'd play along with you for a while until he got bored. It amazed me because he was a lot better than some of the others, but he seemed to tire of it quickly. He'd go indoors."

Sunday was literally a day of rest in East Belfast. Pubs, cinemas and playgrounds all closed and the censorious citizens even chained swings and roundabouts to save the children from the sinful temptations of idle pleasure. Observance was absolute and the stray kick of a ball on a Protestant street would prompt the righteous retort "Away and read your Bible." In Presbyterian homes, no radio or television would be played and window blinds were firmly shut. Even Sunday dinner had to be prepared in advance of the Sabbath. "Most of us went to the hall in the middle of Hyndford Street, The Brethren," Gil Irvine recalls. Inscribed in glass above the entrance of the meeting hall were words that would later inspire the title track of *Astral Weeks*: "Ye Must Be Born Again". As Irvine remembers: "There was Sunday School and children's meetings on Wednesday night. Every year they used to take the kids away for the day on a bus run. Everyone went through that phase where you went to Sunday School for a while. It was typical of Northern Ireland at the time that parents wanted to see their children get a religious education of some description."

Less reverent members of the community would plug in the wireless and enjoy the sedate, forbidden pleasures of the BBC Light Programme to enliven an otherwise dreary afternoon. While kitchen aromas wafted through the air, the radio offered a stolid mix of anodyne music and classic comedy: *Two-Way Family Favourites* linked homesick servicemen with pining sweethearts and devoted mothers via an incongruously eclectic selection of chestnut standards and popular tunes; *The Billy Cotton Band Show* offered quickfire comic sketches and brass-laden Tin Pan Alley covers; in *The Clitheroe Kid*, the magically ageless Jimmy Clitheroe pitted his wits against a haughty sister with the unwitting assistance of her gormless boyfriend; in later years the *Kid* would be replaced by the outrageous and incomprehensibly camp Julian and Sandy, who exposed a secret fantasy netherworld of innocent homosexuality in the centrepiece of *Round The Horne.* Some hours after, it was possible to tune into late-night Radio Luxembourg, whose playlist seemed mouth-wateringly exotic. The evening ended with 'DJ BA' Barry Aldiss detailing the contrasting fortunes of the hit parade élite in the Top 20 rundown, courtesy of the *New Musical Express.*

Those were the good days. Sometimes, Morrison would unconsciously trace the steps of Ian Paisley from Beersbridge Road to Cyprus Avenue where the trimmed hedges, red-blossomed trees and large houses revealed another world of unspeakable affluence. More often, the overwhelming mood of a Protestant Belfast Sunday was controlled vacuity. Time passed slowly. If it was raining outside and you were trapped indoors, minutes would seem like hours. That sense of timelessness, initially frustrating, brought unexpected rewards. There was a warm security amid the serenity, an enveloping feeling of calm in which silence itself took on a strange and powerful significance. The tranquillity allowed you to lose yourself in the labyrinthine corridors of your imagination where everything felt in harmonious equilibrium. For Morrison, these heightened experiences became inextricably linked with the Edenic comfort of childhood. He would spend much of his life vainly attempting to rediscover and articulate those evanescent moments of transcendence. It was like trying to catch rainbows.

Undoubtedly, the greatest influence of all on Morrison was music. He had been exposed to music as a source of pleasure since the age of two when his grandparents lulled him to sleep with the recordings of Eddy Arnold, Tex Ritter, Gene Autry and Jimmie Rodgers. Soon, Morrison was tugging at his mother's apron strings, interrupting her routine and urging her to play more records. "My mother [Alice Stitt] used to come up and take turns," Violet Morrison recalls, "because he'd have you playing them morning, noon and night." The most fruitful source of musical education though was his father whose formidable record collection was the talk of Hyndford Street. This well-travelled electrician had originally been a fan of big band and swing, with a liking for Tommy Dorsey, Artie Shaw and Harry James. Gradually, his tastes broadened to embrace country (Hank Williams, Jimmie Rodgers), gospel (Mahalia Jackson, Sister Rosetta Tharpe), jazz (Charlie Parker, Louis Armstrong, Jelly Roll Morton) and blues/R&B (Leadbelly, Big Bill Broonzy, Muddy Waters, Louis Jordan). This melange of influences had a profound effect on Ivan who increasingly looked to America as the mecca of this mysterious, liberating music. When he was a young child, his mother had bought him cowboy songs on cheap red vinyl from Woolworth's. From singing cowboys, Morrison graduated to folk, country and blues and soon discovered the joy of live performance. "My father took me into town one day and there was this jazz band playing on the back of a truck . . . blowing horns and saxophones and singing. I thought it was great that people could do that." Soon, the boy was participating in the sing-songs that took place in his house on Saturday nights. Usually, his parents would visit a pub or social club and afterwards some uncles or other extended family would arrive at Hyndford Street for a late-night session. Shy in other respects, Ivan never felt self-conscious when requested to sing. "It was a natural thing. People would come over and sing . . . I didn't know until I was much older that other people weren't doing this."

Although his home was host to family musical evenings, George Morrison Snr failed to make a lasting impression on his neighbours. Some labelled him dour and distant, but others felt this was a severe misreading of his character. "The father was a quiet, hard-working man, typical of the time," Gil Irvine points out. "It wasn't a strict family, but nobody said anything against him. That was the way families were brought up then. You didn't answer back to your parents." His only son was protective of his father's memory, seldom speaking of him in interviews and correcting those who dared to remark on his lack of sociability. It was only in the song 'Choppin' Wood', written after George Morrison's death in 1988, that he provided a revealing glimpse into the life of quiet desperation endured by his father against the backdrop of Harland & Wolff's post-war decline. Although he fulfilled his paternal duties as best he could, there was a sense of opportunity lost, a feeling expressed in song with the indelible image of George Morrison returning from Detroit, sitting at home in front of the television and no longer wishing to go anywhere.

Violet Morrison was a different creature entirely: effervescent, petite, wiry and the life and soul of the party. While her husband studiously collected records, she was the singer and the player in the family who brought the music to life. Trained as a dancer, she exploded into animation performing high-kicks at parties, a trick later borrowed by her son as a performer. "The mother was always a trouper," Irvine affirms. "She used to do dance classes and tap dancing, and she was a magnificent harmonica player, which is where I think Van got it from." In addition to the harmonica, she played piano and had performed in one of the many Orange pipe bands that dominated the street every summer. "My mother used to play bagpipes," Morrison remembers. At home, she could be heard at the top of the stairs, walking between the landing and the bedroom, practising scales and enveloping the house with that eerily reverberating drone. Listening to the radio, she would always sing along. Affable and conversational, she never had any trouble coaxing one of the relatives to do a 'wee turn' at one of the family's Saturday sessions. It was there that Morrison gave his first performance, impressing the assembled company with a rousing rendition of Leadbelly's 'Goodnight Irene'. He had already singled out Leadbelly, an unlikely idol, and spent many evenings twiddling the radio dial in search of the American Forces' Network, which played records considered far too esoteric by the staid BBC. During daylight hours, state-sanctioned radio offered a meagre selection of durable big bands, light orchestras, homegrown crooners and variety acts, whose obse-quiousness to wholesome entertainment and traditional values would have warmed the heart of any Ulster Unionist still committed to the

cultural supremacy of Great Britain. Even the programme titles –
Workers' Playtime, Music While You Work and *Housewives' Choice* –
betrayed the benign condescension of a wartime, ration book fixated
broadcasting company that prided itself on knowing what was best for
its happy proletariat.

Morrison was not restricted by the confines of the BBC and soon
followed his father around the city's record shops. Along the way, they
would often pass by Wee Willie Winkle (aka Billy The Busker), a street
entertainer who played the musical saw. Born in Ardrossan of Ulster
parents at the beginning of the century, William Campbell lived in
Wesley Street off the Donegall Road, but spent most of his time
regaling shoppers with his distinctive renditions of 'O Sole Mio',
'Danny Boy' and 'The Gentle Maiden'. A favourite source for
imported jazz was Atlantic Records on the High Street, an emporium
managed by Solly Lipsitz, one of several Jewish shopkeepers
specializing in rare discs. Often the Morrisons would lose themselves in
the splendid jumbled chaos of Smithfield Market which prided itself on
selling *anything*. Furniture, books, battered instruments, knick-knacks
and even false limbs for amputees were some of the items on offer. It
was here that young Ivan purchased his first disc – 'Hootin' Blues' by
the Sonny Terry Trio on New York's Gramercy label – which was in
the sale for 1/6d. The trio soon shared a place in Morrison's private
hierarchy alongside Huddie 'Leadbelly' Ledbetter.

Morrison's fascination for Leadbelly was already several years old on
the otherwise uneventful day in February 1956 when he heard Lonnie
Donegan on the radio singing 'Rock Island Line'. Over the past few
months, Morrison had taken a keener interest in popular music
following the rise of Bill Haley & His Comets whose classic singles
'Rock Around The Clock', 'Shake, Rattle And Roll' and 'Razzle
Dazzle' had spearheaded the onslaught of a phenomenon referred to in
the newspapers as "rock 'n' roll". Haley was a revelation, but
Donegan's chart debut was even more startling for Morrison. While the
world was promoting the Glaswegian's 'Rock Island Line' as the most
exciting new disc of the day, Morrison was already familiar with
Leadbelly's original recording. At only ten-and-a-half years old, the
precocious boy from Bloomfield had a head start on many musicians
twice his age.

Rock 'n' roll was seen as an apostasy by the God-fearing Brethren and Unionist elders of the community. The notion that British youth should be transfixed by the sound of white men singing in black voices was an affront to common decency, not to mention the Empire. Morrison, who lived and breathed the blues, saw no such contradiction. While the press paraded and condemned this immoral pageant of grotesque rock 'n' roll deviance – the vulgar, hip-swinging Elvis Presley, the crippled, delinquent Virginian wildcat Gene Vincent, the unspeakably epicene Little Richard and the bigamist Jerry Lee Lewis whose cousin bride would later be exposed as a scandalous 13 years old – Morrison ignored the hysteria and found salvation in the music.

Partly thanks to the iconography of Elvis, sales of acoustic guitars had shot up in 1957. With near full employment in Britain, luxury goods, made more attractive after years of rationing, had never seemed as plentiful. That July, Prime Minister Harold Macmillan cannily transformed the economic boom into a propagandist boast: "Let's be frank about it – most of our people have never had it so good." Badgered parents were bombarded by impassioned entreaties and hangdog expressions in pursuit of the dream instrument, even if it was a bruised second-hand model. George Morrison, acknowledging his son's genuine interest, took him past Harry Hall's bookshop to Joseph Kavanagh's 'I Buy Anything' Aladdin's Cave in Smithfield, and bought him his first guitar. Back at home, the boy practised rudimentary chords while poring over *The Carter Family Style*, a songbook edited by noted folklorist Alan Lomax. Playing guitar enhanced Morrison's appreciation of folk music – from Josh White to Ireland's own McPeake Family.

The summer of 1957 saw Britain gripped by a new sensation: skiffle. Over the past year, Lonnie Donegan's rise in popularity had coincided with a working-class roots-based musical revival partly based on the negro 'rent parties' of Depression-period America. This embracing of musical minimalism meant that every street kid was a potential player – all you needed was a home-made instrument like a washboard and thimble or a double-bass constructed from a broom handle and tea chest. With his fondness for folk and blues, Morrison was eager to form his own Hyndford Street skiffle ensemble. He was fortunate to find an effusive ally living next door. For years, number 123 had been occupied by the Cookes, then passed to a commercial traveller, Walter Riddell.

Then, in 1957, the Blakely family moved in. Young Walter, the son of a shipyard worker, was an athletic child who quickly befriended Ivan and enthusiastically supported the skiffle scheme, even persuading his mother Ethel to surrender her kitchen washboard for the cause. Fellow Elmgrove pupil Gil Irvine rescued a lead pipe from the bed of the Beechie River and transformed the base metal into a woodwind instrument he proudly named a zobo. "He was lucky he didn't get typhoid," quipped Morrison.

The line-up was completed with the recruitment of two other locals: Billy Ruth (guitar) and John McCullough (tea chest bass). They named themselves the Sputniks after the Russian satellite that was launched into orbit that same year. Soon, they were busily rehearsing a selection of traditional favourites inspired by such skiffle notables as Nancy Whiskey, Chas McDevitt, the Vipers and Johnny Duncan. Although too young to venture far from Hyndford Street, they were thrilled by the chance to play in front of their peers at some of the local picturedromes. "There used to be the B-picture or the 'wee picture' as we called it," Gil Irvine remembers. "There was a break for about 10 minutes [before the main feature] where you piled everything on stage. Not that there was much equipment. There were no microphones so you just did what you could. We played some Saturday mornings and afternoons usually at the Willowfield Cinema on Woodstock Road. Van was doing most of the singing and arranging."

During that summer of 1957, Morrison's future schooling was determined. The dreaded 11-plus examination separated those intelligent or fortunate enough to receive a grammar school education from a substantial majority doomed to spend the next few years at a secondary modern, intermediate or technical school. As the MacBeath report of the period grimly concluded: "The great majority of pupils at secondary/intermediate schools probably are not intellectually equipped to pass any worthwhile external examination." Alas, Morrison was not destined for Grosvenor High Grammar but found himself cast among MacBeath's "intellectually unequipped". Normally, he would have remained at Beersbridge Road, but Elmgrove had recently closed its doors to secondary pupils and now specialized in primary education. Instead, he was bound for the newly-built boys' school, Orangefield Intermediate.

TWO

Orangefield

Orangefield was part of an experiment by the Belfast Education Authority to provide larger up-to-date facilities for the bulging post-war surplus of school children. More than 2,400 Belfast secondary school pupils had begun the academic year in bright new buildings, over half of which were equipped for woodwork, netball, science and art. The local authority sanctioned developments on the outskirts of the city where children, although forced to travel longer distances, could avail themselves of fresh air, pleasant scenery and spacious playing fields. Fortunately for Morrison, the LEA included a number of inner city schools in the scheme with Orangefield regarded as the jewel in the crown. "The development of the Orangefield school site is a coura-geous venture," the *Belfast Newsletter* proclaimed. "It means that many thousands of children in the densely populated and rapidly growing district of East Belfast will have all the education the state can provide under the 1947 Act practically on their doorstops. Not only that, but on the vast site they will eventually have more playing space than their predecessors ever enjoyed."

Orangefield might never have lived up to its promise were it not for the appointment of a dynamic headmaster capable of pushing through a modestly progressive agenda while retaining the respect and confi-dence of the strongly Unionist school council. John Malone, the son of a peripatetic woodwork teacher from Downpatrick, Co. Down, had initially been involved in primary education, then moved into youth work with the Council of Churches. Working with unemployed boys in the hungry Thirties had a profound effect on his outlook. He wrote a report that was mildly critical of the Unionist government's policy, but it was suppressed for over 40 years. Self-financed, Malone subsequently studied for a BA at Cambridge just after the War, then taught around the Shankill area. Eventually, he was appointed vice principal at Ashfield Secondary School before securing the post at Orangefield. "He was an unusual man," one ex-colleague reflects. "He was very fixed and he had a candid expression, but there was an aura of goodness about him. His family were highly respected, churchgoing people. The word most used to describe him was 'integrity'. He didn't dissemble and looked straight at you. He was very generous with his time and money, but not behind in correcting you if you were wrong or there was a misjudgement that affected the children."

Malone was one of the first people Morrison encountered when he walked through the school gates on 2 September 1957. After morning assembly the 570 pupils spent most of the day familiarizing themselves with the layout of the new school and helping teachers with a variety of tasks including filling stock cupboards with text books, chalk and piles of exercise books. By the time the morning bell went for playtime, the pupils were already aware of their place in the school hierarchy, having been divided into streams according to ability. Unlike English secondary moderns, Orangefield Intermediate offered a type of education that, in certain respects, anticipated the comprehensive revolution of the early Sixties. In addition to the standard A-B-C-D-E streams, there was 1G (a grammar stream) and 1T (a technical stream). This catch-all system presented the illusion that some pupils at Orangefield were receiving a grammar school education, although of course the most able children had already been creamed off elsewhere via the 11-plus. Malone maintained some links with other local schools, though how effective this proved was debatable. "I think the concept was that even though the children had been damned by failure at the 11-plus, there was still the possibility of access," one former teacher notes. "If a child recovered and did well he might be introduced into a grammar stream with a transfer after the first or second year. There was something called the Review Examinations and with recommendation a child could be fed into a grammar school and that did happen with certain people. But most of them didn't want to anyway." Indeed, such transfers were rare and for Van Morrison, largely irrelevant. Already academically mediocre, he did not even reach the grammar stream at Orangefield.

Like most schools of the era, Orangefield operated a house system which divided pupils, largely for the purpose of competitive sports. In order to foster closer relations between the school and the Belfast industries in which most of the pupils would ultimately find employment, the savvy Malone named the houses after leading local firms: Bryson, Davidson, Musgrave and Hughes. Morrison, along with his younger contemporary Gil Irvine, was assigned to Davidson, a firm that was part of the Sirocco Works. Within weeks of the school's opening, the publicity-conscious Malone invited representatives from the companies to plant ornamental trees in the school grounds while the four heads of house stood in the background waving flags.

Amid the many new faces, Morrison was relieved to discover some old familiars, including the good-humoured Mr Cummings, his English teacher from Elmgrove. One prominent staff member was Bruce Weston, who taught History and would later replace Malone as head at the end of the Sixties. Probably the most feared teacher was Rodney Usher, head of Physical Education. For many of the pupils who had never seen a tool kit in their lives, metalwork and woodwork with Pop McGarry provided a timely reminder of what awaited them in the working world. The emphasis on technical subjects ensured that music was low on the curriculum list. "It was all based on classics like *Peter And The Wolf*," Gil Irvine recalls. "We had basic drums, triangles, the odd instrument. It was mainly percussion instruments that would be handed out – wooden blocks and xylophones – things you couldn't easily break." Morrison remembers many boring hours attempting to master the recorder in a military atmosphere. "The way they taught music was enough to put you off for life," remembers guitarist Eric Bell, a younger contemporary. "They used to give out these recorders and I couldn't come to terms with it. The teacher would call out, 'Bell – it's your little finger, not your third.' We had a piano teacher who taught us hymns and that put me off as well." Often, Morrison found himself longing for a more sympathetic approach and wondered why the teacher couldn't simply play a record or display some enthusiasm for a piece. Wisely, he kept such thoughts to himself.

It was outside the school gates that Morrison sought greater musical satisfaction. In nearby Greenville Street several kids from the Belfast Technical High School had started a group which attracted his attention. Nobody is in entire agreement about the precise evolution of the ensemble which began as a makeshift skiffle group. Billy McAllen, who lived on a local council estate, remembers it all starting when he teamed up with fellow pupils George Jones and Brian McCusker. After McAllen took some guitar lessons, he passed on his rudimentary knowledge to Jones, sometimes lending him the instrument for the weekend. With assistance from his sister, Jones then acquired an acoustic guitar on hire purchase. At the height of the skiffle craze the boys bought more guitars on mail order from England. "They were only cheap," says McAllen, "but we were all kids and didn't know any better." With several other friends in a frequently expanding line-up that included four or five guitarists and the obligatory tea-chest bass, they named themselves the Javelins. Soon they were joined by Evelyn Boucher, described by McAllen as "a lovely girl and a fine chanter". Once she started performing with the boys they renamed themselves Deanie Sands & The Javelins, as if they were some American high-school surf combo. The arrival of Boucher was a godsend as she was already a minor local celebrity and an exemplary organizer of young talent. Crippled from polio, she wore callipers but never allowed her disability to cloud her pleasant disposition. Working closely with the Hospital Stage Productions, she was brilliant at commandeering aspiring young singers, musicians and comedians to provide free entertainment for the patients. One of her early recruits was guitarist Billy Harrison, who remembers nervously walking to Belfast City Hall where a small crowd of novice entertainers were whisked away on an orange bus provided by the Hospitals' Entertainment Authority. "I'd known Evelyn for years, she was a very good chanter. She'd got two other girls she was friendly with to sing harmony and they asked me to be the guitarist. We used to do 'Moonlight Bay' with lovely harmonies. I did that for quite a while – probably a year and a half. I enjoyed it. It was all amateur talent with maybe one or two semi-professionals topping the bill. There were comedians, singers and musicians entertaining the patients – kids of 11 and 12 singing and tap dancing. You'd get tea and biscuits out of it and that was it. But it got you on stage, got you playing, got you experience. The patients were so glad to see somebody that it didn't matter if you were shitting yourself with nerves. Consequently, after a few shows and sensing their appreciation, your confidence grew. Not confidence in your playing, but standing up in front of people. That's what it was all about."

Once Evelyn joined the Javelins they attracted envious looks from other kids in the area. Fellow "Tech" pupil Roy Kane was an interested onlooker who listened attentively as McAllen and Jones related their latest hospital appearance with Deanie Sands. "I didn't even know where Evelyn came from, but they always used to say how great these gigs were. I came along one night to listen and the guy that played drums with them wasn't around. There was a snare drum there and I just started beating out the time on the drums with my hands. They more or less said, 'You're better than the guy we've got – ever think of playing?'" Kane was quick to take encouragement. Soon after, he persuaded his grandmother to take him downtown to a music shop where she bought him an Eric Delaney drumkit. "It was a plastic drumkit, with a wee tripod and cymbal hanging on the end of it. That was it. I started banging away on it and suddenly I was in the band."

At this point, Morrison had yet to approach the group, but duly noted their progress. Meanwhile, he was adjusting uneasily to school life. After eight months in existence, Orangefield was still in the midst of a £1 million expansion programme. In May 1958, its long delayed opening ceremony finally took place. A choir of 60 boys accompanied the arrival of the Lord Mayor Alderman Cecil McKee who was received by the chairman of the governors Reverend Whittaker, then introduced to the headmaster John Malone and various members of staff. Amid the pomp, McKee addressed the pupils with the revolutionary advice that factual knowledge was less important than "the building of character you will obtain through the influence and the calibre of the men who will be your teachers".

Morrison was not very good at listening to the sage counsel of his teachers or concentrating on his school work. By his own admission he spent much of his time staring out of the classroom window, lost in daydreams. Sometimes, the flights of fantasy had a disconcertingly darker hue. "I think I did have delusions," Morrison later confessed. "At one time I thought I wasn't going to live very long. The thing that saved me was my interest in music." He could often be found at home sitting alone in his bedroom, strumming an acoustic guitar or serenading the family sheepdog Maxie. "A lot of people didn't understand Van and thought he was totally cracked," George Jones sympathizes. Morrison was preternaturally shy, and his introspection was becoming increasingly noticeable, as was his selfishness. Nancy McCarter, who lived at number 131 Hyndford Street, remembers an afternoon when she inadvertently left her door key in the house; stranded outside, she asked Morrison if he would mind climbing over the garden wall and unlocking the door from the back. He merely shook his head in silence and coldly walked on.

By this time, Javelins' guitarist Billy McAllen had struck up a conversation with Morrison and their shared musical interests cemented a long-standing friendship. The Morrisons liked McAllen and he frequently attended their Saturday night music sessions, joining in on guitar. Often he would visit Van at home after school and listen to obscure blues recordings. Like others in the community, he was amazed to discover that the Morrisons actually owned a television set. On one of his early visits, the ever hospitable Violet Morrison suggested he stay for his tea. Emerging from the kitchen, she sat the two boys down, then politely served Billy first. At that moment, Van took umbrage, abruptly left the table and retired to his room. "He was very huffy," says McAllen, "very moody." Other kids would have been thrashed to within an inch of their lives for such infuriating petulance, but Morrison's parents were remarkably patient and supportive of their precious only child. McAllen was always impressed, if not envious, of Morrison's bountiful good fortune and the ease with which he acquired possessions. "They gave him everything he wanted," he muses.

Unfortunately, Morrison's lamentable social skills showed little or no sign of improvement. Even in the presence of Walter Blakely's mother Ethel, he remained terribly uncommunicative. If he saw her on the street, he would keep his head bowed and avoid eye contact. When she visited his mother for a chat he evinced all the warmth of a cowering dog. Violet Morrison was exceptionally tolerant of his foibles, but also concerned about his manners. "I'd have guests at home and Van would have been sitting and not speaking or anything." Eventually, even she felt obliged to take him aside and offer some stern advice. "I would have said he wasn't very sociable and would have to learn to talk to people and so on." Later, the wily child managed to counter such criticisms by pleading that his moods were the product of an artistic temperament. As his mother patiently explains, "One time he said to me it wasn't that he didn't want to talk but tunes were running through his head all the time. He said he didn't know whether he'd been blessed or cursed because the words and music wouldn't go out of his head. So I told him he should write it down, put it down on paper and maybe that might get rid of it . . . In fact, when he started that's how I knew what was happening to him and what he was doing."

Having befriended Billy McAllen, Morrison infiltrated Deanie Sands & The Javelins towards the end of their spell together. Like the Sputniks, they played at the Saturday minor matinee performances at the Strand Cinema, once receiving a startling 30 shillings fee. More often, it was the Hospital Stage Productions run by Desi Heaney and assisted by Evelyn Boucher that provided much-needed experience. "We mostly went to mental hospitals," says Roy Kane, "But I don't know if there was any significance in that. We used to play Antrim regularly. We worked with other acts and sometimes I'd be called upon by a magician to provide a drum roll or crash a cymbal. Many's the time his pigeons would crap on my cymbals, which always got a laugh. Sometimes, there was a semi-pro backing band and their drummer would ask, 'Would you like to play my drums?' I was completely afraid of them. I used to stand up playing one snare drum and cymbal and didn't know how to handle a drum kit at all."

Eventually, the in-demand Evelyn Boucher moved on to other projects, leaving the Javelins to ponder a new start. They renamed themselves the Thunderbolts and became devotees of instrumental music. In order to strengthen the act, they added another Tech pupil, Wesley Black (Blackie) whose speciality was Jerry Lee Lewis-style flourishes on the piano. Among their newer influences were Duane Eddy and Cliff Richard's backing group the Drifters, who had just signed a contract with EMI and were about to record their first instrumental, 'Chinchilla'. "The reason we were an instrumental group is that we had no money for a PA system," McAllen insists. At odd times, they experimented by inserting a small speaker into a concrete shore pipe or placing buckets in front of a borrowed amplifier to achieve an echo. What little equipment they owned was kept in George Jones' back bedroom in Greenville Street. McAllen usually stayed there at weekends and became such a regular visitor that Jones' parents started calling him "son number two". "It was Mrs Jones who really kept us all together," McAllen admits. "She was a great one for the groups and a fine wee woman."

Occasionally, for a laugh, the group would use an alternative alias, the Jokers (or other card names such as the Jacks and Aces) and cheekily charge friends in the area threepence to watch them play. Most of the time, they travelled by public transport, lugging their equipment aboard buses as bemused passengers looked on. Fortunately for Wesley Black, most of the venues they played had a piano on the premises. Over a period of months, they appeared on a parochial circuit that included the Brookborough Hall on Sandown Road, the Hut or East Belfast Working Men's Club on Chamberlain Street, the Harriers Hall in Hyndford Street, the Pigeon Club in Dee Street and the Belmont Tennis Club.

In the spring of 1959, they were attempting to perfect the eerie bass-string rumble of Duane Eddy's twangy guitar aboard a furniture van outside Jones' house when Morrison appeared armed with a tenor saxophone bought by his father. Inspired by the Jimmy McGiuffre 3's startling sax-driven 'The Train And The River', he was now ready to fatten the group's sound. With support from his parents, Morrison next contacted a local tutor, George Cassidy, a devotee of jazz tenor saxophonist Lester Young. The pupil was impressed by Cassidy's love of the instrument and patiently progressed to become an adequate player.

By the autumn of 1959, there was a brief hiatus as several of the boys entered their final year at school and were obliged to spend a little more time studying. In Orangefield, the often inspirational John Malone was energetically pursuing his own educational agenda. As pupil numbers rose, Malone became concerned about those at the bottom of the heap. Always on the lookout for potential, he recruited an old friend, whom he had once taught at primary level, to oversee the remedial department and assist with additional English lessons. David Hammond miraculously escaped inspection by the school committee and was given a remarkably free hand in organizing events and entertaining classes: "The school was enormously dynamic. In those early days Orangefield wasn't an institution, it was a place of great inspiration and zeal on the part of the teachers. There were a few malcontents but almost everybody was willing to work all hours of the day. John Malone was an extraordinary man of great vision and a source of inspiration. He would take risks and recruit people on instinct and most of the time he was right. He was very democratic in the way he ran the school and some teachers felt that the children got too much voice. He devoted a lot of time to the remedial department. Those kids got a fair crack of the whip and an equal amount of money and good teachers."

It was not Hammond's teaching alone that impressed the kids. His exotic image was soon the talk of the playground – and no doubt the staffroom. Dressed in a corduroy jacket and flowing scarf, he was considered daringly subversive by his impressionable charges. "This guy was a beatnik and bohemian to us," remarks Eric Bell. "He was like a celebrity." When Malone declared a war on truancy, it was Hammond who dutifully cycled around East Belfast scouring the streets and calling on startled mothers to enquire about their sick or wayward offspring. If there was a bereavement in a poor family, the headmaster would often entrust Hammond to offer some emergency provision from the school fund. Hammond's reputation as the school's most colourful character was confirmed when he appeared one evening on television playing a guitar. Even Van Morrison, who was then daydreaming his way through school, sat up and took notice. "David Hammond was a big influence on him," Gil Irvine concludes, "simply because he played the guitar." Morrison later recalled Hammond singing a sprightly, impromptu 'Casey Jones' in front of the class, which was much appreciated by the pupils.

Unfortunately for Morrison, the intimidating teacher/pupil divide was never breached. Hammond had no idea that the boy had recently won an audition at the local BBC studios after replying to an advertisement searching for young talent. Morrison had submitted a folk song, which included some tentative lyrics of his own. "It was about a bird," he noted vaguely. "The BBC never wrote back!" The only visible display of Morrison's musical ambition at Orangefield was an appearance at their Christmas concert where he sang Leadbelly's 'Midnight Special' backed by several of the Hyndford Street skifflers. "I don't think they knew what to make of it," he concluded.

Hammond's abiding memory of Morrison is a blurred vision of a furtive creature scurrying around the place like a frightened rabbit. It was not until years later that Morrison would reconnect with Hammond, by which time the teacher had become one of Belfast's most respected folklorists. "I don't think Orangefield engaged him," Hammond notes. "He slipped through the school. I keep protesting that I knew very little of him then, and when I talk to other teachers none of them have any striking memories of him at all. When he tells me what it was like from his experience the way he relates it, it was a childhood of some alienation."

Orangefield School was situated fairly near the home of Gloria Gordon and her husband Thomas. Morrison was still close to his cousin but by the time she was in her twenties, she was suffering from ulcerative colitis with inflammation of the large intestine. It was a condition that medical textbooks claimed often affected highly-strung young women. Psychological factors frequently played a part in the disorder, prompted by or resulting in stress. Excessive bleeding would lead to anaemia and the debilitating effects were alarming; often those affected, although young and strong, would be left so weak that they could barely walk to the bathroom. A progressive disease punctuated by periods of remission, it usually required a spell in hospital. Whether Morrison ever visited Gloria in hospital he has never revealed, but the theme of fatal illness in some of his late-Sixties compositions may well originate from memories of this period. Although tuberculosis and many other diseases had been all but conquered by medical advances, mortality rates in Belfast were still high and death came in many guises.

The East Belfast of Morrison's boyhood was delicately poised between the old world and the new. Enjoying post-war affluence it seemed a far more peaceful community, Ian Paisley's presence notwithstanding. The mass unemployment that had provoked sectarian violence in the Twenties and Thirties was now long past. Yet, the ancient shibboleths remained firmly in the minds of the elder members of the community who still preached the doctrines of eternal vigilance. Beneath a deceptively placid exterior, the politics of 'No Surrender' were still fomenting .

Even Orangefield, with all its airs of social progress, could only be as liberal as East Belfast would tolerate. "In the divided community here, Protestants would always accuse Catholics of being priest-ridden, both

north and south of the border," David Hammond contends. "But there
were plenty of clergymen on all the Protestant school committees and
on the boards of hospitals. The Church was exercising that power."
Both Church and State in the North ensured that the curriculum had a
Protestant bias, with an exclusive emphasis on British history and a total
absence of Irish culture. "I didn't study poetry or read Irish writers,"
Morrison confirms. "We didn't get Irish writers at school. All we got
was Shakespeare, no Irish writers. There wasn't one book by an Irish
writer in our school." Youngsters educated in East Belfast were never
under any illusions about the degree of the sectarian divide. "It was
*Orange*field," Eric Bell stresses. "You need only look at the name. The
words Orange and Catholic do not mix. I never saw a Catholic there."
Indeed, a Catholic presence among the pupils would have been
frowned upon by both sides of the community, the one issue that
united Protestant and Catholic clergy being the absolute importance of
religious segregation in state schools. The Catholic Clerical Managers
offered both denominations the reassuring mantra that "the only
satisfactory system of education for Catholics is one wherein Catholic
children are taught in Catholic schools by Catholic teachers under
Catholic control."

Orangefield included several evangelists on the staff, yet prided itself
on a secular, quasi-liberal agenda that was not always warranted or
unchallenged. Sometimes the local community intervened with a
Paisleyite wrath. "If you live in a divided society, you're lulled by it,"
Hammond admits. "I knew a lot of people in the Catholic community
at that time because of my other interests. One of them was a senior
man at a training college. He was much more Catholic than John
Malone was Protestant, but he sent children from his remedial
department over to Orangefield because I was there. The first time
nuns appeared and people saw these hooded figures walking around the
school, it caused a flurry. There were complaints from parents. I don't
recall whether the teachers complained, but they could have done
without me knowing about it."

The shocking vision of visiting nuns roaming the corridors of
Orangefield occurred during Morrison's last months at the school. By
that time, he had already experienced many of the religious rites of
passage peculiar to Northern Ireland. Chief amongst them was the

annual Orange celebrations, culminating in the colourful parades of the
Twelfth of July when battalions of Unionists marched in honour of
William of Orange's 1690 victory over the Jacobites at the Battle of the
Boyne. Dressed in dark suits, orange sashes and bowler hats in sartorial
memory of their loyalist forefathers of 1912, the participants provided a
tribalist pageant, re-enacting centuries-old conflicts and proclaiming
the present and future Protestant supremacy in the North. For outsiders, particularly from the South, it seemed a perplexing or offensive
spectacle, briskly dismissed by one aggrieved commentator as "an
uncouth mixture of ignorance, xenophobia, self-deception, suspicion,
rabble-rousing, fear and aggression".

For Protestant children, the Orange Order offered the opportunity
to join the flute and pipe bands and learn a musical instrument. The
nearest lodge to Morrison was the Albertbridge Road Orange Hall in
Templemore Avenue. "They had what they call juveniles, 11–16 or
11–18," Gil Irvine remembers. "We were playing cricket one day and
this man approached and asked us to join the Orange lodge. He was
scouting for members. Some did join, some stayed awhile, and some
didn't. Van didn't." Morrison's demurral was unsurprising. He was
never a great club man of any description. "When I was growing up in
Belfast I was lucky because I knew all kinds of people," he later pointed
out. "I wasn't on any side when I grew up so consequently I never
really thought about it . . . I never had any of the ingrained hatred inside
of me. I was conscious of it in other people, but it was very foreign to
me."

Like everyone else in the community, of course, he was involved in
the festivities celebrating the glorious Twelfth. "We'd go and collect
wood for bonfires in Orangefield," Irvine confirms. It was on the eve
of the Twelfth when youngsters hit the streets in earnest, dismantling
old sheds and carrying creaking wardrobes and woodworm rotted back
doors as the search for kindling intensified. "The whole of our lives
were galvanized to the sacrificial fire," remembers future Beirut hostage
Brian Keenan, a new arrival in Mayflower Street, East Belfast, who was
about to enrol at Orangefield, just as Morrison was preparing to leave.
Keenan enjoyed the primitive rituals of the Eleventh and Twelfth as a
boy, the fierce protection of the stacked pyre from rivals and the daring
swig from a flagon of cider or the illicit drag of a Woodbine cigarette.

"The atmosphere moved swiftly from festive abandon to the hallucinatory," he recalls. "Streets were dark, people were moving towards the burning ground on what must have been rivers of alcohol. From the tiny kitchen houses, record players blared out 'The Sash' and 'The Billy Boys' and all the triumphalist marching tunes we were to witness for real the next morning." Anti-papal slogans filled the air and Catholics living in the area kept a low profile. "Living is the wrong word," Keenan qualifies, "existing might just fit my meaning. I can imagine their fear in that terrifying long night as drunken passers-by hurled abuse and spat at their home . . . a home that for many weeks was a prison to them."

"It was East Belfast," Billy Harrison concludes philosophically. "If you're going to talk Orange and Green, East Belfast was as Orange as anywhere else, but maybe not as openly bigoted. Maybe not as recognized a stronghold as the Shankill or Sandy Row, but Orange, for sure. Marches? Kerb stones? Flags out? Christ, yes! If you didn't put your flag out somebody would put your name in a black book."

Orangefield pupil Eric Bell was also caught up in the spirit of the Twelfth. "All my uncles were in the Orange lodge," he confirms. "They all had a sash and a wooden hammer with an orange ribbon on it and the white gloves. Every year you'd look outside and there was a full size Union Jack flying from every house in our street. We put ours up as well in Jocelyn Street. There were red, white and blue flags flying from my aunt's window across the road. They'd put tables out, have parties in the street and paint the kerb stones red, white and blue."

The provocative kerb stone painting was the most public display of sectarian signposting. According to Gil Irvine, this defiant tradition of territoriality stopped just short of Hyndford Street. "They did that further down the Beersbridge Road," he points out. "Those were harder, tougher places. Although Hyndford Street was only a couple of hundred yards up the road, we thought it was a bit beneath us to do that sort of thing. It was never drummed into us that we had to prove our Protestantism. There were no rows with neighbours or fighting in our street. It was a nice place to live."

Despite the fireworks of the Twelfth, neither Irvine nor Harrison can recall witnessing any serious troubles with Catholics in their area during this period. Some might say this was because they were a cowed and intimidated minority. "There were only a few Catholics in the street," admits Morrison's neighbour Nancy McCarter, "and no Catholic churches nearby." Irvine maintains that religious conflicts never played a part in the cultural life of the street, at least for the children. "We got on very well," he remembers. "It was a subject that was never really raised. You went and played with them if they were there." Perhaps those viewing from the outside inevitably saw matters in a harsher, less charitable light. Gwen Carson, a relocated teenager with an atheistic impatience, felt she had suddenly arrived in an aggressively sectarian Protestant heartland. "I lived in Hyndford Street," she says. "I know what it was like and I remember the way people talked. They never mixed with Catholics in their workplace nor in their daily lives. The one line that people would always give you was 'the Catholics are breeding like rabbits and trying to take away our constitution.' And if you asked them what a constitution was, they never knew."

This was the East Belfast that moulded Morrison – an environment where politics and Protestantism were pervasive. Brethren halls, lodges, Orange parades, evangelical meetings, Presbyterian platitudes and born again testimonies – an entire panoply of religious references crowded his consciousness. Small wonder then that religious imagery and snatches of Protestant vernacular would feature so prominently in his music. There was also the unresolved mystery of his parents' religious viewpoints. According to Morrison, his father showed little or no interest in religion, whereas his mother joined the Jehovah's Witnesses, a fundamentalist sect marked by a fiery evangelism. Her conversion must have had a profound effect on her family but its implications have been consistently understated. For a time, she brought her son to services at the local kingdom hall and he recalls being a little overawed by the intensity of it all. A visit to a faith healing meeting was a complete turn-off for the boy although it must have left a deep impression. How he reacted to Bible study or apocalyptic warnings is not recorded. Looking back, Violet Morrison insists "I brought him up to think for himself – to be a free thinker." Interestingly, Morrison later referred to his mother by the same epithet, adding that religion "was never shoved down my throat, whereas most of the people I grew up with or went to school with, it was really imposed on them. They didn't have any free will." How this can be reconciled with the necessary evangelism of a Jehovah's Witness is both unclear and perplexing. Morrison himself later corrected one writer who suggested that his mother "indulged in doorstep evangelism", but it was a very unusual JW that did not sell the *Watchtower* door to door, or seek to convert the public. Her involvement evidently lasted "a couple of years" and any evangelical fervour was modified by the need to "check things out and read about things". "If my mother had been *very* religious, I doubt whether it would have interested me," Morrison concludes. "I'm more likely to reject things people impose on me." The mother's alignment with the JW movement was, of course, perfectly acceptable in the East Belfast community where religious sects flourished and Presbyterian breakaway groups were frequently forming their own churches. "Protestantism takes in everything," remarks one former resident. "Just *not* to be a Catholic was almost enough for the real adherents. Nobody would have thought very much about a Jehovah's Witness – it wouldn't have been noticed really."

Although the late Fifties was a time of relative peace in Belfast, this did not mean that the streets were safe from sectarianism. Common sense and urban suss were necessary to avoid undesirable confrontations and schoolboy tortures. Eric Bell's journey from Orangefield to his home in Jocelyn Street was fraught with hidden dangers. "If I didn't have my bike I'd have to do a detour past a Catholic chapel," he remembers. "The Orangefield badge was pure orange on a black blazer and you could see it a hundred yards away. If Catholic kids saw me I'd have to walk across the road and put my knapsack over my badge. You'd always get a vibe in Belfast then – nothing amazing like guns and knives – but you could get beaten up. If they got you they'd take you down an alley, take your school books and throw them around, beat you up or take a match, blow it out, then burn your hand and say 'What do you think of King Billy? He's a bastard, isn't he?' "

Morrison also suffered such an encounter which evidently had a marked influence on his outlook. "I saw so many Catholics and Protestants for whom religion was a burden. There was enormous pressure and you had to belong to one or the other communities. Thank God my parents were strong enough not to give in to this pressure . . . I wasn't even aware of religious prejudice until one day a couple of kids I'd never seen before came up to me and two friends and started swinging. They were going around punching out Catholics or Protestants, I forget. It was weird because at the same time we were asking why they were trying to beat on us. They stopped when we said we weren't whoever they thought we were. The whole thing was unreal."

Morrison's anecdote may have been coloured by exaggeration as such mistakes were rarely made. Identifying a Protestant usually only took a matter of seconds. A person's name, address or school were often enough to confirm their denomination. "Catholics all went to schools named after saints and Protestants went to schools named after streets," a Catholic contemporary of Morrison points out. Deceit could be exposed by additional interrogation or slips in vocabulary. Catholics were taught Irish history and spoke of "the six counties", whereas Protestants learned English history, called Northern Ireland "the province" and used the phrase "the mainland" to underline their connection with the Crown. Even when they uttered the prayer common to both communities and all Christians – *The Lord's Prayer/Our Father* – the wording was subtly different with Catholics preferring a "who" rather than "*which* art in heaven" and Protestants adding an extra line, "For thine is the kingdom, the power and the glory", omitted from the RC version. Occasionally, it wasn't even safe in your own community, as Eric Bell discovered after a visit to the cinema. "My local fleapit was the Winkie in Woodstock Road or the Castle Picture House in Castlereagh Road, where Van went as well," he remembers. "At the end of the film, they'd play the *National Anthem* and if you didn't stand for it that meant you were obviously a Catholic. Sometimes though you'd be busting for a piss or need to go home and could edge out if you were in the back row. One night, I did this, but as soon as I got outside four guys called me over. They said, 'Did you just walk out while 'God Save The Queen' was on? What are you?' You could tell by looking at somebody if they were a Protestant – Catholics were rougher looking and generally less well off. When I replied 'Protestant', one of them said, 'Leave him.' Then another interrupted, 'No – fuck him! Listen, mate, you *never* again walk out on the Queen – now fuck off!' That was part and parcel of growing up in Belfast."

Against this backdrop, Morrison was continuing to play low-key gigs while waiting to finish school. Orangefield brought a reassuring, if dull, routine to his daily life without overstretching his intellect or imagination. Above all, it taught him the art of invisibility. Stronger personalities and louder voices fought for attention while he was content to sit in the background, secure and unthreatened in his inner world. Sporadic bursts of animation ensured that he was never ostracized, but the terms of engagement were his alone. While some responded to his behaviour with the hoary maxim "an only child is a *lonely* child," Morrison never accepted that description as an accurate summary of his character. Adjectives like 'shy' or 'reserved' better suited his self-image, while solitude evidently provided empowerment rather than spiritual or emotional poverty – at least from his point of view. He would later express some of those complex feelings obliquely through his songwriting. The lack of pressure to conform meant that he could drift happily, choosing his own moments to connect with teachers or casual companions. It was not a strategy designed to win popularity contests or lifelong friends but ensured his survival in a potentially hostile environment. "There was no school for people like me . . . I educated myself," he later insisted in a forlorn attempt to salvage some merit from academic underachievement and anonymity. Instead of leaving school at Easter, he decided to stay on and complete his Junior Technical Certificate – the lowest qualification available. Several of his contemporaries had already found employment. Billy McAllen was taken on at a builders' merchants before working as a compositor for just under £2 a week; Roy Kane had his grandmother to thank for a £4-a-week start at the Co-op; and George Jones and Blackie (Wesley Black) secured jobs at the Post Office. A work colleague responsible for placing Crown transfers on Royal Mail delivery vans passed on some stickers to Jones. Like loyalists entrusted with a symbol of Her Majesty, they proudly attached the image to the front of Roy Kane's drumkit. Thereafter, they were known as the Monarchs.

THREE

The Monarchs

Billy McAllen's much younger cousin Eric Wrixon saw the Monarchs rehearsing one evening and felt they showed promise. "They were OK," he recalls in measured tones, "a good band, but not a great one." Indeed, throughout their four-year existence, the East Belfast ensemble would be outshone in Ireland by a rival Monarchs established in Limerick by Waterford musicians Ray and Dermot Heraty on 15 May 1960. This showband would remain in existence for the entire decade. Such was the division between the North and the South that both bands could operate in their respective territories without causing confusion. "I can't ever remember playing in the South as the Monarchs," says Roy Kane. "We didn't have the connections. I don't know whether to read anything political into that, but no-one wanted to know Belfast bands."

Gradually, the Monarchs enlivened their stage act with McAllen and Jones playing guitars behind their heads and Morrison frolicking around with the sax. His exuberance was soon attracting attention. "A lot of people thought he was simply mad," says his old friend Gil Irvine. "Obviously, there was, shall we say, some lubrication taken and whether it was overly taken may have been conducive to throwing oneself around." So, Morrison's athletic prowess was not fuelled solely by enthusiasm. By the age of 15, he was drinking wine regularly. Other musicians, like Eric Bell, also indulged, albeit in his later teenage years. "We used to buy this very cheap wine called Mundie's Full Strength South African," he remembers. "This stuff was lethal. It was a very cheap way of getting smashed." Such hedonism may have been prompted by insecurity, stage fright, teenage bravado or a combination of all three, but the Monarchs found it difficult to tolerate. For a brief period, Morrison fell out of favour and was no longer invited to every gig. "George Jones didn't like drinking," McAllen points out. Kane was also concerned about "the wee bit of controversy" concerning Morrison and admitted, "a lot of us weren't that fussy about having him in the band". Pressed on the drinking issue, Kane coyly concluded, "Maybe he needed that to loosen up, but then again some people need more than others and that can lead from one thing to another and over-exuberance turns into recklessness . . . I think it was more a fear of it affecting the gigs than it actually affecting the gigs. Bear in mind, we were still kids working under reasonably puritanical upbringings. This was the start of the Swinging Sixties, but they hadn't actually begun yet."

Morrison's banishment from the Monarchs ultimately worked to his advantage, encouraging him to seek work elsewhere. The most obvious course was to take advantage of the showband boom that was gripping Irish youth culture at the dawn of the Sixties. Its origins could be traced back to the Belfast-based orchestra leader Dave Glover, who coined the term 'showband' in 1955 after injecting a variety routine into his act, complete with onstage dancers. However, it was Strabane's Clipper Carlton who popularized the new format throughout the island. Others, including the Johnny Quigley Band and the Melody Aces soon followed. Their strong visual appeal provided an energetic alternative to the old-fashioned orchestra leaders like the evergreen Mick Delahunty and Gay McIntyre. Canny entrepreneurs and building contractors – most notably future Taoiseach Albert Reynolds and his brother, Jim – saw financial potential in the showband game and constructed ballrooms of romance throughout Ireland. By the end of the Fifties, younger outfits were challenging the Clipper Carlton, spearheaded by Waterford's Royal Showband, who boasted their own chunkier version of Elvis Presley in Brendan Bowyer. Under the astute management of T.J. Byrne, the Royal performed six nights a week to audiences of 2,000 plus and eventually took 60 per cent of the door receipts. Before long, they were wealthy beyond their dreams and they inspired a catalogue of lesser rivals over the next few years, including the Dixies, the Capitol, the Miami, the Freshmen and the Cadets.

Morrison would never join this showband élite but paddled in shallower waters. First there was a spot in the Harry Mack Showband, the Great Eight. It was here that Morrison first encountered the baritone saxophonist Harry Megahey and another brass player whose personality and world view would leave a deep and lasting impression. Years later, Morrison was asked to name his biggest influences and reeled off the usual candidates – Leadbelly, Howlin' Wolf – before suddenly adding, 'G.D.'. The mysterious G.D. was Geordie Sproule, a former shipyard worker, nine years Morrison's senior. As Eric Wrixon candidly notes: "I would honestly say that Geordie Sproule was the one person who overtly influenced him: music, image and attitude. The famous Morrison trick of taking his shoes off on stage, that was something he learned from Geordie Sproule. Lying on his back playing saxophone, some choices of material. The first time he met G.D. was quite an experience for him."

Born in 1936, the youngest of 11 children, George Sproule had felt the bitter deprivation of the hungry Thirties. His father, a painter and decorator, died aged 38, leaving the family destitute. During the worst of times eight of the children had to share a single egg for breakfast, accompanied by a tantalizing lick of a bacon rasher. Sproule's musical education came from his mother serenading the children to sleep at night, accompanying herself on mouth organ. Before long, Geordie appeared on stage at an Orange hall and enjoyed the attention. At the end of the Forties, he teamed up with his talented elder brother James, playing pubs for pints and acting like a Shankill toughie. "We'd go out, sing, have a nosh-up and a fight," Sproule recalls, "then end up invading a carry-out party, do more singing and more fighting. That was the *craic*."

Still a young teenager, Sproule was taken on as a 'catch boy' at Harland & Wolff and worked in the double bottoms of the large vessels. With rats running around his feet, he would sing as loudly as possible, competing with the metal din of the riveters and corkers. At lunchtime, he would socialize with the heater boys, toasting sandwiches on the ship's scorching hotplates and singing to the heavens while his co-workers harmonized like slaves on a chain gang. As his voice grew stronger, he became adept at impressions, expertly mimicking vocalists as varied as Al Jolson, John McCormack, Mario Lanza, Louis Armstrong, Frank Sinatra, Perry Como, Paul Robeson, Eddie Fisher and Sammy Davis Jr.

The post-war slump at Harland & Wolff and the decline of riveting in favour of welding forced Sproule to seek new employment. Now married with a young son, he continued to combine back-breaking work with late night music sessions. "I took on two of the worst jobs you could do, singing in front of an audience and steel racking." Chasing the money, Sproule found short-term contract work in England and Scotland and always remembered to take his guitar. Whether in Edinburgh, Glasgow, Inverness or Strathpeffer, he would invariably approach pub managers after a session with the same cocksure line: "I'm a better singer than him – book me."

Back in Belfast, Sproule appeared in Orange halls, hotels and clubs, singing whatever was required. During the skiffle boom, he teamed up with the Spitfires, entertaining the public on the streets surrounding the Shankill Road. What he enjoyed most were the continuing pub sessions with his brother James. A regular stint at the Duke Inn on the Old Lodge Road was notable for their extraordinary blues improvisations. "We were singing blues in the Fifties before any of them thought about it over here," he brags, "a mile ahead of anyone. When we sang blues, it wasn't taken from any record because we didn't have a radio. It just came from the head. We sang about people we knew but gave them spade names. It was Belfast blues we were singing." The reaction was predictably ambivalent. "We went down a bomb, but what musician would say different? Of course there were guys who'd turn around and say, 'you're crap' – so you'd give them a dig in the gob."

Sproule's steel racking, street scrapping and singing adventures even took him to Germany. After a brief spell in Frankfurt, his work crew were forced to seek assistance from the British Embassy for their fare home. Drunk from whiskey binges, they boarded wrong trains, slept rough and were threatened with arrest, but after an odyssey lasting several days finally reached Liverpool. Faint from hunger, they stumbled into a café, ordered full breakfasts, then did a runner, eventually evading their pursuers by finding sanctuary at a seamen's mission. Still penniless, they masqueraded as porters, sneaked aboard a boat bound for Belfast and arrived home exhausted.

After the showbands emerged to claim Ireland, Sproule was ready, clutching an alto saxophone having taken lessons from John Duncan of the Avonaires. "It was then that I met the wee man," Sproule recollects. "Van was running all over the place with me and Harry Mack. I was a lot older than Van and I think he looked up to me. I was doing a lot of headcase stuff that others weren't doing. I was my own advertisement machine and a face about town."

It is difficult to overestimate the effect that Sproule's presence had on Morrison who was entranced by his offbeat humour, brash devil-may-care exterior and outrageous showmanship. Sproule's stunts included being pushed on stage at the George VI Hall while lying on a brass bed or swaying uneasily on a miniature toy truck, waving to the audience, then unexpectedly eating a banana or raw onion. Reaching the microphone, Sproule would announce, "We're just back from New York," before adding the bathetic one-liner, "the New York Dry Cleaners in Hatters Street." At one show, Morrison was astonished to see Sproule remove his shoes and socks and throw them into the crowd. That particular gimmick had happened spontaneously. "Nobody knew it at the time," Sproule says, "but working on a building site you don't ever want to admit that you've walked on a rusty nail because they'd call you 'nail on the boot'. But that day I'd walked on a nail and it went up through me. I still have the scar. So I just took off my shoes and socks and threw them forward – they never came back." Sproule's presence always ensured that a performance was eventful and he also knew how to enliven a long drive home. "We used to have a race to the next town with other showbands. If they'd got their heads out, somebody would piss on them. It was stupid what we did, but it was good camaraderie."

Although playing music was a pleasure, few of Morrison's contemporaries considered the possibility of transforming this enjoyable pastime into a career. Like every other young school leaver, Morrison was soon encouraged to find a proper job. The Morrisons were a hard-working family and understandably felt that their son needed work experience, preferably a trade. The energetic Violet Morrison had already displayed a certain ingenuity in acquiring unlikely employment as a detective at a C&A department store. In contrast to other burly security officers, she was petite, ferociously alert, fleet of foot and remarkably adept at wandering unnoticed through teeming crowds, spotting suspicious shoppers and petty thieves. Well-liked, she was quick to contact George McDowell in nearby Abetta Parade and recommend her son for a job at the engineering firm Musgrave, which had connections with Orangefield School. McDowell, who was employed as a foreman, agreed to take Morrison on as an apprentice fitter, but it proved an unhappy experience for all. During the brief period he was there, the surly Morrison failed to establish any relationship with his work colleagues and displayed that same infuriating lack of sociability evident from his early adolescence. Later attempts at seeking employment, including a spell working as a cleaner of carcasses at a bacon-curing factory, proved equally unrewarding. Morrison's apparent unwillingness to knuckle down to the rigours of an apprenticeship was not unusual among the free-spirited youth of the early Sixties. Increased employment in the commercial sector meant that it was relatively easy to drift from job to job without the fear of a permanent place on the dole queue.

Morrison's Belfast contemporary Eric Bell was pursuing an uncannily similar path in which musical passion was threatening to overcome good sense. Like Morrison, Bell had formed an instrumental group, the Atlantics, which included schoolmates Rodney Howes and Tom Patterson. They too had performed at Orangefield. Bell subsequently played in several different groups over successive months while working in a garage as an apprentice motor mechanic. Civil war broke out in his household when he announced that he was packing it in. Echoing Morrison's adolescent isolation and immersion in music, he retreated to his bedroom and lost himself in the blues. "The music was so earthy, it depressed me," he remembers. "I'd put on blues records late at night, draw the curtains and the room would be in darkness except for the red light on the record player." Often, Bell's sole companion was a bottle of Mundie's red wine. Increasingly withdrawn, he eventually ceased going out during evenings or weekends and spent endless hours perfecting his guitar technique. "I learned more in those eight months than at any time in my life." Seeking casual work that would leave him free time to play, Bell drifted through a series of jobs, most notably as a lamplighter and window cleaner.

The secret benefits of window cleaning had also been brought to Morrison's attention by the ever industrious Geordie Sproule. As soon as a steel racking contract ended, G.D. would offer his services as a handyman in order to support his family. Improbably, he began cleaning windows in the company of a friend with a missing hand. The amputee was unable to climb ladders with a bucket and chamois, so Sproule came up with a workable system. "He couldn't do the top windows, so I did those and he'd do the bottoms. I used to wear this big, long leather coat everywhere. The hardest part of the job was carrying the ladders. They were big wooden jobs." When the cleaning round expanded, Sproule suggested Morrison should join in. "I set it up," he insists. "I said, 'There's a job window cleaning, do you fancy it?' He said he'd do it. He'd been an apprentice fitter and never liked it." Morrison soon learned that the job was not entirely free of danger. After a hard night's boozing, Sproule was cleaning some first-floor windows when he allowed himself to be distracted. Leaning too far across a window ledge he slipped and plummeted to the ground. "I'd had a late night. The next thing I knew I was picking myself up off the ground." His one-handed assistant was amazed when Sproule scrambled to his feet and insisted on completing the job. Years earlier he had fallen 50 feet while steel erecting and his colleagues had forced him back up the ladder immediately to conquer any fear of heights. His lucky escapes merely added to his legend.

When a new steel contract came his way, Sproule abandoned his ladder and bucket, but Morrison continued with the round, working with various locals, including Billy McAllen and Sammy Woodburn. The latter was later immortalized in the song 'Cleaning Windows' in which Morrison vividly recalled his days as a working man, scoffing Paris buns, smoking Woodbines, listening to Blind Lemon Jefferson and reading the beat novels of Kerouac. There was even a closing reference to the Belfast tradition of leaving a 3d bit in the window sill for the cleaner.

Sproule's friendship with Morrison continued throughout this period and for a time they seemed inseparable. On stage, they developed some amusing routines, banging their saxophones together in unison and performing goonish stunts. Sproule effortlessly brought out Morrison's better humour by sharing silly jokes, dry wit and red wine. "There was always a bottle of hooch in the saxophone case," Sproule points out. "A bottle of old wine. Mundie's. Red biddy. I drank QC and old scrumpy from the Spanish Rooms. I slept in Van's house a couple of times with the drink and all in me. Lovely people.

The mother wanted the best for her son and the father was pretty quiet and a gentleman who treated me with great respect, as did the uncles. Van seemed to be thinking the same things I did. He seemed a cut-down version of me, a younger version."

Morrison was not usually an impressionable person, but several people noticed how much he appeared to model himself on Sproule. They shared a similar gait and facial expression, with Morrison even adopting Sproule's familiar tilt of the head in conversation. "That was the hard man look," says G.D. "A lot of those mannerisms happened from the environment you came from." Sproule's other great merit was a total obliviousness to Morrison's shyness, unsociability and darker moods. "Geordie was a character," remembers fellow musician Rod Demick. "There were a lot of people like that in Belfast then who were larger than life. They almost spoke their own language and had a unique sense of humour. Van was very quiet, very insular and didn't mix well with people. But all this just passed over Geordie. If you mentioned it, he'd say, 'What are you talking about? What's the matter with him?'"

Sproule's exhibitionism and cocksure confidence was evident to all, but it served to mask insecurities about his own worth as a performer in a Sixties pop world in which looks and image were becoming paramount. "Me and Van were the ugly ones, but we had talent. I felt I was a better singer than most of them. I had an ego trip walking on the stage. Nobody frightened me. But the looks later sold most of these guys. If I'd have been good looking, I'd have been up there. My voice was good and if you'd put a big sheet in front of me, they'd have said, 'This guy's not bad!' I'd say I had more confidence than Van but I was tied down being married, whereas he could take a chance. Van worked his dues. I've got respect for him. He worked very hard and he was always trying to learn. He would listen and then maybe he'd use something later. He learned through daftness too. Like everything else it was trial and error."

The point about disguising plain looks and lack of stature through onstage exhibitionism was not lost on Morrison and neither was Sproule's unfortunate distrust of managers, agents and entrepreneurs. Hearty, zany and outgoing among fellow musicians, Sproule also had a truculent streak and a quick temper. "I didn't trust enough," he admits.

"I was brought up to be suspicious of everybody from the point of view of perverts, fly men and dirt birds. I was brought up in that environment and always questioned what they wanted." Sproule's caution may have sounded sensible and streetwise but it could also be self-defeating. After one show an agent approached Sproule and was bluntly told, "Decorate the table." The puzzled entrepreneur returned with some drinks, span his spiel, then suffered sudden humiliation when G.D. poured a pint over his head. On another occasion, somebody produced a contract for Sproule to sign but he tore it up in indignant, petulant exasperation.

Such stories were no doubt amusing to Morrison but reinforced negative images of the music business which would endure. Like Morrison, Sproule also displayed a worrying tendency to remember old grudges, even when he might have been the one at fault. Recalling his break from Harry Mack's showband, he made an unflattering remark about the talented band leader, adding with see-sawing contradiction, "I never liked him, but he was all right. But he did the dirty on me. It was the story of my life. I didn't have money to lift the amplifiers out of the pawn shop. Van and him just drove off and left me sitting in the house and I really needed the rent. I think, to be honest with you, they'd use you as a human being. Mack would and even Van to a certain extent. Van would have used you. But for all that there, I liked him. He was just like a kid brother to me."

The kid brother's experience was growing steadily. Morrison's window-cleaning exploits afforded him the opportunity to play in different bands on a freelance basis. Partly thanks to Sproule's connections, he appeared briefly in the prestigious Avonaires, but they promptly let him go. Another short-lived venture was a spot in the Olympics, a precusor of the Regency Showband. Their saxophonist Phil Denver, formerly of the Great Eight, had broken his wrist and was incapacitated for a month. Group leader Harry Baird and manager Tommy Bodel desperately needed a substitute at short notice and were relieved when Denver recommended Morrison who agreed to the temporary arrangement.

The Olympics were then a semi-pro band on roughly the same level as the Monarchs, with a regular itinerary of dances, Orange and parochial hall dates within easy reach of Belfast. Although one of the better bands on the local circuit, they too seemed trapped in the insular world of small-time gigs and low aspirations. "I was serving my time as a spark," says Baird. "We saw playing as a bit of fun, getting out as young fellows, doing what we wanted. It was a hobby for a few quid." One way of transforming their lives as fee-earning musicians would have been to secure a sizeable following down South, but as they quickly realized there was no easy way of competing with such giants as the Miami and the Royal Showband. "The showbands in the South knew what they were doing," Baird points out. "They were totally geared up to be an industry down there. When you consider the people that made the suits, did the photographs and publicity, it *was* an industry. I don't think we realized that or needed it as much." Old prejudices, cultural stereotyping, suspicion and a dash of sectarianism also precluded any serious attempts to challenge this great divide. "It was very difficult for a Belfast band to break into the South," Baird insists. "People in the South considered people from the North to be a different breed. 'They're from the Black North' – that's how they think of it. They don't appreciate that we're a different type of people. You never got, 'Oh they're from Belfast – isn't that great?' It was always 'Jesus Christ, they're from *Belfast* – they've got two horns.' That was the feeling I always got."

The culture clash was not entirely one-sided. Southern showbands, even those as popular as the Royal, sometimes had to take account of local differences. "One of the funniest things was when the Royal Showband played the Ulster Hall," recalls a Belfast resident of the time. "Singer Brendan Bowyer decided to sing 'Ave Maria' and said, 'No dancing.' Of course, the Catholics all stopped and moved off the floor because it was deemed sacrilegious to dance to 'Ave Maria', especially when leaning against a bird. But the Prods all got up and they got the birds. They were groping them and basically giving two fingers, as if to say, 'How dare you come up here and sing that?' So there were divisions, even with the music. That was the only time I ever saw sectarianism at a dance – with the Royal Showband!"

Van Morrison suffered a similarly rude awakening with the Olympics. What they offered him was quick money, experience and a rather unedifying Friday night gig at a parochial hall on the Neilsbrook estate in Randalstown, Co. Tyrone. "It was a five-hour show in the wilds," Baird remembers, "a notorious culchie gig with real farmers that came straight out of the fields with shit on their boots. One of our singers wasn't too well so we were already struggling. Van was blowing and doing his best, then halfway through the night someone said to him, 'Can you sing?'" Morrison nodded gratefully, then took the microphone for a frantic rendition of 'Blue Suede Shoes'. "The whole hall came to a standstill," Baird continues. "Everybody looked up because they'd never heard anything like it. We'd been doing country 'n' western to suit these people and give them what they wanted. Now Van was freaking out and all the hall stopped. I thought, 'This guy has some nerve.' I was band leader so I walked over to take a look at him and his eyes were bulging like organ stops. I'd never seen anything like this before in our world. Anyway, we didn't let him sing anymore."

The remainder of Morrison's stay in the band passed without incident but ended on a frosty note following a Sunday show at the Borderland Ballroom in Muff, near Derry. Since it was a long drive, the band usually made a fun day of the trip, meeting other musicians, playing a game of football and enjoying a meal before turning up refreshed to perform at 9pm. Presumably, nobody had briefed Morrison on the need to be ready to leave at noon. At the appointed hour, singer Alfie Walsh drove the wagon into Hyndford Street, parked alongside number 125 and knocked on the door. After a brief communication with Violet Morrison, he returned to the minibus shaking his head in disbelief. "Yer man can't play," Walsh told his colleagues, "his mammy says he's not coming out." At first they assumed Morrison must be sick or injured until Walsh, barely able to suppress a smile, revealed: "No, his mammy says he's not sick – he's upstairs in his room writing poetry." The exasperated Baird then bolted from the front seat, scurried around the gravelled road for a handful of pebbles and threw them at Morrison's bedroom window until he responded. Eventually, he was coaxed from his poetic doodlings, informed of the impending show and quietly ushered into the bus. It was not a pleasant day. As Baird candidly concludes: "We did the gig at Borderland, came home around 3am and I told him, 'We won't need your services anymore.' I couldn't be bothered with guys like that. I considered Van a total lunatic, an idiot and a weirdo and I had no time for the guy at all."

Perhaps one reason for Morrison's uproarious behaviour, drinking spells and self-absorption was that he was a young man in pain. It was over the Christmas period of 1961 that he suffered a bereavement which was to leave a lasting mark. His favourite cousin Gloria had been severely ill with cancer and was now in the Royal Victoria Hospital. On 28 December, while everyone was still in festive spirit, she died from "carcinoma of the jejunum due to ulcerative colitis". She was only 29. Her husband Thomas, now working as an electric welder, registered the death that same day. Although she had been diagnosed with cancer some time before, the death came as a great shock to the family. Her grandmother Alice Stitt was particularly upset and learned of the death while enduring a bout of chronic bronchitis. Exactly one week later on 5 January 1962, she died suddenly at her home in Lamar Street from a brain haemorrhage due to auricular fibrillation. She was 72. Apart from his mother, these two women – Gloria Gordon and Alice Stitt – were the closest female relatives Morrison had during his childhood and adolescence. They had been his babysitters and had offered unconditional support and familial friendship to the young boy. When he later sang 'Gloria' it was surely memories of such touching, reassuring moments that made him chant "Lord, she makes me feel all right". Now, within the space of a week, both were gone. For the 16-year-old, it was a salutary introduction to an adult world in which the idyllic pastimes, later lovingly recalled in 'Cleaning Windows', were already memories from a better place, briefly enjoyed some months before, but now poignantly distant.

Morrison no doubt needed some healing at the beginning of 1962. His unhappy encounters convinced him that it would be a good idea to be among friendlier faces. He missed the easygoing Monarchs and regretted their falling out over his drinking. Confused and dejected, he decided to seek the counsel of Mrs Jones, who had always been a sympathetic figure. "Totally out of the blue he came to my house," George Jones recalls. "My mother was very fond of Van and said 'Come in son, what's the problem?' He told her he wanted to come back into the group but he didn't know how to go about it." Mrs Jones offered some kind words and cups of tea and ensured he stayed until her son and Billy McAllen reappeared. As they entered the kitchen, Morrison muttered, "Will you let me back into the group?" assisted by Mrs Jones's reassuring refrain, "He's a nice wee lad, give him another chance." Now that Morrison had promised to curb his drinking, there was no longer any reason to leave him out of the band. His re-emergence was timely as the Monarchs were about to evolve into a fully fledged showband. As Morrison had already discovered, promoters were uninterested in Shadows-style instrumental groups and many demanded a horn section to please the legions of dancers flocking to newly-built halls. The Monarchs initially attempted to improve their sound by recruiting bass player Noel Clyde, who looked resplendent in suit and cuban heels. Clyde knew a number of brass players in South Belfast and before long the Monarchs added Ronnie Osbourne (trombone), Leslie Holmes (trumpet), Davy Bell (saxophone), plus vocalist Jimmy Law. "We were never going to get big gigs without the brass," says Roy Kane. "We'd practise a song for one night and on the next we'd perfect the steps. It may sound stupid but as much time was spent on the choreography as the songs."

At first, the Monarchs continued to play tough venues like Thompson's Restaurant and the Willowfield Orange Hall but Jimmy Law, who worked for British European Airways, provided new contacts and expanded their itinerary. However, even his organizational skills could not secure them a booking south of the border. Like their rivals in Belfast, the Monarchs tailored a set which was dominated by the hits of the day. Lead vocalist Jimmy Law specialized in mellow ballads from such housewife heartthrobs as Craig Douglas, Johnny Tillotson and Bobby Vinton; Wesley Black was the featured player on Johnny And The Hurricanes numbers, and Morrison revealed an unexpected comedic appeal worthy of G.D. on Neil Sedaka's 'I Go Ape'. "Van liked a good laugh," George Jones reminisces. "A lot of showbands were doing comedy. Ours was more spontaneous. We used to do the Coasters' 'Yakety Yak'. He'd dress up as a caveman and start jumping over tables. At first we did prerehearsed comedy, 'Along Came Jones', two saxes, each guy doing the same movements. Then it became spur of the moment." Kane noticed that whenever the chubby Morrison rolled around the floor, the intense pressure of his outstretched legs threatened to loosen the zip of his trousers. They egged him on constantly in the vain hope that something embarrassing might occur. "He used to get into a frenzy which we encouraged for a laugh," says Kane. "He used to crawl under Billy or George's legs, then jump up on someone's shoulders – it was just a bit of *craic*."

Morrison's confidence seemed sky high and he enjoyed adding little touches to the Monarchs' set such as the blues instrumental passage on their cover of Bobby Darin's 'Things'. It was around this time that he wrote his first song, the country-tinged 'I Think I'm In Love With You'. Billy McAllen was spending more time than ever at 125 Hyndford Street and proved the perfect sounding board for Morrison who acted out his fantasies as both a bluesman and an evangelical disc jockey. "The mother and father were at work all day so we'd listen to records and try to copy them," McAllen remembers. "I would get the chords off the record and we even tried to write something. We were just messing about. Van knew what he liked. He'd say, 'Wait till you hear this one' and play a record. I remember one in particular that we decided to do on stage – 'Turn On Your Lovelight'. No-one had heard of it, but it had a great feel and used to drive everyone along."

By the summer of 1962, the Monarchs had a promising repertoire with a few surprises, but it was still mainly showband fare. "The punters here didn't want anything else," McAllen complains. "It was a load of crap but you got paid a few quid for playing and that was it. We were just like mercenaries." They also dressed the part in smart, silver suits. After Noel Clyde moved on, the nine-piece unit trudged down to Jackson's tailors in Donegall Street and purchased some shocking pink jackets, offset by Jimmy Law in canary yellow. In promotional photos of the period Morrison had even mastered the art of the showbiz smile. He was reliable in his professional commitments but sometimes slow to emerge from his bedroom. "I'd call for him to hurry," Roy Kane remembers. "I've got this feeling of unpunctuality with Van – he was that type of person, not very together. I seem to remember that if we were going anywhere you always had to remind him, wake him up or call for him."

FOUR

Germany Calling

At the beginning of 1963, the Monarchs were still playing the local circuit, seemingly content with their lot but burdened by the most severe winter on record since 1740. A blanket of deep snow stretched disconcertingly across Britain and Ireland, driven by blinding blizzards and numbing temperatures which had already succeeded in freezing rivers, demobilizing public transport, escalating the instances of hypothermia among the poor, aged and infirm, and encouraging eccentric religious prophets and failed meteorologists to herald the arrival of an apocalyptic Ice Age. In popular music, the incongruously titled *Summer Holiday* reminded cinema audiences of warmer times while one of its many songs, 'Foot Tapper', provided the Shadows with their final number 1 hit; they were unaware that the instrumentals which had kept their career afloat since 1960 and inspired hundreds of groups like the Thunderbolts and the Monarchs were about to be superceded by a new phenomenon. An impressionable young audience, barricaded in their homes by the weather, witnessed four, young, mop-haired musicians whose chirpy effervescence and melodic infectiousness rendered the climate irrelevant. Thereafter, the Beatles would change everything in pop music and fashion, spearheading a year which was later celebrated as marking the apotheosis of the British teenager.

As spring approached great changes were taking place in Northern Ireland. On 25 March 1963, 75-year-old Lord Brookeborough (Basil Brooke), who had once boasted proudly of never having employed a single Catholic during his premiership, was succeeded as Prime Minister by Captain Terence O'Neill. The new leader of the Unionist Party was of solid, Protestant stock from a family with historical connections to the

Red Hand of Ulster. His father had drilled in the Ulster Volunteer Force and was the first Member of Parliament to be killed in action during the First World War. O'Neill was himself a member of the Orange Order but a committed modernist who promised liberal reforms and foreign investment for Belfast's ailing industries.

O'Neill's dream of a new tolerant Northern Ireland was tested early in his premiership. On 3 June, the reformist Pope John XXIII died at the age of 81. The most revered Pope of the century, his demise inspired tributes throughout the world and particularly in Ireland where his photograph would remain on display in Catholic households for a generation and more. Northern Ireland journalists noted incredulously that his death was privately mourned even in some liberal Protestant homes where acknowledging the papacy had previously been synonymous with apostasy. O'Neill joined several Protestant leaders in sending a letter of condolence and allowed the Union Jack to be flown at half-mast. In East Belfast, Ian Paisley was quick to respond. During a rally at the Ulster Hall, he condemned O'Neill and his cohorts as "the Iscariots of Ulster" and, referring to the Pope's death, assured his followers that "this Romish man of sin is now in Hell". Thereafter, he led supporters on an illegal march to City Hall for which he received a salutary fine of £10.

While Paisley denounced Rome, the Monarchs set their sights on new adventures. Their career direction shifted abruptly after they encountered some visiting Scottish musicians one of whom, Bill Carson, briefly took over the bassist position left by Noel Clyde. A more palpable driving force was singer George Hethrington, a brash young Scot and devotee of Ray Charles. Morrison was impressed by his vocal pedigree and soulful musical tastes and the others listened with varying degrees of attention to his pep talks and advice about breaking free from Northern Ireland.

Hethrington had a plan. In return for a lead vocal spot in the band, he promised to introduce them to his manager Frank Cunningham and arrange a six-week tour of Scotland. After conquering his home country, they could descend in triumph on London and seek some exotic dates on the Continent. No longer mere Monarchs, they could then call themselves the International Monarchs. It all sounded terribly exciting to the starry-eyed Billy McAllen who was among the first to agree to the scheme. Waltzing into his parents' house one afternoon, he proudly informed his mother, "I'm packing my job in, I'm going to be a professional musician." Mrs McAllen was too shocked to give a coherent reply. She was not alone. Over the next few days several other parents were confronted by equally rebellious boasts. The protective Violet Morrison was profoundly concerned about her precious boy leaving the country and spent the best part of a week warning him of the dangers of life on the road. "I tried to tell him that it was a very hard life and about the jealousies that go on and the badness . . . but nothing would put him off. You couldn't deter him at all. He was still determined to go, so his father and I talked it over and we decided to let him go. It would either kill him or cure him." Morrison was pleased to receive their reluctant blessing. "We all had great ideas about being big time," McAllen beams, "all kids have."

Alas, McAllen's illusions were not shared by everyone in the band. Roy Kane dismissed the entire enterprise as a "crackpot idea" and pointed out that he had no wish to risk his safe and lucrative job at the Co-op in the pursuit of Scottish rainbows. The brass section were equally sceptical, so suddenly the Monarchs were down to five – Morrison, McAllen, Jones and Blackie, with Hethrington installed as lead singer. In order to bolster the line-up, Morrison turned to Harry Mack, the baritone saxophonist and multi-instrumentalist from the Great Eight, who promised to lead the expedition in his minibus.

The grand summer odyssey to Scotland was no feast of cakes and ale. Manager Frank Cunningham was not the great entrepreneur they had imagined but a small-time booker with limited resources. They spent much time at his home on a council estate in the Pollok district of Glasgow, half-heartedly rehearsing in the garden while curious children and querulous shoppers stared, mocked or encouraged their endeavours. An urgent need for a drummer was answered when Hethrington introduced them to former bandmate Lawrie McQueen, a burly 6'2" docker with a handsome quiff, an intimidating stare and a seaman's love for hard liquor. The septet finally hit the road for a fractured series of gigs, which included a spa in Strathpeffer and a performance somewhere in the Highlands that threatened to leave them lost and penniless. Petrol money consumed their meagre funds and they became more ravenous, sweaty and crotchety with each passing hour. "I remember driving through the Highlands and it was a really hot summer," McAllen relates. "It was so warm, we stopped at the side of a road, went down to a bank amongst the trees and there was a big pool with a waterfall, so we all stripped off. Then we picked up some girls. I think they were Chinese – they made us this egg soup meal with water from the stream."

Such simple pleasures left them refreshed and optimistic. Soon they secured several dates, including a support slot to Don Charles, a minor league singer who had previously enjoyed a couple of low charting hits, 'The Hermit Of Misty Mountain' and 'Walk With Me My Angel'. At one date, they were even afforded the unprecedented luxury of a booking at a plush 300-room hotel. It was so exciting that Morrison regressed into childhood fantasies, re-enacting celluloid Wild West adventures with his hombre George Jones. "At 4am, Van and I were playing Cowboys and Indians up and down the long corridors," Jones laughs. "The manager happened to walk around the door of one of the bedrooms and Van, myself and one of the other guys were in our Y-fronts. We thought he was one of the group, so we ambushed him. Needless to say, we got chucked out. Before the police came Van and I made an exit out of the back window of the hotel, clutching our suitcases."

After their closing date at the spacious Beach Ballroom, Aberdeen, they had saved enough money to finance a trip to London in search of greater glories. Mack and McAllen drove the Austin minibus through the night, stopping only for a toilet break and a fish and chip supper. They arrived in London, bleary-eyed and uncertain how to proceed. Most of the time they hung around Soho, forlornly hoping that something would happen. Within days their money had dwindled to a pittance and they were reduced to sleeping in the crowded minibus while suffering harassment from patrolling policemen. Moving constantly from one car park to another was a depressing experience, but there were some moments of comic relief that lightened their spirits. One night they were driving around central London in the midst of a summer fog seeking a parking space. Weary, impatient and frustrated, they eventually spotted a sign directing them to a subterranean car park. Safe and snug on a summer's night, they stripped to their underwear, lining their shoes and socks along the roof of the wagon. They were a gross spectacle, unwashed and stinking to high heaven. The Scottish giant Lawrie McQueen slept with his feet protruding through the vehicle's side door while Morrison wisely decided to sleep beneath the minibus. Early the next morning, they were woken by the deafening sound of a gong. Scrambling out of the van, the Monarchs found themselves surrounded by Rolls Royces, Jaguars, Daimlers and important-looking gentlemen in bowler hats and pin stripe suits, carrying briefcases and exclaiming in posh voices "Good Lord, what is *that*?" Unwittingly, they had spent the night in the peers' car park at the House of Lords. The ensuing panic was reminiscent of a Keystone Cops sketch. Revving up the wagon, they drove off pursued by the near naked Morrison who was clinging to a blanket while their shoes and socks were strewn across the car park.

Surviving in London was soon proving a nightmare. At one point they attempted to win a residency at an exclusive club with a frenzied audition, but the haughty proprietor told them they lacked class and objected to their dishevelled appearance. Reduced to a diet of drinking chocolate, they were close to conceding defeat and returning to Belfast. Morrison, however, was spared some hunger pangs when he received a small sum of money from home. He immediately treated himself to a slap-up breakfast. Tellingly, none of his bandmates was invited along. They required a more accommodating angel of mercy.

A propitious reunion with singer Don Charles resulted in a dramatic change of fortune. He took pity on the boys, offered them money and food, dry cleaned their shabby suits and even arranged a photo session in Regent's Park. The newly-spruced showband were next taken to Ruby Bard, then manager of Kenny Ball, the Temperance Seven and several other trad jazz ensembles. "We booked them into a few Irish dance halls," she says of the Monarchs. "They weren't an easy band to deal with – they were a right bunch of tearaways." After appearing at some British US bases, the Monarchs expressed an interest in visiting Germany so Bard arranged an audition at the Flamingo Club where her latest clients Georgie Fame & The Blue Flames had a residency. "I dealt with a German promoter who booked a few of my jazz bands and he decided to take the Monarchs following an audition. It was good experience for any young group to play Germany at that time. They'd have to develop their set in order to survive."

For many young musicians of the era, the German experience was a thrilling rite of passage that offered unspeakably illicit and dangerous delights. At this time London's Soho was still perceived as the ultimate emporium of exotica by starstruck teenagers in excited search of coffee bar pop fame or sly glimpses of disrobed showgirls. Few could have imagined what awaited them in the more permissive cities of West Germany where an influx of American servicemen had transformed the sex and entertainment industries. Soda bars and hamburger joints were augmented by strip clubs whose censor-free displays titillated the debauched and pornographic fantasies of an already unshockable clientele. In the Grosse Freiheit, the notorious cabaret district of the Hamburg Reeperbahn, almost every conceivable and aberrant taste was catered for. As the sex club wars intensified, competitive proprietors introduced mud-stained women wrestlers and showed hard-core sexual acts involving pythons, dogs and donkeys. On these same neon-lit strips were cellars blaring live music. The publicity surrounding Elvis Presley's arrival in 1958 had not gone unnoticed in German clubland and impresarios were eager to entice rock 'n' roll acts from Britain's major cities. Bruno Koschmider, owner of Hamburg's Kaiserkeller, had already signed up beat groups like Derry Wilkie & The Seniors and the Beatles as early as 1960. Such was the enormous appeal of Merseyside's embryonic beat merchants that clubs in other cities began to offer residencies to R&B ensembles, jazz musicians, showbands and any other artistes that could provide cheap entertainment and survive marathon, stamina-sapping performances. The excited Monarchs learned that their destination was not to be wicked Hamburg. What awaited them was a more restrained but nevertheless thrilling tour of Heidelberg, Frankfurt and Cologne.

Prior to their departure, the International Monarchs had to over-come a bureaucratic hurdle. Since Morrison was still a few weeks short of his eighteenth birthday, the band were obliged to sign a surety on his behalf and gain special permission from the British Embassy before he was allowed to work in Germany. They also had to surmount the reservations of the ever protective Violet Morrison who was extremely concerned about allowing her innocent son to taste the forbidden fruits of a country whose language he did not even understand. "He said he wanted to go to Germany – well, he was still a boy," she exclaims. Unswayed by the band's enthusiasm, the doting mother again attempted to persuade her son to abandon the idea. When that failed, she conducted her own investigation before satisfying herself that the agent was a reputable person. "We had a friend in the police and he made enquiries for us. He made sure everything was above board. We got a copy of the contract. His pay was to be around £42 a week which seemed to us good money for a boy. I advised him what to do with the money, to put some by and so on – and he agreed."

The International Monarchs travelled by train to Dover, boarded a ferry to Calais, then journeyed by rail across Europe, finally negotiating their way to the Odeon Keller in Heidelberg where they were booked to play from 8pm to 3am, seven nights a week, with two matinees over weekends, for a month. After inspecting the cellar where they would perform, they were directed to their rooms on the first floor, adjacent to a cinema whose soundtrack would constantly interrupt their sleep. Upstairs was a solitary bathroom. The seven shared two twin bedrooms, with Billy McAllen acquiring a special privilege: "I was the guy with the single room, so if the boys were picking up a bird I used to charge them for using my room. There were prostitutes in the room next to me. I'd be half asleep and you'd hear the Americans bargaining with the birds for a price. There were strip clubs too. We were local boys from Belfast, so this was unbelievable."

Sex and violence were par for the course in the local clubs and amid the throng of prostitutes, pimps, soldiers and gangsters were a drunk and disorderly clientele prone to spontaneous combustion. "The Germans didn't like the Americans much, so you were always assured a big punch-up," George Jones recalls. Another facet of exoticism was the presence of free-spending black servicemen, a thrilling revelation to Morrison who became uncharacteristically animated in their presence. He vividly recalls befriending a GI who introduced him to the sounds of Bobby Bland. Morrison was familiar with Bland's 'Turn On Your Lovelight', a Monarchs favourite, but was astonished to hear other great songs by the performer, plus a treasure trove of R&B gems. "I don't like talking in biblical terms, but it was like the road to Damascus," Morrison enthuses. "I really wanted to do songs like these." Such was Morrison's confidence that he started playing harmonica on stage for the first time during a rendition of Sonny Boy Williamson's 'Elevate Me Mama'. "That was where Van became the basis of what he is today," Jones adds. "For the first time in his life he met American coloured GIs who dug soul, blues and all the music he was weaned on. Van drifted away every day to get near coloured guys who talked the same language as him – 'Yeah, man, it's crazy, let's dig it' – all that caper. He suddenly became a big influence on the Monarchs. We started to play all this soul music and we began to like it. Van really achieved a childhood ambition by playing for coloured guys."

With resident Ray Charles fanatic George Hethrington also pushing for a more soulful direction, the Monarchs abandoned their suits, began dressing casually on stage and performed lengthy versions of 'What'd I Say', 'Sticks And Stones' and 'Turn On Your Lovelight'. Occasionally they were joined by Booker T.-style keyboardist Jim Storey and Jim James, a powerful black R&B vocalist whose contribution added grit and a touch of drama to their spirited repertoire. Morrison, who had never been seriously considered as a lead singer, was slowly finding a place for his blues excursions. Nicknamed Duff by the band, he was given a more flattering, if condescending, nomenclature by his black friends: 'the Little White Negro'.

On 31 August 1963, the band organized a surprise party to celebrate Morrison's 18th birthday. Their exuberant stage show was preceded by a zany ritual in which Lawrie McQueen was lifted on to their shoulders and carried forward like a corpse in a coffin. It was an exciting time for Morrison who frequently found himself in the right company at the right time. At one point, he was even invited to appear as an extra in a German television movie, *Glide*.

Morrison was not the only Monarch transformed by Germany. Wesley Black, their own wild Jerry Lee Lewis pianist, suddenly became the object of female attention. His ever present smile and sad, expressive eyes melted hearts while his mischievous personality endeared him to the band. Blackie was the magpie of the group, always on the lookout for a useful item to complement their sparse household inventory. One night while walking through a street near the Odeon Keller, he spotted a smoothing iron resting on a window sill. "We need one of those for the room," he exclaimed. In a flash, he spirited the iron beneath his open coat and walked briskly back to the club. On another occasion, he appeared astride a 'borrowed' motor scooter, much to his fellow Monarchs' amazement.

The Monarchs' popularity at the Odeon Keller prompted the proprietor to offer them an additional month's work. They referred him to Ruby Bard back in London who agreed to a four-week extension of the contract after rearranging their dates in Frankfurt and Cologne. Midway through the second month in Heidelberg, their easygoing camaraderie was spoiled by bitter dissent in the ranks. The hard-drinking Scottish musicians were reprimanded by the bossy George Jones and did not take kindly to his killjoy attitude. After a heated argument, they were ignominiously sacked. McQueen was so infuriated that he wrecked his room, leaving Jones in fear of a retaliatory beating.

With commitments to fulfil, the Monarchs sent out a distress call to Belfast for replacements. Drummer Oliver Trimble from the King Oliver Showband was the first to respond, but they still needed some- one else to cover the vocal gap left by Hethrington. A message was passed on to erstwhile Monarch Roy Kane, who had previously dismissed their odyssey as madness. Seduced by their exaggerated boasts of minor stardom in Germany, he now reconsidered. "I'd had a row with my boss at the Co-op, so I thought, 'To hell with it, I'll go to Germany.' They asked me to come over to do the singing and to bring a snare drum as yer man Trimble had broken his one." Their need was urgent enough for Kane to be flown to Frankfurt on 25 September where he was collected by a German driver and taken direct to Heidelberg to appear at the Odeon Keller that very evening. As he entered the cellar, five figures jumped on him from the shadows. "The boys scared the devil out of me," he laughs. For most of their long set, Kane was neurotically removing imaginary fluff from his jacket having never previously encountered ultraviolet lighting. Relaxing afterwards, he questioned them about their recent adventures. "It was only after the gig that I learned all the hassles they'd been having with the Scottish boys, and all the fights and threatening. They were over the top with drinking and George Jones had wanted them out and eventually got his way. They were still hanging about though and they were trying to get back in the band. There were some near misses that I didn't want to get involved in. It wasn't until we cleared from Heidelberg that they disappeared from the scene." At the end of an exhausting evening, Kane was directed to his bed. He was alarmed to discover a bottle protruding from the headboard and was told it had been lodged there by Lawrie McQueen who had been drunkenly aiming for George Jones' head.

In spite of the recent friction, the Monarchs were still sorry to be leaving Heidelberg. On their final date, there was an emotional farewell from the girls they had met and a last drink with their GI friends who duly sold them a large quantity of cut-price American cigarettes. The next morning the Monarchs took their equipment to the railway station in Heidelberg, then found themselves with time to kill. "We sat on top of our amplifiers, made a little table from one of the speakers and played cards," McAllen remembers. "We were betting with packets of cigarettes. There was a guy there with a cine-camera who thought this was great and he started to film us." The Monarchs then boarded a train to Cologne. Upon arrival, they hailed a taxi and headed for the Storyville jazz club. They had already carted their equipment down to the cellar and onto the stage when the harried club manager rushed forward asking them: "What do you think you're doing?" The revelation that they were "the International Monarchs from Belfast" prompted further exasperation. "No, no, you don't play here!" he shouted. "It was the wrong place," McAllen recounts. "We should have gone to Frankfurt not Cologne. We'd got mixed up."

After a frantic rush, they finally arrived at Frankfurt's Storyville very late that evening. The club was already packed and the manager berated them for their unpunctuality as they sheepishly set up their equipment. Following a troubled start, they discovered that Frankfurt was the equal of Heidelberg in terms of exhilaration. Black American servicemen were once more in evidence along with a cavalcade of showgirls. "We had dancing girls in the next room," McAllen recalls. "I don't think they were strippers but they were always inviting us to this club where they worked. They were friendly girls." Unfortunately, the band were too tired after finishing work to sample what remained of the night life and their flirtation with the dancers did not extend beyond some playful experiments with hair dye. At one performance McAllen, Jones and King Oliver emerged with their hair coloured jet black, much to their colleagues' amusement. More dangerous japes came courtesy of their GI associates. One night, a US soldier offered them a firecracker which was actually a fake grenade used on military manoeuvres. "Throw it into the crowd when everyone's dancing and it will make a big bang and cause a laugh and a sensation," he enthused. McAllen was impressed but then had second thoughts fearing that the spectacle might prove hazardous in the limited confines of the club. Early one morning after a late show, he and Jones decided to ignite the GI's "banger" in a tree-lined square, adjacent to their lodgings. "We lit the fuse then ran across the road," McAllen remembers. "It was like a bomb going off. If we'd thrown it into a crowd it might have blown somebody's leg off. The next thing sirens were sounding and police cars arrived. We just closed the door and went to our beds."

Musically, the Monarchs continued to improve despite the recent shake-up in personnel. Kane and King Oliver alternated on drums and vocals and soon everyone, bar Blackie, was allowed a lead vocal spot. This was good news for Morrison, who was still finding his range as a blues shouter. Years later, he looked back at the Monarchs and concluded that it was a tough but invaluable apprenticeship. It allowed him to enjoy the occasional spotlight without the attendant pressures of pop stardom. This was a time of innocence when ambition was subservient to camaraderie. Morrison always knew his place in the Monarchs. He was a valued but far from indispensable member whose absence would have made little difference to the band's overall sound or career prospects. There is no evidence of any secret desire on Morrison's part to challenge the band hierarchy, let alone push himself as a likely lead singer. Freed from any administrative responsibility by the more assertive George Jones and Harry Mack, Morrison was happy simply to play the sax and enjoy his cameo vocal spots. He could fade into the background or perform wildly, depending on his mood. The same applied to his relationship and interaction with his comrades. Morrison was quite capable of playing the fool with the rest, but he was also allowed to withdraw from the fun at any moment and settle into a more comfortable role as a detached observer. No serious demands or expectations were foisted upon him. He was neither analysed nor judged. He was accepted.

There were any number of talented musicians playing the local circuit and McAllen was especially enamoured of the Taelman Brothers, an Indonesian group with a fantastic guitar sound. During their short hourly breaks, the Monarchs often frequented nearby clubs and beer cellars but the Storyville management was alert enough to monitor their movements and ensure that they were promptly back on stage. Most of their wages were spent on drink and everyday living expenses, but suggestions that they were "starving" were somewhat wide of the mark. "We had money," Kane insists, "and we lived on hamburgers, bacon, eggs and chips." Morrison painted a grimmer scene when reporting back to his mother. "I didn't know until two years later that he'd been on the verge of starvation over there," she says. "He was telling me that all the boys were absolutely starving and hadn't had anything to eat for ages." Mrs Morrison was also under the mistaken impression that "all the boys were living together in one room". Her enduring memory of her son's spell in Germany was revealingly food centred. "They hadn't enough to live on and Van used to go into these supermarkets where they were giving away free samples of cheese just to get something to eat . . . Another time, he said they only had a stale loaf of bread between the lot of them and had to eat it. If I'd known that, I'd have had him back home right away." Period photographs nevertheless picture Morrison with a sizeable girth and a visible tissue of fat beneath his chin.

The gruelling nightly schedule inevitably produced some tensions within the band, but these were usually alleviated by their earthy Ulster humour. "After the Scotch boys left, we all lived in each other's dirt," Kane recalls. "I think there was a wee bit of a crisis between Geordie Jones and Harry Mack about who was leader, but I never looked at it that way at all." Jones regarded Mack as "the scapegoat of the group" and joined the others in mocking his speech impediment. "Harry was a funny guy," Kane stresses, "and also an object of fun. It was innocent fun, although we'd think better of it today. We used to shout at him 'say speakers' and he always said 'seekers'. It sounds bloody childish but we got a great laugh out of this."

Although the Monarchs tormented Mack, he usually rose above the slagging and concentrated on his fine playing. As baritone saxophonist he worked closely with Morrison on Sounds Incorporated material and was one of the first to recognize his potential as a songwriter. Jones praises their joint contribution to a cover of 'Daddy Cool' in which "Van would start off and from the centre solo until the end he would totally ad-lib – he'd change the song every night making up all these different verses." The performance was reminiscent of G.D.'s blues improvisations several years before.

Morrison's interaction with the other Monarchs in Germany was remarkably trouble-free. Unlike McQueen and Hethrington there were no problems or complaints about drinking and he avoided the verbal taunts suffered by Harry Mack. It no doubt helped that he was part of the original gang along with Jones, McAllen, Kane and Blackie. "Throughout it all Van was his own master," George Jones muses, while admitting that "people didn't understand him".

"He was just a bit strange compared to the rest of them, but I always got on with him," McAllen adds. At the time, Morrison's detachment and aloofness went largely unobserved. It was only later, when confronted by journalists or writers, that his friends even attempted to understand or articulate his feelings and motivations. "Van was always a weird wee fellow," Kane concludes. "I always looked at myself as a gregarious big fellow who could get on with anybody, but I never took to him. He was obviously different from everybody else and I don't mean that in a disrespectful way. I don't know how to explain it. Probably someone will say it was because he was so talented and all that – but I think it was just because he was weird. You tried to get a *craic* out of him more than anything else – hence the egging him on to do daft things. In those days we were all just ambling along – the next girl, the next beer, the next fag, the next gig – nothing was that deep."

At the peak of their success in Frankfurt, the Monarchs were obliged to complete their contract with a residency at the Storyville, Cologne. It was an arduous schedule, similar to that experienced by the prototype Beatles in Hamburg three years earlier. The Liverpudlians, with the exception of drummer Pete Best, had conquered their exhaustion by taking the stimulant Benzedrine and the popular slimming tablet Preludin. Such drugs served the double purpose of removing hunger and stimulating the metabolism to induce hyperactivity. A side effect of Preludin was the drying of the mouth which produced an insatiable thirst. Fortunately, German audiences took great pleasure in offering beer to foreign musicians and there were apocryphal tales of people showering the apron of the stage with pills. Nothing that wild happened in the clubs where the Monarchs played, but beer and amphetamines were available. McAllen decided to experiment with amphetamines which were then legal in Germany. "In Cologne, I started taking Dexedrine, and some other thing. There was an RAF station there and we got friendly with the airmen. One was a medic and he had access to these pills."

This dalliance with dexys was very short-lived after McAllen heard of a fatality involving an English musician. "We got a real fright," says George Jones. "The British medic started giving out these tablets that were supposed to keep you going for hours and hours. Three weeks later this fellow was dead. He'd gone on the tablets for a week and when he tried to come off them he collapsed. We were very naive and it put the fear of God in us."

The move from the American to the British sector was depressing for the Monarchs, not least because the Cologne servicemen were more restricted in their movements and relatively few could spend all night in a jazz club. Morrison was upset to discover that his new audience consisted largely of 17-year-old German kids, newly obsessed with the embryonic British beat boom. In deference to their tastes, the management insisted that the Monarchs smarten themselves up and once again don suits, in imitation of the Fab Four. Suddenly they were a showband again forced to play bland covers of current hits to teenagers. "I think it really frustrated Van a lot," Jones stresses. "We didn't go down well in Cologne because we were averse to playing Billy J. Kramer and Gerry And The Pacemakers numbers."

One person who was impressed by their copycat style was a middle-aged, dark-cloaked Dracula lookalike at the back of the audience. He remained there for their first hour on stage evidently out of place among the teenage throng. During their break, he approached George Jones with the clichéd proposition: "I want to make you a star. Make a record for me." The Monarchs were at first dismissive, ridiculing the man as a crackpot and a Hammer Horror reject. They were later taken aback to learn that he was Ronald Kovacs, a respected A&R person and producer at the German branch of CBS Records. He offered them the chance to record a single at Cologne's Ariola Studios insisting that it must be credited to Georgie & The Monarchs in order to focus attention on Jones. There was some concern in the band that the recording might breach their contract with Ruby Bard, but they could not resist such an opportunity. Unfortunately, the resulting single 'Boo-zooh (Hully Gully)' was a bland composition consisting of little more than a series of repetitions of the title phrase. The flip side 'O

Twingy Baby' was little better. Kovacs patiently explained that German teenagers preferred songs in English that were undemanding and these certainly fitted the bill. Billy McAllen was even reprimanded for playing too elaborate a guitar accompaniment and had to re-record his part. Prior to the single's release, Kovacs took George Jones to a restaurant and offered him fame and fortune as a soloist but, suspicious of the producer's excessive interest, Jones responded with endless prevarication. Even after returning to Northern Ireland, Jones was subtly pursued by Kovacs, who despatched copies of the single followed by a note congratulating the Monarchs on reaching number 4 in the German pop charts. This was false flattery, for the single was conspicuously absent from any known listing.

The Monarchs' closing nights in Cologne were less than pleasing. A disgruntled customer took exception to Morrison after the wee man declined a request to play 'Petite Fleur'. "In the big band scene sax players also played clarinet, but Van was a self-taught blaster," says Kane. Morrison was little better at keeping up with the current pop scene. When asked if he had heard of the Dave Clark Five his response was a bemused and dismissive shrug of the shoulders.

After four long months in Germany, the International Monarchs were relieved to be heading home. A few of them stopped off in London to continue the adventure for a few weeks, but everybody was back in East Belfast in time for Christmas. They were accompanied by the piano-playing GI Jim Storey who had decided to use part of his leave to visit Northern Ireland. The homecoming was brutally anti-climactic. Tired of each other's company, they soon drifted into other projects and suddenly the Monarchs were no more.

FIVE

The Sectarian Divide

January 1964 was a pivotal moment for Morrison, Belfast and the pop world. On the return trip from Germany he had experienced a strong feeling that everything would somehow be different in the future. What he could scarcely have imagined was the speed of events – cultural, political and musical – in those few months while he was abroad. The death of Pope John XXIII had been followed by a startling succession of news events including the Profumo scandal which threatened to bring down the Tory government and culminated in the resignation of British Prime Minister Harold Macmillan. Sandwiched between these two dramatic political stories was the Great Train Robbery, the intricacies of which transfixed newspaper readers. But these headlines were made redundant by the world-shattering announcement of John F. Kennedy's assassination on 22 November in Dallas, Texas. It left a feeling of helplessness and an encroaching sense that the events of tomorrow were nothing more than a frightening empty page.

Harbingers of the cult of youth rightly observed a sudden erosion of the old order as teenagers paraded their discontent, demonstrating publicly against racial discrimination and other institutional injustices. That mood was evident in Ireland with the birth of the civil rights movement in January 1964 when a group of middle-class Catholics established the Campaign For Social Justice. It was there too in the clubs, coffee bars and boutiques of Belfast where Catholic and Protestant youth mixed freely and sought to distance themselves from the old shibboleths of their forebears. "The bigotry was dying," Billy Harrison remembers. "There were still strongholds and there always would be but the youth was coming together and not thinking about religion. Sectarianism was definitely on the wane. The youth of the early Sixties wasn't interested. Having already played all over Belfast, I knew people from all walks of life. They were all out mixing together and enjoying themselves – it was probably the best chance we ever had."

Such optimism was far from unfounded. For many, this period of Belfast's history was the beginning of a progressive new era and there was no reason to believe it would end in violence and death. In spite of all its inherent flaws, a strange peace descended upon Belfast. The once feared IRA, which had conducted a largely ineffectual border campaign in the Fifties, was virtually obsolete with little support from Catholics north or south of the great divide. Remarkably, there had been no murders at all in the North during 1963, either politically motivated or otherwise. Over the next two years, there would be only two killings recorded. Few other regions in the British Isles could boast a more impressive example of concord.

The youth of Belfast were no longer mouthing the tired lines written long ago. They saw themselves as players in a new drama where even the stage setting was constructed from different materials. "Sectarianism wasn't an issue for us," Eric Wrixon notes. "The Fifties IRA campaign was a total flop. There was post-war development and a baby boom generation interested in new-found wealth and employment. It was the first chance to really enjoy something since the War. Even I was old enough to remember ration cards. Now there were jobs, money, clothes to buy. Plastics arrived. Working–class people burnt their own furniture so that they could buy formica which was shiny and new. It was a social revolution."

Concomitant to the social revolution was a musical one. The Beatles' chart-topping conquests over the previous few months had opened the gates of the Hit Parade to a legion of groups from Northern England, including Gerry And The Pacemakers, Billy J. Kramer With The Dakotas, the Searchers, the Hollies and Freddie And The Dreamers. Beatlemania had overwhelmed the nation. The strident 'She Loves You' was breaking all previous UK sales records and its successor 'I Want To Hold Your Hand' entered the charts at number 1. Even their album *With The Beatles* was defying nature and steadily climbing the *singles* charts.

When 'I Want To Hold Your Hand' was at last replaced at number 1 by the Dave Clark Five's 'Glad All Over' in mid-January, the national press talked up the achievement, prematurely proclaiming the arrival of "the Tottenham Sound". Morrison could no longer claim that he had never heard of the Dave Clark Five. Nor was he unaware of the Rolling Stones who had just released a Beatles composition, 'I Wanna Be Your Man', and were causing pandemonium on their first national tour. Their long hair outraged columnists still coming to terms with the Beatles' well-groomed mop tops but there was a growing feeling that their hard Rhythm & Blues style might provide a dynamic contrast to stylized Merseybeat. Morrison was eager to pursue an R&B direction and felt he had the right credentials. His immersion in blues since childhood, fraternization with black musicians in Germany and instinctive understanding of the Rolling Stones' feral appeal ensured that he was months ahead of most of his contemporaries. Excited, he dutifully contacted Billy McAllen, George Jones and Roy Kane with the idea of forming a new group, wearing mod clothes, growing their hair and "causing a sensation in Belfast". All three were already committed to showbands and declined.

With no immediate takers, Morrison was anxious to find work and accepted a reciprocal invitation from Billy McAllen to join the Manhattan Showband. Morrison was introduced to their manager Andy Bogle, a colourful character who had seen action during the Second World War and cheated death when a German deposited a grenade in his tank, blowing away both his feet and right hand. "He had artificial feet and his hand was a metal claw," McAllen remembers. The indomitable Bogle trusted McAllen's judgement in selecting musicians and went along with the idea of incorporating an R&B element into the Manhattan's conservative repertoire. Much to Morrison's delight, McAllen agreed to add saxophonist Geordie Sproule to the line-up, thereby guaranteeing some fun adventures. "We went down well," Sproule says. "Billy McAllen and Van were doing Beatles sets and a mixture of numbers like the Searchers' 'Needles And Pins' and Manfred Mann's '5-4-3-2-1'. I was doing a wee bit of country and anything that came into my head. The main singer Junior (Harry Smith) concentrated on Brendan Bowyer and Elvis stuff. There'd be a big finale – usually a Chuck Berry number."

Andy Bogle boasted some impressive contacts, including broadcaster Éamonn Andrews, and introduced the Manhattan to work in dance halls and hotels south of the border, an itinerary that had always eluded the Monarchs. Starting off at the Clifton Orange Hall, the band next played a memorably fractious date in Drumshanbo, Co. Leitrim, and then were thrilled to hit the centre of Dublin, appearing at the Four Provinces, the Television (TV) Club in Harcourt Street and Clery's ballroom, O'Connell Street. Their raucous act proved a little too exuberant for the strict-tempo-loving hotel patrons. "We nearly got thrown out of Clery's," Sproule recalls. "We came out doing this head-banging stuff – throwing ourselves on and off the stage, jumping on each other's backs. Billy McAllen was playing the guitar behind his head. When we came off yer man said 'You're a disgrace. Don't come back. Take yourself off to the Black North, you dirt birds.'"

The Manhattan also played regular weekend dates in Irish clubs in London where the irrepressible Sproule frequently displayed his offbeat humour. "I was singing 'The Irish Rover' in which I'd tell how the poor dog drowns. I was fed up with the same song, so I started barking. Then Van took it up and he was barking all over the place, right in my ear and all. It was a good *craic*, but the audience thought we were nuts."

Sproule's madcap antics allowed Morrison to express his own zany humour without feeling self-conscious or embarrassed. But G.D. was not merely a kindred spirit and comic ally. The remarkable voice that had boomed through the double bottoms at Harland & Wolff made a strong impression on Morrison whose soulful singing was at best an acquired taste and at worst largely ignored. As a vocalist, he had been probably fourth or fifth in line within the Monarchs and even after their main singer George Hethrington had left, it was George Jones who was chosen as soloist on their only recording. Morrison's position in the Manhattan was only marginally better, but this latest collaboration with G.D. was to have far-reaching consequences. "We did a wee tape one time," Sproule remembers. "I was acting the maggot, kidding myself on, putting on different voices. I started doing a cross between Hank Williams and Big Bill Broonzy and the next thing I knew Van was singing like that. He caught on to it. I should have kept it. Me and Van seemed to be on the same parallel but he went further. He was a good man for sitting and watching. He takes it all in."

In February 1964, a vacancy for a guitarist arose in the Manhattan and the search began for a suitable candidate. The favourite was Herbie Armstrong, who lived in Glenmachen Street in the Protestant community of West Belfast. As a young teenager, he had founded the Twilights, a skiffle combo whose popularity was eclipsed only by their more intimidating rivals the Black Shirts who beat them in a battle of the bands competition hosted by Belfast rock 'n' roller Brian Rossi. The defeat dented Armstrong's confidence, but the Twilights survived the skiffle craze and proved surprisingly durable. By the early Sixties they were supporting visiting chart luminaries including Kenny Lynch, Tommy Roe and the Allisons. After five years Armstrong was ready for a new challenge but seemed sceptical about joining a showband. He was soon won over by the exuberant, proselytizing presence of Geordie Sproule. "That guy was as mad as a hatter," Armstrong enthuses. "Crazy. A real character. Van loved him. Geordie introduced me to Van and they said, 'We're like a showband but we do some pretty hip stuff – Beatles, Stones, the blues.'" After a meeting at the music shop Crymbles, outside of which G.D. liked to interview gullible members of the public with an unplugged microphone, Armstrong accepted their invitation.

The predominantly Protestant Manhattan rehearsed at a rented chapel hall in Milltown Cemetery, surrounded by the graves of Republican paramilitaries. Morrison's knowledge of Irish nationalism was tested soon after at a rural gig south of the border. "We finished our set but no-one left," Armstrong recalls. "They just stood looking at us. Then someone came over and said, 'You've got to play 'The Soldier Song'.'" With their limited experience of performing in the Republic, none of them had bothered to learn the words of the Irish national anthem. Eventually, the ice was broken when Morrison volunteered: "I know it on sax." As Armstrong concludes: "Van played it on sax and we all stood to attention and got away with it. We could have been strung up that night."

The Republican theme continued when the band returned to London for a St Patrick's night show at a ballroom in Camden. "It went down well," Sproule says, "until the bass player Ken Armstrong walked through the crowd and got a punch in the eye. Some wee girl was looking at him and her boyfriend objected." In the early hours, Morrison, G.D. and Herbie returned to their lodgings above the Regency Rooms and had a cider party. "We were bouncing on these iron-sprung beds like kids, laughing, singing and getting drunk," Armstrong recounts. "Then Van turned around and said, 'I've written a song, what do you think?' It was called 'Could You Would You'. I told him, 'Wow, you should record this'. He said, 'Where would I do that?' I said, 'I don't know'."

A valuable clue to the solution of Morrison's dilemma was provided when several of the band spent an evening at Ken Colyer's Studio 51 on Great Newport Street, off Leicester Square. The jazz venue was offering a "Rhythm & Blues" night featuring the Downliners Sect. "Van was smitten by them," G.D. remembers, "they were doing a lot of R&B covers. They should have been big." At first glance, the long-haired Sect were mistaken for female musicians by the Belfast boys. "We said, 'Great – girl guitarists!'" Armstrong laughs. It was only the sight of Don Craine sporting a Sherlock Holmes deerstalker hat that put them right. At the end of their set, Morrison asked if he might accompany them on harmonica but was curtly informed, "Sorry – we've finished." Before leaving the club he obtained their manager's phone number and called him early the next morning. This was the strongest evidence yet of Morrison's growing confidence and self-belief. Whereas in the past he had been swept along by events or led by others, he was now unusually proactive in pursuing his musical ambitions and publicizing his talents. "Van was really enthusiastic," Armstrong recalls. "He told him, 'I'm into blues and wouldn't mind a manager.' Then he was asked where he lived – and we never even got to meet the guy."

After returning to Belfast, Morrison could not get Studio 51 and the Downliners Sect out of his mind. The idea of a club presenting a Rhythm & Blues night was a revelation. G.D. wondered why they could not open their own version of Studio 51 and came up with an unlikely venue. Rather than an established address like the Betty Staff Dance Studios or Sammy Houston's Jazz Club, Sproule suggested the Maritime Hotel on College Square North, near Queen's University. Originally a police station, the building had been revamped in 1945 by the Sailors' Friendly League and served as a rest home for visiting mariners. It included a 200-capacity hall which was frequently booked by Christian organizations and the Mothers' Union. There were Tuesday night trad jazz get-togethers, but these were poorly attended and about to be discontinued. "They had a hospital show on a Sunday night then, but little or nothing else," G.D. points out. "I went to the Maritime and said to Joe Harper, the caretaker, 'I want to open a club.' He said 'No problem, G.D.' But then I couldn't get a PA system. It was the story of my life."

While G.D.'s entrepreneurial scheme was foundering, the Manhattan were suffering another of their periodic shake-ups. Recent recruit Herbie Armstrong had barely unpacked his bags after the London trip when he was offered the chance to audition for a place in the Golden Eagles, the resident showband at Belfast's Mecca-owned Plaza ballroom in Chichester Street. What really excited Armstrong was the opportunity to work alongside the band leader Brian Rossi, the local iconic rock 'n' roller who had once presided over the Twilights during their skiffle days. Rossi was already a minor celebrity in the city with a career stretching back to the mid-Fifties. A former cloakroom attendant at the Jig in Townsend Street, he had launched himself as a jiving disc jockey backed by a Dansette record player. For a time he toured Britain on rock 'n' roll bills featuring acts such as Gene Vincent and Billy Fury. As assistant manager at the State Kilburn, he was notorious for upstaging performers in mid-act and was known to swing across the stage on a rope, Tarzan-like, before treating the spectators to a demonstration of frantic jiving. Back in Belfast, he worked with Joe McGee & The Ambers and appeared regularly at the Maritime's Sunday hospital shows. However, his main gig was the Plaza residency where he worked as an afternoon disc jockey entertaining the factory girls who congregated there during their lunch hours. The ballroom had insisted that cross-Channel bands supply the evening entertainment, but manager Bob Herron petitioned for the opportunity to promote local talent. Under Rossi's tutelage, the 11-piece Golden Eagles were formed, complete with two teenage female dancers, a full accompanying orchestra and some of the best players from Northern Ireland's multifarious showbands.

Morrison was mightily impressed when he learned that Armstrong might be working with Rossi and asked his bandmate to put in a good word on his behalf. When Armstrong phoned Rossi to confirm the time of his audition, he requested casually: "You're not looking for a saxophonist, are you?" Rossi paused then said, "No, but we're looking for a singer." Standing beside Armstrong in the phone box, the animated Morrison hissed, "Tell him I can sing!" Armstrong duly went into rhapsodic ecstasy comparing his small friend to Little Richard and Chuck Berry, concluding with "and he sings the blues like you wouldn't believe, and that's what's happening now."

Rossi was phlegmatic but happy to allow Morrison to attend the audition. The bad news was that another local chanter, the impressive Frankie Connolly, was also intending to try out. "I told Van, 'you might not have much hope here,'" Armstrong remembers. "He said, 'Oh well, we'll give it a try.'" Morrison then volunteered a friend from the meat-curing establishment where he had worked to provide transportation to the Plaza. The following afternoon, Armstrong was sitting at home strumming his Fender Stratocaster when a butchers' delivery van pulled up outside. As there was only a single seat in the front, the two musicians were forced to huddle in the rear among the carcasses, desperately rehearsing blues songs. When they arrived at the Plaza they were confronted by the predominantly middle-aged orchestra, several of whom were wearing Aran sweaters and smoking pipes. "We were still teenagers," Armstrong says. "They asked us to try something so we did 'Hoochie Coochie Man'. Then Van started blowing a harmonica and singing in a gravel blues voice."

By lucky coincidence, the overwhelming favourite Frankie Connolly had another engagement that day and pulled out of the audition. Morrison's timing had been perfect. The showman Rossi wasted few words, simply observing, "OK, you've got the job, you start tonight." The two were then taken aside and kitted out in showband-style white suits laced with shimmers of gold thread. Morrison's short arms left his sleeves dangling several inches over his fingertips so Rossi called for pins. While the uniform was crudely fitted, Morrison learned from his new mentor that he would be receiving under £10 a week. "The singers were paid half the rate of the musicians," Armstrong remembers. Still in a flurry, the new recruits spent the remainder of the afternoon rehearsing Chuck Berry's 'Roll Over Beethoven' and 'Bye Bye Johnny'.

That evening they witnessed Brian Rossi at his best. Resplendent in gold lamé suit he conducted the orchestra with a baton while surreptitiously taking swigs from a flask of whiskey. Over the succeeding nights, Morrison adapted quickly to his new role. "It was quite a step to be a vocalist in the Golden Eagles along with Brian Rossi," Armstrong stresses. "Rossi was the ballad singer and Van sang the blues. It was really something to hear a showband orchestra backing him on songs like Ray Charles' 'Hit The Road Jack'. Rossi really got off on him."

In spite of his prestigious spot in the Rossi band, Morrison could not rid himself of memories of the vibrant new R&B movement he had witnessed in London. "He kept saying to me, 'Blues is the thing and groups are going to happen,'" Herbie Armstrong remembers. "All I heard was – 'The Stones are happening, groups are happening.'" Morrison's conviction about the fashionable potency of R&B was vindicated with each passing week. The Rolling Stones, under the canny guidance of their young, charismatic manager Andrew Loog Oldham, were inspiring column inches of earnest debate about their outrageously long hair, raucous live performances and recent run of hits, which now included an inspired adaptation of Buddy Holly's 'Not Fade Away'. Meanwhile, the Stones' original mentor Giorgio Gomelsky was promoting his new find the Yardbirds, who regularly appeared at the Crawdaddy Club and Studio 51 and had just signed to EMI's Columbia label. Another Stones alumnus Dick Taylor had formed the Pretty Things, who were generally regarded as the wildest and most uncompromising group on the circuit, a reputation which helped win a contract with Fontana Records. The London-based Kinks could be seen performing their first Pye single 'Long Tall Sally' on television's *Ready Steady Go!* Meanwhile, Newcastle's Animals furthered the R&B cause on the BBC Light Programme's *Saturday Club* and were about to issue their blues-adapted debut single, 'Baby Let Me Take You Home'. Additional proof of the commercial power of R&B was demonstrated by the continued chart success of Manfred Mann whose '5-4-3-2-1' had already been incorporated into Morrison's brief repertoire.

The fantasy of finding or forming a Stones-styled R&B group became more concrete when Morrison noticed an advertisement on 6 April in the *Belfast Evening Telegraph* requiring musicians to start a Rhythm & Blues club. After phoning the number, he was told that auditions were taking place at a pub in the Old Lodge Road. He wasted no time in contacting G.D., who offered to tag along, clutching a bottle of his favourite Mundie's wine. As it turned out, only a couple of people attended the auditions, neither of whom had any R&B credential. At the pub, Morrison was introduced to the young entrepreneurs Jimmy Conlon, Jerry McKenna and Gerry McCurvey – collectively known as the '3Js'. The trio had already promoted television folk favourites Robin Hall & Jimmy McGregor at the Ulster Hall and felt there was a niche in the city for an R&B club. Initially, they had approached the marginally more experienced Sam Smyth, who had attended the Technical High School with Billy McAllen and George Jones and now managed the College Boys. The wunderkind Smyth was quick to offer his boys for any opening night, even though they were a straight showband with no intention of pursuing an R&B direction. Being young, everyone concerned wanted the club to start as soon as possible. Morrison claims he helped them find an appropriate venue at remarkably short notice by following the footsteps of G.D. towards the Maritime Hotel.

Discovering a suitable R&B group to launch the enterprise was the next urgent task. After giving notice to the Golden Eagles, Morrison set about assembling his ideal line-up which he envisaged as Herbie Armstrong (guitar), Billy McAllen (guitar), McAllen's young cousin Eric Wrixon (keyboards), Gerry McIlroy (drums) and an unnamed bassist, probably George Jones. Alas, this dream team proved resistant to Morrison's entreaties. Safely employed in various showbands, they were unwilling to surrender steady money for the questionable rewards of playing R&B in a sailors' rest home. "Van said, 'I've got some great ideas,'" Armstrong recalls, "but I wouldn't get involved. I'd bought my Vespa and had my girlfriend on the back and as much wine as I could drink." Fortunately, Morrison had an alternative plan. Recently, he had been introduced to another promising outfit sorely in need of fresh inspiration.

The Gamblers had originally formed in East Belfast during 1962 when drummer Ronnie Millings encountered Chuck Berry fanatic Billy Harrison (vocals/guitar), who had just been discharged from hospital after straining his back lugging milk crates at a dairy. Harrison in turn recruited his friend Alan Henderson whom he taught to play bass. The group's repertoire was standard rock 'n' roll fare, mingling Elvis Presley and Chuck Berry hits with a dash of rockabilly, country and popular radio favourites. Although it was difficult to compete with the plethora of slick showbands in the city, the Gamblers persevered, moving successively from hops at the tennis club in Ormeau Road to bigger dates at Sammy Houston's Jazz Club and Betty Staff's. Harrison's musical tastes tended towards the eclectic and he was keen to break free from the familiar rigid group formula of the time. "My mind was still working on what I called rock 'n' roll, although I was playing a lot of R&B without calling it that. I was looking more towards the American style of Johnny And The Hurricanes rather than the standard guitar, bass, drums and singer. I wanted a keyboards and saxophone player."

The idea of emulating Johnny And The Hurricanes, whose career as instrumental hit-makers had peaked several years before with the honking 'Red River Rock' and 'Rocking Goose', was a decidedly passé notion in 1963–64. Nevertheless, Harrison felt he was on the right track. On Saturday mornings he regularly frequented Crymbles music shop in Wellington Place where young players exchanged gossip and discussed the latest vacancies in rival bands. It was there that Harrison discovered Eric Wrixon, a precocious schoolboy who had recently played piano with Frankie & The Echoes and was eager to gain additional experience.

Within weeks, Wrixon had provided, via his cousin Billy McAllen, the link to Van Morrison, whom Harrison knew by reputation as the former saxophonist of the Monarchs and a fellow recruit in Evelyn Boucher's late Fifties hospital entertainment shows. At this point, Harrison envisaged Morrison merely as the Gamblers' sax player, but before long it was evident that his gruff vocal style might prove compatible with the material they were performing. From Morrison's perspective, the Gamblers were instrumentally rough and unpolished but they were evidently pursuing a musical direction which was new and exciting. "About the time I arrived they'd just gone R&B,"

Wrixon points out. "Billy had always wanted to do that. He'd already been playing Chuck Berry and Bo Diddley numbers." Morrison was quietly impressed to discover that Harrison's tastes extended far beyond the limited confines of chart radio pop. Like every other group in town, the Gamblers had covered the Swinging Blue Jeans' current hit 'Hippy Hippy Shake' but Harrison owned a copy of the original US version by Chan Romero. He was also familiar with Bob Dylan's work and liked to strum 'House Of The Rising Sun', then a relatively obscure blues cover from the folk singer's 1962 debut album. "A lot of songs that later became R&B standards, including stuff by Chuck Berry and Bo Diddley, were known to us as rock 'n' roll," Harrison stresses. "R&B became a much bandied and later maligned expression for anything that was marketed. Suddenly, it was all R&B – everything recorded by anybody with a black face was instantly brilliant."

Despite his distaste for genre classifications, a frustration later shared by Morrison, Harrison had been happy to relaunch the Gamblers as R&B specialists. Their new repertoire was honed in a room above a bicycle shop in Victoria Street owned by blues enthusiast Dougie Knight. "We disappeared off the scene, unintentionally really, to do some practising and rehearsing together," Harrison recalls. "We knew the numbers we wanted to play. Van was a good horn player and he was introducing an even stronger blues influence. He knew all that stuff from his dad's record collection because he'd been playing it at home for years. I knew Muddy Waters and others, but he introduced me to people like Howlin' Wolf."

Revealingly, the Gamblers were still functioning as a unit independent of Morrison as late as 20 March when they supported the Stratotones at the Whitehall Restaurant in Ann Street. That same evening the Maritime had opened its doors to the Dominos, fresh from a stint in Hamburg. The scene was far from static and things were happening fast. If Morrison had merely been having a blow with the Gamblers up until this point, he now knew that they were the only candidates whom he could recruit for the 3Js' R&B evening, which was merely days away.

With their new musical direction, the Gamblers also decided on a name change in advance of the Maritime debut. In common with Wayne Fontana's backing group, the Mindbenders, they christened themselves after a Fifties horror movie – *Them!* Young Wrixon felt that the missing definite article 'the' would distinguish them from the legions of rival new groups. It certainly made the quintet sound different, as if they were so alien and unclassifiable that no suitable noun or adjective was available to do them justice.

SIX

Maritime Blues

On Friday 10 April 1964, Them played their first date at the Maritime Hotel, supporting the in-demand College Boys. Approximately 60 people turned up, including some remnants of the old trad jazz audience that the venue had once attracted. This low-key, largely unpublicized performance was historically significant, not least because of the conspicuous absence of Van Morrison from the line-up. That evening he was obliged to fulfil his final outstanding date with the Golden Eagles at the Plaza ballroom.

Within days of Them's unheralded Maritime debut without Morrison, a cryptic advertisement appeared in the *Belfast Evening Telegraph* asking, "WHO ARE? WHAT ARE? THEM?" The following evening, the same column read: "WHEN? AND WHERE? WILL YOU SEE THEM?" And so it went on. "The ads created a mystery from the very start," remembers Gil Irvine. "Other people were cagey with their money and wouldn't do an advertising campaign. Nobody had thought of that angle to create a hype." The tease continued until the Friday evening of their second Maritime show (17 April), where the group were billed as "THEM – Ireland's Specialists In Rhythm and Blues". This was a clever ploy by the 3Js whose concept of an R&B club for the kids was seen as a novel venture. "The Maritime was probably the first time that a band and its management had run a venue for its own benefit," Wrixon claims. "It was a breakthrough in those terms." Few saw Them's first show with Morrison as there was stiff competition that night with Tony & The Telstars playing Betty Staff's and the College Boys appearing at the Cavern Club.

Nevertheless, over successive weeks word spread rapidly among local students and musicians about Them's tempestuous stage performances. Rod Demick, a member of Tony & The Telstars and an entrant for television's *Ready Steady Win!* battle of the bands competition, was studying for his O-level exams at Grosvenor High Grammar when he first heard about the Maritime residency. Accompanied by a Salvation Army trombonist, he attended one of their earliest shows and was transfixed. "I'd never heard anything like it," he says. "Them never sounded as good since. It was so new, so different." Gwen Carson, then lodging in Hyndford Street, was of similar mind. "Van was wild, Van was the best. Back then he was very bluesy. When he came on stage he was out of his head. He was wonderful." Ann Denvir, a Catholic schoolgirl, was also an early convert. "We used to sit on the wooden chairs with our feet up on the stage," she remembers. "Occasionally you'd be pushed under the stage by the crowd. The floor was quite wet. Van would be pushed on stage and come gliding across out of his brains, but once he stood up and sang it was absolute magic. Then he'd start to play the sax and we were all transported into another dimension. I knew those days were special and everybody there knew those days were special. There was such an aura about that time in Belfast – and it was never to be repeated. Ever."

The sense of a lost era encapsulated in those magical nights at the Maritime was a frequent refrain among the spectators lucky enough to witness Them at their rawest. Like the Beatles' early appearances at the Cavern and the Stones' first forays at the Crawdaddy Club, there was an embryonic intensity about Them's shows which was fresh and unique. "We were playing for a certain bunch of people," Morrison noted. "It was really like a cult following. It wasn't in any way a commercial trip." While many of their contemporaries would translate their promise into greatness, Them seemed to thrive on the closeness of their original clique in a small, sweaty seamen's rest. In the beginning there was a purity and a sense of purpose that would later be compromised or insidiously worn away. The intangible power emanating from the stage of the mission hall would never be captured on tape and would live on only as folk memory. For Morrison, at least, it was so evanescent that it was exhausted even in the moment of creation. "Them lived and died as a group on stage at the Maritime," he concluded.

"There's a great difference of opinion between Belfast and the rest of the world," Eric Wrixon observes portentously. "People here have a memory of a certain band that they never saw reflected in the singles releases or the later history. They don't remember it as Van Morrison and Them. Those people remember it as Them. It was a composite – but they were the only ones who saw it live for any length of time. It's pointless discussing the levels of competence of the various musicians in that band, but Billy Harrison was the guy to make it happen. He was one of the most formative people I met in those early days. Billy was *de facto* leader. That was reflected on stage where he would've been singing about half the numbers, which were R&B standards."

"It was about 50/50," Harrison confirms. "I was doing a lot more chanting at the Maritime. I was chanting; Van was chanting. Whenever he sang, I played guitar and when I sang he was either blowing harmonica or saxophone or we'd come in together on things. He knew more songs and was leaning more towards blues and R&B. Gradually, it came about that since he knew more of the stuff he did more singing and I stepped back because it allowed me more time to play."

Soon after their debut at the Maritime, Them extended their itinerary, appearing at small venues that were willing to accept an R&B group. Chief amongst them was an afternoon show at Sammy Houston's Jazz Club on Great Victoria Street and a regular Saturday evening appearance at Inst (The Royal Belfast Academical Institution), which attracted both school kids and students. Janet Martin, then a 15-year-old innocent at Victoria College, was forever pestering her father about attending a dance. Her desire was heightened when she was invited to Inst by her first boyfriend Teddie Palmer, co-leader elect of the showbands the Exiles and Teddie & The Tigers. A prize catch, Palmer was so popular with besotted teenage girls that they would shower the stage with teddy bears in eponymous honour of their hero. "This was my big night," Martin reminisces. "I was going to a dance in Inst with Teddie Palmer. Wow! When I arrived I was showing off to my mates. I remember standing in the middle of the floor and the group started playing before the curtains opened. They began with 'Green Onions' with Van on the saxophone. Then the curtains slowly opened. It was so sexy. The next thing I knew I was at the front of the stage saying: 'Who are these guys?' It was brilliant. Once I saw Them I went every week. No matter where they went, we were there. I went to parts of Belfast I'd never seen before." Fellow classmate Joan McClelland happened to be dating a boy from Annadale Grammar who helped organize a show at his school in June. "It was an end of term concert for the school and he was setting up the lighting. I went with him. I hadn't heard of Them. It was just a school dance for fifth and sixth formers. But it was fantastic. All the girls stopped dancing, rushed to the front of the stage and screamed. We thought, 'What is this? Who are these people?' It was long hair, wild music and Van Morrison making love to the microphone. At the age of 15 in Belfast, this was exciting."

From Annadale and Inst, Janet, Joan and their mates followed the trail back to the Maritime. "We were there every Friday," McClelland says. "We'd go to the Spanish Rooms and buy scrumpy beforehand. You could get a milk bottle full. There was a lot of chatting up from boys, good fun, music and dancing. Them were unique here. They were our equivalent of the Stones with the long hair and the rebel look. It was rock and sex personified. Van Morrison was magnetic on stage. Very sexy. In himself he had nothing to offer. Let's face it, he wasn't good-looking – he was a wee runt of a guy. Offstage you wouldn't have looked sideways at him. But on stage it was different. There was an animalistic sexuality that he didn't have in his person. That was the attraction. There was a song called 'Lovelight' and when he sang that into the microphone it was as if he was making love. If you're talking about Mick Jagger you can appreciate sex but with Van you thought: 'Where does it come from?' But there was no doubt he had it in those days. He was certainly a sexual animal on stage and was able to portray that and that's what we wanted."

"It was a classic period," claims Billy Moore, another local scenester. "I can't ever remember a fight at the Maritime. These days they'd be at it hammer and nails. This was an innocent time. Van would jump on pianos and was very lively. The doorman, Joe Harper, was a kindly old boy who took to the teenagers and was a real character."

Both the Maritime and the Jazz Club were unlicensed, but the clientele were often fortified upon arrival after trips to the Spanish Rooms. Crowds would gather in College Square North from teatime onwards, stretching down the road, eager to sample the evening's entertainment. They were seldom let down. Them were rapidly gaining notoriety as R&B wildcats with a lifestyle to match. In the long queues, knowing voices would tell tall tales of the group's saturnalian drinking exploits, claiming that they secretly stashed a barrel of cider in their van. Such stories heightened expectations of a rollicking performance. On certain occasions, Them lived up to their sybaritic billing. Orangefield alumnus Eric Bell, then playing locally, was eager to hear these new sensations. "They'd only just started and there was this buzz around Belfast, 'Have you seen Them?' Me and Billy Moore went to see them one night. We were standing in the queue and suddenly they arrived." In the distance, Bell saw Harrison and Henderson supporting Morrison, who was draped across their shoulders like a beaten prize fighter. "He had his head down," Bell remembers. "The toes of his shoes were scraping as they trailed him down the road into the club where he was going to play in half an hour. He was blitzed! Then he came on stage. You wouldn't believe what they were like in those days. Morrison would come out, take his shoes off and throw them into the audience. Then he'd get the maracas and throw them into the audience, run up and down the stage, trip, fall into the drums, totally out of his head, and the bass drum went flying. I swear to God this is what Them were like. You'd never seen anything like it in your life. The sheer energy coming off that stage was remarkable."

There was nothing contrived about Them on stage, but they sometimes enjoyed playing up to the mythology of the waiting crowd. "Half the time, the wee man would have done these things pretending," says Billy Harrison of the spectacle witnessed by Bell. "In those days he was offbeat, what you'd have called 'weird' in the Sixties. The guy was different. He had a very dry sense of humour. He used to do things like that, pretend he was half-cut. I'm not saying we didn't get pissed – we did. There were plenty of piss-ups coming back from gigs. But the wee man could act the maggot, throw his arms around you and say, 'Oh, I'm out of it – here we go!' Maybe it was a bit of showmanship if you think about it, creating more interest. He used to do odd things like that at the drop of a hat. Of course you fell in because it was all good fun. The punters would've been thinking 'Van's pissed' and rushed in expecting to see him lying dead on the stage or staggering about like a lunatic."

Harrison's explanation notwithstanding, the behaviour of Morrison left some indelible imprints on the memories of those in attendance. Terry Davis, another young member of the hip clique, was captivated by the hedonistic high jinks. "When I saw him at the Maritime my memories of Van are that he used to perform better when he was drunk," he insists. "I remember a bottle of wine being passed around and he took a fair swig of it – and off he went. They'd take bottles in there. It was fairly heady stuff. He'd rip into it. I remember one occasion at the Jazz Club. He was falling down offstage and hanging on to the microphone stand, trying to pull himself up. Billy came over, lifted him, and propped him up properly. If he was drinking he was better. And if being drunk was his way of getting it over good and proper then he was doing it well."

The local fuss caused by Them would soon attract interest from aspiring entrepreneurs, especially when it was discovered that the 3Js had no management interests in the group. One candidate who failed to act was the aforementioned Sam Smyth. Although still a teenager, a mere five days older than Morrison, Smyth was remarkably well connected. A friendship with Vincent Hanna, then a young solicitor and later political correspondent for BBC's *Newsnight*, coincided with Smyth's introduction to Peter Dempsey, manager of the Freshmen, the most popular Northern showband. Before long Smyth was doing part-time PR work for their company, Pentagon Promotions. Smyth also helped manage a chain of ballrooms and was eager to push the College Boys into the showband stratosphere. He was impressed by the excitement emanating from the Maritime ("It was a cross between a Billy Graham revival and the Apollo in Harlem"), but at that point R&B was outside his sphere. "Sam was a showbander," says Janet Martin, "and the two shall never meet."

A greater missed opportunity was suffered by Eddie Kennedy, later manager of Rory Gallagher's group Taste and a leading promoter of R&B acts in Belfast. In 1964, Kennedy was a dapper dance instructor, whose musical tastes centred on the strict tempo of Victor Sylvester and the ageing orchestras of the era. Improbably, he ended up at the Maritime, saw its financial potential, and was transformed by the experience. "I was enthralled. Van was a phenomenal performer even in those days. He would be singing and he'd lay down on his back and play. And even when the crowd was choc-a-bloc you could hear a pin drop when he played the sax – and then he'd go berserk! But he was such a peculiar guy. He didn't show any emotion, even when the audience applauded him. He was so cool you couldn't believe it. I cannot accept that Van is better today than he was at the Maritime. Back then he was at the start of an era which he created as far as Ireland was concerned. I don't think he knew the power he had over those kids. He was so far ahead of his time. I'm green with envy that I didn't handle him from day one because I was in the perfect position. But at that point I wasn't into management, I was a dancer."

The sudden minor fame that was thrust upon Morrison at this early stage of his career had some unexpected benefits. Reserved by nature, he had been restricted to a small social circle all his life, but suddenly found it was expanding. The Maritime spectacle had placed him in the orbit of upmarket grammar school girls and college students, many from upper middle class backgrounds. These new bohemians offered an alternative world view and a superficially flattering attention which roused Morrison's curiosity and no doubt appealed to his vanity. Eric Wrixon, who might easily have been part of such a privileged clique, watched Morrison's reactions with a detached, jaundiced amusement. "Van hung around with a seedy crowd of failed art college students who were beatniks. They wore duffle coats and corduroy trousers, liked being hip and talked of selling Christmas trees. They were an influence on him." Despite his modest upbringing, Morrison was surprisingly unfazed by their presence. Eric Bell, who always found Morrison quiet and introspective offstage, was impressed by the colourful circle that congregated around Them. "There were a few chicks," he recalls. "I went to Sammy Houston's to see Them play and after the gig a lot of people were hanging around. I saw Van standing at the tea bar where they served coffee and buns, no alcohol. He was talking to this girl who was one-and-a-half times his size and she had a dagger down her boot which I thought was incredible. These were arty people."

It was during this time that the other members of Them learned the extraordinary news that Morrison had actually found a girlfriend. Her name was Jane Adams. "She was tall, slim, had a very pale complexion and red hair," Wrixon remembers. "The girl was respectable and very different from the people Van normally hung around with. She was very attractive. I knew her before she went out with Van as part of a coffee house crowd." Billy Harrison, who vaguely knew her brother Harry, was surprised by the unlikely match. "She was a beautiful looking girl. We were very much a case of the wrong side of the tracks."

The relationship would not last long but many were astonished that it had happened in the first place. "The first time I ever met Van was at the Plaza," Ann Denvir remembers. "I used to go there with Jane, this beautiful girl. She was absolutely stunning with an early Cilla Black red haircut. She seemed so pale and interesting. In my 17-year-old mind I wanted to be just like her because she was so beautiful. I hated her because she was one of those upper class Belfast girls who seemed to have gone to finishing school or something. And Van was going with her! I used to look at them and say 'My God, what does she see in him? He's obnoxious!' He wasn't at all pretty and hasn't improved with age but she was his steady girlfriend for a while."

Sam Smyth held little hope for this improbable union. "Jane was a bit like Jane Asher," he adds. "Terribly respectable and nice. The Adams family lived somewhere off Donegall Park Avenue in North Belfast. They weren't particularly well off. They had a couple of kids who attended grammar school which made them a cut above others there. The finishing school analogy is understandable because she had that sort of cool and elegant persona. She was very well brought up and was always neatly dressed. This was not the normal type of girl Morrison would have been used to. Jane looked the organized, sensible type and probably made her own chutney, like an earlier version of Delia Smith. I'm sure her attraction to him was more a case of sociological curiosity than romantic interest. The one thing I would bet next year's wages on was that the relationship was never consummated. Every time I meet Van, he always asks, 'Have you seen Harry Adams?' and 'Any news of Jane?' I always tell him, 'She ended up marrying a Church of Ireland clergyman.'"

While Morrison's love life was taking tentative flight, Them received a lucky break when they were introduced to 24-year-old Peter Lloyd, a former electronics student at Queen's University who ran a demo studio in Cromac Square. He had been interested in recording a song for the university's rag week and subsequently offered Them the chance to cut some test recordings. Among the favourites was their startling rendition of Bobby Bland's 'Turn On Your Lovelight', the grand finale of their set. Since first introducing the song to the Monarchs, Morrison had transformed the number into an elongated exercise in erotic emotion which climaxed in a manic, frenzied howl after which he would leave the stage drenched in sweat. With Lloyd at the controls, Them attempted to capture some of its spirit in truncated form via three R&B standards: 'Stormy Monday', 'I Got My Mojo Working' and 'Don't Start Crying Now'. Soon after, a copy of the tape was sent to Mervyn Solomon.

The Solomons were already a legend in Irish showbusiness. Maurice Solomon was head of the record distributors Solomon & Peres and a significant shareholder in Decca Records. His son Mervyn was involved in a record label and managed several record shops in the city. A known jazz enthusiast who had previously worked in New York, Mervyn was invited to the Maritime with a view to assisting Them in finding a record deal. "I arrived there and Van was absolutely tearing them apart. 'Lovelight' was terrific. He was running across the stage and down on his knees. The kids were going crazy. I was very impressed." Mervyn wasted no time in taking Them under his wing and even allowed them to rehearse acoustically at his home. What happened next was the most important event in their career to date. Sensing a sensation, Mervyn contacted his brother Philip in London and informed him of the madness at the Maritime. The big time beckoned.

Philip Solomon was one of the most ambitious, aggressive and historically undervalued managers of the entire era. The contrast with his brother was frequently noted by business associates. Mervyn was urbane, modest and quietly spoken, whereas Phil preferred to take the music business by the throat, less like a patron of the arts than a ruthless entrepreneur. During his 40 years, he had carved out a *curriculum vitae* that testified to the spirit of an adventurer. Oddly enough, he had originally hoped to become a vet, but his father declared, "It wouldn't be proper for a young Jew." There were youthful exploits, including a period in Australia still spoken about in hushed whispers by old lags in the music biz, and business ventures that provoked critical comment. Solomon had first come to prominence in the pop world during the mid-Fifties when he was involved in the career of Irish singer Ruby Murray, who dominated the charts in early 1955, notching up six Top 10 hits in less than seven months. The following year, he brought over Connie Foley for an Irish tour, then entered the entertainment industry in earnest. By 1958 he and his glamorous wife Dorothy had settled in London where they concentrated on promoting acts as diverse as Bridie Gallagher, Nina & Frederick, Louis Armstrong, Kenneth McKeller and Cliff Richard. Solomon's fortunes took a decisive turn when he was introduced to Dick Rowe, A&R manager at Decca Records. "Philip first came in my direction originally through his father's connections with Decca," Rowe remembers. "When young Philip began all he knew was that the family were closely connected with Decca and that the person he ought to meet was Dick Rowe." It was to prove a mutually rewarding relationship.

The Solomon brothers invited Rowe to check out Them in their natural habitat and the Decca man responded eagerly. He already had Solomon to thank for providing him with the Harmonichords, a Dublin trio whom he had renamed the Bachelors and fed a steady diet of chestnut standards perfect for the adult, easy listening market. Over recent months, they had infiltrated the upper echelons of the chart with songs like 'Charmaine', 'Diane' and 'I Believe' and in the democratic mood of the time seemed equally suited for summer season shows and beat group package tours. Beyond the Bachelors, Rowe had another agenda. Like any good A&R manager, he was alert to new trends. Decca needed to keep pace with its rival EMI in the battle of the beat groups and had already signed Brian Poole & The Tremeloes, the Rolling Stones, the Nashville Teens and the Moody Blues. The most powerful and influential managers of the era – Larry Parnes, Don Arden and Andrew Oldham – spoke of Rowe in glowing terms noting his key involvement in the careers of numerous stars from Billy Fury to the Stones. For all that, Rowe harboured memories of the near misses over the years. Like virtually every other A&R manager in the country he had turned down the Beatles a couple of years before. He had not warmed to Brian Epstein and felt the group's audition tape was rather amateurish. But at least he had acknowledged their promise and provided an opportunity to record, unlike his myopic peers at Philips, Pye and the myriad of labels under the EMI banner, excepting Parlophone.

Rowe's reputation remained exemplary until he was made a scapegoat for the music industry's conservatism. During the spring of 1964, Brian Epstein was completing his ghosted memoir *A Cellarful Of Noise* and, in one of the most casually vindictive acts ever perpetrated on a British executive, lambasted Rowe for his failure to sign the Fab Four. He even credited the A&R manager with the ludicrous assertion, "Groups of guitarists are on the way out." Not one of Rowe's rivals at the other labels was mentioned, leaving him forever branded as the man who had turned down the Beatles. Other managers were critical of Epstein's display of spite but Rowe reacted with a saturnine shrug of the shoulders. It seemed to make him more determined. Since signing the Rolling Stones, he had monitored the R&B scene with passing interest and was prepared to add a similar act to the label as insurance. Who knew whether the Stones would prosper or implode under the exciting but anarchic stewardship of Andrew Oldham?

Rowe arrived in Belfast with the air of a man unwilling to miss the next big thing. In order to impress his host, Mervyn ensured that fainting kids were being carried out of the Maritime just as Rowe was entering the club. The Decca man merely offered a wry smile. It was a trick he had seen many times on his travels. Although impressed by Them's performance and Morrison's showmanship, Rowe was still cagey and seemed more concerned by Phil Solomon's reaction and commitment. The entrepreneur agreed to take Rowe to Peter Lloyd's studio over the weekend so that he could hear more of Them's demos, after which they would formally audition the group. The following Sunday morning, Them, the College Boys and four other local groups were lined up for Rowe's inspection. "Mervyn appeared in his Sunday best and Phil patronized him dreadfully," recalls College Boys manager Sam Smyth. "Philip's a showman. Peter Lloyd was there and Dick Rowe, who spoke mainly to Philip. Back then you didn't really count as anything. People spoke about you as if you weren't there and treated you as if you were something they'd picked up on their shoe on the way in." Remarkably for someone later so publicly pilloried for failing to sign the Beatles, Rowe never claimed any credit for signing Van Morrison. "I didn't want Them without Philip," he frankly admitted. "It's the same with any group – without good management the chances are that they'll never finish the course. I'd been messed around a lot by groups with bad managers. It was crucial for us that they had good management and I loved Philip as a manager with any act I dealt with. I can't say anything against Philip Solomon. Whenever I leaned on him, he was there. Record companies in those days weren't very bright and he was important and good for us."

Rowe was relieved to learn that Solomon was committed to the group. At that point Dorothy Solomon Associated Artistes was a thriving agency and management company and Philip was looking to gain total autonomy with his acts through publishing and in-house production. Indeed, it would only be a matter of time before he formed his own record company and moved into pirate radio. The young Belfast musicians had good reason to feel overawed when they were next presented with contracts. These were taken away and perused, with the involvement of guardians where necessary, and a time was set for their completion prior to Solomon's departure. Cannily, Solomon was signing the group directly to his own Hyde Park Music and effectively licensing their recordings to Decca. Dick Rowe remembers a subsequent meeting in Belfast where the increasingly impatient Solomon told them "You can have another night to think about it but if you want me to sign you, you'd better be at the airport tomorrow. Please your bloody selves, but don't bugger me about." The next day, they duly turned up, contracts in hand. "They wanted to ask him a few more questions," Rowe recalls. "He casually said 'Well, you'd better be quick – the plane leaves in 30 minutes.' I just stood in the background. I wouldn't have dreamed of speaking to anyone like that. He was ruthless with them. But they signed."

One name missing from the contract was Eric Wrixon. His parents were unimpressed by the proposals, having marked out their son's future as a member of the professional classes. Unlike the others, Wrixon was privately educated and it was a mark of his privilege that he attended the same school as Mervyn Solomon's children and others from their extended family. Although he looked up to Billy Harrison as a rougher, elder brother figure, he felt no such rapport with the wee man. "I wouldn't have socialized with Van," he admits. "We were from opposite ends of the spectrum. He left school at 14 and cleaned windows, I was doing A-levels in a public school. We didn't have much to talk about apart from music."

Wrixon was allowed to continue working informally with the group until the new school term started in September. He was also invited to attend their first recording session in London at Decca's Number 2 studio in West Hampstead on 5 July. As a warm-up, the group agreed to play their first show in London, a nervous and inauspicious appearance at Beat City, near Solomon's office in New Oxford Street. It was poor preparation for their all-important recording date. Typically for a mid-Sixties beat group, there was a need for session musicians to fill out the sound and ensure that expensive studio time was not wasted. "There was a problem with Them's drummer," Mervyn Solomon recalls. "He was very bad. We brought in Arthur Greenslade on organ and session drummer Bobby Graham. At that point the group would do anything. They were determined to get on. Van always knew what he wanted and he sulked if the others didn't do it the way he liked. But he wasn't a prima donna — not at that point." Rowe oversaw the recording as producer, with Greenslade acting as musical director. The session produced seven songs: 'Groovin'', 'You Can't Judge A Book By Looking At Its Cover', 'Turn On Your Lovelight', 'Don't Start Crying Now', 'One Two Brown Eyes', 'Philosophy' and 'Gloria'. The last song captured Rowe's attention and he urged Morrison: "Shout! Make it aggressive!"

Rowe was enthusiastic about Them's prospects after seeing that week's *New Musical Express* chart where the Animals had risen to number 1 with 'House Of The Rising Sun'. It was a good omen. Even better news followed days later when Decca's major R&B asset the Rolling Stones displaced their EMI rivals with their first chart topper, 'It's All Over Now'. The cause of long-haired R&B beat was advanced by the Stones' controversial appearance on television's *Juke Box Jury*. Rowe also smiled with grim satisfaction while reading that Granada Television had received a number of complaints after 19-year-old student Nicholas Austin had appeared on that bastion of middle-class, academic respectability *University Challenge* sporting shoulder-length hair, rakish sideboards and dark glasses. As if to compound these sins, he even had the audacity to chew gum throughout the broadcast. "Gum, dark glasses and hair as long as Mick Jagger's can hardly be considered suitable for a television appearance," opined one complainant. Clearly, there was a detectable shift in pop style and allegiance from the politely suited Beatles towards a harsher species of urban, post-beatnik chic. That summer it seemed that the Olympian flame of Merseybeat had been momentarily passed over to a rival breed of R&B exponents, a view cemented when Manfred Mann's 'Do Wah Diddy Diddy' and the Kinks' 'You Really Got Me' also ascended to number 1.

Them returned to Belfast in exultant mood and continued playing the local circuit while awaiting Decca's next move. Rod Demick saw them at the Plaza that summer and laughed out loud when Morrison rolled on the floor during one song and exclaimed, for no apparent reason, "I'm really Eartha Kitt." Eric Bell started staying so late at the Maritime that he constantly missed the last bus home. "I was enjoying myself too much," he says, "but then I'd have to walk through the city centre, over the Queen's Bridge, down by the slaughterhouse and the Markets, which was predominantly Catholic. There'd always be guys standing around late at night looking for trouble. I'd walk quickly or run, then you'd hear 'Hey you, come here' and half a brick would be thrown at you. Once four guys chased me and it was a nightmare. They kept throwing stones and shouted 'We'll get you next time!' When I got home I was shaking and my heart was pounding. That was part of Belfast."

Such isolated incidents went against the spirit of the modern model Belfast promoted by Prime Minister O'Neill and celebrated by the youth in musical clubs and coffee houses throughout the city. Sectarianism lingered, even in this time of peace. That September, Ian Paisley was incensed when the Irish tricolour flag was displayed during an election campaign at the offices of Sinn Féin in Divis Street, West Belfast. After pressurizing the RUC to intervene, he addressed a rally in which he threatened to descend upon Divis Street and remove the offending item himself. The Minister of Home Affairs urged Paisley to call off the march but he barked back his favourite riposte, "No Surrender!" Gerry Adams, then a teenage schoolboy, had heard about the commotion and was doubly intrigued when his Christian Brother teachers had ordered their classes to walk straight home that afternoon and not dally in Divis Street. "Our curiosity led dozens of us to gather and peer into the window of what we were to discover was a Sinn Féin election office. Further encouragement was supplied by the RUC who sledgehammered their way into the premises and seized the flag. It was with some satisfaction, therefore, the following day when we witnessed a large crowd replacing it, an occasion for a most defiant rendering of *Amhrán na bhFian* [the Irish Republic's national anthem] and the subject of some schoolboy speculation upon what might happen next."

What did happen next were the worst riots Belfast had experienced in nearly 30 years. A cavalcade of armoured cars were met with petrol bomb reprisals, leading to 50 civilian injuries and protests in Dublin where demonstrators stoned the British Embassy in sympathy. Fortunately, the incident did not lead to further civil unrest, but it provided a salutary warning shot and was a precursor of events to follow five years later. Paisley's parade prefigured the arrival of the Troubles and simultaneously sparked the nationalist fervour which would ignite in the creation of his great nemesis and future leader of Sinn Féin, Gerry Adams. "We were beginning to get a sense of our essential Irishness," says Adams, "and events on the Falls Road served to whet our political appetites." For that he owed much to the Big Man.

The unrest in Belfast coincided with Them's first assault on the British mainland. Prior to their departure, they had found an organist to replace Wrixon. For those who dared call Them "a Proddy band" it was noticeable that the new recruit was a Catholic from Ross Street, near the Falls Road. Patrick John McAuley was part of a large musical family whose senior members had toured the North playing céilís and mixing Irish folk tunes with popular songs. As a child Patsy had attended a special school for asthmatics which, unusually for Belfast, enrolled both Catholic and Protestant pupils. One of his best friends was another breathless sufferer and Morrison acolyte, the Protestant Herbie Armstrong. McAuley was a musical magpie and soon took up piano, harmonica and drums before forming the Blue Angels, who played Cliff Richard and the Shadows material. He later founded the Yaks, a more fashionable outfit combining rock 'n' roll, pop and R&B. "Patsy was my musical mentor and the mainman in the Yaks," says their guitarist Billy Hollywood. "We'd busked together since school and in the parlour of his house. He played a variety of instruments and was a damn good artist as well. He was one of those arty people who could turn his hand to anything." McAuley was also a friend of the 3Js and a regular at the Maritime where he first encountered Them. When the drummer vacancy arose in the group, he was perfectly placed to take advantage. "He was enthralled by the group and bowled over by it all," Hollywood recalls. "Van Morrison made a big impression on him. He was one of the few people I knew who was able to talk to him in a very friendly fashion. They got on really well and laughed and joked together a lot at that stage. I was there a few times while McAuley was talking to him, but he didn't speak to me. Van was extremely selective. I admired him but I think you'd have to have been a bit off the wall for him to take a shine to you. Certainly I'd have been too ordinary for him to bother about."

Paisley's voice was still reverberating across Belfast while Them were opening at London's hip 100 Club. Their first single, a cover of Slim Harpo's 'Don't Start Crying Now', was issued that same month. It was backed with the Morrison original 'One Two Brown Eyes', a track distinguished by Harrison's use of a thimble to create a bottleneck guitar effect. With chart R&B seemingly at its apex, the choice of A-side was logical, but regrettable. The single was neither commercial nor particularly distinguished, and duly bombed. Meanwhile, Them were playing around the clock, appearing at R&B venues, ballrooms and working men's clubs. The Solomons had even booked them to appear at some Irish dance halls, which sparked their first rebellion. "There was an Irish club, the Galtymore, Cricklewood," Harrison recalls. "We just turned around and refused to play it. As far as we were concerned it was an Irish club, a showband situation. We were the last thing an Irish club needed, especially with expatriates. They didn't want five wild long-haired guys who were as far away from showband music as possible. So we didn't even get out of the wagon."

When Phil Solomon learned that they had failed to fulfil this engagement, he was furious. Never a man to be crossed, Solomon demanded absolute professionalism from his acts and cared little about their opinions on the suitability of venues. "The Bachelors never missed a date in their lives," he roared. "One of them even had an accident on their way to do a pantomime in Bristol and went on with his leg in plaster and 21 stitches in his head. *That* is professionalism." Solomon's managerial clout was devastating to witness and his business acumen was exceptional for the period. Unlike many other managers, he was never humbled by any of his acts or over-tolerant when faced with artistic caprice or insubordination. Neither Harrison nor Morrison was ever a match for his imperious self-belief. "Van Morrison and Them would *never* have made it without Phil Solomon," insists Larry Page, then manager of the chart-topping Kinks. "He was very shrewd. Phil owned the BBC and [it seemed like] he had Dick Rowe in his pocket." Rowe had already expressed his confidence in Solomon's wisdom and judgement and continued to add his acts to the Decca roster, including the Irish twins Elaine & Derek and the 17-year-old blonde ingenue Twinkle. Privately, he regarded Solomon as the shrewdest manager of the era and never ceased to be amazed by his fearlessness. "I was in a hotel with him up north and the phone rang at one in the morning," Rowe remembers. "He was almost crying with rage. Don Arden was on the other end shouting, 'I'll have your wife's ears off!' And there were tears in Philip's eyes. He was furious beyond words. 'Don't threaten me!' They were at it hammer and tongs. But Philip was much cleverer than Don Arden. You see, Philip Solomon is a winner. He just can't lose. He wouldn't care what he said or did. I've heard him have a row with a priest on the phone. I roared with laughter. He stood no nonsense."

Undeterred by the failure of Them's first single, Rowe suggested that they employ the services of the famed New York producer Bert Berns. Bronx-born Berns, the son of Russian Jewish immigrants, was a music-loving hustler who had worked as a mambo dancer, sheet music copyist and session pianist, before finding his niche as a songwriter, performer and producer appearing under such pseudonyms as René St Charles, Bert Russell and Russell Byrd. Solomon was well aware of Berns' reputation, having seen him working earlier in the Sixties for music publisher Bobby Mellin at the 'hit factory' on 1650 Broadway. Such was Berns' drive that he had been appointed songwriter and producer for Atlantic Records in 1963, replacing the legendary Jerry Leiber and Mike Stoller. Berns' CV included a run of US Top 40 hits for the Jarmals ('A Little Bit Of Soap'), the Exciters ('Tell Him'), Garnet Mimms & The Enchanters ('Cry Baby') and Solomon Burke ('Goodbye Baby'). On an international level, Berns was better known for his production credits on the Drifters' hits 'Under The Boardwalk' and 'Saturday Night At The Movies', and co-authorship of the Isley Brothers' 'Twist And Shout', made even more famous by the Beatles in 1964. Rowe's plan was to maximize Berns' time in England by booking sessions for several Solomon acts, including Them and Elaine & Derek, plus Decca's Lulu & The Luvvers, and other lesser lights. Rowe hoped that a series of quality A-side singles might benefit the label. "I told Philip what I had in mind, but it was going to cost a lot of money. I wasn't sure Decca would see the wisdom of it. But that's where Solomon was good. He followed success." Berns was flown over and ensconced at the Albany Hotel in Birmingham, with Solomon paying his expenses and Decca footing the bill for the recordings.

Solomon's organization was expanding at this point. Apart from his recent signings, he had plucked the talented Derry-born Phil Coulter from Queen's University and hired him as a writer, arranger and musical factotum. One of his first tasks was transcribing lyrics and music from Them's demos onto lead sheets for registration purposes and deciphering Morrison's broad East Belfast accent. "I remember labouring over them for hours," Coulter says. Another protégé affiliated to the company was Tommy Scott, who had recently penned Eden Kane's 'Boys Cry' and was intending to record with Berns. Solomon sagely advised him to pursue his writing and they soon established a joint production company: Scott/Solomon Productions.

Meanwhile, Berns worked his magic on Morrison's adaptation of John Lee Hooker's version of 'Baby Please Don't Go'. "That's when the Them situation turned around," Coulter concludes. "Berns came in with a very heavy reputation. At that period record producers were very few and far between in England. Anyone who wanted to produce became an A&R man working for a record company for £30 a week. Bert was a very creative, dynamic guy. He beat the band into shape. It was a little off the wall before that but, without diluting their rawness, Bert gave them a lot of cohesion. Obviously, Bert was aware of the fact that some of the group weren't cutting it musically. He saw that Van was the man and he was an American producer into making hit records. I don't think Van felt any intense loyalty to the guys in the group. As far as he was concerned he wanted the best record." In order to bolster the musicianship, Berns added another session player to their ranks, the talented teenage guitarist Jimmy Page who doubled the distinctive riff already worked out by Billy Harrison. Almost as an afterthought, one of the songs from the July sessions with Rowe was resurrected to provide a "too good to waste" B-side.

'Gloria' would belatedly emerge as one of Morrison's most memorable compositions of the era. Its title was a veiled tribute to Gloria Gordon, who had died from cancer three years before at the age of 29. "It was about my cousin Gloria," Morrison confirmed. "I dug her." In transforming her name into song, Morrison avoided funereal reverence or sentimental elegy in favour of a thrilling, life-affirming drama that brimmed with a smouldering undercurrent. It was a song of seething passion, performed with a controlled desperation and arrogant defiance, as if the ritualistic incantation of the name Gloria was in itself enough to raise the dead. The melody, which Wrixon believes may have been inspired by Bo Diddley's 'Bring It To Jerome', was enlivened by Harrison's mesmerizing lead guitar riff. A primeval slice of British R&B, Rowe's production of 'Gloria' transcended its humble debut as a B-side to become a garage group, punk rock anthem, later providing a US Top 10 hit for the Shadows Of Night and inspiring notable cover versions from acts as varied as Patti Smith and Eddie And The Hot Rods.

'Baby Please Don't Go' was released at the beginning of November and Them were immediately booked for a television appearance and ordered to buy some Carnaby Street suits. Solomon even suggested, perhaps ironically, that Morrison should wear pink tights for the occasion. Ever rebellious, Them threw aside their polite apparel and kitted themselves out in army surplus gear. "I met them afterwards and they were delighted with themselves," Sam Smyth remembers, "but Philip was horrified when he turned on the TV to see them looking like army commandos." Despite the prestigious exposure, initial sales of the single proved disappointing. To make matters worse, another song from the recent Berns session, his own composition 'Here Comes The Night', had been passed over to fellow Decca act Lulu. Them had earmarked this as a likely follow-up and were bitterly disappointed by the decision. "They bitched to me about it a lot," says Phil Coulter, "but they wouldn't dare to have said anything to Solomon." It was with a certain grim satisfaction that Them watched the rival recording enter the charts at number 50, then disappear.

After a few weeks Them abandoned hopes of achieving a chart

breakthrough with 'Baby Please Don't Go' and feared that their big adventure might be winding to a close. Without a hit record, revenue from performances was pitiful and surviving in London had bled them dry. Reluctantly, they returned to Belfast to face their peers who weren't slow to scoff. "Everybody was pointing their fingers and saying, 'You didn't make it!'" Harrison laments. Drummer Ronnie Millings, who had the added responsibility of a wife and three children, felt he could no longer justify continuing with Them. "He opted to leave and get a job," Harrison notes. "I'd like to think I would've had the integrity to do the same thing but back then – no. We were still young enough to be living in a dream. We were all naive. We weren't even fledglings, we were scaldies."

Millings left behind his equipment and Them resolved to continue as a quartet with the versatile Patsy McAuley switching to drums. Relations between Morrison and the rest seemed increasingly strained as over-familiarity slowly festered into disdain. "You just had to take Van as he came," Alan Henderson remembers. "You couldn't be real sure what mood he'd be in on any particular day. You were always prepared to think, 'Should I stay away from Van today or talk to him?'" Local boy Terry Davis attended several of their gigs at this point, occasionally cadging a lift home with the group afterwards. The atmosphere was strained. "Van wasn't that friendly with the rest of the group," Davis says. "He and Billy weren't getting on terribly well. They were always at each other's throats and having rows in the back of the van. There were harsh words spoken. That didn't bother me too much though because I knew Van was a difficult person anyway."

In order to assist his former friends, Them's erstwhile organist Eric Wrixon volunteered his services for a few dates, including Saturday dance nights at Inst, and McAuley's former group the Yaks were offered a support slot at a hall in Donaghadee. Left alone for the afternoon while Them squeezed in a couple of 40-minute sets elsewhere, the Yaks disgraced themselves by getting bored drunk. "It was more drink than we'd have had in a night," Billy Hollywood admits. The episode did not prevent the Yaks' Jackie 'Griff' McAuley receiving a surprise invitation from his brother to join Them as their new organist. His audition consisted of a trial by silent torture at a local coffee bar where Patsy and Van offered a masterclass in non-communication. "I sat there for an hour and nobody spoke," Jackie recalls. "Nobody was speaking to Van and I was rabbiting on because I'd be out of my head on pills and I got told to shut up more than once." The pained interaction was a sign of things to come, but at least Them had survived their first membership change. By the end of November, they were five strong once more.

In the brief period Them had been away from Belfast there had been only subtle changes in the local music scene. R&B was still a relatively minor interest, not without gimmicky appeal. Queen's University Glee Club had launched the Arabs (an acronym for A Rhythm & Blues Sound) as the most academically qualified group in history with a total of two degrees, 20 A-levels and 45 O-levels between them. Elsewhere, there seemed to be more talk about Sammy Houston's dance team appearing on *Come Dancing* that Christmas than the prospects of his eponymous Jazz Club. Morrison's old friends Brian Rossi and Herbie Armstrong had been sacked from the Plaza for playing R&B at the 'Over 21s night' and were forming a new group, the Wheels. It was still a relatively conservative scene. Those pioneering R&B advocates the 3Js had lost their club at the Maritime and were opening a new venue at Tommy McCarthy's studio on Royal Avenue. Morrison and Them duly offered their support and took up a residency there during December. That same month, Eddie Kennedy launched a rival attraction at the Maritime, introducing the Mad Lads, a group whose sound echoed that of Them. Eager to establish himself as a junior Phil Solomon, Kennedy was ready to take advantage of any new trends. He was probably unprepared for the spectacle of Morrison's old friend G.D. taking the stage at the Maritime and delivering a surreal evening of impromptu blues numbers. "Eddie Kennedy was amazed to find himself this fashionable figure," Sam Smyth smiles. "He was a working-class man, entrepreneurial by instinct, who clicked on to something."

Back in London, the indefatigable Phil Solomon had not given up on 'Baby Please Don't Go'. Having spent money on wining and dining Bert Berns, he was loath to see his investment squandered. When the Rolling Stones entered the *NME* charts at number 1 with a startling revival of Willie Dixon's 'Little Red Rooster' – an incredibly adventurous and inspired choice of single – it underlined the continued potency of the blues in a pop format. Ever the gambler, Solomon pumped in more promotional money so that Them's record was played on the recently launched pirate station Radio Caroline and broadcast nightly on Radio Luxembourg. Using his wife Dorothy's connections, he pulled off a magnificent coup by ensuring that 'Baby Please Don't Go' was used for eight weeks as the signature tune of *Ready Steady Go!*, an honour more famously bestowed upon Manfred Mann's '5-4-3-2-1'. Even the often adversarial Billy Harrison was impressed. "That was a biggie. Solomon spun that deal. There's no denying that it helped immensely." In spite of their recent setbacks, Morrison was bullishly confident that Them would succeed. "We were doing great and we'll do even better when we go back in January," he told Belfast music paper *City Week*.

Not everyone, though, was enamoured of Them and that Christmas they encountered hostility, which rapidly turned to violence. In areas like Strabane and Derry, audiences reared on Irish traditional music and crowd-pleasing showbands were unimpressed by sullen musicians who played obscure R&B tunes. "We were the last thing they needed," Harrison admits. "We'd get a lot of verbal abuse and then they started throwing pennies. Over here, if a guy came along to a theatre or cinema queue and tried to make a few bob playing a harmonica you threw a few pence to him so that he'd go further down the line and you didn't have to listen to him. So they started throwing pennies at us in the country areas. We annoyed them even more by picking the bloody money up. Money's money. Plus we had that attitude of 'whatever you expect, we'll do the opposite'."

On 26 December Them were booked to play a double header in Lurgan, Co. Armagh, and Cookstown, Co. Tyrone, supported by the Stratotones, who specialized in pop covers and benign instrumentals like 'The Flight Of The Eagle'. Their set passed without incident, but Them were greeted with antagonism from the outset. In Cookstown expectant fans, eager to hear the popular tunes of the day, were outraged when Them stubbornly ignored requests and persisted in playing R&B standards. A steady thud of slow handclapping greeted each number as Morrison prowled the apron of the stage leering menacingly at the spectators. Morrison was often aggressive in performance and became downright belligerent when faced with a hostile audience. As the show was reaching a tense climax and pennies started landing on stage, he bellowed into the microphone "Goodnight pigs!" It was a thrilling spectacle. "Van took control and was his own man," Jackie McAuley says. "It was very heavy, a Klondike-like atmosphere. There were people there who wanted to see us but the ugly ones were there in force and stirred the whole thing up. We were very frightened. People tend to forget you're human beings and these pennies could take your eyes out. I was the youngest and Billy was the eldest so I hid behind him. Billy basically ran the group and he wouldn't take any shit from anybody." Unfortunately, even Harrison could not appease this crowd and the unrest soon degenerated into a near riot. Morrison's vitriol and porcine putdown had so incensed the spectators that they started throwing chairs at the musicians. "When the chairs came flying we dived into the dressing room, locked the door, and stayed there for about four hours," McAuley recalls. Outside, the rabble expended their wrath by throwing stones at the hall's windows and smashing the windscreen of Them's minibus. The innocent Stratotones were also caught up in the mêlée and found that their van had been damaged amid the confusion. Afterwards, their lead guitarist Jackie Middleton told the press: "One thing is certain – we won't ever play alongside Them again if we can help it."

The so-called 'riot' provided Them with some unexpected publicity and Morrison could even be seen for a few seconds attempting to explain himself to a news reporter on Ulster Television. Instead of playing the acquiescent pop star he already resembled a mean-looking article with an attitude problem. Them had not yet reached the charts, but they were already emerging as the new bad boys of pop. "A lot of people then booked the band just for the controversy," McAuley notes, "because the places were always packed. I could never understand why people paid money to come to gigs to throw pennies."

The ever alert Sam Smyth, then booking the College Boys in the South, wasted no time in contacting Them with an offer to play the Stella in Mount Merrion, Dublin. "They had to hire a car and turn up in the middle-class suburb of Stillorgan where they were an enormous success. I remember speaking to Van, and surly was the mode. Surly on stage and I suppose it spills into one's private life. They were fairly disagreeable, and not just with me, but with each other. There were tensions. I don't think Van liked the band that much as musicians or thought they were as good as he was. Billy was pushy but, in my view, dealing with Them, the real power emanated from the wee man. He certainly seemed to have a veto on everything."

Morrison was relieved to discover that Dublin audiences were sophisticated enough to keep their pennies in their pockets. Them played several other gigs in the city over the next couple of weeks and caused a minor sensation when 11 girls injured themselves trying to climb on stage. "You can put us down as preferring girls to pennies," Harrison told the press. This latest demonstration of fan mania coincided with the shock news that 'Baby Please Don't Go' was finally climbing the UK charts and heading towards the Top 10. Harrison remembers that moment as one of the highlights of his life. After months of struggling for a pittance, it seemed that Them were about to emerge as genuine pop stars and enter the public consciousness, joining a pantheon that already housed the Rolling Stones, the Animals and the Nashville Teens.

SEVEN

No Mass, No Lemass

1965 began on an optimistic yet ominous note in Belfast with Prime Minister Terence O'Neill's announcement that he was inviting the Taoiseach Seán Lemass to Stormont. Ian Paisley reacted as if the Pope himself were about to descend upon the Shankill and quickly organized a protest. Unionists took to the streets waving provocative placards proclaiming 'No Mass, No Lemass', 'Down With The Lundys' and inevitably 'No Surrender'. When the beleaguered O'Neill responded by accepting the Taoiseach's invitation to visit Dublin he was greeted with a banner warning 'No Welcome For Him In Sandy Row'.

The members of Them always believed that they were immune to sectarianism and prided themselves on playing Catholic venues such as St Teresa's every other Sunday. However, not all their followers were as broad-minded. When Them followed O'Neill down South and played some dates in Dublin, a spirit of separatism was evident. Playwright Aisling Foster, then a teenager, attended a Saturday night hop in Donnybrook and encountered a clash of cultures and religions. "Every boy who asked me to dance had a Belfast accent. They opened with the question 'What school do you go to?' The answer 'Notre Dame des Missions' was all they needed to hear. There was no next dance. Up North, Them were a Prod band." Back in Belfast, John Trew, editor of *City Week*, saw Them as possible saviours whose success across the water could only lead to good. "They may not exactly represent the 'New Image of Ulster' that Premier O'Neill talks about, but they are succeeding in what is, after all, one of the most competitive fields in Big Business. All the signs suggest that the local brand of music could really knock the Mersey sound off its pedestal.

This is not just of interest to teenagers, it would make a big contribution to the prosperity of the whole province. Look what the Beatles have done for Liverpool."

As Them were preparing to leave Belfast for London, the Rolling Stones arrived for a show at the ABC Cinema, supported by the Banshees. The combined appeal of Them and the Stones momentarily transported the city centre into R&B heaven. The Mad Lads, the Alleykatz, the Fugitives and Styx were all jostling for prominence among the new hierarchy, while Queen's University celebrated rag week with a marathon blues session in the window of Hart & Churchill's where Unit 5 played for 14 hours non-stop. Looking on were the Kentuckians, Group 66 and the Teddie Palmer-fronted Spectres, fresh from recording a single, 'The Facts Of Life'. The Spectres' manager David Parkinson had even formed the first Them fan club with the help of secretary Viv McNeekin, who was about to take fandom to its fairy-tale limit by getting engaged to Billy Harrison. Soon afterwards, Lillian Gore, a youngster from Silvio Street, set up a rival fan club. Expectations were high.

In late January, Them set forth on their second invasion of England, accompanied by their dashing, uproarious, braggadocio road manager, Peter Docherty. Resplendent in his dark suit, cuff links and silver bracelet, 'Doc' looked a far more convincing pop star than the brooding Van Morrison or any of his fellow players. "Peter used to pull the birds," Terry Davis recalls. "I don't think Van was terribly lucky in that department." The musicians soon settled into a semblance of pop star luxury when Solomon allowed them to reside at the Royal Hotel adjacent to Russell Square. Over the next few weeks, the members of Them met other touring musicians passing through London, including several of Morrison's blues deities. Chief amongst them was Little Walter, for whom the usually aloof Morrison displayed unexpected reverence, even running petty errands in the hope of receiving some harmonica-playing tips. He was rewarded one evening when the bluesman allowed him to appear on stage for a short jam. Morrison also betrayed kitten-like tendencies upon meeting John Lee Hooker whose blues recordings had enlivened many an afternoon back on Hyndford Street. Another hotel guest whom the group were thrilled to meet was Gene Vincent, the leather-clad, battle scarred rock 'n' roller whose outlaw status and alcohol consumption were legendary. He seemed particularly interested in hearing stories about the illicit delights of poteen which reminded him of his beloved Southern moonshine. "We used to hang out with him quite a lot," Jackie McAuley remembers. "He'd spend hours in the hotel basement playing the piano. He was great, Gene, a wild man, but he never lost his temper with us."

A more important acolyte was celebrity disc jockey Jimmy Savile who used the hotel as his London base and served as an unpaid PR for those lucky enough to cross his path. Both Morrison and Harrison, then and thereafter, spoke of the garrulous Savile in only the highest terms. "We all got on well with Jimmy," Harrison says. "Jimmy Savile had a philosophy which was 'If you can't say something good about someone then don't say anything.' He was a great one for helping all the groups. He punted their records, talked about them and did everything he could for everybody. He did a lot for us, including write-ups in his column for the *People*, mentioning us or saying things like 'those mad Irishmen Them have been in again annoying me' as we shared the same hotel."

Solomon was happy for such patronage as it introduced Them's name to a wider audience and allowed him to promote the group with a series of newspaper profiles, a commendable feat for a period when coverage of pop music in the mainstream media was relatively slight. Decca's Head of Publicity, Tony Hall, was impressed by Them's music but failed to convey his enthusiasm to the group having hit a verbal brick wall with the determinedly silent Van Morrison. Their inter-action did not extend beyond a few garbled sentences in the *Ready Steady Go!* canteen. Unfortunately Them proved equally ill-equipped to deal with even the most sympathetic journalists and soon earned themselves a reputation for cynicism, sarcasm and bad manners. "A lot of the interviews were surly," Harrison admits, "but we didn't intentionally play up. We may have had an attitude problem because we felt the Irish had never had a good reputation on the mainland, especially around London. They were thought of as fighting drunks. We were just concerned with our playing and we were very anti-establishment." They certainly showed their worst side to Fleet Street journalist Ron Boyle who had never encountered such a blatant lack of cooperation and civility. "One of them even refused to answer simple personal questions like 'What age are you?'" he marvelled. "I just got fed up and left them." Despite Harrison's claim that Them were responding to anti-Irish prejudices, they proved no better behaved when confronted with one of their own. The *Irish Independent*'s Des Hickey was flown over by Phil Solomon but left his offices in New Oxford Street a beaten man. "They were the most boorish bunch of youngsters I'd come across in my short career," Hickey recounted. "Each question just got a couple of grunts in response." Solomon hoped that the attractive, chain-smoking young *Daily Express* columnist Judith Simons might soften their approach, but she too was treated with arrogant disdain. Phil Coulter, who sat in on her interview, was mortified. "It was the most painful 15 minutes I have ever spent. She was trying to extract information from them and it was like trying to pull teeth. They would just sit and mutter monosyllabic grunts to themselves and give her off the wall answers. Poor Judith was absolutely flummoxed. They were certainly not a publicist's dream." Tommy Scott, also in attendance, remembered the climax of that interview with a wry smile. "Eventually, she said, 'Well who actually formed you?' And Billy Harrison said, 'British Plastics fucking moulded us.' It was a great line. It killed everyone. It was so embarrassing. But that was Them. While everyone else was trying to curry favour, they didn't give a shit."

Them's irksome press encounters – which Morrison would later raise to the level of a negative art form – were conducted between short breaks in a busy itinerary. Decca, meanwhile, sought to exploit the chart success of 'Baby Please Don't Go' by issuing an EP featuring the brooding 'Philosophy' from the Dick Rowe sessions. It was followed by the belated appearance of 'Here Comes The Night', their second Bert Berns production and their first written by their American mentor. Despite the song's jaunty tone, it was a dark, introspective composition of obsessive jealousy and encroaching loneliness. Berns ensured its distinctive pop appeal with a spirited arrangement, assisted by guitarist Jimmy Page, whose contribution to Them's two hit singles was later over-praised in the music press and subsequently downplayed by the group. "He played rhythm guitar on one thing and doubled a bass riff on the other," Morrison impatiently noted. "That's all he did. I mean it was nothing. It was just zero bit. I don't think it's a big deal now . . .

he was just goofing off." A less contentious contribution came from Andy White, the drummer who had replaced Ringo Starr on the Beatles' first hit 'Love Me Do'. Perry Ford, then in the charts with the Ivy League, joined Tommy Scott on backing vocals while Phil Coulter appeared on keyboards. For Coulter, the recording was a defining moment in his early career. "One of my abiding recollections of that or any other period was walking into Studio 2 at Decca and hearing Berns routining the group on 'Here Comes The Night'. I knew I'd heard a smash. It was the first time I'd ever heard a hit record in its emerging state."

On its first day of release, 'Here Comes The Night' sold 16,000 copies, an impressive number which prompted another PR push, including key television appearances on *Ready Steady Go!* and *Top Of The Pops*. Morrison already hated the formal requirements of these performances which inhibited his movements and made him feel self-conscious. "Them were never meant to be on *Top Of The Pops*," he insisted. "I mean, miming? Lip syncing? We used to laugh at that programme, think it was a joke. Then we were on it ourselves. It was ridiculous. We were totally anti that type of thing. We were really into the blues . . . and we had to get into suits and have make-up put on and all that shit." Harrison was of similar mind. "It was very clinical," he points out. "On television you were given an 'X' to stand on and had to face a particular way. You were a dog's balls if you moved. They actually sprayed my guitar with this matt stuff to make it dull so that it didn't flash back in the camera. That's the way the world was in those days."

A week after St Patrick's Day, 'Here Comes The Night' entered the charts alongside two other R&B-tinged Decca acts, the Nashville Teens and Dave Berry. Them barely had time to savour the moment as they were scuttling across the country in their Morris 100 with its faulty gear stick, playing a delirious succession of one-nighters. During a show in Scotland, Morrison surrendered his shoes, cuff links and tie to frenzied fans and was kidnapped by prankish rag students in Elgin. Such fun episodes were eclipsed by an enveloping gloom and insidious irritation as the road slog took its toll. Bleary-eyed, Them edged their way to Wolverhampton's Civic Centre, then on to Margate's Winter Gardens and Scarborough's Futurist. "We were shredded," Jackie

McAuley groans. "We were absolutely wrecked. It was starting to crumble. We were overworked, underpaid and undernourished. We used to go up to Bed & Breakfasts in some places and they'd say 'No Irish, no blacks'. They had specially made plaques – some said 'No Jews'. We couldn't always get digs, so we slept in the van. It was a joke. There were all sorts of stories going down. We were going to get rid of Van. We were going to get rid of everybody. Van wouldn't communicate. At one time it seemed he wanted to leave. There was no communication. We'd be driving along and nobody would be talking. It was a total mess." The attritional silence ensured that even a tentative, innocuous comment could be misconstrued, culminating in an ugly spat or threatened rebellion, usually followed by another period of prolonged silence. "We all started arguing and fighting about everything," McAuley says. "It was general weirdness." At such moments, the Morris van would grind to a sudden halt after which somebody would explode through the back door and disappear in a huff until they'd cooled off. "We were at each other's throats," McAuley admits. "There would be a huge row, then 'Stop the van'. One day Van got out and I went with him. We walked for miles. He was saying things like 'I'm just going to keep walking forever and ever' – crazy things like that . . . There was one time Van didn't say a word for three days. Twenty-four hours a day, not one fucking word. 'Hi, Van' and he'd nod. He was somewhere else. He wouldn't even mumble. That would just drive everybody mad."

The frustration with Morrison's silences was exacerbated by McAuley's pill popping. In order to stay awake, he had lined his bathroom kit with a handy supply of amphetamines. Overindulgence was repaid with bouts of exhaustion, which could prove costly. "I was in the basement of our hotel and I crashed out," McAuley remembers. "The band couldn't find me and they had to leave to do a gig. When I came to, they'd gone. I had a lashing from Billy. Then we went to a gig near Liverpool, an ice rink. It was a Teddy Boy place, not for us. It was murder. Teddy Boys on skates! There was a massive fight and the gig was stopped. Our van had been broken into and the suitcases were taken. I was livid because I had a shaving kit full of pills. The police came back and said they'd found a suitcase, but fortunately they didn't open it."

McAuley was doubly lucky not to be drawn into more dangerous drug escapades. As he admits, "The guy who used to give me the pills said 'Try a bit of this – heroin'. Not long afterwards he walked under a bus . . . The heroin was a one-off thing. People would give you anything in those days." Although soft drugs were par for the course among many groups of the period, Billy Harrison claims he has no memory of any serious incidences of experimentation. "There may have been the odd grass blown, but it's not even considered drugs now. It would have been reserved for a wind-down. You might have been to a party and took a few blows and had a draw. I'm not trying to come across as a goodie goodie – it wasn't a big thing then." As for Morrison, both he and his solicitors have confirmed that he never took any hard drugs at any stage of his career.

Them's often casual, devil-may-care attitude would soon prove their undoing. An important opportunity to appear on *Ready Steady Goes Live!* was squandered when the group failed to reach the studio on time. The scapegoat was their charismatic road manager Peter Docherty, who had overslept. "We weren't too pleased and he told us to piss off," Harrison claims. "There was a bit of a ruck and then it was goodbye Doc." The Doc left with a bloody nose and immediately returned to Belfast where he threatened to shake up the music scene by launching himself as a P.J. Proby imitator at the Plaza. Phil Solomon was outraged by Them's failure to appear on *Ready Steady Go!* which he saw as another example of their lamentable discipline and lack of profes-sionalism. "How long can you keep accepting this nonsense?" he railed. "Life's too short. I can only say that if Morrison had to be at a studio on a certain day at a certain time then I expected him to be there. And if he wasn't there, I would expect some very good reason, which I think is correct. You book studios, you book producers, you book musicians, you book gigs – everybody is waiting for the man who doesn't turn up. I would be *very* upset."

Remarkably well informed, Solomon had even heard rumours that the group were taking drugs. When Bert Berns told him that someone had been smoking marijuana in the toilet of his New Oxford Street office, Solomon was ashen with rage and indignation. "Pot may not be harmful, but if the police had come in we would all have been arrested." Concerned about the reputation of Dorothy's agency, which after all booked the clean-cut Bachelors, he demanded that Them pull themselves together, knuckle down and fulfil every engagement without fail. His anger coincided with their growing resentment towards any authority figure. Now that 'Here Comes The Night' was in the charts, they were complaining among themselves about the lack of revenue in their accounts. Like disgruntled trade unionists, the group made a collective decision to confront Solomon and demand more money and better working conditions. Naively, they assumed that their current chart successes would weaken their manager's resolve. Given their recent behaviour, it was not the wisest moment to challenge Solomon on the issue, but Them were seldom blessed with good sense or delicate timing. "I reckoned Solomon was on the fiddle," Harrison claims, without proof. "We went into the office and faced him with it and he faced everybody down one by one and I was left standing on my own. It was a real egg-on-the-face job. When you're young you have principles. You don't ask if you can afford them, you go for it. You make a decision, you stick with it. Solomon was imposing and a great one to browbeat you. I was the eldest. I'd grown up without a father who'd done a runner, so responsibility was heaped upon me quite early. I was probably a hell of a lot more mature than the other guys and I'd always been a fighter. If I saw a cause I'd bloody well fight. It was just my nature at the time – an argumentative bastard."

"It was a disgusting experience dealing with those people," McAuley adds. "Even thinking about it all these years later, it's thoroughly distasteful. Here's these young kids from Belfast being sent out into the big bad world and what did we get for it? We worked very hard and never saw the money." Alan Henderson was a little more realistic, admitting "When I dealt with Philip he was straight with me. He just said it like it was and if you didn't like it you could go."

Of course, at this point money was only starting to trickle in from record sales and concert bookings and the group still had expenses that were legitimately deducted. Solomon felt that they had already let him down badly and regarded their demands as impertinent and nonsensical. A roar of indignation and a firm reminder that they were under exclusive contract was sufficient to quell their paltry mutiny. "The Solomon business got sorted out," Harrison acknowledges. "I felt I'd presented Phil Solomon with my head on a plate like John the Baptist.

He made sure the others fell in line. He said, 'If you don't work for me, you'll never work again' and the others believed it. They thought, 'Shit, Disneyland is about to close.' Even if somebody else had handled us, Phil would have retained the publishing. You'd never have got that off him. So he was going to make his bread anyway." Crestfallen, Them contented themselves with the conviction that better times lay ahead.

Solomon calmed troubled waters by farming out some bookings to a subsidiary agent, Maurice King, whose roster included the Rockin' Berries and the Walker Brothers. King was a sharp, no-nonsense manager/agent variously described as a loveable rogue and a con merchant. The latter epithet was provided by no less an authority than his long-suffering wife, Mary. King ran the Starlite Club in Stratford Place, off New Oxford Street, a favourite haunt of East End villains and minor showbiz celebrities. For a time Them regarded the club as a second home, revelling in its understated glamour and easy access. "If we came back to London we usually ended up there," Harrison recalls. "Many's the night we dragged our gear on stage and played till two in the morning. The place was officially closed but food was served and the odd punter was about. We played for ourselves. I suppose that was as near as we ever got to bloody practising. We used to work things out on the Starlite stage." Young Jackie McAuley was astonished to learn that several of the well-dressed onlookers were genuine gangsters, supposedly carrying guns. Harrison was typically unfazed by such whispers and established his own hard-man reputation with a street fighter's aggression. "Someone was mouthing at Alan Henderson and I seemed to do all the battling for everybody so I jumped in hot-headed. There was a rumble outside and I gave this guy an awful hammering. It was normal fisticuffs. I'd been brought up in East Belfast where there was fighting on the streets. If anyone said anything wrong, I jumped on them straight away. There was always a mixture of people at the Starlite but we never had any real trouble. We got on well with Maurice King – at least you could talk to him. Philip let him deal with the group more and more, but he kept control. If we had any complaints they went through Maurice." It said much for Solomon's innate self-confidence that the arrangement worked so effectively, with King willingly accepting a subordinate role.

For Morrison and Them, the tetchy tour dates and flickering flare-ups that threatened their future were balanced by some career high points. The promising chart progress of 'Here Comes The Night' was crowned by an appearance at the most important and star-studded UK pop show of the Sixties. On Sunday 11 April, the *New Musical Express* presented its annual Poll Winners' Concert at the Empire Pool, Wembley, where 10,000 spectators could enjoy, for as little as seven shillings and sixpence, a line-up that brought together the Beatles, the Rolling Stones, the Kinks, the Animals, the Moody Blues, Freddie & The Dreamers, Herman's Hermits, Wayne Fontana & The Mindbenders, the Rockin' Berries, the Seekers, the Ivy League, Georgie Fame & The Blue Flames and Sounds Incorporated. Among the solo performers were the two best UK female singers of the era – Cilla Black and Dusty Springfield – and recent chart topper Tom Jones. Phil Solomon ensured that his stable was represented by Twinkle, the Bachelors and Them, whose performance prompted compere Derek Johnson to enthuse: "Let there be no doubt about their popularity. Lead singer Van Morrison led the audience to fever pitch through the cymbal-clashing 'Here Comes The Night' followed immediately by another number that had many of the audience jumping from their seats. The title: 'Turn On Your Lovelight'. The tempo went faster and faster like some ecstatic pop version of a Cossack dance."

That same week, the Beatles released their new single 'Ticket To Ride' which entered the charts at number 1, displacing Cliff Richard's 'The Minute You're Gone' and leaving Them stranded at number 3 where they remained for a further fortnight. This sudden elevation into the pop élite prompted Solomon and Decca to recall Bert Berns in order to prepare Them for a fresh series of shows and complete work on their first album. Before the sessions commenced, Jackie McAuley was dismissed from the group. Alan Henderson was given the task of informing the youngster that they would prefer a more accomplished keyboardist. Some harsh words were spoken, with Henderson insisting he had nothing against Fenians. "When he said, 'We don't want you in the band anymore', I just said, 'Fair enough!' and they went off to the next gig," McAuley remembers. "Afterwards, when I realized what I'd said, a shock wave hit me."

Within days of McAuley's dismissal, Billy Harrison returned to

Northern Ireland to marry Vivien McNeekin at St Columbanus' church in Ballyholme. Alan Henderson served as best man at the 20-minute ceremony which attracted over 70 fans. A chicken and ham luncheon was served at the reception in the Spanish Lounge of the new Mount Royal Hotel in Donaghadee. Morrison was not in attendance, but Harrison was happy to receive telegrams from Jimmy Savile and various friends in the Pretty Things and the Animals. The couple were allowed a brief honeymoon after which they planned to move into a 16 guineas a week, five-bedroomed flat in Willesden, where Henderson would also lodge.

During this short hiatus, Morrison visited his parents, who had recently opened a record shop on the Beersbridge Road. His mother told him that he was now a local celebrity. Teenagers visiting Hyndford Street would often congregate near their house and bow their heads as if they were passing a church. When Violet enquired about this, she was told they were saying, "Hail Van, King of the Blues", a phrase that echoed the derisive chant directed at the crucified Jesus: "Hail, King of the Jews". Reverence and mockery were often indistinguishable in Belfast humour, as Morrison was quick to discover. A Protestant mural proclaiming 'No Pope Here' had prompted one wag to scribble the addendum, 'Lucky Pope'. The 'King of the Blues' was also the butt of some humour. Violet Morrison was amused to see her dustbin sprayed with the message 'Them's Ma's Bin'. When she took the family sheepdog Maxie for a walk there would be shouts of 'Them's Ma's Dog'. "If I went to the shops, I was always 'Them's Ma'," she says. "They thought I was the mother of the whole group." Even the name 'Them' provided a good excuse for some homosexual humour, typical of the time. Neighbour Gil Irvine remembers people falling about in mirth after delivering the silly one-liner: "Did you know that Van Morrison's *one of them.*"

In search of superior humour, Morrison visited his old friend Geordie Sproule who was preparing for a gig at Queen's University. "I had a wee spot singing R&B, rock 'n' roll, 'Summertime', 'Georgia', all that caper," G.D. recalls. "He was still in the charts with 'Here Comes The Night' so I got him up to do a song. He went on and some guy threw a pot of paint over him. A can of emulsion. There was a right drop in it. People do things like that at the university." Morrison's response to this student jape is not recorded.

Wandering around Belfast, Morrison observed that it was still a lively centre for R&B. The Alleykatz were playing 'Here Comes The Night' at the Maritime, having taking over from the Mad Lads. At the Plaza, erstwhile Them roadie Peter Docherty was sporting a £70 French suit, which was ceremoniously ripped to pieces during his P.J. Proby routine. More impressive were the Just Five, a powerhouse R&B outfit led by 19-year-old Sam Mahood, a pork butcher from Banbridge, blessed with a voice steeped in gospel. From solid Protestant stock, Mahood was a rebel with long hair and a love of soul music, just like Morrison. "The long hair was frowned on then," Mahood reflects. "My aunt caught me by the scruff of the neck, shook me and said, 'You're a disgrace to the family.' I refused to cut my hair, then resigned from the meat factory." Mahood was the great hope of post-Them Belfast but without top-class management his prospects were little better than Morrison's before the arrival of Solomon. Even the local press which had always supported the plethora of blues musicians now sounded a premature note of doom. In an article titled "Is the Belfast scene dying?", columnist Johnny Robb concluded, "Them have gone, the Wheels have gone. More particularly, the influence of Van Morrison and Brian Rossi, among others, has gone with them . . . Them are not here and – with perhaps one or two exceptions – there are no groups with such inventive potential left. Which will mean that the scene will stagnate. Just like what's happened in Liverpool."

Back in London, a replacement had been found for Jackie McAuley. Peter Bardens, a former member of the Cheynes with an impressive R&B résumé, had been working at the Marquee club in Wardour Street when the call came through. Within hours he was playing on stage with Them at the Rikki Tik, followed by a date in Windsor. Bardens was quick to psychoanalyse the group dynamics, suggesting ethnicity was the key issue: "It was because they were all Irishmen that they didn't get on with one another."

In order to introduce the music press to the new line-up, Solomon appointed showbiz publicist Les Perrin who arranged an interview with the *NME*'s star feature writer Keith Altham. The journalist suffered three cancelled appointments before tentatively making his way to a rehearsal studio in Soho's Berwick Street only to discover that the premises was now a strip club. "They have a natural talent for not being in the right place at the right time," he noted, unwittingly echoing the words of Phil Solomon. The bemused reporter finally tracked down Them in the backroom of a nearby pub where he was curtly told "You're wasting Bert's time" and urged to come back in a couple of hours. A photo session was reluctantly agreed to, although not before Billy Harrison ridiculed a request for a posed shot. "By posed, he apparently meant that he objected to being placed near the other four members," Altham quipped. While Bert Berns strummed a Spanish guitar loudly in the background, the interview commenced on a frosty note with Harrison announcing that they were tired of answering "stupid questions" and expressing annoyance that journalists failed to know all their names. Altham pointed out that the members' penchant for changing instruments and the presence of two brothers in the group called John and Jackie hardly helped matters. "Harrison spent most of the interview cleaning his nails with a jack-knife while talking to me in a very broad and bored Irish accent," Altham remembers. An attempt to discover why Them were so uncooperative was met with stony silence. Similar enquiries about the reasons behind their failure to appear on *Ready Steady Go!* and the recent departure of Jackie McAuley were dismissed with scathing, evasive insults. Altham then told Harrison he sounded like "an angry young Irishman". Even this brought an enraged rebuke. "I'm not Irish," Harrison insisted, "I'm an Ulsterman. Why does everyone insist on calling us Irish?" A passing reference to the recruitment of the non-Belfast Bardens prompted a suspicious "What's that got to do with it? There's nothing racial about this." Altham fared little better with Morrison, a study in surly detachment who remained on the sidelines with Bert Berns. The introspective McAuley also provided a good imitation of a zombie. "Pat's gimmick is that he says nothing, even when asked," Altham later wrote. Eventually, Altham slinked away, largely unnoticed. "No-one said goodbye as I walked out," he complained, "but that figured – no-one had said hello." Afterwards, Them's publicist coyly observed, "They're different, aren't they? I'm thinking of building up a mystery image for them. The group that no-one knows."

Altham had his own image of the group which was rather less flattering. "I came away very disenchanted with Them and I wrote a fairly scathing piece in the *New Musical Express* headlined 'Billy

Harrison Gets Mad When You Call Them Irish!' I'd come to write a good piece but I'd been sent up and ignored. The article was a personal reflection on Them as individuals. The following week Phil Solomon rang my editor, Andy Gray, and asked him to sack me because he felt the piece was an extreme attack on the artiste but it was merely an attack on their insulting attitude to me." Fortunately, Solomon's power did not stretch quite as far as the offices of the *NME* and Altham retained his job.

Interestingly, it was not the group dynamics that excited the music press readership but Harrison's sectarian banter about the definition of Irishness. "Billy Harrison is only showing his ignorance when he says he is not an Irishman but an Ulsterman," a reader from Co. Monaghan wrote. "Perhaps if he ever did geography at school he would recall that Ulster is a province of Ireland and that makes him an Irishman whether he likes it or not."

EIGHT

The Angry Young Them

Phil Solomon was unreservedly appalled by Them's unruliness, poor reliability and devilish disregard of the music press. He had neither the time nor inclination to enrol them in a finishing school to tame their manners but realized that it might be possible to exploit their ignoble savagery and possibly even market Morrison's natural sulkiness. As lead singer, Morrison was Them's focal point and the man most responsible for attracting their audience. Yet he was the complete antithesis of the traditional pop star. With his unattractive personality, plain looks, wavy red hair, fluctuating weight and diminutive stature, Morrison was a publicist's nightmare. The *NME* had even remarked on his uncanny resemblance to the small, balding, middle-aged comedian Charlie Drake, a comparison that infuriated the singer. Morrison had neither the sexuality of a Jagger nor the boyish good looks of a Paul Jones or McCartney. Like Eric Burdon, he had vocal power and aggression in abundance, but they were restricted to onstage performances and never translated into verbal dexterity. Burdon was known as the friendly Animal, the life and soul of the party and a supreme socialite in London clubland, an image far removed from the pained truculence of Morrison.

Desperate measures were required to present Morrison and Them as more palatable or at least to turn their negativity into a saleable commodity. Solomon reluctantly accepted that the notoriety of the Rolling Stones and the dreadful appearance of the Pretty Things had assisted their record sales. Teenagers, it transpired, were now seeking anti-establishment figures to complement the clean, antiseptic image projected by the Beatles and embodied in Solomon's major act, the

Bachelors. Solomon, Les Perrin, Dick Rowe and Decca had seen it all before in the Fifties when the evil Elvis was challenged by the anodyne Pat Boone and playwright John Osborne shocked an older generation with *Look Back In Anger*. Osborne and his contemporaries had been dubbed "The Angry Young Men" so Decca adapted the phrase to create The Angry Young Them. Suddenly, it seemed that Altham's reference to Them as "angry young Irishmen" had become a self-fulfilling prophecy. Morrison, whose personality fitted the billing perfectly, nevertheless felt uneasy about being promoted exclusively as a bad boy of pop. "I was just being a street cat from Belfast," he protested, "and was probably like thousands of kids from Belfast who were in bands. But the management built an image around that – 'The Angry Young Them' – the punk image, when in fact there were lots of people like me in those days. Everybody's got different sides to them but an image is like taking one thing and saying a person is *that*."

While their press profile was developing an increasingly cynical colour, Them continued working with the excitable chain-smoking, wig-wearing Bert Berns. "He'd done a super job recording 'Baby Please Don't Go' and 'Here Comes The Night' and he had a lot of charisma," Harrison enthuses. "By a British way of thinking, Bert broke all the rules. In studios then, you set up and everything was pristine and exact. Bert would just grab a drumstick, start beating on a cymbal and say, 'Let's get this thing cooking'. It created an atmosphere and made you feel good. That's how he got those performances." Certainly, Berns' approach had a liberating effect on Morrison, who responded eagerly to his suggestions and displayed a respect and quiet reverence rarely seen in his dealings with others in the mainstream music business. Unfortunately, with only a handful of recordings attempted, Berns was obliged to return to America, leaving Tommy Scott to take over as producer. "That was like giving a kid candy for a fortnight and then not only taking it away but locking him in a room," says Phil Coulter. "It must have been very tantalizing for Them to have worked with a hotshot American producer. He knew what they were trying to say and encouraged them musically. Tommy was less a musician than a writer. It was a totally different approach. Tommy simply wasn't good enough for the gig." Coulter's harsh appraisal was echoed by Morrison, who concluded, "Except for Bert Berns I felt

those people who said they were producing Them didn't have a clue . . .
Bert was the only guy who had any conception of what we were trying
to do but unfortunately he only did a few things with us. All those other
people had some weird conception about what we were at. I never
quite found out what it was."

Scott's appointment made perfect sense to Phil Solomon, who rated
him highly as a professional producer. The fact that he had recently
brought the questionable talent of Twinkle close to number 1 with
'Terry' underlined his commercial acumen. For Morrison, of course,
such considerations were unimportant. What he required was a
sympathetic producer who could relate to his work. Morrison prized
spontaneity and feel, elements that were all too easily lost without
Berns' touch. "It was a very loose thing that the band was into," he
explained, "but in the studio it became very tight with Tommy Scott.
He didn't want anybody to get stoned." Scott was astute enough to
prepare material at Regent Sound, the small studio in Denmark Street
often used by the Rolling Stones. There, at least, Morrison was able to
improvise at will and select the compositions likely to be included on
the album. "Half the stuff was ad-libbed," Harrison claims, "because
Van was magic with that. If there seemed to be a lull you started a guitar
riff and the rest of the boys fell in. The next thing you knew Van was
blowing harp and words were flowing. In those days, it didn't much
matter what they were. I remember him coming into the recording
studio without a song in his puff. He had ideas written down on
cigarette packets. He made them up and refined them as he went
along."

Morrison was never strong on communicating his ideas or objections
so accepted the prevailing conditions with Scott as producer. Despite
lingering reservations, the three short studio sessions passed without
incident and were completed on time. Scott seemed happy with the
results and Them spoke positively about the record in contemporary
interviews. "I appreciated their efforts and didn't at the same time,"
Harrison concludes with hindsight. "Phil Coulter's a super musician
and played piano on some tracks. He was very mild-mannered and
Tommy was more cocky. Songwise, I always felt he was going to get
his share of the action because he was more aware of the money than
we were. We were naive. But we got on fine. I didn't have anything

against them but I always had the feeling that whatever they thought about us, they were still Solomon's boys. They'd answer to him at the end of the day."

Them's fortunes took a decisive turn that spring when their fees from live performances hit an unexpected high in the immediate aftermath of 'Here Comes The Night'. For a brief period, it seemed that they might yet emerge as rich pop stars. "We were getting £300 each," insists Harrison. "There's no argument about that. Groups didn't have the outlay they have now and we were playing seven shows a week. With five guys that's £1,500 after expenses. Certain promoters paid you in cash, others sent cheques to the office. I wore a money belt with nearly £2,000 in it. I'd have killed anybody that came near me – you could've got your throat cut for £2 then, let alone £2,000. I remember dividing up the money on a Monday and taking £250–£300 at a time when I know your mother was getting £6 a week. Today that £250 would be worth several grand. Jesus, £1,000 a year was the goal for years – you were worth millions if you had that." Like all businesses, Them needed to sustain profits in order to survive and thrive. Their concert receipts were entirely dependent upon their drawing power which, in turn, was determined by their chart position. "When you're on the road, money doesn't last long," Alan Henderson remarks. "It was fleeting and we spent it."

In the rapacious mid-Sixties pop world, singles were akin to lifeblood. Careers could be ended overnight by successive chart misses and once a group ceased to hit the Top 20, media exposure evaporated. There was no underground rock press to provide cult credibility or sustain groups in times of crisis. For Them, everything was resting on 'One More Time', the follow-up to 'Here Comes The Night', which was readied for release in June. Decca and Solomon took out a half-page ad on the front cover of the *New Musical Express*, then looked on in disappointment as the single failed to pick up airplay and flopped spectacularly. Even the music press reviews were decidedly lukewarm. "It's very slow indeed," complained *Disc*'s Penny Valentine, "with Mr Morrison singing very insinuatingly as though he had hot potatoes in his mouth . . . It doesn't strike me as being as good as their other records." For Morrison, its chart failure was almost poetic justice as he had no love for the finished product and scorned Tommy Scott's sterling attempt to transform the composition into a hit song. "I remember going into the studio and cutting it," Morrison says. "A soul ballad. It sounded great. A couple of days later I got the dub. He had added echo to the vocal and the guitar sounded like sandpaper with wah-wah fuzz. It was just polluted with echo. Echo on everything – this was his image of the group. This is what he thought we should sound like – totally commercial. And that's not what the group was." Morrison's promotion of the record matched his scathing appraisal. When *Record Mirror*'s Richard Green enquired how he had written the song, Morrison scowled: "I got a pencil and wrote it on a piece of paper." At the end of that interview Green was ushered out by an apologetic Dorothy Solomon who had long since tired of this ridiculous charade. Them would never enjoy another UK hit single and their live earnings plummeted immediately thereafter.

That same month, Them's debut album was issued. Following Andrew Oldham's bold gesture on the Rolling Stones' first long player, Decca ensured that Them's name was conspicuously absent from the front cover. On the rear, they were introduced as The Angry Young Them and subject to a portentous essay which proclaimed "These five young rebels are outrageously true to themselves. Defiant! Angry! Sad! They are honest to the point of insult!" The 14-track selection was reasonably impressive for the period, spoiled only by some predictable covers such as 'Route 66' and 'Bright Lights Big City'. There were three Berns numbers, including an ill-conceived reworking of the traditional chestnut 'I Gave My Love A Cherry' and a brooding version of John Lee Hooker's 'Don't Look Back' which Morrison considered his finest vocal to date. What really transformed the record, however, were the superior Morrison compositions on display. 'Little Girl', a song of schooldays eroticism, had already been the subject of controversy when an earlier released version on a Lord Taverners' compilation was censured for containing an offensive four-letter word. Morrison's ability to tackle raucous and soulful material was emphasized on the contrasting 'I Like It Like That' and 'If You And I Could Be As Two', but the best new song on the record was the opening track.

'Mystic Eyes', like 'Gloria', remains one of the most fascinating compositions from Morrison's early career. A magical piece of spontaneous creation, it was recorded virtually by accident. "We didn't plan a note," Morrison revealed. "We were just busking around. Someone started playing a fast riff and we all just joined in." After blowing his harmonica for about seven minutes, Morrison remembered some lyrics from another song he had written and threw in some lines about "walking down by the old graveyard" and other cryptic allusions. Overall, it was the closest Morrison had come to recapturing the elusive spirit of the Maritime. A stunned Tommy Scott was left with a 10-minute track that had to be edited severely in order to fit on to the album. Like the elongated 'Gloria' played live back in Belfast, the unedited version of 'Mystic Eyes' remains one of the tantalizingly lost R&B workouts of the mid-Sixties.

The other stand-out track from the album was 'You Just Can't Win' which emerged as Morrison's 'Positively 4th Street', a bitter protest about a gold digger. Morrison spat out the lyrics in Dylanesque fashion and introduced his trick of using specific geographical references from Camden Town to Tottenham Court Road. Significantly, the milieu was London rather than Belfast, echoing the Rolling Stones who had alluded to St John's Wood on their equally scathing 'Play With Fire'.

Morrison's adoption of Dylan-inspired protest was well-timed. Over recent months, the master had infiltrated the singles charts with 'The Times They Are A-Changin'' and 'Subterranean Homesick Blues', introducing teenage record buyers to a lyrical landscape previously beyond their imaginations. A preponderance of Dylan-composed protest hits followed, including Manfred Mann's 'If You Gotta Go, Go Now', Joan Baez's 'It's All Over Now, Baby Blue' and Johnny Cash's 'It Ain't Me Babe'. In Belfast's Smithfield Market, sales of acoustic guitars, harmonicas and tin whistles rose markedly, confirming a sudden resurgence in folk. Local musicians Paul Murphy (Murph) and Speedy Mullan combined blues and folk influences and were acclaimed as Belfast's answer to Donovan and Bert Jansch. Murph soon moved across the water, busked at London tube stations and occasionally sang with Morrison at a jazz club in Greek Street before playing the starving folkie in Beckenham. In this time of rapid change, reinvention or blatant commerciality seemed the only options for chart survival. During the past year most of the promising Merseyside groups, including the Searchers, Gerry And The Pacemakers and Billy J.

Kramer With The Dakotas had been frozen out of the charts. Recent R&B faves like the Pretty Things and fellow Decca act the Moody Blues had suffered the same career reversal as Them. The Moodies had hit number 1 with 'Go Now' but failed to dent the charts with the Bert Berns-composed follow-up, a cover of the Drifters' 'I Don't Want To Go On Without You'. Now the competition was even stronger.

At the precise moment they needed to be most united, Them found themselves systematically torn apart from within. The relationship between Harrison and Morrison, never close at the best of times, seemed to be deteriorating with each passing week. Recent recruit Peter Bardens noticed how the petty arguments festered into lingering antipathy. "Van and Billy had vehement fights over who was leader and sometimes Van's eyes got all glassy. You knew he was about to erupt." In interviews, Harrison still styled himself as the group's spokesman and spiritual leader. "I play the father confessor," he told music journalist Penny Valentine, "it's important to me that the boys tell me their troubles. Not because I can help or anything – just so they can get it out of their system." He certainly seemed to have Morrison's psychology sorted and confided in Valentine: "He worries a lot – he's very moody because of that. He doesn't really know how people will accept him . . . He'll be in a terrible mood then immediately he goes on stage he's fine and he snaps right back into a bad mood when he comes off." This understated appraisal for the pop press barely scratched the surface of the tensions at play in the group. Harrison was the last person that Morrison was likely to turn towards as his counsellor or confidant. Increasingly distant, the singer insisted on travelling separately from the group whenever possible, and found a sympathetic ally in a new girlfriend of independent means based in Notting Hill Gate. "When things started to go to hell he had this girl Dee that he was knocking about with," Harrison recalls. "She was considerably older than him and drove him about. He started splitting into the star scene and it became 'I'm a star – I don't travel with the group.' In my opinion, she was a bad influence. She filled his head with rocking-horse shit and made him think he was something he wasn't."

Morrison always denied that he fell victim to the vanities of pop stardom at any stage of his career, even claiming that he never wanted to be famous. That viewpoint was not shared by his contemporaries who felt that Morrison coveted success, albeit on his own terms. If his ego had become inflated, as Harrison argues, then it was hardly surprising in the context of the times. Lead singers were always afforded more attention than musicians, particularly in the image-conscious Sixties. The fact that Morrison was the only songwriter in the group also enhanced his reputation, sometimes to the detriment of his colleagues. By contrast, Billy Harrison's standing in Them as leader, guitarist and occasional vocalist had been subtly eroded since the formation of the group in 1964. Sam Smyth had first noticed Morrison's strength of will when negotiating terms for Them's debut appearance in Dublin. In the back of the van, it was Morrison's opinions that were heard and acted upon, more often than those of his colleagues. That power and self-belief only grew stronger once he moved to London.

Harrison and the rest were sometimes intimidated by the presence of session musicians in the studio, but Morrison knew that his vocal spot was never under threat. Phil Solomon made no secret of the fact that he considered Morrison the focal point of Them. Oddly, he never credited Harrison for his undoubted organizational skills which were largely forgotten amid complaints about unpunctuality and bad behaviour. During the all-too-brief period of Them's reign as chart stars, Morrison alone was seen as a true contender for possible fame. Discerning fans, pop critics and backstage flatterers liked to compare him with Eric Burdon or even Mick Jagger when discussing who was Britain's best white blues singer. Evidently, the new girlfriend Dee shared such views and boosted his ego accordingly, much to Harrison's disgust. The other members of Them treated the mysterious and aloof Dee with suspicion. At one point, there was even a crazy conspiracy theory put forward that she might have been deliberately recruited to secure some form of psychic control over the singer. There were already wild rumours circulating among the group about Maurice King's gangster connections, so the fanciful notion of Dee as a putative Mata Hari, conscripted solely to influence Morrison and manipulate Them, was at least a great pub anecdote. Seemingly, nobody was too quick to point out that neither Morrison nor Them was an important enough investment to warrant such intrigue. It was only many years later that Morrison learned of the scurrilous gossip about his former girlfriend and he rightly dismissed the story as a ludicrous fantasy. What it demonstrated was the extent of the breakdown in communication between the various parties.

Like Morrison, Harrison had also become frustrated with his role in Them and sought to distance himself from the psychodramas. Previously, he had been the man to pacify promoters if the group was late for a gig and ensure that box offices paid the correct amount in advance. A strong personality, Harrison could be intimidating if crossed and had already shown a fearless confidence in challenging Solomon's hegemony, albeit unsuccessfully. Playing a combination of sergeant major and nursemaid in Them was all too often a thankless task and the continuing silences, consuming rivalries and sudden explosions of temper eventually took their toll. "I don't know what triggered me off," says Harrison, "but something did. One morning the guys came to pick me up for a gig up north – a double bumper, Saturday and Sunday night. I said, 'I'll tell you what – fuck off! Go on your own.' They played without me and that put the cat among the pigeons."

When Phil Solomon discovered this latest drama he was as exasperated as ever but left Morrison to sort it out. "After that they didn't want me," Harrison concludes. Over the next few days rumours spread that Harrison was leaving and Them were splitting up. Cornered by the press during the first week of July, the guitarist acted like a seasoned politician, confidently denying any rifts between himself and his fellows. "We've no intention of breaking up," he insisted. "It's just another rumour by people with no idea what they're talking about. You know the sort of trouble we've had before from some pop writers. They are looking for sensation all the time and I'm afraid they pick on us more often than most. It's all becoming a bit of a bore."

Hubris awaited Harrison the following week when the music press confirmed that he had been sacked. The Solomons released a statement distancing themselves from the execution. "These boys take their own decisions on a cooperative basis. Billy was not getting along with the other four and they voted him out." The statement was somewhat disingenuous, ignoring the critical rivalry between Morrison and Harrison which had undoubtedly prompted the split. "My brother wouldn't have voted anybody out," Jackie McAuley notes. Indeed, Patrick John McAuley was so disenchanted that he left of his own volition two weeks later, having concluded that Them was "a complete shambles". His departure appeared to confirm that prognosis. Bassist Alan Henderson remained but found his loyalties severely tested as he was still lodging at Harrison's home. The music press, already weary of Them, paid little attention to the specifics of their disintegration. It seemed as though the group had merely confirmed their stereotyping as angry young Irish rebels – wild, mad, unreliable, drunk and disorderly.

Nobody in London bothered to follow up the story, but back in Belfast Billy Harrison eventually broke the silence with a devastating and frank reappraisal which emphasized the extent of his disillusion. "Things were OK for a while," he told the local press. "Then Van began to get 'kinky'. He didn't want a group. He wanted a backing group. He became aloof. He wanted musicians whom he could hire and sack as he wanted. He began to get rude to promoters. All of a sudden he developed a mania against me. He said I was creating trouble. I was accused of stealing the limelight from him on *Ready Steady Go!* He told me to tone down my act as I was attracting too much attention to myself. I began to get the push. Then I heard through a friend that Van was auditioning guitarists to replace me. I refused to go on the next date. They went without me. I got a polite letter saying my services were no longer required. Nobody had the guts to tell me to my face. Alan said he was going to leave . . . out of sympathy. I told him to stay on." When asked his reaction to Harrison's barbs, Morrison replied that he was not annoyed by their content but simply regarded them as pathetic. Clearly, he had moved on.

It was another couple of years before Morrison reflected publicly on the disintegration of the original Them line-up, for which he evidently accepted some of the blame. "Everything just got out of proportion," he admitted. "In the beginning the thing was great because everybody dug it. There was no motive behind anything you did. You just did it because you wanted to do it and you enjoyed doing it. That's the way the thing started, but it got twisted somewhere along the way and everybody involved in it got twisted as well, including me."

Some indication of the twisted feelings is underlined by the knowledge that Harrison and McAuley seemed content to show two fingers to the group just as an international breakthrough was underway. That same month, 'Here Comes The Night' entered the US

Top 30 and 'Gloria' was also receiving acclaim as a regional West Coast hit. The group had been tentatively earmarked for a lengthy American tour as part of Dick Clark's Caravan Of Stars, but problems with work permits, a familiar bugbear for artistes in the Sixties, delayed the invasion for the best part of a year. "Phil Solomon screwed that up royally – we could have made millions," was Henderson's view. "That would have opened everything for us. Maybe he thought we weren't ready. I don't know. It doesn't make sense." Given their parlous state, the postponement was probably a blessing. Although America was the stuff of dreams, the reality could often prove nightmarish. Contrary to Henderson's fantasies of "making millions", such expeditions usually lost money in the short term and could often bring a group to its knees. The Kinks, for instance, toured the US that summer encountering countless problems culminating in a four-year ban.

With all momentum lost, Morrison looked to his Belfast past for salvation. Reviving the idea of re-creating his original vision of Them, he contacted Billy McAllen. "I don't think he was ever happy with Billy Harrison who did the job OK but wasn't a great player," McAllen says. "He wanted me to come over and join the group and offered me £30 a week from Solomon's office. I was earning more money here in the Stan Lynn Showband. I reckoned I'd be travelling all over the country with Van doing seven nights a week for £30, so I said no. I wasn't really tempted by fame." Morrison's future was so uncertain at this point that any number of minor musical collaborations might have been discussed over an evening drinking session. During a brief visit to Dublin he socialized with Paul Brady, even suggesting vaguely that they might collaborate on some project, but knew it was unlikely. Instead, Morrison was forced to accept unfamiliar musicians at short notice in order to fulfil outstanding bookings and complete record company photo shoots. Bardens recommended guitarist Joe Baldi and drummer Terry Noon, neither of whom was known to Morrison. Initially, they were described as 'temporary' replacements and placed on a weekly retainer of £30–£35 per week. Their recruitment inevitably prompted cynical asides from former Them members. Eric Wrixon felt that the entire set-up was now geared towards Morrison. "Phil Solomon was paying people a living wage but not the sort of money that would keep them there. All he had to do was go out and find four world-class musicians and stick the money into the band. It's a wonder it never occurred to him."

While on the road that summer, Morrison enjoyed a reunion with Belfast friends the Wheels, who had relocated to Blackpool before finding accommodation at a farm occupied by the outrageous, party loving Rockin' Vicars. With the shaven-headed Brian Rossi as front-man, the Wheels were enjoying a reasonable living on the northern club circuit playing pop and R&B while occasionally masquerading as a showband performing 'Danny Boy' for cabaret audiences. Morrison envied their innocence and confided in Herbie Armstrong that he hardly knew the names of the characters that constituted the revamped Them. Armstrong assisted Joe Baldi with some guitar tunings but could not help noticing that the new member was far more interested in jazz than R&B. "We weren't in competition, but the Wheels was really the band that Van should have had as his group," Armstrong concludes.

Such a scenario might indeed have been possible, for the Wheels had just joined the Solomon organization. On a whim they had despatched a tape to his New Oxford Street office and were thrilled to receive a reply inviting them for an audition at Maurice King's club, the Starlite. Nervously, they noted that the club was full of music biz notables, but responded positively to the pressure. "We tore the place apart," Armstrong boasts. "Scott Walker, who was sitting dead quiet, was smashing a beer mug on the table crying 'More'. The whole place erupted. I remember Phil Solomon came up, gave us money and said, 'Go out and buy yourself a slap-up meal.' That was amazing." Still in a daze, they signed a contract soon after and met their immaculately-dressed agent Dorothy Solomon who politely asked "Who are you?" before returning to more pressing engagements. The Wheels were next taken to Regent Sound where Tommy Scott and Phil Coulter arranged some demo recordings. Ever astute, Solomon was grooming the Wheels as a surrogate Them. Encouraged by Scott, Herbie Armstrong enquired tentatively whether Morrison would object to their recording 'Gloria' as their first single. "I don't give a shit," Morrison deadpanned. He seemed beyond caring.

Memories of Them's postponed West Coast tour were rekindled when they were booked alongside Donovan, Kenny Lynch and Charles Dickens as support act to the visiting Byrds. Billed as

"America's Answer To The Beatles", the Byrds descended upon England that August for one of the most controversial tours of the era. They had recently climbed to the top of the charts on both sides of the Atlantic with the mesmeric 'Mr Tambourine Man' and were at the forefront of a new phenomenon christened folk rock. Its arrival signalled a sea change in pop attitudes rendering Them's lively R&B passé overnight. A new single, 'Half As Much', written by Bert Berns, proved a commercial failure. Morrison was aware that Them needed to change tack but displayed little empathy with his latest recruits. The exuberant Kenny Lynch found Them a miserable bunch who often seemed uncertain of their geographical location as the tour traversed the country. Road manager Bobby Hamilton remembers Morrison fortifying himself with sizeable shots of vodka as the debilitating procession took its toll. In striking contrast, the hipper Byrds preferred illegal substances and consumed marijuana with abandon. Over the next few weeks, it seemed that folk rock was about to rule the world. Sonny & Cher's 'I Got You Babe' became another transatlantic chart topper, while former New Christy Minstrel Barry McGuire was preparing the ultimate catch-all protest anthem with P.F. Sloan's 'Eve Of Destruction'. Elsewhere the Beatles dominated with 'Help!', their most literate and articulate record to date, while the Rolling Stones had found their own career anthem with '(I Can't Get No) Satisfaction'. Other acts continued the trend of covering Dylan songs for credibility and quick profit. The master himself was not to be outdone by his disciples and challenged for the top of the *singles* chart with the groundbreaking, six-minute 'Like A Rolling Stone'. 1965 was probably the most spectacular summer that pop music had ever known.

Morrison's unhappy troupe did not survive that remarkable season. After the Byrds' tour, the new membership lost heart and by the end of August only Morrison and Henderson remained. They returned to Belfast once more, spending a month auditioning local players and rehearsing a fresh set at the Maritime. The solicitous Mervyn Solomon was again called upon to oversee matters and assist with the new direction. "I always had a great belief in him," he says of Morrison. "I felt he should have been taken away and made a soloist. We needed a modern jazz group behind him with flutes. He was always coming up with snippets of lyrics and melodies but he wasn't always with us and that was his weakness." At one point, Mervyn considered bringing in the Misfits as a possible backing group, but instead recruited their young drummer John Wilson. It was a big break for the teenager who had only recently won a place in the Misfits when their madcap drummer Dino Martin had elected to become a DJ at the Plaza. A more experienced player was the accomplished guitarist Jim Armstrong who, since leaving Harry Baird's Olympics and the Regency, had sensibly worked in a bank while moonlighting with ageing showband the Melotones. Completing Them's new line-up was jazz keyboardist/saxophonist/flautist Ray Elliott, a beatnik with a Neptune beard, late of the Golden Eagles and the Broadways.

The presence of Morrison in Belfast attracted interest from various quarters. Several musicians attempted to check out the Maritime rehearsals, among them Billy Hollywood who was surprised by the move away from R&B. Eddie Kennedy's son Billy watched Them briefly routining Dylan's 'The Times They Are A-Changin'', which was soon dismissed. "Van was a strange person," he remembers. "He would see someone and half an hour later he'd look through them." Morrison did manage to reconnect with older friends and found that they were faring well. George Jones and Billy McAllen were in the Silhouettes, a colourful showband who dressed like kinky executioners, complete with masked hoods, knee-high black leather boots, dark trousers and black zip-up tops. Sweating profusely on stage, they attempted to invest their act with a certain mystique by referring to each other by a designated number rather than a name. Across town, Geordie Sproule was driving up a storm in the saxophone-led Federals; Gil Irvine was playing in the Elms and the Idiom; Eric Wrixon was veering between the People and the Kings, and former Them roadie Peter Docherty was now managing the Aztecs and the Set. The Milk Marketing Board was sponsoring several Bangor groups, including the Hoods, the Continentals, and the A-Side whose ranks included Billy Harrison's brother, Mike. Even Morrison's mother was working as a secret publicist for her nephew Sammy Stitt's group, the Other Ones. "I have heard the Other Ones twice at the Harland & Wolff Social Club recently and they have improved out of all recognition," she informed the local music press. "Van sang with them once or twice before he went to England with Them and thought they had lots of feeling."

The legacy that Morrison had left Belfast was reflected in the formation of the Blues Foundation, a co-op of groups that included the Luvin Kind, Styx, the Other Ones, the Suspects, the Blue Angels and Memphis Blues. They even found their own version of the Maritime at the Boat House on Balfour Avenue. Belfast kids had not forgotten Morrison's contribution to the city and a sizeable number turned out for the new Them's first outing at the Top Hat Club on 24 September. The group performed a 40-minute jazz-tinged soul set which went down surprisingly well. As *City Week*'s laconic columnist noted: "The sight of Van Morrison and new boy Ray Elliott chase-chorusing their way through a two-tenor version of the Jimmy Giuffre/Bob Brookmeyer duet 'The Train And The River' would even have stimulated a Royal Showband fan who had arrived a night early at the hall."

A week later, Them departed for England with Misfits' manager P.J. McGuire tagging along as a temporary roadie for regional dates at Huddersfield, Nelson and Dunstable. Morrison was also reportedly scheduled to record some solo vocals at Decca. Them were barely back on the road when they received one of their most exciting bookings to date, a coveted appearance at the Olympia, Paris, alongside Bo Diddley and Barry McGuire. Unfortunately, John Wilson was too young to obtain a work permit so Terry Noon agreed to deputize as drummer. "It was a really hot show," Alan Henderson recalls. "They blamed us for getting the crowd too riled. Van invited them up on stage to dance. It was a huge hall and the place started coming apart. Brilliant." Jim Armstrong, already showing his banking background by bitching about the Solomons' agency commission, was thrilled when the crowd continued chanting "T-H-E-M" during Barry McGuire's succeeding set. Representatives from French Decca treated the Belfast group like real celebrities, arranging photo sessions and accompanying them on a shopping expedition. "The clothes over there are a ridiculous price," noted the fiscally-conscious Armstrong. "Van paid out £6 for a pair of trousers and I fancied a shirt that cost £4 which I could get in London for 39/11d."

After returning to London, Them were expected to record a new album as soon as possible. Tommy Scott was exceptionally busy at the time working with other Solomon acts. The Wheels' Rod Demick was impressed by Scott's industry and attitude. "In those days the producer ruled the studio," he explains. "He decided what was done. At first, I didn't even know what double-tracking meant. But he was great for us. He sang backing vocals on our version of 'Gloria' and wrote songs with Phil Coulter. Tommy was a real hotshot, Tin Pan Alley guy. We did four singles in an afternoon."

Compared to the malleable Wheels, Morrison and Them were always a handful. Deciding upon a suitable direction was no easy task as a new strain of self-penned beat group protest had completely transformed the pop landscape by the autumn of 1965. Although still at the cover version stage, Them's closest rivals the Animals had success-fully voiced a sense of social and personal unrest with their hits 'We Gotta Get Out Of This Place' and 'It's My Life'. The Rolling Stones' '(I Can't Get No) Satisfaction' and 'Get Off Of My Cloud' also sounded disgruntled enough with the world to be classified under the protest banner, even if the targets were suitably vague. The Who had adroitly commandeered the moral vacuity at the centre of mod culture to proclaim the triumph of selfish youth in 'My Generation'. And then there were the chancers and clever pretenders. Jonathan King, a Cambridge undergraduate and therefore an instant pop intellectual in class-conscious Britain, had charted with 'Everyone's Gone To The Moon', a quaint collection of simple, bleak images that nevertheless fulfilled the criterion of sounding like a pseudo-profound commentary on the human condition. King also managed Hedgehopper's Anonymous, whose hit 'It's Good News Week' opened with the sardonic observa-tion "Someone's dropped a bomb somewhere". It was a wonderful comment on the times that this anti-establishment litany should be written by musicians still in the secure employ of the Royal Air Force.

In this more literate climate, Morrison was eager to expand the range of his writing, but met resistance from his commercially-minded producer. "Van went dry for a while," Scott insists. "In all our opinions, his writing had taken a lapse. He went through this period of writing protest songs . . . stuff like 'Down By Queensway'. It seemed strange and it wasn't really commercial material." Like everyone else on the pop scene in late 1965, Scott readily acknowledged the importance of Bob Dylan and was eager for Morrison to cover 'It's All Over Now,

Baby Blue'. After several hours' work on the Dylan track at Regent Sound, pianist Phil Coulter went home and Scott called a break. "The number wasn't going down," Scott remembers. "Van wasn't sure. Then the guys said he didn't fancy it and thought it was cheap because I'd tried to go after the 'Here Comes The Night' tempo." Scott reconsidered and after picking up a blues riff, a new arrangement emerged, apparently with added piano work from Peter Bardens. Engineer Bill Farley modulated the sound and Morrison provided one of his most expressive vocals. It was a rare example of Scott and Morrison in productive communication.

After the preliminaries at Regent Sound, Them were booked into Decca's studios to record their next album. During three sessions, spread over two days, they completed a batch of songs including a large number of Scott compositions, several of which were also recorded by the Wheels. It sounded like conveyor-belt pop, a view amplified by Scott's occasional partner Phil Coulter. "I don't think anyone with half an ear could say it was strong material. That was a great bone of contention. They were definitely pushed into doing that stuff by Scott backed by the might of Phil Solomon. Scott was an aspiring producer/ writer and his priority was to get his songs on there." Although ambitious, Scott maintained that he was innocent of unreasonable self-promotion. "I think I recorded everything Van wrote during that period," he maintains. "We used to do as much of his material as possible. I could come up with a reasonably commercial song so that we'd have as many copyrights as possible back at the company."

As publisher, Phil Solomon stood to benefit whether Morrison or Scott was the named writer. His priority was to ensure that product was available for Decca and when the politics of evasion and taste prevented their completion, his response was ruthless. "The second album was not thought of as an album," he points out. "We couldn't get Them back in the studio so we finished some of the Scott songs that were only done as demos. We wouldn't normally have considered them. Anything that Morrison wrote on his own we were only too happy to record but if Morrison didn't give us the songs or demo them with Tommy Scott then we didn't know of their existence. Van did a lot of things in his head but never got them down on paper or made demos of them."

Ironically, the group's next single was a track previously released on album by the Harrison line-up: 'Mystic Eyes'. It was well received in the US, climbing as high as number 33, but met a mixed critical response in Britain. The *NME*'s Derek Johnson praised its frantic tempo, but *Melody Maker* concluded that the approach now sounded a little dated. Over at *Disc*, Them suffered an unexpected and premature burial from one of their keener supporters. "Goodness, the surprises I get," sighed Penny Valentine. "Since Them aren't any more I hardly expected a record to appear by them this week . . . It's better than many they've made but its chances of getting into the chart when there's no group around to play it seem more than doubtful." Contrary to Valentine's valediction, Them were touring the backwaters of Britain that November, although her ignorance of their existence was understandable. Without a hit they were yesterday's men, which meant small gigs and meagre promotion.

With 'Mystic Eyes' providing aural memories of the old Them line-up, it was appropriate that Billy Harrison should suddenly reappear on the scene. Ray Elliott was staying at his home for a spell and Henderson was still lodging there. Between sessions and hanging out with the Pretty Things, Harrison was also frequenting Them's late-night stomping ground, the Starlite. Always forthright, particularly after some post-pub drinks, the guitarist could be heard complaining about the booking fees Them had received from Maurice King. The proprietor was not amused to learn of such griping taking place in his own club and neither were some of the shadier elements present. "I got a few phone calls where people hung up," Harrison confides. "I was still a troublemaker when I left the group. Al, a Geordie who managed the Starlite, was very friendly but warned me that the Krays were getting my name. I didn't even know who the Krays were then. He thought I was going to be turned over. I was still digging – that's something I'd rather keep quiet. But I always got on well with Maurice King."

The spectre of Harrison was also present when Them played an embarrassing performance at St Mary's College in Strawberry Hill. Turning up with the Pretty Things' Viv Prince, Brian Pendleton and Phil May, Harrison found himself in the strange position of experiencing Them for the one and only time as an observer rather than a participant. "We went there for a laugh," he recalls. "Although I'd left the group, I was still bloody curious and wanted to see what it was like. Armstrong's a superb guitarist, better than me, man. But what happened that evening wasn't down to him, it was down to the wee man." As the audience waited expectantly, the group took their places behind the stage curtain and began playing the introduction to James Brown's 'I'll Go Crazy'. Morrison appeared in the wings, seemingly uncertain how to proceed as the group struck up the intro yet again. "He had a glass of wine in one hand and a joint in the other," Armstrong remembers, "and he didn't know which one to set down. Then he started pacing up and down and we started the intro yet again. He then downed the drink, took a run forward and jumped over the amps." At this point, the curtains opened to reveal Morrison in full flight, sailing over the two-feet-high speakers like one of Phil Solomon's racehorses. "When he took up that run he was sliding to grab the mike but he slipped, fell on his back and slid into the mike stand and hit his head," Alan Henderson adds. Armstrong retained an everlasting vision of Morrison careering across the stage, straddling the microphone stand and then blacking out. "The roadie came out, slapped him around the face, brought him around, put the mike in his hand and when he looked out in the front there was Billy Harrison. There was no love lost there."

"It was laughable," Harrison gleefully recounts. "After three intros he'd suddenly appeared like a flying demon, leapt on top of an amplifier and fallen on his face. He thought he could fly. The instant arrival was an absolute farce. I think he was out of the lid. Armstrong unplugged and walked. After the disastrous intro we pissed off. I felt I've got nothing to worry about here – goodbye!" After Morrison recovered and Armstrong returned, further humiliation awaited. Midway through their climactic rendition of 'The Train And The River', the college caretaker casually ambled across the stage and pulled the plugs, ending the evening prematurely. "Wilfie [John Wilson] was totally embarrassed by the whole affair," Armstrong remembers. For the drummer, it was a timely warning not to bank his future on the group.

Them's tempestuous live career continued its wayward course through December. While driving from a show in Scotland, their van expired on the M6 and Morrison decided to seek assistance. He gave up, hailed a taxi and returned to London leaving his colleagues stranded and puzzled. They abandoned the vehicle, not even bothering to return for the PA equipment which Armstrong scorned as useless. Morale was low. Phil Solomon was not amused by Morrison's epic taxi trip but the singer was beyond caring. As John Wilson remembers: "He was mad. He really was, like the manager would be giving him a chewing for something Van had done wrong and Van would listen quietly to him. When the manager would finish, Van would get up and say something like 'How would you like me to drop a bomb on your head?' and he'd walk away."

Two weeks before Christmas, the *NME* published its annual readers' poll and neither Them nor Morrison appeared in any category. As far as the pop world was concerned, they hardly existed. Later that month, in an unexpected turn of events, the exiled Harrison was stunned to receive a call inviting him to rejoin Them for a visit to France and Sweden. Jim Armstrong had been rushed to hospital in Liverpool for an appendix operation and was convalescing over the Christmas period. With young John Wilson still unable to work abroad, Terry Noon re-emerged to join this unique line-up. "We went to Paris, then Stockholm," Harrison recalls. "We were in Stockholm on New Year's Eve. Getting a drink in Sweden was difficult for some reason so I drank the New Year in with a glass of water, which was a bummer." The end of the year seemed a suitable time for the dissatisfied Wilson to bow out. Quietly critical of certain members' excesses, he rejoined the Misfits after which he received a pay-off from Solomon.

By the time Jim Armstrong emerged from hospital, Them had yet another drummer: David Harvey. An engaging personality with a slightly aristocratic air, the Englishman was a steadying influence, a role he achieved simply by getting on with everybody. His arrival coincided with another bizarre twist as the McAuley brothers re-emerged with their own version of Them, adding Ken McLeod (guitar) and Mark Scott (bass). A cheeky ad appeared in *Disc* promoting the new group and, when challenged, their Belfast manager Ray Henderson produced documents revealing that they had registered the name "Them" for copyright purposes two months before, on 4 November. Maurice King was outraged and instructed solicitors Bernard Sheridan to seek an immediate injunction. "It is quite ridiculous for any other group to claim that they are Them," King fumed. "This is the name that the group led by Van Morrison had been using – without a break – for the past two years. The McAuleys were connected to it at one time but they have no right to the title." Battlelines were drawn.

NINE

Hollywood

Amid the name-game fiasco, Decca issued Them's second album in January 1966. *Them Again* boasted some amusing liner notes, not least the public revelation that the singer "sometimes throws his advisers into a frenzy of hair-tearing despair: moody, unpredictable, perverse, often downright wilful – but always creative". Alas, the finished album was a major disappointment which merely confirmed the extent to which Morrison had lost control of the group as a recording unit. Only five of its 16 songs were written by him, the rest consisting of cover versions and a sizeable number of Tommy Scott (aka M. Gillon) compositions. Apart from the driving Scott/Coulter rocker 'I Can Only Give You Everything', a spirited attempt to recapture the magic of 'Gloria', the producer's material was weak. With the exception of the impressive 'It's All Over Now, Baby Blue', the covers were merely average and even the legendary 'Turn On Your Lovelight' had lost its lustre. A lengthy version of 'Stormy Monday', which Henderson felt was the group's finest performance to date, was edited then chopped from the final listing. Even Morrison's contributions were not entirely satisfactory. Both 'Could You Would You' and 'Bad Or Good' were derivative and dull, especially when placed alongside the powerhouse 'Bring 'Em On In' with its distinctive use of local place names and the elegant, lachrymose 'My Lonely Sad Eyes'.

The great find on the album was surely 'Hey Girl', one of several Morrison songs in which an unnamed girl is fondly remembered. Jim Armstrong added a pastoral flourish on guitar which brought out the best in Morrison as he sang this deceptively innocent celebration of holding hands in the fog while watching sailing boats. As the vocal intensifies, the fascination with the child's innocence appears to be supplanted by an ambiguous sexuality of almost *Lolita* proportions as Morrison implores: "You're so young – I don't know what to do." Although ostensibly a moving ballad of young love, it was delightfully equivocal, finally leaving the listener wondering whether Morrison had unwittingly written one of the earliest examples of paedophiliac pop, pre-dating the Union Gap's chart-topping 'Young Girl' by two years.

Despite recent setbacks, there was still hope at Decca that Them might mount a chart comeback. Although R&B was past its popular peak, the Spencer Davis Group had recently emerged as late front runners with two consecutive number 1 hits: 'Keep On Running' and 'Somebody Help Me'. Several other contemporaries, including the Animals, the Yardbirds and Manfred Mann, had suffered line-up upheavals, negotiated changing fashions and shifted musical styles yet still retained their position among the pop élite. Morrison's group had displayed sufficient stylistic diversity – incorporating blues, soul, pop and folk – to warrant another crack at the charts, but their material still lacked the necessary quality and commercial edge. Minor success in America had elicited promises of television spots on *Shindig* and *Hullabaloo* and the group were lined up on London's Embankment to mime three songs, including their next single – an alternate take of Tommy Scott's 'Call My Name' from the recent album sessions. Unfortunately, it sounded like a desperate attempt to emulate the success of the Animals' 'Don't Let Me Be Misunderstood' and proved a resounding failure on both sides of the Atlantic.

The ongoing dispute with the McAuleys' incarnation of Them reached new heights when Phil Solomon entered the fray. He was aggrieved to learn that the group had signed with Reg Calvert and Terry King, who represented several chart acts including the Fortunes and Pinkerton's Assorted Colours. At the time, Solomon had just won 20 per cent control of Radio Caroline and was well aware of Calvert, who owned the rival pirate station Radio City. In a wonderful example of brinkmanship, Solomon informed the music press that he intended to launch two obscure Birmingham groups under the names Fortunes Ltd and Pinkerton's Assorted Colours Ltd. He even notified Decca's MD Sir Edward Lewis, demanding the withdrawal of all recordings by those hit groups with the attendant threat of a legal suit for substantial damages. Music journalists stood in awe as the entrepreneur decreed: "Our group Them have lost work all over the world because of the confusion caused by this other group. Now I intend to cause similar confusion by booking out duplicate Fortunes and Pinkerton's Assorted Colours. After all, I've registered the names." Solomon's powerplay had the desired effect of cowing his opponents. Terry King backed down and the doomed Reg Calvert returned to his pirate radio exploits. Within four months he would be shot dead in bizarre circumstances by Major Oliver Smedley, a former member of the Liberal Party Executive. Meanwhile, the McAuleys made themselves scarce, moved to Scandinavia and relaunched their replica Them as the Belfast Gypsies.

Morrison slowly retreated from Them as apathy festered into antipathy. He spent much of the time at his base in Notting Hill where his relationship with girlfriend Dee veered from loving to volatile. As well as driving Morrison to gigs, she mothered him, running errands for wine and cigarettes and ensuring that he was wrapped up well in a scarf. "She was just right for him," observes Them's cockney roadie Bobby Hamilton, without a trace of irony. "He loved her, he did. Thought the world of her." Jim Armstrong witnessed the darker side of the affair. "Van was contrary," he stresses. "We went around one day to pick him up. He was having a fight with her and the radio went through the window and onto the street. Then he didn't want to go to the gig because he was feeling ripped off. The tortured genius! Our roadie just lifted him, put him in the van, chilled him out and that was it."

Backstage, Morrison was often subdued but would psyche himself up with a stiff drink. "He'd drink a bottle of vodka before he went on," Hamilton exaggerates. "Not a few mouthfuls, but a bottle." The roadie's most visually striking memory is witnessing Morrison removing some false teeth, then rubbing his gums with vodka. "He'd put the teeth back in again, then he'd go out there and play the saxophone like you've never heard."

During this period, Rod Demick and Herbie Armstrong visited his home in Notting Hill where they also witnessed his vodka consumption. The Wheels had been working with Tommy Scott on a cover of 'Call My Name' and increasingly felt as though they were being dressed with Them's cast-offs. "It was a shame," Demick regrets. "A lot of songs we did were written by Tommy Scott and they kept giving us songs Them had already done. We were accused of copying Them." Forgetting their woes, the pair accompanied Morrison to a London club where they bumped into singer Long John Baldry and ended up watching a performance by Belfast's Paul Murphy. Later, the Wheels duo returned to Morrison's flat for a session. "We sat up half the night," Demick recalls. "Dee went out and left us with a bottle of vodka and Van. He and Herbie took out their guitars and I played harp. Van was singing off the top of his head. We were all drunk and out of our heads, then he phoned someone and said, 'Listen, this is what we should be doing.' He held the phone over the table as we played. Then we crashed out and Van was sitting there with his guitar and a Grundig open-top reel to reel singing his heart out in streams of consciousness, drunk as a lord. He was still singing and playing after the tape ran out. That night it was a bottle of Smirnoff. He wasn't very happy at all then."

Jim Armstrong also visited the Notting Hill abode for some late-night music sessions and found Morrison tolerable enough "when he had his guard down". The singer's fondness for interrupting people with odd calls at unsociable hours can also be traced back to this period. "He used to ring in the middle of the night saying 'Man, someone followed me home,'" Armstrong remembers. "I said, 'So?' I think he wanted someone to come up and hold his hand or something. But I got on with him." Morrison's unpredictable behaviour was no doubt influenced by the state of his career and his relationship with Dee. He did not confide in colleagues about the state of his love life, but over the next few months Dee's name would disappear from conversations. Later, it transpired that she had subsequently died, reportedly from a brain tumour.

In times of trouble, Morrison often looked to Belfast for solace, reconnecting with old friends from a time before he was in the spotlight as a pop star and part of the Tin Pan Alley circus that now included Them. That March, he arrived in the city and attended the Queen's University Blues Festival. Alexis Korner was present, but the real highlight for Morrison was a musical reunion with his pals. The irrepressible Geordie Sproule and fellow Federals Ricky Maitland and Eddie Campbell had teamed up with Billy McAllen and George Jones of the Silhouettes, plus Keith Donald of the Greenbeats, to form a one-off showband supergroup mischievously named the Half Cuts. Morrison joined them on stage for some rock 'n' roll and R&B covers that enlivened the student audience. The performance was a reminder of happier times when he was running around with G.D. in the Manhattan or learning to play saxophone in Hyndford Street with the Monarchs. Although he had escaped and outgrown Belfast, its appeal as a sanctuary, as home, was undeniable.

Witnessing G.D., Jones and McAllen settled and happy in their respective showbands, Morrison could not help wondering who were the real winners. In contrast to the hectic pace of life in London, Belfast was relaxing and endearingly parochial in its cultural life. Looking around, it seemed that everything was the same as when he had left – except for a few name changes. Instead of Them, it was now the Just Five, featuring Sam Mahood, that were mobbed every week at the Maritime. With a repertoire featuring blues classics and the latest Rolling Stones songs, Mahood strutted across the stage like Mick Jagger while guitarist Billy McCoy carefully retuned his instrument to imitate the sitar sound of the chart-topping 'Paint It, Black'. As a tribute to Them, they regularly included a version of 'Baby Please Don't Go'. Their set was so frenzied that Mahood was sometimes accompanied from the stage by a couple of bouncers. Among their rivals were up-and-coming group the Few, a quintet of hip school kids managed by aspiring starmaker Norman Cowie. Morrison grimaced sardonically upon seeing that the Solomons were still in control of the city. Mervyn had established Emerald Records and corralled several R&B groups including the Alleykatz, the Luvin Kind, the Just Five, the People and the Bats into a package recording released as *Ireland's Greatest Sounds – Five Top Groups From Belfast's Maritime Club*. Retailing at 19/11d, it was promoted as the "lowest priced album of Irish pop in record history". This was the true legacy of Them – cut price, cheaply recorded R&B from those left behind. It was enough to drive Morrison back to London where his group were about to enter the final stages of their tortuous and tortured history.

By the spring of 1966, Them had lost almost all of their original motivation. Their rapport with their record company, producer and management had deteriorated as the hits evaporated. Some managers

fulfil the role of surrogate father figures but Phil Solomon was more like
a Victorian patrician or headmaster: stern, feared, distant and godlike.
"Philip wasn't too keen on their discipline," Tommy Scott points out,
with delightful understatement. "They were wee bad boys, turning up
late at gigs. They would ask me to ask Phil things. They were afraid of
him – the impresario image! One time, Van put his problems to me and
I told him, 'Phil's your manager – if you want me to tell him I will, but
it's really up to you.'"

Morrison's poor communication skills and inability to articulate his
misgivings ensured that matters worsened. It seemed as though he no
longer cared whether Them fell apart before his eyes. Viewing from the
wings, Phil Coulter realized that the group was in irreparable decline.
"The relationship had been deteriorating. The band were having
internal troubles, guys bickering, leaving, getting a hard time on the
road, not having hits, not even enjoying being in the studio." Even
former members now regarded Them as a bad joke. Pianist Eric
Wrixon, who had recently moved to Blackpool to join Morrison's
mates in the Wheels, was appalled by their lax approach, poor discipline
and flagrant disregard for everybody. "Ray Elliott and Van Morrison
went completely senseless. We met them a few times when I was in the
Wheels and the one thing they weren't was slick professionals. They
were a 'Let's go and get it done' band. All the backbone went out of
Them when Billy Harrison left." Jim Armstrong, the sober-blooded
ex-bank-clerk, spent every available weekend in Belfast in blessed
retreat from Them's increasingly erratic exploits and boorish boozing.
"The thing was falling apart," he admits. "There was so much
infighting and the band were failing. Ray Elliott used to get his money
on Monday, get blocked and pawn his saxophone. We had to get the
saxophone out of the pawn for the next gig and things like this. They
just drank themselves stupid to get away from all the fighting."

Phil Solomon's reaction to this impudence was felt in harsh words
and a lingering contempt for Morrison's demeanour, conduct and
personality. He regarded as laughable the notion that the singer was
merely an over-sensitive creature with an artistic temperament. In his
opinion: "the man is as thick skinned as a crocodile. Morrison would
do these things to suit Morrison because he's not a professional. He
never was and he never will be. That's the tragedy of Morrison. He was

a genius who never reached fulfilment. He couldn't be big because of himself. He was his own worst enemy."

Solomon retained flickering hopes of reasserting some control over Morrison and his mutinous crew by sanctioning further work in the studio. Under Scott's tutelage, they recorded more demos while searching for a likely single. A cover of Paul Simon's 'Richard Cory' was selected as topical fare, although such material already sounded terribly dated. "We did a slow version of the song with harmonica, where Van was able to think about the lyrics," Armstrong remembers. "We were trying to be creative. Then we went back and did it uptempo." They all agreed that the slower tempo was an exceptional performance but Scott preferred the more commercial uptempo arrangement. A bitter impasse followed with Scott insisting that they record the song his way. Armstrong rebelled and decided to take his case to the ultimate authority: Phil Solomon. Like Billy Harrison before him, Armstrong was determined to play the union leader and help Morrison enforce his will in the studio, achieve greater autonomy and perhaps even secure an improved deal. All the talk came to nothing. "We arranged the meeting with Philip," Armstrong explains, "and Van, of course, did his usual thing. He didn't bother. He was hot-headed for one minute and then he just thought 'Nah'. He didn't even appear at the meeting. It was just the four of us, so Philip didn't give a shit." Solomon did not even have to raise his voice over the matter. A withering look was enough to convince Armstrong that he was out of his depth. "I was finished with that game by then," he concedes, "and I felt, 'Ah, I'll just get it done.'"

Like Armstrong, Morrison also felt disillusioned and defeated. "It became a trial, a sort of endurance test like [when] the Indians used to make people walk while they hit them with sticks. It was no longer people making music and grooving together. It became sick. There was no point in caring about anything because there was nothing to care about."

The minor insurrection over 'Richard Cory' – another predictable flop – disguised the greater problem of lost inspiration and lack of direction. A few protest records were still charting but the angry voice of youth represented by Them had lost its resonance, grown shrill with political hectoring. More sophisticated acts like the Byrds, and Dylan himself, had long since moved on.

The demoralized Armstrong left Them before the release of 'Richard Cory' and returned to Belfast. Ever practical, Phil Solomon simply contacted Billy Harrison and asked him if he wanted his old job back. Morrison blocked that proposal without delay, not wishing to open old wounds. Temporarily minus a guitarist, Them seemed set for a spell off the road until Solomon intervened with confirmation of an imminent American tour. With the group in disarray, it was even suggested that Morrison should tour with musicians he had never met. "They wanted me to go to the States with four guys that they picked out and called Them. I took the group with Henderson, Armstrong and Elliott." Of course, they still had to contact Armstrong in Belfast and tempt him back. The guitarist voiced caution about the financial arrangements on offer but could not resist the adventure and said: "OK, see America and die." Aware of the many tales of money lost by British acts on first American tours, Morrison sought cast-iron guarantees. Solomon had offered a percentage of door receipts but the singer refused to risk losses and demanded a weekly salary and set fee. Such caution sounded like good sense but would turn out to be a miscalculation with bitter consequences.

Towards the end of May, Them flew into New York where they were met by Tommy Scott who was responsible for paying their wages and ensuring that they arrived punctually for radio interviews and performances. Scott had arranged some minor promotional activities in the city and visited Bert Berns with a view to recording Them in America. "I felt it could all be regenerated," he says. "Bert wanted to arrange a deal with Phil Solomon." With their underground success in the USA as a calling card, there was every possibility that the influential Berns could provide the contacts and, more importantly, the hit record that might yet catapult Them towards mainstream success.

After flying to San Francisco, they were whisked away on a local flight to appear at a tiny theatre, then onwards to Phoenix, Arizona, where they were treated like presidential candidates and placed in an open-top Cadillac. Pursued by delirious fans, they were driven straight from the airport to a local football arena. Like the Beatles at Shea Stadium, Them found it difficult to compete with the racket generated by the audience. Accustomed to 100-watt equipment at home, they were astonished when presented with a single Fender amp issuing 20 watts. "I've used bigger stuff to practise with," Armstrong curtly informed his backline.

Excitement followed with a lengthy series of bookings through early to mid-June at the famous Whisky A Go-Go on Sunset Strip. The prospect of visiting Hollywood was a dream to be savoured as the Strip had recently become a teenage paradise. Legions of bright young things arrived daily, fed with fantasies of seeing the Byrds or encountering one of the visiting British musicians, preferably a Beatle or a Stone. There was a boom in music venues and an endless supply of all-night eateries and health food stores for the sleepless hordes and early risers who were busily marshalling the hippie movement which would reach its apotheosis the following summer at the Monterey International Pop Festival. Morrison was ready to offer some new songs, in addition to the standard Them set, and found time to work on a couple of fresh compositions. At one point, he approached Tommy Scott and recited the lyrics to 'Walking In The Queen's Garden', which included the line: "See the Duke in drag waving a yellow flag". Aware of Unionist Ulster's reverence for the Crown, he worried that it might prove controversial and enquired of the producer: "Do you think it's too disrespectful?"

Scott's role as advisor and fee dispenser barely lasted beyond the first few days in Hollywood. At that point, the group was receiving $2,000 a week (less 35 per cent commission), which sounded like excellent money. All that changed though when they discovered that Solomon was to receive a cheque for $10,000. Armstrong was appalled by this discrepancy in their respective incomes. "If he'd said 'I'll take 35%' [of $10,000], we'd have said 'Thank you, Santa Claus.'" Of course, Solomon could justifiably point out that Morrison had accepted a set salary instead of a percentage and was now merely complaining after the event. What might otherwise have been sorted out in Solomon's New Oxford Street office took on far more serious implications when the absent Them elected to take a stand. Deprived of the benefit of Solomon's browbeating logic, they discovered the foolhardy courage to rebel. The issue later became clouded in bitterness, but Solomon never lost sense of the financial facts. "The truth is 101 per cent as follows," he patiently explains. "When Tommy Scott went to ask for the money he was told Van Morrison's taken it. As Van had some money before he went to the USA, he'd actually had it both ways. He had the money from us and the money from the promoter in America. We asked for the money back and he wouldn't give it to us. A court case eventually came and it was settled out of court. In the end we lost thousands of pounds because we'd paid Van Morrison, and by the time the lawyer's fees were paid we'd lost very heavily on it. And that was the cause of the break-up."

Before the legal skirmishes began, Them enjoyed their stint at the Whisky where they were supported by several sterling acts – Captain Beefheart, Buffalo Springfield, the Association and the Doors. Morrison entertained the audience with his stage antics which included standing unsteadily on speakers while waving his arms and pretending to fly. Another trick was flailing the microphone to create feedback and distortion in imitation of the Who's Pete Townshend. What most people remembered, however, especially those on their tab, was Them's extraordinary alcohol consumption. The Doors' John Densmore was astonished by Morrison's capacity but even that paled alongside the intake of the hedonistic Ray Elliott who supplemented the Whisky's beer supply with tumblers of gin from a local liquor store. "On our first night at the Whisky A Go-Go, Van wrecked £900 worth of microphone equipment," Elliott remembers. "I just got drunk. At the end of the week, Them's drinks bill was $5,400." Elliott was an exotic specimen to the anglophile Whisky clientele who adored his striped blazer, Rupert Bear trousers and Sherlock Holmes deerstalker. After the first Whisky show, Elliott woke up the next morning to find himself in what turned out to be Frank Zappa's house, where he stayed for the remainder of his time in Hollywood. Morrison, meanwhile, was ensconced at the Sunset Palms, where he combined sporadic socializing with bouts of sullen isolation. He sent starstruck postcards back to friends like G.D. and once phoned Belfast to say he was enjoying himself at a party with members of the Mamas & The Papas and the Lovin' Spoonful. Armstrong recalls a less savoury incident when he was ejected from a club along with Doors vocalist Jim Morrison after catcalling "Johnny Rivers is a wanker". This fraternization with the L.A. pop élite was consummated in a startling duet at the final Whisky date where the two Morrisons traded verses on elongated versions of 'Gloria' and Wilson Pickett's 'In The Midnight Hour'.

After Hollywood, Them returned to San Francisco, then played at a roller rink in San Leandro. It was there that Morrison first met 19-year-old Janet Rigsbee, a California-raised Texan whose beauty, innocence and optimism proved instantly alluring. Rigsbee had never been to a pop concert before and her favourite act was the folk duo Simon & Garfunkel. For a time, she had aspired to become a serious actress, having played Juliet at a Shakespeare festival and performed in a production of *Peer Gynt*. After signing to a casting agency, she was given some work modelling and appearing in television commercials, both of which she found unfulling. A new road beckoned. Over the next year, she would metamorphose into Janet Planet, embracing the flower power hippie trappings of the time, with an attendant interest in astrology. Her first encounter with Morrison only hinted at the intensity to follow. "We didn't see much of her," says Armstrong. "She was very quiet, a nice kid. I don't think she was known as 'Planet' then. I thought she was only about 17 – *very* young looking and not a hippie. She was more like the all-American college girl. And she certainly didn't look like an actress."

While in San Francisco, Them also played at Bill Graham's Fillmore Auditorium. By this time, they had become more daring and were accompanied by an imposing heavy provided by the Whisky's owner Elmer Valentine. "This was the sort of guy you'd see in a film," Armstrong remarks. "He played cards with us in his shades, vest and boxer shorts with a gun on the table. His original job had been collecting debts and breaking arms and legs. He was a great bloke but we were totally in awe of him." Emboldened by their muscular companion, they refused to play the Fillmore unless Graham paid them upfront.

Word was gradually spreading that Them were without a manager. Cast adrift in the shark-infested waters of the American concert circuit, they soon discovered establishments which were controlled by Mafia-affiliated characters. The group had shown some bravado in defying Solomon but now they were targets for unscrupulous, if not dangerous, poachers in search of a profitable investment. "We did gigs with the Mafia, sure," Armstrong admits. "We were asked to sign with them and they'd make sure we had hits. We'd just collect money on the road and they'd collect royalties." The request was politely declined. One evening Armstrong made the mistake of pouring his heart out about the break with Solomon and its likely implications for the future of Them. His listener nodded sympathetically, then casually remarked: "Well, for a certain sum and a round-trip first-class air ticket, a contract could be taken out to shoot this Phil Solomon." "You're joking," the flabbergasted Armstrong spluttered nervously, before swiftly taking his leave. It was clear that Them were totally out of their depth.

After appointing a solicitor, Morrison and the group did their best to relegate the Solomon dispute to the back of their minds, but it was no easy task. They had always been humbled by the presence of the man whose authority, confidence, leadership and charisma could seem overwhelming when he was in full flow. Morrison feared terrible repercussions. It was difficult to determine how badly such a serious rift with management might derail his career or to calculate the full wrath of Solomon. "I was emotionally intimidated by him myself," admits Phil Coulter. "It's no big confession. Remember that for all the hit records, they were still small-town boys." Other managers might have rushed to the States to confront their mutinous charges, but Solomon, even in this highly volatile situation, retained a cold professional distance and dealt with Morrison with scrupulous efficiency worthy of a High Court Judge. "I'm not a violent man" Solomon points out. "I only fight with the help of a legal representative in a court. If I have a case, I take legal action. I don't threaten people because I think that's a stupid way of reacting. You've got the law to protect you and if something's wrong you've got to fight through the law. I take exception to the word 'intimidated'. That was a figment of Morrison's imagination. If Van had any problems he could have walked into our offices with witnesses. We weren't hiding from him. It doesn't add up. All I did was instruct an American solicitor, Walter Hofer, to take action. He represented the Beatles among others. He was a very honest solicitor. He certainly wasn't the Mafia – and he was very expensive. I was 6,000 miles away in London. What could I do?"

For Solomon, the relationship with Morrison and Them was already history, irrespective of their ultimate court settlement. He had better things to do with his life. Them, by contrast, chose to lose themselves in a haze of alcohol. As Solomon might have feared, they went wild without the restraining hand of Tommy Scott. In July, they received a unique opportunity to visit Hawaii where they were booked for a series of shows at the Waikiki Shell. Upon arrival, they were presented with garlands of flowers and driven to Honolulu's Hilton hotel only to learn that there had been a mix-up with their booking. Instead, they were offered a beautiful beach house and the opportunity of a non-stop party. Ray Elliott remembers that they arrived with $17,000 from the recent Whisky and Fillmore bookings and then proceeded to spend the equivalent of £7,000 – an incredible sum for the period – in the paradisal setting of Waikiki. A large amount was spent on colourful cocktails, much to the pleasure of their promoter who found them much more animated on stage when they drank. "Van jumped and fell into the drums," Armstrong laughs. "We were totally blocked." The spectators were nonplussed at times, which was hardly surprising given the incongruous supporting act. "It was Them and the Ramsey Lewis Trio," Henderson points out. "Anyone who came to see Ramsey Lewis wasn't interested in us. Hawaii was a failure in that respect."

Despite the exotic attractions of Hawaii, the boys had not forgotten their Protestant upbringing and were momentarily drawn back into old rituals as the glorious Twelfth of July approached. Back in East Belfast, Morrison's local lodge in Templemore Avenue was the starting point for the 276th anniversary celebration of the Battle of the Boyne. Some 54 lodges and 45 bands, comprising 3,000 flag-waving Orangemen, marched to the field in Finaghy, accompanied by the strains of 'The Sash', 'Waltzing Matilda', 'Dolly's Brae' and 'Star Of The County Down'. That evening in Hawaii, the ghost of Ulster was conjured up by Ray Elliott who climbed a palm tree and began playing the loyalist anthem 'The Sash' on his flute. Morrison seemed transfixed by the music and his memories wandered back to the streets of Belfast. Suddenly, he turned to a Hawaiian girl and asked her, in all seriousness, "Do you know G.D.?" The chances of anybody in Hawaii having heard of his former window-cleaning colleague and showband mentor were beyond remote but Morrison was too lost in the moment. "It's etched forever," Armstrong reminisces. "The Twelfth, Waikiki Beach, big flames illuminating the beach, sipping drinks, Ray playing 'The Sash' and Van talking about G.D. Strange!"

The Hawaiian sojourn ended with a casualty. After drinking countless cocktails, the usually reliable Armstrong went surfing, then allowed his pale skin to be frazzled by the afternoon sun. The following morning he woke in intense pain and was alarmed to find his body covered in grape-sized blisters. Unable to walk, he was forced to convalesce while the group took off for some shows in San Francisco, where Moby Grape's guitarist was hired as a temporary ringer. Armstrong rejoined the crew for the remainder of their tour which took them to Washington, Arizona, Oregon and Seattle before returning to California. Morale had now hit a record low as the full implications of the split with Solomon were hitting home. They had squandered most of their concert fees on lawyers and ended up in a far worse financial position than if they had accepted their manager's original terms. Their single 'Richard Cory' was receiving little or no airplay and hopes of extending their trip and making a profit were scuppered when they could not obtain the necessary work permits.

Morrison's moods took on a darker hue towards the end, culminating in some unusual behaviour at a show in San Luis Obispo on 24 July. "He didn't talk to anybody at this time," Ray Elliott remembers. "He would just sit there in a deep depression . . . On stage, he'd just go mad and start attacking the band with a mike stand." Like a Free Presbyterian preacher exhorting the expulsion of the serpent from Eden, Morrison stalked the stage menacingly, ever ready to flail the ungodly. "He was singing away, then he lifted his mike stand and took a swing at Ray Elliott," Armstrong marvels. "There was a wee bit of tension and he was all wound up. He'd come over to me and look and I just looked back at him. We wondered what was going on. There was no warning. Ray was playing all right and so was the band. He never explained it. Ray just laughed and said, 'The wee man's gone mad!' 'Gloria' was the last number, then they pulled the curtains."

Soon after, Morrison took his money, bought an expensive tape recorder and returned to London with Alan Henderson. David Harvey decided to marry a girl in Los Angeles and stayed on. Armstrong and Elliott were flat broke and had to beg their American solicitor to stump up the money for an air ticket home. On arrival at London Airport, Armstrong turned to Elliott in astonishment at the sight of crowds of screaming teenagers. "I didn't know we were this popular," he joked. Another happy illusion was shattered when they discovered that the reception was for the Beatles who were travelling on the same flight, albeit in first class.

With members of Them scattering in every direction, Morrison and Henderson were anxious to resolve matters and seek some kind of rapprochement with Solomon. "We were hitting a brick wall," Henderson admits. "We didn't even get a meeting with Solomon." The entrepreneur preferred to conduct his dealings with Morrison through his solicitors. Far from fretting about the loss of Them, Solomon turned a bad situation to his advantage. His wife Dorothy had already thrown up her hands and said "Philip, no more groups!" Reflecting on Them's tempestuous past two years, he acknowledged that she was right and contented himself with the knowledge that he still retained their royalties. Thereafter, he diversified his interests successfully.

While Morrison and Henderson were foundering in confusion, Solomon had already confined Them to the dustbin of history. His view of the wee man was provided with the cold precision of an auditor adjusting a balance sheet. "There comes a time when you have to say, 'Is it worth it?' And in the case of Van Morrison in the end it *wasn't* worth it, even though we poured a lot of money into him." He admits that he regarded the aberrant Morrison as little more than an animal in a chain of evolution which no doubt placed Solomon on a considerably higher level. "I regret that we couldn't have controlled Morrison better. You've always got regrets with an artiste whom you believe in very sincerely but who doesn't do as well as he could. I think his career has come to a complete halt. If I was writing a book about him, I would say 'Morrison small' and 'Morrison big – that might have been'. I think he would have been big if he'd been straightened out at the start of his career. He wouldn't have been overdrinking and he would have learned to be a professional." While Solomon felt that Morrison had squandered his talents, the singer was equally contemptuous of his old master. He seldom mentioned the man by name in his later career but his feelings were displayed in occasional asides. "He was an Irish Jew," he obligingly informed one interviewer. "The worst kind, that's what they say." Regrettably, Morrison did not enlighten us as to where we might find a better quality of Jew.

Phil Coulter attempted to console Morrison by reassuring him that there was life after Solomon. What neither knew was that Solomon had already found a promising singer-songwriter whom he regarded as a far greater talent than the flawed Morrison. Such was the tycoon's confidence that he was financing this latest prodigy to the tune of £20,000. At a time when Solomon was at his entrepreneurial peak, his rebellious charge was thrust into a downward spiral. Like a beaten dog, Morrison returned home to East Belfast to face an uncertain future.

TEN

Belfast Before The Troubles

The Belfast awaiting Morrison had not changed drastically over the previous two years, but subtle and significant cultural and political shifts were detectable. It could hardly be otherwise in 1966, a year that everybody had pinpointed as a likely trouble spot in the province's already inflamed history. The two-forked 50th anniversary celebrations of the Republican Easter Rising and the Battle of the Somme, combined with news that the Queen and Duke of Edinburgh were conducting a state visit, focused external media attention on Northern Ireland for the first time in years.

The Republicans' Easter parades had caused such concern to the Unionist government that all trains from Dublin to Sandy Row were cancelled for the duration of the celebrations. Wild headlines appeared in Belfast newspapers warning "IRA Threat". The Protestant-owned newspapers were apparently unaware that the organization was dormant, its available arms few. Nevertheless, the armed B-Specials were mobilized and in the background lurked the menacing presence of the recently formed Ulster Volunteer Force, a paramilitary organization which took its name from Edward Carson's 1912 loyalist defenders and pledged "a declaration of war against the IRA and its splinter groups". The founder and first commander of the revamped UVF was 32-year-old Gusty Spence, a Shankill resident and near contemporary of Morrison's friend Geordie Sproule. Like Sproule, Spence had suffered a childhood marked by poverty. He had worked barefoot in a Belfast mill for a pittance and was naturally resistant to the prevailing notion that loyalists were a privileged caste in a corrupt state. Spence followed the party line of Orange politicians, believing "the border was likely to fall, the Jesuits would move in and all hell would break loose". Working with the Royal Ulster Rifles in Germany and as a military policeman for the British forces in Cyprus only hardened his resolve and after returning to Belfast he was ready to defend the province.

Remarkably, in such a potentially explosive climate, the Easter parades passed peaceably. Unionist fears of a resurgence of Irish nationalism in the North and South seemed largely unfounded. Most of the marchers were interested in reform rather than revolution. Many Northern Catholics, although the victims of institutional injustices, were still wary of a united Ireland in which health, welfare and pension allowances would surely all be lowered. Conversely, Catholics in the South, although weaned on dreams of unification, were not yet ready to inherit the economic and political encumbrance of Northern Ireland. The Taoiseach Seán Lemass, despite his strong Republican roots, was a pragmatic reformist whose major aim was establishing a strong economy in the 26 counties.

By summer, tensions had heightened. It was no great surprise that Ian Paisley, then aged 40, was at his most rancorous that year, denouncing foes real and imagined. He now had his own newspaper, the *Protestant Telegraph*, his own church and his own political party. At a time when other Christian churches were promoting concord and unity, he took to the streets demonstrating against the "Romanizing tendencies of the Presbyterian Church". His 'No Surrender' politics exacerbated the siege mentality of his zealous following and the protest ended with skirmishes, a near riot and the arrest of the Big Man. As in 1964, Paisley's invective not only inspired a new, fiercer loyalism, but also provoked political reaction from the nationalist community. Rita and Gerry O' Hare, later prominent figures in the IRA, saw this as a pivotal period in their lives. "There had always been a heavy nationalism within me," Gerry recalls, "but like every other guy growing up I just wanted to have a few jars, get married and have kids. I was able to tolerate the situation because I had a decent job. I wasn't hungry. I hadn't been deliberately discriminated against because I never went to a Protestant company to look for a job. I never wasted my time. I went straight to a Catholic company . . . But there was an election and Paisley came. That started me . . . My mother was a very strong nationalist and my grandfather owned the famous Gladstone Bar on the Falls Road. 1966 was the anniversary of the Rising and we had tried to hold a decent commemoration parade but the RUC weren't allowing it. In 1966, I couldn't have envisaged the way it was going to turn out, but I saw that we were basically saying, 'Look, we're entitled to our culture. What's wrong with celebrating Easter 1916?' My mother was born in 1908 and she woke up in 1921–22 to discover that she was British at the stroke of a pen. Nobody had asked *her*. So after that I gradually became involved in issues."

Premier O'Neill was concerned about Paisley's omnipresence and even more troubled by the rise of the UVF. In a speech at Stormont, he remarked: "To those of us who remember the Thirties, the pattern is horribly familiar. The contempt for established authority; the crude and unthinking intolerance; the emphasis upon monster processions and rallies; the appeal to a perverted form of patriotism; each and every one of these things has its parallel in the rise of the Nazis to power."

The UVF's grim progress was charted in several sectarian killings that summer, none of which could be justified even by the cold logic of vengeance. A firebomb, intended for a Catholic off-licence, succeeded in killing a 77-year-old Protestant widow Matilda Gould in her bed. Her son Samuel was awarded £336 compensation. Soon after, John Patrick Scullion was assassinated in the Falls while returning home from a pub. The merciless killings culminated in the infamous Malvern Arms murder, in which four Catholics were mistakenly identified as IRA leaders and shot, one fatally. He was identified as Peter Ward, a Falls Road bar worker and political innocent. This outrage prompted a massive murder hunt, ending with the arrest of three UVF men, including loyalist icon Gusty Spence, who were each sentenced to 20 years' imprisonment later that year. Harold Wilson denounced the murder and described the UVF as a "quasi fascist organization" in the House of Commons. Reacting swiftly, Premier O'Neill invoked the Special Powers Act and had the UVF outlawed. It was an embarrassing prelude to the arrival of the Queen, not to mention an unprecedented number of bemused British journalists.

For years, the British media had ignored Northern Ireland, partly through indolence but also as a reflection of government policy. Broadcasters were encouraged to leave reporting of Northern Ireland affairs to the locals, who better knew the region and its difficulties. News features tended to promote reconciliation rather than criticizing government policy or exposing corruption. Hard, investigative journalism was not welcomed. When Fleet Street belatedly caught up with modern Ulster that July, its journalists were shocked and appalled. Some arrived in time for the Twelfth and witnessed blazing bonfires and banners proclaiming 'Only By Eternal Vigilance Shall We Overcome The Threat Of Papist Rule In Ulster'. The *Sunday Times* adapted George Bernard Shaw's *John Bull's Other Island* into a sneering headline, 'John Bull's Political Slum', then announced: "There is a part of Britain where the crude apparatus of political and religious oppression – ballot rigging, job and housing discrimination, and an omnipresent threat of violence – comfortably co-exists with intense loyalty to the Crown." The paper's Sunday rival, the *Observer*, was even more critical and wondered why the Queen's route took her "past the lavatory-wall patriotism of the fiercely Protestant Sandy Row, with its viciously offensive anti-Catholic slogans". The old loyalist conviction of being misunderstood, patronized and perpetually in danger of being sold out by Westminster was no doubt reinforced by such reports. For nationalists, it must have sounded like a sudden end to a conspiracy of silence. What came across most forcibly was the sense of disbelief among English journalists when faced with Orangeism at its most virulent. At a time when the cult of youth was in the ascendancy and the spirit of the Swinging Sixties espoused the gospel of fab and the epistle of optimism, the realization that sectarianism was on a neighbouring doorstep in all its anachronistic splendour was a spectacle too terrible to confront without lapsing into adjectives of disgust. After reasonably describing Belfast as a "time-honoured powder-keg into which the wearing of the wrong colour, the whistling of the wrong tune, or the waving of the wrong flag in certain areas could throw a match," the *Observer* concluded with a devastating appraisal of its general populace. "They are a touchy people. A London socialist who carelessly said something rude about royalty in the city centre this week had to be rescued from the crowd which promptly attacked him. Bigotry is a casual, unchallenged reflex here: it is difficult to find any institutions, even individuals, it has not tainted. This is a sick, sick country."

The British media's dire diagnosis took no account of the carefree youth of Belfast, many of whom did not regard the Queen's visit as a heart-stopping event and saw bigotry as anachronistic and counter to the spirit of the age. Optimists perceived hope beneath the depressing headlines and concluded that Paisley's protest was an increasingly desperate attempt to reverse the liberalization policies which had been underway since 1963. However, there was one chance moment that summer when Ulster might have exploded in violence. A Catholic workman, acting on impulse, threw a block of concrete from a building which crashed onto the bonnet of the Queen's limousine as it passed through Great Victoria Street. Nobody was hurt and the government immediately issued a statement confirming that there was no political motive behind the attack. By later Ulster standards, 1966 was still relatively peaceful. Neither the Easter Rising celebrations nor the Orange parades had provoked rioting. Paisley's protest had ended with a court appearance and a charge of unlawful assembly. While some extremists stoned the Catholic-owned International Hotel and attempted to ignite a bookie's in Sandy Row which dared employ Fenians, other major disturbances were avoided.

Morrison was well aware of the religious divisions in his midst but, like his young contemporaries, remained optimistic, even turning a blind eye to the old prejudices encountered in everyday conversation. "That was always going on. But this was before all that bigotry got really big. Everybody was just too busy getting on with what they wanted to do and what they were interested in. The people that I grew up with, my peer group at the time, weren't into that stuff. They were into sharing ideas; they had energy and they saw a bright future. All that changed later on." As Morrison walked around the city that August, he heard transistor radios blaring out the latest chart-topping hit: 'Out Of Time'. The song was both an ironically apposite anthem for Unionist Belfast and a curt reminder to Morrison that he had now been eclipsed in popularity by Chris Farlowe, a gravel-voiced R&B singer who had never previously seemed a promising candidate for *Top Of The Pops*. The worlds of politics and pop were in constant flux and Belfast was buzzing with the esprit of a people who had defied cultural commentators by surviving their summer of danger intact. Paisley was in Crumlin Prison serving a three-month sentence, which simultaneously pleased his critics and galvanized his hard-line supporters. Ever ready to play the humility card he celebrated his release later that autumn by emerging in a car bearing the slogan 'Behold The Lamb Of God'.

Writer Donald S. Connery, a visitor to Belfast that summer, was struck by how powerfully the place had been influenced by "the permissive manners and morals of Britain in the age of pop and plenty . . . Belfast and the Ulster resort towns seem to me to have an extraordinary number of dance-mad youngsters, long-haired beatniks, motorcyclists bearing guitars and pathetic groups of boys and girls just drifting about looking for something to do." Among this anti-establishment aggregation was former Them employee Peter Docherty, the self-styled 'greatest showman in the city' who said "Belfast? The town has had it. It's out. It's nothing, boy."

The beatniks and "pathetic groups" had good reason to be cynical but their impatience with the old order was producing more than mere indolence. There was a dramatic rise in the number of clubs and boutiques catering for young tastes as Belfast displayed its own determination to be part of 'Swinging Britain'. In Wellington Street, the city's first men's boutique John Patrick was teeming with crowds every Saturday afternoon and soon found a rival in Douglas Wilson, a classier outfitters that sold fashionable John Michael clothes. Meanwhile, the girls flocked to the smaller Flair, also on Dublin Road, and Mark Anthony on Church Lane, where loud music drowned out the patter of sales staff. Art students hung out at the Coffee House in Queen Street which provided Continental-style post-midnight dining, usually consisting of coffee and mini-steaks. A more plebeian clientele frequented the Crow's Nest or Kelly's Cellars for bacon, egg, chips or a stout and a sandwich. Musicians preferred the Wellington Street café Isabeal's where dreams of fame on the mainland were woven amidst an endless supply of coffee and buns. The Plaza in Chichester Street still ruled as Belfast's premier ballroom but the enterprising Sam Smyth was busily promoting Romano's in Queen Street, which offered a regular supply of visiting English groups and a distinctive mod evening every Wednesday. Showbands dominated at the Astor in College Court, while a younger set frequented the Orpheus on York Street and the Boom Boom Room on Arthur Square. The more modish preferred the Jazz Club, with its ultraviolet lighting or the cavernous, dimly-lit Elizabethan on Royal Avenue.

By the summer of 1966, the city centre had attracted a unique clique of heads and hipsters who resembled a motley microcosm of the hippie hordes regularly seen on Sunset Boulevard, Carnaby Street and the King's Road. Even Morrison, usually so introspective, recognized that his hometown was a place apart. "It doesn't have much to do with the Irish scene either," he observed. "It's just Belfast. It's got its own identity, it's got its own people . . . it's just a different race, a different breed of people."

With time on his hands and no place to go, the 21-year-old Morrison was uneasily reconnecting with that "different breed of people" for the first time in several years. Coincidentally, most of his old colleagues and rivals were either residing in or returning to Belfast as autumn reared. The Wheels were back with Brian Rossi after a brief rift in the ranks and plotting new adventures after a stint at the Jazz Club. Roy Kane had recently joined Billy McAllen in the Silhouettes, an offshoot of the Stan Lynn Showband. Another Silhouette and ex-Monarch, George Jones, was already planning the showband super-group Tara while awaiting the arrival from England of *Crossroads* television star Deke Arlon as the charismatic frontman. Meanwhile, the indefatigable Geordie Sproule (G.D.) was enjoying unprecedented success with the Federals who were chosen as the support act at the Floral Hall and the Ulster Hall for visiting chart stars the Kinks, the Troggs and the Rockin' Berries. That autumn, the Federals became a clearing house for a number of ex-Them members. When talented guitarist Eddie Campbell announced that he was moving to the Stellas, G.D. recruited Jim Armstrong and then found the perfect soulmate in Ray Elliott. "He was a great musician," G.D. recalls. "We used to go to a club off the Markets called the Golden Gate Bar. I'd get wee gigs for me, Jim and Ray. He would play flute and sax. Me and him were drinking really hard." Morrison's old adversary Billy Harrison was officially off the scene, living with his wife back home in Bangor and working for the General Post Office with plans to qualify as a communications engineer. "I think Them are finished!" he informed the local music paper *City Week*. "They are pathetic now. There is no showmanship. They can't announce numbers. And they fiddle about for about five minutes between each song . . . As far as I'm concerned Them don't exist." Technically, Harrison was correct, although the

group's name continued to be bandied around amid rumours that
Morrison might revive the outfit. That same month, the Belfast
Gypsies, still living on a boat in Stockholm, released 'Gloria's Dream',
the title of which provoked a wince from the wee man.

Looking to the future, Morrison realized that a variant of the brand
name Them might still prove useful in promoting some local gigs. In
order to clarify matters, he allowed *City Week* a brief interview in
which he revealed: "We want to play our original music now. We've
had this sick pop. We objected to the release of our last three records.
But what is the use?" Alan Henderson, also in attendance, added
"People are finished making their fortunes out of us. Now we're going
to make our own." The piece concluded with the optimistic message,
"Them are the most mucked-about group in the business. But that's
finished now. They are looking for a new manager. They are looking
for a new life. They are going back to their roots."

Morrison's fraternization with the local music magazine introduced
him to several of Belfast's hip élite, most notably *City Week*'s colourful
columnist Donall Corvin. A scenester par excellence, Corvin was a
complex character with a fascinating history. His Republican father
Hugh Corvin, a respected accountant, had taken part in the 1916 Easter
Rising and the family settled in Antrim Road, later moving to
Ormonde Park in the Belfast suburb of Finaghy. Born on 22 February
1946 and christened Domhnall Gearóid Corvin, the boy was brought
up in a Republican Northern Ireland household where Gaelic
remained the first language. "He never spoke English until he was
seven," Sam Smyth marvels. After leaving boarding school Corvin
looked set for a promising career in the Insurance Corporation of
Ireland but, much to his family's consternation, fell into the pop scene,
working evenings as a disc jockey, moonlighting as a photographer,
then joining *City Week*. When he wasn't judging supermod contests at
the Jazz Club, Corvin could be found drinking heavily in Belfast's
hipper haunts or inviting starstruck girls to his flat on the pretext of
getting them into some spurious showbiz production. Late-afternoon
visitors to his home were occasionally taken aback by the sight of
scantily-clad young women parading around the front room. When
music scene gossip was dull Corvin created his own sensations, the
more bizarre the better. He once persuaded a teenager to pose for a

photo swallowing sugar lumps, then submitted an article claiming Belfast was the new mecca for LSD. Spontaneous and reckless, Corvin acted as though he was the leading character in some imaginary movie and cultivated a *carpe diem* lifestyle that usually meant he was penniless and hungover. One friend casually asked Corvin out for a drink one evening, fully expecting to visit a local hostelry. Instead, Corvin announced, "Let's go to London!" Hours later they were on the plane and spent a drunken night in Soho before cadging the fare back home.

Corvin's great ability was to sell himself in print as the ultimate avatar of cachet. "It was very important at that time if you wanted to do something in Belfast to get the word from Corvin," Sam Smyth attests. "That was his lifestyle. He used to wear purple suits, act the fool and write cryptic things. He always had literary aspirations." Corvin's circle was impressively wide, and included such relatively straight arrows as the avuncular ex-Monarch Roy Kane. "I had a lot of time for Corvin," Kane recalls. "He knew everyone and was very well read. He was brilliant. But he was also a sorrowful character. At that time drinking was a preoccupation with a lot of people and Donall was an expert at it." Journalist Colin McClelland sometimes imbibed with the expert. "There was a dark side to Corvin," he notes, "a deep cynicism about life in general. He was a notoriously heavy drinker. I remember being out with him on one or two drinking sessions. God, it was very hard to keep up with him. One night he had us drinking Brandy Alexanders. I'll never forget the hangover after that." Former Them keyboardist Eric Wrixon regarded Corvin as "a fascinating character, but slightly less fascinating in the flesh. He was a great column writer, a spectacular one given the period. As a person he wasn't quite so outgoing or witty – he was a lot deeper than that. There was a dark side to him. But he was an educated, intelligent guy and we all took to him."

Corvin became a great advocate of Morrison in *City Week*, championing his talent without ever lapsing into sycophancy. He encouraged the singer to play some local gigs and rekindle memories of the glory days at the Maritime. After making some cursory enquiries, they learned that the Elizabethan in Royal Avenue was closing and a new club was to open on the same premises called the Square One. "It'll be good to play in a Belfast club again," Morrison told Corvin at the time. "I thought the only places in town who'd consider booking us would be one of the draughty ballrooms. I didn't much relish the idea. It looks as though Square One could be the start of something."

While awaiting Square One's opening, Morrison had a free month which he spent monitoring the local scene, with Corvin occasionally acting as tour guide. One night in late September, they went to see Teddie & The Tigers at Sammy Houston's Jazz Club, watching with amusement as singer Teddie Palmer teased the girls who responded by throwing teddy bears onto the stage. Midway through the opening number, Morrison's thoughts turned to food and he and Corvin disappeared into the night.

At the time, Corvin was living in a flat in University Street which he shared with the pink-haired Dino Martin, the original drummer in the Misfits, who had taken over from Brian Rossi as the resident disc jockey at the Plaza. Martin was an in-demand character with an intimate knowledge of the local music scene and a drinker's thirst for post-pub entertainment. After the Plaza closed, he would often take visiting groups to Heaven, an illicit drinking den situated above a shop in the Markets area. A motley bunch of musicians would jam through the night while booze flowed and impressionable youngsters from Queen's University looked on in awe. Mattresses were scattered around the room and it was not uncommon for the police to arrive in the early hours in the hope of finding drugs, but all they discovered were empty bottles and bleary-eyed revellers. Martin's social and DJ-ing engagements had recently encompassed regular visits to the Dublin club, Scene. He was surprised to see Morrison turn up in the city one evening, having taken the train from Sandy Row. What struck Martin was Morrison's lack of money during his brief stay. "I had to pay his 30 shillings fare back. He always seemed short of money. He was looking for a drink or anything that was going, somewhere to crash when he was down there."

Perennially suspicious of people's motives, Morrison was vigilant when approached by well-wishers. "When I went back to Belfast I'd meet people in the street and their whole concept of the thing was totally money. 'How much money are you making? You must be making a lot of money.' And you aren't making any money . . . I was totally broke because I got a little money from the stuff that I'd written. I got a little – I didn't get it all and I didn't get anything from the recordings." There was no doubt that the recent break-up of Them and resulting litigation with Solomon had proven costly. As part of his settlement, Morrison had lost the revenue from his work with Them and there was no guarantee that he would ever enjoy another hit as big as 'Here Comes The Night'. This meant that he was a local celebrity but not the kind who could be relied upon to treat everybody to a round of drinks. Sometimes he felt like an ordinary worker wandering around Belfast but, even among friends, he could not completely escape the unwanted burden of pop stardom. "Some of them acted very strange. They expected me to have a lot of money and throw it around. You really know who your friends are. But a lot of them treated me just the same."

The cooler kids and local musicians soon adjusted to the prescence of Morrison without making a fuss. One night he visited the Maritime, which Eddie Kennedy was soon to rename Club Rado, to see the Few, another Them-influenced band with a penchant for Chicago blues. As he had done with the Downliners Sect two years before, Morrison expressed a desire to appear on stage for a brief jam, but again he was turned down. "I wouldn't let him on," recalls the Few's Brian Russell. "It's terrible when I think of it now. He'd come into the club and wanted to play harmonica. In those days harmonicas were 4/6d and I didn't want him playing one of our harmonicas so it never materialized." Russell's future wife recalls a more salty exchange. "You're talking to somebody from Northern Ireland here. I only say what's true and don't embroider anything. Brian said, 'I don't want your filthy spittle in our harmonicas, you wee cunt!' If Van Morrison wanted to play, he wanted to play and if he didn't he would sit on his own or interrupt somebody else's conversation. He was a real bore." Soon after, Russell caught up with Morrison at Isabeal's coffee bar in Wellington Street, but their conversation was again strained. "I asked him why he didn't get the boys together and go out and tour, but he didn't seem interested at all," Russell recalls. "He didn't say why. It was very hard to get anything from him."

Janet Martin, the schoolgirl who had followed Them around the city two years before, frequently sat opposite Morrison in Isabeal's, knowing it was best to be seen but not heard. "I never rubbed him up the wrong way," she says. "I respected his privacy. Van knew he was special and on some level we all knew it too. When he was offstage he was very quiet and withdrawn. He wasn't the most forthcoming of people. If you were a friend of his, as we thought we were, it was because you didn't hassle him. We'd sit in Isabeal's all day over a cup of coffee then. People like to discuss what they're going to do but Van wasn't like that at all. He was pleasant enough to me but he could be awfully nasty to other people. That's one thing I remember about him. He was not the kind of person you could take liberties with. *Ever.*"

Even Dino, who was among the pop élite of the city, was careful not to force himself on Morrison and soon learned that it was best to ignore the man in public. "Even if you were in a bar drinking, he wouldn't say anything. You might say to someone 'There's Van,' then go back to what you were doing. You never made conversation with him. You just nodded your head. We always thought he was on a different level – that was the impression he wanted to give. With Corvin, Van was more open."

The rapport between Corvin and Morrison was a combination of friendship and mutual expediency. "Obviously, Corvin was looking for a way to sell Van, as a publicist or whatever," Dino notes. "Maybe Corvin was hoping to be his manager but Van was still somewhat tied up with the Solomons and I'm sure it would have cost money to get out of that." Such niceties were no impediment to Corvin's vivid imagination. Inflamed with the idea of becoming a young svengali in the tradition of the charismatic Rolling Stones manager Andrew Oldham, Corvin convinced himself that he could relaunch Morrison, cause a sensation, and possibly make a fortune. "Van and Donall went drinking together," Sam Smyth remembers, "and Corvin told me he was going to be his manager. I said 'Good luck, Donall!' Jesus Christ, it was like wrestling crocodiles. I knew it would be difficult and probably wouldn't work. Donall wasn't the person. He was clever enough to do anything he wanted to do, I imagine. But the organization and discipline required for that job were not for him. At least Solomon knew who to ring. Donall would pick up the phone and ring me! So it was never that serious. It was more that Van liked Corvin, respected him and was shrewd enough to spot that he had a good mind and was a smart guy."

With the opening of Square One ("Belfast's newest and kinkiest club") approaching, Morrison urgently needed to hire some musicians. Initially, he approached Roy Kane and Billy McAllen, but they had other commitments. They directed him to Mike Brown, a young bass player they were auditioning for the Silhouettes as a replacement for George Jones. Brown was playing in the Alleykatz, one of the more promising groups on the circuit whose line-up included former Yaks' guitarist Billy Hollywood, rhythm player Jim Ross, vocalist Brian Godfrey, and drummer Joe Hanratty. The drummer and bassist were both happy to join Morrison, but they were forced to look elsewhere for a suitable guitarist. One Saturday afternoon, Morrison ventured to the music shop Crymbles and tracked down his former Orangefield alumnus Eric Bell. At the time, Bell was playing in Unit, an R&B offshoot of the Castaways, and another minor group, the Legends. His friends were impressed when Morrison called him aside and invited him over to Hyndford Street that very evening. "I went home and told my folks," Bell recalls. "They'd heard of Them and were pleased for me. I went to his house that night and his mother and father were there. As soon as I went in they put on their coats and went out with the dog." Bell was ushered inside and confronted with the expensive tape recorder that Morrison had purchased a few months before in America. "It was like nothing I'd ever seen in my life. It had wood veneer and meters like something you'd see in a recording studio. Before that I'd only seen a Bush recorder with a plastic mike. He had a few songs and wanted me to listen to them. I was told, 'Plug in your guitar and play whatever you want.' He sat there, chain-smoking. Then he put on these songs. They were very strange. Some of the lyrics had lines like 'Silly little policeman laughing'. It was Dylan-like and completely different from Them with him finger-picking on acoustic guitar and singing. I didn't know what I was doing, so I just played off the top of my head and tried to get into the mood of the songs. He said 'That's nice, man!' He was the first person to ever call me 'man'."

After unveiling the new line-up, Morrison invited Bell for a coffee the following day at Isabeal's. They then spent the evening at a nearby folk club whose beatnik in-crowd intellectually intimidated the working-class guitarist. "People were giving out nuts and raisins in bowls and there was a lot of talk about art, painting and blues music.

The girls had long hair and wore polo necks. I was way out of my depth and felt like a fish out of water. I left but he stayed on and seemed comfortable enough. Corvin was around then, and this artist, Cecil McCartney."

It says much for Morrison's changing social status that he felt relatively at ease with the proto-hippie crowd and art students around the university area. Cecil (later Cezil) McCartney was already a local cult figure variously described as "Belfast's answer to Andy Warhol" and "the original space cadet". Both epithets had some merit as McCartney was an innovative painter with an off-kilter bohemian view of life and an oft-stated ambition to become an astronaut and fly to Mars. A New Age convert before the term had been invented, McCartney studied at the Belfast School of Art and had a keen interest in Beat poetry, Buddhism, mysticism and meditation. He gained some local notoriety when the education committee in Omagh ordered the removal of a commissioned mural he had painted which featured such provocative slogans as "I got scrotian in my bones", "Stop the radiation, man" and the strange "Evolution explains the nature of man's origin and the word sterility". After befriending some pop stars in London, he travelled extensively. While Morrison was performing with Them at the Whisky, McCartney was outside the venue standing on his head promoting Buddhist meditation and vegetarianism. He ended an eventful summer surfing with astronauts on the West Coast before returning home.

Hearing that Morrison was back in East Belfast, McCartney invited him to the art studio at his home in Bangor. "I was one of the first intellectual, thinking people that he met," McCartney observes proudly. A great proselytizer of vegetarianism with an inexhaustible supply of wild theories about the cleansing properties of various minerals and herbs and the importance of fasting, McCartney could talk endlessly, but not always completely coherently, about astrology, alchemy, spiritual transformation, comparative religion, the properties of interplanetary light, space travel and the road to ultimate transcendence. Sometimes he would casually throw jaw-dropping boasts into everyday conversation such as "I'm one of the most advanced people" or "I was probably the first person that really knew anything about what a mystical experience is." For Morrison,

McCartney's mindscape must have seemed as far removed from the buttoned-down earthiness of East Belfast as was imaginable.

During one of his early visits to McCartney's home, Morrison was intrigued by a book on display titled *Mysticism* by Evelyn Underhill, a study of the importance of contemplative prayer, first published in 1911. But what really stuck in his memory was a sketch or poster on the wall which alluded to 'Astral' travel and would later inspire the title of his most famous album. "It was a painting," McCartney corrects. "There were several paintings in the studio at that time. Van looked at the painting and it suggested astral travelling to him. I don't think I went into very deep explanations as to what the paintings were about. Most of my painting at that time, the misty stuff, was based on atmospheric effects like Turner would have painted but it was also very heavy, biological, metaphoric shapes . . . probably the influence of psychedelia, although I didn't use psychedelic drugs. I was on a natural high."

McCartney's mind may have been fixed towards the astral plane but he also owned a less cosmological means of transportation in the form of a mini-van. He soon found himself recruited in a variety of roles, helping out Morrison as driver, roadie, artist and light-show projectionist. Unexpectedly, his first assignment followed Morrison's rarest request: "I want you to take some photographs of me." McCartney drove to Hyndford Street, met Morrison's mother, then set out on this curious fashion shoot. "Van had a blue velvet suit or cloak and looked somewhat like Little Lord Fauntleroy. I got my camera and we drove out into the country, stopping in a little wood that had about 10 trees growing in it. It was like a fairy circle. I took some pictures of him and it was hilarious. There was still paint on my trousers from trying to paint like Leonardo de Vinci and Vincent Van Gogh. I was delighted and exhilarated by Van strutting around in his little blue suit. I don't know why he wanted me to photograph him. I suppose he thought he was an Irish king or something."

On another drive, McCartney took Morrison to Cave Hill, telling him that there was a stream on the summit. "Van came panting up, he was about 100 feet behind," McCartney smiles. The artist ripped off his shirt and pants with the intention of bathing in the stream but it was dry. Wisely, Morrison had remained fully clothed throughout.

As he had done with Eric Bell, Morrison allowed McCartney to hear some tapes he had been making which sounded like a cross between the Goons' verbal nonsense and avant garde experimentation. "I thought it was really weird," McCartney concludes. "All I could hear was what seemed like his lip being pulled back and abstract sounds. He thought this was totally and utterly amazing. I felt it was just somebody making abstract sounds with his lip, so I didn't pay much attention to it. He was enthralled by it. Maybe it had been made when his perception was heightened by a little smoke or something." Then again, Morrison may simply have been attempting to out-weird McCartney by proving that he was more eccentric. Back in Bangor, their conversations sometimes took a surreal turn when Morrison got stoned. "He would just sit there and roll a joint," McCartney recalls. "I'd never seen hash in my life before. I would get a whiff of it across the table and then Van would take a couple of drags and go into a trance-like state. When he came out of that he'd be talking about the fact that the subconscious mind only knew what was visible around you." When McCartney countered with an alternative view, Morrison merely mumbled "That's right, the subconscious knows everything."

Some of the other ramblings were so off-the-wall or ill-informed it is difficult to imagine that Morrison wasn't just amusing himself by deliberately putting on his colourful host. "He was trying to explain to me how Hitler got his name," McCartney remembers, "about some publicity guys in the German government making him a hot politician. He punched his hand into his palm and said 'Yeah, *Hit*-ler! That's what we'll call him.' Then he was talking about the Pope and Judaism and implying that the Pope was very involved in Judaic teaching . . . that's as much as I will say."

Morrison's cultural pursuits included occasional forays to local picture houses. With Bell, he whiled away the afternoon at a cartoon cinema, sitting stony faced while all those around him erupted in laughter. Another newspaper cutting from the period documents him attending Fellini's *8½* in the company of McCartney. Morrison was also in the habit of hanging out with various teenage art school students, including several posh girls – Debbie Thompson, Cynthia MacHenry and Ursula Graham-White – whom he encountered when they were painting a mural for the opening of the Cavalier Club on the site of the old Fiesta ballroom on Hamilton Street. "The Cavalier was in the Markets area," MacHenry points out. "If our parents had known that we were even near that area we probably would have been banned from going out for about three years." The girls were not easily impressed but knew the wee man's reputation from the Maritime days. Morrison wasted no time in asking out Debbie Thompson, who politely declined, pointing out that "he was not a good-looking boy".

"Och, he tried that with everyone," says Cynthia MacHenry. "He didn't like to be seen to ask people out. It was 'You're either with me, or you're not'. He never really approached girls as such. But he liked to get into their company, as if to say, 'You're with me, tonight.'"

As he had shown with Jane Adams back in the Maritime days, Morrison was attracted to good-looking, respectable, upper middle-class women. Debbie Thompson was articulate, well-educated and discriminating. Her classmate Cynthia MacHenry was the goddaughter of Lady Moyra Hamilton, one of the Queen's ladies-in-waiting. With well-heeled parents – her father a solicitor, her mother an antiques dealer – and a brother who swanned around in a bright orange hearse purchased from the Duke of Westminster, MacHenry was quite a catch.

Morrison was even more taken with Ursula Graham-White, arguably the most glamorous girl among the arty set. The daughter of a Second World War spy, psychiatrist and university lecturer, Ursula was supposedly attending Belfast College of Art but spent much of her time in the company of visiting English pop groups such as the Kinks, who attended a party at her parents' palatial home. She was also fondly admired by the young promoter Sam Smyth, who was quick to exploit her good looks. "I was great friends with Sammy and Corvin," she reminisces. "I didn't have a relationship with either of them – we were just good friends. Sammy brought groups in and became the promoter of a ballroom [Romano's]. He wanted something to happen so he brought me in as 'the hostess with the mostest!' It was ridiculous. I was freezing outside the door of the ballroom with a skirt up to my navel saying hello to people." An exotic dresser, Ursula picked up all the latest gear in London and scoured the markets for Victorian dresses which showed off her statuesque figure. "I used to dress unusually and often walked through town in these long skirts with everybody giving me real stick."

Her first memory of Morrison is a fractured conversation at Isabeal's coffee bar where all her art school friends congregated. "We also used to hang out at the Jazz Club," she adds. "He actually used to dance with me at the Jazz Club. He didn't dance very often, but he did dance with me. Van was very fond of me – he fancied me, basically. I could say all the things that people say about him and they would be true because he is difficult to communicate with. It was never easy trying to have a conversation with him. He didn't say very much. His humour would consist of tongue-in-cheek comments – that sort of thing. He used to hang out a lot because he didn't have that much to do. He was waiting. It was a waiting period."

Morrison's attempts to ingratiate himself with the art school goddesses proved gauche and sometimes embarrassing. He held no physical attraction for Ursula Graham-White or Debbie Thompson and was dismissed by Cynthia MacHenry as an irksome oddball. "He was a total bore," she complains. "We couldn't get rid of him. He followed us around the place. We used to say, 'Go away!' " In a crude attempt at zany humour, Morrison re-enacted a sketch from his favourite radio comedy *The Goons*, taking on the role of Neddie Seagoon, the Harry Secombe character who spent much of his time in a dustbin. "If you were walking along University Road, he used to jump out of dustbins," MacHenry recalls. "He'd say, 'I can't get out.' " Unimpressed, Cynthia retorted, "Just stay there" and closed the lid over his head.

Unfortunately, Morrison's Goonish humour was lost on MacHenry who failed to recognize the classic Seagoon routine and was nonplussed by his eccentricities. "He used to do dreadful things. They weren't pranks. This was Van. He was incredibly odd. He wasn't drunk and he wasn't on drugs. It was just – he was quirky. I remember the jumping out of bins because he did that on and off for about a fortnight. Maybe he didn't have anywhere to stay! You'd be walking past an alleyway and a bin would open and Van would pop his head out and say 'I'm stuck, can you help me?' 'No!' If he asked 'Where are you staying?', you'd never say because you knew perfectly well that he'd probably get out of the dustbin and follow you. That's not a joke. It wasn't done in any way as a wind-up. If you knew Van in those days, it was the sort of thing he would have done just because he was Van – and he was odd."

Unsurprisingly, Morrison soon found that he was frozen out by

MacHenry on those rare occasions when he attempted to engage in conversation. "He was a loner, definitely," she concludes. "He liked to choose his own company. But he used to muscle in on other people's conversations and sit down and try and add a word or two. He'd say something and nobody would pay any attention to him. There were times when he was so fly-ish, so sticky that you'd have to say, 'Look, have you nowhere to go?' Then he'd move on to another group. He was just hanging around."

Morrison enjoyed friendlier communication with Ursula Graham-White but she too saw him as a soul adrift in the new Belfast. "Van was always very much the same," she says. "Very laid-back, low-key, never coming forward. I don't think he was particularly happy at that time because he didn't know where he was going or what was going on. He felt misplaced. Although he had been brought up in Belfast and it was his hometown, when he went back he didn't fit. He felt that people didn't recognize him and that he wasn't given the credit he was due for what he had so far achieved. But he was always a difficult person to give anything to in that way anyway."

Morrison soon discovered the extent to which he could no longer rely on past glories. With his new, shorter, modish haircut, he appeared at the gala opening night of the Cavalier Club for the Rockin' Vicars' set and, as press reports confirm, was summarily ejected. "We'd been painting the club," Ursula remembers, "and when Van came along the guys chucked him out. They just didn't know who he was. I remember him being very put out. I'm sure if they'd known who he was they wouldn't have done that." The waspish Cynthia MacHenry offered little sympathy, adding, "Van not getting into places and not being allowed to be around other people doesn't surprise me. It happened so frequently."

At least Morrison was allowed the chance to regain his dignity the following week when advertisements appeared for the much anticipated opening night of Square One on 28 October featuring Van Morrison & Them Again. Corralling his new band into a rehearsal room, Morrison put them through their paces with aggressive aplomb. Eric Bell had already been familiarizing himself with material from Them's two albums which Morrison had told him would constitute the bulk of the set. The guitarist was expecting a relatively relaxed run-through, but Morrison had other ideas. "It was really strange," Bell says, "we started playing and I didn't think he was going to sing. He just stood there, eyes closed. I didn't know what he was into but then he started singing 'Gloria'. Then he came up to me and Mike and said 'Shout! Shout it!' It wasn't 'Oh, do you think you could . . .' but 'Shout' – and a look that said 'Do it!' It was very intense with no joking like you'd see in other bands. I was a bit intimidated by the guy. It was very heavy."

There was no let-up in tension on the night of the performance. The new club was jam-packed as Morrison and the group were ushered into the dressing room which already contained support act the Blue Angels and several reporters, headed by Corvin. In the midst of the scrum, Alan Henderson appeared clutching his bass guitar, much to Mike Brown's bemusement. Bell was convinced that Henderson was attempting to muscle in and reinstate his importance in the line-up for this well-publicized event, but no adequate explanation was forthcoming from Morrison. He simply turned to the others and said "Alan's playing with us tonight." The small hall was so tightly packed that people were almost spilling onto the stage. A couple of mischievous girls tied the laces of Bell's shoes to one another ensuring that he spent the evening waddling around like Donald Duck. The rest of the night was a nerve-racking experience for Bell as Morrison re-enacted the crazed performances that had previously bemused Ray Elliott in Hawaii. "I had a list of all the songs on the top of my amplifier," Bell remembers. "I was looking at the first one to psyche myself up and Morrison turned around and said 'Start a blues in E, man.' I said, 'What about the list?' He said 'Fuck the list.' I thought 'Here we go.' The drummer counted in and we made it up as we went along. Morrison was doing things I'd never seen him do before and haven't seen him do again: playing the harmonica, scat singing, eating the microphone, running up and down the stage like someone demented. It was incredible – like a happening . It was as if he'd brought it from America to Belfast. No-one in the band knew what was going to happen next. We did a few of the songs but there was a hell of a lot of improvising. He was seemingly making up lyrics on the spot. He played an ice blue Stratocaster that he'd hired from Crymbles and wore a paisley suit with a blue satin cape. Unreal."

Throughout the set, the musicians were bombarded by Cecil McCartney's extravagant light show, which was projected on to white cloths hung at the rear of the stage. McCartney ran a monochrome silent film featuring Charlie Chaplin and employed three more projectors each showing slides of his paintings. "I'd simply run back and forth between them and superimpose the paintings on top of one another. My paintings were biomorphic and metamorphic and swirling with thousands of brush strokes like Vincent Van Gogh's work. When I projected them, they segued with the music."

Brian Russell and several members of the Few were totally taken aback by the spectacle. "It was very weird," Russell relates. "It was more like San Franciscan Acid Rock. I don't think anyone in the audience knew what was happening, let alone the band. Obviously, he'd seen this stuff out there, but nobody else had. Everyone was saying 'Why isn't he playing 'Here Comes The Night' or 'Gloria'?' He wasn't doing much that anybody could recognize."

The redoubtable Corvin was left with the task of summing up the evening for the readers of *City Week* and proclaimed: "I don't think Belfast will ever produce a 'show' to equal the opening night of Royal Avenue's Square One. Van went on stage wearing a very out-of-character shiny blue uniform with brass buttons and a flowing cape. Looking more like Little Lord Fountenroy [sic] than a hippie singer, he had two bass players . . . The sound was too much . . . Van was scheduled to play 45 minutes. He stopped after an hour and a half."

One person less than impressed by the Square One show was Alan Henderson. Having seen it all before in America he insisted "it wasn't real hot" and declined to appear again. The next date at Carrickfergus Town Hall on 4 November, although ignored by city reviewers, was equally remarkable. Previously a showband bastion, the hall had only recently allowed R&B groups to perform. Despite sterling support from the Carpetbaggers and the Fugitives, Morrison's drawing power was limited and the show was poorly attended. At the back, a row of fierce-eyed local Teds seemed intent on giving Morrison a hard time, the more so given his unwillingness to play jukebox hits. "It looked pretty deserted," Bell recalls, "just a smattering of Teddy Boys in drape coats. We were playing and suddenly Morrison took off his guitar and brought this book over to the microphone. Then he said 'Take it down!' He looked at this book and as far as I could see it was upside down. It was a book of poetry, I think. He shut the book, put up his arm and said, 'To wank or not to wank, that is the question.' And then he said it again. You could feel something in the air. He's going 'Hands up all the wankers in the hall.' I looked over to Mike Brown and we both put up our hands just to break the ice. A few Teddy Boys started throwing pennies at us and shouting, 'Get off you dirty wee cunt!' Morrison just went insane, eating the mike stand and bringing up the excitement. The guy running the gig stopped the music and said, 'If there are any more outbursts, Van and the boys are leaving the stage.' We played another number and fucked off." A flustered McCartney, who had witnessed the affray, was lucky to escape with his film projectors undamaged.

On the way home from Carrickfergus, Morrison was still indulging in the naughty schoolboy humour that had characterized his onstage banter. Sitting in the back of McCartney's car, Brown and Bell were subjected to behaviour they had not seen since reaching adolescence. "Morrison was in the front and he'd turn around, twist his finger and stick his tongue out, then turn back again," Bell says. It was no wonder that some people were amused or perplexed by Morrison's minor eccentricities.

Six days later, the group was back in the safer environs of Sammy Houston's Jazz Club, but even there all was far from well. Morrison and Bell were now at loggerheads and appeared to be intent on drowning each other out. Billy Moore attended the performance and came away disappointed. "I think Morrison was a bit jealous of Eric, who was such a good guitarist," Moore stresses. "There was a clash of egos. Eric went over to turn up and Van told him to turn down. Morrison always wanted to be the star. I don't think they clicked temperamentally. Bell was a natural guitarist, very single-minded, strong willed and went his own way."

Events reached a head in mid-November when the boys were booked to play the Festival '66 Happening in the Old Students' Union at Queen's University. When they arrived for the soundcheck, they discovered several art students rolling around on the floor covered in paint. Others were throwing paint against a wall to create a psychedelic mural. The musicians did their best to rehearse but their feet kept sticking to the floor. Eventually everyone retired to the changing rooms where drink was plentiful. At that point, the organizers appeared and brought in three members of the Patricia Mulholland Irish Ballet Company who had agreed to provide some choreography. The trio comprised dancer Joyce Ann Henry, the teenage Frances Tomelty (later a celebrated actress and Sting's first wife) and future IRA freedom fighter Gerry O'Hare. "They'd booked Van to do the gig, but they wanted to expand it, so they came up with this idea," O'Hare explains. "We did traditional Irish dance music and stories like Cuchulain – dancing, miming and spoken word. I was a decent dancer and could shift on the floor between Irish dancing, ballroom dancing and rock 'n' roll. Your man Morrison was playing and we were basically introduced to each other. Meeting him, I think I got a grunt and a hello and that was it. He said he would play such and such and we came up for a couple of tunes. There was talk that it [the dance] should be suggestive, but none of us wanted to expose our faces. That was Belfast at the time. So somebody came up with the idea of a screen and a silhouette behind it. The theme of the dance was two women chasing one guy and him dallying with both of them. We laid on the ground and as the music started we rose one at a time and improvised. We just got into the rhythm and danced. It was a night out and we got a few pints. Everybody seemed to like it."

Fusing traditional Irish dance with hard-edged R&B was distinctly odd, but this was a strange night. The university's generosity with refreshments ensured that the remainder of the set was something of a free-for-all with onstage egos clashing violently. "I was so drunk that I turned up my guitar," Bell admits, "then I saw Morrison go over to Mike Brown who said 'Van says you're too loud, turn it down.' I had a real chip on my shoulder in those days. I turned down a bit but then Van turned his guitar up and I took the needle. I turned my amp up to full volume and Morrison kept turning around. By the end of the gig I'd had far too much to drink and had a hangover and didn't feel good." On the drive back from the university, there was a sullen silence, which was finally broken by Bell who said: "I'm leaving the band." Morrison showing no emotion replied, "There's your money, man." As Bell concludes: "That was all he said. That was it. I then buggered off home."

Well known for his mood swings, Bell relented the following

evening and called over to Hyndford Street. He was taken aback to see the Federals' former guitarist Eddie Campbell auditioning for the next date. Slightly embarrassed, Bell said, "See you later!" and left the room. A few days later, Corvin submitted a scathing review of the Queen's University gig, slamming Bell for attempting to upstage Morrison with "noisy instrumentation", lamenting the musical infighting and concluding that the "whole thing sounded like Tea Time With Tommy". Even Cecil McCartney and his colleague Dave Wallace were ridiculed for a light show which Corvin called "a three and sixpenny peak at Blackpool illuminations gone wrong". Finally, he turned on Morrison for mistakenly "dumping" Alan Henderson, "the only one left who could understand Van".

Unsurprisingly, the review prompted a purge which left Morrison in need of a new set of backing musicians. Rather than prising Jim Armstrong and Ray Elliott from G.D., he returned to Romano's and temporarily enlisted Roy Kane and Billy McAllen from the Silhouettes. With George Jones unavailable, Mike Brown was retained as bassist. Sadly for all concerned, their next date was a repeat of the Carrickfergus debacle. Kane collected the musicians late in the day and they drove to Newry Town Hall, where the warm-up band was just finishing their set. With no time to rehearse, Them took the stage and soon found they were in hostile territory. "They wanted showband material at Newry," McAllen remembers, "they threw pennies at us." Roy Kane felt uncomfortable from the outset and became more frustrated as Morrison refused to accede to the wishes of the increasingly angry spectators. "I just used my snare drum with my drumkit, which I couldn't get into at all. Of course everybody was shouting for Them's hits and he absolutely refused to do them. We could have played them fine. In the Silhouettes we'd been doing 'Here Comes The Night' and 'Gloria'. The next thing, the pennies came flying onto the stage. We said to him, 'Go ahead, do the hits', but he just said, 'Fuck them.' Consequently, we got booed off the stage. I was hit in the face with a penny. After we went off, that was it. I can't even remember if we got paid. I just drove the boys back home. I'll never forget that night."

As Christmas approached, Morrison found himself in a peculiar position as a former pop star who could not escape his past. Moreover, his public performances were prompting violent scenes seldom seen since the anarchic, early days of Them. It cannot have been gratifying to play town halls where shows ended in chaos and fellow musicians concluded that the evening was a waste of time. The arrival in Belfast of Chris Farlowe and the Pretty Things for shows at the Floral Hall underlined that R&B was still popular, but Morrison was no longer one of its leading lights. His commercial standing had slipped to an all-time low, even in his own birthplace. Local pop polls trumpeted the promise of the Interns, the Misfits and the Fugitives as the great white hopes of Belfast R&B, but there was a steady, if unstated, realization that the scene was now in terminal decline. On Christmas Eve, the Royal Showband played to a packed Ulster Hall and were followed on New Year's Eve by Joe Dolan & The Drifters. It was a timely reminder of where the real money was to be made on the Irish pop scene and proof positive that showbands still reigned triumphant even amid the much touted R&B boom.

ELEVEN

Fitzroy To Manhattan

1967 began with the founding of the Northern Ireland Civil Rights Association (NICRA), a movement inspired by the civil rights campaigns in America. Among its membership were veterans of the Campaign For Social Justice, university students, liberals, workers, trade unionists and enlightened Republicans, several of whom had forsaken militarism for Neo-Marxism. NICRA's emergence emphasized the continued frustration with a corrupt system that legalized discrimination and disenfranchised the poorer nationalist community through ward rigging and gerrymandering. Subtenants, youths or adults living at home with parents, and people living in lodgings who were not ratepayers, had no vote at all, whereas those owning a business (predominantly middle-class Protestant Unionists) were allowed a staggering six votes. NICRA promoted regular marches demanding one man/one vote, an end to gerrymandering, public housing on a points system, the disbanding of the B-Specials – widely condemned as a sectarian police force – and the repeal of the Special Powers Act under which citizens could be imprisoned without charge.

These were fast-moving times, yet there was still an innocence among the Belfast youth who moved freely between sectarian divides and clung to the belief that religion and pop culture were antithetical. Many of the leading showbands and groups featured both Catholics and Protestants in their line-ups without any sense of tension. Theirs was the perfect mixed marriage. Bands performed in Orange lodges, Catholic parochial halls and ballrooms while dancers attended all three, irrespective of their denomination. In certain venues there were occasional flare-ups between different parties but most regarded these territorial games as Ulster's equivalent of the mods and rockers' clashes in Brighton or the tribal rivalries between opposing football supporters. This was sectarianism on Saturdays only. "When we played the Plaza ballroom in Chichester Street every weekend the Protestants and the Catholics beat the shit out of each other," recalls Harry Baird, leader of the Regency Showband. "It was a ritual. The Shankill beat the Markets and the Markets beat the Shankill. And when the cops came, they beat the cops. But if a boat came in from Canada or New Zealand and the navy visited the ballroom, all of a sudden there were no Protestants and Catholics. They closed ranks and were all Belfast men and they beat the shit out of the Canadians or whoever, and chased them up the high street and back onto their boats. This was a family feud."

Belfast youth turned a jaundiced eye to such happenings, which they saw as over-familiar, outmoded rituals, signifying nothing. It was simply a part of everyday life, like the annual marches. What really mattered to most of the ballroom patrons or denizens of Isabeal's was the latest news from Swinging London, the fashion and music capital of the world. Although civil rights was undoubtedly a hot topic among students at Queen's, it had yet to impinge upon the music-mad, party-loving kids in Morrison's immediate circle. Even the politically conscious tended to look outwards, focusing on events abroad. Local boy Terri Hooley was namechecked in the press, but the subject was CND not civil rights. The outspoken Cecil McCartney, who was pointedly phoning the White House from his home in Hamilton Road to protest against the Vietnam War, showed no interest in confronting the institutionalized injustices that permeated everyday life in Northern Ireland. The Unionist equation of the fledgling civil rights movement with hard-line Catholic and even subversive Communist interests prevented many young Protestants from embracing the cause, even though they were radical in other areas. "I was a pacifist," McCartney stresses. "Probably because of the brainwashing and the way I was brought up, I didn't see a need for civil rights. I didn't see anybody lacking in civil rights. I didn't want to be involved with anybody that was doing violence."

In some respects, mid-Sixties Belfast was a youth-obsessed city in the closing years of adolescence. Elsewhere in the province there were harbingers of trouble ahead but few saw the signs. "The Troubles were smouldering long before 1969," Harry Baird insists, "although I didn't realize it then." Looking back, he remembers odd incidents in 1966–67 that suggested times were changing for the worse. During an appearance in Portadown, his band were reprimanded for not playing the Orange anthem 'The Sash' in its entirety. "We did this medley of 'kick the Pope' stuff and this guy came up and actually complained that we hadn't sung all the verses of 'The Sash'. We said, 'Look mate, it's a medley, we only do it all on the Twelfth.' He said 'Well, you better sing the whole of 'The Sash' tonight or you're not getting out of here alive.'" Amid the tension, nobody could remember the words. "Jimmy Green, who was a good Catholic, sang the whole lot," Baird laughs. "And him a Catholic. You should have heard the slagging on the way home in the bus. In the band there was Alfie Walsh, past master of the Orange Order, and he didn't know 'The Sash'."

Perhaps it was a prescient fear of the civil rights campaigners that led some of the Orange halls to close ranks. "The Protestants danced in the Orange hall one night and the next they'd be down the parochial hall," Baird points out. "When we went back to Portadown Orange Hall there was a big notice saying that no-one of the Catholic persuasion was allowed to dance in the hall. I went up to the caretaker wee Jack and said, 'What's this?' He said, 'Well, our boys went to a dance at the parochial hall the other night and there was a wee bit of tittle-tattle and they told us not to come back.' I just said, 'Well, Jack, you've a bit of a problem here.' 'What's that?' says he. I said, 'We're not playing! If you think I'm playing in there with a notice like that on the door and half my band are Catholics, you've no hope.' We packed up the wagon. We never played there again – and that was 1967."

In other areas there was pressure from Republican dissidents. The Regency's occasional Friday night bookings at Armagh Orange Hall coincided with the strange disappearance of their saxophonist Ignatius Hughes. "He didn't want to play," Baird recalls. "When it got blatantly obvious, I said, 'Iggy, what's going on? Every time we play Orange halls near you, you're not there.' Then he told me, 'The boys in my town are saying that if they catch me playing that hall again, they'll knuckle me.' Being hot-headed, I said, 'Come on, we'll talk to them!' He shook his head and said, 'Harry, you can't talk to these boys – they've threatened my family.' I hadn't a clue what he meant – now I do. I'm convinced this was the Troubles slowly manifesting itself in our world."

Van Morrison shared this ignorance. Back in Hyndford Street, his priority was to kick-start his career and get out of Belfast. His mother looked on patiently as he attempted to translate some ideas into song, filling up tape. "He'd usually start off by playing and just humming a note and then the words would come," she recalled at the time. "He'd play the chords at first, and he'd go on and on maybe for about an hour. He'd work on a basic idea . . . then he'd work on it the next day and it might have a different tempo and the words could change. It just flows." He continued to make tapes and send them to England but few record companies were interested. Decca's Dick Rowe remained loyal to Phil Solomon and regarded Morrison as a lost dog without his master. The A&R head who would never have dreamt of signing Morrison without Solomon's involvement was not about to take another chance on such an apparently minor talent. The smaller Philips Records were at least listening, but greeted Morrison's entreaties with a steely unwillingness to close any deal. Composer Phil Coulter, only months away from winning the Eurovision Song Contest with Sandie Shaw's 'Puppet On A String', noted the decline of his old colleague with a shudder. "He was on a downer and he was drinking. He wasn't the most bankable of artistes. He had been the frontman for yet another of those R&B bands that had gone up the Swanee and there were three or four versions of Them touring. It was a joke. He was no gift. There weren't record companies falling over themselves to sign him up."

Stuck in Belfast, Morrison urgently needed some escape route and it came unexpectedly when he learned that Bert Berns had been enquiring about his whereabouts. Since producing Them, Berns had launched his own publishing company and record label with Atlantic Records' executives Ahmet and Nesuhi Ertegun and producer Jerry 'Gerald' Wexler. Bang Records and Web IV publishing (the titles an acronym of its owners' first and last names, respectively) already had a promising roster of talent, including the McCoys, Neil Diamond and Freddie Scott. Berns was confident that the maverick Morrison could be remoulded into a hit act and contacted Phil Solomon to enquire about his contract. Solomon explained that he had washed his hands of Morrison after the US tour fiasco and confirmed that the singer was no longer with Decca.

Over the transatlantic phone, Berns offered Morrison a recording session in New York and a contract with Bang. Morrison needed little convincing. This was the best news he had heard since returning to Belfast the previous summer. "I'd been wanting to go to the States for a while," Morrison explained. "When I called him up, he said, 'Let's get together and make an album.' There was another record company [Philips] that I was hoping to sign with in England but I couldn't wait on them any longer. They weren't doing anything except talk. But Bert gave me money, a good advance [initially $2,500], and he paid my way. I really respected him."

It says much for Morrison's financial state of mind that he considered Bang's advance a good deal. The one-year contract he signed on 9 January 1967 was typical of the time and heavily weighted in favour of the record company. It included the standard stipulation allowing them the option to retain the artiste for up to four more years. They agreed to pay a 5 per cent record royalty based on the US retail price, and half that figure for recordings released overseas. Morrison was obliged to record a minimum of 12 songs per calendar year. However, the company had the power to call upon him to cut another 50 songs per annum, if necessary, which may seem remarkable, but was not untypical of the time. Even major American labels contractually demanded as many as three or four albums per year, although the onerous terms were seldom enforced. Many artistes were thankful if a record company even released their product. Indeed, an addendum to his Bang contract reveals that one of Morrison's main concerns was that the company would definitely release the equivalent of six double-sided singles within a year.

With time to kill, Morrison took to jamming with some of the musicians that hung around Isabeal's, most notably Mick Cox, a Royal Air Force recruit stationed in Northern Ireland. Cox had recently established himself on the Belfast scene, playing in the End, hanging out with Sam Mahood and replacing Billy Hollywood in the Alleykatz. Cox's brother John was another promising player who shared a flat in University Street with Mahood and was hotly tipped to join his band the Just Five, who were still one of the city's hottest R&B acts. They all congregated at Isabeal's and over the next few months gradually wandered into the bohemian lives of a cavalcade of girls living in Fitzroy Avenue.

Schoolfriends Janet Martin and Joan McClelland had recently started work and along with Gwen Carson, Ann Denvir and art student Ursula Graham-White rented a house in Fitzroy that became famous as a drop-in centre for some of the hippest musicians in Belfast. "You might come home and find 20 people around," McClelland remembers. "Van used to be there a lot. He'd potter in and out like a lot of the guys did. It was a good scene. There was an innocence then which people have lost nowadays. This was before the Troubles so you didn't have to worry about who the people were."

The house in Fitzroy Avenue was a hotbed of loud music, late-night partying and intense teenage romance in which several of the girls played leading parts. Janet Martin, who'd already had a much-discussed relationship with Dino, would later marry, and divorce, Sam Smyth; Ann Denvir was engaged for a spell to the irrepressible Corvin, who later became involved with her best friend Gail Owens; the glamorous, upmarket Ursula Graham-White entranced visiting musician Mick Cox, who would soon become the first of her three husbands. And so it went on. "We were all girls because mixed flats weren't the thing," notes Gwen Carson. "But it was open house on Friday and Saturday night. People used to turn up and parties ensued. These girls were very beautiful and minor celebrities on the dance floor. It was all very Sixties. By today's terms it wasn't that wild, but we partied a lot."

One of the attractions of Fitzroy Avenue for Morrison was the presence of Ursula Graham-White. "Van was very keen on Ursula," Joan McClelland points out. "All the men were. She was a very good-looking girl, tall and very wild. There wasn't a man in Belfast that didn't fancy her." Fellow art student Debbie Thompson, whose father had refused her plea to join the Fitzroy sorority, appreciated Ursula's heart-throb reputation. "Ursula was great fun," she enthuses. "She had long legs, wore short mini-skirts, had an English accent and really wowed all the boys." Cynthia MacHenry concurs: "Ursula in her day was drop dead gorgeous. Stunning. She was almost Spanish-looking with straight black hair, a round, pale face and very high cheekbones, which was unusual for Northern Ireland. Her family were English and had loads of money. She stood out in a crowd. She was very sophisticated in her own way but could fit into most people's company." White was aware of Morrison's infatuation, but retained a platonic distance. "He was in love with Ursula," Ann Denvir states matter-of-factly. "Van was madly in love with her," Gwen Carson adds fancifully. "This was a great contradiction for him because Mick was his great friend and Mick was beautiful and charming and we all thought the sun rose and set on Mick Cox. With Mick and Ursula getting together, it must have been very strange for Van. There he was caught in a dilemma with his love life."

"It was a one-off time," Ursula Graham-White concludes. "We were all stuck in Belfast. I was supposed to be at art college! There was a closeness that built up because I'd known Van before and Mick knew him and he was very fond of Mick and he fancied me. There was some sort of bond at that point. Mick and I were very spiritual beings and Van was too. He was telling stories about seeing flying saucers from the windows of planes. He had this spiritual side. Mick was into astral travelling and spiritual search and all sorts of things. Their talks leaned towards that. We were drawn together. He later sang about Fitzroy on *Astral Weeks*."

"Van and Mick Cox teamed up as a kind of songwriting team, fiddling about with guitars," Carson remembers. "I'm not sure exactly what they were doing because I wasn't particularly interested in them. He'd sit in the flat and play the guitar and mouth organ. Because we were so used to musicians we'd say, 'Oh there's that bloody Van Morrison off again.' I remember him playing something in Fitzroy Avenue that later appeared on album. It's a dreadful thing to say but he was such a disliked character that we used to think he was a bloody nuisance. There were wee moments when he'd come round and we'd say, 'Ah, he isn't that bad after all', but he was an unattractive person and that was his downfall."

"Offstage he had very little going for him," Joan McClelland adds, "and that's the sad thing. I felt he was fairly morose and depressed of nature. He used to sit in corners and was always whingeing because he couldn't get a woman." Ann Denvir maintains, "Because he was so ugly he was always infatuated with beautiful women."

"He would fall in love with somebody different every single week, but he would never approach them," Carson stresses. "It would always be at the end of the party you'd find him crying in the corner saying, 'I love you Avril' or 'I love you, Janet'. I thought he was always so wretched back then. We used to find this funny because at 17 you have no insight into psychology or any understanding of the sadness of life. I just thought he was pathetic and a really sad man."

"At Fitzroy, he would call around but it was very much to sit and have a cup of tea or coffee," Janet Martin recalls. "All our mates were there and he would talk to the boys a lot more. He definitely wasn't into women as far as I knew. He was probably falling in love with these women but he never took it anywhere. He was very much a person unto himself who knew he had potential and what was in him. I honestly think he felt he was a man of destiny."

"We had a 1920s fancy dress party and he wore a boater hat and a striped jacket," McClelland adds. "I remember us walking around the streets of Belfast, he in the boater and me in some long dress. He was saying how miserable he was. He had all the admiration and acclaim but on a personal level he was morose. He always seemed lonely. I think he was in a depression, not knowing what was going to happen next."

The emphasis on astral travelling, spooky happenings and similarly airy notions were the only subjects that seemed to animate Morrison during visits to Fitzroy. After one late-night party, he, Mick Cox and Janet Martin found themselves visiting the grounds of a small church opposite Fitzroy Avenue. "There was a sunken pool there," Martin recalls. "We went out into the gardens and Mick and Van had a jamming session. There was a lot of talk that night – philosophical discussion. It was the most I'd ever heard Van talking."

Gwen Carson remembers another night when they all went for chips, piling into a sports car owned by one of the party guests. After driving back, Morrison had an unusual request. "He had this thing about graveyards so we went to this graveyard. It was probably to frighten the daylights out of us. At one point the car broke down and we were pushing it. The next thing from out of nowhere a sports car appeared and we couldn't see anybody driving it. It followed us for miles and miles but there was nobody behind the wheel. Then it just disappeared. I'm not at all mystical but Van was really caught up in this. He talked about it for hours saying 'That was strange' and 'I wonder what that was.' We said, 'Och, it's just a practical joke' or 'somebody crouched down.' But it was quite strange at the time."

Back at Fitzroy, such occurrences were recounted to fellow revellers, most of whom had their own mystical tales to tell. The weekend was a non-stop party with a seemingly endless supply of booze on tap. "Everyone we knew was drinking and we were often very drunk," Joan McClelland admits. Morrison was no exception and when inebriated would encourage the girls to play blues records, usually Sonny Boy Williamson and Leadbelly. They did not seem to improve his mood, which often worsened as the evening went on. It was a blackness which had been increasingly noticeable in the months following Them's doomed tour of America. "Van was a mess," Sam Smyth concludes. "A lot of the time he was drinking far too much and was clearly very unhappy . . . He was hanging around with Corvin and a few of us and going up to Janet's flat in Fitzroy Avenue. There were always guys around there drinking. Van was a regular and often got drunk up there. I would imagine it was one of the lowest periods of his life. Van's relationship with drink I always put down to Indians and firewater. The two don't go very well. He was a bad drunk. He really was very messy . . . He would get rat-arsed drunk, falling down drunk."

Terry Davis, then part of a dance troupe at the Plaza, attended the Fitzroy parties and was taken aback by Morrison's drunken state. "You could never get close to him. He was always very difficult, an isolated character. Even at parties he wouldn't have a great deal to say about anything. He was having a bad time in Belfast. As regards drinking, I often remember Van being absolutely blind drunk. But these were heady days. The worst I saw him was at the party in Fitzroy. He was crashed out on the stairs and everyone was falling over him. Me and a friend picked him up, dragged him upstairs and dropped him on a bed in one of the rooms. He was absolutely, completely gone at that point."

"Everybody drank, and he did," Gwen Carson notes. "I have held him over a toilet being sick, and I presume it was drink. Nobody we knew didn't drink. It was a drinking culture." Indeed, within this young, party-loving social and musicians' circle, Morrison's consumption was evidently not seen as exceptional.

"He always reminded me of a soul in torment," Ann Denvir adds. "Not a happy chappie. The more he drank, the more obnoxious he became. I saw him drunk loads of times, but we were no saints."

One afternoon, Janet Martin came home to find her boyfriend Dino in the kitchen with Morrison "drinking anything that came to hand". She was astonished to see Dino demonstrating the alcoholic wonders of

Old Spice. "We spent a lot of time there," Dino reminisces. "I was into dope then, just shit and pills, you know. The aftershave? Yeah. It was one of those crazy things!" When the mischievous Sam Smyth heard this story, he dubbed Dino and Morrison "the sweetest smelling drinkers in town".

Another occasional Fitzroy visitor who enjoyed a drink and a musical session was John Cox's flatmate, Sam Mahood. His first encounter with Morrison was during an inebriated evening in the centre of Belfast which ended with a snowball fight outside a maternity shop. "Sam was a one-off with wild red hair and staring eyes," Ann Denvir coos, "but he was the sweetest and gentlest guy you'd ever meet. He and Van used to drink the cheapest red wine and some people joked that they drank hair oil on one occasion. But mostly it was Mundie's wine." Janet Martin, who worked in a bank, remembers being kept up all night when Mahood arrived late one evening for an extended jamming session with the Cox brothers, overseen by Morrison.

That January, a couple of weeks after signing his contract with Bang Records, Morrison attended a Friday night dance at Annadale with the intention of guesting with the Just Five. The resplendent Mahood arrived looking like a deranged pirate in an orange corduroy, double-breasted, three-quarter-length frock coat that he had recently bought for 17 guineas from a boutique in Ann Street. "We were the main band," Mahood remembers. "Another band was doing the warm-up for us. Morrison borrowed a guitar from one of their members and proceeded to break it for some reason and stomped off with a bottle of vodka in his pocket. One of our VOX amplifiers went on the blink at this point. The curtains were drawn and I was pushed out front and had to do about half an hour with harmonica and talk and sing before a thousand people in that large gymnasium." Debbie Thompson, who attended the show with Corvin, recalls Morrison's initial reluctance to take the stage that evening. "The audience started booing but he went on and in the end it righted itself." An anonymous newspaper report, no doubt penned by Corvin, mentioned how "all the gear had packed up except Van's whereupon somebody got angry and tossed a mike about . . . Great image building."

The image that Morrison projected on stage was uncontrolled aggression combined with the self-belief of a performer always ready to challenge his audience. Away from the lights, he maintained a detached arrogance and the selfish streak that had marked him out since childhood. Mahood's girlfriend and occasional backing vocalist Rusty encountered him at a house party in unhappy circumstances. "He walked in, slipped down the wall and sat on the floor. He didn't want to know anybody. He shunned everyone, was very rude to me and nobody really bothered with him, so he just went off after an hour and a half." Even Donall Corvin, who was regarded as an acolyte, was critical enough to recognize certain contradictions in the man. Employing some amateur psychoanalysis, he wrote of Morrison as "a cryptic person. Gentle and quiet at the best of times but given to sudden fits of anger. His physical appearance may have given him an inferiority complex. Or maybe even a persecution complex. Whatever it was, it mustn't have been very pleasant for him."

This stress on Morrison's appearance was echoed in the comments of many of his Belfast contemporaries, who saw this fragmented self-image as his true fatal flaw. "He was a victim of his looks more than anything," insists Gwen Carson. "He emerged in the Sixties when everyone was beautiful and he wasn't. He had nothing that made him beautiful. He didn't even have a beautiful personality. When Them came back home Van was still the wee, fat, ugly man. He had this great chip on his shoulder about his looks. He had a pair of white trousers that he wore constantly until they were filthy grey. It seemed like he was desperately trying to have a pop star image and he really didn't look the part. In those times that mattered. He had all these hang-ups about his looks. It made him very cranky."

Some of that cantankerousness was experienced by the unfortunate Ann Denvir. One night after a party, she found herself cramped in the back seat of a car next to Morrison. During the drive, the pair became involved in an intense conversation that became more animated with each passing mile. As they gesticulated to argue a point the car turned abruptly and they inadvertently collided. The following morning Denvir discovered an unwanted souvenir of the previous night's discussion. "He'd given me a black eye! It smarted the next day . . . There was a lift home and I'd called him 'a window cleaner'. A lot of cider was drunk . . . I must have been 17. I suppose it was my fault for 'insulting his talents'. That was Van. I should have known better."

By this point Morrison was acutely aware of all he had lost over the past year. Although pop stardom had brought many unwelcome burdens and pressures, it also provided a status and a sense of purpose that was now absent. With Them, Morrison had recorded albums, performed regularly, appeared on television and toured America. He had even met a beautiful girl whom he had been forced to leave behind in California. They still corresponded. Although he hoped to connect with her again, there were no guarantees that the relationship would develop, particularly given the geographical distance beween them. Much depended upon the outcome of his dealings with Bert Berns. Whatever else, it was paramount that he left Belfast to re-engage with the music business before it was too late.

Morrison kept his own counsel about the Bang contract and the imminent trip to America. In the meantime, he had continued writing rough sketches of songs, borrowing freely from recent experiences, observations and childhood memories of his life in Belfast. Compositions like 'Madame George' contained splintered mirror images of lost souls and what some saw as descriptions of transvestism or even the dramatized sadness of homosexual longing. These stream of consciousness creations contained distorted reflections of mundane everyday events, such as the ritual visit to Isabeal's with its assemblage of aspirants, beatniks, hipsters and desperates. A gay waiter completed the cast. "Isabeal's was a fabulous place," Ann Denvir notes. "We all used to congregate there. There was a waiter called Matthew and he used to scream abuse at everybody. We all loved him. He was the only gay I'd ever met."

"Matthew was the queer boy," confirms Brian Russell, who also recalls the kindly, middle-aged manageress Joyce who would feed the starving art students with free buns and ignore the new sign that insisted 'Minimum orders, 2/6d'. Billy Moore, a Friday regular, remembers "the queer there, Matthew," embarrassing Eric Bell whom he always called "my little blond Beatle boy". Since his recent departure from Morrison, Bell was displaying the moodier side of his personality: "the life and soul of the party, then a deep depression the next day".

The long afternoons in Isabeal's were a pleasure to many, but some of the more soulful characters on the scene were subject to melancholic thoughts as they sipped their coffee. Like Eric Bell, Donall Corvin could easily slip from manic enthusiasm into quiet introspection. "Van got on very well with him," Corvin's first fiancée Ann Denvir recalls. "Donall was very clever, but he was also a con merchant of the first degree. He was a loveable rogue and a lot of fun. He had a very dry sense of humour. We'd do daft things all the time and you never knew what to expect. I just adored him. He didn't give a toss for authority or anybody in charge. He hated that. He was an absolute rebel. Donall and Morrison got on amazingly well."

"Although he and Corvin got on well, they never seemed to say much to each other," Sam Smyth elaborates. "They just silently empathized at that time. Corvin was a completely different personality. He was a social creature. I felt Van always had difficulties socializing."

Smyth's synopsis was something of an understatement. "He's a very troubled person and always was," Ann Denvir says of Morrison. "I remember vividly in Isabeal's me and Corvin and all of us used to sit there for hours and he was always morose and wouldn't talk to you. You'd just sit there and think 'Christ, what's he doing with us?' Nobody had the heart to tell him to go away."

Like others in the community, Janet Martin was struck by the startling contrast between the wary, taciturn Morrison and the outgoing, superficially confident Corvin, but she also recognized that they shared deeper, darker thoughts. "I think they were joined at that time in sadness," she notes with hindsight. "It was almost like two lost people together. Corvin was highly intelligent and literate, like a poet waiting to be born, only he didn't have the savvy. I always got the impression that Corvin was an isolato. He would have lots of friendships, but they were not deep. I don't think Donall ever had people to hang on to, to keep him centred." Cynthia MacHenry, who had not a single good word to say about Morrison, was positively reverential when asked about Corvin. "A nicer or more human guy you could not have met," she eulogizes. "He looked after me – like a babysitter. He didn't really want me to be on my own or going off with strange people. He seemed to know what you were thinking before you thought it and could foresee things before they happened. A deep thinker and a fantastic person. If he had to be a show[-off] personality he could – other than that he was very introvert. He called himself a journalist, but he was actually writing books as well. He did his own thing completely. That guy had a heart of gold." Debbie Thompson, who also regarded Corvin as her best friend in Belfast, enjoyed talking with him in a private language they perfected which baffled and bemused outsiders. "Corvin was always good fun," she stresses, "and a lovely man. But very occasionally he would be sulky or seem upset. The eyes would go quite dark."

Whatever darkness descended over Corvin at such bleak moments would dissipate once his lively imagination was inflamed by another mad scheme. Sitting across the table, Van Morrison maintained his unassailable reputation as Isabeal's moodiest customer. "When we used to go to Isabeal's with Donall Corvin and Sammy Smyth, Van would sit there," says Gwen Carson. "He was really grumpy. He was one of the grumpiest people I'd ever known. Everybody loathed him. He was the most disliked person I can ever remember. There must have been some who liked him. People looking back now may say he was wonderful but I can remember everybody saying 'What a wee naff he is. Who does he think he is?' Not only did he have hang-ups but it was made worse by the fact that he was so disliked by people and he had no way of communicating at all . . . He wasn't attractive in the Sixties when being attractive was really important. And he wasn't a communicator. He had nothing really going for him. And coming from Belfast where so many people are articulate in a garrulous sort of way – he was not."

The wry sense of humour that Morrison occasionally displayed had evidently deserted him during those final desperate days in Belfast. More than anything, he resembled the little kid who had once selfishly ignored a plea of help from his neighbour Mrs McCarter when she couldn't gain access to her house. Now, truculence, aloofness and indifference were everyday Morrison traits. "If you said black, he'd say white or he just wouldn't talk to you," Denvir insists. "You'd see him and say 'Hi, Van' and he'd look at you and just walk on. He was very moody and he got away with that sad behaviour."

Perhaps the only person capable of cutting through Morrison's sullen demeanour was Isabeal's irrepressible waiter whose camp humour could instantly transform macho egos and mood merchants into figures of fun. "Oh Matthew really fancied Van," laughs Rod Demick. "He'd say: 'You've all been sitting there too long with your coffee. Now, you can all get the hell out of here – but wee Van can stay.' He liked Van, but that didn't go down too well with Van either!" Debbie Thompson recalls one afternoon when Morrison turned up after a session at the Spanish Rooms. "We used to call it the Scrumpy Rooms, and it wasn't even scrumpy, just the dregs of cider and beer. I remember Van Morrison coming from the loo and falling down . . . He was pretty drunk when he fell down the stairs. Matthew was a bit cross, but you had to take him with a pinch of salt."

Morrison was spared any further blushes when the first recording date with Bert Berns was confirmed for March. Meanwhile, he celebrated by undertaking a surprise semi-promotional appearance in the Netherlands, where Them's records had always sold well. During his brief visit, Morrison appeared with local group Cuby & The Blizzards wearing a candy-striped suit similar to that sported by Ray Elliott on Them's US tour. Morrison also conducted a radio interview which revealed that he had once followed the example of Scott Walker and Andrew Oldham by going on a short retreat at an unnamed monastery. "It was just to get away," his protective mother later confirmed, "not for religious purposes."

Back in Belfast, news spread quickly that he was heading for New York. Relieved that the recordings were actually happening, Morrison could not resist some small gloating over his good fortune and returned to Fitzroy Avenue just before his departure. "He was in the kitchen talking to all the boys and we were all lying around in the front room settling down for the evening," Janet Martin remembers. "Then Van walked in and came out with this big speech. Everybody just sat there in shocked silence. He said, 'One day you'll see my picture up on the wall and you'll all say, 'I knew him.' It was just silence after that. But he was bloody right!"

Gwen Carson confirmed Martin's account verbatim but remembers a vicious punchline directed at one of the musicians in their company. Turning to his victim, Morrison sneered: "And I'll just say 'Fuck you!'" Nobody was particularly surprised at the rebuke. "That gives you a good insight into his character," Carson notes. "He couldn't even say anything nice when he was going. I still think it's funny because it was prophetic. He knew he was destined for big things even though he was insecure in other areas of his life. He knew he was different and his music was good." Reflecting for a moment, she added, "But I thought he was such a nasty character; always rude and quite vulgar."

As Morrison gathered together his tapes in preparation for the Big Apple visit, Belfast was celebrating the arrival of blues legends Cream for a show at the Ulster Hall. Local promoters Sammy Houston and Eddie Kennedy seemed determined to maintain the city's standing as a bastion of R&B and added a number of local acts to the bill including the Interns, the Group, the Few, Styx and the Recordites. For Morrison, the R&B boom now seemed very much in the past. Since the closing days of Them, he had been compiling recordings of stripped-down blues and extended improvisations that would reach fruition on *Astral Weeks*. It was these that he took to Berns' Manhattan office, along with some more conventional material. Morrison played the tapes for Berns, who listened carefully to the rudimentary arrangements, which featured a sparse guitar/vocal backing and some tambourine percussion. "They're great – we'll put them out like that", he quipped. Enthused, Morrison added, "Yeah, that's the way I want to do them", before cautiously pointing out that they should retain the original, impromptu feel during the actual recording.

"It never happened," Morrison lamented. "When we got to the session, it was a big production number." As he had proven with 'Here Comes The Night', Berns' speciality was conjuring hit singles perfect for Top 40 radio. In spite of the growth of album sales over the past couple of years, Berns knew that the single was still the major market for the record-buying public. The producer assembled a team of highly proficient players to assist Morrison, including engineer Brooks Arthur, the renowned flautist Artie Kaplan, jazz guitarist Eric Gale and the Sweet Inspirations on backing vocals. Brill Building legend Jeff Barry was on hand to sing, play tambourine and offer advice. Also sitting in was Al Gorgoni, co-composer of the Hollies' 1966 *NME* chart topper, 'I Can't Let Go'. This was a veritable academy of musical stylists whose presence would have flattered any visiting singer.

From the eight songs cut during two sessions on 27–28 March, one stood out as eminently commercial. 'Brown Eyed Girl' (originally titled 'Brown-Skinned Girl') was an exuberant combination of R&B and pop with a nostalgic lyric celebrating the euphoria of young love. Berns was impressed with the vocal and Gorgoni's guitar work, but Morrison felt the polished arrangement was a little too pop-oriented. The remaining songs sounded rougher but still lacked the spontaneity that the singer desired. His limited ability to read or write music meant that the musicians had to follow his fingers on the frets in order to grasp his suggestions. Musical empathy on both sides was evidently lacking despite the wealth of talent and experience present. At one point, Morrison's frustration poured out with the plea "I think it should be freer, you know? At the minute we have a choke thing going."

By the time Berns got around to mixing the tracks Morrison was already on a plane back to Belfast. There were insufficient funds to warrant keeping him in New York. By his own admission, Morrison had simply turned up and sung, leaving Berns to direct the band and determine the outcome of the session. Before leaving, he signed a five-year publishing contract with Berns' Web IV Music on 31 March for a non-recoupable advance of $500. It could have been worse if Morrison had not deleted Clause 5 of the publishing agreement which allowed Web IV the option of retaining his services for an additional five years, from 1972–77, for a mere $1,000 advance. Morrison also agreed to be handled by his new mentor's production and management company, later describing the arrangement as "professional suicide". It was remarkably similar to the all-encompassing deal he had signed with Phil and Dorothy Solomon three years before. While Morrison's decision appeared to disprove the proverb 'once bitten, twice shy', the truth was that Berns and Bang offered the best, perhaps the only, route back from Belfast oblivion. Even Janet Planet felt that he was "lucky" to secure such a deal.

A period of limbo followed during which Morrison concentrated on writing more of the impressionistic prosopography that would dominate *Astral Weeks*. His mother occasionally offered some musical accompaniment, thereby risking the screaming rebukes of her snappy son. "I play harmonica and I used to play guitar and a bit of organ and piano," she explains. "I never pleased Van the way I played organ because it was too square. We always ended up having rows about it . . . He always said I played organ like I was in a church."

After his New York trip Morrison spent less time hanging out with Corvin and the Isabeal's crowd, but he occasionally travelled to Bangor, popping in on painter Cecil McCartney. Evidently, such visitations usually occurred after a hard night's drinking. "He'd come over to our house at 2 o'clock in the morning and scare the wits out of my mother," recalls McCartney. "He'd grab the telephone and dial numbers with no reason at all behind them. I'd gently ease him away from the telephone, make him a cup of tea and go up to the studio. He'd collapse and sleep on my bed and I'd sleep on the studio floor next door. Then I'd get him up in the morning, take him downstairs and try to get him to eat some breakfast. I would make him drink a lot of orange juice because even back then I was getting a very sharp, clear mind from drinking the juice of about 50-60 oranges a week. He'd take some and it would take a long time to sober him up. He would put his arm on my shoulder and I'd put my arm on his shoulder and I'd walk him." McCartney recalls one occasion when he took Morrison to the nearby Broadway Golf Course behind the Savoy Hotel on Hamilton Road. As the sun shone, the painter and the singer inspected each other's auras, with McCartney no doubt explaining the phenomenon at length.

In America, the fabled Summer of Love had begun in earnest during mid-June 1967 with the Monterey International Pop Festival, an event that represented the ultimate flowering of youth culture at a period when the divisions between chart pop and underground rock were still blurred. Beverly Hills based chart stars the Mamas & The Papas and LA colleagues the Association seemed perfectly at home on a bill with San Franciscan radicals the Grateful Dead and the Jefferson Airplane. Morrison's old rival Eric Burdon, now transformed into a fully-fledged hippie, helped fly the flag for Britain. The synchronicity of the event was uncanny. Two weeks before, the Beatles had issued the epochal *Sgt Pepper's Lonely Hearts Club Band*, Paul McCartney was on the cover of *Life* proselytizing the wonders of LSD and the Rolling Stones' Mick Jagger and Keith Richards were battling the British legal establishment after their arrest on a drugs charge. The festival even provided its own flower power anthem courtesy of Scott McKenzie's worldwide hit 'San Francisco'. Looking on, the canny Bert Berns seized the moment by issuing Morrison's 'Brown Eyed Girl' which he figured rightly would reach the same audience entranced by McKenzie's effervescent summer single.

When he received a copy of the record, Morrison rushed around to Mick Cox's flat in Limestone Road, Belfast, and proudly played the disc on the guitarist's Dansette gramophone. Cox was already familiar with the song having played it live with Morrison during some low-key gigs a few months earlier. "He was really pleased with it," Cox confirms, although that opinion would soon change.

In July, Morrison's friends the Wheels returned to Belfast almost broken and defeated. With Rossi gone, Herbie Armstrong and Rod Demick suddenly found themselves the sole remaining members, but were determined to carry on. Morrison, who had always expressed an affection for the group, provided moral support by suggesting the possibility of taking Rossi's place in the line-up. "We stood outside a fish and chip shop in Belfast and he said he was coming to join us," Armstrong remembers. "He should have been vocalist in the Wheels. That combination would have been the crème de la crème." Unfortunately for Armstrong, Morrison added a caveat: "I need to phone Bert Berns."

After contacting Bang, Morrison learned that 'Brown Eyed Girl' was receiving extensive airplay and steadily climbing the charts. A transatlantic phone interview was hastily arranged with a New York radio station newspaper, much to Morrison's satisfaction. After all the slagging he had taken in Belfast of late, the prospect of returning to the States in triumph was something to be savoured. "I'm into a completely different thing now," Morrison gushed. "Now there is no limit to what I can do. I plan to use the type of instrumentation I like and be completely free. This is only the beginning for me. Writing and singing are just as important to me and I'll always be an artiste. I'm not planning to fall into the background. My material is my own and whatever I do now will be completely solo."

Morrison had seldom, if ever, sounded so excited, self-confident and unequivocally positive. Within a month, 'Brown Eyed Girl' was in the US Top 10 and his presence was urgently required. With promotional duties and the likelihood of further recording commitments, this was not going to be a short trip. Indeed, it would culminate in Morrison's emigration. Before leaving, he turned to childhood friend Gil Irvine for support. "He asked me to go over with him just to have somebody there that he'd know so that he wouldn't go bananas," Irvine reveals. "He didn't know anybody really, except Bert Berns. I would be his companion, personal manager or roadie . . . As I say, he just wanted somebody there. With him being a very shy person, it must have been a hell of an experience to go to the States on your own knowing one person and expecting to do business." Regrettably, Irvine was forced to decline the offer as he was due to be married in October.

Once in New York, Morrison was housed in a hotel opposite Berns' Broadway headquarters. Before long, the singer was joined by Janet Planet, the girl he had met on the West Coast during the 1966 Them tour and kept in contact with by letter. Clearly, the romance that had begun in California was now more serious. It certainly came as a surprise to her photographer friend Michael Maggid. "We were hippies and she was rooming in a place where I ended up staying. Then she went and had a romance with Mr Morrison. Her name then was Janet Gauder. Peter Gauder was her husband. She was married, separated, probably divorced by then. She had met Morrison and there were some sparks flying, then nothing happened and then she moved away. She was thinking of him and he was thinking of her. They were romantically involved. But she was a single mom raising a child when I knew her. She was very lovely, very beautiful. A young flower child. Everyone was in love with her. I'm sure they were very interesting to each other, culturally." When Planet arrived in New York, she was accompanied by her young son, Peter. Her presence brought some stability and responsibility to Morrison's life at a crucial moment and ensured that he would stay in America. This was good news for Bert Berns who was keen to harness Morrison's raw talent. The producer was effusive about the success of 'Brown Eyed Girl' and suggested that they collaborate on some songs aimed at the singles market. Morrison was predictably resistant, thereby missing the chance to add his name to a new work in progress, 'Piece Of My Heart'. Instead, Berns took the song to Jerry Ragovoy (composer of the soul classic 'Cry Baby') and after completion it became a hit for Erma Franklin and an impassioned highlight of Janis Joplin's live performances.

The clash between Berns' entrepreneurial instincts and Morrison's artistic notions was soon evident. With the brand name profile provided by a hit single, there was a golden opportunity to develop Morrison as a serious artiste by producing a stunning album that would reveal the full range of his talents as a writer and performer. However, Berns could not resist the lure of a quick buck and hastily assembled a patchwork, cash-in album from the sessions recorded back in March. *Blowin' Your Mind!* sounded like a collection of adorned demos, passed off as a fully-realized album. Even the title and cover artwork were an embarrassment. Morrison was not consulted about the release and claimed he first knew of its existence when a friend phoned informing him that he had just bought a copy. Upon seeing the shoddy psychedelic cover, Morrison said he felt like throwing up. He was similarly dismissive about the musical contents. "I wasn't really happy with it. He picked the bands and tunes. I had a different concept of it. I had a hard job convincing him what I wanted to do and he didn't want to listen anyway." This was not the entire truth. Berns at least had the foresight to feature a sample of Morrison's more intense work. "I give [Berns] a lot of credit for letting it happen, for not filling the album with his songs," says Janet Planet in mitigation. "For somebody of Bert's stature to allow Van's material to be heard at all was a big deal." Unfortunately, the released work was erratic in both content and quality. The material ranged from the flamenco-styled 'Spanish Rose' to what sounded like the tree-lined avenues of East Belfast on 'Ro Ro Rosey' with its references to an idealized 16-year-old girl. The bluesy 'Who Drove The Red Sports Car?' suggested a similar provenance with the admonition "who read your bible" and the character Jane, who may or may not have been inspired by Morrison's first known girlfriend, Jane Adams. Even the song's title recalled that strange evening in Fitzroy when the party-goers had encountered a driverless sports car on the road.

Morrison has always maintained that the eight-song *Blowin' Your Mind!* was a bastard creation of material originally intended for release as four singles. However, the length of at least two of the cuts, not to mention the terms of his Bang contract, suggests otherwise. 'He Ain't Give You None', a spoken blues, was a rambling narrative with a passing reference to troubled times spent in Notting Hill Gate and Morrison's favourite sexual euphemism, the backstreet jelly roll. Its sparse backing was rescued by Eric Gale's extended guitar solo. Of the remaining tracks, the undisputed standout was the extraordinary 'T.B. Sheets', a bitter requiem painfully detailing a young woman's slow death from tuberculosis. Given the preceding references to Notting Hill, some were tempted to speculate that the 'Julie' mentioned in this composition was the doomed Dee, Morrison's girlfriend during the final days of Them. Her tragic death, reportedly from a brain haemorrhage, may have partly inspired the elegy on a subliminal level, but few of Morrison's songs are transparently autobiographical. He could just as likely have been subconsciously re-enacting the trauma of Gloria Gordon's final days in hospital or simply imagining the entire episode. The provenance of 'T.B. Sheets' is wider, conjuring up memories of old blues songs and a disease that once wiped out a frightening proportion of Belfast's population. It was a composition that seemingly emerged whole from Morrison's subconscious after spending a night at Hollywood's Tropicana Motel. In the song, he makes no attempt to romanticize the death, instead concentrating on his anger and grief which pour out in a vocal torrent of emotional intensity. The song's execution was so draining and cathartic that he reputedly burst into tears after the performance. As a distillation of pain, it is extremely moving, almost grotesque, like a lurid phantasmagoria. Significantly, Violet Morrison remembers the composition emerging after a troubled night's sleep, as if implanted by a succubus. "That's a dream he had," she reveals. "A nightmare. In fact it was over an hour long, the original [home-taped] recording. He felt it so strongly that he couldn't eat breakfast the next morning. He started to tell me about it and he ended up singing about it. The original version was absolutely marvellous, the verses just went on and on."

Phil Solomon was well aware of Morrison's surprise success in the US charts and, like Bert Berns, was quick to cash in by releasing old material. The same week that *Blowin' Your Mind!* came out in the States, Solomon's new record label Major Minor issued the self-referential 'The Story Of Them, Parts 1 & 2'. "It was done with me in Denmark Street in early 1965," Billy Harrison remembers. "It started off as a guitar riff and we just fell into playing while the engineers were changing tapes or setting something up. We were just amusing ourselves and the next thing Van started singing and Tommy Scott recorded it." Although never likely to be a hit, the song was a fitting epitaph to Them's career with a bluesy guitar backing echoing the Rolling Stones' 'Little Red Rooster' and a rambling seven-minute discourse on the trials and tribulations of the group during their spell at the Maritime. Its closest contemporary counterpart was the Animals' nostalgic Tyneside homage 'Club A Go Go'.

Although the memory of Them was now distant, Morrison suddenly found himself re-enacting the pop star life that he had last experienced at the peak period of 'Here Comes The Night'. Berns celebrated the success of 'Brown Eyed Girl' with a lavish launch party aboard a boat on the Hudson River. Promotional eyeglasses were given away as Morrison played a short set surrounded by well-dressed socialites, songwriting pals of Berns and record company executives. "It was just a boat full of revellers," Janet Planet remembers. "In the midst of all this a heartbreakingly young Van [was] singing his heart out. He was so great back then. He really had something to prove." A promotional tour was arranged with a band comprising Charlie Brown (guitar), Eric Oxendine (bass) and Bob Grenier (drums). Morrison had no special empathy with the musicians and his disillusion festered when they were booked to play venues he considered unsuitable. Morrison had been brought up on the club and dancehall circuits of Britain and Ireland where the patrons were thoroughly engaged with his performance. In America, apathy was a more common reaction. Worse still was the prospect of appearing on television shows where he was forced to mime 'Brown Eyed Girl'. For a man who once regarded BBC's *Top Of The Pops* as a sell-out, this was the ultimate embarrassment. Having arrived in the States with limitless ambition and new-found confidence, Morrison was again crushed by the relentless pop machine and seemed ready to spurn chart fame for a quieter life. "Sometimes I feel I may be just an underground thing, but if that's the way it has to be, that's it," he concluded. "I'm not really too commercial because I don't come across. I can't mix, you see, that's my problem. You have to be able to mix if you want to be in show business . . . Right now, I just want to do my thing and groove with it. I want to turn people on." For Bert Berns, dutifully schooled in the American Dream, Morrison's anti-commercial attitude was both perplexing and frustrating.

A series of bookings in Greenwich Village intended to mollify Morrison and win over local journalists brought further controversy. In order to enliven the stage act several backing singers were employed. "He hired these three Bronx girls who had never been in the Village before," recalls Jake Holmes, a musician and local scenester. "They didn't know anything about rock 'n' roll or folk music. They were R&B backing singers." The set was dominated by a frantic, scary rendition of 'T.B. Sheets' during which Morrison surrendered control to his demons and began "kicking the microphone stand over, smashing into the drum set, crashing into everything." Meanwhile, the Bronx girls continued to sing "ooh, T.B. Sheets" in a high gospel falsetto that merely added to the weirdness. "He was swinging the microphone over the girls' heads and they were ducking and their eyes were getting bigger and bigger," Holmes remembers. "They didn't know what the hell was going on". Finally, they departed the stage, leaving Morrison to carry on – "screaming and yelling and kicking and breaking shit and just going nuts". This unruly season of gigs ended on a sour note. Berns' wife Ilene has made some unspeakable allegations about Morrison which, although partly substantiated by similar testimony from Phil Solomon, remain unproven and unprintable. Of course, Solomon was never entirely happy with Morrison, whose uncompromising and sometimes confrontational live appearances had a feral appeal for R&B fans which contrasted markedly with that of the more mainstream acts in his stable. "When somebody pays to see you they're entitled to get value for money," Solomon pontificates, "and when somebody goes on and acts like . . . In my opinion, he was an animal, but if he'd learned to be a professional, all these things would have been forgotten. People have risen from mediocre backgrounds to become captains of industry and professionals in their career. Morrison could have done this – he could have been big."

While Morrison was on the road, Bang issued a follow-up single 'Ro Ro Rosey', an innocuous rock-blues piece which sold abysmally. Back in the UK, 'Brown Eyed Girl' received little airplay and failed to appear anywhere in the charts. Meanwhile, Phil Solomon was exacting his ultimate revenge by launching a new talent whom he was convinced would eclipse Morrison and rewrite pop history in the process. David McWilliams, a 22-year-old singer-songwriter from Ballymena, had been groomed with a degree of care usually reserved for the entrepreneur's fabled prize-winning horses. A known gambler, Solomon invested a fortune on one of the biggest star launches in the history of British pop music. A poster campaign flooded major cities with buses and billboards screaming the words: "Are you ready for the sound of David McWilliams? The album that will change the course of music". Music press readers were astonished to discover pages of ads proclaiming the genius of a singer whose voice they had never heard. In the *NME*, McWilliams occupied the entire front page, back page and middle pages, leaving little room for anyone else. Incredibly, yet another page was reserved for a long list of testimonials, a biography and a presumptuous explanation of the methodology of stardom. His single 'The Days Of Pearly Spencer' was played incessantly on Radio Caroline, the pirate station whose playlist Solomon controlled. Fellow entrepreneurs were amazed by Solomon's nerve, commitment and endeavour. "If Philip had done to Morrison what he did to McWilliams, it might have been a different story," Eddie Kennedy notes waspishly. Amazingly, McWilliams' single failed to infiltrate the UK charts, although it sold well in France and Germany, thereby recouping most of Solomon's investment. Critics compared McWilliams to Bob Dylan and Tim Hardin, but his aversion to live performances proved his undoing and Solomon's conviction that he was a far greater talent than Morrison was never vindicated.

Meanwhile, Morrison's American adventure was taking a new and unexpected turn, thanks to the career crisis of Neil Diamond. The Brooklyn singer was experiencing similar problems to Van Morrison in dealing with the steely Bert Berns. Although Diamond would later emerge as one of the best-selling albums artistes of the Seventies, he could not persuade Berns of his potential as a cerebral singer/ songwriter. Berns had convinced himself that Diamond could become the next Elvis Presley and spent a large amount of Bang's budget on aggressively promoting his singles. Albums sales were dismissed as negligible. By this point, Berns had already rushed out two Diamond long players without adequate advertising or marketing. They were laden with unexceptional cover songs and, in a further slight to the record-buying public, *both* works featured the hit singles 'Cherry Cherry' and 'Solitary Man'. Relations worsened when Diamond demanded that Bang release the pensive, autobiographical 'Shilo' as his next single. He was firmly told to concentrate on more commercial material in the vein of 'Cherry Cherry'. Frustrated, he rebelled and told Berns that he intended to leave the label. "When I informed Bang of this," he claimed in a court affidavit, "Mr Berns began to threaten me. He told me that he had the power to ruin my career . . . He said that he 'owned' an artiste named Van Morrison and that it would be a simple matter for Bang to advance Morrison's career and stagnate mine by promotion, advertising and selection and timing of recordings to be released."

For a moment, it seemed that Diamond's misfortune had become Morrison's opportunity. In November, Berns made good his threat to "advance Morrison's career" by persuading him to record some new songs with the carrot of total artistic control. "I did another session with him that wasn't really an album," Morrison explained. "He had this studio in New York that he wanted me to try out. It worked out real bad." Morrison was hoping for a more sympathetic, less cluttered production but when he entered the studio he was confronted by an array of session musicians. When he attempted an acoustic ballad, a 10-piece rhythm section appeared and at one point there were several rhythm guitarists all vying for a place in the line-up. The studio atmosphere resembled a Phil Spector session without Phil Spector. Berns' role as musical co-ordinator was sometimes compromised by his numerous business interests which proved distracting. Although he was still positive and polite, this was not the same Berns who had tirelessly drilled Them into shape in an upstairs pub room. "Van dug being in New York and the whole Greenwich Village scene," Phil Coulter recalls, "but the initial euphoria wore off during those sessions. Bang went wrong for Van because he wasn't getting the personal attention from Bert that he wanted. He was being fobbed off and just became another artiste on the label."

The sessions rapidly degenerated into pantomime with Morrison finally pulling the plug amid scenes of anger and frustration. "I'd write a song and bring it into the group and we'd sit there and bash it around and that's all it was," he complained. "They'd say OK, we've got the drums, so let's put drums on it and they weren't thinking about the song . . . but it was my song and I had to watch it go down. So there was a point when I had to say, 'Hold it! Stop!' I couldn't see my songs go down like that all the time. It was wrong."

Morrison never expected to hear those sessions again but three years later, when his profile was much higher, Bang took advantage by issuing several of the recordings, along with some selections from *Blowin' Your Mind!*, under the provocative and misleading title *The Best Of Van Morrison*. Appalled by the production, the singer retorted that it

should have been called *The Worst Of* . . . Its contents were
unmemorable apart from the intriguing Dylan-influenced 'Joe Harper
Saturday Morning', whose title was a tribute to the fatherly caretaker of
the Maritime Hotel. In 1974, Bang were to return to the vaults in
another excavation exercise entitled *T.B. Sheets*. This time, they
unearthed two songs that were crude blueprints of *Astral Weeks*
material: 'Beside You' sounded undeveloped instrumentally, but the
real shock was 'Madame George'. Here, Morrison's classic meditation
was swamped by backing singers and a bizarrely inappropriate party
atmosphere. Perhaps the idea was to capture the moment of Morrison's
departure from the party-loving Fitzroy Avenue crowd. It remains one
of the strangest items in his canon.

Whether Morrison could have prevented these releases from
reaching the public by appealing to Bert Berns' better nature was never
tested. Their sometimes stormy relationship abruptly ended on 30
December 1967 when the 38-year-old producer suffered a fatal heart
attack in a New York hotel room. "We were just mortified," Planet
recalled upon hearing the news. "Van felt really bad because I guess
they'd parted having had some big fight or something . . . It was a
strange relationship. It was really a relationship that lived and died in the
studio." Significantly, Morrison did not attend Berns' funeral, which
Planet later concluded was a mistake and may have alienated his already
embittered widow.

"I really respected him," Morrison concluded by way of distant
elegy. "I dug him. I really don't know whether he was into my music.
I knew him as a person and could relate to him that way. But he was
also a big businessman. He had a big business trip going on and I
couldn't figure it out. What did I know? I was 21."

Morrison never fully resolved his ambivalent feelings about Berns.
Over the next three decades, whenever he mentioned the producer in
print, he would offer a conditional tribute, frequently laced with
poison. "He's deeply conflicted," says San Francisan-based writer
Joel Selvin. "On the one hand the whole thing's a sad memory and an
ugly time, but there's part of it that really makes him feel like he was
one of those R&B guys that he really admires. At the very same time
Berns was working with him, he was making records with Freddie
Scott and Solomon Burke. That appeals to a romantic element of

Van's self-image. So part of him is fascinated and part of him is repelled."

Ultimately, Berns remains a paradoxical figure in the Morrison story, but his importance was central. He transformed Them into an effective recording unit and arguably saved Morrison's career from artistic oblivion by establishing his name in America. Although reluctant to allow Morrison to pursue his purist vision as a singer-songwriter, Berns had a profound knowledge of the US pop marketplace and understood the crucial importance of singles in establishing brand name recognition among the record-buying public. And without the commercial success of 'Here Comes The Night' and 'Brown Eyed Girl', it is quite possible that Morrison might never have secured the record company contracts and long-term commitment that subsequently enabled him to produce such a formidable and uncompromising body of work.

TWELVE

The Recording Of *Astral Weeks*

The death of Bert Berns sent Morrison's career spiralling into uncertainty. He had fallen out with Bang Records and antagonized Berns' widow Ilene, who was still coming to terms with her husband's sudden death and had given birth to a son only weeks before. The new mother was a neophyte in the record business, having relocated from California to New York a few years before as a teenager. For most of her short marriage she had been pregnant and had only a scant knowlege of her much older husband's various business interests. Suddenly, she found herself with a record company that was about to lose its two major signings: Neil Diamond and Van Morrison.

One of Bert Berns' occasional employees was the charismatic Carmine 'Wassel' Denoia, a Broadway music veteran and former bookmaker who operated at Jack Dempsey's restaurant on the ground floor of the Brill Building. More recently he had been involved in the management of singer Freddie Scott, who recorded for Berns. Fiercely built, Wassel had a presence that demanded submission, and it was not wise to incur his wrath. He wore a large, expensive ring which could cut through flesh if it connected with somebody's face. Not that he needed such a weapon; his bulky frame was intimidating enough. "He was a piece of work," Janet Planet recalls. "Carmine was the kind of muscle that was always there [at Bang] and he just did 'stuff'." Among the 'stuff' Denoia admitted to doing was breaking up bootlegging pressing plants with baseball bats, smashing a publisher's desk with a pipe wrapped in a newspaper, and taking to task a corrupt, double-crossing DJ by hanging him upside down from an open ninth-floor window. "One guy pulled a knife," Denoia remembers. "I didn't care.

I was wild then. But we were trying to make a living, that's all we wanted to do." As another commentator observes: "Everybody was trying to shake down everybody. Among the Jews that ran the business there was treachery without end in the Temple." "I used to help them," Denoia adds. "I was the only Italian guy on Broadway and I didn't take no shit from nobody. I respected everybody."

Wassel was well connected and knew some of the leading gangsters in New York. He was a great raconteur, full of stories about the underworld and the colourful characters he had known since childhood. Once, he had introduced Berns to the retired Mafia boss, Frank Costello, whose criminal empire extended to control of the jukebox racket with fellow gangster Meyer Lansky. "The record business is a *good* business," the paternalistic Costello had said.

When Wassel learned that Morrison was intending to defect from Bang, his anger and indignation could hardly be contained. In his moral scheme, this smacked of treachery and betrayal. He had already felt obliged to respond to what he considered the singer's insufferable impudence by hitting him on the head with an acoustic guitar. Clearly, another lesson in good manners and discipline was now required. "Carmine's a wonderful guy," one of his dinner companions enthuses. "Loyalty is a real issue. Wassel has a world view that's unique to his lifestyle. You see it portrayed in television movies, but Wassel's the real deal. And all his values were formed in that crucible." One of the cardinal sins in Carmine's moral scheme was a person's failure to remain "a stand-up guy". Morrison had evidently transgressed this unwritten law on more than one occasion. In order to let off some steam, Wassel paid Morrison a surprise visit. As Janet Planet recollects with a chill: "One of the memories I'll take to my grave is Carmine pounding on our hotel-room door at the St George Hotel in Times Square, saying, 'Van, you're finished in the [music] business.' It was scary . . . Van has this lifelong ability to forget that he can't act out, and every now and again he runs into somebody he can't act out with, and Carmine was one of those guys. We figured out really quickly that this was a serious situation and that we were in big trouble . . . The unholy hell that was unleashed upon him when Bert died was really horrible . . . It was a very stressful time. We had just gotten back together after a year, so we were still getting to know each other again . . . It was an odyssey." For a time, Morrison and Planet stayed in cheap hotels in Greenwich Village including one joint where a parade of transvestites emerged every evening like extras from a movie version of 'Madame George'.

With his visa status unresolved, Morrison faced the ongoing threat of deportation and found himself stalked by former associates of Berns, who felt they owned a piece of the man's subsidiary interests. "Bert was eclectic, a tireless go-getter and hit-maker," producer Jerry Wexler observes. "But then things started to get funny . . . Only later would I learn of his obsession with power. He was intrigued by the wise guys, loved hanging with hoodlums and trading gangster stories." Towards the end of his life, Berns was keen to secure total autonomy and had parted company with his original partners from Atlantic Records in order to run Bang alone. "He sued us for breach of contract and the whole deal blew up," Wexler recalls. "We said goodbye to Bert and Bang – not cost-free: Neil Diamond, Van Morrison and the McCoys remained with him."

It was well known in New York circles that Bert Berns had entered into clandestine arrangements with underworld figures after breaking away on his own with Bang. Working alone, he felt a need for such muscle and financial clout, and his gangster friends were certainly capable of providing both. Berns could hardly have picked a more dangerous companion than Tommy Eboli, then acting head of the Genovese family and one of the most feared Mafia men in New York. Eboli had a fierce temper and once served a prison sentence for assaulting a boxing referee who had dared award a points victory against his fighter Rocky Castellaini. There was nothing subtle about the assault. Eboli had simply climbed into the ring and laid out the official in full view of the spectators and the police. Since his promotion to surrogate boss of the Genovese clan, Eboli had acquired interests in various restaurants, night-clubs and gay bars, but it was vending machines and jukeboxes that pulled in the income. He saw the vast amounts of money generated by the music business and took a large slice himself after purchasing a share in Promo Records, whose primary output was 'cut-out' albums. After purchasing deleted LPs from the major record companies, Eboli could maximize profits by counterfeiting the stock, safe in the knowledge that nobody would make a fuss over product that had already been declared unsaleable at full retail price. Investing in Bert Berns must have seemed a reasonable proposition given his recent run of hits.

Berns enjoyed the excitement of Eboli's company and regularly visited him on his boat. Eboli was also a guest on Berns' vessel, *A Little Bit Of Soap*, named after one of his early hits. Another Berns associate was Paddy Pagano, brother of Mafia boss Joseph Pagano. The Paganos were also interested in the music world and among Joseph's close friends was Phil Solomon's old sparring partner, Don Arden, and his young son David. Later, when the Ardens were brought to trial at the Old Bailey for allegedly blackmailing and falsely imprisoning their accountant, Joseph's son Danny appeared as a witness. Clearly, Berns was mixing with some heavyweight villains, but he was a man quite capable of recklessly courting danger. As a boy, he had suffered a bout of rheumatic fever which left him with a damaged heart. A further legacy was hypochondria manifested in impulsive behaviour, *carpe diem* risk-taking and a constant awareness of the likely arrival of the grim reaper. Berns had no reason to fear any gangster when his own body was a time-bomb ready to detonate.

The precise terms of Berns' unwritten and undocumented business deals went with him to the grave but his fraternization with New York Mafia heads meant that there was always a debt to be paid by any money-making artiste who dared challenge the entrepreneur. Neil Diamond had recently discovered this to his cost and, just before Berns' death, one of his shows was disrupted and his new manager was badly beaten. Diamond felt so intimidated that he borrowed a gun, sent his family into temporary hiding in Long Island, and asked to be placed under the protection of the New York Police Department. The shady, anonymous men who claimed a passing interest in Berns' legacy were not to be crossed, but precisely what they required of Morrison was still unclear. "Bang was a horrible experience for him," claims one former signing of the company. "It might have been that his life was threatened. Believe me, they were not rumours. Bang was, from the information I'm getting, a dangerous outfit. Van had to get out of town, literally. He tells a couple of tales and it's not my place to really get into the details, but it was a nasty thing. He didn't want to work with them anymore and obviously felt he wasn't getting paid. It's still a thorn in his side." Many of Morrison's suspicions and grievances were later aired allegorically in the testy 'Big Time Operators', released in 1991. Safe in the fictional realm of songwriting, his narrator could look back at the New York music business and pour forth all sorts of conspiracy theories about unnamed individuals who bugged phones, threatened deportation and arranged to have adversaries blacklisted and framed for possession of drugs. If this was any indication of Morrison's attitude towards Bang's mysterious underworld affiliates, then it is small wonder that he elected to cut all ties and start afresh.

Accompanied by his fiancée Janet and her son Peter, Morrison left New York and took up residence at Green Street, a bohemian enclave of Cambridge, Massachusetts. There, he was able to relax in the company of local musicians, most notably Peter Wolf, a part-time disc jockey and established singer in the Hallucinations, an R&B group that would evolve into the J. Geils Band. Wolf first met Morrison during an afternoon rehearsal at the hip club, the Boston Tea Party, where Howlin' Wolf was topping the bill. Sensing kindred spirits and a shared musical background, Morrison turned up looking for work or at least some advice about where to play in Boston. Wolf, who had been a fan of Them, was taken aback to see the singer and composer of the recent hit 'Brown Eyed Girl' reduced to scrounging gigs. He was also struck by Morrison's bleak mood and the extent to which he seemed lost and out of place in his new locale. Their mutual love of blues cemented a friendship and before long they became late-night drinking partners. Sometimes, Morrison would drop by the FM station where Wolf worked and request a selection of obscure blues tunes. He even agreed to be interviewed, although no tape of that encounter has ever surfaced. Morrison also spent a lot of time at Wolf's house, devouring his record collection and endlessly spinning songs by old favourites such as Louis Jordan, Hank Williams, Ray Charles, John Lee Hooker and Gene Chandler. Those listening sessions seemed to provide a therapeutic escape from all his worries and problems. On at least one occasion, Morrison joined the Hallucinations on stage at the Tea Party for a frantic, extemporary version of 'Gloria' in which he scatted like a jazz musician. This unorthodox reading of the song provoked a hostile reaction and Wolf felt obliged to chide the audience for their lack of respect. The experience did little to improve Morrison's confidence and no doubt made him feel even more adrift. Time was passing slowly.

For several months, Morrison waited patiently as he weighed up the full implications of Berns' sudden demise. He was gripped by the same uncertainty that had followed his painful break with Phil Solomon. While recent label mate Neil Diamond was busily entertaining lucrative offers, Morrison slipped into a malaise. "He had no skills to extricate himself from that situation," Janet Planet observes. "He's a difficult personality . . . He's not in any sense positive about his life or what's going to be happening in the future. It was like pulling teeth to get anybody interested. Basically, the interest came from people who responded to the music. But in terms of having meetings and talking people into things – forget it."

One surprise visitor during this uncertain spell was his old friend Mick Cox whose group Éire Apparent had recently released a single 'Follow Me' on Track Records and were touring America with the Jimi Hendrix Experience. Morrison was keen to rekindle the loose collaborations that had proved so enjoyable back at Fitzroy Avenue and invited Cox to help him form a new group. Alas, Cox's commitments put paid to such dreams and his stay was all too brief. "It was a choice between Hendrix and Morrison," Cox reflects. "I think I made the right decision."

Eager to start afresh, Morrison took stock of his finances. Despite the chart success of 'Brown Eyed Girl', he was disappointed to discover that most of his earnings had been swallowed up by promotional and related expenses. An injection of capital and record company commitment was urgently required to save his career. At last it was time to talk business. After a short period of negotiation he signed with Inherit Productions, a company formed by producer/engineer Lewis Merenstein and Brill Building alumnus Bob Schwaid. Given his problems with Phil Solomon and Bert Berns, it was surprising that Morrison again chose to place himself in the hands of individuals who would control his production, management and choice of record company. Possibly the ongoing dispute with Bang Records left him with no alternative. Fortunately, his new backers had much to recommend them. Both had strong track records and Morrison was particularly impressed with Merenstein's credentials, which included work with jazz giants Thelonious Monk and Art Farmer.

Finding a sympathetic record company required the inspiration of a young talent spotter. Andy Wickham, a music-loving English expatriate, then working as an A&R executive at Warner Brothers, expressed a keen interest and duly alerted his vice-president Joe Smith to the likely availability of the Belfast singer. One of Smith's colleagues had been responsible for recommending Schwaid and Merenstein to Morrison, so a valuable link had already been forged. The influential Smith had been instrumental in the signings of such mavericks as Van Dyke Parks and Randy Newman and regarded Morrison as an exciting challenge. From the outset, there was high drama. "There were immigration problems and he was holed up in Massachusetts," Smith remembers. "Using my Boston sources, I found him living in a hotel in Cambridge, about to get deported." Smith succeeded in pacifying the immigration hounds and any remaining concerns about Morrison's green card became irrelevant later in 1968 when he married his fiancée Janet in a quiet ceremony in New York.

An equally pressing task facing the various parties was freeing the singer from his outstanding publishing and recording agreements. Contractually, Morrison still owed a number of songs to Bert Berns whose estate was now controlled by his wife Ilene. The young widow was proving a formidable adversary, having wisely decided to place the Morrison problem in the hands of her solicitors. While the argument over publishing dragged on, a settlement over Morrison's release as a recording artiste proved less complicated. Or so it seemed. Suddenly a third party entered the proceedings. The unnamed 'wise guys' who had once fraternized with Bert Berns still felt they were owed some compensation. The tenacious Joe Smith was aware of gangland protocol and decided to secure Morrison's freedom through the most straightforward and expedient method. "There was speculation about Morrison's contract status because of suspicions that the Bang label was financed in part by some 'wise guy' money in New York," he explains. "I made some contacts to get to the people who could deliver the contract release and the terms were ominously spelt out – $20,000 cash, which I had to take to the third floor of this deserted place in New York City. I was told to come alone. I had 20 $1,000 bills in an envelope when I got up into this tiny room and there were two unpleasant guys there who were not common to the record company world. We looked at each other, the contract was signed and witnessed and the money counted out. My concern was that as soon as I turned for the door, I was going to be hit on the back of the head and wind up with no $20,000 and no contract. So when I left I went flying off that landing, almost jumping one whole floor and running over to 8th Avenue to find a cab and get the fuck out of there. I put the contract in the Warners safe and then began my journey with Van Morrison."

By the spring of 1968, Morrison was auditioning several players from Boston's Berklee School of Music with a view to forming an electric band. Among the candidates was student Tom Kielbania, who was soon recruited as bassist. Several stand-in drummers appeared in the line-up, including another student Joey Beebo. Their first guitarist was a studio musician who soon met a grisly end. "He was murdered in Boston by his room-mate who flipped out on acid and killed him," Kielbania recalls. Another local player, 17-year-old John Sheldon, allowed them to rehearse in his basement. "Van tried to move into my house," he jokes, "but my mom wouldn't let him." Kielbania was impressed by Sheldon's abilities, but he was considered too young to tour. Usually working as a four-piece, Morrison and his band played at local clubs and bars without making any serious impact. "There were people coming and going all the time," Kielbania stresses. "We didn't have a lot of work and were just picking people up and then they'd leave. Peter Wolf would come to the rehearsals. It was like a transit as far as living conditions were concerned. We were playing blues. There was 'Brown Eyed Girl', a few things from the Bang album and stuff that he'd done with Them. The club dates weren't really much of anything."

Peter Wolf came to the group's rescue by connecting them with an Italian agent friend who secured them some bookings at various high schools and amusement parks. They even appeared on a Boston public broadcast television station with Berklee teacher Charlie Mariano guesting on saxophone. Mostly though, it was a slog that offered little beyond beer money. As summer approached, Morrison took Kielbania aside and confided: "I'm tired of this rock 'n' roll, electric stuff, I want to play acoustic." The band members were summarily dismissed, but Kielbania was retained and reverted to playing stand-up string bass with Morrison on acoustic guitar. This allowed for greater vocal improvisation and a freer, folkier feel.

In addition to performing as a duo with Morrison, Kielbania occasionally jammed with a jazz ensemble that congregated at an old warehouse near Boston harbour. One of the players was clarinettist and flautist John Payne, a philosophy student who had just completed a year at Harvard University. Kielbania casually invited him to sit in at a Van Morrison date, an offer which elicited a lukewarm response. Payne, a strict jazz buff, had never heard of the singer. Nevertheless, the flautist was happy to show up at the Catacombs, a basement coffee house adjacent to the Berklee School of Music. "It was a weekday night," Payne remembers. "There were about 30–40 people there. One of the guys that hung out was Peter Wolf who I knew, but he was the only 'celebrity' there. I'd only been playing flute for six months but I wanted to be a musician really badly. I didn't think I could become one. I was only getting a paid gig here and there." The polite Kielbania introduced Payne to Morrison who reacted with the warmth of an iceberg. Watching the opening set with the audience, Payne was unimpressed. "I have a way with singers of not appreciating them until I've played with them," he now admits. "It's because my background is jazz. During the first set, I was thinking 'He sings nasally and doesn't do that much for me.' I almost left! When I started playing with him on stage it was entirely different from any singer I'd ever played with before. I'd never played with someone of that calibre and emotional depth. One of the things I could feel was that he'd heard what I was doing and had responded to it. At the end of the first song, I thought 'Wow I felt that!' I couldn't articulate it at the time but it was real different!" Payne was even more taken aback when Morrison began singing the second song, 'Brown Eyed Girl'. "I'd heard the song before. It was a big favourite on the jukebox back at Harvard. So suddenly I'm playing with the guy who was on the jukebox. It was freaky. I thought 'This guy is big!'"

The starstruck Payne was still recovering from the realization that the singer was a famous recording star when Morrison asked him back the following evening. "He offered to pay me and I said, 'No, I'm just sitting in – it's cool.' The next night I took some money, maybe $20 or something. Then he asked, 'Do you want to join the band?'" Payne needed no persuading. Disenchanted with his studies at Harvard, he was looking for an excuse to leave and upon learning that Morrison had a new recording contract with Warner Brothers, he was thrilled. "I figured I'd finally made it," Payne laughs. "It was just the naiveté of someone who had no understanding of the music business. I'd hooked up with a guy with a record deal!"

Morrison's status as a Warner Brothers recording artiste was not reflected in his lifestyle or world view. "He was very confused," Kielbania recalls. "He didn't trust anybody and he was always looking over his shoulder. So many things had gone on in his life. All of a sudden he found himself in Cambridge, living in a dumpy little apartment house in Green Street in a rundown section of town. He couldn't figure out what had happened. He was trying to put the pieces together. We weren't part of a group. We worked for Van. He was paying us from his money, which was fronted, and he was always paying people back. He never really knew where he stood."

Peter Wolf was also struck by Morrison's evident penury. The singer was barely scraping a living and could only afford a street-level apartment which housed himself and his new family. Their sole luxury item was the expensive reel-to-reel tape recorder that Morrison had purchased in the dying days of Them. "They lived in one room," Wolf remembers, "with a mattress on the floor – no telephone, no money. He would come over to my home [a few blocks away] and use the telephone. He was putting together this business deal and finishing these songs that would later become the album *Astral Weeks* . . . I would come by and he would be so discouraged. We would go out drinking and I couldn't tell you how many times we threw up on each other."

Morrison spent much of the summer in New York, attending meetings with Merenstein and Schwaid and laying the groundwork for the recording of *Astral Weeks* in late September. In the meantime, the lingering dispute with the Berns estate over his publishing was finally resolved. A document of release was drafted and signed on 12 September 1968, but it came with a stiff price tag for Morrison. The onerous clauses, far from freeing him, left him bound and gagged to his old agreement with a number of compensatory demands. Amazingly, he agreed to submit to Web IV three new original compositions per month over the next 12 months, totalling 36 songs. Even for an artiste as prolific as Morrison, this was a frightening work rate to undertake. He was also obliged to include two Bang-period songs on his next album (*Astral Weeks*) and remit 2 per cent of his first year's royalties from Warner Brothers. And, just in case he came up with another hit like 'Brown Eyed Girl', there was a clause requiring him to assign to Web IV Music half the copyright of any self-penned single released in the next year, up until 12 September 1969. Ilene Berns could seemingly rest easy in the knowledge that she had extracted the best possible terms imaginable.

However, once free, Morrison showed no intention of honouring the spirit of the agreement. Just before starting work on *Astral Weeks*, he booked some recording time and unveiled a plan of sabotage. In a cynical attempt to undermine the terms of the Web IV settlement, he submitted 32 songs of calculated gibberish. The contents were a grotesque burlesque of Berns' songwriting and production techniques, including moronic parodies of 'Twist And Shout', 'La Bamba' and 'Hang On Sloopy' and an oft-repeated criticism of the excessive use of session musicians, particularly drummer Herbie Lovelle. 'Blow In Your Nose' lampooned the album title *Blowin' Your Mind!* with the line, "It's got a psychedelic jacket . . . it's a gorgeous album cover". 'The Big Royalty Check' complained about monies allegedly owed, while 'Ring Worm' commented unfavourably on Berns' complexion. Several titles alluded to Berns under the name 'George', apparently a pun on the actor George Burns. The most explicit lyric was the fragmentary, 83-second 'Dum Dum George' which detailed Berns' drive from New York to Boston ("He was freaky and he wanted to record me and I said, 'George, you're so dumb' and he said, 'I know, why do you think I make so much money?'"). Tuneless, spiteful and inane, the tapes are a lasting testament to the bitter dregs of Morrison's resentment. As one critic noted: "It was some present to give to a grieving widow." Burdened with children, one recently born, Ilene Berns was in no mood to parlay with Morrison, who was extremely fortunate to escape without contesting another lawsuit. "You couldn't even copyright them," she said of the tapes. "I had too much going on in my life at the time to even bother to sue him. I just let it go. I did once think of putting them out as a record myself. I was going to title it *Garbage Van*." Her words turned out to be a self-fulfilling prophecy when the unlistenable tracks finally filtered into the marketplace some 25 years later under the titles *The Lost Tapes* and subsequently *Payin' Dues*.

While Morrison was reorganizing his life and career, Mick Cox breezed into New York for another visit and was invited to contribute to the new album. Unfortunately other commitments forced him to decline the opportunity. Eventually, Kielbania and Payne were flown in from Boston and booked into the Chelsea Hotel. They used the offices of Morrison's new management as a meeting place and rehearsal venue, then found some local gigs. "We started playing at the Cafe Au Go Go on Bleecker Street," Payne remembers. "Some nights nobody would come in. Literally nobody." As a solo artiste, Morrison was no more than a one hit wonder at this point which meant that most promoters used him as a support act. Fortunately, the headliners tended to be compatible. Among them was John Lee Hooker to whom Morrison showed considerable deference. Tim Hardin, a luminary of the Greenwich Village folk scene, and one of the most accomplished and moving singer-songwriters of the era, also played several nights. "Live, we were more folkie," Kielbania stresses. "*Astral Weeks* would be more on the jazz side. But all the stuff on that album we played over and over. He was writing a history of his past. He would ad-lib and the forms of the songs were very loose. I just stood at the back and followed him. I knew all the songs. He wouldn't even say what he was playing. I could tell by the introduction and went with it. John Payne would always follow his vocals."

Morrison's love of improvisation, increasingly evident since the Square One happening in Belfast, was tailor made for the new material intended for *Astral Weeks*. Onstage, he paid little homage to the literal reproduction of his lyrics, preferring to use scat vocals to convey the emotional impact of a composition. It was a technique familiar in jazz, but there were also examples from the rock 'n' roll era. During the Fifties, songs such as Gene Vincent's 'Be-Bop-A-Lula' and Little Richard's 'Tutti Frutti' had emphasized the divide between articulation and emotion. Buddy Holly, the undoubted master of the extended syllable, had the capacity to transform a banal and repetitious exhortation like 'Peggy Sue' into a profound declaration of his affection simply by manipulating the pitch and accent of his voice. Some educationalists ridiculed these songs for their infantile lyrics but they were worthy attempts to express emotion by using the voice as an instrument of onomatopoeia. Like Morrison, Little Richard borrowed freely from the blues tradition and when he screamed the words

'AwopBopaLooBop ALopBamBoom' the listener was not alienated by the apparent incoherence but rather astonished at the singer's innate ability to transcend the normal requirements of sense and language. Morrison realized as much when he asked "What does 'Tutti Frutti' mean? Nobody to this day can say what 'Tutti Frutti' means."

It was already clear that the forthcoming album would combine folk and jazz elements in a fashion unusual in pop music at the time. Morrison was determined to stretch himself and look beyond the boundaries of contemporary rock. He later explained: "I just wanted to get back to playing and singing really − it was like getting rid of everything and starting again. *Astral Weeks* came out of this desire to break out of this rigidity, to extend the lines and chop it up and move beyond 1-2-3-4 beats to the bar." John Payne, struggling to categorize this new style, even started calling Morrison's performances 'chamber music'. The only performer Morrison ever namechecked as an influence on the construction of *Astral Weeks* was King Pleasure, the champion of vocalese − the method of fitting lyrics to well-known jazz solos. With the 1952 album *King Pleasure Sings*, a generation of listeners, including Morrison, had been introduced to the art of vocalese, which later featured in the work of many performers from Annie Ross through to Georgie Fame and Al Jarreau. What no doubt attracted Morrison to King Pleasure was the vocalist's exclusive fondness for the work of saxophonists, particularly those whose improvisations displayed a strong melodic undercurrent. Although the name King Pleasure would not feature either in contemporary interviews or appraisals of *Astral Weeks*, Morrison nevertheless paid subtle tribute to his source by allowing himself to be photographed holding one of the singer's Prestige label albums while pointedly staring away from the camera lens.

The *Astral Weeks* project soon took on far greater significance thanks to the inspired intervention of Merenstein and Schwaid whose backgrounds in jazz brought Morrison into a new league. It was to the singer's everlasting benefit that his mentors could call upon some of the finest players in contemporary jazz and that they were willing to lend their services to an album aimed at the pop/rock market. "They were business-type people there to make a killing," Kielbania says of Schwaid and Merenstein, "but they were interested in Van's career. Merenstein produced *Astral Weeks* and they fronted money for it." Payne read their motives differently, insisting that "Schwaid and Merenstein were definitely into Morrison and thought he was great. There's no question about their sincerity. Their concept was to do it that way. It was a pretty uncommercial thing to attempt. They were doing it for artistic reasons. I don't remember any feeling that they were trying to cut costs. I could be wrong, but I don't think so."

The recording of *Astral Weeks* commenced at Brooks Arthur's Century Sound Studio on New York's West 52nd Street on 25 September 1968. Tom Kielbania attended the session but soon learned that his services would not be required. "Van knew I'd be upset. He took me aside and said, 'Don't take this personally, but they're putting a lot of money into this and they want to use their own bass player and drummer.'" Any indignation disappeared when Kielbania learned that his replacement was the great Richard Davis, a member of the Thad Jones-Mel Lewis orchestra, whose résumé included appearances with Miles Davis, Eric Dolphy and Sarah Vaughan. "I idolized him," Kielbania acknowledges. "He was the premier bass player. I showed him the lines I was playing and he picked them up." A formidable line-up was completed with the arrival of guitarist Jay Berliner who had previously played alongside Charles Mingus, percussionist Warren Smith Jr and the Modern Jazz Quartet's drummer Connie Kay.

"It was an amazing session," says Kielbania. "They jammed and it was three times the length of the album. They had to cut all the solos out. Every song was a whole side. It was a big jam and I really enjoyed it. I even got paid as an advisor." According to Payne, who was also there as a spectator having been replaced by an uncredited flautist, the first session produced 'Cyprus Avenue', 'Beside You' and 'Madame George'. The last two songs were the Bang-period compositions that Morrison was contractually obliged to record for the album. Had this not been the case, the epic 'Madame George' would probably never have been featured on *Astral Weeks*. The first session was a breeze for the jazz players who were allowed to roam free, unchallenged by Morrison's structurally simple compositions. Although no-one remembers him feeling intimidated by the quality of the players, he must have been aware that he was the least experienced musician in the studio. Evidently there was no visible rapport between Morrison and the others, who looked to Merenstein and arranger Larry Fallon for any advice. "I can't remember him having a conversation with any of the musicians at any time," Payne stresses. "Maybe he did, but I don't remember it. In my experience as a musician that was unusual. He might have been a little in awe of these guys, or just shy." Richard Davis felt Morrison was "very remote", stressing, "He never had a thing to say to us and we never said anything to him. The guy was expressionless." Joe Smith sat quietly in the background, moved by the music he was hearing, yet unable to rid himself of the fear that he was about to deliver Warners another Van Dyke Parks.

Larry Fallon was a crucial presence at the session and later faced the tricky task of adding colour to Morrison's minimal compositions without spoiling their fragility. Given Morrison's lack of formal musical training, there could easily have been major problems. "All the other guys were seasoned studio players and read music," Payne notes. "I can remember Larry running out with all these chord charts for these tunes. The tunes were real simple but they got screwed up once in a while because Van would do them a little differently. If you listen carefully you can hear Richard Davis go for the wrong bass note on a number of occasions because Van had done it differently from the last time. Later, I would point that out to students who were worried that pros never made mistakes. 'Hey, he went to the wrong place, but they put it on the record and nobody noticed. Relax!'"

Producer Lew Merenstein was sufficiently impressed with the outcome of this initial session to encourage the players to try one more number. Morrison proffered a new composition, a two-chord song played in 3/4 time which later took the name 'Astral Weeks'. The tired flautist, having completed some fine work, elected to go home at this point. So it was that John Payne was offered the chance to contribute to the album's title track, adding tonic and subdominant flute interjections. "I hadn't even brought my flute," Payne remarks, "because I knew I wasn't supposed to play. So I asked the other guy if I could use his and he said OK. He was a good player. 'Astral Weeks' wasn't supposed to be on the record. It wasn't on the agenda at all. It was just one take, I'm pretty sure, as were most of these things."

A second session was booked soon after, but apparently nothing was salvaged from the tapes except 'The Way Young Lovers Do'. "It was done in the morning," Payne recalls, "because everyone was working around Richard Davis's schedule. But at 9am, it wasn't happening. I don't remember them using a single thing from it and I can't even remember what was played." Morrison vaguely recalled a couple of outtakes, including a long narrative about trains. At a later session, there was also an obscure song titled 'Royalty' and an ode to Jesse James. The latter could conceivably have been a blueprint for Morrison's 'Crazy Face', an unknown original or a variation on the traditional 'The Ballad Of Jesse James'.

On 15 October, the ensemble reconvened to record 'Sweet Thing', 'Ballerina' and the aforementioned outtakes. "They put the chart in front of me, but I didn't look at it," Payne confesses. "I can read chords but for stuff that simple harmonically, I thought I'd just feel it. I don't know how much the other guys were looking either. Jay Berliner had some inspired moments but I don't know how much they were into it or whether it was just another session, another day, another dollar. They never talked about it."

As with the first session, there was enough time left at the end to throw in another new number, 'Slim Slow Slider'. "That was the tape on the floor," Payne remarks. "I'd never heard the song before and I'm sure it wasn't intended for the album. It was an afterthought. Lew got a real echoey sound on my soprano saxophone. That was the first time I'd ever played soprano with Morrison. I just happened to bring it that night – I don't even know why. I'd only ever played flute with him up until then. It's weird because it felt very intimate even though Van was in a separate vocal booth and you couldn't see him." Merenstein held back Morrison, Davis and Payne for a final section in which they let fly. "It was five to 10 minutes of instrumental jamming, semi-baroque and jazz stuff," Payne marvels. "Where he sings 'Everytime I see you I just don't know what to do' is where they cut the tape. It'd be interesting to hear. It's a whole other side of Van Morrison. When he dies and a boxed set and all the outtakes come out I hope they still have it and it wasn't just thrown away."

Soon after the final session, Larry Fallon was called upon to overdub strings and horns at a studio near Times Square. "Larry did a great job with great sensitivity," Payne concludes. "So many times things can be over-arranged. Especially with a guy like Van, you could overdo it easily. But he did an incredible job. He was really modest. He played the harpsichord part on 'Cyprus Avenue' and when he was putting it down he was really shy about it. Van was going 'No, that's great man!' "

During the same period of recording *Astral Weeks*, Morrison was playing a support slot at Steve Paul's Scene on West 46th Street and 8th Avenue. Paul was then managing Tim Hardin who was still in convalescence following a serious bout of pleurisy. John Payne remembers Morrison and himself travelling by subway and devouring hamburgers at a joint near Times Square prior to the show. The Scene attracted a hip clientele, including Jimi Hendrix, who witnessed a Morrison performance one evening. "I'll never forget that as long as I live," Kielbania says. "I idolized Hendrix." More often, Morrison was playing for the early crowd whose interest was cursory at best. "We weren't headlining there," Payne points out. "At midnight the place was barely getting started. Different people would play a set for an hour and that was it. Around 3am, musicians might jam, but I never stayed that late. One Friday we were opening for Tim Hardin and there were some high school kids in there with their girlfriends. For the first set they were just talking and paying no attention. After a couple of numbers all we heard was 'yak, yak, yak'. In the middle of a number Van stopped and just sat down. Eventually, there was quiet. He then said something about how this was disrespectful, turned to Tom and said, 'Play an E-minor'. He vamped on it, started playing, then sang this song which was a subtle putdown of the audience which they probably didn't get. It went on and on. We figured he made it up on the spot. It was stream of consciousness, like Bob Dylan. I wish there was a recording of it."

Apart from apathetic audiences, Morrison continued to suffer the occasional radio and television appearance. "We did Channel 11," Payne recalls, "where they introduced him as 'the Irish soul singer'. He really hated that. They wanted him to lip sync one of his records but he refused." Radio shows were also regarded as torture, particularly if the subject wandered into areas other than music. According to Kielbania, the topic of Northern Ireland was broached by some stations, even at a time well in advance of the formation of the Provisional IRA. "They'd always get into politics," he claims, "and he didn't want to talk about the problems in Belfast. They'd bring that up – that he was a Protestant.

Van the baby.

The Belfast cowboy.

With parents George and Violet, and sheepdog Maxie.

Sir Edward Carson signing the Ulster Solemn League and Covenant on 28 September 1912. Standing either side of him are Lord Londonderry and Sir James Craig.

WHO SAID WE'RE TO HAVE
HOME RULE?

COME TO
BELFAST
AND WE'LL
SHEW 'EM.

"Ireland Sings her Old Songs"

HOME RULE

ULSTER'S PRAYER

Dont let go!

NO SURRENDER FORTS

FREE SOUND

SCOTLAND

PROSPERITY
PROVINCE

POVERTY
PROVINCE

MAYOOODLE
PROVINCE

LAND LEAGUE
PROVINCE

MOLLY MAGUIRE
POINT.

UNION CHANNEL

BUDGET
BAY

LORDS
HEADLAND

LABOUR
HEAD

UNIONIST
ROADS

ENGLAND

LIBERAL STRAITS.

HOME RULE ROCKS.

GULF OF
SOCIALISM

TARIFF
REFORM
CHANNEL

RADICAL SOUND

Registered.

Belfast Blitz kids.

The Monarchs with the doomed Wesley Black on piano.

The Monarchs in Germany with producer Ronald Kovacs.

The Monarchs with Morrison smiling, second from the left, front row.

Them, late 1964.
Left to right: Alan Henderson, Pat McAuley, Billy Harrison, Jackie McAuley and Van Morrison

Them, mid-1965.
Left to right: Joe Baldi, Alan Henderson, Morrison, Terry Noon and Peter Bardens.

Them, late-1965.
Left to right: John Wilson, Ray Elliot, Alan Henderson, Morrison and Jim Armstrong.

Ian Paisley, ever the theological provocateur.

Sam Smyth (*left*) and Donall Corvin in the Swinging Sixties.

Left to right: Jeff Barry, Bert Berns, Morrison, Janet Planet and the charismatic Carmine 'Wassel' Denoia smoking a cigar.

He didn't want to get involved in that at all. A thing that came up once in a while was the thought that he was running away from it. Did he really leave to make it big in the United States or did he leave because of the problems at home?" The fact that Morrison had left Northern Ireland long before the beginning of the Troubles answers Kielbania's question.

Nevertheless, the fuse that was to ignite the Troubles was now burning fast and even Morrison could not escape the conflagration. While he was putting the final touches to *Astral Weeks*, Northern Ireland was making international headlines. The socialist Éamonn McCann, supported by the Civil Rights Association, led a protest march in Derry on 5 October which loyalists regarded as a provocative attack on the Unionist hegemony. The demonstrators suffered savage treatment from the police in scenes televised across the world. Stormont and Westminster MP Gerry Fitt was captured on camera with blood streaming down his face. Soon after, students in Belfast marched angrily to the City Hall demanding reform. Paisley, meanwhile, amplified Protestant fears and organized counter demonstrations fuelled by the immemorial cry of 'No Surrender'.

That same month, Morrison's former spiritual sidekick Cecil McCartney (now rechristened King Om) achieved an impossible dream with the launch of his own album on EMI Records. *Om* was a predictably strange record, accompanied by a press release confirming that its creator was born "on the edge of infinity where space curves". Celebrating its release, King Om sought oneness on a mountain where he consumed life-enhancing herbs. "The molecular structures I absorbed were more complex than LSD," he told reporters. *Om*, a concordance of New Age mysticism, animal rights militancy and spiritual enlightenment, was far more astral in its subject matter than anything emanating from Morrison's sessions in New York. The exotic vegetarian pacifist King Om might have been expected to make some radical statement supporting the students and civil rights demonstrators in the North but, like Morrison, he had been brought up as a Protestant and remained ambivalent on the issue. His one contribution was a polite call for peace: 'Orange And Green'. For McCartney, pop and politics were inextricably linked, but his favoured target was the world stage, specifically President Johnson. While batons bruised youngsters in Derry, Om sent LBJ "a direct command from the neo-god of love to cease fire in Vietnam and form a coalition government composed of Red Chinese, Americans and North and South Vietnamese members working for the total good of Vietnam. If this message is ignored for more than six months, the youth of this planet will strike by paralyzing education and industry if senile politicians cannot achieve peace by civilized methods."

Om did not ignite the world, but then again neither did *Astral Weeks*, which was issued in the US soon after without fanfare. It arrived at a time when Americans were still grieving after the assassinations of Martin Luther King and Robert Kennedy earlier in the year and coming to terms with rioting in Chicago and civil unrest from anti-war demonstrators. Big Brother & The Holding Company featuring Janis Joplin (*Cheap Thrills*) and the Jimi Hendrix Experience (*Electric Ladyland*) held sway at the top of the album charts. Both singers would be dead within two years. Morrison's meditative work was an appropriate record to sum up the times but few mainstream listeners heard the album which sold abysmally. Its lukewarm reception confirmed the worst fears of Warners' Joe Smith who was again left wondering whether Morrison would remain on the cult fringe. Foreign interest was equally tepid. Amazingly, it would be the best part of a year before the album was deemed suitable for release in the British market. Most of Morrison's Northern Ireland contemporaries remained completely unaware of the record's existence. In any case, those among the student fraternity had weightier matters on their minds.

In Belfast, Christmas was a time of planned militancy for civil rights advocates. At Queen's University, the People's Democracy was founded. Among its leading lights were Michael Farrell and the vibrant 21-year-old Bernadette Devlin. A resident of Cookstown, the penny-throwing scourge of Morrison's Them, Devlin had been a staunch Republican who, even before her teens, had won a prize for a powerful recitation of Pádraig Pearse's famous blood-sacrifice speech: "The fools, the fools, the fools! They have given us our Fenian dead, and while Ireland holds their graves, Ireland unfree shall never be at peace." After attending a civil rights march from Coalisland to Dungannon she was converted to a ticket of non-political social reform. Partly inspired by Martin Luther King's famous long walk from Selma to Montgomery,

Alabama, the university students planned something similarly news-worthy for Northern Ireland.

On New Year's Day 1969, Devlin led a student peace march from Belfast to Derry. Among the retinue was Gerry O'Hare, a non-student who would rise to treasurer in the organization. "Rather than joining the Civil Rights, I joined the People's Democracy," he points out. "I had a trade union background and a lot of people in the PD liked that. I looked at the Civil Rights as middle class. Whenever the Civil Rights Movement seemed to get soft on issues the PD would take a harder line. That's why the march took place. The Civil Rights people didn't want it to. Then they took it over. They were smarter than us, probably. More mature, plus there was a big business element there. We were the young Turks so we were to be pardoned for our foolishness, as they saw it." Even before the marchers left Belfast, they met fierce resistance from heckling Paisleyites. Inflamed by egalitarian zeal, the PD attempted to convert their armed adversaries with a perverse display of extreme democracy. "Every time you met you had to vote to confirm what you'd already gathered to do," remembers the socialist Éamonn McCann. "It was ridiculous. The chairman said, 'I *now* propose we march to Derry'. That was after we'd already assembled at Belfast City Hall and I'd travelled from Derry to join them. There were loads of loyalists at the back carrying sticks and clubs and they were asked to vote too! 'Hold up your cudgels,' they were told. Even *they* were seen as part of our 'People's Democracy'. I thought, 'This is mad, what sort of lunacy is this?' Luckily they wouldn't vote! I always remember that as the ultimate expression of both the blithe revolutionary spirit of the PD and the impracticality of it all."

Paisley maintained his vigilance. The Big Man, still the ultimate personification of hard-line Protestantism, had galvanized Orange opposition, denouncing the demands for reform and condemning civil rights as a coded campaign to achieve a united Ireland and destroy Unionism. Not for the first time, acerbic loyalist graffiti spoke volumes: 'Civil Rights Association = Crafty Romanist Agitators'. The march was haunted by the bizarre presence of ex-army officer Major Ronald Bunting, who had been converted by Paisley following a near-death experience, and now emerged as the Big Man's chief lieutenant. He had seen off the marchers with a virulent display of Union Jack waving before moving ahead of them to Derry, where he joined his master for a religious meeting which soon turned into a riot. During the disturbances, Bunting urged people to join the Ulster Protestant Volunteers and arm themselves in preparation for the invading Romanists. A section of this loyalist paramilitary force lay in wait for the marchers, clutching stones, brandishing chains and wielding cudgels crudely reinforced with spikes or long nails. On the fourth day of the march the protesters reached Burntollet Bridge, seven miles from Derry, where they were ambushed and savagely beaten by the Ulster Protestant Volunteers and a number of off-duty B-Specials while uniformed constables looked on approvingly. "Strangely enough the safest place to be at Burtollet was in the front line," recalls Éamonn McCann. "When the attacks started we put our heads down and ran. We were OK, but the people behind us were cut in two as the ambushers erupted through the hedges. The marchers headed across fields and into the river while we were up the road. We'd just got through by the skin of our teeth. One of my most vivid memories was of Bernadette Devlin urging people to *go back*. I thought, 'Go back on your own, Bernadette!' She was braver than I was . . . We regrouped as best we could and then marched towards Derry. To this day, I can still feel the thrill of just looking at the crowd running towards us. There were hundreds of ordinary people that came out to form a ring around the marchers as stewards and protectors." The violent assaults were far from over. Later that evening, a number of inebriated RUC officers entered the Bogside district of Derry, damaging property, assaulting Catholics and chanting sectarian slogans. In the early hours they assembled outside a row of houses and launched into a macabre version of '(Theme From) *The Monkees*': "Hey, hey, we're the Monkees and we'll monkey you around . . . till your blood is on the ground." One female resident later informed a British government enquiry: "I looked out the window and one shouted, 'Come on, you Fenian, 'til we rape you'." Such actions were widely condemned, but the events that day merely reinforced the conviction among Northern Catholics that the police were nothing more than loyalists in state uniform. Many of the civil rights marchers left that blood-splattered affray at Burntollet convinced that they required something more potent than a fatalistic rendition of 'We Shall Overcome'.

THIRTEEN

The Politics Of *Astral Weeks*

Warner Brothers publicly voiced their commitment to Morrison as an albums artiste, but privately they knew that a hit single would boost his profile and sales. Clearly, *Astral Weeks* was bereft of singles potential. Morrison was capable of writing more commercial material and already had a new composition that fitted the bill. His ambivalence was demonstrated by the fact that 'Domino' remained unissued for the best part of two years. "We did 'Domino' in the same studio as *Astral Weeks* with John Payne," Kielbania claims. "I played bass and it was a big drum session, possibly Connie Kay, with congas and everything. To me that was the best 'Domino' I ever heard. Van didn't like it for some reason. He didn't think it was 'in' so it wasn't released." A more pressing reason from Morrison's point of view was the knowledge that any single issued during this period would allow Ilene Berns a 50 per cent cut of the publishing. That proved reason enough to procrastinate.

With 1969 barely underway, the restless John Payne announced that he had embraced Scientology, the cult founded by the controversial science fiction writer L. Ron Hubbard in 1950. Hubbard was a fascinating character whose public pronouncements and publications promised cures for a variety of ailments ranging from asthma to arthritis, polio and leukaemia. At the height of the Cold War, he had even marketed a pill that supposedly combated radiation poisoning. In 1959, he had moved from America to England and bought a maharajah's estate in East Grinstead, West Sussex, that became the world centre of Scientology. The following year he published the clumsily titled *Have You Lived Before This Life?* which documented reincarnation experiences revealed by his subjects during the therapeutic procedure known as 'auditing'. Their testimonies were amplified by Hubbard who claimed to have lived many past lives, some on other planets. Such was the influence of his cult that American students were descending in droves on East Grinstead in search of enlightenment. In 1968, Britain's Health Minister declared Hubbard an "undesirable alien" and banned Scientology students from entering the UK. In a damning report, the Minister informed the House of Commons: "The government is satisfied, having reviewed all the available evidence, that Scientology is socially harmful. It alienates members of families from each other and attributes squalid and disgraceful motives to those who oppose it. Its authoritarian principles and practices are a potential menace to the personality and well-being of those so deluded as to become its followers; above all, its methods can be a serious danger to the health of those who submit to them."

Payne was unfazed by Scientology's bad press, most of which could only be read abroad. To many young Americans, it seemed a worthwhile pursuit, particularly in the hippie era when alternative therapies were embraced with wide-eyed faith rather than cold reasoning. Surprisingly, given his interest in different systems of thought and his later advocacy of Hubbard, Morrison expressed scant interest in Payne's Scientology adventure. Instead, he took the flautist aside and offered the pragmatic opinion: "I think you're more psyched about this than you are about music." Burning with the zeal of the newly converted, Payne elected to "follow his bliss". Morrison wasted no time in recruiting a replacement – Graham 'Monk' Blackburn – an English player and resident of upstate New York.

Monk's arrival encouraged Morrison to relocate to Woodstock, the artist-friendly colony that served as a hip retreat for the rustic-minded. Populated by painters, sculptors and boasting the presence of Bob Dylan, it seemed well-suited to Morrison's reclusive temperament. Settling in a house on Ohayo Mountain with Janet and her son, he enjoyed the company of some sympathetic musical neighbours, including folk singers Artie and Happy Traum and several members of the Band. Bob Schwaid, who drove him to Woodstock in a station wagon, still failed to break through his characteristically steely reserve. "Van was never open with anybody," he concluded. "The only one I ever saw him open with was Janet and even then he was guarded. It was

like somebody watching you with a third eye all the time." Tom
Kielbania also made the trip to Woodstock but lived in an apartment
downtown and seldom visited Morrison in his "house on the
mountain". Nevertheless, Kielbania noticed that he seemed more
relaxed away from the madding crowd, a view echoed by John Payne
who, on a rare visit, saw brief glimpses of a more secure, family man.
"Janet was very centred, very sweet and very outgoing," he emphasizes.
"She had a tremendous, unbridled faith in him. She believed in and
really cared for him. When he was in the right mood, he would play
with her son, Peter. It was the only time I could see warmth in him."

During the early months of 1969, Morrison promoted *Astral Weeks*
with a series of dates across America. In February, he returned to
Hollywood's Whisky A Go-Go, the scene of Them's greatest triumph
on American soil. Kielbania was thrilled to meet Jim Morrison there,
who was rehearsing with the Doors in a studio near their motel.
Unfortunately, the much anticipated Whisky show proved a mini-
disaster. "It wasn't the kind of music they really wanted to hear, so we
didn't go over that big," Kielbania admitted. Hollywood correspondent Judy Sims, reporting for *Disc & Music Echo*, was one of the first
journalists to review Morrison's *Astral Weeks* material in a live setting.
"Poor Van Morrison," she lamented. "He opened at the Whisky last
week and played to a big crowd which was fêted by his record
company; lots of important people crammed into booths and tables,
drinking and talking and generally ignoring Van on stage. After three
numbers I wished I were able to ignore him – it was simply awful. He
played an acoustic guitar, backed by a saxophone player and an upright
bass player, and sang loose rambling songs which all sounded alike.
They went on for ever, rising and falling monotonously, and Van's nasal
voice did nothing to vary the pace or inflection. At first it was merely
embarrassing, and finally it was painful. We left after what must have
been a solid hour of this torture, and he still hadn't finished his first set."

Morrison persevered with the *Astral Weeks* set, securing a prestigious
spot on a Jeff Beck bill at Chicago's Kinetic Playground in March.
Money was tight, the shows were often unrewarding and nervous
tension was always in the air. "Janet was always concerned about his
health," Kielbania points out. "She'd say, 'Take care of yourself, you
worry too much.' She tried to encourage him a lot. He had problems

with his neck and was so uptight all the time that he couldn't relax. He was seeing a chiropractor in New York. He'd always have a couple of drinks – Johnnie Walker Black Label – before we played, and occasionally wine, just to loosen up." Kielbania noticed that Morrison, despite his regular consumption of whisky, showed no interest in drugs throughout their time together. "There were always people smoking grass and stuff and he never did anything. It was almost like he was afraid of it, as if he'd had bad experiences in the past and didn't want to have anything to do with it at all. I never saw him touch anything."

During this period, Morrison still kept in touch with events in Northern Ireland via correspondence with his mother. He wrote her an upbeat letter claiming that he had established several close friendships and Janet added that she was planning to write a book titled *My Husband – Van Morrison*. Meanwhile, political headlines about the North continued to seep into the American press. On 23 April 1969, the fiery, militant, mini-skirted Bernadette Devlin caused a sensation when she was elected at Westminster as Member of Parliament for mid-Ulster. That morning she was celebrating her 22nd birthday, which appropriately coincided with both St George's Day and the eve of the 1916 Easter Rising. It was a revealing snapshot of the period that as many were scandalized by the length of Bernadette Devlin's skirt as by the whirlwind force of her political statements. Her maiden speech electrified the House of Commons and was universally applauded for its power and sincerity. Journalists and photographers, besotted by her youth and moral certitude, documented her exploits, building up her image as the 'swinging MP', 'Irish Joan of Arc', 'mini-skirted Castro' and 'babe' of Parliament. Paisley, in one his more subtle sideswipes, dubbed her 'International Socialist Playgirl Of The Year'.

That same month, a sit-down protest in Derry was broken up, after which the police pursued stone throwers into the Catholic Bogside area, entering a house and beating up an innocent family, one of whom, 42-year-old taxi driver Samuel Devenny, subsequently died. No RUC officer was prosecuted for the killing. Over 30,000 people attended the funeral. It would not be the last fatality that year. Within a week, Premier O'Neill, already stung by Devlin and on the run from hard-line Unionists, resigned from office in disillusionment. The thermometer of the Troubles was rising steadily.

By the spring of 1969, Morrison's group urgently required a boost in morale and a serious musical rethink. "We weren't getting too good a response from the audiences," Kielbania admits. "They wanted electric." Morrison's road manager Thomas Reynolds recommended New York guitarist John Platania, a former Bang Records signing, whose group the Silver Byke had recorded a one-off single for the label, 'I've Got Time'. Coincidentally, Platania was then living near Woodstock in Ulster County. Uniting the two 'Ulstermen' was no easy task. Platania's girlfriend Beth Nussbaum pleaded with him to attend the audition and it was only after considerable coaxing that he drove to Morrison's home in Ohayo Mountain. "I just jammed and then Van scribbled my name and phone number on a piece of paper," Platania recalls. "He was quiet, but I liked him. He didn't come across as being the eccentric everybody thinks he is. He was into his music and that was it. Whatever plot he had for the future, he kept to himself."

Along with former Fugs' drummer Bob Mason, Platania joined the expanded line-up, but confidence was low. They were forced to play demeaning gigs, performing alongside bubblegum nonentities the 1910 Fruitgum Company and even warming up the crowd for a screening of Cream's farewell concert film. Media exposure was severely limited. "We did one television show in New York," Kielbania remembers. "Van did a couple of radio shows. He didn't like talk shows. They'd get into politics and he didn't want to talk about Belfast."

Sporadic attempts at recording new work continued during the late spring. Graham Blackburn remembers Morrison endlessly tinkering with a new tune, 'Moondance', and there was a further shot at 'Domino'. "After we went to Woodstock, we went back to New York and recorded it again," Kielbania recalls. "This time it was all electric. That one wasn't bad but Van said, 'I don't know.' It was almost like he was in some kind of business hassle with the record company and was playing a game and didn't want to release it, holding out for something, playing a little political. It got to be that way just before I left." Kielbania's suspicions were well founded. The obvious reason Morrison failed to release 'Domino' as a single at this point was due to the settlement with Web IV Music which would have acquired a 50 per cent share of any 45 rpm disc issued within 12 months of the resolution, until the expiry date in September 1969.

Morrison's group did not survive the summer. "The reason I left is that I'd just got married and my wife was pregnant," Kielbania explains. "I didn't want to have a kid on the road. Secondly, it seemed that we were getting nowhere. Van was always in some kind of disarray with the record company and the management. He never let me in on the business side, which was good. After I quit, he got rid of virtually the whole group."

By July, Morrison and Platania, now working as an acoustic duo, appeared at the prestigious Newport Folk Festival, which featured several key Warner Brothers acts, including the Everly Brothers and Joni Mitchell. Joe Smith dutifully attended and by the close of the event had verbally secured another signing, James Taylor. Morrison, visibly nervous onstage at such a big date, preferred to hang out with Sonny Terry & Brownie McGhee, whose blues had enlivened his childhood and adolescence. Soon after, he hired saxophonist Jack Schroer and keyboardist Jeff Labes, then playing in the Colwell-Winfield Blues Band, a Boston outfit that had recently relocated to upstate New York. "We did this gig together in Woodstock," Morrison elaborates. "That was the original Woodstock festival . . . It didn't have anything to do with the movie at all. It was in a little field, a muddy field. They had the festival every year and it was really mellow . . . It was musicians and artists." Sound Out, as the event was called, also featured the Montgomeries, a New York country blues outfit that had recently relocated to the area. "That's how we first met," says their guitarist Jon Gershen, recalling the get-together at the Peter Pan Farm. "He hung out watching us play and we stayed around to see him do his thing. Needless to say, we had never heard anything like it. He was in the *Astral Weeks* mode at the time and it was something to witness. The next day, he tracked us down and asked if he could come over to our place and play. Our answer was 'Of course.' From that point on, a special bond was formed." Over the summer, the Montgomeries could be seen on stage with Morrison at the local Sled Hill Cafe or hanging out at Rose's Cantina. He seemed happy in the company of Woodstock's artistic community, proudly pointing out, "They weren't into commercial things and they weren't into that whole hype scene."

What Morrison referred to as "that whole hype scene" was nothing less than the most momentous gathering in the history of rock music.

The Woodstock Festival, which took place at nearby Bethel, swiftly entered modern folklore when the expected audience of 200,000 mushroomed into a veritable nation. By the eve of the event there was an estimated one million people on the road. Those forced to turn back were greater in number than any previously recorded festival audience. For their glimpse of heaven, the remaining half-million had to endure three days of stifling weather, overflowing toilets and limited supplies of food and water. Among the illustrious names appearing at the festival were Morrison's Woodstock neighbours the Band and the Paul Butterfield Blues Band. Dylan was conspicuous by his absence and Morrison probably did not even merit an invitation, which he would likely have declined. Although the festival was only 60 miles from his home, the international focus on the spectacle, which spawned a best-selling treble album and a lucrative movie, proved disconcerting. "The town of Woodstock did not like hippies," Morrison insisted. "And when the movie came out the town couldn't believe it. They just could not believe their own town was going to be ripped apart the way it was. The movie wasn't even [filmed] there."

Woodstock was promoted as the ultimate flowering of Sixties youth, a haven of love, peace and music. Back in Belfast, Morrison's acolytes Donall Corvin, Sam Smyth and Dino Martin had staged their own Woodstock two weeks earlier at the Minnowburn Pop Festival on 4 August 1969. The overreaching Corvin had even invited John and Yoko to appear but had to be content with a message of support from the peaceniks and a less radical headlining act – chart-topping pop stars Marmalade. Whether Morrison would have participated had he still been in Northern Ireland remains a provocative question. Despite the festival's non-sectarian agenda, its subtext was perceived by Paisleyites as a rallying cry for civil rights which, crudely translated, meant an attack on Unionism. "Minnowburn was Corvin and Sammy's idea," Dino admits, "and it was successful in the number of people that came there and the publicity that it got, but it didn't achieve its aims. This was Pop For Peace. They had just started throwing stones around the Falls and the Shankill and up in Derry. It was just before the British came in. Nobody had been shot and killed but buses were being burned and people were throwing stones. It was the Catholics against the police. This was the time of the march – Bernadette Devlin and all."

If Minnowburn and Woodstock promoted peace then Northern Ireland was surely no longer listening. The People's Democracy spoke of social revolution, but its egalitarian, non-sectarian ideals appealed to relatively few Protestants, not least one suspects because its leftish sloganeering echoed the Marxist rhetoric of the Official IRA. Newly radicalized students, more militant in the wake of anti-war protests in America, France and Britain the previous year, had lost patience with a corrupt police force and a paternalistic government whose reforms seemed timid and half-hearted. By contrast, hard-line Unionists spoke of IRA intrusions, communist sympathizers and enemies of the state. Paisley, ever the great theological provocateur, offered speeches laced with apocalyptic imagery and rich, biblical rhetoric. The peace train was about to come off the rails.

In Derry, the annual inflammatory Orange parades went ahead at a time when civil rights marches had been outlawed by Stormont. Amid heightened tension, stone throwers were again out in force, prompting the B-Specials to chase them into the Bogside. Locals erected barricades and established 'Free Derry', resisting armed police with petrol bombs and paving stones and establishing first aid posts and fire brigades. Assisted by Protestant Volunteers, the police continued a fierce onslaught over two days, firing tear gas for the first time in the history of the province. "Bernadette Devlin, seemingly immune to CS gas, was in the thick of the fighting, an inspiration to the young people of the area," Gerry Adams recalls. A number of other prominent Republicans were radicalized by the Battle of the Bogside, including Martin McGuinness and future Sinn Féin president Mitchel McLaughlin. In Dublin, the Taoiseach Jack Lynch, convinced that Stormont had finally lost control, despatched the Irish Army to the Donegal border and set up field hospitals and refugee centres. "The Irish government can no longer stand by and see innocent people injured and perhaps worse," he informed television viewers. "It is obvious that the RUC is no longer accepted as an impartial police force."

Protestant militants were predictably outraged and rioting spread. In London, Harold Wilson, fearing civil war, reluctantly ordered the British Army onto the streets of Derry. Within a day, they would also be deployed in other areas, including Belfast. Initially, they were greeted as liberators by the Catholic population and could be seen on television receiving cheers of jubilation and an endless supply of tea, cakes and sandwiches. "You're giving them tea now," Bernadette Devlin sneered from the Bogside. "What will you be giving them in six months?" For Unionists, the presence of British soldiers defending Catholics represented a humiliating betrayal of their political heritage.

While the Bogside was burning, the rioting spread overnight to the streets of Belfast where sectarian conflicts were even more pronounced. Before the arrival of the Army, the RUC had attempted to maintain order but, goaded by loyalist agitators, they soon overreacted. The dreaded B-Specials entered Divis Street in armoured cars killing a British soldier home on leave and a nine-year-old Catholic boy, Patrick Rooney, who was shot through the head while asleep in his bed. In Bombay Street, 15-year-old Gerald McAuley was killed by a sniper and two Protestants suffered gunfire wounds in Sugarfield Street. Catholics in Conway Street and Cupar Street were burned out of their homes as the conflict reached its height. Heavily outnumbered, Catholic families fled as hundreds of houses were razed. Journalist Colin McClelland, a friend and contemporary of Sam Smyth and Donall Corvin, was sitting downstairs in the Abercorn bar with a group of friends when the first fires erupted. When they left the pub, they were alarmed to find the streets deserted. A column of smoke rose in the distance as the conflagration continued. "This was unheard of," says McClelland. "Belfast, a British city. Evacuated. There were about 12 of us in the group – Catholics and Protestants. We had to get home. Nobody said anything but the Catholics who lived in the Catholic areas went home together, and so did the Protestants. I remember looking around and thinking 'My god, what's happening here?' The ghettoization had started even among us who were middle-class people. We became very aware of what religion we were that afternoon." Eventually, the fires burnt out, but the embers of bitterness remained. In West Belfast, graffiti decorated walls lambasting the impotency of the men who had proclaimed themselves the defenders of the beleaguered Catholic population. It read: "IRA – I Ran Away".

August 1969 signalled the grim advent of the Troubles proper as Catholic families continued to flee from loyalist strongholds. Over the succeeding months, the streetscape of Belfast was redrawn more starkly than any gerrymanderer could ever have envisaged. For many, life would never be the same again. The golden age was over for Belfast. It was as if the Sixties had been a waking dream, a surface illusion, which had been stripped away like a bloodied bandage to reveal the institutions, injustices and intransigent dogma utterly unaltered after 50 years. O'Neill's reforms, the civil rights movement, the idealistic youth who had bonded across the sectarian divide and promised not to make the same mistakes as their forebears – all this was blown away. Paisley's star continued to rise in line with Unionist fears, which would soon be vindicated by the emergence of the Provisional IRA.

Less than a month after the Belfast pogroms *Astral Weeks* finally received a release in the UK market. The timing was eerily appropriate. This was Morrison's farewell to Belfast, his personal requiem for a city that seemed increasingly lost to him. Now, it served as a painful soundtrack to an era that was no more. "The songs came out of some inner expression of trying to cope with what was happening around me," Morrison revealed. "It came out of people I knew and snatches of conversations, snatches about people's lives. Parties. It came out of the spirit of what was happening. Most of it was capturing the spirit of what was going on with my peer group at the time in Belfast." Listening to the album conjures many evocative images: the cherry trees of Cyprus Avenue, the six bells of St Donard's Church, the biblical placards and signs with their fundamentalist slogans, the parties at Fitzroy, the head games with Corvin at Isabeal's, the astral theories of Cecil McCartney, the longing for beautiful, unattainable girls, the fleeting glimpses of childhood bliss and countless other flashbacks which Morrison could never fully articulate when discussing the work. In his more grandiloquent moments he called the album a "rock opera", but later referred to the work as consisting of "multiple visual sketches". "The album's full of sketches and that's why people read more into it, whatever they want," he concluded.

If *Astral Weeks* is a blank canvas, it is nevertheless an intriguing one. For many, it remains an enduring mystery, a song cycle that resonates with a profound sense of longing for a state of rapture that appears alternately tangible and elusive. Its title track is dominated by the lament "to be born again", a reiteration of the Calvinist conviction, advocated by Paisley, that salvation cannot be achieved by good works but only through being reborn via the intervention of the Holy Spirit and God's sovereign grace. The talismanic streetscapes of Belfast echo through several songs, usually serving as a reassuringly familiar backdrop for an unfamiliar and evidently troubled journey towards transcendence. Along the way, a sense of temporal and geographical distortion is ever present. Cyprus Avenue, home of Ian Paisley, is recognizable from the passing reference to its tree-lined pavements. Everything else seems out of kilter as images rush by and a narrative unfolds involving schoolgirls, a wine drinker and an arresting final meditation on a seemingly forbidden love for a 14-year-old. It is increasingly unclear how much of the action is taking place on Cyprus Avenue or even what time scheme is employed. This is dramatically underlined halfway through the song when Morrison exclaims: "My tongue gets tied every time I try to speak/And my insides shake just like a leaf on a tree", a direct quotation from Elvis Presley's 1957 hit 'All Shook Up'. The words shift the time frame back to the Fifties, allowing the listener to re-enter a world when Morrison himself was 12 years old and walked to school down the avenue. The part-fictional landscape of 'Cyprus Avenue' is transitory and the connections between its constituent parts have all the logic of a half-remembered dream.

A similar technique is noticeable in 'Slim Slow Slider'. As in 'Cyprus Avenue', the street location is fixed, yet strangely alien and contradictory. Morrison sings of a girl walking in Ladbroke Grove, catching pebbles by a sandy beach, accompanied by a boy riding in her Cadillac. Of course there are no beaches in Ladbroke Grove and, even if there were, we wouldn't expect to see a Cadillac in the vicinity. The geographical dislocation dramatizes the narrator's own mental anxiety and confusion. For as the song concludes we learn that he is witnessing the death of a loved one who also realizes that her demise is at hand.

The rapid movement of a mind under stress continues in 'Madame George'. Once again, we are taken to Cyprus Avenue and the Protestant stronghold Sandy Row, but in the middle of all this a character jumps up and screams a line that would be more appropriate in an episode of Kojak in Harlem: "Lord have mercy, I think it's the cops!" Of all the songs on Astral Weeks, 'Madame George' is the most mysterious. Oddly compelling, it invokes fractured visions of a sad transvestite. "Dry your eyes for Madame George", Morrison sings, with feeling. During one interview, he mischievously, or obtusely, attempted to deflect attention from the composition's homosexual undertones with the ludicrous suggestion that he was actually singing "playing dominoes is a drag" instead of "in drag". Somewhere along the line, for reasons he claims he cannot recall, Morrison made the decision to alter the title of the song from 'Madame Joy' to 'Madame George'. Perhaps he was subliminally influenced by the controversial 1968 film *The Killing Of Sister George* which featured a powerful performance by Beryl Reid as a cross-dressing lesbian. Whatever its origin, Morrison's 'Madame George' is a moving, enigmatic picture that comes to life not through any literal transcription of the lyrics but courtesy of the vocal phrasing, accentuation and repetition. Towards the end of the song, Morrison chants "And the love that loves the love" over and over, stopping only after 15 exclamations of love, like a hypnotist's captive subject emerging from a reverie. This was part blues, part Protestant testifying, as the singer urges his congregation with the insistent verve of a Presbyterian preacher. Like many of Morrison's songs, 'Madame George' is an impressionistic piece of automatic writing which even he could begin to fathom only retrospectively, and then none too confidently. Pressed on its meaning by one critic, he replied laconically that it was about "a Swiss cheese sandwich".

The redoubtable Donall Corvin, no doubt intrigued by the Belfast references, pushed Morrison for an explanation and was rewarded with a surprisingly revealing account of the origins of 'Madame George'. "The song is actually 'Madame Joy'," Morrison corrected. "Sometimes I write the music first and then the lyrics. But 'Madame Joy' was a straight poem with music added. It was just a spontaneous thing and I didn't really dig what it was about until after I wrote it. It was a stream of consciousness and then later – flash! I *knew* what it was about. I had a great aunt whose family name was Joy and she lived in the Cyprus Avenue area. I only met her once when I was little. She was supposed to be very clairvoyant or psychic and lived in this old Victorian house. I just heard stories about her. That's part of it. It's about other things too. It's a sketch about a lot of various moods. The feeling of that song is very important because that enables the lyrics to come through."

The lyrics were the least significant aspect of *Astral Weeks* and no word sheet was included with the album. This was surely a wise decision. On paper, Morrison's verbal tics, repetitions, peculiar phrasing and chaotic musings would seem overblown or meaningless. Nevertheless, there were unconvincing attempts to market Morrison as pop's latest poetic genius. The artwork featured a suitably misty, out-of-focus shot of a pensive Morrison in striking contract to his previous incarnation as the Angry Young Van. Promoting the singer as a mystical, romantic poet seemed as blatantly unconvincing as the tactics once used by Solomon and Decca to manufacture Them as Belfast punks. Similarly, Merenstein's ordering of the two sides of the record into 'In The Beginning' and 'Afterwards' deliberately suggested a thematic structure reminiscent of Blake's *Songs Of Innocence And Of Experience* or Wordsworth's *Prelude* and *Excursion*. In reality this was poetic pretension, for *Astral Weeks* had no such structure. Morrison later pleaded that the album was incorrectly sequenced, but failed to suggest what the correct order should have been. Perhaps this was because even the most ingenious sequencing could not provide a series of songs that fitted neatly into a before and after concept. Morrison confirmed as much years later, adding: "Well, I think the concept was suggested to me after it was done . . . There wasn't really a concept. The producer of the album saw it as a concept . . . that's how the idea came about that it *was* a concept."

Morrison may well have been the first songwriter to introduce Belfast place names into the rock marketplace. At a time when Swinging London, New York, Hollywood and San Francisco were the epicentres of pop culture, it was strange to hear Belfast streets mentioned as if they were as well known to the average listener as Sunset Boulevard, Washington Square or Route 66. The naming of Sandy Row must have gladdened the heart of many a staunch Unionist, particularly at such a sensitive time. Not that everyone was impressed. Playwright Aisling Foster attended a party in Dublin at which Bernadette Devlin was present. When *Astral Weeks* was placed on the turntable, Devlin immediately left the room. "She had a lot on her mind I suppose," Foster reflects, "because when we put on Van she moved to another room where she remained for the night, singing sad rebel songs with her Northern friends and looking disapproving."

"Bernadette's a fierce Republican," says her former party colleague Gerry O'Hare. "She was into the Irish language and probably wouldn't have been intrigued by rock 'n' roll, or anything like it. Her party piece was the lament 'Down By The Glenside'. She had a beautiful voice and she would stop a room full of people talking when she sang that. The first time I heard *Astral Weeks* was when somebody sent me a copy. One song I loved was 'Ballerina' – that always connected me with my dancing with Van Morrison [at Queen's University]. I loved the flute and the strings. We'd never heard music like that before, someone from East Belfast with a full orchestra behind him. With Belfast Republicans of my era, we were into everything. If there was music on a dancefloor we were there whereas Protestants wouldn't even go to a céilí which was considered 'Catholic music'. It never bothered us. I think we were always one step ahead of them there. We enjoyed ourselves more."

Socialist Éamonn McCann had similar impressions growing up in Derry. "When I was a teenager young Catholics seemed more into rock 'n' roll. They were more outward looking. Whereas Protestants may have looked down on Catholics socially, economically and politically, I think Catholics looked down on Protestants culturally. Consider the sheer ugliness to Catholic ears of the lambeg drum compared to the sound of the Uilleann pipes. It's a generalization, and may be unfair, but Catholics certainly had the impression that Protestants were a bit tuneless and had no melody in them." McCann sees Morrison's work as an unconscious cultural expression of something larger. "*Astral Weeks* is a bit like the 1916 Easter Rising. Everybody who was around was supposedly into it big, but I remember very few who were alert to it. The people I knew who were took pride in the knowledge that somehow our place had generated this fine work. Later I thought, fancifully perhaps, 'Wow, while we were calling for revolution in Northern Ireland, Van Morrison was in America and had it in his head . . .' [His revolution] was expressed through popular culture."

Critical reaction to *Astral Weeks* was surprisingly muted, echoing Bernadette Devlin's evident disapproval. Although it had already achieved cult status as a fashionable import, its much anticipated British release failed to provoke dancing in the streets. The *NME*'s Nick Logan responded coolly to the work: "The album is as far removed from Them as possible, Morrison sounding for all the world like José Feliciano's stand-in on eight of his own compositions. The comparison rather deadens the impact of the album because Morrison can't better Feliciano's distinctive style. The songs themselves aren't particularly distinguished apart from the title track and suffer from being stuck in the same groove throughout."

Given *Astral Weeks'* later critical standing, it is easy to scoff at Logan's gibe, but a listen to *Feliciano!*, one of the best-selling albums of 1968–69, reveals some surprising stylistic similarities, both vocally and musically. While Logan perhaps missed the troubled beauty at the heart of *Astral Weeks*, his complaint about the songs being "stuck in the same groove" was understandable. The arrangements were certainly repetitive, relying on melodic improvisation around two or three chords, without hooks, choruses or harmonies. Proselytizers would no doubt argue that the sparseness and repetition provided the songs with their distinctive mood and allowed Morrison's yearning, soul-searching singing to emerge more powerfully. Surprisingly, Morrison made no such claims himself and seemed to agree with Logan's harsh assessment of the album's limitations and lack of musical pace. Questioned in 1970 about how he might alter *Astral Weeks* if he could travel back in time, Morrison answered unhesitatingly: "I would change the arrangements because the arrangements are too samey. Guys like Richard Davis and Jay Berliner have got a distinctive style, and they're groovy for like two songs and they can really do it, but four or five other songs should have had a change of mood. That should have happened, and it didn't. I didn't have the same mood in mind for the whole album."

Astral Weeks became both a blessing and a curse for Morrison. Lauded as a hippie adjutant, it was subsequently acclaimed as one of rock music's greatest albums, appearing frequently in pre-millennium music press polls. Unfortunately, its legendary reputation tended to obscure and diminish many of Morrison's later recorded achievements. Whereas there was no firm critical consensus on what constituted Bob Dylan's or Neil Young's greatest album, Morrison's canon of work was all too often crystallized in a single moment. Like the Beach Boys' *Pet Sounds*, *Astral Weeks* was perceived as a one-off whose critical standing allowed little discussion for other equally fascinating musical forays that followed. For Morrison, the critical ballyhoo over *Astral Weeks* ultimately became so tiresome that he dismissed the entire debate about its supposed cultural importance as just another myth.

FOURTEEN

Internment

By summer 1969, Morrison was already preparing the follow-up to *Astral Weeks*. Disappointing sales encouraged him to record a more accessible album that would attract audiences and radio listeners. "I make albums primarily to sell them," he noted, "and if I get too far out a lot of people can't relate to it." Years later, he added, "I had to forget about the artistic thing because it didn't make sense on a practical level. One has to live." A number of crude, unreleased demos surviving from this period capture Morrison in transitional mode. Chief amongst them was 'Lorna', another composition which alludes to a narrator's fascination with young schoolgirls, a motif already familiar from songs like 'Hey Girl' and 'Cyprus Avenue'. Equally impressive was 'I Need Your Kind Of Loving', an attractive melody that deserved a better fate than consignment in a tape vault. Several other songs – 'Really Don't Know', 'Hey, Where Are You?', 'Rock 'n' Roll Band', 'Nobody Really Knows', 'Funny Face', 'Tell Me About Your Love', 'Bayou Girl', 'Magic Night', 'Mona' and the stunning 'Wonderful Remark' – were duly registered or recorded, then either ignored, deferred or abandoned. Remarkably, one of Morrison's most celebrated compositions – the compelling 'Listen To The Lion' – was also recorded in 1969, but its intimidating length ensured a long-delayed release.

Sessions for this new album began at Mastertone on New York's 42nd Street with Lew Merenstein at the console. It wasn't long before Morrison became disenchanted both with the producer and the musical direction. "He did a few songs," John Platania recalls, "and some of the musicians from *Astral Weeks* were involved, but he didn't want them. He wanted me and the other boys and he fought for that. Merenstein seemed to be a nice guy but Van was struggling financially. On that basis alone he had to get rid of him." As a compromise, Merenstein accepted the role of 'executive producer', leaving Morrison free to work with the engineers.

According to Joe Smith, Morrison was feuding with his co-manager Bob Schwaid throughout this period. Andy Wickham intervened by recommending a mediator, Canadian Mary Martin. A former booker for manager Albert Grossman, Martin was already enshrined in rock folklore for introducing his premier client Bob Dylan to the Band. Her close friendship with the quartet ensured that she was pleasantly received by Morrison. "He rattled around with all those good guys in the Band," she fondly recalls. "Richard Manuel was truly a soulmate. They used to terrorize the roads of Woodstock." When Morrison enquired about Martin's intended role, she told him firmly: "I manage you – you manage the band!"

Disentangling Morrison from his deal with Inherit Productions was Martin's first task. She had no affection for Merenstein or Schwaid, referring to them contemptuously as "those creatures". Schwaid still hoped to retain Morrison and with true chutzpah tried to win over Martin to his side. "He said 'If you make sure Van Morrison re-signs I'll make it worth your while,'" she laughs. "When I told Van that, he got very male!"

Dismissing the musicians previously chosen by Merenstein, Morrison recruited his own team. Former Colwell-Blues Band flautist Colin Tilton was added to the trio of Platania, Schroer and Labes, along with John Klingberg (bass), Gary Malabar (drums), Guy Masson (congas), plus a trio of backing singers: Jackie Verdell, Emily Houston (from the Sweet Inspirations) and the renowned Judy Clay (of 'Private Number' fame). After strenuously rehearsing the band, Morrison took them to New York's A&R studios while they were still fresh. "We did our jaunts into the city and it was a lot of fun," Platania confirms. "Most of the album was done live, mistakes and all."

Moondance emerged in February 1970 and after reaching the US Top 30 and UK Top 40 confirmed Morrison's standing among the new élite of rock. Without sacrificing any of his strengths, he produced a more upbeat work that largely dispensed with the poetic, lyrical self-consciousness of its predecessor. Even the cover artwork offered a starker, almost aggressive image of a more intense Morrison. There was little of the vocal abandonment that characterized *Astral Weeks* and the songs were more clearly defined. Instead of rambling, stream of consciousness epics, Morrison concentrated on compositions with commonplace themes, counterpoising spirituality with earthiness. There was the familiar synthesis of blues, folk and jazz, but the material was highly arranged throughout with choral accompaniment and a strong horn section. At a time when many of his contemporaries were discovering the indulgent use of brass and gospel augmentation, Morrison seemed perfectly suited to a big band.

The opening 'And It Stoned Me' is a wonderfully understated remembrance of a childhood fishing expedition to Ballystockert during which Morrison experienced a sense of timelessness. "For five minutes everything was really quiet and I was in this other dimension." There is no pat moralizing or sentimentality in relating the story and even the water symbolism that unifies the piece is introduced without ostentation. There are other deft touches such as the clever use of inversion ("bottle two") to prevent a jerky rhythm and one of his best sax solos.

'Moondance', with its jazzy walking bass line, first emerged as a soprano sax instrumental before Morrison added some sensual lyrics. Another celebration of nature, this time expressed through a lovers' union in the night air, the song became both an FM radio favourite and something of a standard on the cocktail jazz circuit. Its success was mirrored by the gospel-styled 'Crazy Love' which worked particularly well when handled by a female vocalist and was soon covered by both Rita Coolidge and Esther Phillips.

'Caravan', a romantic portrayal of gypsy life and a testimony to his love of radio, featured some of Morrison's most attractive vocal dynamics and became a stage highlight. Even better was the first-half closer 'Into The Mystic', one of his finest compositions of the period. Originally titled 'Into The Misty', the song was written orally and featured an alternative set of lyrics ("I was born before the wind/Also younger than the son" versus "I was borne before the wind/All so younger than the sun"). Although its province sounded like the astral plane, it also conjured images of the shipyards of East Belfast with Morrison's tenor sax imitating the sound of a fog horn.

The second side of the album commenced with 'Come Running', a US Top 40 single that gained Morrison considerable commercial airplay. Vibrant sax hooks also underpinned 'These Dreams Of You' whose lyrics were inspired by a dream in which an assassination attempt was made on Ray Charles. Rather than employing elements of dream psychology as he had done in 'Slim Slow Slider' and 'Madame George' with their distorted spatial and time schemes, Morrison retains a naturalistic setting, focusing on the painful deterioration of a relationship. What emerges most forcibly is his own tribute to Charles' resilience.

Closing the album were three songs of unrestrained joy. 'Brand New Day' was written in Boston after Morrison had heard the Band's version of Dylan's uplifting 'I Shall Be Released' on the radio; 'Everyone', with its catchy 6/8 arrangement and frilly flute flourishes led into the equally light-hearted and lightweight 'Glad Tidings', which ended the album on a positive, optimistic note.

Unlike *Astral Weeks*, *Moondance* was widely reviewed and well-received. *NME*'s Nick Logan concluded that it was "near to being a brilliant piece of work" and breathed a sigh of relief that Morrison had abandoned his Feliciano imitations, even if he now sounded like Curtis Mayfield.

American critics were even more reverential. *Rolling Stone* afforded the album a full-page review with Lester Bangs and Greil Marcus providing twin insights into Morrison's grand significance. No longer an obscure troubadour, he now had "the striking imagination of a consciousness that is visionary in the strongest sense of the word". His greatest asset was supposedly the "authenticity of his spirit" and a verbal magic as inventive as that of Dylan. Writing in the *San Francisco Chronicle*, the senatorial Ralph J. Gleason was even more rhapsodic and placed Morrison alongside Dylan, the Band, the Beatles, John McCormack and even the cartoon character Charlie Brown. Seeking an ever-expanding historical framework, Gleason gushed: "He wails as the jazz musician speaks of wailing, as the gypsies, as the Gaels and the old folk in every culture speak of it. He gets a quality and intensity in that wail which really hooks your mind, carries you along with his voice as it rises and falls in long soaring lines." This slobbering assessment finally lurched into pastoral stage Paddy purple prose: "He sounds like a young Irishman haunted by dreams, a poet, one of the children of the rainbow, living in the morning of the world."

The ecstatic American response indicated how rapidly Morrison was being reinvented and remodelled. Gleason's enthusiastic appraisal treated the singer as though he had just emerged from the Gaeltacht. The fantastical imagery was Erin-laced, wild, pastoral and green, whereas Morrison was Northern, Orange-hued and urban. He was a child of the shipyard rather than a child of the rainbow. He had never been exposed to Irish poets or Irish writers and knew nothing of the Irish language. The rebellious literature that Morrison read came not from Ireland but America. It was the Beat Poets that fuelled his imagination, not Brendan Behan or Seán O'Casey. Unable to draw on the cultural traditions of the North, American commentators lazily located Morrison in a misty-eyed, romanticized Celtic twilight populated by Irish stereotypes. From their descriptions he sounded something like a cross between *The Quiet Man, Darby O'Gill* and an extra from *Finian's Rainbow*.

The myth of Morrison as American rock music's mad Irish poet-in-residence seemed too alluring to resist. By 1970, US singer-songwriters were in the ascendant and, unlike many of his rivals, Morrison offered a gritty soulfulness that added a welcome edge to the soprano sensitivity of the traditional confessional wordsmith. His foreignness, inscrutability, obscurantism and lyrical waltzes into stream of consciousness terrain were all exotic assets that differentiated his work from the laid-back, easy-lay fixated expostulations of the new LA aristocracy. Unfortunately, just as a fresh cloth of green was being cut for Morrison, his art was moving far from the Irish landscape. The gypsies, the shipyard fog horn, his childhood allusion to Ballystockert – all these were fading traces of an Ireland that now seemed far away. The Belfast streets, Orange place names and Northern vernacular so dominant and palpable on *Astral Weeks* had all but disappeared on *Moondance* and would become more distant over the next few years.

Morrison had good reason to feel a sense of detachment from his native city. Although his parents still lived in East Belfast, there was an increasing sense of tension among the Protestant community, ever fearful for the future of their province. Dire predictions were commonplace. Just weeks before the release of *Moondance*, there had been an historic break in Republican ranks. An increasing number of working-class nationalists regarded the Official IRA's Marxist ideology as nothing more than the opiate of left-wing intellectuals. After the recent pogroms, more reforms had been promised but the Catholic community felt increasingly ambivalent towards British troops and hostile towards a police force they felt was little more than the armed wing of the Unionist élite. What they required was a more convincing and protective presence that provided military not verbal ammunition. The breakaway Provisional IRA would fulfil that remit, albeit at a terrible cost.

One of the early recruits was Gerry O'Hare, the dancer who had once appeared with Morrison after his return to Belfast in 1966. "There wasn't much ideology involved in why you joined the Provos or why you joined the Official IRA," he recalls. "A lot of it tended to be where your parents were from or your area or parish. I had no problems about it in my time. Because I had a bit of a political background, I was always aware of the Stalinists that were involved in the Official Republican movement and I didn't like that. I went the other way. People always said that we were sectarian but I would deny that vehemently. With me, it was a pure political choice."

The evidence of a divided community was manifested in the increasing number of no-go areas as people turned inwards and sought solace in tribal solidarity. Entertainment was an early casualty. Former Monarch Roy Kane was playing in the Tara Showband, which included both Catholics and Protestants in its line-up. Their saxophonist Seán Fox was a young victim of the Troubles. "Seán was shot dead," Kane reveals. "It turned out that he was Official IRA at the time of the IRA split. There were the Officials (the Stickies) and the Provos, and the Provos shot him dead. It was in the flats at the bottom of the Falls Road. They've fallen down since."

The cynical but loveable Donall Corvin tried to rise above the tribalism despite his Republican upbringing. Ironically, he was placed in danger after foolishly attempting to sell a gun on behalf of a friend to a member of the Official IRA. "There was no patriotism involved," Sam Smyth stresses. "They wanted to sell it for money. Given Donall's family credentials and so on, they tried to sell it to somebody in the Official IRA for a few hundred quid. These fellows got the gun and tried it out. The bullet exploded in the chamber and nearly took the hand off someone. They could have killed Corvin because that's the way those guys worked. But one of them said, 'Ah he's just an eejit, he's involved in rock music'. So he got the Fool's Pardon from those IRA people."

For Morrison's old pal G.D., the onset of the Troubles spelt the beginning of the end for many aspiring Belfast players. "Things were getting off the ground in the late Sixties, then it was slapped down. It was ghettoized. Bands were breaking up. Then synthesizers came in and ruined a lot of guitarists and drummers. You couldn't go out. You were afraid to go to different places. Gigs were hard to get and there was a drinks curfew when they closed everywhere at 10 o'clock."

Forced to travel, the showbands found that they could not even gain work in the South. The ballrooms that had catered for thousands of dancers throughout the Sixties were now falling into disrepair. Many were transformed into amusement arcades or bingo halls, or simply abandoned. "Those ballrooms were barracks, cold and wet," Harry Baird recalls. "Plus they only sold soft drinks. Once discos started in the hotels it killed the showbands. The hotels offered plush surroundings, a bar and central heating – and everyone drifted in that direction. The ballroom owners have a lot to answer for. They made lots of money out of it, but they never reinvested it. There was nothing to stop them building lounges." As a result, several of Morrison's former bandmates were forced back into non-musical employment. Many prayed that life might return to something approaching normality. It would not be long before those hopes were dashed.

While Belfast smouldered, Morrison's life was changing for the better. His wife was about to give birth, but a heavy snowfall in Woodstock almost prevented her from leaving their mountain home. "Given that it took a mile of narrow road to get down our hill, a recurrent nightmare was that Van would have to deliver the baby," she shuddered. "Not a good thing!" Fortunately, Morrison was spared the embarrassment of playing midwife. At Kingston Hospital, he was joined by his former Woodstock friends, Jon and David Gershen. "David and I sat up with Van all night long while Janet was giving birth," Jon recalls. "We were the only people he called to be with him that night. You would think a whole entourage would have been seeing him through what was a long drawn-out labour. No, it was just the three of us."

In April 1970, the Morrisons were blessed with a daughter whom they christened Shannon Caledonia Morrison. Her middle name betrayed her father's fascination with his Scottish Presbyterian roots. He had already recorded a 15-minute instrumental titled 'Caledonia Soul Music' and the name would reappear frequently in future projects ranging from his publishing company to his next band. Bert Berns had once told him that soul music had its origins in Irish and Scottish traditional music. After learning that Scotland was known by the Romans as Caledonia, Morrison saw himself as embodying a tradition that embraced both Celtic folk and American R&B.

At the time of his daughter's birth, Morrison was pursuing the Protestant work ethic with conviction. On 3–4 April, he appeared at the Fillmore East, sandwiched between Quicksilver Messenger Service and the ludicrously hyped Brinsley Schwartz. In a legendary example of record company largesse, United Artists had flown over a hundred journalists to New York at a cost of £40,000 simply to hear the British group's much-touted debut performance. The stunt backfired for the Brinsleys, leaving Morrison the unexpected beneficiary. *Melody Maker*'s senior critic Richard Williams provided a glowing review, indicating that Morrison's American reinvention was now solidly underway.

Three weeks later, Morrison played the Fillmore West, San Francisco, and the show was broadcast on radio KPFA. In order to ensure her husband was happy, Janet had agreed to travel with the new baby. The Fillmore's proprietor Bill Graham was quick to notice Morrison's potential drawing power. Thereafter, he would book the Ulsterman with a relish that he usually reserved for the Grateful Dead.

Despite the Fillmore triumphs, Morrison still felt ambivalent about live performances and was prone to stage fright if the venue or audience was to his mind unsuitable. "I don't ever remember playing to empty halls," Platania stresses. "He definitely had a following. But, yes, I think the stage fright was there. At that point his motto was 'The show must not go on.'" Mary Martin was all too aware of his aversion. "He was holding his own in concert," she concedes, "but he didn't like to do it. He disliked the road immensely. He had these demons which used to dictate he was Van Morrison and it was difficult to go out and play a record. From *Moondance* – its promotion and marketing – you saw the rise of a guy who at one point had nearly burnt out a lot of promoters. Thanks to Bill Graham, he proved himself to be an able ticket-draw on both coasts."

Morrison's least favourite experience was performing at the large rock festivals which were coming into vogue in the aftermath of Woodstock. Playing on a bill with a dozen other acts in front of a rowdy and easily distracted audience seemed like a nightmare. A reluctant showing at Randall's Island Pop Festival that July confirmed Morrison's worst fears. It proved a bizarre and hilarious occasion. After belting out a couple of songs, Morrison felt deflated by the unexpectedly muted response. Upon further investigation, he noticed that some spectators seemed more intent on a paper-plane throwing contest. Incensed, he ordered the group to stop playing and sat down in protest like a rock 'n' roll Gandhi. Even then it took several minutes before the audience noticed and order was restored. After the show, Morrison made a promise to avoid the festival circuit whenever possible. "In America when I went solo I was sometimes playing huge places that I didn't think I should be playing," he later said. "Large venues and large sit-down audiences did not suit my performances and my low-key approach."

The same month as the Randall's Island debacle, Morrison appeared on the front cover of *Rolling Stone* in his first major American interview. Bypassing the usual critical interrogation, he submitted to a friendly Q&A session with his Woodstock neighbour Happy Traum. The interview offered a welcome career overview for those unfamiliar with the singer's history, and the only noticeable castigating comments in the piece were directed at Bert Berns. For Warner Brothers, the high-profile promotion was further proof that Morrison had arrived and they quickly encouraged him to complete a new album, preferably with a harvest of radio-friendly singles.

Morrison did not disappoint his record company. A pilot single, 'Domino', featured some startling Stax-styled sax work and a strident R&B riff that propelled the tune into the US Top 10. "The record company was asking me for singles," he said, "so I made some like 'Domino', which was actually longer but got cut down." The attendant album *His Band And The Street Choir* was a less focused work than its predecessors with a troubled history. Originally, Morrison had envisaged recording a pure a cappella album, featuring a select group of friends and musicians, including his wife Jànet. "I had a group of people in mind who were the Street Choir. They were living around Woodstock and we used to play together. I asked them if they wanted to sing . . . then people's personalities got involved in it and then the old ladies [wives and girlfriends] got involved in it and it ruined the whole thing . . . By the time I finished with it I didn't like it because it put me through so many changes. I was doing a lot of gigging and I was under pressure to get the album finished."

In order to ensure that the album was shipped before Christmas, discussion of the artwork was necessarily brief. This much was evident from the sleeve with its incorrect ordering of tracks and the promotion of an alternative title *His Band And Street Choir*. The gatefold shots of Morrison surrounded by the group with their wives and children were taken at a party for Planet's son Peter and were dismissed by the singer as "rubbish". Far worse was the visionary style front cover which included an hilarious image of Morrison in a full-length kaftan – the ultimate hippie apostle. "I was never a hippie," Morrison complained. "A lot of people think you're a hippie because of long hair and a beard. It's not true. I had long hair and a beard because where I lived it was extremely cold. That's the truth! Why are you laughing? I never had it in the summertime. I always had it in the winter because where I lived – upstate New York – there was snow for five months of the year." And the kaftan? "Well, I'd bought that in Woodstock, and that's what people were wearing. There was nothing else in the shops . . . The whole album package was very misleading. Even the title." Completing the effect were the sleevenotes from hippie nirvana, courtesy of Janet Planet, who implored "This is the album you must sing with, dance to, you must find a place for the songs somewhere in your life. They belong to you dear listener . . . There is so much light here, and incredibly I have seen Van open those parts of his inner self – his essential core of aloneness I had always feared could never be broken into – and say . . . yes, come in here. Know me."

Mercifully, the songs were superior to the artwork, but a severe disappointment when compared to the material on the previous two albums. Following 'Domino', there were a couple of upbeat singles

('Blue Money' and 'Call Me Up In Dreamland'), some passable R&B ('I've Been Working'), a failed attempt to recapture the spirit of 'Caravan' ('Gypsy Queen'), an insistent gospel refrain ('If I Ever Needed Someone') and some striking ballads ('Crazy Face' and 'Virgo Clowns'). Only the concluding 'Street Choir' hinted at the original a cappella concept and its closing words served as a reminder to critics and fans that the kaftan-wearing singer was no guru ("I just can't free you at all").

Morrison continued to tour, but was eager to downscale his live commitments. His favourite tipple on the road was still Johnnie Walker whisky. "I think he'd gone through a serious amount of alcohol before I'd managed him," Mary Martin considers. "There was a period of time before we got together where he was not taking good care of himself. But I know for sure he never did drugs. I can remember quite distinctly that he liked to drink. If there was a desire for Johnnie Walker some of us always tried to do in half the bottle before he got to it. Your job is to make sure half the bottle is gone. But he was not excessive. He had some demons that caused him to have a fear of the stage and sometimes his concerts were not as great as other times, but you could never tell. Some were absolutely magical and if you caught him on a good night you would remember it as long as you lived." Like other American commentators, his manager romantically imagined drinking to be part of his Celtic heritage. "He's Irish!" she cried. "All Irish 'poets' like to have a few little nips. Yeah, maybe he needed a few little drinks of Johnnie Walker and that's fine. He's outlasted so many people."

During his final days in Woodstock, Morrison was visited by former neighbours the Band and duetted with the doomed alcoholic Richard Manuel on the whisky-soaked '4% Pantomime', which later appeared on their album *Cahoots*. As he carefully noted, the '4%' referred to the difference in strength between Johnnie Walker Red Label and Johnnie Walker Black Label.

The Woodstock adventure ended in disillusionment for Morrison, who complained that the hamlet had become a tourist attraction since the release of the festival movie. Encouraged by his wife, whose family lived in California, he agreed to move to the West Coast. It made perfect sense to be closer to Warner Brothers headquarters and also signalled a new start for his own family.

Before departing for the West Coast, Morrison agreed to play two farewell shows at New York's Fillmore East (26–27 February) which proved notable for their energetic choreography and eccentricity. The set, which included a novelty cover of 'Buona Sera Senorita' and that favourite of Irish-American exiles 'Danny Boy', culminated in a dramatic reading of 'Cyprus Avenue'. Morrison lost himself in the song as if its meaning was unfolding for the very first time. Singing the lines inspired by Elvis Presley "My tongue gets tied . . .", he accentuated every syllable, distorting his features into a pained expression of self-awareness. After a short silence, he shrouded his face with his left arm, as though fearful of the audience. Then, finding himself caught one more time on Cyprus Avenue, he abruptly announced "I'm extremely wasted and I'm pouring spaghetti bolognese over you." A bizarre interlude followed with Morrison chiding the spectators for talking, then admonishing the lighting crew. "Can we turn the lights off?" he requested, prompting one wily patron to retort that it might be a better idea to turn off the amps. Apparently amused by the quip, Morrison teased the crowd with the words, "We could stop anytime. We could just stop." Then, in a frenzied finale, he ran across the stage, tripped over a lead en route, returned to stage centre, shook his head with such force that his shades flew from his head, then coldly stared at the audience before uttering the familiar litany: "It's too late to stop now." And that, ladies and gentlemen, was Morrison's goodbye to New York.

In April 1971, the Morrisons arrived in Marin County, approximately 10 miles north of San Francisco's Golden Gate Bridge. Their spacious three-bedroomed house was an impressive retreat, perched atop a hill and surrounded on all sides by redwood trees. Soon after moving in, the family acquired an array of pets including a cat (Sherbert), a dog (Tupelo) and a horse (Moondance). It sounded like rural bliss, but business concerns were never far away. Mary Martin had already sorted out Morrison's publishing, negotiating with Warner Brothers' Ed Silvers. Now it was time to renegotiate his record contract and ensure that his concert commitments were not too demanding. Unfortunately, rumours had already leaked in the UK music press that Morrison was intending to play at London's Royal Albert Hall and record a show for the BBC's *In Concert* series. A preposterous report in Ireland even suggested that he might return to Belfast to direct a film.

Anticipation remained high until 15 May when music press headlines screamed: "Van's Tour Off". Impresario Jo Lustig had received a call from Morrison's agent Ron Harriman informing him of the cancellation but no reason was provided beyond a vague allusion to management problems. Lustig duly hit out at Mary Martin accusing her of being "completely irresponsible, with no regard whatsoever for British audiences".

"I took the heat on that one," she says. "I can think of a million reasons why he was pissed off . . . Van had a difficult time contemplating going 'across the pond', as he would say. Whatever demons operated in him, there were certain things he would do and certain things he wouldn't do. Going across the pond held a great deal of fear for him. Perhaps he didn't feel successful enough. I don't think we ever properly discussed that." It later transpired that they had been unable to assemble a suitable group of musicians in time to make the visit economically viable. At this point, even the faithful John Platania was reluctant to join Morrison on the West Coast. "I didn't want to go out there," he admits. "It was too fragmented and I didn't see that it was a lasting situation."

Mary Martin vainly attempted to salvage some positive PR by convincing concert-goers and music press journalists that the cancellations were proof of Morrison's exemplary standards. "He decided it would be best for everyone concerned if he didn't go," she told the press. "It's only because he is so much of a perfectionist, that's the only reason. He wanted the best thing possible to go to England, which he couldn't do under the existing circumstances."

The manager fared considerably better when renegotiating Morrison's record deal with Warner Brothers. Briefly moving to Sausalito, she met the singer's lawyer and they agreed that it was crucial to secure a sizeable advance plus favourable royalty rates in order to allow him more time in the studio and remove the burden of financing his career through endless touring. "We got him such a substantial record deal that he decided that there was no need to have a manager, so I quit," she remembers. "That was my demise. I'd moved back to New York and it was difficult to manage someone in California if you like to be hands on . . . The fondest memory I have is of a young man who grew into a man. He'd married Janet and just had a child and that put a wholly different perspective on his life . . . I don't harbour bad feelings towards Van Morrison one bit and I'd venture to say that he doesn't towards me either."

History may have proved Martin correct but, within months of her leaving, Morrison was on the attack, railing against managers whom he appeared to regard as anachronistic, tin-pot svengalis. "I'm not the type of person who can have a manager. So right there that puts the music business through quite a few changes. It means that they have to deal with somebody who's not a puppet, who doesn't function like a clockwork robot. It's an old show business trend that we should get rid of. The sooner the better." Clearly, since his troubled relationship with Phil Solomon, Morrison had never been entirely happy with any manager. Although he demanded a high level of aggressive professionalism, he simultaneously clung to the reins of power, often withholding complete cooperation. Consequently, the manager's brief went way beyond merely administering the artiste's affairs. Often, it entered the more complex area of interpreting artistic caprice and contradictory needs. The role required the managerial realpolitik of a Phil Solomon or Don Arden combined with the sympathetic appreciation and psychological understanding of a Brian Epstein. In short, it was probably an impossible task.

After settling into his new home, Morrison tentatively opened his doors to several like-minded musicians. Pianist Mark Jordan fondly remembers one such evening when he and guitarist Doug Messenger played into the early hours. Morrison amazed them by ad-libbing lyrics in a way that they had seldom seen. Looking on, Planet played the dutiful wife. In the back of her mind was a wry, throwaway comment from the departing Mary Martin: "Don't let him get too happy – the music will start to suffer." "I thought at the time that it was a most shocking sentiment, and naturally paid no attention to her point," she remembers. "My one and only obsessive activity during my time with him was this fool's errand: to make him happy." For a time, she was successful. The relaxed, laid-back lifestyle and musical camaraderie obviously impressed the singer who said that the West Coast experience reminded him of his carefree early days in Belfast.

Such nostalgia was bitterly appropriate as every bulletin from Belfast sounded a foreboding note. The brief honeymoon period between the

Catholic community and the British Army had ended. Provisional agitators hardly needed to point out that the troops were acting for loyalist interests and sustaining an anti-Catholic statelet. When the Falls was raided and two Unionist MPs, accompanied by British troops, swanned around with triumphant smirks, the message was abundantly clear.

The assimilationist aspirations of the civil rights movement had been replaced by the new reality of separatism, with each community retreating to their respective enclaves and battening down the hatches. Paisley, who had correctly predicted this outcome, had meanwhile risen to unimaginable heights, winning the Westminster parliamentary seat previously occupied by O'Neill. Tension on the streets increased after the Provos began bombing in earnest. Soon there was retaliation followed by rioting in the Clonard. Confrontation between the IRA and the British Army escalated. In February 1971, the army had suffered their first casualty at the hands of the IRA. One month later, three soldiers were escorted from a Belfast pub and shot dead by the Provos. O'Neill's successor James Chichester-Clark resigned. Meanwhile, loyalist gun clubs emerged, spearheaded by the newly-formed Shankill Defence Association. That July, there was more outrage when the British Army shot two unarmed men in Derry. Worse was to follow.

In Belfast, many people avoided the city centre whenever possible. Snipers, exploding bombs, arson attacks, armed robberies, curfews and searches were now a part of everyday life. It was difficult to escape the conclusion that the province was heading towards a complete state of anarchy. Roy Kane still attempted to play during the early years of the Troubles, often appearing at the Trocadero in Cromac Street in the Republican Markets area. His world changed one evening while playing at a venue on the corner of Springfield Road and Falls Road. "There was a riot," he remembers. "Some guy didn't stop for the army at Springfield Road barracks and they shot him in the car and he was killed. That started the riot. A couple of guys on the door deserted the place to take part. Then the rioters got in and tried to come for some of us because we were Protestants. To my eternal thanks, the people and staff in that bar put us in the back room and defended us until some of the powers that be came down and sorted it out. When I say 'the powers that be' I don't mean the guys in the peaked caps, but the godfathers whom we never knew, saw or wanted to see. They got things quelled enough for us to get out. That was the day internment was brought in."

It was the morning of 9 August 1971 when British troops began Operation Demetrius. Under the Special Powers Act, the government was able to arrest, detain and imprison members of the public indefinitely without trial or recourse to legal representation. As a means of defeating terrorism, the policy proved disastrous. Intelligence, based on outdated lists supplied by the RUC, was appalling. Provisional IRA personnel were young, mobile and still largely unknown to the forces. Farcically, they knew of the intended sweep in advance and remained untouched by the operation. Those initially rounded up consisted of some old Official IRA men, long out of service, and a number of civil rights activists, socialists, and nationalist supporters whose only crime had been to question the status quo. The rest were predominantly political innocents, relatives of Republican sympathizers or those unlucky enough to be living at an address or a street where the army turned up at daybreak. Many others were dragged in for no apparent reason. The heavy-handedness of the forces provoked much bitterness, made worse by the realization that the arrests were sectarian in intent. Significantly, not one loyalist paramilitary or Protestant was arrested during the operation.

There was a grim triumphalism in the Shankill that evening manifested with typically raw Belfast humour. During the summer the UK charts had been dominated by Middle Of The Road's singalong 'Chirpy Chirpy Cheep Cheep'. Loyalist supporters now adopted its chorus as a chant and stood outside Catholic houses singing "Where's your daddy gone?" to distraught children. There was no humour in the riots that followed. Within days, 22 were dead in Derry's Bogside area alone. There were more casualties in the 96 hours following internment than there had been in the whole of 1970. The viciously partisan round-up was not only inflaming Catholic opinion but provoking loyalist institutions into ever stronger defence measures against imagined reprisals. In Sandy Row and the Shankill, a pamphlet was distributed urging "responsible citizens" to form platoons using "whatever weapons are available".

Gun battles and rioting increased and attitudes hardened as news filtered through of police brutality during interrogations. A number of detainees were subjected to routine beatings, forced to run barefoot across ground covered with broken glass or thrown blindfolded and screaming from helicopters, which they assumed were hovering in the clouds above Belfast rather than three feet from the ground. Others had liquid funnelled into their ears, their heads held under water, their testicles agonizingly squeezed, objects inserted into their backsides, plastic bags placed over their heads and their bodies burned on radiator pipes or electrically shocked with cattle prods. Deep interrogation techniques were also employed, with prisoners forced to stand spreadeagled against a wall for hours, sometimes days, while being bombarded with white noise and assaulted at the first sign of any movement. Sleep and food deprivation were accompanied by bizarre rituals. Interrogators climbed aboard men's backs and rode them like horses, some were forced to wear soiled underpants on their heads or subjected to sudden manic dramas such as the appearance of an aproned butcher, complete with bloodied cleaver. The brutal techniques, seemingly designed to unhinge detainees, provoked condemnation from several unexpected commentators, including novelist Graham Greene, who wrote: "'Deep interrogation' – a bureaucratic phrase which takes the place of the simpler word 'torture' and is worthy of Orwell's *Nineteen Eighty-Four* – is on a different level of immorality than hysterical sadism or the indiscriminate bomb of urban guerrillas. It is something organized with imagination and a knowledge of psychology, calculated and cold blooded . . ." Families were also targeted as part of the interrogation process, and some women detainees claimed they were threatened with rape. Five years later, the European Commission of Human Rights found Britain guilty of torture. An appeal to the European Court of Human Rights overturned that charge but upheld a decision of "inhuman and degrading treatment".

Far from quelling terrorism as intended, internment radicalized a large proportion of the Catholic population and served as a recruiting campaign for the Provisional IRA. The following month, a bomb exploded at the Four Step Inn on the Shankill, killing two people. Paisley was quick to appear on the scene, informing an angry crowd that he was forming a new political organization – the Democratic Unionist Party. Loyalists responded with the paramilitary Ulster

Defence Association, which paraded in the streets and promised to take on the British as well as the Provos in the event of any sell-out.

By now the religious communities were completely polarized and the once thriving Belfast music scene shrank into insignificance. Gerry O'Hare, who had been appointed press officer of the Provisional IRA's Belfast Brigade, set up Radio Free Belfast in response to internment. "It was a radio station that moved around the place. We would play rebel music and provide news bulletins with our slant. We were trying to keep one step ahead but my luck ran out. We'd only got it going for a few weeks when I was grabbed." On 9 September 1971, O'Hare was interrogated at Long Kesh. His superiors instructed him to say nothing and to resume his pirate radio propaganda after his release. "I was held for 48 hours and got the shit kicked out of me like everybody else. It was fucking hard enough, I can tell you. I was pinned, two fingers against the wall, feet spread out, and they'd put a foot out and bring you down. They were saying things like 'You won't be telling any more lies' and all that old shite. I was bollixed by the end of it. The British were happy to see me out of the way because there weren't many involved in PR. There was a great mistrust of the media [among the IRA]. But guys like myself, and later Danny Morrison, saw the value of using the media."

By this point, Belfast had changed beyond recognition. All the old faces from Morrison's past had either moved on, given up or found themselves straitjacketed in a moribund, culturally impoverished wasteland. Corvin had been manhandled by B-Specials, then fell out with *City Week* after submitting a piece on Australia which he foolishly insisted must be accompanied by a photograph printed upside down. Frustrated, he moved south to Dublin, where he was joined by his old friend Sam Smyth a few months later. Morrison's mentor G.D., unable to find work at home, joined a North Sea oil rig. "I was the only man in the world ever to sing or play guitar at the bottom of the North Sea. I had it filmed. I made a few old daft songs up about rigmen." Gil Irvine, once an R&B rebel, was now performing a staid repertoire at the Harland & Wolff social club to an older, predominantly Protestant audience that included Morrison's mother. "You'd play light pop, country and ballads and a couple of Van's songs if his mother was in the audience, maybe 'Brown Eyed Girl', but nothing too heavy," he stresses. "The punters would complain if you went into 'Gloria' – they'd call for a cardiac machine." Roy Kane, large of stature and heart, found his world diminished. "The Troubles killed the music scene," he concludes. "It'd make you cry talking about it. It was so sad. It was amazing how quickly it happened. Clubs closed and because of all the killings these shebeens opened. People didn't travel outside their areas, so there were extensions of football clubs and community clubs. The Protestants all went to the Protestant clubs and the Catholics all went to the Catholic clubs. It was a captive audience, they weren't going anywhere else. For me it ruined creativity in bands. People not only ghettoized themselves, they ghettoized music. Even people like myself who were cross community – we were afraid. We could play a Proddy club and knew we'd be safe. But we didn't know for certain that someone might not come around the corner and throw a bomb into the place because it was a Proddy club and we'd get blown up. There was fear."

Kane's fears were well-founded. Not long afterwards, a bomb left by the Ulster Volunteer Force at McGurk's Bar in North Belfast killed 15 people. Stormont denied that loyalists were responsible and alleged that Republicans had stored explosives in the Catholic bar. Years later, the truth emerged when a UVF man was jailed. At the time, of course, the British Army needed this disinformation to justify their failure to round up suspected loyalist paramilitaries in the Operation Demetrius debacle. Propaganda, pub closures, fear, bitterness and recriminations were now part of the everyday Belfast experience. It was not a pleasant time for a home visit.

As a panacea to the Troubles, Morrison focused his songwriting on his recent experiences in America. When he looked back nostalgically, it was no longer to Belfast but to 'Old Old Woodstock'. Increasingly, his new family life would take precedence over childhood memories. Not that mysticism and superstition were ignored or forgotten. Sometimes Janet Planet played the part of spiritual guide, a role previously allocated to Morrison by the American rock press. On one occasion she was awoken by a disturbing dream in which their house was destroyed by an earthquake. Convinced this was a prophecy of imminent doom, she immediately relocated the family to Albuquerque until rationality prevailed. Upon their return, Morrison made an unlikely attempt to ingratiate himself into polite society. "The funniest thing was when he wanted me to vouch for him to join a country club outside San Francisco," Joe Smith laughs. "He was taking up golf. I said, 'Somebody would want *you* in a country club?'"

With his five-year record contract signed and delivered, Morrison appeared more relaxed. While working on his new album during September at Wally Heider's San Francisco studio, he collaborated with his idol John Lee Hooker on two songs, 'Never Get Out Of These Blues Alive' and 'Going' Down'. Emerging from the sessions, Morrison offered the memorable tribute: "He could play the guitar until it talks."

That same month, Warners rush released 'Wild Night', a sax-dominated single intended to repeat the success of 'Domino'. It failed to set the charts alight despite featuring a rare collectors' B-side, an alternate take of 'When The Evening Sun Comes Down'. While his new album was in production, Morrison undertook some promotional appearances, including an informal show in front of 200 people at Pacific High in San Francisco. The small gathering were treated to some choice moments including a rendition of Doris Day's 'Whatever Will Be Will Be (Que Sera, Sera)' which segued into a raucous version of Elvis Presley's 'Hound Dog'. Even stranger was a tense reading of Dylan's 'Just Like A Woman' which took poetic licence with the lyrics ("Please don't let on that you knew me when I was weird"), even adding a homosexual element ("Your long-time curse hurts but it's clear there's this queer in here"). Unsurprisingly, there would be no sign of any queers or Madame George-like drag queens on his next album.

Tupelo Honey, released in November 1971, was probably Morrison's most accessible album to date and soon sailed into the US Top 30. Predictably, the ever restless Morrison had again reshuffled his studio group bringing back Connie Kay (*Astral Weeks*), Gary Malabar (*Moondance*) and Jack Schroer (*His Band And The Street Choir*). Ted Templeman, a former member of Harper's Bizarre who had recently worked with the Doobie Brothers, was appointed assistant producer. According to Morrison, they had intended to record a pure country & western album before diluting the work with older songs. What finally emerged was a far more commercial product.

The original concept was captured, probably unintentionally, in the inner sleeve artwork which displayed Morrison perched precariously atop a fence looking like a refugee from the OK Corral, complete with a cravat, Wild Bill Hickok-styled hair and a sizeable paunch. Janet's old friend Michael Maggid was the photographer chosen for the session, much to his surprise. His cover shot remains one of the few attractive images of Morrison ever captured on a record sleeve, although that was largely due to the presence of Janet Planet looking resplendent in flowing dress and cascading locks, riding a snow white horse, just like the romantically doomed character in 'Slim Slow Slider'. "They were very much in love," Maggid remembers. "She was a lovely girl, so pretty. The shot was taken in a town called Fairfax in Marin County. They owned a horse, Moondance, and it seemed a good idea to go to the local boarding stable where it was kept."

The idyllic pastoral scenery accurately reflected the country-tinged music on the album. 'Starting A New Life' sounded like a homage to Marin County and, significantly, followed Morrison's farewell to 'Old Old Woodstock'. 'Tupelo Honey' and 'You're My Woman' were both supplications to an idealized woman, probably Janet, but the emotional responses in each were subtly different. The former oozed tenderness and sweetness while the latter built upon a smouldering intensity which reached passionate proportions as Morrison offered a strangely pro-prietorial veneration ("I am your guiding light"), sounding not unlike a Free Presbyterian minister. There was a whimsical sheen to 'I Wanna Roo You' and a comic element to 'Moonshine Whiskey' with Morrison attempting to re-create the sound of fishes blowing bubbles.

Tupelo Honey was no masterpiece, but it was a considerable improvement upon *His Band And The Street Choir*. At a time when the rock élite were seduced by the lovelorn laments and steel guitars of country rock, Morrison emerged with a work that offered a soulful romantic veneer without lapsing into banal sentimentality. The album both celebrated and created a pastoral utopia that was as far removed from the brutal realities of Belfast life as could be imagined.

Locked up in Long Kesh, Gerry O'Hare had no opportunity to savour Morrison's latest work. Only weeks before, O'Hare's militant wife Rita had been shot during a gun battle with British soldiers in Andersonstown. One of the few women to achieve prominence in the overwhelmingly male world of the Provisional IRA, the former Rita

McCulloch was unusual inasmuch as she was the product of a mixed Catholic/Protestant family. Her Protestant father Billy McCulloch was an old-school Communist and her political education was forged in the years leading up to the Troubles. On Christmas Eve, Rita was released on compassionate bail due to the severity of her injuries and swiftly fled to the Republic, much to the embarrassment of her captors. Securing freedom might have been considered a propagandist victory for the IRA but their recruits were never encouraged to retire gracefully. The struggle was ongoing. Nearly four years later O'Hare was still active and displayed reckless audacity with an act worthy of a spy novel. Amazingly, she was caught attempting to smuggle a stick of gelignite inside herself while visiting an IRA prisoner in Portlaoise jail. The Special Criminal Court in Dublin sentenced her to three years' imprisonment. This established her reputation as one of the most notable female Republicans of the modern era, continuing a tradition that stretched back to the nationalist icon and champion of the Women's Prisoners' Defence League, Maud Gonne MacBride, and that towering, aristocratic socialist, founder of Fianna Éireann and president of Cumann na mBan, Countess Constance Markievicz. Rita O'Hare's story of political awakening, violence, capture, exile and incarceration was a salutary paradigm for the times.

FIFTEEN

Marin and Dublin

The same month that *Tupelo Honey* was released, Morrison announced that he would be retiring from major live performances for the foreseeable future. His farewell show at Winterland was a nervy affair which ended with support act Taj Mahal coaxing him back onstage for an encore. Weeks later he could be seen appearing alongside Rambling Jack Elliott at the Lion's Share, a small folk and blues club in San Anselmo. Thereafter, he played some low-key shows which were boosted by the presence of several guest stars. One night John Lee Hooker jammed, along with the Band's Rick Danko and Dylan's former sidekick Bobby Neuwirth. Morrison seemed to siphon renewed confidence from these impromptu appearances and undertook a major East Coast tour which culminated in a critically acclaimed performance at New York's Carnegie Hall. At some shows, Morrison was photographed wearing a Cossack hat, similar to the one famously sported by Ian Paisley.

Early in 1972, Morrison agreed to be interviewed by *Rolling Stone* magazine. He admitted feeling tense and uncomfortable throughout. One of his bugbears was the manufactured image that surrounded his media persona. He denied that he had any cult following but the magazine suggested otherwise by padding out the piece with a series of testimonials from *Astral Weeks* freaks. The participants in this pseudo-sociological aside included a depressed New Yorker who swore the album saved her sanity; an art student who drove a bus named 'The Van Morrison' through India and Afghanistan; and a psychologist who claimed to have discovered "higher truths" while listening to Morrison under the influence of "exotic gas". The accounts sounded apocryphal but perpetuated the myth of Morrison as the mystic guru of the West Coast. Although he resisted the claims of mystical status, Morrison nevertheless made himself sound pretty far out with tales of astral projection. "Every now and then I'll be lying down on the bed with my eyes closed and all of a sudden I get the feeling that I'm floating near the ceiling looking down."

The mystical image was combined with the pastoral poet, rural hippie look in a double-page spread borrowed from the *Tupelo Honey* photo shoot. In an attempt to deflate some of this iconography, Morrison allowed himself to be photographed with a coffee mug on top of his head. "That was certainly his idea of a clever joke, goofing around," photographer Michael Maggid notes. "I had a studio in my house then and he was in a good mood when he came over. He has a rather forbidding reputation, deservedly so. He was a private person in many ways and he was public property. Anyone who achieves celebrity status deals with it in their own graceful or not so graceful way. You're imposed upon by groupies or people who think they know you. I think he felt they were a pain in the ass and didn't want to be nice to them if he didn't feel like it. When I went to visit him some guy wandered into his home, just walked through the back door saying, 'I heard you playing and thought I'd come by and tell you how much I love you.' Van threw him out!"

One subject that Morrison could no longer avoid was the dreaded Irish question. It had become even more pertinent in the wake of the tragic events of Bloody Sunday (30 January 1972) when British soldiers shot dead 13 unarmed civilians during an anti-internment demonstration. The soldiers later claimed that they shot civilians aiming bombs at them, a charge completely unsubstantiated by forensic tests. At the inquest in Derry, Coroner Major Hubert O'Neill offered the chilling conclusion: "I say without reservation – it was sheer unadulterated murder." Violence escalated thereafter with Catholics rioting in the ghettos. The unrest even inflamed moderate opinion in Dublin where an angry mob burned down the British Embassy. In the House of Commons, the firebrand MP Bernadette Devlin physically assaulted Home Secretary Richard Maudling. In London's Oxford Street, 1,500 marchers turned out for a demonstration opposing British involvement in Northern Ireland. At the centre of the crowd was John Lennon carrying a placard which read 'For The IRA Against British Imperialism'. "The mood of the crowd was a happy one under the circumstances," he noted, "considering we were all there to show our sympathy for the 13 people who were mercilessly shot down by British imperialists." Lennon gave money to the civil rights movement and provided some forthright and ambivalent comments on the IRA. "If it's a choice between the IRA and the British Army, I'm with the IRA, but if it's a choice between violence and non-violence, I'm with non-violence."

A number of prominent civil rights and Republican speakers attended the demonstrations, among them Bernadette Devlin, Ivan Cooper and Gerry O'Hare. "I went because I was one of the first internees to be released," O'Hare remembers. "I was going to give a speech on behalf of the prisoners because my wife Rita had been shot." Lennon's pro-IRA comments did not go unnoticed by the Provisionals who were anxious to recruit his services for propagandist purposes. Although it has never previously been documented, Lennon agreed to a meeting with a member of the IRA in New York and promised to play two concerts in Dublin and Belfast in support of the movement. "Lennon was taken *very* seriously," O'Hare confirms. "There was nobody bigger than the Beatles. Paul McCartney had also written [about Ireland]. These were powerful people to have on your side. We were up to speed with Lennon because he was very interested [in the IRA]. In New York there were Irish Americans who kept him briefed. I was over on a speaking tour and within two days I was in his presence. I met him through a contact whose name I do not want to divulge. Lennon gave me the impression that he was genuine. He said he'd like to do the concert in Dublin but he insisted on doing one in Belfast too. I got the impression he wanted to do an additional show for the Protestant community. His problem was that if he left America he might not be able to get back in again and he was frightened by this." There was no easy answer to Lennon's dilemma and the concert plans were ultimately scuppered due to his immigration problems with the US authorities.

After Bloody Sunday, the Provisionals inevitably stepped up their terror campaign. In Belfast, the Abercorn Bar was bombed, killing two people and leaving over 130 injured. With opposition leader Harold

Wilson demanding an end to internment and even secretly meeting members of the IRA, Conservative Prime Minister Edward Heath needed to show a firm hand. Resisting Unionist protests, he suspended the Northern Ireland government at Stormont and introduced direct rule from London. Having determined Ulster policies for 50 years, the Unionists had finally lost their own parliament.

Soon after, Morrison was approached for an interview by the Dublin-based magazine *Spotlight*, whose readership was still predominantly showband-orientated. Questioned about Northern Ireland, he proved predictably evasive. "I'm definitely Irish," he pointed out, as if it were in dispute. "I don't think I want to go back to Belfast. I don't miss it with all the prejudice around. We're all the same and I think it's terrible what's happening. But I'd like to get a house in Ireland . . . I'd like to spend a few months there every year."

The Irish dimension was also explored with Janet Planet. "He is incredibly Irish to live with," she observed, without explaining what that vague statement actually meant. "And he's different too, he is . . . he's Irish. He comes from that whole thing. And of course he has a temper and he is always moving. He has to be doing something." Planet's characterization of the Irish as "different", ill-tempered and restless was worryingly close to the prejudicial Paddy stereotype. But what followed proved an illuminating and disconcerting description of a domestic life on the edge. "He doesn't like a lot of people around. With more than two people he gets uncomfortable. He doesn't like the idea of all those people looking at him. Really, he is a recluse. He is quiet. We never go out to parties, we never go out. We have an incredibly quiet life and going on the road is the only excitement we have." These comments betrayed the fragilities of a marriage heading for the rocks.

Since moving to Marin County, Planet had put her own acting career on hold, a sacrifice far from unique for rock wives of the period. Coincidentally, Neil Young's partner of the time, actress Carrie Snodgress, also went through a period of turning down acting auditions and living in seclusion at their remote ranch. Planet's sense of isolation was similar. "Janet wanted to get into acting but Van wanted a traditional woman at home and I know that bothered her," one associate recalls. "People used to offer her modelling assignments and

acting roles, but Van flatly refused to allow her to do these things. The
lack of socializing drove her crazy." Increasingly worn down by her
husband's darker side, bad temper and negativity, she grew tired of
playing the domestic goddess and longed for freedom. "I wanted more
than anything to make him happy, but I just couldn't do it. I was
confusing the music with the man. The music was everything you
could hope for as a romantic. The man was a prickly pear."

While the relationship foundered, Morrison was preparing his most
important and consistent album since *Moondance*. For a time, it went
under the working title *Green*, named in part after a song which would
be held over for a subsequent album. Whether Morrison fully realized
how provocative *Green* would have sounded to those of the Orange
persuasion back home in Belfast is uncertain. Fortunately, he was saved
from such controversy after completing a stream of consciousness
composition which bore the title 'Saint Dominic's Preview'. "I don't
know what 'Saint Dominic's Preview' means," he mused. "The words,
the syllables, just came out of my mouth and I wrote them down. I was
messing around with the guitar. But a funny thing happened after I'd
written the song. I was in Nevada and I picked up the paper and saw
an ad about a mass for peace in Belfast which was to be held at St
Dominic's Church, San Francisco. So to me that *wasn't* coincidence
and I worked out in my head that 'Saint Dominic's Preview' was me
seeing that before I looked at the paper. That's what I thought it
meant."

This spooky experience convinced Morrison to retitle his new
album *Saint Dominic's Preview* and photographer Michael Maggid was
again commissioned for the cover shoot. "We found a beautiful little
church in San Anselmo, Marin County," he recalls. Bizarrely, from the
various posed photos taken, the one chosen featured Morrison with his
legs akimbo, revealing a visible tear in his jeans just below the crotch.
"Oh my goodness," Maggid recoils. "We didn't even notice that
looking at the proofs. It was entirely unintentional, I can assure you."
The other distinctive feature of the artwork was the ominous absence
of Janet Planet. There were no unctuous liner notes or testimonials and
not even a picture of the woman whose model looks had glamorized
his recent record sleeves. "I got the feeling that he and Janet may have
split up then," Maggid reflects, "because she was nowhere to be seen.

I assumed they were no longer an item." Although nobody was keen to quiz Morrison about the impact of sensual artwork, let alone the state of his marriage, the sudden eclipse of Planet as an icon was significant. "I know to a certain extent my physical appearance played a part," she admits. "I was a sweet-tempered innocent; many beautiful pictures were taken and the people at Warners were always very eager to use them on the covers of albums. They also believed that my image, precisely because it was so enigmatic, was the perfect visual to describe what was going on musically. Everybody knew that I played some part in what was going on creatively, but nobody knew exactly how it worked. Van wasn't talking, and couldn't be pressed for details."

The emergence of *Saint Dominic's Preview* in July 1972 confirmed that Morrison was creatively at the peak of his game. Combining the pop R&B familiar from 'Domino', the gypsy apotheosis of *Moondance* and the improvisational aspects of *Astral Weeks*, the work was an expert distillation of all his musical strengths. The opening 'Jackie Wilson Said' was a powerful tribute to the soul singer whose catchy 'Reet Petite' would pass through the ages, entrancing listeners unborn at the time of its original release in 1957. Morrison's homage took on a new meaning three years later when Wilson suffered a heart attack on stage. While in transit to the hospital, an oxygen machine malfunctioned resulting in permanent brain damage. After weeks in a coma, Wilson recovered consciousness but was unable to walk, talk or feed himself and remained in a nursing home until his death in 1984. Morrison's sprightly memorial was subsequently issued as a single, but failed to reach the Top 40 despite including a rare B-side 'You've Got The Power'.

There were many other strong songs on *Saint Dominic's Preview*. The puzzling title track combined thoughts on a variety of subjects from Edith Piaf's soul to Safeway's supermarkets and even a reference to window cleaning in Belfast. 'Gypsy' was a reasonable attempt to recapture the excellence of 'Caravan'; 'I Will Be There' was nightclub blues; 'Redwood Tree' enshrined the beauty of Marin County. Impressive as these tracks sounded, they were dwarfed by the magisterial epics that closed each side of the album. 'Almost Independence Day', an evocative meditation on San Francisco harbour, was full of crescendos and vocal pyrotechnics that created an enthralling trance-like feel. Drawing on two chords, Morrison repeated lines and phrases, accompanied by the haunting Moog synthesizer work of Bernie Krause. The startling 'Listen To The Lion' was even better and ranks amongst Morrison's greatest work. A personal odyssey in the style of 'Madame George' and 'Cyprus Avenue', its execution was musically more sophisticated than either of those tracks. The dynamic range was impressively diverse, moving from forte crescendos to pianissimo diminuendos. Far removed from the Belfast landscape, it embraced Celtic mythology, using selected symbols, most notably the English national emblem, the lion. This was Morrison's attempt to capture the utopianism of Blake's 'New Jerusalem' in the mythical vision of Caledonia. During the 11-minute voyage, he sings, shouts, improvises lines, delays and omits them, until he symbolically re-creates the sound of an unleashed lion within himself. It remains a considerable achievement.

Saint Dominic's Preview provided Morrison with his first US Top 20 album and secured fulsome reviews. Even his old adversary Phil Solomon, who had good reason never to stomach listening to Morrison's work again, spoke warmly of the record. The singer had more pressing matters on his mind, not least the deteriorating relationship with his wife. That summer his parents arrived, ostensibly for a holiday, but also to offer moral support. After bloodstained Belfast, Marin County must have seemed like heaven. Obviously aware of their son's marital problems and determined to see their granddaughter while she was growing up, they decided to emigrate the following year. The Troubles played a key part in their reasoning. When they flew out to San Francisco, there was still hope of a breakthrough in Belfast. The IRA had declared a ceasefire and members of its political wing, including the young Gerry Adams and Martin McGuinness, attended a secret meeting with the new Northern Ireland Secretary William Whitelaw at his home in Cheyne Walk, London, on 7 July 1972. IRA Chief of Staff Seán MacStiofáin proceeded to read out a set of hard-line demands: the withdrawal of British troops from Northern Ireland; an end to internment; the release of political prisoners, and recognition that the people of Ireland should determine their future. Ultimately, the talks came to nothing and by the time the Morrisons returned to Belfast, the Provisionals had extended their bombing campaign prompting more working-class Unionists than ever to turn towards paramilitarism. It proved the most violent few weeks in the history of the Troubles. Drunken loyalists stormed into a Catholic house, murdered a mentally handicapped boy and then raped his mother. Days later was the horrific atrocity of Bloody Friday, 21 July, when the IRA planted 22 bombs in Belfast, killing 11 people and injuring scores more. At the end of July, nine people, one a child, were killed by IRA car bombs in Derry. Bloody Sunday, Bloody Friday and countless other incidences of British Army, IRA and loyalist violence had brutalized the province during the first seven months of 1972. "One of the reasons he moved his mother and father to the West Coast was because of that," John Platania confirms, adding that Morrison always preferred not to speak about the Troubles. This was not entirely correct. That summer, the singer was asked by an Irish journalist whether he would ever return home. "I think about going back," Morrison reflected, "but I know it's all changed. And I think of why I split – the hatred and the violence and the not caring. But I had friends there – and I'll go back to visit sooner or later."

Platania was regularly visiting Morrison in late autumn as preliminary work began on the next record. This time the sessions took place at the 16-track Caledonia Studios, which Morrison had built at the rear of his house. Recent tensions were evident during these recordings. "His back was hurting," Platania recalls. "He was lambasting the music business with 'The Great Deception', and he was on his back singing the song off the top of his head. Later, he revised the lyrics." Janet Planet was still around but by November she finally left Morrison, never to return. "By then our life together was very traumatic and horrible," she later confessed. "I couldn't stand any more of his rage as my daily reality. I worried about its implications on the children . . . I couldn't reconcile the fragile dream with the emotional chaos which kept intruding and crashing everything down."

As she drove away from the Morrison home, Janet literally underwent a change of identity. "Janet Planet was never my name until I met Van and it just came out of his mouth one day. Pretty much the minute we parted and divorced, that was the end of Janet Planet. It was a four-year deal." Planet's departure did nothing to help Morrison's temper. Still conducting business without a professional manager, he was often at loggerheads with the world. When the US label Parrot decided to release a compilation album titled *Them With Van Morrison*, the singer became so incensed that he wrote an indignant letter to the Assistant Attorney General of the United States insisting that the public was being defrauded and requesting help. It sounded like a massive overreaction.

Morrison's anger was not restricted to repackagers but also descended upon his record company, Warner Brothers. "There were points when he seemed certifiable," Joe Smith jokes. "He was so angry at everybody and everything with no grace or charm. You couldn't have a conversation with him, but he was always calling: 'Need a lawyer. These guys are doing this to me.'" His aggressive attitude was also evident from casual tirades in the music press. "It's ridiculous," he complained. "If I'm going to work with somebody, they're going to be working for me and not the other way around. The word 'product' keeps coming up. And if I'm the product, then these people are supposed to be an extension of how I operate. And if they're not, they're operating against me. And that's what happens to a lot of artistes. It's part of an older generation set up that has nothing to do with this generation. There's a brand new world now – our generation. I want to do it the way of right here and now. I don't want to live by anyone's old philosophies."

As Christmas approached, Morrison readied himself for a stand-off with Warner Brothers' Joe Smith in which he would unveil a list of petty grievances. Smith was not in the best of moods, having not yet done his Christmas shopping and the last thing he wanted was a visit from Morrison, accompanied by his lawyer and his agent. "They arrived late," he complains, "Van grunting. None of this bullshit list of crimes sounded so terrible. I couldn't do anything about these gripes until after the holidays, which is what I told them. One thing Van Morrison had never done was yell at me. Rule one: Don't yell at me! But Van did. 'You're a fucking liar,' he yells. 'I thought you were different.' I said 'Sit down! I don't want to hear from *you* again. You've got these guys, you pay them money, let them talk.' I turned to his men and said I would check this stuff out, but it would take 10 days and if we'd blown it I'd try and make it up to them. Van then slammed his hand down on my desk and broke this pen set there, both pens snapping off. Suddenly I got crazy. Van was leaning over the table and I grabbed him by the tie and I yanked his head down against the table.

He can't move and I'm choking him! I picked up the pen set and I'm about to hit him with it . . . and I flash on a *Rolling Stone* headline: 'Executive Kills Artiste With Pen Set!' I stopped, realizing what I was doing and said 'You guys get out of here!' They got up and walked to the door and Van stopped, turns around and says: 'Merry Christmas!' I snapped and threw the pen set, which stuck into the wall next to him." Immediately after the meeting, the still seething Smith phoned his colleague Mo Ostin and said, "I don't want to deal with Van Morrison anymore. Period."

Alas, Ostin fared little better in negotiating with the inflammatory singer whose rage was fiercer than a Shankill loyalist at a Sinn Féin meeting or a Falls Republican at a unionist rally. "He was as difficult as anyone I ever dealt with," Ostin admits. "He would explode on stage, in your office, having dinner at the house. I remember we almost came to blows because he kept insisting that I guarantee him a number 1 single."

Unsurprisingly, Morrison's ire with record companies increased after learning that Bang Records intended to issue another of their barrel-scraping compilations of his 1967 work. He reacted swiftly by instituting legal action claiming unpaid royalties. His solicitors Martin E. Silfen and Goldberg & Gershon calculated that the outstanding monies owed from Web IV for his musical compositions amounted to $50,000 and that a further $25,000 in royalties was due from Bang, each amount subject to interest. Ilene Berns responded forcibly in May 1973 by issuing a counter claim in the New York State Supreme Court on behalf of Web IV and Bang against Morrison, his publishing companies Van-Jan Inc and Caledonia Music, and Warner Brothers Records. A key point in the counter claim was the 'gibberish' recordings submitted by Morrison to fulfil his obligations to Web IV publishing. They were described as "completely unpublishable" due to their "vulgar and coarse language" and "devoid of any substance or originality or artistic merit". By reason of Morrison's "bad faith" Web IV had not accepted these compositions and were now arguing that his release was void and that he still owed them a substantial number of songs. In a humorous twist of the knife they kindly offered to return the 32 unpublishable 'compositions' that he had given them. As a consequence, they could lay claim to all the songs Morrison had written between 21 March 1967 and 21 March 1972. Additionally, they held Warner Brothers liable for copyright infringements in recording and releasing such material. They also pointed out that, under the terms of his release, Morrison had agreed to pay Bang 2 per cent of his royalties from any subsequent record deal for a period of one year. They insisted that Morrison "wholly failed" to account for these sums. These ripostes were very serious with potentially damaging consequences if upheld in court. The counter claims dragged on, with Warners denying the allegations. In the end, Berns held firm and released the album, *T.B. Sheets*. It was the first opportunity the public had to hear the original versions of 'Beside You' and 'Madame George'. The latter song proved a frightening revelation with its party-style arrangement in marked contrast to the more solemn rendition on *Astral Weeks*. Curiosity aside, *T.B. Sheets* added little to any serious appreciation of Morrison's work. The album also signalled an end to Ilene Berns' interest in the singer. Within a year, she would conclude this unhappy chapter of her life by selling her interest in Bang to CBS Records.

Meanwhile, Morrison faced more legal action, this time from his wife. In January 1973, Planet had instituted divorce proceedings citing "irreconcilable differences". She claimed a 50 per cent share of their property – which Morrison listed in court as a home studio in Marin County, a new Mercedes, $40,000 in savings, plus publishing and recording contracts. The biggest prize of all, of course, was custody of their two-year-old daughter, which Planet was expected to secure.

Morrison, meanwhile, struck up a relationship with Carol Guida, a waitress then working at his favourite restaurant in Marin County. He was also collaborating with Jackie De Shannon, who recorded his 'Sweet Sixteen' and their joint composition 'Sante Fe'. Despite reports of a planned duet album, nothing appeared, although she did join him onstage at some dates and added backing vocals to one of his new compositions 'Flamingos Fly'.

Selecting material for the next album was proving problematical. Since signing to Warner Brothers, he had stockpiled various songs, some of which were passed over to other artistes. Art Garfunkel listened to a batch and chose 'I Shall Sing', while Johnny Winter recorded 'Feedback Out On Highway 101'. Other titles like 'Bread Winner', 'Foggy Mountain Top', 'Coming Down To Joy', 'The Street Only

Knew Your Name', 'Try For Sleep', 'There, There, Child', 'Down To Earth' and a cover of Little Milton's 'Grits Ain't Groceries' were consigned to the tape archives. "I'm going to have to start doing double albums," he complained. "You put a lot of energy into it and then somebody at the record company tells you: 'Well, I think the promotion calls for a single album' and then you have to start editing everything. Take this song out, take that song out. It's hard to choose which to take off because they're all so different. You just guess or something."

Hard Nose The Highway, released in July 1973, testified to Morrison's artistic dilemma. In addition he faced the quandary of considering how much of his publishing interests might pass to his estranged wife at the conclusion of their divorce settlement. The album that emerged was an inconsistent affair of musically unconnected songs, blighted by a second side that seemed part of a separate concept. It began promisingly enough with the atmospheric 'Snow In San Anselmo', a meditative piece augmented by the Oakland Symphony Chamber Chorus, which celebrated the first local snowfall in over 30 years and included a veiled reference to his new girlfriend. By contrast, 'Warm Love' was a jaunty Top 40 hit and the title track an oblique and impassive commentary on his career and the state of the music industry. 'Wild Children', a celebratory roll call of post-war anti-heroes including actors Rod Steiger, Marlon Brando, James Dean and playwright Tennessee Williams, was a sparse, jazzy piece in 3/4 time which sounded oddly restrained. The opposite was the case with 'The Great Deception', one of the bitterest and, to later listeners, most dated songs in the Morrison canon. A sustained attack on plastic revolutionaries, pampered rock stars and hypocritical hippies, it resembled a parody of a mid-Sixties, Dylanesque protest song. "That's about things that I know about," Morrison said, "like the hippies who aren't hippies and the showbiz syndrome that's just raping people." Whether intentional or otherwise, the pointed allusions to John Lennon ('Power To The People') and Sly Stone ('Dance To The Music') added a personal sting to the commentary.

After the almost Paisleyite wrath of 'The Great Deception', the second side proved a strangely enervating experience. The insubstantial 'Bein' Green', the first non-Morrison composition to appear on one of his albums since *Blowin' Your Mind!*, was written by Joe Raposo and had been originally performed by the puppet Kermit the Frog on the children's television show *Sesame Street*. 'Autumn Song', a light jazz excursion with an indulgent, heavily drawn-out coda, led into a pleasantly innocuous rendition of the McPeake Family's 'Purple Heather', a traditional tune already recorded by artistes as varied as the Clancy Brothers, Judy Collins and the Byrds, often under the alternative titles 'Will You Go Lassie Go' and 'Wild Mountain Thyme'. Although it was possible to see subtle links between these songs via their autumnal imagery or the vaguely symbolic association of green with regeneration, the material was generally weak.

The saddest aspect of *Hard Nose The Highway* remained a secret for many years. Warners' tape vaults later revealed the extent to which it was a deliberately compromised work of self-sabotage. Included among its outtakes was the intriguing 'Madame Joy', an upbeat sequel of sorts to 'Madame George' that had once been intended for a film, and the reasonably good 'Contemplation Rose'. The piano-driven 'Not Supposed To Break Down' sounded like it was inspired by his divorce, as did the bitter 'Drumshanbo Hustle', whose title was inspired by a contentious gig that Morrison had played in Co. Leitrim during 1964 with the Manhattan Showband. Its lyrics were a bitter litany of unfair publishing and recording contracts, complete with a reference to a meeting with a judge, after which a curtain descends, possibly on the Morrison marriage. For personal or financially pragmatic reasons, the singer elected to confine this material to his archives thereby creating a false impression among fans and critics that his songwriting was on the wane.

Fortunately, Morrison was in the midst of what was arguably his greatest phase as a live performer. With the Caledonia Soul Orchestra, he had the perfect backing band, whose personnel included key players who had contributed to his recent albums. A brass and string section was added during some shows at the Troubadour in Hollywood, after which Morrison embarked on a major US tour. This was immediately followed by a European jaunt which brought even greater acclaim. Many fans had been waiting years to see Morrison in concert and he did not disappoint. His entourage first arrived in Amsterdam for a show at the Carre Theatre, which was preceded by a press conference.

Morrison proved cagey throughout, predictably dodging questions about Ireland and his recent marital problems. "I'm an artiste, a musician," he informed his interrogators, "and believe me there's a great difference. As far as I can see most so-called entertainers have what amounts to a canned show . . . the whole show business trip. That's definitely not our scene. We're a music band . . . To tell you the truth I wish I could just work clubs. But with a band of this size, it's not economical. I wouldn't even break even."

The shows in England, culminating at London's Rainbow Theatre, were a revelation. Morrison combined familiar songs from his recent albums with several blues workouts. The unreleased 'Paid The Price' was featured, alongside the epics 'Listen To The Lion' and 'Cyprus Avenue'. There was even room for the old hits 'Here Comes The Night' and 'Brown Eyed Girl'. "He had a funeral for a lot of his old songs onstage," John Platania quips. "With Caledonia, he really got off on performing. There was definitely joy getting onstage at that point. That was a wonderful time for everybody. It was really like a family. Ordinarily, with rock 'n' rollers, jazzers and classical musicians in the band, you'd think it was a three-headed serpent but everybody got along famously."

The family image was completed when Morrison's three-year-old daughter wandered on stage and was captured by photographers in a baby dress that barely covered her knickers. The only dampener on the tour was the cancellation of two concerts in Dublin. It was not until four months later that Morrison, in a signed statement, insisted that the shows had never been scheduled and blamed a representative of Warner Brothers for leaking erroneous information. Strikingly, nobody even mentioned the possibility of adding Belfast to the itinerary. It was difficult enough to see G.D. perform in his hometown these days, let alone an international star like Morrison. Civil unrest and IRA explosives were undermining Unionist supremacy and many working-class Protestants felt bitter towards an English and foreign media that still portrayed them as a privileged ruling élite. Gusty Spence, leader of the banned paramilitary Ulster Volunteer Force and a 20-year lifer in Long Kesh, made the pertinent point that living in Belfast was no Protestant picnic. "One has only to look at the Shankill Road, the heart of the Empire that lies torn and bleeding. We have known squalor. I was born and reared in it. No one knows better than we do the meaning of slums, the meaning of deprivation, the meaning of suffering for what one believes in, whatever the ideology. In so far as people speak of 50 years of misrule, I wouldn't disagree with that. What I would say is this, that we have suffered every bit as much as the people of the Falls Road, or any other underprivileged quarter – in many cases more so."

After returning to Marin County, Morrison faced familiar administrative headaches. Danny Cowan, manager of Alice Stewart & Snake, a Bay Area band who had accompanied the singer on the European tour, recommended his next-door-neighbour as a likely adviser. Stephen Pillster had just ended a spell managing Dan Hicks & His Hot Licks and after meeting Morrison agreed to take on the role of general manager of Caledonia Productions. "At that time he wasn't planning any touring," Pillster recalls. "He was finishing the mixing of his double live album." Pillster soon found there was much work to be done and hired Morrison a specialist tax accountant, a West Coast-based lawyer and a new agent. Among his first tasks was finding a way to alleviate his client's problems with the press. "I don't want to do any interviews," Morrison had insisted, then went on to complain tediously about how he had been misquoted and misrepresented. Pillster's solution was to hire a publicist, Cynthia Copple, to assist with the production of a 'media guide'. *Reliable Sources*, a booklet filled with flattering library clippings, was immediately sent out to journalists as an educational tool. Nobody pointed out the irony that Morrison's people were relying largely on the press they were denouncing in the first place. Originally, it was intended that the publication would be constantly updated but this novel, if hubristic, idea remained undeveloped.

A more worrying problem for Morrison was the denouement of his marriage. "He and Janet were separated and he was living at the house up in Fairfax which he wanted to get out of because there were so many bad memories there," says Pillster. "But he had a recording studio as well. When I first came on board a custody battle was going on. Van had a divorce attorney looking to make the case that he should get custody of his daughter. In the end, they got what they expected, which was visitation." Although Morrison was deeply hurt by the divorce and the loss of his only child, he soon came to terms with its inevitability. "It preoccupied him, "Pillster admits. "He has a tendency to focus on one thing at a time for whatever period. He seemed a little preoccupied with it for a few months, then the custody hearing came and went and he'd go on to the next thing." One relaxing activity that Morrison briefly enjoyed was playing his favourite records on a local San Rafael radio station, KTIM. While all this was happening, his parents completed their move to the West Coast and opened a retail outlet named Caledonia Records in Fairfax. "Part of it was the Troubles, and it was something they wanted to do," Pillster reckons. "I didn't get to know them too well. I think they mistrusted everybody around Van – me included."

In need of a holiday, Morrison unexpectedly returned to Ireland on 20 October 1973, spending most of his time hanging out with Donall Corvin, who was then living in the Dublin suburb of Sutton. It was Morrison's first appearance in Ireland since 1967. Within days, a road trip was underway. "I relaxed and toured," Morrison told the press. "I hired a car and drove to Cork, Cashel, Killarney and even saw the Blarney Stone." Returning to Dublin, Morrison was spotted at Gonzo's Rock Palace and other music haunts. He spoke vaguely about publishing a collection of poems he had written but subsequently admitted that he burnt the contents, which was probably a wise decision. Promising to return in the New Year with the Caledonia Soul Orchestra, he consulted with Corvin and then abruptly decided to make an impromptu appearance on Radio Telifís Éireann's *Talk About Pop*.

Producer Bill Keating was excited by the news. "We were delighted that he should want to appear on *Talk About Pop* and, recognizing his position in contemporary music, we paid him the courtesy of giving him the 30 minutes to do exactly what he wanted. If Morrison wanted to sing, dance, stand on his head, anything at all, all he had to do was let us know and we would arrange it." One condition RTÉ had insisted upon was that compere Tony Johnston should be allowed to open and close the show and ask Morrison a few questions. At the appointed time, Morrison turned up with Corvin and informed them that his friend would be conducting the interview. What followed was a televisual nightmare. Five numbers from a 13-song set were broadcast, including the rare 'Drumshanbo Hustle', an amusing, acerbic condemnation of the music business. It was not the music, however, that attracted attention, but Morrison's curt treatment of his host. Irate viewers bombarded RTÉ with complaints about Morrison's unsavoury display, forcing Bill Keating to make a defensive apology: "What you saw was one of the worst shows in the series. It was dreadful television and unforgivable rudeness on Morrison's part. Tony Johnston was made to look like an idiot, with Morrison strumming loudly and turning his back on him when he said anything. It wasn't even clever. It was just downright rudeness."

After the RTÉ calamity, Morrison returned to Sutton for the remainder of his visit. Corvin invited his friend Sam Smyth along for a possible interview, which never happened. Smyth was nevertheless entranced by Morrison's female companion, Carol Guida. "She was a one-woman metaphor for California. She would appear and give him some form of physiotherapy, massaging his neck to take the tension away. He spent a lot of time doing exercises, rolling his head around to unknot. He got his picture taken by my friend Tom Collins and there were two wolfhounds in the Sutton House Hotel. Tom got these dogs to put in the photograph and I think Morrison got a bit freaked out by it and thought, 'Symbolism! What is the symbolism of this? What are these people doing to me?' "

One new aspect of Morrison that Smyth and Corvin both noticed was that he appeared to be a teetotaller. "He'd given up drink," Smyth recalls. "It was a very good idea because he was really bad at it. He was never a social drinker insofar as people sit in a group and drink at roughly the same pace and get pissed together. He was snappy and argumentative with drink. Disagreeable. He was always a difficult guy. He wasn't relaxed socially."

Corvin, who was hoping to write a book on Morrison, grilled him at length about his career, even coaxing some information about the origins of 'Madame George'. Focusing on his Belfast past, Morrison became animated. Journalist Colin McClelland received a strange phone call from Sam Smyth asking for a favour. "He said Morrison was with Corvin in town and they didn't want anyone to know. He wanted somebody to find his Auntie Joy, who was apparently Madame George, and I was sent to find her. I was told to give her a message which was the phone number where he was staying." The only lead

McClelland received was a suggestion that one of the older residents of Hyndford Street might know of her whereabouts. Alas, his search proved fruitless.

As well as reminiscing about his childhood, Morrison reluctantly confided some political views. While he was in Dublin, three leading Provisional IRA members had escaped from the city's Mountjoy jail in a daring rescue during which a helicopter had actually landed in the prison yard. Gerry O'Hare, who was then in charge of ground control at Mountjoy, received an additional 12-month sentence for his part in the audacious adventure. Republican sympathizers the Wolfe Tones rushed out a single 'The Helicopter Song' to celebrate the event and it topped the Irish charts. Irish politics was on everyone's lips. As ever, Northern Ireland was back in the news with confirmation of plans for a power-sharing executive. A meeting at Sunningdale, Berkshire, at the end of the year would provide another false dawn for peace. Where Morrison stood on such matters was an intriguing question. "I think a musician who gets involved in politics is way out of his depth," he insisted. "Unless it's someone like Pete Seeger who really knows what he's talking about. Guys like Pete Seeger have been through all that and that's why they can talk about it. I think it's terrible for musicians to use their position to influence people like that. They don't have any right. Music is universal. It's not for one side or the other. Black. White. Music is for people. There's no sides."

Morrison's apolitical pronouncements were decidedly out of kilter with those of his great contemporaries such as Bob Dylan, John Lennon, Paul Simon and Neil Young, all of whom had included political songs in their repertoires. Dylan had built his career on the civil rights movement and although he abandoned protest songs in the mid-Sixties, his radical conscience could still be pricked by perceived injustices, as his statements and recordings in support of George Jackson and Hurricane Carter indicated. John Lennon, whom the Americans were currently attempting to silence with the same heavy-handedness they had used against Pete Seeger in the Fifties, had embraced left-wing politics with a vengeance. His pronouncements on Irish politics in 'Luck Of The Irish' and 'Sunday Bloody Sunday' were pure agit-prop and featured lyrics as venomous as any speech by Ian Paisley. When the IRA-supporting Lennon sneered "You Anglo pigs and Scotties sent to colonize the North/You wave your bloody Union Jacks . . .", he was not only attacking British imperialism, but laying a firm blow against the Protestant hegemony. "Repatriate to Britain all of you who call it home" was as anti-Orange as anything ever voiced in popular song. Even the PR-conscious Paul McCartney joined the campaign for a united Ireland with the characteristically polite 'Give Ireland Back To The Irish'. Morrison's old friend Phil Coulter, best known for composing winning or runner-up Eurovision Song Contest singalongs, found his political voice with one of the best and most moving laments of the Troubles in his paean to Derry, 'The Town I Loved So Well'. Countless other artistes have commented on the situation in Ireland, often with eloquence, passion and power. Indeed, it is possible to argue that, contrary to Morrison's statement, the removal of politics from popular music would neuter a potent form of art.

So what did Morrison really think about the Troubles? "What I'm not part of is the hatred thing," he volunteered. "Well, I *hope* I'm not . . . I don't think I have a specific country to be patriotic about. As for dying for my country, I wouldn't do it. I don't know what that means . . . What difference does it make where you were born? It's just a piece of land." Pressed for a political viewpoint, he concluded: "All I can say is that I'm neutral."

Morrison's professed neutrality might have sounded admirably apolitical to some, but others viewed such fence-sitting as a political comment in itself. Civil rights campaigner Michael Farrell argued the case with conviction. "No compromise is possible in the North any longer," he noted in the mid-Seventies. "To get power and hold on to it, the loyalists must detect and destroy minority resistance. To avoid enslavement the minority must destroy loyalism. No-one can be neutral in this struggle."

Of course, Morrison was in a very difficult position and any comment from him on Northern Ireland entailed certain risks. His musical silence on the issue spoke volumes about his own upbringing in Orange Belfast. What was he to do? Whether he was truly as 'neutral' as he claimed was impossible to ascertain. An apolitical stance enabled him to avoid many unpleasant questions and considerations about his birthplace. If he had any sympathy towards Catholic and nationalist grievances, his former neighbours or family friends in East Belfast would most likely have preferred not to hear them. Alternatively, if he was a fainthearted loyalist or a closet Orangie with a secret sash and a bowler hat, there was little to be gained and much to be lost from eulogizing the Union Jack. Not only would this have been counter to the gospels of John (Lennon) and Paul (McCartney), but beyond the proscribed sympathies of the rock world where radical chic was all. A pro-Unionist voice would have been akin to a rock singer supporting Spiro Agnew and Richard Nixon at the height of the Chicago riots. Whatever Morrison's true politics, it would always be less troublesome to play the neutral card. Invariably, he followed the famous Northern Ireland dictum: Whatever you say, say nothing.

Despite his political elusiveness, Morrison retained powerful and unresolved feelings about Belfast. Although these would normally have remained concealed, the memory of his final days there in 1967 stirred up bitter memories and angry thoughts. "I felt the antagonism, but not only in religion," he admitted. "I felt the antagonism in everything. No matter what you try to do in Belfast they're down on it. Everything I tried to do in Belfast, they put the screws on it immediately. That's just the way people are brought up there. I don't know."

It was ironic that after returning to Ireland for the first time in seven years, Morrison should leave behind a sense of disappointment and, thanks to his television appearance, a lasting impression of his boorishness. At least the vacation had a positive effect on his songwriting. In the space of three weeks there, he completed eight new songs destined to form the backbone of his next album.

SIXTEEN

Veedon Fleece

The visit to Ireland had a profound effect on Morrison at a time when his life was at a crossroads. Increasingly, he began to question everything, including his place in the American rock culture. Ever the pragmatic Protestant, he had fallen in sufficiently with Warner Brothers to be promoted successfully as a singer-songwriter for the hippie generation. Championed by both Bill Graham Enterprises and *Rolling Stone* magazine, he represented the soulful Irishman in exile for a media in search of such a stereotypical image. Even the British music press tended to see him more as an American artiste than as one of their own. Not many would have wagered that he would ever return to the UK. Even his accent was now an odd hybrid of East Belfast drawl lightened by traces of West Coast American argot. In interviews, he spoke of recording an American-style country album and claimed to have completed covers of such standards as 'Banks Of The Ohio', 'Wild Side Of Life' and 'Crying Time'. There was even desultory talk of a possible Christmas album of festive favourites.

The public focus on all things American distracted attention from Morrison's parallel fixation with Ireland. Significantly, the compositions he had sketched during his recent visit now took on considerable artistic importance. At the time, Morrison was seeking relief from the break-up of his marriage and the pressures of the music business by undergoing Gestalt therapy, a Zen branch of psychology that promoted self-awareness and emphasized the importance of obliterating the pain of the past through immersion in the present. Its therapeutic techniques were primarily concerned with filling in holes in the personality by owning the qualities that you project upon others – for example, imagining a friend is jealous of you, whereas you are actually jealous of them. Gestalt therapists believed that by reclaiming such projections and combining fractured aspects of the personality into a resolved organism, the individual could realize its full potential. An emphasis on the self, as opposed to the self-image, was intended to make the patient feel an active rather than a passive performer in the drama of their life. Morrison later admitted a sense of frustration with his public image at the time, which he felt had been projected upon him by the media, particularly the US rock press. What no doubt appealed to him about Gestalt was the stress on 'awareness' and 'potential' in place of any attempt to adjust the individual to the needs of society. Thus, instead of a certain behaviour being called neurotic, it might be seen as a strategy that the person has adopted to survive the rigours of a particular situation. Equally important was the realization that the Holy Grail of Gestalt seemed to be a state of consciousness similar to that experienced by healthy young children who tended to live in the moment, largely unencumbered by an awareness of passing time. This was the type of visionary experience that Morrison had been attempting to articulate and capture on *Astral Weeks*. It all led back to his childhood in Belfast.

Morrison was still willing to keep his promise and return to Ireland for some concerts in March. Promoter Noel Pearson had flown out to Marin County to finalize arrangements for the singer to appear at the Olympia Theatre as part of Dublin's Music Week festival. British dates were subsequently booked but Belfast was again conspicuously absent from the itinerary. Stephen Pillster claims he spoke with an Irish promoter, but was warned off. "The reason he gave was that they couldn't guarantee Van's security and that there had been death threats, or some threats against him. Whether that was true, I don't know. It may have been that they just didn't want to do dates in Belfast. When somebody says to me 'there are death threats' in a place where you read every day about bombs . . . I'm going to listen."

The safety issue may have had some validity as the ongoing debate over power-sharing and the proposed implementation of the Sunningdale Agreement had galvanized Unionist opposition. Paisley was busy disrupting meetings of the Assembly and calling on Protestants for "drastic action" to end the "perfidious agreement" which he dubbed "a massive confidence trick". Edward Heath had replaced

Harold Wilson as Prime Minister, thereby adding more uncertainty to the future of Northern Ireland. Meanwhile, the IRA had extended its bombing campaign to the British mainland. It was an emotive time as four Provisional prisoners, including Marion and Dolours Price, had started a hunger strike and were being force-fed. Tensions were high.

In advance of Morrison's arrival in Britain, Warner Brothers issued the celebrated double live album *It's Too Late To Stop Now*. Even as it reached the public, the shock news filtered through that Morrison had parted company with the Caledonia Soul Orchestra. "He makes life very difficult for himself," Phil Coulter observes. "He's very restless – physically, emotionally and creatively. He's totally unpredictable. Look at Caledonia. In Van's book, the way to react to that success was to dismantle it." At least the album served as a tribute to the ensemble and was rightly acclaimed as one of the best double live sets of the era. Carefully compiled from performances at London's Rainbow Theatre, the Troubadour in Hollywood and the Santa Monica Civic Hall, the work featured material stretching back to the Them days and beyond into blues, jazz, soul, gospel and R&B. Effectively, it was a live anthology of Morrison's musical history and a testimony to his longevity and maturity as a performer. Revealingly, none of the band heard its contents until they received completed acetates. "It's common practice to go back and fix things, but not with Van," says bass player David Hayes. "I think that's what helped make it one of the best ever. When I speak to him about that album he still talks about it as having marked the peak of his career. He really feels he was on to something very special."

Back in the States, Morrison announced the formation of the new style Caledonia Soul Express. He retained the Orchestra's rhythm section (David Hayes and Dahaud Shaar), but added James Rothermel (horns), James Trumbo (keyboards), and Ralph Wash (guitar). They played some warm-up gigs, including a show in Cambridge, Massachusetts, attended by Morrison's former flute player John Payne. "I went to the soundcheck, walked up on stage and said, 'Hi, Van'," Payne recalls. "He looked kind of spaced. I said, 'Remember me?' As I'm saying this, he looks up, turns around and walks away. I felt my stomach going. I was standing there trying to figure out what was going on, not knowing what to do. The guy I used to see every day for months had just walked away from me. Then he turned, came back and put out his hand. It was a real limp handshake. He made the gesture. I started talking, then I noticed he was looking glazed and wasn't really paying attention. He just didn't seem interested. I maybe asked him a couple of questions and he didn't answer much, so I said, 'Good to see you' and walked off." Later that evening, Payne placed himself near the front of the stage and was quietly amazed when Morrison played a set dominated by the twin epics from *Astral Weeks*, 'Madame George' and 'Cyprus Avenue'. "I swear he was looking straight at me from the stage," Payne concludes. They would never meet again.

Following a St Patrick's Night appearance at New Jersey's Capitol Passaic Theater, Morrison flew to England and promptly fell victim to a bout of flu. The English shows were cancelled and the much-anticipated Dublin appearances were jeopardized. Acutely aware of the disappointment and resentment resulting from the postponed Dublin shows the previous year, Warners took the unusual step of submitting a signed doctor's certificate to the music press for publication. It confirmed that Morrison had a "high fever and a respiratory disease".

Although in a severely weakened state, Morrison decided to avoid any further flak from the Irish press by fulfilling his obligations. Unfortunately, playing Dublin in favour of Belfast had already provoked criticism from Northern journalists. "People regarded him as a traitor," remembers Colin McClelland, who penned a preview which ended with the words "How can you stand up an entire nation?" Music and political reporter Chris Moore wrote an even more critical piece in the Belfast press which so outraged Violet Morrison that she sent a testy response from California insisting that she and her husband had begged their son not to risk his safety by playing in his home city.

The Dublin concerts inevitably proved troublesome. A large contingent of fans travelled down from Belfast, many of them disgruntled. "Has he gone over to the other side?" was a question proffered by some of the Protestant spectators. One denizen of East Belfast spent much of the show vainly screaming out a request for 'Cyprus Avenue'. Originally, Morrison had intended to include an acoustic segment at the start of his set, but that idea was abandoned. Instead, he moved into a tentative 'Astral Weeks' backed by the Caledonia Soul Express. He sang in short, sharp gasps and continually glanced towards the wings. As the number ended, he walked off for an unscheduled break, leaving the band to play an instrumental version of 'Moondance' during which David Hayes apologized to the audience. "They just put me on stage while I was sick," Morrison later complained. "I didn't know what was going on. I'd just got out of bed and taken a bunch of stuff that was supposed to make me feel good. I didn't feel good at all." After re-emerging, Morrison completed a one-hour set which ended with 'Here Comes The Night' followed by lacklustre applause. He returned for encores of 'Come Running' and 'Gloria', then retired to his sick bed before completing a second set at the venue later that evening. Sam Smyth, who attended the gigs with Corvin, was struck by the number of Ulster accents around him. "There was a huge crowd down from Belfast. He felt enormous pressure on him. Anybody who was there will remember it. They were a terrific band and very American in style and sophistication."

Outside the Olympia, visiting journalists were nonplussed by the negative reactions of some of the Belfast fans. "I didn't come here to enjoy Van Morrison," one volunteered, "I came to criticize him. You've got to understand it, man . . . my girlfriend lives around the corner from Cyprus Avenue in Belfast and I still live there and that should tell you why I came here. I don't want to enjoy Van Morrison . . . I hate him. Tell me . . . why didn't he sing 'Cyprus Avenue'? Where's his head at not to do something like that? Why won't he play up in Belfast?"

On Saturday 30 March, Morrison returned for two more sets, culminating in a lengthy 'Listen To The Lion'. A rowdy crowd from Belfast in the balcony area demanded another encore, then a bottle was thrown onto the stage, prompting instant chaos. "The last train to Belfast had already gone, so they weren't in any hurry to leave," Pillster recounts. "We had the house-lights up and figured it would end of its own accord. They threw bottles and knocked over a saxophone." At this point, road manager Ed Fletcher walked on to appeal for calm, then became involved in a fracas with some unruly patrons. "Eddie was off the stage, which wasn't good," Pillster frowns. "A big mistake. I went into the crowd to try and get him out and there was pushing and shoving, then somebody called the police. When they arrived it was over and I had strong words with the promoter, Noel Pearson. We got into a shouting match and he said 'Arrest them!' So Ed and I got taken away by the police. They were very nice to us and brought us tea and biscuits. An hour later, Donall Corvin, who was the publicist, turned up and told the police his version, which matched ours. I think Noel was on his way down to drop any charges. He walked in, saw Corvin and asked him what he was doing there. Donall said, 'I'm here to tell the truth.' Noel replied, 'I don't pay you to tell the truth – you're sacked!' Then a sergeant came in to tell us, 'Mr Pearson has dropped the charges.' I said, 'That's very generous of Mr Pearson.' Van, meanwhile, knew nothing of this. He was already back in his hotel asleep." After the garda released the captives, they were driven to Corvin's cottage where they stayed up till dawn listening to Boz Scaggs records. "It was quite an evening," Pillster concludes.

For the second time in under a year, Morrison left Ireland amid gossip and petty controversy. Retreating to the continent, he played several more dates, including a memorable appearance at the Falconcenteret, Copenhagen. Prior to the show, Morrison moaned about having to regurgitate over-familiar songs. "There was a full moon," Pillster recalls. "He told the band to tear up the set list. He went onstage and did some songs that had never been released, plus covers he hadn't done before. It was a really eclectic set and he was very into it. The audience was extremely reserved. I was thinking, 'They hate this.' But when it was all over they gave him a standing ovation." After completing a couple of rescheduled nights at London's Hammersmith Odeon, Morrison returned to the States. Throughout the Irish tour, he had been comforted by his girlfriend Carol Guida, whom the press referred to as his fiancée. "I think you could call her a fiancée," Pillster says. "It was her idea but Van went along with her and got her a ring. She was his masseuse. Later, there was a period of time when I didn't hear from him and when he popped up again she was off the scene. She called herself his fiancée and sported a ring but I never knew or got the idea that Van was very much into it." If Morrison was on the rebound, then it was not only his personal relationships that were affected. Within months he decided to dismiss the Caledonia Soul Express, close Caledonia Productions and discharge Pillster.

Taking stock, Morrison played another of his low-key gigs at the

Lion's Share in Marin County, a venue that always provided solace during periods of personal or musical upheaval. Backed by the club's piano tutor John Allair and drummer Steve Mitchell, Morrison performed a soulful set which included covers of 'Rock Me Baby' and Lenny Welch's 'Since I Fell For You'. Throughout the evening, he lost himself in powerful harmonica workouts, seldom heard since the glory days of the Maritime.

By now, the Maritime was a distant memory for Morrison, who had no plans to visit Belfast in the near future. It was just as well since Northern Ireland was about to come to a standstill. The 'No Surrender' siege mentality that always characterized Unionism reached a potent peak during May when the Ulster Workers Council elected to take on the British government and end the political power-sharing plotted at Sunningdale. An all-out strike threatened to render the province ungovernable. At first, it seemed that grimmer news might distract attention from the strikers. The UVF chose this moment to launch a twin bombing campaign in Monaghan and Dublin. In one of the most sickening episodes of the Troubles, 32 people, including two baby girls, lost their lives. The bombers were never apprehended. The paramilitaries were determined that the Workers' strike in Belfast would not be marred by violence, although in order to ensure its success they were obliged to threaten scabs at gunpoint and menace shop owners with promises of petrol bombs. Within days, the UDA were overjoyed to discover that the populace were on their side. In Catholic communities the IRA took on the unlikely role of mobile grocers, providing milk and bread for those trapped in their homes. In London, the recently re-elected PM Harold Wilson lost his patience and addressed the nation on television with the memorable phrase "Who do these people think they are?" In a damning and provocative summation, he referred to loyalist men and women as people who were "spending their lives sponging on Westminster and British democracy." His comments fanned the flames of support for the strike and, in a typical example of Northern humour, many started wearing little sponges on their lapels. A few days later, the Executive foundered and Sunningdale was history. Paisley was practically dancing in the streets and celebratory bonfires were lit in the Shankill. The politics of 'No Surrender' had prevailed.

One month later, Morrison was back in Europe for another tour with a new line-up of musicians featuring keyboardist Pete Wingfield (an alumnus of Jellybread, the Keef Hartley Band and Colin Blunstone), Motown bassist Jerome Rimson (formerly of the Detroit Emeralds) and ex-Crosby, Stills, Nash & Young drummer Dallas Taylor. Once again, Belfast was not included in the itinerary. In order to promote the visit, Warner Brothers issued a surprise single, 'Caldonia (What Makes Your Big Head Hard?)', a song made famous by Louis Jordan in 1945. Recorded with the Soul Express during their recent stay in Holland, this retitled adaptation of Forties Swing was quite unlike anything Morrison had previously recorded. The B-side 'What's Up Crazy Pup?' also echoed the jive/city blues style of Jordan, Slim Gaillard and Cab Calloway, a form that Bill Haley had later modified in the Fifties on hits like 'Shake, Rattle And Roll'. An album of Dixieland Swing would have proven an interesting concept at this stage of Morrison's career, but 'Caldonia' was a single rarity bought only by dedicated fans.

The summer tour began with a controversial appearance at the Montreux Jazz Festival during which Morrison was derided by a female spectator and responded with a frightful obscenity. His foul language was enough to secure a headline in the British music press: "Van Gets The Bird". It was unfortunate that more attention was not focused on the music. With Peter Van Hooke replacing Dallas Taylor, the band continued their European tour, which featured a formidable selection of new compositions including 'Boffyflow', 'Heathrow Shuffle', 'Naked In The Jungle' and 'Mechanical Bliss'. Several of these songs were recorded in Holland for an album that remained unreleased. "I'm really happy with this one we just cut," Morrison noted at the time. "We just went in and did it the way it should be . . . It's everything, it's like blues, jazz and R&B."

Following an appearance at the Knebworth Festival in Hertfordshire, Morrison and his trio embarked on a 25-date American tour with a small crew and minimal sound equipment. Improvisation was the norm and audiences showed due respect. "They put up with a lot," Pete Wingfield recalls. "Sometimes Van would suddenly decide he didn't want to play the set we'd worked out, and he'd launch into a number he'd just written and which we'd never heard before . . . We had to just busk along in front of thousands of people with him calling out the chord changes to us between the lyrics . . . there were very little formal arrangements. Van controlled everything with hand signals."

By the autumn, Morrison was winding down his touring commitments in anticipation of an extended period of absence. Since establishing himself as a major concert draw in America, he had been lionized in the US music press to such an extent that the image of Van Morrison as the 'Irish mystical guru' was pervading his own sense of self. "It all became completely unreal insofar as what they were putting out about me," he complained. "They were putting me on this pedestal, writing all this stuff that really had nothing to do with me . . . Even the way people were reacting at gigs, real silly. So I had to get away."

This eventful period was punctuated by the release of *Veedon Fleece*, an exemplary album that perhaps represents his greatest and certainly most underrated achievement. It was the most penetrating distillation of the Irish experience since *Astral Weeks*. Inspired by his visit to Wicklow and interest in Gestalt readings, Morrison shifted the landscape from Ulster to Southern Ireland and, instead of reflecting on an idealized past, concentrated more on his experiences in the present. Northern Protestant fans who had asked the provocative question "Has Morrison gone over to the other side?" would have found much to exacerbate their paranoia on this album. There were no allusions to Sandy Row, Cyprus Avenue or any other Orange strongholds here. Instead, the territory featured place names that Ian Paisley would have damned as distinctly foreign: Killarney, Arklow and, most controversially, "God's *green* land".

The album opens with 'Fair Play', a title inspired by Donall Corvin, who had a habit of repeating the Irish colloquialism "fair play to you" as a wry compliment. After praising the blue lakes of Killarney and name-checking Oscar Wilde, Edgar Allan Poe and Henry David Thoreau, Morrison takes this well-arranged 3/4 ballad into a stream of consciousness rap conjuring phrases plucked from his memory such as the familiar loyalist/Republican euphemism 'tit for tat', the playground chant 'Geronimo' and the Lone Ranger's famous cry to his beloved horse, 'Hi Ho Silver'.

'Linden Arden Stole The Highlights', the tale of an Irish expatriate in San Francisco, inevitably recalls Morrison's own move to

California. However, Linden Arden is essentially mythological – the Irish warrior transposed to American soil. A fighter, a hard drinker, a lover of children who still attends church on Sunday, and a vengeful law breaker, Linden Arden emerges as a cross between Desperate Dan and John L. Sullivan. If there is a subtext to the song, it lies in the extremely violent imagery, particularly the gruesome allusion to decapitation, a method of execution that was attempted by extremists within the UVF.

The refrain about being lonely and living with a gun which segues into the succeeding 'Who Was That Masked Man?' is another ambiguous allusion. Once again, the title refers to the masked hero of the television series *The Lone Ranger*, whose exploits invariably closed with a grateful recipient of his frontier justice speculating about his true identity. However, the theme of the song is totally detached from its catchy title and, as its identical melody indicates, this is Linden Arden, Part II. Here the heroic Irish emigrant is demythologized and presented as an ossified icon: fearful, suspicious and isolated. There is also the chilling sense of a contemporary parallel with Irish paramilitarism familiar to anyone witnessing masked, balaclava-clad UDA or IRA men.

'Streets Of Arklow' features a dominant recorder playing a Celtic melody line augmented by textured strings. It is clearly a tribute to the Wicklow town that Morrison, his girlfriend and Corvin visited during the 1973 homecoming. The idealization of Éire here as God's green land, combined with the unforgettable cover artwork featuring Irish wolfhounds at Sutton House, completes this rare example of Morrison embracing an Ireland outside Ulster.

The side-closing 'You Don't Pull No Punches, But You Don't Push The River' remains Morrison's most accomplished composition to date, an experimental peak which took a step beyond even his most ambitious work. By his own admission, its inspiration owed much to his recent readings in Gestalt therapy. The song's elusive and allusive title was adapted from Barry Stevens' *Don't Push The River (It Flows By Itself)*, a journal of her experiences at the Gestalt Institute of Canada on Lake Cowichan, British Columbia, at the end of the Sixties. What begins as a love song reflecting on a girl's childhood moves gradually into a journey to the West Coast of Ireland in search of the "real soul people". Without warning, Morrison suddenly transmogrifies the geographical landscape taking us beyond the naturalistic scenery of Ireland with its beaches and cathedrals into a new realm inhabited by William Blake, the Eternals from *The Book Of Urizen*, the silent guru Meher Baba and the Sisters of Mercy. At this point, Morrison's personal odyssey takes on a mythological status as he begins the search for the Veedon Fleece. Whereas Yeats would have populated the mythical landscape with Irish heroes such as Cuchulain, Conchubor or Fergus, Morrison typically uses his private mythology in which he becomes the Jason-like figure leading the quest. Musically, the song combines a decorative woodwind section with the dramatic use of strings, both played in block chords. Moving along in 6/8 time, it reaches a musical crescendo even before the arrival of Morrison's vocal. The transition from an organic to a mythological landscape is translated musically in dramatic fashion through the successive use of plaintive flute and soaring strings. These dynamic contrasts are echoed in the narrative technique which employs external description and interior monologue along with naturalism and magic realism, as if challenging the listener to synthesize the various parts into some kind of impressionistic whole. At times, the entire song sounds like an eccentric musical exercise in Gestalt therapy but it is never less than thrilling.

The second side of *Veedon Fleece* is a more understated meditation on Ireland. 'Bulbs' continues the theme of emigration with its references to a woman embarking on a trip to America to be reunited with her family; 'Cul De Sac' reflects on a homecoming; 'Comfort You' seeks catharsis in childhood memories; the Tim Hardin-influenced 'Come Here My Love' and 'Country Fair' both use the traditional Irish ballad style to contemplate the passage of time and recognize the importance of focusing on the natural world in all its pastoral glory. Partly influenced by Gestalt, Morrison concentrates on capturing the quality of the moment rather than providing details of the characters within his songs.

Unfortunately, critics on both sides of the Atlantic at first reacted coolly to the album. An overfamiliarity with Morrison's more popular R&B and soul leanings ensured that the subtle, contemplative beauty of *Veedon Fleece* was either severely underrated or completely ignored. In the US, *Rolling Stone* praised the least adventurous track 'Bulbs', lambasted the brilliant 'You Don't Pull No Punches, But You Don't Push The River' as "pompous tripe" and dismissed the entire album as "self-indulgent . . . mood music for mature hippies". Back in the UK, *Melody Maker*'s review bore the headline "Van Ordinaire" and concluded that the album's first side (which arguably stands as Morrison's most sustained creative achievement) featured "some of his least memorable shots at songwriting since *Tupelo Honey*". *NME*'s Nick Kent proved a notable exception, acknowledging that the work was "probably his most intriguing project since *Astral Weeks*" before launching into a peculiar argument, making extremely tenuous comparisons between *Veedon Fleece* and Dylan's 1968 album *John Wesley Harding*. Nobody, it seemed, was ready to champion *Veedon Fleece* as Morrison's finest work. Yet, at a time when he was facing burn-out and semi-retirement, its contents provided a perfect complement to *Astral Weeks* and an unintentionally apposite conclusion to this stage of his career. If Morrison had never recorded again, *Veedon Fleece* would have served as an exquisite requiem and epitaph.

SEVENTEEN

Linden Arden and the Shankill Butchers

The fantasy Ireland that Morrison had presented on *Veedon Fleece* bore little relation to contemporary realities. As listeners lost themselves in the pastoral tones of 'Country Fair' and 'Comfort You', the IRA were intensifying their mainland campaign with the infamous Birmingham and Guildford pub bombings. The UVF were also ready with explosives. David Ervine, who had attended Morrison's old school, Orangefield, was arrested in a stolen car carrying a bomb which had been constructed in his home territory of East Belfast. The army forced him at gunpoint to dismantle the device and he was subsequently sentenced to 11 years' imprisonment in Long Kesh, where he received a new political education under the tutelage of the august Gusty Spence, who was keen for loyalists to develop a political strategy to rival that of Sinn Féin.

The spirit of Linden Arden, the hatchet-wielding, head-chopping anti-hero of Morrison's imagination, lived on in Belfast in the more macabre form of the Shankill Butchers, a menacing gang of UVF members whose speciality was dismemberment and torture. Other Protestant paramilitaries used similar tactics. Back in 1972, Francis Arthurs was abducted and slashed with a knife for over an hour; SDLP politician Paddy Wilson was later brutally stabbed by the UFF while his girlfriend had her breasts cut off; Thomas Madden, a likely UDA victim, was stripped naked, hung upside down and slowly skinned alive; Francis Crossan had his cut throat as far as the spine. And so it went on. Many of the killings were arbitrary and usually executed after a fortifying drinking session at a Shankill pub. The murderers' *modus operandi* was picking up innocent Catholics off the street, bundling them into black taxis, then cutting them into pieces with butchers' knives, cleavers or axes, before slitting their throats and dumping the corpses. Such psychopathic behaviour had a Brothers Grimm quality which characterized the darker side of the new Protestant paramilitary. As psychologist Ken Heskin observed, this descent into barbarism was likely to occur "more easily in organizations which lack the cultural traditions and historical respectability of the IRA".

For most of 1975, the IRA maintained an uneasy ceasefire while secret talks took place between the Provos and the British government in the vain hope of an army withdrawal. Progress proved too slow for the rank and file of the movement and, apart from the ending of internment, the IRA concluded that they had gained little. Their special category status as political prisoners, a right granted by William Whitelaw in 1972, was about to be abolished, a decision that would have unforeseen consequences. The ceasefire failed to bring peace to the streets of Belfast and sectarian disputes escalated. Throughout the year, the opposing paramilitaries were conducting tit-for-tat killings which produced a strangely symmetrical annual fatality rate. It was rather like witnessing brutally calculated exchanges on a chess board heading inexorably towards sectarian stalemate. The upsurge in Protestant assassination gangs, spearheaded by the Shankill Butchers, ensured that conflicts were more violent and senseless. It was not only Catholic nationalists who had reason to fear this latest terrorist incarnation. Morrison's old friend Wesley Black, the gregarious keyboard player in the Monarchs, was performing at paramilitary drinking clubs and this later led to false claims that he had been a member of the UDA. A born-again Christian, recently separated from his wife Karen, he betrayed the zeal of the newly converted. "Whenever I used to see him he'd scream across the road that I was going to hell, for no apparent reason," Roy Kane recalls. Once the religious ardour cooled, Blackie had started playing organ at the nearby Highfield Community Centre. On 27 February 1975, the 32-year-old ex-Monarch entered the grim annals of Troubles folklore. Kane believes that Black was innocently caught in the middle of a feud between the UDA and the UVF. "He had his daughter out for the day and she'd asked Wesley to stay for his tea but he was playing at the Highfield so he went down to the local chipper for a fish supper. There was a loyalist feud at that time and I can only assume he recognized them or shouted at them and they just shot him dead. A woman came to his assistance and he said, 'Why did they shoot me?' " In fact, it was a sole Republican gunman who was responsible for Blackie's death. The real target was a former UDA commander who lived on the West Circular Road. When he answered his door he was shot in the head and stomach. As the Republican raced away, he passed Blackie and shot him, presumably in fear of being identified. Karen Black later wrote a heartfelt letter thanking those who had helped her and her five-year-old daughter in the wake of the murder. "Wesley didn't know how loved he had been," she concluded. She harboured no thoughts of vengeance against her husband's killer, insisting "that would be a matter for God's hands". At the funeral, several of his former bandmates carried the coffin. "I was very fond of Wesley," Kane laments. "I'd introduced him to his wife Karen. It meant a lot to me. I had some photos of us in Germany way back in 1963 with Wesley sitting at the front on a piano. I showed these around once and a woman said, 'There's death in that photo.' It turned out that she was talking about Wesley and she didn't know him from Adam."

Morrison did not fly over to attend Black's funeral. Increasingly distant from old friends, he was still recuperating from the pressures of the record business. He seemed more interested in Gestalt therapy than the psychology of terrorism and set forth on a private odyssey during which he intended to spend more time reading, relaxing and contemplating the silence. Aside from some shows in San Francisco during the spring, he withdrew from public performance. "I got to the point where music just wasn't doing it for me anymore, a point I never thought I'd reach. I hadn't taken time off before and something was telling me to knock it off a bit. I caught up on years of sleep . . . when you're committed to a series of concerts you lose all the spontaneity – it's not jazz anymore. The reason I first got into music and the reason I was then doing it were conflicting. It was such a paradox."

At first, the music press found it hard to believe that Morrison had gone away. A new album, recorded the previous year in Holland, was consistently rumoured for release under such titles as *Mechanical Bliss/Naked In The Jungle* and *Stiff Upper Lip*. However, Morrison felt it was incomplete and would not sanction its release, later dismissing the entire project as nothing more than an extended jamming session.

During May, there were confident reports in the music press that Morrison was intending to return to Ireland and buy a house not far from Donall Corvin's home. It never happened, but that did not stop Corvin from dreaming that he might yet end up working with Morrison in some unspecified capacity. When he subsequently received an invitation to visit Marin County, he seemed upbeat. For an adventurer like Corvin, a move to San Francisco represented an opportunity to unleash his talents in spectacular fashion. "Donall never had any money," recalls Sam Smyth, who once shared a flat with him. "He'd spend it as quick as he got it. He was rooting around for money and he was on the phone to Morrison a lot of the time. Eventually, he went out to be with him as an 'in-house counsellor'. He flew to San Francisco, went to his house and they sat down for two to three days. Nothing was said and there was no food in the fridge. Corvin was a good man in his own company. He was an avid reader and had brought lots of books. One of them was about UFOs, flying saucers and all that nonsense. Morrison said, 'What's that you're reading?' There was another silent day and then Van said, 'I saw one of those things in the garden.' Corvin said, 'What?' He just thought it was daft. Corvin didn't think for a second that there was ever a UFO in the garden. Van didn't really talk to him. Corvin would have been wise enough to know that there was no point in talking because there wasn't going to be a lot said. There didn't seem to be a lot of point being out there. They didn't have words or an argument, just a week of long silences." Corvin left Morrison to listen to his silences and cadged some money from a friend in San Francisco for the flight home. Clearly, there was no advisory role to play in Morrison's life.

If Morrison had any vague notions of settling in Dublin or any part of Ireland, they were soon forgotten. The Troubles, which had always been a consideration, were now a specific threat. Musicians, once regarded as a neutral body in the sectarian wars, had recently become targets and victims. Five months after the murder of Morrison's former friend Wesley Black, Ireland was stunned by another outrage. In the early hours of 31 July 1975, the Miami Showband were driving back from an engagement in the North when they were stopped by several UVF men disguised in army uniforms. After lining up the musicians in a field, they planted a bomb in their van which they intended would explode in the Republic, thereby working as black propaganda against the IRA. Instead, the bomb detonated immediately, killing two of the UVF bombers. Amid the carnage, the remaining paramilitaries turned their weapons on the Miami, coldly assassinating Tony Geraghty and Fran O'Toole as they begged for mercy. A third Miami member, Brian McCoy was also killed. A fourth, Stephen Travers, was found barely alive in a field with bullet wounds in the abdomen and chest. An arm with the tattoo 'UVF' was discovered among the debris. The massacre shocked both communities and was felt strongly by many of Morrison's former showband colleagues. "Showbands faced extinction," recalls journalist Vincent Power. "The massacre helped to put the final nails in the coffin . . . The Miami outrage was different because the North's showband and ballroom scene seemed to transcend sectarian hatred."

Within days, the killings destroyed various Protestant/Catholic links as Southern bands refused to cross the border. Dickie Rock, once leader of the Miami, insisted that he would never play in the North again. The Miami's promoter Mervyn Solomon condemned the massacre while his brother Phil cancelled a booking in Belfast for his young star Lena Zavaroni. Back in America, Morrison was distancing himself ever further from his homeland. For several months, he ceased listening to music altogether and showed no interest in meeting musicians or discussing his future. "I just had to stop," he confessed. "I'd had enough. I was mentally exhausted and I just needed to get away from music completely. . . . I just had a total aversion to everything about it." During this period, he was reportedly attending special sessions with a pupil of the Swedish 'tension expert' Ada Rolf and devoting attention to selected tomes on Celtic history, Jungian psychology and supernatural phenomena. Meanwhile, the music press was playing a game of 'Spot Van Morrison', dutifully reporting rumoured sightings at gigs and documenting studio appearances including his contributions to Bill Wyman's *Stone Alone*. A session date with Joe Sample wrongly convinced many that he was recording an album with the Jazz Crusaders, produced by Stewart Levine. There was even hearsay that Morrison was intending to cut a skiffle album, a project which would not reach fruition until his collaboration with Chris Barber and Lonnie Donegan many years later. Irritated by all the speculation, Morrison finally issued a public statement in May 1976 clarifying his position: "As far as the past year was concerned things simply came to a grinding halt. Everything just came to a standstill as far as being into music and being into the trip. I simply stopped doing it for a while in order to get a new perspective on what it was all about. I wanted to change the way I was working. I wanted to get more of a solid business trip together. I wanted to open new areas of creativity so I had to let go of everything . . . I went through a lot of personal changes – there were a lot of things within myself that I had to sort out. . . . I've been trying out various experimental projects at various times and places. It's likely that a wide cross section of these sessions will be released at a later date on a 'history of' sort of album."

The press release also revealed that Morrison had made the eventful decision to return to Britain. "I want to get back to the roots, back to where I started off. And that also is what's happening now with my music as well. I'm getting back to basics – basic rock 'n' roll stuff." Apparently, all he needed was a manager to organize his business and personal affairs in England.

Promoter Harvey Goldsmith was involved in a lucrative Rolling Stones tour when Morrison first entered his orbit. As a favour to Bill Wyman, Goldsmith had agreed to draft a list of trustworthy managers for the singer's consideration. During a subsequent dinner date, Morrison casually announced "I've thought about it – I want *you* to be my manager." Goldsmith was nonplussed, not least because he had no managerial experience whatsoever. After politely declining the offer, he was rapidly won over by Morrison and agreed to take the reins for a trial period. "Everybody told me I was nuts!" he stresses. "Every single person that had been involved with him, be it record company, publishing, promoting, agency or whatever, had a tremendous respect for him but everyone also said that he was the most difficult person in the world to deal with."

During the spring of 1976, Morrison started a new album at the Manor Studios in Oxfordshire. He seemed determined to break free from the singer-songwriter tag that had marked his career during the first half of the Seventies. What he required was a rootsier sound and a fresh set of musicians. His choice of collaborator was New Orleans legend Mac Rebennack (Dr John) and Ray Parker Jnr. "After two days, Morrison decided that he wasn't satisfied with Ray who's got a jumpy, flamboyant style," Goldsmith recalls. "He tried out all sorts of things. We had Chris Barber's jazz band down there doing some New Orleans stuff. It never got used but it was fun. I thought the sessions ended up pretty well."

The combination of Dr John and Van Morrison was a potentially explosive partnership, but the experienced Rebennack proved a surprisingly calming influence. He admitted that he sometimes felt like "punching out" Morrison when the sessions proved irksome, but successfully suppressed his anger. During the late Fifties, he had worked with the manic, self-professed king of rock 'n' roll Little Richard, whose temper was legendary. "Van is more of an expressive person," Rebennack considers, "whereas Little Richard likes to whoop and holler. Morrison can whoop and holler too, but that's not what he digs doing. However, they both do have one thing in common: the ability to express a lot of feeling without using a lot of words." The lyrical minimalism would later prove a stumbling block for several critics, but confidence was high that the completed work would be well received.

While the album was at the mixing stage, Morrison and Dr John accepted an invitation from the Band to participate in their Thanksgiving Day farewell extravaganza at Bill Graham's Winterland in San Francisco. Filmed by Martin Scorsese, the event became a celluloid classic featuring numerous music legends including Bob Dylan, Joni Mitchell, Eric Clapton, Neil Diamond, Muddy Waters, Ronnie Hawkins and Emmylou Harris. Before the show, Morrison seemed in good spirits. "He was really up for it," Goldsmith remembers. "On the night, everything was laid out and everybody had turned up. But 20 minutes before he was due on he disappeared. He'd ran back to the hotel, decided he didn't look right, changed. Then he wasn't going to do it. I literally went over to the hotel, got him back and virtually pushed him out on stage." Morrison emphasized his Celtic heritage with a surprise reading of the traditional 'Tura Lura Lural (That's An Irish Lullaby)' (credited to his daughter 'Shannon') and a powerhouse version of the showstopper 'Caravan', complete with high-kicks reminiscent of a superannuated Tiller girl. "It was one of the most magical performances I've ever seen him do," Goldsmith says. "It was electric. He went out there and stormed the place. Clapton, Dylan and Joni Mitchell were out there in a little area on the side and everybody came out to watch. They all stood up and roared with the audience. And that's where he's at. When he's onstage there's no-one to touch him, but when he's offstage he's unbearable." Morrison later joined the entire ensemble for a rendition of Bob Dylan's 'I Shall Be Released'. It was the first time he had ever played on stage with the master.

The Last Waltz re-established Morrison's name in the American media, but increasingly his thoughts were turning to England, which he spoke of as a more "happening place". Goldsmith found him a luxurious residence in Kensington but after picking him up at the airport, events took a characteristically strange turn. During the drive to central London, Morrison decided that he no longer wanted to live in Britain and flew back to America as abruptly as he had arrived. He was only in the country for a matter of hours. With the new album set for release, Goldsmith was forced to commute between countries every fortnight in what was already becoming a managerial nightmare.

In April 1977, the long-awaited *A Period Of Transition* appeared and was roundly pilloried by critics. Most were hoping for a work of primeval vocal aggression that would challenge the emerging élite of Morrison pretenders, whose ranks included Bruce Springsteen, Bob Seger, Phil Lynott, Graham Parker and Elvis Costello. Instead, the 'comeback' album proved a masterclass in mediocrity. Only on 'The Eternal Kansas City', which blended the lily-white sound of the Anita Kerr Singers with strong gospel overtones, was there evidence of Morrison's mysterious majesty. The closing tracks, 'Heavy Connection' and 'Cold Wind In August', were evocative in places, but overall the album was terribly anti-climactic and one of the most demythologizing rock artefacts since Dylan's *Self Portrait*. Many concluded that it was the worst album of Morrison's career and certainly his most ill-timed. Rather fittingly, it was soon followed by one of the weirdest and most excruciating interviews ever heard on British radio.

The nightmare confrontation between Morrison and Capital Radio disc jockey Nicky Horne commenced the moment the singer entered the station's building. Upon being greeted warmly by Horne, Morrison curtly enquired "Who are you?" "He was obviously in a bad mood," Horne recalls, "and you couldn't talk to Mac Rebennack because he didn't know what planet he was on. I distinctly remember Mac standing there with a shillelagh in order to stand upright. Van didn't say a word to anyone. He was looking very morose." Horne's opening gambit was to ask how Morrison and Mac had got together. Morrison deadpanned "Well, I was going along the freeway one day and I saw this sign for an advertisement." The words sounded like the beginning of one of Dylan's surreal mid-Sixties songs, albeit without the lacerating humour. "Er . . . fine," Horne replied, before swiftly placing a Them record on the turntable while a McDonald's advert blared in the background. After further misunderstandings, Horne decided to tackle the controversial issue of Morrison's mystique. "There's no mystique about me," Morrison interrupted. "The only thing that's around me is this microphone . . . there's things up on the wall, tape's here [bangs on the wall] . . . I can't see no *mystique* anywhere."

"The whole interview was perpetuating the mystique," Horne insists. "I do think there was a touch of Machiavelli about it. When your manager asks you to promote an album and you arrange an interview with the largest commercial radio station in London, you therefore put yourself in a position where you are actively promoting yourself. How can a man who writes such sensitive lyrics, whose music is so powerful and who is so creative in the studio be so naive when it comes to promoting a record? I cannot believe that . . . He must be sympathetic to the power of radio. When he was behind that microphone he must have known the power of the media with which he was dealing."

If Morrison was aware of such power then he was evidently unconcerned about creating a positive impression. "The interview went on until I started to lose my cool," Horne reflects. "He was blowing it. There were thousands of people who wanted to hear this man talk, who had listened to and loved his music and who wanted the man to say something." In desperation, the DJ turned to Dr John who merely uttered a couple of half-completed sentences in a slurred New Orleans drawl. Reverting to time checks, album tracks and more radio ads, Horne then attempted one last question but was cut off by Morrison, who hissed: "I was born with a natural gift to play music and to write songs and that's all I know – the rest of this stuff, I haven't got a clue what it's about."

After a rather unconvincing "thanks very much for coming" and "good luck with the album", the programme ended on an enigmatic note with 'Into The Mystic'. Morrison made no apology for his embarrassing performance. Without even saying goodbye, he walked from the building, leaving Horne to mull over the worst interview of his professional career. "I have never done an interview that bad. I've done interviews where I perhaps asked the wrong questions or the interviewee might not have wanted to talk. But nothing on that scale . . . I was really upset that a man I had admired for so long could blow it so totally. He really did destroy my feelings for him as a man."

Morrison's reticence was also on display in a strange but memorably comic interview with *Sounds* journalist Vivien Goldman. Printed in brutal Q&A fashion, it was most notable for its mind-blowing banality. Among the topics discussed was the food he ate on the plane and his views on the Queen's Jubilee. "It's good to see the Queen and the Duke of Edinburgh waving," he quipped, like a jocose loyalist. Anything more earnest, including information about his reading habits, was summarily dismissed. "Can't tell you," Morrison teased, "it wouldn't be right for this paper. It would throw the whole thing into a totally different context and people who are interested in pop music would not be interested . . . I mean what they want to hear is, like, me saying, you know, it's all groovy and isn't it really fabulous, they want to hear me say I'm a rock 'n' roll star or something . . . They don't want to hear about reality." When he wasn't insulting the intelligence of the paper's readership, Morrison was complaining about the media and wearily asking "What's the point?" His exasperation took on new heights when discussing his recent break. "This is nothing new we're talking about because people do take time off and people don't even know they took it off, but, you know, like, who works nowadays? I don't know anybody who works nowadays." Profound social commentary indeed.

Morrison's barbs were a baffling mixture of sarcasm and comedy. Although the sarcasm was cutting and the humour possibly unintentional, there was a defiantly satirical edge to the proceedings. It was even evident in one of his recordings. That July, the single 'Joyous Sound' was released with a surprise B-side dating back to 1974. 'Mechanical Bliss' saw Morrison momentarily transformed into the Noël Coward of rock, complete with an affected upper class English accent. It was akin to hearing Bob Dylan attempting vaudeville. "That was a big disappointment for me because I was trying to break into comedy," Morrison improbably claimed. "That was the only comedy song I had out. I played it for Dudley Moore and he flipped over it. I thought, 'This is it . . . my big chance'. But I guess Warner Brothers buried it."

Morrison's media truculence and dark sarcasm might have made perverse sense if he had been drinking heavily, but he was at this point a teetotaller of several years' standing. "He had a very strict diet," Goldsmith remembers. "He'd gone through a heavy drinking period in his life and when he stopped he changed drastically. I think he was nervous about going on the road and the possibility of lapsing back into that environment." During the same period, Morrison even provided a rare insight into his journey towards abstinence. "One day the switchboard lit up and I saw where it was all going. I saw what alcohol could do to people and I saw that it wasn't a good thing anymore. Plus I wasn't a teenager anymore myself. It wasn't 1964 . . . I realized I was growing up or something like that. You have responsibilities . . . you've got to think about getting your act together. I didn't even know what it was doing to me. I didn't know how dangerous it was. People talked in terms of drugs and I used to think 'Well, in Ireland everyone drinks. Nobody gives it a second thought.' You're Irish number one and you're a drinker number two. That's the first two things about us Irish. And that's cool if you're not allergic to it. If you *are* allergic to it, that's another story altogether. And I happened to be allergic to it."

Harvey Goldsmith was soon encountering problems in his attempts to promote Morrison. The singer seemed reluctant to undertake a stadium tour, but he had been appearing at showcase gigs, including Maunkberry's in London's Piccadilly, and the Speakeasy. With a backing group featuring Dr John, Mick Ronson, Mo Foster and Peter Van Hooke, Goldsmith felt he had found a likely unit for a future tour. That hope soon evaporated. As Goldsmith reveals: "Suddenly, one day, he said, 'I don't want to work with this lot anymore, I'm off.' He wanted to do it but when it came down to it he wasn't ready for it. He felt a bit uncomfortable here in Britain." After returning to the States, Morrison continued to badger his manager incessantly. "He got to the point where he got crazy," Goldsmith explains. "He wasn't bowled over by the sales of *A Period Of Transition*. He thought it was going to be an absolute killer. When he was in America he called me every day – 2am and 8am. It was driving me nuts. But it was an experience and a challenge. If the record had been a big hit, he would have eased up a bit more." Events reached a head when Morrison demanded that Goldsmith quit promoting in Britain and emigrate to America. The entrepreneur baulked: "When I can earn as much money out of you as promoting, that's when I'll pack it up." Thereafter, Morrison terminated their relationship. "In some respects I'm surprised our thing lasted as long as it did," Goldsmith reflects. "But in other respects we were just beginning to work out a relationship. He knew what he wanted. It was always black and white; absolute definitive statements . . . We had a fight once. He was in one of his moods. But I'm a bit like that – get really excited, scream and shout – and then it's over. I think I got into him too much. He had a girlfriend, a film editor, who felt I was getting too close to him. She started sticking the knife in."

Morrison's departure to America occurred just as the IRA was transforming itself from within. The 1975 ceasefire had created serious internal divisions which threatened to bring the movement to its knees. Many young northern nationalists in Long Kesh were convinced that the Dublin leadership had been duped by the British. Morale was low, sectarian disputes were damaging resolve and resources, and the new Northern Ireland Secretary Roy Mason was proving a formidable foe intent on portraying and treating the IRA as ruthless gangsters rather than committed freedom fighters. Even the traditional American support for the movement had been eroded by the SDLP under the inspired leadership of John Hume. Stranger still was the transformation of the modern UVF founder Gusty Spence, who had educated himself in Long Kesh and reached the conclusion that the armed struggle was no longer tenable. Interviewed in prison, he declared: "All warring factions must put aside their weapons. Eventually, Loyalist and Republican must sit down together for the good of the country." Within four months of that plea for reconciliation he would be replaced as commanding officer of the UVF. Sectarian killings continued.

The IRA was close to defeat during this transitional period, but all that was about to change. Following his release from prison in spring 1977, Gerry Adams, with support from the Northern Command, advocated a new strategy – the Long War. This challenged the illusion that ceasefires and concessions would bring an early end to the conflict. Equally importantly, Adams saw the need for a new political base to reinforce the armed struggle. The emergence of a revitalized Sinn Féin would fulfil that remit while the reorganization of the IRA into a cell structure successfully blocked infiltration from British Intelligence.

In Adams' attempt to usurp the IRA's Dublin leadership, one of the first victims was Van Morrison's one-time choreographical accompanist Gerry O'Hare. Between 1975 and 1977, O'Hare edited the Republican newspaper *An Phoblacht*, working with IRA veteran Dáithí O Conaill. During this period, O'Hare became involved in a relationship with O Conaill's sister-in-law Gráinne Caffrey, who was also the cousin of IRA Chief of Staff Ruairí Ó Brádaigh. The marriage of Gerry and Rita O'Hare had been severely strained during their long periods of imprisonment. But it was the Caffrey controversy which led to his expulsion from the IRA. In an extraordinary series of events, he was brought to a Revolutionary Council meeting which took the moral highground pointing out the immorality of his conduct and insisting that he honour his marriage vows. The notion of the IRA conducting its business with the self-righteous sanctimony of a church council assessing a sexually active priest was not as odd as it sounded. "I was a bad example," O'Hare admits. "Guys were in jail and their wives were out running around with other guys and it was causing a lot of upset. I was given an ultimatum to end a relationship, which I refused. Then I was told 'You have to go.'" As one of his friends later quipped: "He's the first person I know to leave the IRA because of sex, drink and rock 'n' roll, and the only one I know to have been in every prison on this island – North and South." Behind O'Hare's removal was the political rivalry between Dáithí O Conaill and Gerry Adams, who was determined to take control of *An Phoblacht* in order to establish his leadership on both sides of the border. "It was a smokescreen," O'Hare says of his removal. "There was a lot more politics to it . . . they were trying to get at Dáithí O Conaill. I knew exactly what they were doing . . . They wanted control of the PR arm and to do it they had to get rid of me. This was all part of the game plan." Eventually, Belfast-born Danny Morrison emerged as the IRA's director of publicity and, a few years later, Adams was elected President of Sinn Féin, suc-

ceeding Ruairí Ó Brádaigh, who would later form the breakaway
Republican Sinn Féin. "Adams was the man of the moment for
the Republican movement," O'Hare now acknowledges. "His direction was between carrying on a full scale guerrilla war and/or moving
into politics. It took somebody with his weight to do that, to bring the
movement to where it is now. And he was ably assisted by Martin
McGuinness who was extremely important because he brought the
North West with him. Danny Morrison was also vital in a supporting
role to both Adams and McGuinness. And my ex [-wife] Rita too."

While the IRA was writing a fresh chapter in its history, Van
Morrison was carefully reassessing his career and attempting to
reconnect with an audience still sceptical of his recent comeback. He
was keen to record a new album early in 1978 as if to distance himself
from the public humiliation of *A Period Of Transition*. Consciously or
otherwise, he brought together musicians from every phase of his past.
Belfast was represented by his old showband pal, Herbie Armstrong; the
London R&B scene of the mid-Sixties was recalled via former Them
associate Peter Bardens; the New York Bang period was revisited via
the remix engineer Brooks Arthur; and the spirit of Woodstock was
embodied in the eccentric Garth Hudson from the Band. Completing
the line-up was drummer Peter Van Hooke, who brought in bassist
Mickey Feat and guitarist Bobby Tench.

The album was recorded over several months at the Manor in
Oxfordshire and completed at the Band's American studio Shangri-
la. "We stayed at the Manor," Tench recalls. "We'd wake up and
have breakfast. It was 9 to 5 really. He didn't drink at all when we
were recording. This was a period when he hadn't had a drink for
ages. He just had gallons of coffee which I didn't think was too good
for him. I'd rather you have a drink because you get all twitchy with
coffee. He didn't know it, but he was wired. He was twitchy, pacing
around and couldn't sit still. I don't think he knew the coffee was
doing it."

Perhaps as a reaction to the market failure of *A Period Of Transition*,
Morrison seemed willing to record a more accessible and commercial
work. Both Bobby Tench and Peter Bardens would receive additional
credit for 'Special Assistance In Production'. "He'd just got the songs
on acoustic and it was all in his head basically," Tench points out. "I've

got to tell you it sounded nothing like it became on vinyl. He strummed away and I started taking him in a different direction with Peter Van Hooke – he didn't seem to mind. He seemed to enjoy going somewhere else on the production side. I quite liked the songs 'Natalia' and 'Wavelength' because I had a lot to do with them. They came together quickly. He's a very quick worker and once it's there he doesn't see why you can't record it. He let us get on with it, really. It was a good band."

Wavelength, released in September 1978, was an upbeat effort which became the fastest selling album of Morrison's career, achieving gold status within three months. It was far from classic Morrison and may even have been a commercial compromise of sorts but it had a musical consistency and glossy production that pleased contemporary listeners. Initially, Morrison spoke of the work in portentous terms, announcing: "Every time you deliver an album that's a year or two of your life. It's taken me 15 years to deliver *Wavelength* and all the albums before that. It ain't easy to keep going. It's still a struggle for me, and it's still a struggle for most people." Later, he would blithely dismiss the work, insisting that it was a step in the wrong direction.

The presence of musicians from every stage of his career was reflected in the song titles and lyrics. 'Kingdom Hall', a celebration of dance and song, was inspired by his childhood experiences as the son of a practising Jehovah's Witness. 'Wavelength' fondly remembered his adolescence, listening to Ray Charles' 'Come Back Baby' on the Voice of America. Other lyrical references to boats sailing into the harbour recalled similar images in songs such as 'Hey Girl' and 'Into The Mystic'. Despite these allusions, critics understandably tended to see the album as strongly American in influence. In a damning review, *Melody Maker* interpreted *Wavelength* as evidence of Morrison's "drift into the American Dream". No doubt this perspective was partly formulated from the song title 'Venice USA', the Voice Of America reference in the title track and the refrain "lost dreams and found dreams in America" on the concluding 'Take It Where You Find It'. Apparently oblivious to these cumulative citations, Morrison insisted: "The only real reference to America in the whole album is a couple of lines, 'Lost [dreams] and found dreams in America', right? Which has nothing to do with any American Dream; it's not about the country, it's about my personal experience. A lot of people think I went to America and now I'm involved in some American Dream. That's like saying all black people have got rhythm . . . it's clichéd . . . garbage."

Despite Morrison's objections, many now saw him primarily as an American recording artiste. Since leaving Harvey Goldsmith, he had been briefly involved with former Doors manager Bill Siddons, before appointing promoter Bill Graham, who was then handling several high-earning acts, including Santana, Ronnie Montrose and Eddie Money. "It was like going from the frying pan to the fire," Goldsmith says. Under Graham's tutelage, Morrison agreed to an ambitious 10-week tour, which would provide its fair share of controversy. It started promisingly enough with a sell-out concert at San Francisco's Old Waldorf during which Morrison stormed through a 75-minute set featuring songs from almost every period of his career. "Loads of people came to see that one," Tench recalls. "San Francisco was always a good stronghold for him. He was really singing his arse off. It was a great night for the band. He's a strange chap. Some nights he'd be in the mood for it and other nights he wouldn't, even though we'd be playing well."

The night where it all went wrong happened in November at the Palladium, New York. Midway through the second set, Morrison abruptly left the stage without explanation. At first, the musicians assumed he was merely taking a break. "If we were doing 'Help Me', he used to go off and have a coffee and a cigarette at the side of the stage while Bobby Tench played lead and Pete Bardens did a solo," Herbie Armstrong explains. "But all of a sudden he wasn't there." Convinced that Morrison had gone for a toilet break, they continued playing, with each member taking a solo. "I kept looking in the wings," Tench recalls, "and eventually I had to end it. The audience went berserk. They were stomping and shouting and weren't very happy." Backstage, Tench heard that there had been a noisy conflict between Morrison and their tour manager, Mike Bridgen. "While we were onstage and still finishing, chairs were being thrown backstage. There was a big argument going on."

Amid the mêlée, Armstrong learned that Morrison had been spooked by a glaring spotlight and was now back at the hotel. A frantic Bill Graham hovered uneasily, fearful of the consequences. Morrison had been booked to appear on *Saturday Night Live* soon after and that television promotion was regarded as crucial. Despatching Armstrong to track down Morrison, Graham hissed: "Go quick! Tell him if he does *Saturday Night Live* then we can cancel the whole tour if he wishes!" Jumping into a waiting Cadillac, Armstrong was soon surrounded by an angry crowd demanding to know what had happened. Several wanted an immediate refund. The guitarist told them Morrison was suffering from exhaustion and should not have played the gig. Eventually, the crowd parted and Armstrong reached the hotel, wary of what he might find. "I know Van and I know what he's like. I knew he was wired up. I knocked on his door and when he opened it he was white as a sheet. He just said, 'Hi, Herbie.' I thought I'd better crack a joke. We were overlooking Central Park so I said, 'Fancy going for a walk in the park?' because Van loves walking. I knew no-one went into Central Park after dark and it was nearly two in the morning. But he said, 'I'll get my jacket.' He was steaming ahead of me and I was thinking, 'How do I get out of this one?' I couldn't say I was just joking because he was so wired up. While we were heading for the park I saw a delicatessen and I said, 'Hey, Van, fancy a coffee?' So, there we were in the deli with all these tramps and down and outs. There was a guy with no legs, wheelchairs, and tramps begging along the roads. I said 'Van, at least we can fly out of here tomorrow – these people can't go anywhere.' "

Having calmed down, Morrison explained what had happened at the Palladium. "You know what freaked me out?" he said. "Coming to New York. Every time I've been in New York there have been problems." After hearing Bill Graham's ultimatum about *Saturday Night Live*, Morrison announced that he did not wish to cancel the tour but added sheepishly: "I wouldn't mind taking a week off." As a result, four dates, including Chicago and Washington, were cancelled. After completing the all-important television engagement, the musicians returned to England and Morrison recuperated in San Francisco. Before long everyone reconvened in Texas and, according to Armstrong, "the rest of the tour was brilliant". Morrison's favourite show was a club date in Boulder, Colorado, where "it was all happening". "He was more comfortable in smaller venues," Tench points out. "The tour was quite subdued really. There was a big studio in Boulder with cabins and we rented the whole place, but it wasn't to record. Instead of staying in hotels, we stayed in these log cabins. It was fantastic. They had horses and mountain bikes. We had a week off. There was a big canteen there and they cooked for us. Good eating was something I normally didn't do. Overall, with the gig and the setting, he was very comfortable and so was the band. He liked the fresh air and quietness, as we all did. He had to have a masseur on that tour to relieve stress and we had this health person with us. We'd wake up in the morning and he'd have all these vitamins laid out and if you were a bit tense, he'd give you a massage. He kept everybody in shape. That was one of Van's ideas."

The health regime did not save the band from some bad reviews. An appearance at UCLA's Royce Hall in December was lambasted by *Sounds'* LA correspondent, who concluded waspishly: "Maybe it's a good thing he's been walking out before the end of some of his shows. If he's not careful, he'll be racing the audience to the exit."

Facing a busy itinerary, Morrison had not made himself available for interviews, but Warners agreed to send over Corvin who had been asked to produce a feature for a West Coast journal. After a friendly greeting and a brief chat, Morrison announced that he was too tired and retired to bed. Corvin came away empty-handed, although not before Morrison had tried a media experiment of his own. "Corvin told me stories that Van would give him a drink but Van wouldn't take a drink," recalls Brian Russell. "What he was trying to say was that he was rehearsing this. He was getting someone to interview him to see what kind of questions journalists would ask and therefore have the answers himself. When Corvin came back he was very low."

EIGHTEEN

Belfast Revisited

At the beginning of 1979, Morrison's long-suffering fans in Northern Ireland read a news flash which they could hardly believe. During a 21-date UK tour, the singer was booked to play Belfast for the first time in 12 years. Safety was no longer a major issue as the most violent phase of the Troubles was over and death rates had decreased significantly. As it turned out, Morrison faced far greater danger from music press snipers than from any member of the IRA. Two months before, *Melody Maker* had printed a small news item about the troubled Palladium gig, which had miraculously escaped Morrison's notice. Previewing his forthcoming tour, they repeated the story on their front page, once again highlighting some ill-advised comments from a Warner Brothers publicist.

When Morrison belatedly read these words, he was apoplectic. An immediate retraction was demanded and the unfortunate publicist Gary Kenton was sacked for his indiscretion. Warners' chairman Mo Ostin was sufficiently alarmed by Morrison's reaction to issue a mortified apology and letter of support from his Burbank office. "I am very embarrassed by the quotes attributed to Warner Brothers," he wrote. "Furthermore, I am very sorry for any misgivings or embarrassment that this statement may have caused Van personally. His popularity remains at a peak . . . his Belfast show sold out in just half-an-hour . . ." Morrison was still seething about the affair after arriving in London and insisted on using an outside public relations agent rather than risk further treachery from his record company.

The person chosen to mastermind Morrison's media relations was none other than Keith Altham, the former *NME* journalist who had written the most scathing interview with Them ever published in the British press. Since leaving the *NME*, he had established himself as a towering PR, whose clients included the Rolling Stones, the Police, the Who and the Cure. Altham's first meeting with Morrison since 1965 took place at Kensington's Inn Of The Park Hotel. "I walked into the restaurant and there was the hero of an era just past, sitting at the table cleaning his teeth with tooth floss, which he continued to operate for the whole time I was talking to him. He had a great many apprehensions about the press." Altham faced the onerous task of convincing Morrison that his fear and suspicion of the music media were not justified. Seeking a sympathetic journalist, Altham approached his Sixties counterpart at *Melody Maker*, the genial Chris Welch. An interview was arranged, but it proved a daunting encounter.

Morrison's relationship with the press was by this stage uncannily similar to Ian Paisley's relationship with the Catholic Church. Every comment, no matter how sincerely expressed, could ultimately be interpreted as a form of Jesuitical deception. It was as if he was transforming the words 'No Surrender' into a psychological weapon to be used against his adversaries. Faced with the disarmingly avuncular Welch, Morrison responded as if he was being interviewed by Judas Iscariot. "You're just stroking me," he chastized his interrogator. "You've got plans. The front page will look perfect, but in the article you'll definitely catch me. You'll have something on me by the time this is all over. What else are you looking for? Really? Are you looking for *dirt*? I know journalists and they look for dirt, so I don't let them interview me. You nodded your head, right?"

Altham next persuaded Morrison that a photo session was required to update the material in Warners' files. Morrison acted as though he had been asked to break the first two Commandments by worshipping graven images. Nevertheless, portrait photographer Brian Aris, who had visually documented the Troubles in 1970, was commissioned and a time set for the shoot. After waiting two hours, Altham tracked Morrison down at his hotel, only to discover that he was suffering from toothache and had abandoned Aris in favour of the dentist. Eventually, he was coaxed into making a late appearance. "He turned up and staggered up the stairs disgruntledly," Altham recalls. "After about 10 minutes he re-emerged with a great clatter of indignation, exclaiming,

'I finished with all this fucking posing years ago.' I explained that it was a *posed* shot. So, at that point, we had an altercation." Sensing Morrison's penchant for confrontation, Altham forced the issue by demanding what he required of a press agent. "I'm employing you to say 'No! No! No!'" Morrison retorted. Altham then told him: "You should get a parrot. If you don't want to do anything, get a secretary or an answering device to say 'No comment, no interviews, no photographs, no nothing'." Morrison growled, "I'll think about it", then disappeared for the remainder of the week. Meanwhile, Welch's interview appeared and was not as bad as Morrison expected. Altham was politely told to carry on. "It was as near to an apology as I could expect," he mused.

The highlight of the tour was Morrison's shows at Belfast's Whitla Hall which had sold out in under 30 minutes. As soon as he set foot in his home city, the singer could feel a sense of anticipation among the populace. Bizarrely, the day of his arrival coincided with the long-awaited sentencing of the Shankill Butchers, who were responsible for the most notorious and gruesome killings in the history of the province. Eleven of the gang members were indicted on over 100 charges including 19 murders and various other offences. They received 42 life sentences amounting to over 2,000 years. Passing sentence, the judge noted: "Many of the murders you have pleaded guilty to were carried out in a manner so cruel and so ruthless as to be beyond the comprehension of any normal person."

The sensation surrounding the sentencing of the Shankill Butchers did not dissuade Morrison from visiting his favourite Protestant haunts. Filmed by freelance director Mike Radford, the singer stopped off at Sandy Row and Stormont, then the Beersbridge Road and Cyprus Avenue, the streets that, coincidentally, also featured in the life story of a very different Belfast icon, Ian Paisley. Back at the Whitla Hall, touts were greedily demanding £100 for a pair of tickets. Fans were not alone in complaining about a raw deal. Journalists were appalled by the cursory treatment they received from both the promoters and the record company. The *Irish Press*' Alan Murray was flabbergasted to discover that he would have to pay five pounds for a ticket to review the concert. In protest, he declined to provide his paper with a write-up. As another reporter railed: "Those who didn't see the two shows don't know any more about their homegrown superstar now than they did before."

Thankfully, the concerts went spectacularly well. At the post-gig reception, Phil Coulter turned up to join Morrison and Herbie Armstrong for a sing-song. The following day, the entourage set forth for Dublin, where Morrison was booked to perform, after which he intended to complete an interview with the *NME*'s Tony Stewart. They shared a car on the journey, but the anticipated rapport was embarrassingly absent and hardly a word was spoken. The Dublin performance brought back bad memories of Morrison's last appearance there, complete with a violent incident which had ended with bouncers beating an irate punk. Back at the Shelbourne Hotel, Altham assumed that Morrison would postpone the *NME* interview, but he seemed devilishly keen to proceed. He then announced that the confrontation was to be filmed and even asked Altham to introduce the programme. Any levity was soon forgotten when the cameras started rolling and Morrison retreated into what Altham referred to as "his suit of armour complex".

According to Stewart, the singer was "irritable, frequently angry, disparaging and obstinately single-minded." He pontificated endlessly about the evils of the media as Paisley might have done had he been addressing a papal inquisition. Stewart had clearly been set up as a puppet participant in a drama of Morrison's creation. He accused the press of using his name to make money, conveniently ignoring the fact that such publicity both enhanced his career and earned him a considerable income. "It's very hard for me to relate to people asking questions that are not only boring but don't have anything to do with my life, or aren't relevant. It's a waste of time on my part – because it drains me from doing what I really want to do, which is just play music." His life, his music, his personality were all off limits and in a remarkable display of autocracy, he decreed: "I'll do it myself. I'll sit down and I'll write a book and I'll backtrack and I'll go through everything. I'll say this song was about this. But it'll belong to me and I'll have control of it."

Back in 1974–75, Morrison had retreated from the music business, partly to find himself and partly to escape from the public perception of what he represented. Now it seemed that the conflict of identity that bothered him so much then had never gone away, despite his return to recording and touring. "They're not coming to see Van Morrison," he insisted. "They're coming to see the image that was in the movie *The Last Waltz* – and that's not Van Morrison." The recent rumours about Morrison returning to Ireland were also now regarded as laughable. "How the hell can I live in Ireland?" he spluttered "What am I going to do – move to Ireland and open a grocery store? I'm in the music business. I'm not going to sit up on a hill somewhere writing songs that are going to sell 10 or 20 albums. I'm not a 17-year-old rock 'n' roll star." He continued in this vein, complaining that he was seen as little more than a carnival freak by the press. It was evident that he no longer wished to be a pawn in the hands of a Phil Solomon, the *NME* or his record company. Neither good reviews nor sympathetic journalists could sway him from a fundamental belief that the media was hell bent on tarnishing his name. Such was the intensity and finality of his words that Stewart wondered aloud whether this might be the last ever Van Morrison interview. "I wouldn't even dare answer that question," Morrison exploded, "because that's a front-page job. I'd be an ape if I answered that one. I wouldn't be a monkey, I'd be a complete fucking gorilla."

From there, the interview degenerated into a repetitive party political broadcast. Stewart made one last-gasp effort to ask Morrison about his emotions, but was told he must be out of his mind. Finally, the journalist admitted defeat and, visibly shaken, retired to the bar for a stiff drink. For 90 minutes he had sacrificed himself at the altar of Morrison's ego without changing the man's blinkered perceptions one iota. On the contrary, Morrison seemed rather pleased with himself. Evidently, he had discovered a new style of confrontation even more devastating than that witnessed by Nicky Horne. His reputation as a sensitive singer-songwriter may have been dealt a fatal blow by this latest media clash, but that perception was merely deemed another disposable myth. Faced with the demands of playing the media game, his most effective answer had been to embrace the psychology of 'No Surrender' and re-enact in interview mode the aphorisms of Unionist Ulster, which were roughly translated as 'Morrison Says No' and 'Morrison Will Fight And Morrison Will Be Right'. Paisley might well have admired his resilience.

The remainder of the UK tour seemed haunted by the bitter engagement with Stewart. At the Glasgow Apollo, Morrison felt inexplicably intimidated by the height of the stage. "He came on, saw the stage and shoved Peter Bardens off the keyboards," Bobby Tench remembers. "He stayed there all night and he didn't even know the songs on piano. Bardens had to play organ and Van can't really play the piano. I couldn't understand that. It was simply the height of the stage. I didn't see any big deal in it. They put the mikes back, but he didn't come back. Another interesting night." As the tour concluded in Newcastle, Morrison was left to mull over some decidedly mixed reviews, including a vicious panning of the London show in *Melody Maker* which ended with the dark elegy: "The legend dies; a future in cabaret seems the only answer." Although he had recently spent entire interviews denouncing the press as irrelevant, Morrison was still incensed. "He freaked out and got really angry," Herbie Armstrong recalls. "Everybody in the band was pissed off too. He turned around and said, 'Why do you think I don't talk to the press? They twist everything.'"

It did not end there. A week later, the professorial Simon Frith devoted an entire column to the singer's personal failings. "Morrison doesn't emerge as a character of much conviction," he argued. "A tour by someone who doesn't like touring. Concerts to sell records by someone who seeks to keep clear of commerce. Interviews with someone who keeps his self hidden and hates the press. The musical reasons for all this activity buried deep under the obsessive close-to-the-chest calculations of someone doing an unpleasant job as quickly as he can . . . Van Morrison, loser to the last, got everything wrong."

Predictably, publicist Keith Altham was rueful. Watching Morrison in action had proven a painful, if instructive, lesson in the limitations of PR. "It's a pity that he is so lacking in his ability to handle the media and press. Morrison is scared of an intrusion into his personal and private world and there is no reason that any journalist would be able to do that. Paul McCartney, for example, gives the media what they want and at the same time doesn't give them anything. Morrison has never learned to play that game and I don't think he ever will. He's a very aggressive and abrasive personality, but he's also hyper-sensitive. He is unable to relate to people about his lifestyle and his work. And for that reason I don't think he should ever do interviews . . . If anyone ever approached me and if he ever approached me again to do his PR

I'd say forget it because he is the worst PR of his work that I've ever come across."

More than ever, Morrison required a trusted and empathetic journalist like Donall Corvin to enhance his lamentable media persona. Unfortunately, Corvin was no longer a music writer. Since the dawn of punk he had relocated to the west of Ireland and, in one of his stranger career moves, achieved editorship of the *Roscommon Champion*. Corvin seemed determined to place Roscommon on the map and shake up the place, just as he had done in Belfast back in the Sixties. He had recently become involved with a new girlfriend, a fun-loving thrill seeker many years his junior. Ever the wry sensationalist, Corvin once persuaded her to pass herself off as a schoolgirl when meeting her at Roscommon station. After alighting from the train, she was greeted with passionate embraces and erotic kisses from Corvin while scandalized passengers looked on aghast. Corvin's challenges to Roscommon mores soon entered media folklore. On a visit to Dublin, he met up with a well-known regional journalist and broadcaster and casually confided some startling new findings about changing moral attitudes in Roscommon. He claimed to have conducted an extensive county survey through the paper which confirmed that a substantial number of people favoured divorce and many did not object to abortion on demand. Upon hearing this, Corvin's contact went into overdrive. "Television crews appeared in Roscommon," Sam Smyth recalls. "Donall was preparing the front page and he was very plausible on TV. Of course, fools that they were, they were saying, 'This wipes aside normal thinking that people in the country are very conservative and this means Ireland is now one of the most go-ahead nations in the world.' They were all in the green room at RTÉ afterwards, all very pleased with each other, then the telephone went. It was Donall. He started to laugh and said, 'I had to ring you because I made it all up!!'" The ashen-faced broadcaster, fearing ridicule, begged Corvin, "Never ever tell anybody!" Corvin's cultural and political punditry embraced interviews with several politicians, including Republican Sinn Féin President Ruairí Ó Brádaigh and the Fine Gael Taoiseach-in-waiting Dr Garret FitzGerald. The latter confrontation caused a sensation well beyond Roscommon when Corvin printed an extended piece in New Journalism-vein titled "The Return Of The Nutty Professor". "I think it was the first time anybody noticed that Garret FitzGerald wore odd socks," Smyth reflects. "He included all of his dithering and blithering ways. People were horrified but the owners of the *Roscommon Champion* had to print 3,000 extra copies because Fianna Fáil supporters were sending it to friends and relatives around the country as the great putdown of the white hope of liberalism."

While Corvin was establishing Roscommon as the centre of the universe, Morrison had returned to California where he completed a new album, *Into The Music*, released during the same month as Dylan's evangelical *Slow Train Coming*. Inevitably, the works were compared and some critics made the mistake of assuming that Morrison, like Dylan, was a born-again convert. Although Morrison's work did mention the Lord and the Bible on a couple of tracks, it was immediately evident that the composer was more concerned with nature than religion. Since *Astral Weeks* he had employed rebirth as an underlying theme in his work, but there had never been anything explicitly Christian, excepting perhaps 'Kingdom Hall', his celebration of the Jehovah's Witness place of worship. His interest in comparative religion had seen him peruse a bewildering number of esoteric disciplines without committing to anything in particular. Later, when pushed, he conceded that he was a "Christian mystic", without defining the term, subsequently adding that he was "into everything". The songs on *Into The Music* were equally non-committal, mixing Christian and pagan imagery on successive tracks. 'Full Force Gale' praised the Lord, whereas 'Rolling Hills' was essentially pantheistic with a *carpe diem* philosophy. Many of the songs were upbeat celebrations of love and life, most notably 'Troubadours', 'Stepping Out Queen' and 'You Make Me Feel So Free'. The cheerful mood was encapsulated in the minor hit 'Bright Side Of The Road', an answer song to the country soul classic 'Dark End Of The Street', featuring the brass work of new recruits Mark Isham and Alfred 'Pee Wee' Ellis, with strong vocal support from Herbie Armstrong and Katie Kissoon. The emphasis on spiritual healing which would dominate Morrison's work hereafter was subtly introduced with 'And The Healing Has Begun'. With its references to Muddy Waters and walking down the Avenue, the composition looked back to the singer's Belfast youth, a period also evoked in a revival of Tommy Edwards' 1957 chart topper, 'It's All In The Game'. The latter segued

into 'You Know What They're Writing About', which served as
Morrison's musical reply to all those unanswered interview questions.

Spiritual healing was also a subject entertaining the thoughts of
Corvin, who was now back in Dublin with a new agenda. Having
failed to find a post with Morrison and burned his bridges in
Roscommon, he was acting as publicist for the celebrated faith healer
Finbar Nolan. Memorably described by writer Edna O'Brien as "a
young boy whose looks are a combination of Georgie Best and the
Giotto painting of St John the Baptist", the wide-eyed, bearded Nolan
attracted multitudes of the afflicted. "They talked to him in whispers,
imparting more or less similar confidences," O'Brien observed. "There
he was a faith healer, a charmer, telling us he must touch the flesh . . .
Off came jumpers, cardigans, stockings, frocks, corsets, brassieres,
camisoles, vests, bodices and even scapulars. An array of white flesh, fat
flesh, purple flesh, roly-poly flesh, every kind of flesh pitifully exposed
in the weird, torrential rain of a melancholy summer's afternoon in
Ennis, Co. Clare." Such was Corvin's success in publicizing this
"seventh son of a seventh son" that the tax authorities wrote a letter of
enquiry about his income and commission. While Morrison was
veering increasingly towards spirituality, Corvin maintained a cynical
aloofness from what he called "the healing game". His humour was best
exemplified in a letter he wrote to Roy Kane, which was signed
"Corvin – Assistant Faith Healer".

Since leaving Roscommon, Corvin's melancholia had become more
pronounced. Some said his volatile relationship with his younger
girlfriend had taken its toll on his spirits, but those who knew him from
the old days testified to a deeper, darker despondency. "There's no
doubt that he was prone to terrible depressions," stresses Sam Smyth.
"He had a nihilistic streak in him. He destroyed most of his
manuscripts. For a time, he stayed with the journalist Michael Hand
who was very good to him. He came and went as he liked. He never
had any money. Whatever he had, he spent it. He was a very talented
writer and a very intelligent guy. He could have done any job he
wanted but he just didn't seem able to hack it." One evening, Corvin
went for a drink with Smyth and told him in a tone of disconcerting
nonchalance that he had recently attached a hose to the exhaust of his
car and attempted to kill himself. "He spoke to a lot of his friends about

it and told me very matter-of-factly," Smyth confirms. "This was a few months before his death."

On 6 September 1979, Corvin turned on the oven at his home at 5 Lower Mount Town, Dun Laoghaire, and gassed himself. His corpse was discovered by Aidan Hand and a local musician Paul Ashford and he was officially pronounced dead at the local St Michael's Hospital. He was 33. Dr Bart Sheehan, the Dublin coroner, conducted an inquest two weeks before Christmas which confirmed that he had expired from self-induced carbon monoxide poisoning. News of Corvin's death sent shock waves through the pop, rock and showband communities in Ireland. His funeral was held at Mount Argus in Dublin with the famous 'showband priest' Father Brian D'Arcy conducting the service. "I went to the funeral and I was so overcome in the church that I couldn't go to the graveside," fellow journalist Colin McClelland recalls. "There was a vast number of people there and a huge well of emotion. The church was full of grown men crying their eyes out. There were well-known businessmen, politicians and pillars of society in tears. He was such a loved person. What freaked me out was that somebody said a lone piper was going to pipe the coffin up the hill to the cemetery. I couldn't take that. It was too much for me. The way to sum up Corvin was that he was the symbol of freedom and the symbol of hope to many of us from that era. Here was a guy of our age who wasn't married, didn't own a house or have the encumbrances we all have, but he was still happy and surviving. And then to discover No, this wasn't the case. That's why grown men were crying in that church."

Even Morrison was reported to be upset by the tragic circumstances of Corvin's death, but he did not attend the funeral. While Corvin's coffin was placed in the earth, Morrison was continuing his explorations into New Age esoteria, even setting time aside to record an album at Super Bear, a studio on the site of a former abbey in the French Alps. "It had been a monastery-cum-safe house for the secret religious society the Cathars," says Mick Cox. "What had happened was that some of the society were caught and massacred in this very place . . . It's obviously haunted . . . and a few of the guys and Van saw some strange things. It was atmospheric in a slightly unnerving way, and it burned down a few weeks after we left. It gave an atmosphere to the album that was special." Although cloistered, the studio was a modern facility, complete with swimming pool and easy access to the beaches and casinos of San Tropez. The musicians were relaxed and the meditative Morrison felt a new freedom to indulge his explorative, improvisational tendencies.

Common One, released in September 1980, proved the most problematic record in the entire Morrison canon. Uplifting, frustrating, outstanding, banal, deadly earnest and comically bathetic, it was a record steeped in aesthetic contradiction. Strangely riveting, it contained some of Morrison's most inspired moments undercut by a self-indulgence that was breathtaking in its arrogance. The album smacked of hip mysticism, gratuitous literary namedropping, excruciating poetry and elongated jazz riffs that sometimes meandered into the realms of the soporific. Most of the reviews were merciless. The *NME* described the work as so monumentally boring, "colossally smug", "cosmically dull", "vacuous and drearily egotistical" that they recommended hot coffee and regular pokes of a stick in order to stay awake.

Despite its lapses, *Common One* was Morrison's most daring and unclassifiable excursion since *Astral Weeks* and his most intriguing since *Veedon Fleece*. It was an extraordinarily brave and uncompromising work in which he seemed determined to follow his own muse, irrespective of the commercial consequences. The work began with 'Haunts Of Ancient Peace', a spine-tingling song that continued his New Jerusalem quest and stands alongside his finest moments. 'Summertime In England', a 15-minute improvisational piece, was impressive in parts with a delicate string arrangement from Jeff Labes, enlivened by Pee Wee Ellis's expert musical direction. It was also overweening in its ambition. The references to Avalon and other Arthurian allusions seemed designed to provide a spurious epic grandeur to Morrison's musings which included embarrassing lines about Coleridge and Wordsworth smoking dope in Kendal and a self-conscious list of literary heavyweights featuring Blake, T.S. Eliot, James Joyce, Yeats and Lady Gregory. Additional references to Jesus and an archetypal figure in a red robe with a light in her head appeared to be a calculated attempt to add some iconographical significance to the piece. Although Morrison's recitation occasionally resembled a laundry list of impressive-sounding poets, this in itself added a comic undertone to his musings. It may not have been intended, but 'Summertime In England' was funny as well as deadly serious. The fact that it later became a live repository for anyone on Morrison's reading list emphasized its lighter aspects. Ultimately, it served as an endearing entreaty to enter Morrison's universe on his own terms.

The remainder of the album was marred largely by Morrison's lyrical lapses. 'Satisfied', a self-congratulatory statement in which the singer told us he had got his "karma", threw in another gratuitous literary allusion, this time to Salinger's *Catcher In The Rye*. 'Wild Honey' sounded closer in feel to Morrison's familiar repertoire, while 'Spirit' played with sudden tempo changes to dramatic effect. The most peculiar composition on the album was another 15-minute epic, 'When Heart Is Open'. Experimental in form, with no discernible melody or tempo, it pre-empted the era of New Age music. Lyrically strained, with self-consciously archaic phrasing ("you will tarry"), insipid similes and a comic chauvinism (his darling being ordered to fetch his boots), it was nevertheless oddly affecting as a strained piece of musical experimentation.

Common One was, in many ways, a great work unrealized. It still serves as a powerful mood piece and arguably stands alongside Morrison's finer achievements, but it also inhabits a foreign league by itself. Morrison later indicated that the original concept was even more esoteric and heavily influenced by his reading of nature poets. At the time, it seemed as though he was attempting to adopt the mantle of the John Clare of popular music, albeit without the great poetry. Nevertheless, *Common One* was a fascinating and challenging album, which threatened to open an entirely new musical direction for Morrison during the Eighties.

After the best part of a decade living in California, Morrison's parents decided it was time to return to Northern Ireland. Their planned homecoming coincided with the most emotive political events in the six-county province since Bloody Sunday. During the past few years, prisoners at the Maze (formerly Long Kesh) had been seeking to reinstate their standing as political detainees as opposed to common criminals. Kieran Nugent, the first Republican denied special category status, had refused to wear a prison uniform and cloaked himself in a bed blanket. Soon, hundreds of Republicans, and a number of loyalists, were 'on the blanket'. The protest escalated in 1978 with a refusal to empty chamber-pots and the spreading of excrement on cell walls. "I ripped off a lump of the mattress to do it with," recalls Gerard Hodgkins, then a teenage IRA recruit. "You were going against your whole socialization of how you were brought up . . . against everything you'd ever learned about basic hygiene and manners . . . I lived like this from 1978–81 . . . After a time you became accustomed to it . . . You were literally waking up in the morning and there were maggots in the bed with you . . . I think the human spirit can become accustomed to any environment." The prisoners found a zealous publicist in the visiting Cardinal Tomás O'Fiaich who told the world: "One could hardly allow an animal to remain in such conditions, let alone a human being . . . The stench and filth in some cells, with the remains of rotten food and human excreta scattered around the walls, was absolutely unbelievable . . . I was unable to speak for fear of vomiting."

The prisoners subsequently issued their 'Five Demands': the right not to wear prison uniforms; the right to determine their own work in prison; free association with other prisoners; weekly visits; and the restoration of remission lost as a result of the protest. Reinstating the political status disallowed since 1976 proved tougher than anyone expected, the more so when Margaret Thatcher became Prime Minister in May 1979. Amid a stench of maggot-infested beds, vomit and diarrhoea, the dirty protest continued. On 28 October 1980, seven Republican prisoners refused breakfast and a hunger strike commenced. By 1 December, three female IRA prisoners from Armagh jail – Mairead Farrell, Mairead Nugent and Mary Doyle – joined the strike and Bernadette McAliskey (née Devlin) emerged from the political wilderness to add her voice to the campaign.

The omens were not good. On 8 December, the IRA-supporting ex-Beatle John Lennon was assassinated in New York. Ten days later, Seán McKenna, now on the 53rd day of his hunger strike and blind, was given the last rites. That night, his comrades saved his life by ending the strike, having gained certain concessions. But it was not enough. Suspicion remained, not least from Paisley, who was apoplectic at the news that Margaret Thatcher had subsequently met with the Irish Taoiseach Charles Haughey.

The New Year began with fresh drama. On 16 January, three

members of the UDA descended on Bernadette McAliskey's farmhouse at Derrylaughan on the shores of Lough Neagh and deposited seven bullets into her chest and legs. Her husband was shot in the head, stomach and right arm. Miraculously, they survived. Immediately after, a hoax bomb was left on the doorstep of the SDLP's John Hume. Within three weeks, Paisley was back in the headlines having invited journalists to a midnight meeting on a hillside in County Antrim where he unveiled a paramilitary force of 500 men, many waving arms certificates. Addressing his audience, he bellowed "This is a small token of men who are placed to absolutely devastate any attempt by Margaret Thatcher and Charles Haughey to destroy the Union and take from us our heritage." Evoking the spirit of Sir Edward Carson, he proceeded to denounce the Thatcher/Haughey summit as "the most nefarious conspiracy that has ever been hatched against a free people", adding that his men would "resist to the death . . .We will stop at nothing." Soon he was telling police that there was an Official Unionist conspiracy to have him shot.

It was an unsettling time for the Morrisons to return to Ireland, but this was just the beginning. In March, a second hunger strike commenced, headed by a minor league Republican, Bobby Sands. Originally from the Protestant-dominated Rathcoole district of Belfast, Sands had been scarred by the Troubles. When his family were forced from their house by loyalists, he became politicized and, at 18, joined the IRA. Arrested for carrying firearms, he had spent much of his life in Long Kesh, where he studied Irish history, revolutionary politics and the art of songwriting. His nickname was Geronimo, a nomenclature echoed in the opening track of Morrison's *Veedon Fleece*. With his long hair and gaunt features, Sands resembled the archetypal mid-Seventies' singer-songwriter. The image was appropriate as he had already composed a number of striking compositions and poems, written under the pen name borrowed from his sister: Marcella. At the time of the hunger strike, he was serving 14 years for possession of a single revolver. He had never killed anybody. His decision to commence a new hunger strike of 'staggered starvation' was a high-risk strategy. The idea was that other prisoners would start starving themselves every week, creating a chain of martyrs. As each died, a replacement would enlist, thereby ensuring that the spiral of self-destruction would continue, piling corpse upon corpse. It was nothing less than the ultimate commitment to Pádraig Pearse's doctrine of blood sacrifice.

While some dismissed Sands and his comrades as puppets of IRA propaganda, this was far from the truth. Both the IRA and Sinn Féin were firmly against the hunger strike, fearing that its failure would damage the organization. Gerry Adams had already sent a letter saying, "Bobby, we are tactically, strategically, physically and morally opposed to the hunger strike." It was to no avail. The momentum now lay with the strikers. Sands' world changed forever within days of starting his fast. The sudden death of Frank Maguire, the Republican MP for Fermanagh–South Tyrone, provided Sands with the chance to run for the seat under the title 'H-Block-Armagh Political Prisoner'. Amazingly, Sands was elected after a record-breaking turn-out of 86.9 per cent of the electorate. By now it was the 41st day of his fast and tensions were running high. His comrades in the Maze said the rosary for him twice daily in Gaelic. Loyalists voiced their own view in murals stained with graffiti proclaiming 'Let Bobby Sands Die' and the grimly humorous 'Don't Be Vague, Starve A Taig'.

Throughout the strike, Margaret Thatcher remained intransigent. Some assumed that she would not allow a democratically-elected MP the propagandist glory of a martyr's death on the meagre fare of the 'Five Demands', but they underestimated her cast-iron certainty. Jim Gibney, the campaign officer who had first suggested that Sands stand for parliament, knew that his friend would not survive. "Bobby Sands was close to death. I just decided that I was going to go in and say goodbye to him for what I knew was going to be the last time. When I went into his cell, it was one of the saddest scenes that I can recall in my time in the struggle . . . He had a pair of rosary beads around his neck which had been sent to him by the Pope . . . He didn't know who I was because at that stage he was blind, but he said 'Is that you, Jim?' And I said 'Yes it is, Bobby' . . . I took his hand and he said 'Tell the lads I'm hanging in there.' And I wished him goodbye."

Sands died in the early hours of 5 May 1981 after 66 days of starvation. Tributes poured in from all over the world. While the British press, including the *Guardian*, supported Thatcher's obdurate stance, the global response was more sympathetic. Poland's Lech Wałęsa sent condolences calling Sands "a great man who sacrificed his life for his struggle"; students marched in Italy, burning Union Jacks; in Tehran, Winston Churchill Street was renamed Bobby Sands Street; there was a one-minute silence in India's parliament and the *Hindustan Times* concluded that the British PM had "allowed a member of the House of Commons, a colleague, in fact, to die of starvation . . . Never had such an incident occurred in a civilized country." More deaths followed. During the next two weeks, Francis Hughes, Ray McCreesh and Patsy O'Hara perished. Thatcher announced that she would not allow political status to "criminals and enemies of society" and insisted that the IRA had played its "last card".

It was a fatal miscalculation. Sands' funeral attracted 100,000 mourners and more hunger strikers were now joining the spiral of death. Within a month, two won seats in the Irish Parliament *in absentia*. Still more deaths followed. It was only the intervention of prisoners' families some months later that ended the strike, by which time Republicans were claiming a moral victory. Gerry Adams, who had once opposed the great fast, admitted that Sands' death produced the most profound international impact of any event he had witnessed in Ireland during his lifetime. The ten blood sacrifices not only emphasized the IRA's continued commitment to the struggle, but spearheaded an infiltration into mainstream politics. With a battalion of new recruits, the IRA and Sinn Féin began the long road towards a political solution to the Troubles. The next phase was ably articulated by the leadership's director of publicity Danny Morrison who, addressing Sinn Féin's Ard Fheis in Dublin at the close of the strike, announced: "Who here really believes we can win the war through the ballot box? But will anyone here object if, with a ballot box in one hand and the Armalite in the other, we take power in Ireland?"

The hunger strike affected musicians on both sides of the religious divide. Two months after Sands' death, George Jones' showband Clubsound played their final concert in Belfast, linking arms at the end of the evening for 'Peace', an anthem of the Troubles. Moving Hearts' Christy Moore would later keep the lyrics and music of Sands alive, most notably in his haunting version of the anthemic 'Back Home In Derry'.

In the wake of the double deaths of Donall Corvin and Bobby Sands, Phil Coulter visited Morrison in California. It was sad reminiscing about Corvin, but Coulter was surprised how relaxed Morrison appeared. "He's not angry anymore," he told me soon after his return. "He's very mellow. He's straightened out his alcohol problem . . . His hang-up now is coffee. He leads a very simple and straight life. He has a live-in lady and he had his kid staying with him during the summer holidays. I think he's a lot happier." The pair collaborated on some songs for the first time and, perhaps influenced by recent events, Morrison seemed increasingly drawn towards his Irish heritage. Some months before, he had contacted Harrison's Records in Castle Street, Belfast, and ordered a rare recording by Ulster poet James Simmons. Now, the Irish influence was stronger than ever. He even considered featuring a series of Gaelic-styled instrumentals on his forthcoming album. "One of the nights I was there we stopped working and went for a drink in town," Coulter recalls. "He'd discovered an Irish bar in San Francisco where they played traditional Irish music. There was a time in Van Morrison's career where there was no way you'd have got him into a pub, let alone an Irish bar where they played very average traditional music. He has got a thing about the evolution of the Celtic tradition and Celtic culture and he's very aware that he is a Celt. One evening he produced an album of chants in Scottish Gaelic from the Shetland Islands. It was very primeval and he was fascinated by that." Coulter also told me at this time of Morrison's continued interest in spirituality. "Religion has been an ongoing awareness in his life. In his study two of the four walls were bookcases full of tomes on comparative religion. That's one of his great interests in life outside music. He's been into everything from mysticism to psychical experiences through the more organized religions . . . not practising, but studying. The whole comparative religion thing has been there for a very long time."

One esoteric writer dominating Morrison's thoughts was Alice A. Bailey, who had written a number of books which she claimed had been telepathically dictated to her by a Tibetan master, Djwal Khul. Among these were *Esoteric Astrology* and *Esoteric Psychology: A Treatise On The Seven Rays*. The astrological notion of the rays influencing events on Earth partly inspired a new Morrison composition, 'Celtic Ray'. He was even more taken with her 1950 publication, *Glamour: A World Problem* which dealt with the New Age concept of a series of so-called 'glamours' or 'mental illusions' which created a fog, veiling the spiritual wanderer and the Aryan race from a true vision of the world. Illumination came when the dweller on the threshold was engulfed in the purifying light of the soul or Angel of Presence. Morrison distilled some of these phrases in two more songs, 'Aryan Mist' and 'Dweller On The Threshold', co-written with his engineer Hugh Murphy. A virtual album was completed with several songs revealing a strong folk influence but, according to Herbie Armstrong, all of the recordings, excepting the instrumental 'Scandinavia', were either scrapped or reconfigured.

Morrison's New Age interests, esoteric songwriting and low-key recordings met with a tepid response from Warner Brothers (US). Manager Bill Graham was also aggrieved that Morrison was not exploiting his potential to the full by submitting to a nationwide tour. Increasingly, the singer's live appearances seemed restricted to small clubs in the Bay Area. As relations between manager and artiste deteriorated, the volatile Graham was reduced to pounding on Morrison's door in at attempt to force a confrontation. "There was a management dispute," Herbie Armstrong confirms. "He decided to break with Bill Graham. I think he didn't want to pay Graham a percentage. He sacked him onstage in San Francisco and he did a whole rap where he tore management apart. I flew in for that gig. Bill was a nice guy but he was taking Van in the wrong direction. He was trying to commercialize him." Armstrong remembers attending a meeting with Tom Dowd, whom Warner Brothers had recommended to produce the new album. He was sold to Morrison on the basis that he had once worked with Ray Charles, Joe Turner, LaVern Baker, Aretha Franklin and Dr John. It was only after learning about his recent CV that Morrison suspected Warners' motives. "They're trying to turn me into Rod Stewart!" he roared. Dowd was informed that his services would not be required.

Instead, Morrison assumed production duties and *Beautiful Vision* finally emerged in February 1982. It proved a highly impressive album. The songs carefully combined Morrison's metaphysical musings ('Across The Bridge Where Angels Dwell'), religious raptures ('She Gave Me Religion'), Ulster references ('Northern Muse'), love songs ('Vanlose Stairway') and earthy nostalgia ('Cleaning Windows') to create a work that was finely balanced. Those unfamiliar with Alice Bailey's writings tended to superimpose their own interpretations on Morrison's more abstruse lyrics. Phil Coulter, for example, assumed that there was a subtext to 'Across The Bridge Where Angels Dwell', pointing out that Morrison's daughter and former wife lived in San Mateo, which was literally across the bridge from Morrison's home in Mill Valley. Other compositions could be equally appreciated as mystical or corporeal, depending upon the listener's inclinations. And, of course, the catchy 'Cleaning Windows' became a minor UK hit. Well structured and arranged, *Beautiful Vision* was a disciplined work, which offered depth and listenability. It also underlined the extent to which Morrison had moved away from the R&B stylings which had made him such a hit on American FM radio. Increasingly, it was his Irish lineage that propelled his music. "It's important for people to get into the music of their own culture," he insisted at the time. "A lot of that's being missed because of modern forms of music and the influence of the media. When I was growing up in Belfast, I was listening to American music. Irish music was going on all around me, but that was nowhere. I was looking for something different. I was listening to black American music. I think it can be dangerous to not validate the music of where you're from, *for anybody*, whether it's Bulgaria or whatever."

The release of *Beautiful Vision* coincided with the first in a series of celebrated concerts at London's Dominion Theatre. Old friend Herbie Armstrong was chosen as the support. It was his first ever performance as a soloist and he was so nervous that he took tranquillizers washed down with a tumbler of brandy. His impressive set included a fine reading of 'Friday's Child' in which he amusingly altered the lyrics to sing Morrison's motto "It's too late to stop now". Morrison's own performances proved a revelation and are still regarded by many as his most memorable since the glory days of the Caledonia Soul Orchestra. He even made sense of the difficult *Common One*, reinterpreting 'Satisfied' and transforming the indulgent and hilarious 'Summertime In England' into a live *tour de force*, even throwing in references to Christopher Isherwood and alluding to Dylan's dictum 'Gotta Serve Somebody' as a defence of his own spiritual ramblings. His sense of fun was also evident during a show at Belfast's Ulster Hall which included guest Phil Coulter on keyboards. Midway through some stream of consciousness banter, an audience member cried out "What are you talking about?" Without missing a beat, Morrison retorted: "If you don't know who I'm talking about, then why are you here?" The phrase was repeated by MD Pee Wee Ellis in the response section to 'Summertime In England', much to everyone's amusement.

While on tour, Morrison visited George Jones in Bangor, Northern Ireland, attending a party along with Phil Coulter and other acquaintances. He looked back fondly on his showband days, laughing at their comedy routines and reminiscing about a time before the business of music dominated his daily life. "He always wanted to retain his home ties," George Jones told me after the party. "Although Northern Ireland didn't do anything to help his career, he loved the way of life here. We used to rehearse in Cyprus Avenue and he would walk up and down there. It gave him a lot of inspiration. He always loved the mannerisms and colloquialisms of the people. That always made him laugh. I know he calls America his home now . . . but he loves it here. I think when he comes back he's afraid of the hangers-on. He was always ahead of his time and that frightened a lot of people off who didn't understand him, and it still does. I think his next step will be out of music and into movies, plays or comedy. I honestly think that he's given music all that he can give to it . . . He wants to do something different."

The notion of Morrison reinventing himself as a comedian sounded ludicrous, particularly to those who only knew him as a sour puss. But just as Ian Paisley could quickly turn acerbity into ready wit, Morrison had a dry sense of humour, although it was usually reserved for old and trusted friends. Amazingly, he had already toyed with the idea of playing the entertainer but soon realized it was a conceit too far. As he admitted: "If I went out and tried comedy, what would happen? It would be 'What?' The image that's out there is not conducive for me to do comedy."

NINETEEN

Rave On, Ian Paisley

Van Morrison's life had once been a battleground of daily dramas and a seemingly unending struggle against what he perceived as a hostile music business. Back in the Sixties, he had served a tough apprenticeship with the Monarchs and Them, never sure of what was to come. Even after establishing himself with a hit group and touring the States, his career could easily have been finished in the aftermath of his conflict with Phil Solomon. Time passed slowly then. Every decision he made was of potentially huge importance, from accepting Bert Berns' offer to return to America to signing with Warner Brothers and recording *Astral Weeks*. The Seventies had brought international stardom, albeit at a price. Once again event was piled upon event as Morrison entered the cauldron of the American music business, crossing swords with executives, playing huge venues against his better judgement, battling between his twin roles as a singles and albums artiste, and coming to grips with a media image that portrayed him as some form of Irish mystic. On a personal level, he experienced marriage, fatherhood, divorce and a three-year retirement before finally deciding to return to England and restart his career.

By the dawn of the Eighties what he desired more than anything in his professional life was a greater control over his destiny. This autonomy was achieved by negotiating better terms with a new record company, improving his publishing deals and limiting his live performances to concert halls and theatres that he deemed suitable. Later, he would elect to license his recordings to labels of his choice having already paid upfront for recording costs. It was all part of a drive to cut out the middle men whom he had always felt had interfered with or compromised his grander plans. As a result, Morrison was able to continue the familiar album–tour–album syndrome without the attendant melodramas of previous years. This created the illusion of time speeding up, as the mishaps, excesses and incidents of youth were replaced by a less frantic and more prosaic lifestyle in keeping with approaching middle age. With his major achievements already logged and a sizeable bank balance and several properties to his name, Morrison no longer needed to worry about financial hardship or momentary career blips. He spent more time visiting old friends, regularly commuting between London and Belfast. More than ever, he was free to indulge his interests in fringe religions and New Age pursuits, while also reconnecting with his Irish roots. Although he continued to complain about the burdens of being a public figure, he largely escaped the glare of publicity and was able to conduct his daily business without interruption. Often he was seen walking around Holland Park, eating in restaurants or visiting the cinema. To take one example, a friend of mine went to the theatre in London to see *The Mysteries* and found herself sitting a few seats away from Morrison. He remained untroubled throughout the performance and nobody bothered asking him for an autograph afterwards. Although some of his songs suggested otherwise, Morrison had clearly achieved that perfect balance between celebrity and privacy. Journalists were uninterested in discussing his love life and not one of his girlfriends was photographed, interviewed or even mentioned in print. That situation would remain unchanged until the Nineties.

Like many of his contemporaries, most notably Bob Dylan and Neil Young, Morrison would find the Eighties a tough decade in which record sales could no longer be guaranteed purely on the basis of past reputation. Fortunately, Morrison's esoteric spiritual interests fired his imagination and revitalized his recordings, resulting in a solid run of albums that many listeners regarded as a panacea for a more cynical and materialistic decade. His critical and commercial standing in Britain would remain relatively healthy thanks to regular touring, but his profile in America plummeted. Once the darling of *Rolling Stone*, Morrison was rapidly reduced to the level of a respected elder statesman with a small but devoted cult following. Major American tours were no longer a priority and his visits were fleeting. For the whole of the

Eighties, not one of his albums would register a US Top 50 placing, a barely believable statistic considering his immense standing during the previous decade. Morrison displayed no visible concern about this commercial decline. On the contrary, he seemed relieved to find his life on a more even keel.

Such changes could scarcely have been imagined by his followers back in the summer of 1982 when his name was all over the music press. Suddenly, there was renewed critical and commercial interest in Morrison's mid-period work, largely thanks to the success of Dexys Midnight Runners whose 'Come On Eileen' became the year's best-selling UK single and climbed to number 1 on both sides of the Atlantic. Their concomitant chart-topping album *Too-Rye-Ay* revealed singer Kevin Rowland and his colleagues adopting hoe-down gypsy chic and playing a style of music influenced by Morrison's Seventies work. When Rowland's inspired cover of 'Jackie Wilson Said' reached the UK Top 5, the Celtic/soul fusion pioneered by Morrison was now all the rage. There was even press speculation about the pair working together, but it came to nothing.

It was against the backdrop of this renascent popularity that Morrison made the momentous decision to relocate to London on a semi-permanent basis. With his marriage long behind him and his daughter soon to enter her teenage years, he felt the time was right. Fittingly, he chose Notting Hill Gate as his base – a district already immortalized in 'T.B. Sheets' as the fictional scene of his most agonizing and inspired moments. His move back to Europe may also have owed much to a recent love interest: Ulla Munch. "I first met Ulla during the *Wavelength* tour when he was still managed by Bill Graham," Stephen Pillster recalls. "She worked for a promoter in Denmark and came over during that period. She lived upstairs in Vanlose Street, Copenhagen, and he wrote 'Vanlose Stairway' [for her]. It was one of my favourite songs. I think she was a pretty steadying influence on him." Their relationship would last for several years.

During the same period, Morrison became friends with film-maker Peter Hayden, who was working on a documentary about Francis Ford Coppola. Morrison had recently been asked to provide music for Coppola's new movie *One From The Heart* but turned down the offer, explaining "I'm not particularly fond of Las Vegas and that whole thing and that's why I didn't do it. I didn't feel like I could be true to doing that kind of music – although I like Coppola a lot. I think he's a great film-maker." Hayden had previously met Morrison at the premiere of *The Last Waltz* in 1978, but their paths did not cross again until a chance meeting. "He'd only just come back from America," Hayden recalls. "We were on a plane to Copenhagen and we were the only people on the plane. He was visiting Ulla – the tall one. I gave him my business card and when I got back there was a message, 'Mr Morrison rang.'" It took a while before Hayden realized that the mysterious Mr Morrison was indeed the singer. After returning the call, the pair agreed to meet at the Mean Fiddler in Harlesden and became good pals. "I found him friendly," Hayden reflects. "He'd call me and say, 'Let's get together and have a cup of coffee.' He liked movies. He was cultured but he didn't intellectualize things. At the time, he was into Scientology. I'd broken up with my wife and it was a period of disruption. I didn't discuss it much with him but he'd try and help. He'd suggest things to do or books to read. He'd say, 'These things happen.'"

Morrison's reading list expanded during the early Eighties, but one book that stood out was Cyril Scott's *Music: Its Secret Influence Throughout The Ages* (1937). Enthusing about the healing power of music, Morrison revealed: "I've just done some research and there's things I've been finding out. About teachings – ancient teachings – about different keys and what they do. Apparently, in the old days if someone was sick . . . they'd get a harp and play a chord . . . to heal this affliction or whatever. These teachings are still floating around in various religious sects . . . They've been lost but you can still dig them out."

Before long, Morrison found a fellow Cyril Scott devotee in Derek Bell, a musician and spiritual seeker whose accomplishments he had good reason to feel in awe towards. Like Morrison, Bell had been raised in Belfast, but he was no child of the shipyard. His father was a banker with enough money to ensure the boy was educated privately. At the age of 11, Bell had already written his first concerto and even worked part-time for the BBC as a composer; at the same stage Morrison could barely play an instrument and when he wrote to the BBC, they did not even reply. At school, Bell studied hard and won a scholarship to the Royal College of Music; by contrast, Morrison became a window

cleaner and a showband saxophonist. Both subsequently toured the
world, Bell managing the Belfast Symphony Orchestra and Morrison
heading the Caledonia Soul Orchestra. While Morrison spoke of Celtic
roots and the evils of commercialism, Bell had already established
himself as the sole Protestant in Ireland's leading traditional folk
ensemble the Chieftains and recorded a wealth of esoteric music under
his own name. Their approach to matters spiritual was similarly
contrasting. Morrison had taken the equivalent of a crash course in
New Age writings after the break-up of his marriage and career crisis in
1973–75, whereas Bell had been studying Eastern mysticism since his
teenage years and was now a practising Buddhist and Druid who
meditated religiously every day.

Their mutual interest in music as a healing force had brought them
together at a time when Morrison was still reflecting on the shock
suicide of Donall Corvin. As Bell explains: "Van was deeply searching
for an answer. He'd gone into his shell reading and studying theosophy;
the Rosicrucians, Scientology. Every bloody thing he could think off
. . . Van wanted teachings, but he didn't want to do any work. He was
in a hurry. He wanted them *now*." Morrison's belief that music was an
emollient for the body and soul encouraged his interest in producing
instrumental music. Privately, he told friends that his lyrics had become
a distraction for the listener and an impediment to receiving the true
message. "He'd been ringing me at one and two in the morning from
California asking me if I knew of any publishers who would publish his
book of poems," playwright Martin Lynch recalls. "I mentioned the
Blackstaff Press and he rang up to say, 'I wrote another poem last night.'
I said 'That's great Van' . . . He was writing a load of instrumentals at
the time and he said he was fed up with singing and wanted to be a
poet. He didn't want to be a rock 'n' roll singer, he wanted to be
accepted as a literary artiste." Morrison articulated those feelings in a
revealing aside. "I'm trying to create forms that bring some inner peace
and the instrumental music is supplying something for that need.
You've got no attachment to what the person is saying. You've just got
the music and you can meditate to it. The point is that this kind of
music is needed as an antidote to all the thump, thump stuff."

On *Beautiful Vision*, Morrison had closed his album with an
instrumental and left behind two others, a skeleton 'Daring Night' and

the B-side 'All Saints Day'. His next work *Inarticulate Speech Of The Heart* featured four non-vocal tracks which testified to his interest in Irish traditional music. It was a brave departure, but one that tended to diminish his art. Never an accomplished instrumentalist, Morrison's greatest strength had always been his voice. It was his white soul credentials that helped establish his reputation, particularly in America during the Seventies. Although there were enough new converts to ensure his latest work a Top 20 placing in the UK charts, the American response was alarmingly apathetic and the album peaked at number 116, his worst ever showing since appearing in the listings. The importance of Morrison as a vocalist was made most eloquently on the album's key track, the surprisingly successful dramatic monologue 'Rave On, John Donne'. Like 'Summertime In England', the song betrayed a comic element, partly through its title which combined a Buddy Holly song with a metaphysical poet, but mainly as a result of Morrison implicitly placing his meagre achievements alongside those of such literary heavyweights as Walt Whitman and W.B. Yeats. If its roll call was presumptuous, its sentiments were undoubtedly sincere. Originally rumoured to be nearly 45 minutes in unedited form, spread across two reels of tape, this arresting mantra was a potent distillation of Morrison's literary, philosophical and New Age interests. Its appeal lay not in the subject matter as much as the vocal execution. More than any other song in the Morrison canon, this revealed the influence of Ian Paisley in its oratorical cadence, thumping repetition and celebratory fervour. Humility had never been Morrison's strong point, but the same could be said of Paisley, who was nevertheless contrite enough to acknowledge that redemption was an undeserved gift. "If God gave me the due reward for my deeds, he would send me to hell," he once admitted.

Morrison was similarly humbled. There was an almost palpable desperation in his advocacy of Yeats' *A Vision* and the other writings and authors mentioned, as if he knew they were connections of which he was ultimately not worthy. Like a Protestant seeking divine grace, Morrison sounded in awe of a higher power. "I actually think he's a very Protestant artiste with a very Protestant voice," critic Seán O'Hagan agrees. "I think that idea of testifying runs in the Protestant oral tradition from William Blake to Ian Paisley. And there's a lot of the lunacy of Paisley in some of Van's flights of fantasy. In 'Rave On, John

Donne' he's off on this mad testifying. I can't think of any other popular musician who does it."

It was not John Donne, William Blake or Ian Paisley that critics centred on when interviewing or discussing Morrison, but the eccentric and delusional leader of a cult religion, whom the singer had credited with special thanks on his latest album. The controversial L. Ron Hubbard, an impoverished science-fiction writer turned millionaire prophet, had already claimed to have discovered cures for everything from the common cold to cancer, additionally boasting that he could increase a person's lifespan by 25 per cent. He spoke extravagantly about previous lives on different planets and once claimed to have visited heaven 43 trillion years ago, even providing a strangely mundane description of the cosmological kingdom.

Hubbard's theories caused a sensation in 1950s America when *Dianetics* shot to the top of the best-sellers listings. Promoted by its author as a "science of mental health", the book compared the human brain to a virus-contaminated computer whose corrupted files needed to be cleared in order to function correctly. This was achieved through a process called 'auditing' during which the subject (called the 'pre-clear') was placed in a 'Dianetics reverie' and then encouraged to travel along a 'time track' in order to locate the origin of any neurosis, which could then be erased and "positively cured by Dianetics processing". Within a year, Hubbard was proselytizing the related system he called Scientology, which he insisted was an exact science. Central to its philosophy was Hubbard's claim that he had proven by scientific means the existence of the 'thetan', an immortal spirit or soul which inhabited the body and had survived the deaths of innumerable people over trillions of years, even on other planets and in different universes. While the 'clear' was the goal of Dianetics, Scientology aspired towards the state of 'Operating Thetan' (OT). Amongst other qualities, an OT would have telekinetic abilities and be able to move at will through all universes. Hubbard once described this state as being akin to that of God, adding that neither Jesus Christ nor Buddha had achieved OT level, but were "just a shade above clear". Interpreting and understanding Hubbard's myriad theories and writings was a near impossible task given his astonishing productivity, frequently unfathomable postulations and love of neologisms. As one investigation observed:

"He wrote tens of thousands of pages and spoke 30 million tape-recorded words about thetans, operating thetans, past lives, time tracks, engrams, implants, galaxies, events of countless trillions of years ago and a multitude of other similar topics. He propounded axioms, factors, logics and prelogics; and he wrote about dynamics and emotional tone scales."

In February 1954, Hubbard had converted Scientology into a religion, a move which happily provided his church with tax-free concessions. The movement prospered thereafter, despite being lambasted frequently by the medical and psychiatric establishments. Soon, Hubbard began attracting the attention of the FBI, the CIA and, inevitably, the IRS. Often they seemed bamboozled by the labyrinthine nature of his organization with its countless affiliates and sub-divisions. After relocating to Britain in 1959 and establishing the Church of Scientology in the unlikely environs of East Grinstead, West Sussex, Hubbard toured frequently and Scientology continued to make a worldwide impact. It proved particularly popular in parts of Australia, but a backlash of bad publicity prompted the government in Victoria to launch a Board of Inquiry into Scientology in November 1963.

The Board's Report by Kevin A. Anderson, QC, was the most devastatingly detailed and persuasive investigation of Scientology ever published. Protected by privilege, it was free to discuss every aspect of Hubbard's organization without fear of legal reprisals. The Report, published in 1965, consisted of 128,000 words (excluding appendices) and 30 chapters compiled from the evidence of 151 witnesses whose testimonies, spread over 160 days, took up four million words and 8,920 pages. The Board also undertook the unenviable task of reading reams of Hubbard's writings on Dianetics and Scientology and listening to a considerable number of the staggering 30 million words spoken by him on tape, before adding with a note of sarcasm: "The Herculean task of reducing to manageable size the content of these Hubbardian emanations must await the labour of a dedicated Scientologist with the time, money, capacity and compulsion to undertake such a useless exercise."

The tone of the Board's Report was not only critical but contemptuous. Its Preface warned readers that it would be a grave mistake to dismiss Scientology as "silly" or consider the cult's practitioners as simply "harmless cranks": "Scientology is evil; its techniques evil: its practices a serious threat to the community, medically, morally and socially; and its adherents sadly deluded and often mentally ill." The next 30 chapters emphasized these points in exhaustive analytical detail.

Hubbard was vilified as a charlatan, and his sanity seriously doubted. One chapter, provocatively titled "Hubbard's Morbid Preoccupation With Perversion" detailed his interest in sex, rape, abortions and the abnormal behaviour of women. Many of his extreme theories were quoted containing opinions such as "A large proportion of allegedly feeble-minded children are actually attempted abortion cases." The Report continued, "Expert psychiatric opinion is that the many books, pamphlets, articles, bulletins, and the like which bear Hubbard's name, indicate in their author symptoms of paranoid schizophrenia of long standing with delusions of grandeur." Summing up his voluminous writings, Anderson said: "Hubbard continually distorts and mis-represents, frequently asserting as fact propositions which are positively wrong. His writings and theories stand condemned *en masse* as being entirely contrary to conventional learning and experience in the many sciences in which he falsely claims to be knowledgeable. So far as his own theories are concerned, they are unsupported by any proof and are generally contrary to reason. If there is a scintilla which Hubbard has written or said that is justifiably excluded from the foregoing general denunciation of his works, it is of negligible content, and cannot serve as a foundation for the fabric of falsehood, fraud and fantasy which he has forged."

The Report pulled no punches in its language, describing Scientology as "a perverted form of psychology . . . rivalling in fantasy the most advanced science fiction". Its theories were "generally impossible, peculiar and novel to itself" and its practitioners "unqualified with no knowledge of psychiatry or psychology". Anderson was amazed by the reverence shown to Hubbard by his followers, observing that "Scientology students are specifically taught that he is not God, lest they think he is. The adulation and obeisance which they offer him is almost unbelievable." Although a number of Scientologists offered evidence in support of their beliefs, their testimonies proved counter-productive. "Many active Scientologists believe they have obtained benefit from Scientology processing," the Report admitted. "This is not proof that in fact they have obtained benefit, because processing and training are specifically designed and conducted to create in the mind of the preclear the very delusion that benefit has been obtained. The effect of prolonged processing and training is that the critical faculties and common sense of the individual are destroyed, so that he comes to believe that Hubbard is right, Scientology is right and everything else is wrong . . . When asked to explain some of Hubbard's writings witnesses were unable to make any sense out of them."

After damning Hubbard thoroughly, the Board then patronized his followers as dupes or victims, conned by a perverted system of belief. Scientology, the Report concluded, "robs people of their initiative, their sense of responsibility, their critical faculties and sometimes their reason. It induces them mentally to debase and enslave themselves. It has done, and is capable of doing, grave harm to the mental and physical health of its victims by the practice of dangerous procedures and by persuading them that orthodox medical care and treatment, which some of them may urgently require, is evil and to be avoided. It consistently relieves them of large sums of money in payment of fees for processing and training."

After 30 chapters in this manner, the Anderson Report closed on an unambiguous note of opprobrium: "If there should be detected in this Report a note of unrelieved denunciation of Scientology, it is because the evidence has shown its theories to be fantastic and impossible, its principles perverted and ill-founded, and its techniques debased and harmful. Scientology is a delusional belief system, based on fiction and fallacies and propagated by falsehood and deception. While making an appeal to the public as a worthy system whereby ability, intelligence and personality may be improved, it employs techniques which further its real purpose of securing domination over and mental enslavement of its adherents. It involves the administration by persons without any training in medicine or psychology of quasi-psychological treatment, which is harmful medically, morally and socially . . . The HASI [Hubbard Association of Scientologists International] claims to be 'the world's largest mental health organization'. What it really is, however, is the world's largest organization of unqualified persons engaged in the practice of dangerous techniques which masquerade as mental therapy . . . That many Scientologists sincerely believe in the virtues and the efficacy of Scientology is apparent from the evidence. Some have become so dedicated to it and have served it so faithfully that their sacrifices cannot but excite compassion. These ardent devotees, though quite rational and intelligent on other subjects, are possessed of an invincible impediment to reason where Scientology is concerned . . . They seemed to be deluded, mistaken and almost innocent tools."

Anderson's Report failed to destroy Scientology and Hubbard responded with his customary intemperance, attacking the Australian Board as a "kangaroo court", noting that "only a society founded by criminals . . . could come to such a conclusion" before damning them all as the offspring "of the riff-raff of London slums – robbers, murderers, prostitutes, fences and thieves". Nevertheless, the cult suffered a series of serious setbacks over the next few years from legislation in Australia, Britain, Greece and France. Hubbard's novel solution was to take to the high seas, and for several years he became an international outlaw, commandeering a fleet that was monitored closely by the FBI and CIA. His personal liner was said to contain spare cash in excess of $1 million and a regiment of pubescent girls in hot pants who attended his every need in their role as 'messengers'.

After returning to America in the Seventies, Hubbard remained convinced that the enemies of Scientology were plotting his downfall. In an ingenious piece of counter espionage, he instructed some of his supporters to infiltrate the institutions that were hounding him – the IRS, and various government departments – and systematically destroy any incriminating records they held. The subterfuge proved remarkably successful but was eventually discovered by the FBI and ended with nine Scientologists being indicted before a federal grand jury in Washington on 28 counts, including conspiring to steal government documents and conspiring to obstruct justice. On 26 October 1979, they pleaded guilty to one count each of the indictment and received custodial sentences. Hubbard was not among them.

A combination of negative publicity and declining health may have caused Hubbard to retire from view at this point. After 1980, he was never seen in public again. Ever resilient, the Church of Scientology overcame its recent difficulties and continued to thrive in the new decade when the need for spiritual solace, psychological counselling and mind and lifestyle gurus increased in direct proportion to a decline in church attendances and support for conservative religious institutions. By this point, Scientology was attracting some notable figures from the film world and music business. Within Van Morrison's circle, musicians Robin Williamson and Mark Isham both shared his interest. Other rock personalities were attracted to the cult because of its reputation for curing addictive traits. Whatever its alleged short-comings, Scientology could boast many positive testimonies from those who had followed its 'Purification Rundown' programme and related disciplines in the area of drug addiction therapy, most of which had been introduced over a decade after the damning Anderson Report.

Many were surprised to see Morrison's name associated with Scientology, but his involvement was perhaps typical of someone who preferred the mystic hipness of Rosicrucianism, Druidism and other esoteric cults to institutionalized religions. What no doubt attracted Morrison was the emphasis on healing in Hubbard's *Dianetics* and its claim to eradicate 'engrams' ("lasting marks or traces") that were the result of childhood, pre-natal or past-life trauma. If these engrams were erased from the 'reactive memory', then a lifetime's pain was effectively over and the subject was 'clear'. As one writer explained: "To become 'clear' of all engrams was the goal devoutly to be pursued for 'clears' were free from all neuroses and psychoses, had full control of their imaginations, greatly raised IQs and well-nigh perfect memories." Indeed, Hubbard added that such photographic recall had the additional bonus of full "colour, motion and sound" as well as optimum computational ability. It sounded like the Edenic awareness that Morrison had visualized from *Astral Weeks* onwards – a place, a time and a state of mind before the fall that was free from pain.

In thanking L. Ron Hubbard on his album sleeve, Morrison had effectively issued a press statement saying "I am a Scientologist." To his naive horror, this was the one area that everybody wished to explore in interviews over the next few years. It became an even hotter topic after L. Ron Hubbard Jnr sensationally denounced his father as an habitual liar who supposedly practised black magic and thought he was Satan incarnate. A more reasoned, but no less damning, commentary on Hubbard and Scientology was subsequently offered by a California judge in May 1984 who declared: "The organization clearly is schizophrenic and paranoid, and this bizarre combination seems to be a reflection of its founder. The evidence portrays a man who has been virtually a pathological liar when it comes to his history, background and achievements. The writings and documents in evidence additionally reflect his egotism, greed, avarice, lust for power, and vindictiveness and aggressiveness against persons perceived by him to be disloyal or hostile . . . Obviously, he is and has been a very complex person and that complexity is further reflected in his alter ego, the Church of Scientology." A few weeks later, in London's High Courts of Justice, Mr Justice Latey amplified this viewpoint, describing the cult as "immoral, socially obnoxious, corrupt, sinister and dangerous", adding that Hubbard's methods were "grimly reminiscent of the ranting and bullying of Hitler and his henchmen," and concluding, "Mr Hubbard is a charlatan and worse." The words of both judges were uncannily similar in tone and content to the denunciations voiced in the Anderson Report nearly 20 years before.

Between 1983 and 1984, Morrison attempted to ban the subject of Scientology during his interviews, but even then it was still mentioned in print. There were even apocryphal reports that he had not only been visiting but helping out at the Scientology centre in Tottenham Court Road, which was conveniently situated only minutes away from the Dominion Theatre, where he was resident for a series of concerts. Whatever the publicity blackout, there was no doubting his commitment to Hubbard's cult, as Rod Demick discovered at a chance meeting. "I bumped into him at the Festival of Mind, Body and Spirit at Olympia," he remembers. "My wife was working with her mum at one of the stalls and I went for a wander around. I was passing the *Dianetics* stand and I saw him with the headphones on listening to some lecture. We both said 'What are you doing here?' Then we sat down for about two hours and drank a million cups of coffee. He was trying to convince me that Scientology was the answer . . . he really thought it was the answer to everything. He didn't say how he got into it. At the time, he just said he found it a very practical solution. Everybody's searching."

TWENTY

Spiritual Friends

While Morrison continued his spiritual search, he settled into a less stressful performing schedule in more intimate venues. Agent Paul Charles, who had been responsible for 'business arrangements' since Morrison's return to the UK, ensured that the itineraries were to his client's satisfaction, while David Ravden co-ordinated other important office-related and accountancy matters. A couple of performances in Belfast were deemed suitable as a source for Morrison's first live album since the celebrated *It's Too Late To Stop Now*. Released in February 1984, *Live At The Grand Opera House Belfast* testified to Morrison's immersion in the present, with a set list that concentrated almost exclusively on recent material. Its high points included a nine-minute performance of 'Rave On, John Donne' and a sprightly 'Cleaning Windows' which held a particular nostalgic significance for the Belfast audience. The concerts throughout this period were often magical, although there was always the possibility of an off-night. "He's not a natural get-out-there-and-do-it guy," Peter Hayden reminds us. "He's a creature of mood. And if he's in the wrong mood, he doesn't feel it. His performances throughout his career have been up and down. I've seen blinding performances and I've seen some that make you think, 'What's he doing? He's not really here.' Performers are expected to turn it on all the time – it just can't happen. I went to a concert with someone and afterwards they said, 'He doesn't half look rough doesn't he?' I said, 'He looks rough! What's that got to do with it? What about the concert?' They were more interested in what he looked like."

Morrison secured some surprisingly positive profiles and reviews in the post-punk British music press of the early Eighties. In a period before the arrival of such magazines as *Q* or *Mojo*, most artistes of Morrison's vintage were beyond passé. Glossy teenage magazines like *Smash Hits* dominated the marketplace, while the *Face* served style gurus and the ever hip *New Musical Express* concentrated largely on the burgeoning student market and indie music scene. Theoretically, Morrison should have been irrelevant to the readership of all three, but an anomaly in the journalistic ranks of the *NME* worked to his advantage. At this time three of the paper's leading writers – Gavin Martin, Seán O'Hagan and Stuart Bailie – were from Northern Ireland and their shared interest in Morrison ensured that he was treated with respect rather than ignored as a relic of the Seventies. Not that Morrison ever acknowledged his good fortune. He remained a tough interviewee whose spiritual pursuits did not preclude flashes of self-aggrandizement. When asked by Gavin Martin whether he saw himself as part of the blues tradition of John Lee Hooker and Muddy Waters, he replied with supreme arrogance: "No, I transcended all that. I see myself as having transcended the whole thing. I was part of one period but I transcended it. I went through the R&B thing but I transcended that. I transcended folk, transcended every medium. So now I'm just myself."

This solipsism was also evident in his attitude towards his past. On 10 June 1984, former Them member Patsy McAuley died in mysterious circumstances. "I did a lot of investigation and it was a bit of a shock," his brother Jackie reveals. "I checked all his movements. He'd gone out to two bars, saw some friends and came home about 12 o'clock. He'd drank between three to four small bottles of cider during the night so he wasn't really drunk. But he was hungry so he made some soup. Then he went to bed. He felt sick during the night, went to the toilet half-asleep, fell asleep in the bathroom and vomited. He just passed away in his sleep in the bathroom. He had a good heart but his lungs weren't very good because he was asthmatic. The doctor said it was a million-to-one chance and it could have happened to anybody." Former associates were shocked by McAuley's death and Rod Demick decided to pass on the news to Morrison who had always had a good relationship with the quietest member of Them. "I phoned to tell him," Demick remembers. "This was typical Van – he didn't seem that bothered. His attitude was 'Those guys were only in the band for five minutes.' That was when he was on a different plane with the Scientology."

The one-man musical genre may have been on a spiritual quest, but he occasionally revealed something approaching a social conscience. In September he played at a benefit show for striking miners at London's Royal Festival Hall. A few weeks later, Margaret Thatcher, the scourge of the unions, escaped death when the IRA planted a bomb at the Grand Hotel, Brighton, during the Conservative Party conference. According to Sinn Féin publicity director Danny Morrison, an assassination threat had been a long time coming. Since the death of Bobby Sands and his comrades, Thatcher had been a target, albeit a seemingly impossible one to reach. "She was reviled," Morrison stresses. "[She was] very bitter, ignorant, intransigent. This woman, to me, epitomized evil. People in West Belfast, further afield, would have been asking the IRA and demanding of the IRA after the Hunger Strike 'How can you let this woman get away with this after what she has done?' It was obvious if the IRA could have found a way to kill Mrs Thatcher, they would have done so." Their sole opportunity came and went with Brighton, from which the Prime Minister emerged more resilient than ever. "Today we were unlucky," the IRA announced, "but remember we need only to be lucky once. You will have to be lucky always." The UDA no doubt felt the same. Only months before they had almost assassinated Sinn Féin president Gerry Adams. That two of the most prominent figures in the history of the Troubles could so easily have been killed underlined the continuing threat of violence. In the pop world, the ever outspoken Smiths frontman Morrissey callously announced: "The sorrow of the Brighton bombing is that Thatcher escaped unscathed. But I feel relatively happy about it. I think that for once the IRA were accurate in selecting their targets."

Van Morrison, predictably, said nothing. Despite his support for the miners, he side-stepped the political debates that dominated the pages of the music press and the mainstream media. However, he did insist "there's a big part of me that's just strictly involved with the island of Ireland . . . I *belong* to, specifically, Ulster." He wanted to play more traditional music, perhaps work with Moving Hearts, but felt strong resistance from many quarters, later complaining that the media and public still saw him as an American star. Back in Belfast, he was regarded by some as little more than an anachronism. Writing in the *Belfast Review*, the insightful Gillian Russell concluded: "As far as contemporary Belfast is concerned, Morrison has little direct relevance; he belongs – with [George] Best, another Belfast cowboy – to the Sixties, before the Fall. His own concept of his Irishness seems to have been lost somewhere and the image of Ireland conveyed by *Veedon Fleece* and some of his more recent LPs seems to have greater affinities with a Hollywood Glockamorra than with political and social realities."

Morrison reserved his combative skills for those he saw threatening his career. Throughout this period, he could be heard railing against a false report that Warner Brothers (US) had dropped him, complaining about a new biography, insisting that Bruce Springsteen had ripped off his dance movements and then falling foul of W.B. Yeats' estate over his intention to include a musical adaptation of the poem 'Crazy Jane On God' on his next album. Yeats' executors, unaware of Morrison's grand literary aspirations, were understandably unwilling to have the great poet's name sullied by association with a mere pop star and declined permission. "I thought I was doing them a favour," Morrison grumbled, "my songs are better than Yeats's."

The delayed album, *A Sense Of Wonder*, finally appeared in February 1985. Its rear sleeve displayed Morrison in garb which cried 'Zorro chic', an image thankfully not reflected in the music, which was impressively diverse, although far from his best. The strong opening track 'Tore Down A La Rimbaud', which expressed his awareness of the unconscious process of songwriting, had first taken form during the during the lengthy lay-off between *Veedon Fleece* and *A Period Of Transition*. "It took a long time to finish," Morrison remarked. "Eight years before I got the rest of the lines. That's the longest I've ever carried a song around." Along with the Rosicrucian-inspired 'The Master's Eyes', there were two songs inspired by William Blake. 'A New Kind Of Man' (based on Michael Davis's study of the visionary) was complemented by the climactic 'Let The Slave' which incorporated Blake's *The Price Of Experience* (from *Vala Or The Four Zoas*), complete with an arrangement by poet Adrian Mitchell. The idea translated surprisingly well into performance, with Morrison offering an uneasy yet amusing poetry reading at the close. The most prosaic track was a blues reworking of Mose Allison's 'If You Only

Knew' which had been included at the eleventh hour following the removal of the Yeats lyric 'Crazy Jane On God'. Irish elements were also present courtesy of the traditional ensemble Moving Hearts, whose presence enlivened both the instrumental 'Boffyflow And Spike' and the affecting title track on which Morrison conjured memories of old Belfast in a monologue listing such salivating plebeian delicacies as barmbracks, wagonwheels and pastie suppers at Davy's Chipper. That strange combination of the mystical and the mundane would dominate his work hereafter.

In May 1985, the *Daily Mirror* revealed that Morrison had been seen at an Alcoholics Anonymous meeting. Lots of people attend such gatherings for a variety of reasons, even after decades of abstinence. The singer, who had never liked the label alcoholic and had not been seen drinking in public for many years, was chafed by the report and critical of the AA. "Alcoholics Anonymous wasn't anonymous," he growled. "I don't know whether it ever has been anonymous, but I think that's the biggest lie for me. Because people still related to me as what I did, not as an alcoholic. I had to say at meetings to people: 'I don't give a fuck whether you've got the album or not. I'm here because I think I've got a drink problem. That's why I'm here.' To me, that's not being anonymous. That's rubbish. For me the attraction was the anonymity but it doesn't exist. It's a lie. A total lie."

Morrison's steady work rate continued during the mid–Eighties when he spent more time than ever playing dates in Continental Europe. His relationship with Ulla Munch ensured that Scandinavian fans saw him on a number of occasions appearing with the Danish Big Band. There were also a small number of American dates. "I have to thank Ulla for getting me back," states Stephen Pillster, who was recalled as Morrison's US tour representative. "When a round of touring began, he was trying out what to do and Ulla mentioned me. It hadn't occurred to Van. I'm sure she was involved in the Danish Big Band collaboration. Eric Mills, the head of the Big Band, had said 'Tell him to pick out a couple of numbers and I'll do the orchestration.' Van has a fascination for Frank Sinatra. I remember we played a date the night after Sinatra had been there and he said, 'You mean, he was in this dressing room last night?' He liked the idea of going into a studio the way Sinatra did with the band ready and rehearsed. He'd get up, get a level checked, count it off and sing the song. That always appealed to Van – getting up and blowing and not having all the other questions to answer."

The big question that still needed answering was the Irish one. There was fresh hope of a breakthrough with the signing of the Anglo-Irish Agreement in November 1985 which gave Dublin a consultative role in Ulster affairs. In Belfast, over 100,000 Unionists took to the streets in protest. Many nationalists voiced support for the Agreement, despite their distrust of Thatcher, but soon lost heart, as did the Dublin government. Paisley, meanwhile, continued to rave on and was twice expelled from the European Parliament for interrupting addresses by Thatcher and the Pope. Although Morrison seldom aligned himself with political causes, he joined U2, the Pogues and Elvis Costello in May 1986 at Self Aid, a post-Live Aid venture designed to raise funds for Ireland's unemployed youth. Even there, Morrison could not resist complaining about his own lot, announcing on stage: "If I was a gunslinger, there'd be a lot of dead copycats out there." He then sang a new composition, 'A Town Called Paradise', in which he railed against those who had supposedly ripped off his words and melodies. His words were surprising, given his considerable debt to black music. He also seemed to have forgotten the adaptation from 'All Shook Up' on 'Cyprus Avenue'. Accusations of plagiarism later took on concrete form when Morrison sued the pop group Wet Wet Wet for incorporating substantial lyrics from *A Sense Of Wonder* on their hit 'Sweet Little Mystery'. They had evidently intended this as a tribute to the man, but it was a sentiment that clearly backfired.

The old anger was also evident from the title of his next album, released in July 1986. *No Guru, No Method, No Teacher*, a phrase borrowed from the reluctant guru Krishnamurti, served as a tetchy rejoinder to the media mongrels who had branded him a fully-fledged Scientologist. The sessions brought together a triumvirate of Morrison's past colleagues: John Platania, David Hayes and Jeff Labes. "To me, he was still the same Van Morrison," Platania recalls. "Nothing really changed. He still viewed the business with a jaundiced perspective. I just recorded what I needed to record and he let me go. That's what he usually does. He'll give pointers or say he wants a certain thing, but even that's minimal. We did a short tour, which was business as usual, but fun. The tour wasn't that successful, not like the Caledonia one. I loved the album, but I don't know what that means in the scheme of things."

For many critics, the album contained Morrison's most meditative work to date. The longing that had been present since *Astral Weeks* took on a more contemplative tone here. 'Got To Go Back' was an almost neurotic reminiscence about his lost childhood in Orangefield, made more poignant by the oboe work of Kate St John. Religious imagery pervaded the album from the mysticism of 'Foreign Window' to the references to the Protestant Church of Ireland in 'Tír na nóg'. 'Ivory Tower', 'Thanks For The Information' and 'A Town Called Paradise' sounded like petulant songs of self-justification, albeit with a spiritual veneer. 'Here Comes The Knight', a pun on his biggest Them hit, outflanked the proprietorial Yeats estate by borrowing some lines from 'Under Ben Bulben' that were arguably part of the public domain, having also served as the epitaph inscribed on his gravestone in Sligo's Drumcliff Churchyard: "Cast a cold eye/On life, on death/Horseman, pass by!"

Clearly the most important song on the album was the side-closing 'In The Garden'. Its length and power recalled other defining tracks from Morrison's early career such as 'Into The Mystic', 'Listen To The Lion' and 'You Don't Pull No Punches, But You Don't Push The River'. Morrison recognized 'In The Garden' as perhaps the key recording of his Eighties career and spoke at sometimes ponderous length about its significance. "I actually take you through a definite meditation process, which is a form of transcendental meditation. If you're listening carefully, what you should have at the end is some degree of tranquillity. So, when this happens in the song and I say, 'I turn to you and I say, no guru, no method, no teacher – just you and I and nature and the Father, the Son and the Holy Ghost,' you really have the whole line to know what it means." The familiar imagery of gardens washed with rain, described both here and in 'Tír na nóg', combined the myth of an Irish Shangri-la with Morrison's perennial longing for a lost Eden. However, the pragmatic Protestant that lurked within him could not resist adding an awkward footnote to his hymn of mystical devotion. "You can also call this a press release," he insisted, like a cross between an advertising executive and a preacher. "This is making it quite clear that I'm not affiliated with any organization. I don't have a guru, I don't have any teacher, and there's no method that I subscribe to, and that's really what it's saying as well." Coincidentally, this disavowal occurred only a few months after the death of L. Ron Hubbard. Morrison still refused to discuss Scientology and continued to play down his involvement a decade later when he admitted: "I took courses in Scientology over a period of 18 months, but I'm not a joiner. I don't join things."

While Morrison's spiritual musings dominated his recent work, he was also capable of reinvestigating the jazz and blues influences that had preoccupied him earlier. On 6 June 1986, he had made a surprise appearance at London's Ronnie Scott's club where the jazz trumpeter Chet Baker was playing. Morrison sang on the Stephen Sondheim composition 'Send In The Clowns', which had already been recorded by a number of nightclub singers and was also a hit for Judy Collins. The concert was belatedly transmitted on BBC Television following Chet Baker's death in 1988.

Despite a run of successful albums, Morrison was far from content with his life. He had good reason to be pleased with *No Guru, No Method, No Teacher*, but aesthetic pride and favourable critical responses evidently meant nothing. Once again, Morrison allowed himself to be disillusioned by an almost obsessive focus on the philosophy of fame, made worse by an increasing administrative burden which made him question whether it was worth continuing in the music business. "This is my job and all that other bullshit is not my responsibility," he pleaded. "The whole thing of being famous is an illusion and I pay no attention to illusions. I was once in the business where I played rock and R&B, but now I'm as far removed as night is from day. I'm forced to do music part-time now; 95 per cent of my time is taken up with the business of getting the music out. The record company does nothing except distribution. I book the musicians and in most cases I pay for it . . . I have to go through a major record company, so I'm forced into this game. I'm not fond of playing games. Sometimes it feels as though I will never do another album and I've no idea of what may happen next. I enjoy playing the music. The rest is complete nonsense."

In spite of his reservations, Morrison kept busy. In November 1986, he was interviewed on local television in his hometown, Belfast. He also appeared at the Whitla Hall and performed with Nimajazz (Northern Ireland Music Association), whose ranks included former Them drummer John Wilson. During time off, Morrison took his Dublin saxophonist Richie Buckley on a guided tour of his former haunts. The pair quickly received a stern reminder of the sectarianism that still divided Northern Ireland. Only days before, the UDA had planted bombs in Dublin and there had been a huge protest outside Belfast City Hall against the Anglo-Irish Agreement. Undeterred, Morrison wandered into one of his former drinking dens. "It was a loyalist pub," Buckley stresses. "I didn't know it at the time. It was lunchtime and it was real dark but we went in. Van ordered a coffee and he asked me what I wanted. I said 'Oh, I'll have a pint of Guinness' at the top of my voice. Suddenly all these guys just stopped and looked around. The barman came over and said to Van: 'You better leave fairly soon.' So the two of us made a quick exit for the door."

Although Morrison had no guru or teacher, he was collecting what he termed "spiritual friends". The singer also entertained various visitors at his favourite cafés in Holland Park and Notting Hill, near to his London addresses in Aubrey Road and Simon Close. There, they would spend many an afternoon discussing the mysteries of the universe. Among those invited were two journalists in search of transcendence. Steve Turner met Morrison while writing *Hungry For Heaven*, a study of the relationship between religion and rock music. A committed Christian, Turner was nevertheless familiar with comparative religions and seemed relatively at ease when Morrison offered such casual opening gambits as "What do you think of the blood of Christ?" The vision of the cleansing blood of Jesus dripping from the Holy Cross into the Earth had inspired the Christ-centred founder of anthroposophy and radical educationalist Rudolf Steiner, who was evidently at the top of Morrison's reading list. His books included such eye-catching titles as *Christianity As Mystical Fact* and *Occult Science – An Outline*. Mick Brown, a self-confessed spiritual tourist with an enquiring mind and some knowledge of Steiner, was the other music-related journalist and writer offered access to Morrison's inner beliefs. One of the singer's favourite Steiner dictums was that the creative process is unconscious until the age of 28 and self-conscious thereafter. This fitted in neatly with Morrison's own experiences, recalling the year of his marriage break-up and the sense of creative burn-out that had followed in its wake. For someone normally so suspicious of the media, Morrison proved remarkably open with Turner and Brown and would later feel a sense of betrayal when both chose to reveal their experiences of the man in print.

Apart from his periods in London, Morrison frequently visited Northern Ireland, where his parents and childhood friends still lived. While there, he fraternized with other spiritual acolytes including Chieftain Derek Bell and his friend and fellow seeker Clive Culbertson. Ballymoney-born Culbertson was a "mystic, musician and healer", a practitioner of ritual magic, a Druid and member of a dazzling array of esoteric societies including the Old Gaelic Order, the Raven Shamanic Lodge and related Rosicrucian and Martinist organizations. He filled Morrison's head with some of the most airy New and Old Age theories, arcane knowledge and obscure belief systems since the heyday of Cecil McCartney. All of these Ulster-born enthusiasts of the ethereal shared distinctly Protestant backgrounds. Culbertson had been brought up in a strict Presbyterian family. "It's the case nowadays that if you were raised in Northern Ireland as a Protestant Unionist you're supposed to be apologizing all the time," he complains. "I don't make any apologies. It was good for me." At the age of 14, Culbertson had been 'saved' at a Campaign Crusade and religiously attended gospel meetings for nine months. Childhood memories of what he termed "mystical encounters" ("Sitting in my bedroom late at night, guys would walk through walls and stuff – I'd never really sussed what that was all about but I'd always accepted it") stimulated more esoteric interests. After relocating to London's hippie-dominated Earl's Court, he fell in with Buddhists and Hare Krishnas but upon returning to the North he joined the Mormons. Culbertson's free thinking, not to mention his then rock 'n' roll lifestyle, was unsuited to such fundamentalism, so he swiftly moved on through Rosicrucianism and the "robe and swords ritual magic" Martinist Order. Over the years, he had pursued a chequered career in the music business with workmanlike bands including Maybe, No Sweat, and the Sweat. He had even had a legal run-in with Mervyn Solomon and offended his powerful brother Philip by wearing a Star of David medallion. Clearly, he had a lot in common with Morrison and since 1981 they had been good friends, sharing many dinners at the Crawfordsburn Inn, Co. Down.

Culbertson was one of the few people to whom Morrison confided his interest in and eventual disillusionment with Scientology. "I think Scientology did free him," Culbertson argues. "A couple of times he took me through the auditing process which was interesting. I'm sure he was just skipping here and there, but he pinpointed areas in my life that needed looking at and I found it very useful . . . I know he did a lot of work with them and he got rid of a lot of crap. But the financial commitment got bigger and bigger every year which was an awful pity. I said to him, 'But did it work?' 'Yeah, it worked!' I said, 'Pay them!' 'Nah, too much money . . . I'm not paying those fuckers.' I couldn't see it and told him, 'You've got to make another financial commitment. You're so rich it's irrelevant. Give these guys another 100 grand . . .' But the money was always [a factor]." Given the sums involved, Morrison's reticence was understandable.

Like Derek Bell, Culbertson found himself both perplexed and irritated by Morrison's seeming lack of commitment to any belief system. Although impressed by his knowledge of Alice Bailey, Culbertson was dismayed to learn that Morrison seldom practised what he studied. "The only way you can find out if a system works is if you do it for six months," he told him. "Then if you don't like it you can throw it in the bin." Such words ultimately fell on deaf ears. "Probably the stuff I gave him was too simple," Culbertson considers. "But even when I did give him some really heavy rituals and told him, 'You could do this stuff on your own, get five candles', he said, 'What?! Candles? On my own? I'm not doing that!' I told him, 'OK, you don't want to do ritual magic. Here's one for opening your chakras.' 'You mean bring the Kundalini up? Holy shit, I can't deal with my life as it is, how I am supposed to . . .' I would bring in this week's book and this week's theory or something from the Rosicrucians and we would talk about it till we talked it out and the next time we'd meet he'd ask 'What have you got for me?' and I might produce a Martinist thing and we'd talk about that until it was exhausted. I always thought it was pointless."

So what was Morrison ultimately hoping to discover? "The answer to the mystery of being in two short sentences," Culbertson quips. "That pretty well sums up where he was at. He wasn't prepared to work. I said, 'You could be free of this. You've so much free time and so much money, you could do this for a year and nobody would miss you. Have an album sitting ready and you could just go.'" Initially, Morrison was intrigued by this idea and even considered taking Bell and Culbertson on an extended meditative trip to Spain, but in the end it came to nothing.

Culbertson was also invited to accompany Morrison on a house hunt in Ireland with female friend Ulla Munch. "She was a great woman and her heart was as big as a three-storey building and she loved him. She told me 'You're good for Van, it's going to be rocky here and there but I'd appreciate it if you'd stick in.' She thought it was good that he could have somebody he could trust. We went to see a bungalow in the wilds of nowhere. It was absolutely gorgeous and he was saying 'This could be the house.'" After entering the premises, Morrison opened a cupboard downstairs only to be confronted by a Calor gas canister. "What the fuck is this?" he roared, prompting a brief explanation that the heating was gas powered. "What?" he exploded. "Gas! Everybody out! Gas! We could be gassed!" Later in their car, a perplexed Munch asked whether the heating system back in Holland Park was gas or electric. "No, it's not gas or electric, it's *central* heating!" Morrison concluded authoritatively. "He was funny," Culbertson smiles. "He used to have a great repertoire of jokes and funny observations about people and life. The first couple of years I knew him, he was good to spend time with. But by 1986, that was going downhill. If you know somebody's a cunt, OK, but he had been good."

Around this time Morrison liked to relax at the Crawfordsburn Inn, situated in the quaint village of Crawfordsburn on Northern Ireland's 'Gold Coast'. The Co. Down coastline was home to thousands of wealthy Protestants and was something of a privileged spot, seemingly immune to the Troubles. According to a local saying, "There are two types on the Gold Coast – the 'haves' and the 'have yachts'." With its yachts, tennis clubs, fine houses and famous thatched restaurant, Crawfordsburn was a Protestant utopia whose residents ranged from Chief Constable Ronnie Flanagan to Jim 'Jonty' Johnson, leader of the loyalist Red Hand Commando's local battalion. A number of judges, spies and police officers also called the area home, happy in the knowledge that there was only one main road in and out of the village, a feature that acted as a deterrent to the IRA. Morrison loved the place and was known to throw a Christmas party for his mother at the Inn, an establishment where he felt relaxed, confident and free to express himself. Unfortunately, it was also an oasis that occasionally brought out his more aggressive and abusive traits, especially after he took up drinking again following a long period of abstinence. "When he came over to Crawfordsburn, he would drink and get really abrasive," Culbertson recalls. "He'd say 'What have you done with your fucking life, you should have been this.' He'd browbeat you. 'I suffered for my art and you'll never be a star.'" It was during this period that Culbertson endured a devastating verbal assault that left him deeply shaken. Morrison had offered to produce some tracks for his spiritual associate at a local studio in Randalstown and seemed genuinely interested in playing saxophone on some cuts. Culbertson was in seventh heaven, but his dreams were demolished during a troubled supper. "I know there were times when he was a fucker," Culbertson notes, "but there were also times when he was helpful. That's the weird thing. He was getting grumpy and a bit crabby. We were sitting having our dinner in the Crawfordsburn Inn. I don't even remember how we ended up there, but I said to him 'That's grand, my son.' And he said, 'What? What did you fucking say to me? You fucking called me your *son*! Don't talk to me like that.' It was meant to be a term of endearment like 'brother'. By now every person in the Crawfordsburn Inn was looking because he was slamming the table and swearing at me at the top of his voice. 'Who do you think you fucking are?' I apologized and said I wasn't aware it was an offensive term and took it all back. Then he said, 'You can stick your fucking record!'" The humiliated Culbertson stood up, threw some money down and promptly left the table. But that was not the end of the matter. Morrison continued his rant, screaming "Where the fuck do you think you're going?" and pursuing his quarry. "He grabbed me by the shoulders," Culbertson recounts, "wheeled me around and said, 'Go on, you really want to hit me. Hit me!' I told him, 'I don't want to hit you.' 'Go on! You really want to hit me. Fucking hit me.' And this is on the main street in Crawfordsburn! I said, 'What are you doing this for?' Then he repeated 'You can't talk to me like this, who the fuck do you think you are?' He brought his fist up to my chin and said, 'Do you want me to fucking punch you?' I said, 'Van, where are you at?' By now tears were welling up because it had gone from the guy who was producing my record to *this*. If he didn't want to do it all he had to do was say. I think he wanted a way out. It was easier to explode because then he could draw a line under it. If you go, 'Fuck you, fuck your record', it's gone. It's not discussed. And it never came up again. He would have done a lot of that. He drew a lot of things to a close like that."

Back in 1984, American journalist and editor Bill Flanagan had asked Morrison the apparently preposterous question "Have you ever thought of being a teacher?" Even more astonishing was Morrison's positive response, "I've had no offers, but I've thought about it quite a bit. That's the kind of thing I'd like to do, actually." The idea of Morrison, with his poor communication skills, aggressive impatience and absence of empathy ever daring to consider becoming some kind of teacher seemed farcical. It was even more far-fetched than his previous comments about the possibility of reinventing himself as a comedian. Nevertheless, he could not rid himself of the notion of a higher calling. Speaking to Steve Turner the following year, he admitted that his primary aim was discovering "somewhere to put my experiences" and "to find out what they were". Although he continued to see himself as the unconscious repository of some transcendent inspiration, there was now an equal stress on his supposed academic abilities. "There's something inside of me that directs me to do this, and I don't know why myself. It directs me to do my work and my study, to study religion and to study various aspects of this in relation to experiences." By the time he had completed *No Guru, No Method, No Teacher*, Morrison was talking about the need to divorce his "meditative music" from its associations with "rock 'n' roll". "I never had anything to do with rock culture," he blustered. "Rock 'n' roll is not music, it's a lifestyle and . . . people are making a lot of money out of it." Reacting once more against the music business treadmill, he insisted, "I certainly don't want to do this album-tour bit anymore – I'd like to make this the last time I do that . . . it's not working for me anymore." He hoped that the album would "maybe lead me to the next stage . . . and maybe people can come and see me under different circumstances in different places that aren't rock 'n' roll places."

Morrison found an unexpected vehicle for his pedagogical ambitions when he was introduced to the Wrekin Trust, an organization devoted to awakening "the spiritual nature of man and the universe" and helping people develop themselves "for channelling spiritual energies into society". The Trust's founder, Sir George Trevelyan, was a devotee of Steiner, which for Morrison was recommendation enough. The singer became more interested when he learned that one of the directors, Malcolm Lazarus, had headed a conference titled *Music, Mathematics And Consciousness*. It sounded like Cyril Scott and Rudolf Steiner rolled into one. Intrigued, Morrison duly attended one of Lazarus' symposiums in Winchester and although finding it "heavy going", he came away excited by the idea of organizing something similar under his own name.

Meanwhile, he completed a striking new album, *Poetic Champions Compose*, released in September 1987. Recorded in Bath and London, the work emphasized his commitment to creating a more contemplative style of music. Originally, he had intended to record a work of jazz instrumentals, but once lyrics filled his head that idea was abandoned. Nevertheless, three non-vocal tracks were retained, with 'Spanish Steps' and 'Allow Me' bookending the album. There was also evidence of Morrison's philosophy reading list. Alan Watts, the author of *Cloud Hidden, Whereabouts Unknown*, a book which popularized Eastern mysticism for Western readers, was namechecked in the title 'Alan Watts Blues', a song that testified to the singer's perennial need for seclusion. 'I Forgot That Love Existed' mentioned Socrates and Plato and contained a couplet that borrowed Steiner's dictum about the importance of thinking with the heart and feeling with the mind. 'The Mystery', a plea for spiritual liberation, featured a beautiful string and woodwind arrangement by Fiachra Trench. There were also some optimistic love songs ('Queen Of The Slipstream', 'Someone Like You'), another Celtic-inspired instrumental and a controlled reading of the traditional 'Sometimes I Feel Like A Motherless Child'. What came through most frequently on this uplifting album was Morrison's heightened sense of ecstasy, purification and renewal. 'Give Me My Rapture' and the climactic 'Did Ye Get Healed?' were powerful, positive statements of transcendence confirming that the spiritual dimension to his music was now an overwhelming priority. "Psychologists will tell you that artists have to be in a state of despair before they produce great work," he contended, "but I don't think that . . . In my case I know it doesn't create better work. I produce better work if I'm content. I can't create that feeling if I'm in a state of conflict."

The release of *Poetic Champions Compose* coincided with Morrison's collaboration with the Wrekin Trust. He agreed to appear at a weekend seminar at Loughborough University (18–20 September 1987) extravagantly titled *The Secret Heart Of Music: An Exploration Into The Power Of Music To Change Consciousness*. Its aims, as detailed in an accompanying brochure, echoed the sentiments voiced in past Morrison interviews and current album lyrics:

> Since the beginning of human culture it has been known that music can form a bridge between the spiritual and material worlds and help us to reach into realms beyond the senses. Spiritual traditions of the past have made disciplined use of the magical properties of music to induce mystical states of awareness and the transformation of the personality. Nevertheless, 300 years of materialism have degraded our musical inheritance and turned it into a consumer product – a far cry from the ideal function of music as a universal creative power and a vehicle for initiation into the divine mysteries.

The weekend featured a diverse set of speakers and players, including Pir Vilayat Khan (Spiritual Head of the Sufi Order of the West), sitar player Nishat Khan and a Renaissance chorale – Anthony Rooney and the Consort of Musicke. Morrison's own band included two of his closest "spiritual friends": Derek Bell and Robin Williamson. As the programme explained: "This unique gathering has been arranged to help restore music to a central place in our culture as a unifying and transcendent force. It will bring together from many parts of the world musicians and music lovers both amateur and professional who are awakening to a spiritual reality." Asked to clarify what he would wish his music to achieve, Morrison replied: "Ideally to induce states of meditation and ecstasy as well as to make people think."

Morrison's relevance to the seminar was wonderfully overstated in the programme's flattering biography, which claimed:

His passion for music and his bemusement with the contradictions inherent in being famous have led him to deeply question many of the underlying attitudes of our age. In particular, he has investigated the esoteric influences on music with a view to discovering more about its effect on the body-mind relationship. His own work is now increasingly intended as a means for inducing contemplation and for healing and uplifting the soul . . . His struggle to reconcile the mythic, almost otherworldly vision of the Celts, and his own search for spiritual satisfaction, with the apparent hedonism of blues and soul, has produced many inspired and visionary performances.

It was a strange weekend for Morrison who played two concerts in front of a small audience largely unfamiliar with his music. The first of these, billed as *Across The Threshold* in the programme, was preceded by two exotically-titled seminars: *Music: The Bridge Between Heaven And Earth* and *The Effect Of Music On Hormonal Secretions In The Endocrine Glands*. Wrekin's Chairman Malcolm Lazarus introduced Morrison by treating the audience to a plum-voiced recitation of 'The Mystery'. The singer then played a short set with his band, including 'Celtic Ray', 'And The Healing Has Begun' and 'In The Garden'. Robin Williamson contributed a spirited 'Tír na nóg' and duetted with Morrison on 'Mr Thomas'. The following evening's *Alive In The Mystery* was better attended and more ambitious, but not without its problems. Nishat Khan's preceding performance on sitar set the tone for spectators seemingly more at home with classical music. The Wrekin audience included a number of elderly people, several of whom left within seconds of Morrison's appearance complaining about the loudness of the music and its rock leanings. What they missed was a cross section of his more meditative work, culminating in 'Summertime In England' and 'Rave On, John Donne'.

On the final day of the seminar, there was an Open Forum in which delegates were invited to pose questions to a panel that included Morrison, Derek Bell and author Joscelyn Godwin. John Etherington, who had helped promote the weekend, spoke briefly to Morrison but found him very reserved and unapproachable. "Few dared go near him," he remembers. When faced with a difficult question from the floor about the healing effects of music, Morrison informed his inquisitor: "Just read the brochure." His lack of confidence as a public speaker, despite years of performing, was made worse by a brusque manner which alienated his audience. One woman was so offended by his demeanour that she was moved to write a poem of protest which she read out. It must have been an excruciating experience for Morrison to sit in silence while his personal shortcomings were detailed in verse. "She singled out Van in the poem," Etherington says. "The gist of it was that she had come to the weekend hoping to learn about music and consciousness and speak to the musicians. She had found Robin Williamson very approachable but then she spoke of Van Morrison's 'piercing stare' and 'piercing glare'. It was a direct attack on him and how detached she'd felt and how difficult she'd found her non-encounter with him. Something about him obviously got to her. She knew he was at the heart of it, but she implied that she was terrified and couldn't go near him. Nonetheless, he did talk a bit about his music, but he was not terribly forthcoming."

Following this poetic diatribe, both the audience and the panel applauded the woman for articulating her feelings so unflinchingly. The afternoon session concluded with *Back To Earth*, featuring Anthony Rooney's ensemble, who were joined by Morrison for a strained version of 'Greensleeves'. Overall, the conference was a major departure for Morrison the performer, but testified to the seriousness with which he was taking himself as a writer of meditative music. Unfortunately, it also demonstrated his limitations as a public speaker, let alone a teacher or communicator, and cast serious doubts on the efficacy of his ambitions to discover a new role outside the music business.

Speaking shortly after the Wrekin conference, Morrison maintained a defiantly quixotic belief in his power to transcend the reductiveness and compartmentalization of the music business: "I don't suffer fools gladly. To get where I am I've had to fight. It's still a fight. It's still a struggle. I'm not playing the same game I played 20 years ago . . . I've been a star I don't know how many times . . . I went through being a teenage star. Then I went through being a 20-year-old star. Then a singer-songwriter star . . . By the time I was 27, I'd done that one. I'd gone through my second phase of being a rock star. That's what they called it in those days. But I didn't call it that. I'd already wrapped that up by the time I was 28 . . . When I came back into the music business I started a whole new phase because I was no longer that person . . . For the past 12 years or so I've only been in it part of the time. I'm only in the music business part time now . . . I've run the gamut, I took the blows. I realized I've lived that out and I don't have to do it anymore."

TWENTY-ONE

Are You a Proddy?

Irish folk influences were often present in Morrison's work but he had seldom explored them in anything but a cursory manner. That changed when he agreed to record an album with the Chieftains. The legendary Irish ensemble had begun their career in the early Sixties playing informally in the backroom of O'Donoghue's pub in Merrion Row, Dublin, before joining the Ceoltóirí Cualann folk orchestra of the composer and folklorist Seán Ó Riada. They subsequently played a leading part in popularizing traditional Irish music by fusing formal arrangements of familiar material with startling instrumental virtuosity. By the Seventies they had established themselves internationally, winning an Oscar for their work on Stanley Kubrick's film *Barry Lyndon*, appearing with various members of the rock élite and famously playing in front of Pope Paul II at an open-air mass in Dublin's Phoenix Park, which attracted a record-breaking 1.3 million people. It was soon after their papal audience that they had first encountered Morrison when they shared a bill at the Edinburgh Festival during August 1979. Although their musical backgrounds were widely different, Morrison always hoped that they might work together.

In late 1987, Morrison invited leading Chieftain Paddy Moloney for breakfast at his favourite Notting Hill café where the terms of the collaboration were first discussed. The timing was particularly poignant as Ireland was mourning the horror of the Enniskillen bombing in which 11 Protestants had been killed, and many more injured, while attending a Remembrance Day ceremony. It was clear to Moloney that Morrison was interested in searching for his Irish roots and discovering more about traditional music. Soon after, he flew to Dublin for further discussions about touring and recording. Outside the Shelbourne Hotel, the pair paced around St Stephen's Green exchanging views about which songs to include on the album. The garrulous pipe player left Dublin convinced that Morrison was a tense character who felt he had been ripped off in the past and was deeply concerned about his standing in the music business and wary of the perceived danger of "selling out". "Van's not a great one for discussions about music. He'll talk about everything else but music . . . He has a reputation for being awkward but when you work with him you only see this man who's completely involved. Everything else is a distraction from the music."

In order to allow Morrison greater privacy Moloney booked him into the Roundwood Inn in Wicklow. When the Chieftain turned up to meet the singer, he discovered that Morrison had accidentally trapped himself in the bathroom. A locksmith had to be hired to free him. This farcical incident amused Morrison so much that he ended up rolling across the floor in paroxyms of laughter. It augured well for the forthcoming sessions which took place at Dublin's Windmill Lane Studios. Morrison seemed to enjoy recording with the Chieftains and there were many moments of light banter, some of which were unintended. "When we were doing *Irish Heartbeat*, Van was into these long cadenzas, very traditional West of Ireland keenings, long warbling endings," Moloney remembers. "So I said to him, 'Fine, but just before you're going into one of these cadenzas, can you give me the Billy?' That's Dublin slang for 'give me the nod'. So he says, 'Yeah, great, I'll give you the Billy, no problem.' The song is coming to an end and we're about to crash into the last chorus and Van starts shouting, 'Billy! Billy! Billy!' He didn't know what I meant. And he was dead serious."

While awaiting the release of the new album, Paddy Moloney was flattered to receive an honorary doctorate from Dublin's Trinity College for his life's work in music. The 25th anniversary of the Chieftains was also celebrated on a rousing edition of Ireland's *The Late Late Show*, with Morrison contributing three songs. He had even risked censure in the Protestant heartlands of Belfast by appearing in a pre-recorded BBC St Patrick's Day celebration, dressed in a leprechaun green shirt. Although the Chieftains usually shunned political discussions, there was no doubt how they were perceived in the North. Their sole Protestant member Derek Bell once offered a friend a

Chieftains album as a Christmas present only to be told, "Oh, that's Catholic music." The words were said with innocent surprise rather than malice, but the meaning was clear. "It wasn't a joke," Bell stressed. "He definitely felt that anyone who played a harp instead of a flute was Catholic. You'd never get that sort of provincial attitude in the South." For some, Bell's involvement with the Chieftains was almost a subversive act. As he concluded: "They just think 'Why is this fellow from the North down in Dublin playing music with these people when he should be marching on the Twelfth?'"

In this busy period, Morrison, like Moloney, was also university-bound, having accepted an invitation to attend a conference organized by the Literary Society of the New University of Ulster in Coleraine. Playwright Martin Lynch, a fellow guest, was excited to hear that Morrison and Derek Bell had both agreed to appear and it was anticipated that the event would re-enact the Loughborough experience. "Morrison was going to come and talk about his work and not play at all," Lynch recalls. "Then he said, 'No that would be too difficult for me.' So I said, 'OK, play a few tunes. Do your career in an hour-and-a-half.'" Lynch met Morrison for a rehearsal and sat stunned as he started playing 'Madame George', followed by 'Beside You' and much of Astral Weeks. "He went through each LP singing these different songs for about an hour. The format was worked out. Two days before the show was due to open, he said, 'Oh, I don't want to do that.'" Instead, Morrison played half a dozen songs, including the Carter Family-inspired 'Foggy Mountain Top' and Leadbelly's 'Western Plains'. His question-and-answer session was equally unpredictable. Lynch, who still remembered Morrison phoning him at all hours saying he "wanted to be a poet not a rock 'n' roll star", opened the talk with the casual statement, "you've been writing and you're interested in poetry". "Oh, no, not at all," an incredulous Morrison retorted, no doubt to the bemusement of the members of the Literary Society.

Two days after the Coleraine appearance, Morrison received some shocking news. His father had recently been advised to lose weight and, having successfully shed a few pounds, was looking forward to a healthy future. That all changed when he was suddenly taken from his home in Cairnburn Road to the Holywood Arches Health Centre on Belfast's

Westminster Avenue. On 22 April 1988, he was pronounced dead after suffering a myocardial infarction resulting from ischaemic heart disease. He was less than one month away from his 66th birthday. Three days after the fatal heart attack, Morrison registered the death in Belfast. The funeral was a quiet affair and did not feature in the press. For Morrison, this was a time to reflect on all that his father had contributed to his life. Undoubtedly, his greatest legacy had been that unique musical education he first provided during the formative years of Van's life. Exposure to the most arcane blues and jazz records of the pre-War era enabled the singer to find his own distinctive style and establish himself as one of the great white soul singers of his time.

One week after his father's death, Morrison was due to set out on a lengthy series of dates with the Chieftains. The tour simultaneously served as a distraction and a wake. Audiences, unaware of Morrison's personal circumstances, were amazed to see the normally truculent and taciturn singer smiling, talking and even dancing a few steps with guest singer June Boyce. "I think when we did that tour he came out of himself a bit," Paddy Moloney suggests. "He only gets that when he's onstage and there's that magic that comes out of improvising and interplay and reaching some kind of state. That's the only time he feels he can let loose. He's in a cage otherwise." It was evident that the witty repartee between himself and the Chieftains in concert was having a beneficial effect on his mood at a time of sorrow. All that would soon change.

Towards the end of the first leg of the tour, Morrison found himself irritated when Bell and Culbertson spoke of supernatural happenings, including the presence of luminous beings on stage and forces of energy entering Morrison as he sang. "There were nights when you were on stage and you'd see the robed guys, the angelic beings behind him," Culbertson testifies. "There was no doubt in my mind that the holier beings were there to help him with his life's mission. His Dharma. Once it anchored in him I could see the rush coming at me. It was like 'Bang!' You could actually feel it coming through your system, like they were anchoring a power source on stage and on those nights he was breathtaking. The voice was incredible. It was amazing, there were sparks and stars, like fireworks, a proper psychic vision. On other nights you could see it coming down trying to get in. It was sparking around his head and he was almost actively stopping it. I was thinking, 'Come on, send it to me or Derek, let's get a vibe in.' But if it didn't get into him first, it didn't come to me or Derek. Even Derek said to me, 'Did you see the angels last night?' and when it didn't happen he'd say, 'It didn't get into him tonight, did it?' He had a lot more psychic visions and abilities than he let people know." After a show at the Hexagon, Reading, Culbertson regaled Morrison about these visions, assuming from past conversations that he would be intrigued. Instead, the old pragmatic Protestant in Morrison re-emerged with a cutting vengeance and Culbertson was told to keep his visions to himself. Perhaps the brutal reality of his father's sudden death had closed Morrison to lively discussion of such otherworldly manifestations.

The much anticipated Morrison/Chieftains collaboration *Irish Heartbeat*, released in June 1988, represented an opportunity for the Belfast bard to place his work in a distinctly traditional Irish context. "They're all Irish songs basically because that's where I'm from," he pointed out. "Going away and coming back are the themes of all Irish writers, myself included." If the album had a theme, it was the underlying message of Celtic unity, a point punctuated by the title track in which Ireland is seen as a spiritual home. In another sense, the work betrayed the North/South divide with Morrison contributing material that emphasized his Protestant roots. 'Star Of The County Down', 'Carrickfergus', 'My Lagan Love' and 'She Moved Through The Fair' (a traditional air that later provided the melodic basis of Simple Minds' chart-topping 'Belfast Child') were all Northern songs. There was even an uneasy reading of Monaghan poet Patrick Kavanagh's classic 'Raglan Road' and a provocative snatch from 'The Sash' in 'I'll Tell Me Ma'. In contrast to Morrison, Chieftains' vocalist Kevin Conneff seemed far more at home with the traditional material, particularly on the Gaelic 'Tà Mo Chleamhnas Déanta' ['My Match Is Made'], which was enhanced by an appearance from singer Mary Black. Occasionally, Morrison's gruff, soulful vocals sounded jarring and out of place. "From the purist's point of view it's grotesque," Derek Bell conceded. "No purist is going to sing things like 'She Moved Through The Fair' repeating 'our wedding day' three times. The repetition and jazz-like style of words for the sake of emphasis – that belongs to soul. It has nothing to do with our tradition. What Van does with 'My Lagan

Love' is even more grotesque. He virtually makes a Hindu chant out of it in the last note."

It was the stirring, upbeat songs like 'I'll Tell Me Ma' and the exuberant finale 'Marie's Wedding' (with a notable contribution from singer Maura O'Connell) that worked best on the album. The rock media on both sides of the Atlantic applauded while the folk community that Morrison was attempting to reach poured scorn on the work. Even his friend Phil Coulter declared the collaboration a mismatch. More dissenting voices were heard in his hometown, with the *Belfast Telegraph* joking that people would leave early if he dared sing 'My Lagan Love' at a Belfast party, while the ghost of Patrick Kavanagh should have haunted the singer for desecrating 'Raglan Road'. The ultimate irony was that the record was praised universally in the mainstream music press at a time when Morrison was telling the world that he had no connection whatsoever with rock culture.

A year before the release of *Irish Heartbeat*, Morrison had openly admitted that his approach to the media may have been flawed. "For a long time – for years – I didn't realize how important it is to actually explain what you're doing, so that it will be approached in the right way. I'd go into an interview and I didn't really know what it was I wanted to get across; I didn't know what they wanted. So I'd just be playing this game with interviewers where I'd be trying to give them something I thought they wanted, and it wasn't really me."

When it came to promoting the Chieftains collaboration, Morrison evidently forgot those words or perhaps he simply fancied a game of 'torture the reporter' in the excruciating tradition of his Seventies encounters with Nicky Horne and Tony Stewart. Paddy Moloney was mortified when a gaggle of journalists lined up at the Tara Hotel to experience ritual humiliation. The bewigged piper tried to lighten the mood by making constant jokes and telling his favourite stories about the imaginary pig, Micky The Muck, and an assortment of pandas and fairies. Liam Mackey from *Hot Press* barely reached his third question before Morrison announced wearily, "Is it OK if I go to sleep?" Seconds later, he was saying, "Hello, you've got your pound of flesh", then retorting, "I don't have to prove anything." On it went, with Morrison asking, "Do you want me to stand on my head?", repeating his "pound of flesh" gibe and finally collapsing in exasperation. "These questions, God, they're unanswerable. 'Why those songs?' We've been asked that all day. I mean, 'Why get up in the morning? Why, why, why?' There is no why. You just do something because at the time that's the thing to do . . . There's nothing to read into it at all. There's no mystery. What I do is very simple. My songs, my music, my whole shtick, is not something that's mysterious."

The *NME*'s resident Morrison fanatic Gavin Martin fared no better. After proffering an intelligent enquiry, he was firmly put in his place with the sarcastic "Well, if you have all the answers why don't you tell me? I'll just sit here and listen. It will save me work." The only coherent comment about the album from Morrison was the description "it's basically a cross section of Irish music from stage Irish to deep roots going back to traditional Irish and back to New Age Irish to Celtic revival to street songs." Martin's memories of the encounter were decidedly unpleasant. "He was stuffing his face with buns. It was absolutely obscene – and Paddy Moloney was on cloud nine."

"Rule number one, you don't sit anywhere near Van when he's eating," jokes Clive Culbertson. "It's everywhere. He's a real untidy eater. We used to go for the Ruby Murray [curry]. In the middle of this meal he put some stuff in this sauce and throws half of it down his jacket. 'Waiter!' The waiter comes over, but what can he do? We had a gig the next night and he had a big stain down the side of his jacket. The next night we went for a late-night feed and he decorated the other side of his jacket. As we were going on stage I watched him and he looked in the mirror and noticed for the first time that he's got chicken korma down the side. He turned to me and says, 'Do you think they'll notice?' He dressed in the same clothes. On the fifth or sixth date Ulla Munch would arrive and take him out of the hotel where the guys were so that he wouldn't eat the wrong stuff at the wrong time. He needed that. She preferred for him and her to have a meal. She'd get him new clothes and knew what to buy for him. He went onstage the next night looking great . . . he was spick and span for a man of his age. You always knew if she was there – he was sober, dressed and shaved. OK, he'd be a bit quieter, not so much *craic*. The best times were when she came for a day or two. He was brilliant for those few days after she left because he'd got all his clothes, the shoes were clean, the hair was cut, and she'd gone. All the other stuff had been taken care of and he didn't have to worry about that anymore. He could have a ball and he loved going out with the Chieftains."

The tour, which had started so well, gradually deteriorated in quality, amid accounts of friction between Moloney and Morrison. At one point, they drenched each other with wine in a post-gig lounge incident. There was also a starker divide between the sets, the first half of which featured Morrison's predominantly Irish band, including Clive Culbertson (bass), Arty McGlynn (guitar), Richie Buckley (saxophone), Dave Early (drums), June Boyce (vocals) and Derek Bell, followed by the full quotient of Chieftains. "Considering they were so good for him, he really wasn't very nice to them," Culbertson observes. "He treated them like the hired help, which wasn't fair." The mystically-minded Bell and Culbertson soon formed a private two-man club performing their meditations after each show while everyone else got blitzed in the nearest bar. "If Derek Bell hadn't been on that tour I wouldn't have survived it," Culbertson admits. "When we were on the bus everybody was talking shit and the guys drank a lot. We'd just have a couple of Bailey's. He was a genius. A real genius, the most talented human being I've ever met. He could play 11 instruments to world orchestra standard. Eleven instruments. That's frightening. He had a standing invitation from several of the world's orchestras that if he ever left the Chieftains he'd have a job. He could have doubled or trebled his income." Surprisingly, Morrison failed to appreciate Bell's humility and unassuming attitude towards money or career advancement. "Derek knew something else," Culbertson stresses. "He was already living in the presence. The man was totally at peace with himself, no matter what happened. He was at peace with God and Van didn't see that as any bonus. 'Works for the fucking Chieftains, what's he got?' 'He's in the oneness, Van. Every hour of every day, this man shines. God is in him.' 'Yeah, but what's he got?' 'He's got God, 24 hours a day.' 'Yeah, but he only lives in a house in Bangor.' He never caught that, never got that the peace was worth more. Or maybe he couldn't respect it in other people."

During the summer break from touring, Bell and Culbertson attended a seminar in Sussex at which they were introduced to a German Rosicrucian master whose influence on both proved profound. From their very first encounter Culbertson seemed convinced that he was "probably the most powerful human being I've ever met in my life before or since". At a private meeting, the master asked the musicians, "What do you want from me?" Bell, not untypically, requested the ability to write even greater music. "Of course, he went through Derek and they wrote the Violet Flames Symphony which was fabulous," Culbertson effuses. "It will become a major world work. It's an incredible piece of music, but then Derek was a genius anyway." When the master turned to Culbertson, the Ballymoney man had a strange experience. Ever since he was a child, he had noticed that at key moments in his life a theme tune played over and over in his head. Once, he had even written a Mormon hymn using parts of the tune that he could remember. Now, it was back again. When asked what he desired, Culbertson spluttered: "I want to know how to get hold of you any hour of the day no matter where I am." Unfazed, the master produced a pen and paper, drew a symbol and told him, "Visualize this in violet, then sing this tune." "It was *the* tune," Culbertson explains. "I just sat and cried. Where do you go? You've met this guy and he's been singing inside your head for 30 years and he's here. The tune was the ritual tune of the Violet Ray, and this had only been given out to a few people. He said, 'Write it down, you'll need it.'"

Culbertson excitedly told his story to Morrison, who had been invited to attend the seminar, but failed to appear. "Ah, I'm Van Morrison and if I'm there I'll just get letters for money," he complained. Nevertheless, he was intrigued by Culbertson's claims, which rekindled his curiosity about the supernatural. Culbertson became even more apostolic after attending an initiation ceremony presided over by the master. Asked again what he wished to know, he answered, "I would like to know that there's some part of me that exists external to my body, separate but connected, that will be here even if my body isn't." The Rosicrucian responded with the confident ease of a magician asked to perform a familiar trick. "He gave me a visualization to do and we were chanting and stuff," Culbertson says. "Then he got up and said, 'Ignore what I'm doing, just keep on.' He came over and it was just like he pulled me and lifted me out of my body. All of a sudden I'm hovering in the air. I was awake and conscious looking down at my knees and legs. In my spiritual body I looked at him and he could see me. This guy could do all the conjuring tricks – he could solidify. He could be sitting in Switzerland and be here. Finally, he looked at me and said, 'Now do you believe?' Then he just stared at me and laughed."

The Rosicrucian master also seemed to know an awful lot about Van Morrison's spiritual history. After advising Culbertson to appear on the singer's next album, he confided an astounding tale, revealing that Morrison, whom he had yet to meet, was in the grip of an Angelic Knot. "I was told that from a past life through certain occult works he had been involved in, there had been a knot placed in his throat and that had a lot to do with the mood swings. Energy would come in there. That was where he was caught. The German Rosicrucian master told me and Derek all this. He offered, at no cost to himself or no signing to anything, to break this knot of these other beings that were around him . . . The darker parts of him are operating through the throat chakras. That's where his message was coming from. The energy that's coming from there could be used for lighter, holier things. He could free himself but it's a past life committing him, from a ritual commitment he had made [in a previous existence] that's karmically still with him."

This was not the best time to regale Morrison with revelations about past lives, Angelic Knots and Violet Rays. His mood had changed once more and, by the time the tour with the Chieftains recommenced in the autumn, he was in a distinctly unspiritual place. Onstage friction soon threatened to spill over into something more nasty. At one continental date, Morrison became involved in a flare-up with tour manager Dave Whitehouse after seeing a film camera onstage. Infuriated, Morrison grabbed Whitehouse by the throat, dragged him to the apron of the stage and demanded an explanation. "He's got Whitehouse over the edge, shouting and swearing at him 'No fucking filming I told you!' " Clive Culbertson remembers. "I had to get in the middle and get him off Whitehouse. Of course, the guy holding the camera then comes after them! Whitehouse says, 'It's not filming, it's just closed circuit for the big screen . . .' Van almost hung Dave off the side of the stage while being filmed on video and shown on the big screen!"

A replacement roadie was backstage at an even more eventful and fractious date in Finland during which Morrison became irked by

Paddy Moloney, made some unflattering remarks about the Chieftains, then left the stage in a huff. He was swiftly followed by fiddler Seán Keane, who was enraged by his condescending behaviour. "They were about to go at it," says Culbertson, recalling the confrontation. "Mick, the roadie, just walked in and said, 'You're paid for an encore, get the fuck out there! Get out, now!' I couldn't believe this, but Morrison went on and did his encore. 'You're getting one song!' he said. Mick had told him, 'If you don't get out, I'll plant you, I'll fucking clock you!' He always knew that Mick *would* hit him."

Like Culbertson and Keane, the Chieftains' Kevin Conneff was left with some unwelcome images of Morrison's darker side. "There were times when he would get into a mood. Usually alcohol was involved, and I didn't want to be near him. He could be quite unpleasant . . . everybody around him had to suffer." As the tour wound its way towards its final date at the Royal Albert Hall in October, it was obvious to all concerned that the collaboration had continued for too long.

Along the rocky way, Morrison's long-term relationship with his Danish girlfriend Ulla Munch also ended. "She was great, she was a joy," Clive Culbertson enthuses. "I adored the woman. The only problem was he hated her being there when he was having fun because she didn't really drink very much . . . I don't think she ever took any shit and I think that was why it was a bit rocky. They were always at sixes and sevens because she knew he had to be tidy. She knew he was a star. She worshipped the ground he walked on."

It was not long before Morrison was back in the market of romance. His next paramour was Mira Radkovitch, a young woman of Yugoslavian descent, who had been living with his friend Peter Hayden. They had first met in the early Eighties when, according to Hayden, "she was totally unimpressed by him, but he kind of liked her." Over the years, her attitude softened until Hayden suddenly discovered that there was another man in her life. "I went away for quite some time," he recalls, "and she was in the house on her own. She was a lot younger than me. She was working as a waitress in Notting Hill Gate and she ended up meeting him and going out with him. She said, 'I've met this guy while you were away.' I said, 'Do you like him?' She said, 'Yeah,' and I said, 'Good.' We were sleeping together, but she was young and attractive and into projecting how much she loved the particular person she was with. And her projection went on to Van." At first, Radkovitch kept Morrison's identity a secret. "He rang up and obviously his voice was a total give-away," Hayden smiles. "He'd put the phone down unless he got her. I said, 'What's this guy's name?' and she said, 'Johnny.' It was hilarious . . . I liked him and still do but I think he felt slightly embarrassed because he ended up living with a girl who was with me . . . She lived with him in Bath [later] . . . they must have been together for three to four years. Mira's a nice girl."

Along with the change of woman was a shake-up in the managerial ranks. Morrison's long-time agent and business arranger Paul Charles had moved on, later emerging as a writer of crime fiction. Chris Hodgkin, who had briefly taken over from David Ravden, opened an esoteric bookshop in Oxford. John 'Kelloggs', who had been appointed in the mid-Eighties, entered the annals of Morrison mythology as the manager who had famously compiled his own list of choices when the singer was booked to appear on Janice Long's *My Top Ten* slot on BBC Radio 1. Morrison had stormed off and remonstrated with Kelloggs afterwards. It was not a relationship destined to last. More recently, a tour manager had risen in the ranks. John Rogers, nicknamed Harpo, a former roadie for the showband Chips, gradually emerged as Morrison's favoured orderly. Back in America, Stephen Pillster was still called upon to organize the odd tour until he was deemed too expensive. From outside this pack a new appointee arrived – the experienced former Thin Lizzy manager, Chris O'Donnell. His recruitment coincided with an upsurge in Morrison's popularity and a move to Phonogram's sister label Polydor. At a time of great change in his life, Morrison had seized the moment and was about to complete his most commercial work of the decade. With no pre-publicity, he sold out four shows at Broadway's Beacon Theatre, serving up a set which included some R&B covers, memorable renditions of 'In The Garden', 'Rave On, John Donne' and 'Tore Down A La Rimbaud', plus the return of 'Moondance' among the encores. Although Morrison knew he had to maintain some sort of profile in America, extensive touring was never a welcome proposition. "He hated coming to the States because it was so far from home and he doesn't like flying,"

Pillster points out. "I finally got him to fly Concorde but he still thought it was too long by an hour and a half. He liked to work in Europe because it was never more than one-and-a-half hours from home. When he was living in Holland Park, he could fly back to London. He had the best of both worlds."

Pillster was also surprised to find that Morrison was drinking. "I never saw him take a drink until about 1989. The take of the people that were around him more, including the English band, was that – whether it was cause and effect – he began drinking after his father passed away . . . Like me, Van's not a good drinker. He'll drink with you until you pick him up and put him to bed . . . Plus, he's a control freak, so that's got to be complicated for him. To be out of control and want to be in control and so forth. But when he puts it down, he puts it down . . . One of the guys in the band wrote to me and said there was a particularly bad night somewhere in Europe and after that Van never took another drink for . . . maybe another year. And when he came back for the 'shed' tour of the States he wasn't drinking then. It was always Seltzer and water or coffee. He'd drink a ton of coffee, like there was no tomorrow."

Morrison's commercial rehabilitation was cemented in 1989 with the release of *Avalon Sunset*. Over the years, his albums had sold moderately, while his singles success was practically non-existent. Since the brief glory days of Them, he had failed to register a solitary UK Top 30 hit under his own name. What changed that statistic and helped introduce Morrison's name to a mainstream audience was the presence of Cliff Richard. Both artistes shared an interest in religion, but whereas Morrison dipped into various cults like a schoolboy in a sweet shop, Cliff had been a committed Christian since the Sixties. Morrison's hip, New Age flirtations and non-specific spiritual quest had seen him variously dubbed as a rock eccentric, pop mystic and transcendental troubadour. Richard, by contrast, was regarded as conservative and his religious affiliations had been mocked, vilified and even libelled in left wing areas of the British music press.

When it was learned that the lead-off track on Morrison's album was a duet with Cliff Richard, several critics expressed surprise, even perplexity. Typically, Morrison was nonplussed by such perceptions and retorted: "Cliff Richard? You're joking, aren't you? You're kidding. I grew up with Cliff. He'd be on *Saturday Club* [the influential

Saturday morning BBC radio show]. I was a teenager, so I listened to records, television, radio and all that, just like any other teenager." Working with the preternaturally youthful singer was evidently a pleasure. "He's a professional," Morrison proclaimed. "He just goes in and does it . . . It's great working with somebody like that . . . He couldn't be around this long if he wasn't a great singer. I think he plays himself down, though, underestimates himself."

Of course, Cliff Richard *never* underestimated himself and he hardly needed the patronage of Morrison. Over several decades, he had survived every shift in popular music and won some unlikely supporters along the way. Even an inveterate rebel like the Sex Pistols' manager Malcolm McLaren had declared Cliff Richard one of the most important figures in the history of British pop music and argued passionately that he deserved a far better critical standing than Mick Jagger. One of Richard's greatest and most underrated strengths was as a vocal duettist, a point proven on collaborations with both Phil Everly and Elton John. With Morrison, it was a classic example of the sweet and the sour finding harmony. The catchy 'Whenever God Shines His Light' was obviously the most chartworthy song to feature Morrison's name in living memory and the record company wisely held back the single to take advantage of the Christmas market. Although its ultimate success was relatively lukewarm by Cliff standards, the single restored Morrison to the UK Top 20 for the first time in 24 years and resulted in a bizarrely memorable duet on television's *Top Of The Pops*. The Peter Pan of Pop was generally complimentary about Morrison, but sensed an inner conflict in the man. He later admitted that Morrison had a greater sense of self-loathing than anybody he had ever met in the music business. This was a remarkably frank and alarming perspective on a personality whose dogged insularity had baffled and outraged a legion of media commentators.

The remainder of *Avalon Sunset* was surprisingly impressive and a sparkling addition to the Morrison canon. Although it failed as a single, 'Have I Told You Lately' became something of a Morrison standard and was later successfully covered by Rod Stewart. The jazz-tinged 'I'd Love To Write Another Love Song', featuring organist Georgie Fame, curiously addressed writer's block at a time when Morrison's output seemed anything but sparse. Familiar themes such as healing ('Contacting

My Angel'), nature worship ('These Are The Days'), William Blake ('When Will I Ever Learn To Live In God') and childhood reminiscence ('Orangefield') were all present, but what transformed the album were two tracks which testified to Morrison's sense of place. The extraordinary 'Coney Island', a shimmering narrative in which he recounts a trip across Ulster, owes its appeal not to any self-conscious mysticism, but rather through its simplicity of effect and distinctive diction. The use of Irish colloquialisms such as "the *craic* was good" and the sudden lapse into Belfast brogue in Morrison's pronunciation of the word "face" gave the composition added force. There was humility here and humour too, most notably with the reference to stopping off at Ardglass for jars of mussels and potted herrings in case they became famished before dinner. As one reviewer perceptively noted: "You get a great rush of satisfaction here; in knowing that Van Morrison, despite his long, painful progress towards spiritual election, is still a ravenous foodie at heart." The majestic segue into the pastoral 'I'm Tired Joey Boy' effected the transition from one great track into another.

The promotion of the album was a story in itself. There was a launch party at Ronnie Scott's club in Soho where Morrison played a 40-minute set with a nine-piece backing group which included Georgie Fame. His presence encouraged Morrison to feature some R&B/jazz numbers, including a lengthy version of 'Help Me'. Perversely, Morrison failed to play anything from *Avalon Sunset*, thus negating the promotional purpose of the evening's performance. The singer was equally reluctant to be interviewed but agreed to the novel idea of an informal talk with Spike Milligan. Morrison had admired the humorist since the Fifties when he was a devotee of the cult radio comedy show *The Goons*. He had even named one of his compositions 'Boffyflow And Spike' in part homage to Milligan. The pair had met only once before, but Morrison decided it would be congenial to visit his childhood hero at his home for an interview to be published in the upmarket rock magazine Q. The 71-year-old comedian greeted the grumpy singer, departed, then re-emerged wearing a large false nose. Morrison could not contain his mirth and a photographer was well placed to capture the obvious enjoyment etched across his normally surly countenance. Milligan felt free to ask Morrison some provocative questions and neatly summarized the uneasiness experienced by many interviewers by telling him to his face: "You have a very strange charisma. I don't feel quite comfortable in your presence." After discussing their favourite comedians and indulging in some amusing banter, Milligan had the audacity to question Morrison about his religious upbringing. "Are you a Proddy?" he enquired, playfully. "Don't come near me, I don't want to catch it!" Morrison, evidently sensitive about the question, admitted only to being a member of the Church of Ireland. Unperturbed, Milligan bombarded him with the type of personal questions few journalists would have dared to ask: "Van, do you relax? Do you go out to restaurants? Got a wife? A girlfriend? Or a bloke? Got a good pad in London?" Inevitably, Morrison could only offer evasive replies, but at least he responded with good humour. "I'm not into talking about myself with journalists. I talk about my music. The fact is that I do this for a living, and then I have my own life which is separate from that. So Van Morrison makes records, and I'm separate from that. I can't mix my personal stuff with the job, so I just talk about my job. I'm not interested in selling myself. I just sell my records, my music. I have to censor everything I say because if I don't they just use it against me."

Milligan later recounted his encounter with a characteristically acerbic edge. "The man was a pig, looked dirty and scruffy, though it might be an act. I said 'How are you? Are you married?' – just small talk – and he said to me 'I didn't come to talk about all that crap. I want to talk about my new record . . .' Then he left the room and went outside, and he'd spilt coffee all over the floor. So I took all my clothes off and I put on a big black hat and my false nose – the penis nose – and he laughed. I thought 'Fucking hell, you have to do a lot to make him laugh!' "

Three weeks after the release of his album, Morrison appeared at the Glastonbury Festival, scene of New Age hippiedom and, according to the singer, the site of the true Avalon. He had previously appeared at the event in 1982 and 1987 and, despite his dislike of large gatherings, would reappear there several times in the Nineties. Part of the appeal was the avuncular presence of organizer and site owner Michael Eavis who chauffeured Morrison direct from his hotel to the backstage area. Sheelagh Allen, Eavis' personal assistant, remembers: "The timing had to be spot on, literally, so that he would just arrive in time to go onstage. I think he got very nervous before the performance and it was cut very fine, but we always got him there." One of the highlights of his 1989 set was a new song celebrating the late British comedian Max Wall. A review in the *NME* was complimentary but could not resist adding that Morrison resembled "an extremely disgruntled pig". Spike Milligan could not have put it better. Perhaps it was a sign of the times, but there was a sudden emphasis in the media on Morrison's physical shortcomings. A cursory musical appraisal in *Punch* was most notable for its merciless dissection of the man's public persona: "Van's a man that makes your average King Edward spud look svelte by comparison. He's short, fat and almost bald. He has terrible dress sense; dress sense so bad that you wonder how they ever let him out in public. His tubby legs are wrapped in baggy jeans. His belly strains against black Concorde-collared shirts. He tops this off with workmen's overcoats. And this is for his album covers. God knows how he goes around in private."

While *Punch* pondered the singer's lack of sartorial elegance, the *NME* delved deeper into the more relevant question of his notoriously 'difficult' personality. With impeccable Gestalt logic, Morrison insisted that it was his detractors who were transferring their own inadequacies on to him. "They're the difficult ones," he barked, "that's why they put that stuff out. Look, I've got my act together, well together as far as my professionalism goes. And my commitments. And the job I do. I'm very, very, very together. A lot of people resent that. When people are difficult they project it on to people they don't like. These people exist, you know. Professional jealousy or a lot of little guys who run around thinking the world owes them a living, who don't connect with hard work. If they're anyway envious of you, they start putting this stuff out."

It was difficult to reconcile Morrison's insistence about supposed media enemies projecting their jealousy with the stark evidence of his own truculent behaviour. The previous year's interviews in the company of Paddy Moloney had underlined this point and there was no sign of any professionalism in Morrison's latest encounter with *Hot Press*. Journalist Liam Fay, who had flown from Dublin to London to conduct the interview, was taken aback when Morrison terminated proceedings after a handful of questions and switched off the tape recorder. He then started haranguing his inquisitor and ended up virtually chasing him down the road, demanding the tape. Once again, he singled out the paper's editor Niall Stokes comparing him to Shylock and insisting he wasn't getting his "pound of flesh". Although Fay retained the tape, the abusive interview was never published. If this was an example of Morrison being "very, very, very together" then the prospect of him unravelling was a frightening thought. Clearly, he still found the promotional interview irksome, intrusive and intimidating and continued to respond in brutal fashion.

TWENTY-TWO

Don't Call Me Jack!

During the final months of the Eighties, Morrison continued his recent series of collaborations and over the next couple of years he would work or guest with artistes as diverse as Bob Dylan, Slim Gaillard, Roger Waters, Jerry Lee Lewis, Lonnie Donegan, Georgie Fame, Andy Fairweather-Low and Tom Jones. The Dylan/Morrison connection reached its apogee on the Hill of the Muses in Athens in late June 1989, when the two were filmed for the television documentary *Arena*. Two Morrison songs were completed during the film shoot: 'Crazy Love' and 'Foreign Window'. "Dylan didn't want to sing any of his own songs," director Anthony Wall notes. It would be another nine months before the show was broadcast but, in the meantime, Dylan and Morrison continued to display their mutual admiration in concert. While Dylan sang 'One Irish Rover', Morrison would occasionally feature 'Just Like A Woman' and 'It's All Over Now, Baby Blue'. The two even shared a stage together early the following year at Dundonald Ice Bowl near Belfast, when Morrison joined the maestro for a version of 'Tupelo Honey'. The pair would later reconvene on a double bill performing concerts in Europe.

With all this retrospection, it was fitting that the new decade should begin with the first comprehensive anthology of Morrison's work. Released in March, *The Best Of Van Morrison* was well received and sold in sufficiently large quantities to thrust Morrison once again into the pop/rock mainstream. Its appearance allowed new fans and casual purchasers to sample 25 years of his recorded output without having to wade through a vast back catalogue. For collectors, there was one surprise – the rare 'Wonderful Remark', previously only available on the soundtrack of the film *King Of Comedy*.

The combined sales of *Avalon Sunset* and *The Best Of . . .* pushed Morrison into a new stratosphere. Suddenly, his name was plastered across high street stores alongside displays for multi-million selling acts like Phil Collins and Elton John. It was a conscious effort by Morrison to maximize his appeal, but Stephen Pillster rightly credits his new manager for negotiating that tricky compromise between commerce and art. "Chris O'Donnell was experienced and did a good job in terms of getting the company to push the record. Van was into racking up the sales. He was saying 'I'm this level of artiste, how come I don't sell this much – it must be the record company's fault.' Chris told him, 'Well, in part it is, but you need to give them incentives too – there has to be some give and take.' That's what he did for Van Morrison. He was always very vocal about what he'd done – 'Look, the sales have increased 40 per cent over the last year.'"

Although Morrison was enjoying huge sales, he still wished to pursue a more esoteric line of work. Around this time, he reconnected with his old spiritual pal Cecil McCartney, who had turned up at one of Dylan's Belfast concerts clutching a vial containing a potion which he believed might "cure" the bard's increasingly croaky voice. Later, Morrison visited McCartney at his Bangor home where he was entertained by tales of heightened experiences and enlightenment. The aspiring spiritual astronaut and painter had been visiting the Lake Tahoe mountains, wandering around in a white robe and living on a diet of cashew nuts, mangoes, dates and other vegetarian fare. While meditating on the mountain, he claimed to have had a life-changing experience, the details of which he was eager to convey to his host. "I was lying flat on a rock," he recounts. "I'd been up since 6am looking at the light of the planet Venus which, according to thirteenth-century alchemists, is very beneficial to the mind of artists. Each planet has a different chemical composition and when sunlight hits it the light that comes back to the Earth is of a different quality . . . One morning after meditation, I sat up on the rock and suddenly I felt a transformation come over me. I looked at the mountains around me and felt totally and utterly in perfect harmony with the entire universe – that's galaxies, stars, planets, quasars, the earth, the rocks – everything. I'd never felt like that in my whole life. It lasted about three minutes Earth time – but it was an infinity. I said, 'Wow, this is what I've been waiting for my whole life. This is the enlightenment that Buddha received' . . . That three minutes was absolute bliss."

Morrison sat quietly while McCartney told his story. The Bangor painter who had once inspired the title of *Astral Weeks* subsequently became convinced that he had contributed another album name. "He sat in this front room for four hours and listened to my description of my enlightenment in Lake Tahoe. He listened to all this and it was a highly God-conscious conversation and shortly after that he made the album called *Enlightenment*, which was kind of related to the conversations we had."

For all his spiritual, New Age leanings and search for enlightenment, Morrison retained a Protestant pragmatism that would sometimes surface when conversations strained his credulity. Journalist Mick Brown had observed this tendency after accompanying Morrison on a visit to a swami who some claimed might be the reincarnation of Christ. After attending a meeting, Morrison emerged with a wry grin and offered the cynical conclusion "What a fookin' joker." He was equally uneasy when Clive Culbertson had started seeing luminous, robed beings on stage. That same scepticism was evident on the evening he invited McCartney to join him at the local Crawfordsburn Inn for a meal. Even before they entered the restaurant, McCartney's extravagant astronomical pronouncements were beginning to try Morrison's patience. "As we were going through the door of the Crawfordsburn Inn I pointed up to the stars and said to Van that I'd been playing beautiful mental games by visualizing three-dimensional architectural shapes like stars and double pyramids interpenetrating each other, using a star for each point where the form turns. So I was building models that were hundreds of light years across, the largest sculptures that could exist, simply by drawing lines with my mind – red, blue, green, yellow, silver, turquoise and gold lines between stars. This is a very advanced astronomical, spiritual and intellectual exercise. He couldn't accept that so he just sniggered at it and took a look at his friends as if I was crazy. But it was just beyond his understanding what I'd been doing as an intellectual exercise to strengthen my mind."

Once inside the restaurant, McCartney produced a bottle of Norfolk punch which he claimed was made by monks and contained spring water and herbs. "It's really beneficial for the mind and mellows you out," he told them. "It gives you a sense of well-being and it's conducive to good, deep conversation." Unfortunately, McCartney's conversational skills tended to amuse rather than impress those in attendance, despite the presence of the mystically like-minded Clive Culbertson. When somebody mentioned a diabetic colleague, McCartney could not resist offering them his words of wisdom on the wonders of alternative medicine, vegetarianism and herbology. It did not go down well. "They wouldn't believe this," McCartney complains. "They had no trust in the regenerative power of the human body."

By this point, there was no stopping McCartney who was in full flow about the wonders of vegetarianism. As the evening went on, Morrison grew more fractious. "Several times in the conversation I tried to talk about Jack McClelland who is a world champion long distance swimmer and a vegan," McCartney says. "But every time I looked at Van and was about to say 'Jack McClelland . . .' before I could get the name McClelland out, he said 'Don't call me Jack!' " Clive Culbertson, who had once been psychologically demolished at the Crawfordsburn Inn for daring to call Morrison "my son", realized fireworks were imminent when the singer ominously growled "I was fucking Jack a minute ago!"

While Morrison quietly stewed, McCartney ordered a vegetarian meal and complimented the Crawfordsburn Inn's chef. Morrison may have felt he was trying to make a point. "I'd read all the books and found out that a lot of mystics fasted and a lot of them were vegetarians . . . Van said he'd never got into the vegetarian trip, but he did take some bits off my plate, little Indian bits . . ." If Morrison suspected that there was an element of condescension or pontification beneath the vegetarian proselytizing, then he may well have been correct. "I've always wanted Van to go on a vegetarian diet, go to health farms and really take care of his body and get in good shape so that he can keep playing for another 20 years, but he's a very earthy person. He'd never talk to me about how galaxies develop or the residual matter left over from other galaxies and quasars. I've never been able to get him to think deeply about the wonderful things that go on in the universe."

One topic that Morrison was eager to discuss was his old touchstone, the cleansing blood of Christ. He started talking about the Moors Murderers and the apparent conversion of Myra Hindley to

Christianity. "Van was saying how marvellous it was that Myra Hindley had studied at the Open University or something and he said she's a wonderful person now," McCartney claims. "I should have admitted that there's a thing about a person changing their whole life, no matter how wicked they were – but if a crime or sin is so big, it's hard to think of them as a clear person even if they become a Christian. Then he said, 'What about redemption and the blood of Christ?'" What had started as an interesting theological debate suddenly became extremely heated. The normally placid McCartney lost his cool completely and started arguing in the mode of an Old Testament preacher. "I said 'That woman's a monster, she assisted in the murder of young children . . . it would take many gallons of blood to cleanse that woman's heart . . . If an event occurs, it has occurred, nothing can wipe it out.' He seemed to want to think that because of the sacrifice that Christ made – that could completely wipe out the murders, and I said 'No!'" McCartney continued in this vein, apparently unaware that he was provoking Morrison's ire. Perhaps it was the tone of self-righteousness that grated most. As McCartney admits: "He got angry when I said, 'If it's that easy to negate crimes, people would go out and do whatever they want and turn to the [Christian] solution when the guilt got too much.' It's much harder to do what I've done and avoid wrongdoing in the first instance so that I don't have to beg forgiveness from God or anyone for it."

It was at this point that Morrison snapped. "He got very annoyed by that and he threw his keys at me," McCartney alleges. "Then he came around the table and started kicking me in the legs and then started punching my face – and I was still sitting down. I stood up and looked down at him because I'm about a foot taller and said, 'Well, you were talking about forgiveness and Christ, Van, so I'll turn the other cheek. Would you like to hit this cheek too?' He'd already punched one side of my face quite hard. I was stunned . . . but I got up and did a Christ bit . . . He looked at my face, freaked out and turned and ran out of the hotel, up and down the street for 10 minutes to try and cool off . . . That constituted an assault, actually . . . He did attack me and lost control of his emotions and I couldn't even defend myself because there were other people around. I could easily have laid into a dear friend, but I didn't want to do that either. So he left me in a terrible dilemma." Before the evening ended, McCartney did manage to reprimand his host by reminding him of his bad times back in 1967. "I said, 'Look, Van, when you were drinking half a bottle a day and were over the edge and came and recuperated at our house, you were very welcome and we probably saved your life a couple of times because if you hadn't had our base to mellow out and sober up, and if you'd been in that state wandering around Bangor, you could have got into serious trouble." Unimpressed, Morrison stormed off with the punchline, "I'm fucking gone, you fuckers can go where you want." Although Culbertson was familiar with such behaviour he was still shocked after witnessing Morrison's physical assault on McCartney and offered him a lift home. "Poor Cecil," he sympathizes, confirming verbatim the details of the assault. The next day, McCartney phoned Morrison in an attempt to smooth things over, but met with a cold response. There would be no more dinner invitations for him.

Clearly, Morrison's sense of enlightenment did not always extend to his old friends. Soon after the McCartney confrontation, he also broke off contact with Culbertson. They had worked together in the studio the previous summer on what the bassist felt was a stunning version of 'When Will I Ever Learn To Live In God'. "The rehearsals had been much nicer than the recordings for *Avalon Sunset*," he says. "We were feeling the songs, fleshing them out and it was almost a holy process. The sense of spirituality in there was incredible and I really believe he felt it. You could feel he was in there. The Rosicrucian teachers had told me, 'Go work with him' and said they would work through him. But he never got it. He said, 'They're not working through me, I did this all myself.' But those three days' rehearsal in the studio were probably the best days he had in 1988. He was great. We got most of it. There were a couple of rocky bits but I said to him, 'There's no point shouting, we're giving you heart and soul' . . . On one occasion I arrived at his flat and it was awful. He said, 'It doesn't suit' and slammed the door in my face."

Although evidently sceptical about the Rosicrucian master, Morrison was sufficiently intrigued by the accounts of apparitions, Angelic Knots and Violet Rays to learn more. "When I was in the band, he phoned my house one day 24 times," Culbertson claims. "I'd gone shopping. He said to the girl I was going with, 'Where is he? What do you mean gone shopping? You tell him I need to talk to him.'

I came in an hour later – 'Where the fuck were you?' I said, 'Hold on, Van, I'm here' . . . It was unbearable with the phone calls." When Morrison sent his aide Harpo (John Rogers) to convince Culbertson to hand over some esoteric information provided by the Rosicrucians, it led to a bitter impasse. "The master had written out some musical meditations to supposedly let you contact the soul behind the music, the soul in the notes. It was all to do with singing and colours. I asked, 'Can I share this?' and was told 'It's a one-to-one' so naturally when Van said, 'I want this' I gave him the phone number. They didn't want anything from him. But he wasn't going to ask in case he felt beholden to someone. Harpo said, 'You've got to give it to him. He needs to know where your loyalties lie.' I told him, 'My loyalties lie with the path to God and that's it!'" Culbertson's relationship with Morrison never fully recovered from this perceived slight and after a while the phone calls ceased.

Despite their recent troubled tour, Morrison was still keen to work with the Chieftains. For his next project, he recorded a couple of new studio tracks with Paddy Moloney and Derek Bell, then decided that he wanted the harpist all to himself. Bell, who had no interest in working in the jazz-influenced bands favoured by Morrison, declined all entreaties to abandon the Chieftains. Predictably, Morrison erupted. "We had a row about the way I was ruining my life," Bell explained. "Van said I was too much under Moloney's apron strings. He told me that it was no good reading all these books about masters and then not living the life . . . He said I just hadn't got the guts to break out, stand on my own and do something . . . Then he says, 'Look, where do you think I am? I've got to the top of the tree here. Where do you think you are? You're down here. And that's why I can't hold a conversation with you.'" With that, Morrison stormed out in frustration.

A week later, he could be seen on stage in Berlin at a presentation of Roger Waters' *The Wall*. The fall of the Berlin Wall encouraged Morrison to make one of his rare forays into political pop. In the show, he performed 'Comfortably Numb', reading his lines from prompt cards on the floor, backed by ex-Band members Rick Danko and Levon Helm, plus former Amen Corner vocalist Andy Fairweather-Low.

Morrison's busy schedule showed no signs of slowing down, despite advancing middle age. Buoyed by recent successes, he undertook a major US tour in 1990 which proved another high point in his performing career. Stephen Pillster felt its success owed much to the avuncular presence of his friend Georgie Fame as musical director. "Here was a guy that Van idolized and respected as a musician. Georgie has a pretty light-hearted approach to everything. One big change I noticed was hanging out with the guys. Van didn't want to travel with them so much. They'd be in the bus and he'd be in the car but after the show, he'd say, 'Where's the band? Which room are they in?' Prior to that, when the American band was there, he wasn't that comfortable. It was more like he'd step into their dressing room a few minutes before and maybe after the show. But he genuinely liked the camaraderie of the English band. He got back more into touring and did a lot of dates." The odd bout of stage fright that had once spooked Morrison was no longer in evidence. "He'd gotten more reliable in doing a whole set," Pillster confirms. "You may know there's a shitstorm coming when he's had the roadies out 15 times because he can't hear or his guitar strings are breaking. You know he's not having a great time but he's going to do the whole set. There were times in the early Eighties and especially in the Seventies when, if it wasn't going the way he liked, we're out of here and no amount of reasoning or pleading was going to change that."

Although everyone agreed that the US tour was a success, it ended unhappily for Pillster who was finally undone by Morrison's fiscal economies. As he recalls: "Chris O'Donnell was involved briefly at the beginning of this, but then he and Van parted company, so it ended up being me without any management oversight, having to pull the whole thing together. I sat down with his accountant, who was also the treasurer of his corporation, and worked out a deal for myself. Then when Van saw it, he felt it was unfair and that I was getting paid too much money. I wrote back to his attorney in England and said, 'I'm willing to listen to a counter-proposal.' At this point, I had the money in my pocket. All I got back was a letter from his attorney thanking me for my previous contribution but saying that my services were no longer required nor did I represent Van Morrison in any way. So that was the end of me and Van."

In September 1990, *Enlightenment* was released to favourable reviews and strong sales. The album was hardly groundbreaking but consolidated Morrison's reputation as a purveyor of consistently good work. Its title track continued his seemingly unending search for enlightenment, albeit with a tinge of humour. 'Real Real Gone', previously attempted for *Common One* and gifted to Herbie Armstrong for his solo album, recalled the upbeat feel of 'Domino' and 'Jackie Wilson Said', without threatening either. The contemplative 'So Quiet In Here' and 'Youth Of 1,000 Summers' restated the importance of silence while meditating upon paradise. An attempt to find a way forward in the search for spiritual salvation was alluded to in both 'Start All Over Again' and 'Avalon Of The Heart', but Morrison still seemed inexorably drawn back into his own past. There was a lyrical retread of the opening of 'Astral Weeks' on the latter, a composition titled 'Memories' and a song that consisted largely of famous song titles such as 'White Cliffs Of Dover', 'Days Of Wine And Roses', 'Bright Lights Big City', 'Get Down' and 'Baby Please Don't Go'. The spoken word ending of 'See Me Through' was a desperate-sounding incantation in which Morrison attempted to will himself into his own past like a neurotic time traveller. The journey back to the East Belfast of his youth was completed with 'In The Days Before Rock 'n' Roll', which easily stood out as the album's eccentric highlight.

Co-written and narrated by Trinity College writer-in-residence Paul Durcan, 'In The Days Before Rock 'n' Roll' was a powerful distillation of all that Morrison had been attempting to achieve in his own songwriting. Durcan had previously written an effusive piece about the singer in the magazine *Magill*. "I like Morrison because I know that his work comes from the same level as my own poetry," he observed, "the level of daydreaming." This was high praise indeed. The pair spoke several times on the phone and Durcan's patronage clearly appealed to Morrison's literary vanity. They found common ground in their approach to performance, sharing a strong emphasis on accentuation and rhythm. Durcan's strange, hypnotic voice luxuriated in every syllable of his poetry, bringing dramatic life to his writings. Like Morrison, he relied on repetition for effect, creating a droning chant. This effect worked spectacularly well on 'In The Days Before Rock 'n' Roll' with its references to searching for Radio Luxembourg on an old Telefunken, a theme which recalled 'Wavelength'. Georgie Fame's musical contribution was in turn inspired by Durcan's evocative lyricism. "I didn't know what to play on that," he recalls, "then I thought about the waveband, so I played a signal on the organ which is Morse code – three dots, three dashes, three dots [the SOS signal]. You always used to get that Morse code interference on the radio when you'd be trying to tune it in. You'd pick up the ships. It was all completely out of time, but it fitted." What emerged was an eerily ethereal composition which paid tribute to a gallery of musical icons including Fats Domino, Elvis Presley, Sonny Terry, Lightnin' Hopkins, Muddy Waters, John Lee Hooker, Ray Charles, Jerry Lee Lewis and Little Richard. The list was completed by a mysterious character referred to only as Justin, whose significance remained unclear, even to Durcan.

The Morrison road show rolled on for the remainder of 1990, culminating in a 20-date UK tour. Among the highlights was a performance at Wembley Arena which was preceded by the surprise release of 'In The Days Before Rock 'n' Roll' as a single. The song was receiving strong airplay on daytime radio in England where it was perceived as a novelty record. Disc jockeys voiced amused perplexity when confronted by lyrics about letting goldfish go by the stream and other strange allusions. In an attempt to generate more interest, Polydor's marketing department sent sweatshirts to journalists emblazoned with a goldfish logo and even the invitations to Morrison's post-gig launch party were goldfish-shaped. Morrison was evidently embarrassed by the promotional trickery and sabotaged the PR exercise by pointedly removing all references to goldfish when he played the song at Wembley. At the climax of the set, Morrison left the stage to be replaced by childhood idol, Lonnie Donegan. The former skiffle king led the group, which included Georgie Fame and Andy Fairweather-Low, through such classics as 'Tom Dooley', 'Down By The Riverside' and 'Grand Coolie Dam'. Morrison then returned for a lengthy series of encores including a version of 'Send In The Clowns' during which he left the stage only to re-emerge with a gong which he struck, much to the puzzlement of his audience. The show confirmed just how much Morrison was enjoying himself now that he was surrounded by several of his more famous Sixties contemporaries.

Morrison ended the year with shows at the Point in Dublin, which

were most notable for the appearance of the Chieftains and Paul
Durcan. The emphasis on Irish poetry was further demonstrated by
Morrison's narration of the myth of Cuchulain. The Irish warrior
whom Yeats had used as the hero of several poems appealed to
Morrison who agreed to read scenes from the saga, accompanied by
actor Fay Howard and percussionist Ben Norman. Tellingly,
Morrison's delivery was compared to the stentorian oration of Ian
Paisley. The work was deliberately issued without publicity, initially on
tape at esoteric book shops, until the small independent Mole Records
released a limited edition pressing.

Morrison began 1991 on another house-hunting expedition. He
found a country retreat in a £200,000, four-bedroomed single-storey
house in Little Somerfield, near Malmesbury. Keeping up with
Morrison's property purchases was time-consuming. He had recently
purchased the Wool Hall Studios, near Bath, and also owned another
house in Bangor, Co. Down. Investment properties remained an
important part of his financial portfolio.

Morrison's more cerebral side was on display in March 1990 when
he appeared on two television programmes: the much anticipated *Arena*
documentary *One Irish Rover* and *Coney Island Of The Mind*. The
former, described by director Anthony Wall as "an illumination rather
than an exploration of his work", included an appearance by Bob
Dylan. Morrison's disembodied voice was dubbed over shots of sea,
sky, rocks and sunsets, a move designed to make him feel more relaxed
and forthcoming. "I don't think he would have been if the cameras had
been there," Wall notes, with obvious understatement. The singer was
filmed in concert, guesting with the Chieftains, the Danish Radio Big
Band, and jamming with John Lee Hooker in a bayou swamp. Faced
with the tricky task of articulating his 'art', Morrison foundered, leaving
the viewer to interpret vague sentences and proving once again his
limitations as a public speaker. "The songs don't measure your life," he
announced, in one of his more coherent asides. "And the problem is
that people – especially that write about it – think it does. I mean, it
isn't real what I do. It's in a way some kind of entertainment, some kind
of diversion is what it really is. It isn't really reality . . . You see it all
comes back to the music . . . the doing of it is what keeps you going
rather than the thinking of it."

Channel 4's *Coney Island Of The Mind* took its title from beat poet Lawrence Ferlinghetti's celebrated 1958 collection *A Coney Island Of The Mind*. Partly filmed at Irish traditionalist Garech a Brún's palatial home in Luggala, Co. Wicklow, the programme provided another flattering portrayal of Morrison, featuring contributions from poets Michael Longley, Seamus Deane and John Montague. With landscape scenes and visits to such Protestant strongholds as Cyprus Avenue, Orangefield School and Hyndford Street, the programme concentrated on the parochial sense of place and self in Morrison's songs. The presence of poets at least encouraged Morrison to speak a little more coherently about his work, as if it were worthy of some literary significance. Describing his "poetry" as "transcendent" he concluded that he was in a tradition uniquely his own. Ludicrously grandiose though Morrison's assertions might appear, they brought him some of the credibility he had long been craving. For years he had been pleading an unconvincing case that he was more than a rock star and now the liberal, mainstream arts media was partly backing that claim.

Despite his poetic conceits, Morrison still had an engaging habit of fraternizing with fellow Sixties pop stars. His latest find was Tom Jones whom he had approached to record a new composition, 'Carrying A Torch'. The Welsh singer was so impressed that he invited Morrison to play on his new record. After a single day's session, three more songs emerged ('Some Peace Of Mind', 'It Must Be You' and 'I'm Not Feeling It Anymore'). The resulting album, *Carrying A Torch,* released by Jones in April 1991, was as perplexing to some Morrison fans as the collaboration with Cliff Richard had been on *Avalon Sunset*. Once more, however, Morrison's choice made sense and Jones was quick to remind journalists that they shared musical tastes. "Van loved Jerry Lee Lewis and everything about rock 'n' roll just as much as I did in the 1950s, and later when we were both breaking into the music business, American disc jockeys thought I was an R&B singer on the strength of 'It's Not Unusual'. But then there always was that black influence in my music, from Little Richard onwards. If Jerry Lee influenced me in terms of projection and performance it was Solomon Burke who influenced my phrasing and so on. And Wilson Pickett and Otis Redding. That's how I saw myself in the Sixties, as a white rock 'n' roll singer."

It is interesting to note that Jones' litany of influences so clearly correlated with the icons mentioned in recent Morrison songs like 'In The Days Before Rock 'n' Roll'. What was most surprising was Tom Jones' ease of expression in articulating Morrison's religious quest. His plain language contrasted strongly with the guarded musings of the tongue-tied Ulsterman. "Van is always trying to find something. He's forever searching and so religion for him must be seen in that context. He's trying to find what he believes to be the truth, to hold on to some form of light. Yet, although I myself believe in God and pray, I'm not what anyone would call a churchgoing Christian. And I'm not driven by the same craving that fires Van Morrison on that level. If I was, I'd be a songwriter and I'd write about all those things to try to untangle myself, as he does. But I've known him since the early Sixties and even though we hadn't met for years, I know enough about what he's talking about to believe I could take it on board and make those songs sound like my autobiography."

Surprisingly, all four of the songs offered to Jones reappeared later in 1991 on Morrison's next album, the sprawling *Hymns To The Silence*. Originally titled *Ordinary People* it was prepared for summer release, then held over till September. According to the record company press release, the new work was "part of an ongoing search for enlightenment", a view with which the singer predictably disagreed. "It's got nothing to do with enlightenment," he insisted. "It's got nothing to do with making me happy. It doesn't make me happy, it's just a job. Does anybody's job make them happy?" What the album did display was a veritable cornucopia of Morrison's musical interests from jazz and gospel to hymnal. Two contrasting themes dominated the work. Firstly, there was Morrison's uneasy relationship with the music business which had festered into a cantankerous cynicism. 'Professional Jealousy' singled out imagined enemies in the media; 'I'm Not Feeling It Anymore' complained about the empty trappings of success; 'Ordinary Life' and 'Some Peace Of Mind' deplored the search for personal satisfaction; and 'Why Must I Always Explain?' asked a question that begged the reply, "But you've never explained anything!" On this occasion, however, Morrison seemed all too willing to pour scorn on his audience's insatiable thirst for elucidation. "You do the album, you do the music and then, you know, that's it," he growled.

"Why should I have to explain them? That's what I do, that's what it is. If people like it, they buy it, if you don't, that's too bad. If you don't connect with it then you don't need to take it any further, buy some other record! It's not for everybody. That's basically what I'm saying. I don't really want to have to explain myself because I'm not really interested in doing that. If I was I would be somebody else. I'd be a politician or a celebrity. What I'm saying is, I'm just me. I make the records. I make this music and that's it, you know." As for fame, it was a shallow mistress that left him feeling betrayed. "They think you're having a great time. It's all what they would like to have, in their imagination . . . I don't see any advantage in being famous . . . Some people want to be famous and that's what they go for, but I just want to play music. I'm not a celebrity. I don't want to be a celebrity."

The second predominant theme on *Hymns To The Silence* was Morrison's exhaustive search for the lost Ireland of his youth. He paid tribute to the Protestantism of East Belfast by including the gospel hymns 'Be Thou My Vision' and 'Just A Closer Walk With Thee'. The latter was tagged on to the end of 'See Me Through Part II', which sounded like an overwrought reiteration of 'In The Days Before Rock 'n' Roll'. His neurotic lyrical retrospection continued on the incantatory 'Take Me Back' and culminated in the self-mythologizing tribute to his birthplace, 'On Hyndford Street'. Childhood memories of picking apples from the trees in Cyprus Avenue, visiting Fusco's for ice cream and listening to Radio Luxembourg and the Third Programme were now safe havens from an apparently painful present in a music world where professional jealousy, false myths and deceitful images were common currency. In Morrison's fictional landscape, where memory and imagination intertwined, old Belfast was equated with a spiritual awakening which had been all but extinguished amid the experiences of adulthood and could now only be retrieved through contemplation of the past.

Having spent much of the last decade reaffirming his roots in Ireland and reinvoking the lost innocence of his childhood, it was ironic that Morrison should conclude 1991 on a sour note, in conflict with members of his own community. Residents of East Belfast were reportedly proud that Morrison had eulogized his old locale on his latest album. So too was the Belfast Blues Appreciation Society which announced its intention to honour the city's lost son by erecting a plaque at his former home, 125 Hyndford Street. Assuming that Morrison would be flattered by an accolade usually reserved for politicians and writers, the Society invited American blues guitarist Buddy Guy to unveil the brass plaque. Morrison's reaction was swift, scathing and decisive in its cold formality. Always excessively concerned about any exploitation of his name or intrusion into his private life, he instructed local solicitors Cleaver, Fulton and Rankin to write to the *Belfast Telegraph* dissociating himself from this innocuous tribute.

Although he no longer had any direct connection with Hyndford Street, it was still part of his life and he acted as though it was sacred ground about to be violated. His reaction clearly discomfited the Society which diplomatically expressed regret. Spokesperson Rob Braniff sheepishly announced: "If it's caused any embarrassment to Van, we apologize. It was put up in the best of faith." Even those aware of the singer's legendary obtuse behaviour were surprised that he would fuss over such a trivial incident. Predictably, his intervention proved a public relations disaster. It merely brought more publicity for the plaque and a testy rebuke from East Belfast's DUP councillor Jim Walker who suggested: "He should remember that the people of Belfast admire him not just for his music – but as a man, and one of their own. Belfast is part of Van Morrison and what he has done in his lifetime." Local newspaper the *Sunday Life* went further, improbably placing Morrison alongside a small gallery of Belfast hellhounds. "First there was George Best," they lamented. "Then Alex Higgins. And now Van Morrison. Why is it that some of Ulster's most famous faces behave the way they do? Higgins is virtually beyond the Pale. Best is not far behind. As for Van Morrison, he has just snubbed a sincere attempt to mark his musical achievements. They erected a plaque at his childhood home in East Belfast but Morrison did not want to know. A local councillor said the singer should remember that the people of Belfast admire him not just for his music, but as a man of their own. Do we really?"

Bernadette Devlin
on the campaign trail.

(*Left*) Gerry O'Hare, former choreographical accompanist to Morrison, later a prominent figure in the IRA. (*Right*) Rita O'Hare, Gerry's former wife, now a leading light in Sinn Féin.

Van and Janet in Woodstock.

Morrison with the exotic 'Little Lord Fauntleroy' blue cape.

KING PLEASURE
Original Moody's Mood
with Quincy Jones
Lucky Thompson, Kai Winding, J. J. Johnson,
John Lewis, Percy Heath, Kenny Clarke, Dave
Lambert, Blossom Dearie, Betty Carter, Jon
Hendricks and others.

© Elliott Landy/Redferns

King Pleasure was an understated influence on *Astral Weeks*.

Van Morrison – early Seventies Cossack chic.

Ian Paisley – early Seventies Cossack chic.

Morrison during his visit to Ireland, October 1973.

Morrison, late Seventies.

Sinn Féin's 1986 Ard Fheis, featuring the Belfast leadership.
Left to right: Gerry Adams, Danny Morrison and Martin McGuinness.

Former loyalist icon
Gusty Spence.

David Ervine, Orangefield School
alumnus, later leader of the PUP.

Violet Morrison in her autumnal years, still showing off her high kicks.

Van and Michelle.

Michelle Rocca in her beauty queen days.

TWENTY-THREE

Dublin

During the early Nineties Dublin was fêted as the most vibrant and exciting city in Europe. Comparisons with London in the Swinging Sixties or Paris at the turn of the century were not uncommon. People spoke of the 'New Ireland', a strangely paradoxical statelet half in love with Europe but still immersed in its older Celtic traditions. It was personified for many in the form of the radical, young president Mary Robinson, the first woman to hold the position. Emigration was still a burning issue among the young, but the haemorrhage of the Eighties had now been stemmed. Census figures revealed that 44 per cent of the Irish population in the Republic was under the age of 25. Their presence brought a vibrancy that helped establish Dublin as the youth capital of Europe. There was also a whiff of new wealth in the city, buoyed by a revitalized economy and soaring house prices. The winds of change blew ever fiercer against antiquated policies. In January 1992, Albert Reynolds, who had made his name building 'ballrooms of romance' during the showband era, succeeded Charles Haughey as Taoiseach. Unlike some of his predecessors, Reynolds paid more than lip service to the Troubles and soon became involved in secret talks with the British PM John Major, Sinn Féin's Gerry Adams and the SDLP's John Hume in an attempt to find a way forward. In the new Dublin, the old dancehall king seemed a fitting symbol of progress.

For Van Morrison, Dublin had much to offer. In earlier times he would have resented its stifling parochialism and goldfish-bowl familiarity, but he found it was possible to saunter across the city without attracting attention. The inhabitants had a suitably blasé attitude towards celebrity and not without good reason. U2's Dublin-based empire was a magnet for singers and musicians like Elvis Costello, Maria McKee, Marianne Faithfull and Jerry Lee Lewis. Killiney, where Enya lived like a fairy princess in a castle, was now the home of Hollywood stars and aspiring A-list actors. Irish popular culture was about to enjoy a commercial renaissance with Roddy Doyle's *Paddy Clarke Ha Ha Ha* winning the Booker Prize, the musical *Riverdance* breaking box office records and the comedy *Father Ted* scooping numerous television awards. The plays of Brian Friel and the films of Neil Jordan and Jim Sheridan were critically revered and new productions were the talk of Dublin. In hotel lounges and trendy diners, politicians mingled with pop musicians, flanked by playwrights, artists, actors and journalists. It was a closed, insular world that embraced everybody from the horsey Curragh clique to the music-loving, late-night denizens of Temple Bar.

Morrison was financially well equipped to enjoy the high life in this renaissance Dublin. A sneak peak into his accounts reveals that on 30 April 1992 he had cash in the bank totalling £1,701,190. He also owned several properties and the net assets of Caledonia Productions were valued at £1,186,867. Add to this his publishing and recording incomes and other assets and it was evident that he was an extremely rich middle-aged man. No doubt he felt it was time to start enjoying some of that wealth.

Before long, Morrison settled into a townhouse in the affluent Ballsbridge area of Dublin. He was no model of conspicuous consumption and at first tended to avoid the trendy rock 'n' roll haunts, film premieres, book launches and star-studded gatherings favoured by some of his more hedonistic contemporaries. However, there were signs of a subtle elevation towards the privileged élite of Dublin society. Towards the end of the year, he attended a fund-raising dinner party for an ecological charity at Leixlip Castle, home of Desmond Guinness. The hospitable Guinness was the cousin of Garech a Brún, the grand patron of Irish culture who had founded Claddagh Records, the spiritual haven of the Chieftains. The party was a revealing indicator of the old and the new Ireland in easy equilibrium. In among the millionaires, debutantes and members of the chattering classes was a strikingly attractive, tall brunette whose high-fashion looks instantly drew Morrison's attention.

Michelle Rocca was the granddaughter of Italian immigrant Egidio Rocca, who had settled in Dublin after the Irish Civil War. The family had started a business repairing mosaics and their son, Paddy, helped establish Rocca Tiles as a thriving concern. Daughter Michelle was a popular, outgoing girl and the envy of her friends when she began dating the Arsenal and Irish international footballer John Devine at the age of 17. After leaving school, she won a place at University College Dublin, reading Greek and Roman Civilization and Italian and French Archaeology. Her first major brush with the media occurred after she turned beauty queen, winning the Miss Ireland title. Sam Smyth was sent to interview her and was amused and nonplussed by the encounter. "He came back from lunch and sat shaking his head," colleague Colin McClelland recalls. "He said 'I'm finding this hard to sink in but this woman really believes she's the most beautiful woman in the world.' We said, 'No, get away!' But he said, 'No, seriously. It's not an act. She's not stupid or giddy. Becoming Miss Ireland has made her Queen of the World.' She'd totally lost the run of herself when she'd won the title and was God's gift to Earth." An exaggeration no doubt, but it certainly gave her confidence and evidently greater resolve. John Devine, fearful that her new-found celebrity status might end their relationship, was reassured on the evening of her victory when she suggested they get engaged. The following year they were married, and two daughters, Danielle and Natasha, followed in quick succession. Playing the peripatetic footballer's wife in England troubled Rocca, however, who missed her family in Dublin. By 1987, the couple had separated and she returned to Ireland with the children. While working in the family business, she started modelling, subsequently emerging as a television personality when she co-hosted the 1988 Eurovision Song Contest with Pat Kenny. Later that year, she became romantically involved with pilot Cathal Ryan, son of Tony Ryan, the founder of Ryanair and owner of Guinness Peat Aviation. In January 1989, he proposed and she accepted, but the marriage never took place. Rocca's friend, boutique owner Marian Gale, remembers Ryan proffering her a number of rings and demanding that she fling all her other diamonds into the river to prove her love. "I know she didn't throw them in the Liffey," Gale quipped with confidence.

By Rocca's own admission her relationship with Ryan was blighted by "difficulties". They lived together for nearly two years, first in Bedfordshire then in Dublin, but separated during the Christmas holidays in 1990 when Rocca was four-and-a-half months pregnant with his child. According to her sister Laura, Michelle was vomiting in the toilet when she learned the news. Ironically, her divorce from Devine in the English courts had only been finalized seven weeks before. When Claudia was born in April 1991, Ryan attended the birth and later that year they reunited, holidaying in Ibiza. By the following year, the relationship had foundered once more and Rocca gained a reputation as a woman unlucky in love. Gossip columnists loved her emotionally-scarred CV and tended to paint her as a free-spirited bohemian, an image which she felt was inaccurate. "I'm anything but a bohemian. I've been rearing children since I was 20. I come from a very stable background so I certainly wouldn't call that bohemian . . . There's a side to me that likes bohemian people. I like people that are different."

The man she was introduced to at Desmond Guinness's soirée certainly fitted the bill. Despite hosting the Eurovision, Rocca's knowledge of popular music was surprisingly limited. When someone pointed out Morrison to her, she first mistook him for Val Doonican, a vocalist who was nearly 18 years his senior and old enough to be Michelle Rocca's grandfather. Later that evening, they were introduced formally, but even after hearing the name Van Morrison, she said "Who?", then asked "What do you do?" When Morrison told her he was a singer, she cheekily demanded "Let me hear you sing then." Morrison was completely taken aback but, surprisingly, acceded to her request, accompanying himself on piano. It was only at this point that Rocca recognized his voice and enquired: "Are you the guy who sang 'Brown Eyed Girl'?" Obviously in playful mood, she then teased Morrison by asking "Do you own the rights to that? Well I have two brown-eyed daughters, would you give me the rights?" The conversation continued in a similarly flippant and flirtatious fashion.

Morrison was entranced by Rocca, one suspects not merely because of her looks, but also the insouciant impudence with which she addressed the shy singer. Far from being in awe of the man, she saw him as terribly unsophisticated in comparison to other guests at the Guinness table, clearly "no oil painting" and "a little bit obnoxious". Indeed, at one point, she was unafraid to tell him bluntly that he was bugging her. Nevertheless, they spent much of the evening together and soon found that they shared a dry sense of humour. Morrison might not normally have accepted the mordant wit of a stranger with such tolerance, but Rocca's beauty and confidence was a winning combination. And if Morrison retained any of the astrological interests associated with his earlier days, then he probably saw significance in the coincidence that Rocca, like himself and his ex-wife Janet Planet, was born under the sign of Virgo. Even the fact that she had hardly heard of him must have seemed an attractive trait. He always dreaded people's preconceptions, accusing them of having an angle or seeing him through the distorted prism of the Van Morrison myth. Here was a woman who had no such illusions and was willing to treat him like a flawed human being. In the misogynistic music world in which he moved, women were frequently seen as subservient groupies. By contrast, Rocca was a paragon. Three decades before, Morrison had been enchanted by glamorous, middle-class art school girls whose cosmopolitan allure testified to a world far removed from his East Belfast shipyard background. Later, he was attracted to a Hollywood beauty, whose flower-child trappings, endless optimism and devotion to his personal happiness proved the ultimate romantic aphrodisiac. In the Eighties, he had dated girls of Danish and Yugoslavian extraction, figures from foreign realms of experience. Michelle Rocca was different again; at once an assuringly familiar woman of Ireland and simultaneously an impossibly exotic creature beyond his social station. In short, it was a relationship worth pursuing.

Morrison's own social standing went upwardly mobile that year when the University of Ulster in Coleraine presented him with an honorary doctorate. The fashion for awarding degrees to minor celebrities was reaching epidemic proportions during the early Nineties. Pop stars as diverse as Mark Knopfler (Newcastle), Joe Cocker (Sheffield) and Sting (Northumbria) were joining an ever-expanding list of comedians, actors, football managers and local politicians in the degree mills. As one broadsheet noted: "Forget the *Hello!* interview . . . today's B-list celebrity is no one without a doctorate from a B-List university . . . It cannot be long before Mr Blobby becomes Dr Blobby." Morrison, who had recently complained about a plaque in his honour, was happy to attend the ceremony clad in a red robe and gold-tasselled cap. "Belfast childhood and the city's atmosphere, streets, scenes and people were reflected throughout his work," said Professor Peter Roebuc in his citation, adding, "As with the best singers and musicians there is an unremitting integrity in his work and a refusal to admit commercial compromise which, I suspect, has its roots – like his music – in the Ulster soil from which he springs." Such rhetoric notwithstanding, the suspicion remained that this was as much a marketing exercise by the university as an acknowledgement of excellence.

Morrison evidently considered himself a more worthy academic than Dr Blobby. In a priceless example of hubris, he later let slip in a promotional interview that he would "like to develop a philosophy class in a university", insisting, "if I was offered a position I'd do it tomorrow." Never mind the fact that Morrison had no academic qualifications, had never taught, had never written a book or even had a single article published in any journal, respected or otherwise. Indeed, there was no objective proof that he knew anything about philosophy. Whether he was sufficiently qualified even to be taught the subject, let alone teach it himself, was a more pertinent consideration. And even if he really had read certain books or authors, was there any guarantee or likelihood that he could communicate his ideas in a class, lecture or seminar setting? Apparently, such considerations were deemed irrelevant by Ulster University. Within days, a faculty member was excitedly offering the singer the opportunity to fulfil his dreams. It smacked terribly of vulgar PR and grasping tuition fees eclipsing academic merit. Morrison, perhaps realizing he was already out of his depth, ultimately resisted the bait.

Since his first meeting with Rocca, there were telling signs that Morrison was loosening up. Bob Geldof met him on a passing visit to Bangor and spent a long evening in a bar, where they played an impromptu session. Both singers were entertained by comedian John McBlain, whose speciality was impersonating Ian Paisley. On this particular evening, he mimicked both the Big Man and the Wee Man, adding Geldof's Dublin brogue for good measure.

Although Morrison would soon become a regular at awards ceremonies, he began 1993 by turning down the chance to attend the annual Rock 'n' Roll Hall of Fame ceremony in the US, leaving Robbie Robertson to provide the citation and accept the honour on his behalf. It was the first time a living inductee had spurned the institution. One suspects that Morrison would have made the effort if the Hall of Fame in question had been Jazz or Blues rather than a Rock 'n' Roll institution. Instead, the giants of the music world descended upon Dublin and lined up onstage in an impromptu tribute to Morrison at the Point on 6 February. Éamon Carr, ex-Horslips' drummer-turned-journalist, was in two minds about attending the show having been sorely disappointed by Morrison's previous performances which he regarded as tedious. "I went to see him because Dylan was in town. Word was out that there had been tentative negotiations and they might appear on stage together. So we went, and it was an outrageous gig. It started on a high and just kept building. I noticed there was a set list at the mixing desk and the guys there said 'That's just a rough guide for us, even the band aren't sure what he's going to do.' But they were on their toes that night. Everybody played quite brilliantly. Morrison's own contribution suggested something crucial was at stake. He was fighting for his life. You got the impression he'd got something to prove. Sure enough at the end of the set when he did 'Gloria', Bono came on and said, 'This is sacred ground. This is a church. The Church of the Holy Ground.' The audience loved this and it drove Morrison to greater heights. People expected Dylan to come on, then Van waved over to stage right. This character in a glitzy jacket came out from the other side of the stage and grabbed him around the midriff and almost squeezed him. It was Dylan. Then a host of stars appeared: Steve Winwood, Kris Kristofferson, Nanci Griffith, Elvis Costello, Chrissie Hynde, and a hovering Jim Capaldi. There were a million onstage for Dylan's 'It's All Over Now, Baby Blue' but it was Morrison's show, no question about it. Even if they hadn't been there, it would still have ranked as one of the great gigs." Still buzzing, Carr attended the post-performance reception, which resembled a musicians' *Who's Who.* "When I rambled backstage the first words I heard when I got to the hospitality area was an American woman speaking to the promoters and saying, 'We've got to get Van away from the red wine.' He was mingling with the guests with his shades on and the room was very crowded. Subsequently, there was a party at a nightclub and he was fairly out of it by that stage. Obviously, he'd invested so much in the gig that he needed to unwind."

A combination of red wine and Dublin bonhomie partly explains Morrison's greater openness and sociability during this period. He resembled a man keen to rediscover the freedom and wildness of his youth in a city that was fast emerging as the hippest watering hole in Europe. Various members of the Rolling Stones could be seen on Grafton Street and a legendary rock 'n' roller was about to declare himself an honorary Irishman. Morrison was so excited when he learned that Jerry Lee Lewis was arriving in the country that he pre-empted the visit by meeting the singer in Wales. Over the past decade, European devotees of Lewis had held an annual convention at the King's Hotel in Newport. "It was such a great atmosphere and good rock 'n' roll vibe created by the manager Gordon McIlroy that we decided to come back every year to discuss Jerry Lee and forget about our troubles," recalls one of the founders, Tadgh Coughlan. "Van had obviously stayed at the hotel, picked up on what Mac was doing and loved it. They became friends." Performing commitments meant that Morrison missed Jerry Lee's three weekend shows, but he was there for convention day on 15 March. "He turned up to meet his idol," Coughlan stresses. "Basically, nobody there was bothered with Morrison because they were all Jerry Lee Lewis fanatics. A lot of these guys don't listen to anything else. People there spoke normally to Morrison, but it was all about Jerry Lee. Van was talking about obscure songs, lyrics, label covers and all that. He was just a fan. There was no Van Morrison superstar bullshit – he was there for Jerry Lee."

One member of the American clan that attracted Morrison's attention was Jerry Lee's younger sister, Linda Gail Lewis. Prophetically, her first impression of the singer was decidedly negative. "He was rude to me and I didn't really like him. He was not very nice; a grumpy kind of guy. I'm real sensitive so that didn't 'gee and haw' as we say." Linda Gail had no knowledge of Morrison's standing in the music industry, apart from his American chart success with 'Brown Eyed Girl'. Coincidentally, her husband Eddie Braddock had been involved in promoting that single in the Southern states and he happily imparted that information to the frosty singer. Predictably, what was intended as an ice-breaker turned ugly as Morrison was taken back to the bad days of Bert Berns and Bang Records. "He started fussing at Eddie," Lewis remembers, "but Eddie was an independent promotions person, he wasn't working for Bert Berns. Van, instead of taking these things into consideration, just proceeded with his tirade." Braddock was taken aback by Morrison's response and remembers his wife saying, "I think this is a horrible man." She couldn't get away from him quick enough. It would be another seven years before they met again.

On 16 March 1993, Jerry Lee, his wife Kerrie and son Lee took the ferry to Dublin to start a new chapter in a life unrivalled in popular music for its tempestuous eruptions, unrelenting drama and lurid headlines. Since his 'child bride scandal' in the late Fifties, Lewis had totalled six marriages, buried two wives and two sons, and played out the modern equivalent of a mediaeval morality tale in which God and the Devil vied for his soul. "I've been abused, sued, jailed, ridiculed, persecuted and prosecuted," he says, "but I never let it bother me. It was the passing of caskets that brought me down." His other great nemesis was the Inland Revenue Service which had pursued him like a pack of bloodhounds. Recently, they had taken his home and confiscated all of his belongings, including the Stark piano that his parents had mortgaged their house to buy him for him when he was a child. "They not only took the freezer, but the food inside," Kerrie adds.

Tired of the relentless attention of the American media, Lewis made the decision to emigrate to Ireland, enrolling his six-year-old son in a local school in Foxrock. He was amazed to discover how accommodating the people were and even more surprised about the general lack of intrusion into his affairs. Declaring "I've always been Irish," the Killer concluded "I've learned to love Dublin, man, this is one of the finest places I've ever been in my life." Within weeks, he found himself surrounded by a core of hard-drinking pals, including Morrison, Ron Wood and Shane MacGowan. For a time, there was talk of Lewis and Morrison collaborating on a covers album with the Belfast singer producing, but it came to nothing. "They talked about 'Bright Side Of The Road', but it didn't even begin," Coughlan remembers. "When it went to corporate level it fell apart." The real collaboration happened on stage at Bad Bob's, a music venue in Dublin's Temple Bar where, along with Ron Wood, the pair appeared that June.

The Bad Bob's shows coincided with the release of Morrison's new album *Too Long In Exile*, a revealing insight into his current state of mind. Its title track mentioned George Best and Alex Higgins, the Belfast hellraisers with whom he had recently been compared in an acerbic editorial in *Sunday Life*. 'Wasted Years' and 'Big Time Operators' reopened other old wounds, with the latter offering provocative allusions to his troubled time in New York during the Bang period. The archetypal paedophile blues standard 'Good Morning, Little Schoolgirl' and the ameliorating 'Till We Get The Healing Done' reiterated familiar themes. But the key to his future lay in the reworking of old material with John Lee Hooker, including an improbable cover of 'Gloria'. Here was Morrison intent on sharing his load and working with his friends and heroes, just as many of the old jazz and bluesmen had done in their autumnal years. It was the firmest indication yet of his determination to avoid the familiar treadmill of the rock singer–songwriter. From here on, collaborations and partnerships would prove central to his game plan.

Choosing Jerry Lee Lewis and Shane MacGowan as drinking partners was not the healthiest way of spending an evening, but it was certainly fun. By their excessive standards, Morrison was the embodiment of sobriety and he thoroughly enjoyed their company. He frequently visited Jerry Lee Lewis' home and on at least one occasion kept his host awake for most of the night by playing Jimmie Rodgers' yodelling songs. Morrison was also the soul of the party when in the company of MacGowan and his girlfriend, the vivacious Victoria Clarke. At one Irish festival that summer, Van and Vicky were spotted in a flirtatious embrace which prompted one of MacGowan's wittiest one-liners, "So now it's Van the *other* man!" Morrison felt close enough to Clarke to allow her sole access as his interviewer of the season. After years of complaints against journalists, he had at last alighted on the perfect solution of employing a trusted female friend to perform the task. It also meant he had control over the copy. At one stage, there was wild talk of syndicating an interview for a £30,000 fee but in the end it went the usual route, appearing in the rock monthly Q. To her credit, Clarke presented Morrison with some teasing and tough questions about his irascible personality, which he countered well. What Shane MacGowan made of all this camaraderie can perhaps best be gleaned from his later composition, the vexatious 'Victoria' in which he wrote: 'Victoria, Victoria, you left me in opium euphoria and went off with a fat monk saying a Gloria". Whether this was fictional jealousy or something more substantial remains a tantalizing consideration.

Morrison had planned to produce an album featuring MacGowan covering his songs, a project identical to that discussed earlier with Jerry Lee Lewis. After completing one track, the Them rarity 'Philosophy', the collaboration foundered, mainly due to contractual complications. Despite this, the pair remained drinking buddies when in Dublin, but MacGowan's feelings towards his Belfast counterpart became increasingly ambivalent. "Van depressed me. I remember one time I had to pick him up off the floor of the Clarence, which is not an easy job and I'm sure that's not the only time that's happened. I stayed up drinking with him many nights and I always tried to convince Van what a wonderful life it was and what a wonderful life he was living or could live if he stopped being such a miserable fuck, but it didn't work. There's a man who lived up to his public image, he was meant to be a miserable git and he is a miserable git, but he is capable of having a really good laugh."

The lighter side of Morrison was in evidence during a series of summer sightings at various Dublin hot spots, where he was often seen in the company of Michelle Rocca. It was not long before their friendship was rumoured to be romance. After seeing a photograph of the pair together, Sam Smyth said, "It is surely the most unlikely coupling in human history." What added intrigue to the relationship was the emphatic denial that they were anything other than good friends. Unfortunately for the publicity-shy Morrison, this piqued the curiosity of arguably the most waspish and wittiest gossip columnist in the world. Terry Keane, the wife of Supreme Court Judge Ronan Keane, documented the adventures of Dublin's social élite in the *Sunday Independent* with such a wicked turn of phrase, biting sarcasm and beautiful irony that her column was an unmissable hoot. For those in the know, which in Dublin meant even the dogs on the street, her views had an additional secret spice. Here was a woman with a thresher-like humour whose own closet contained a prized skeleton. For years she had been having a clandestine affair with the Taoiseach Charles Haughey, one of the most colourful figures ever to hold office in Ireland. It spoke volumes for her nerve, courage and sheer cheek that she would lend her name to such a provocative column knowing that her own romantic life might make headlines at any moment.

Keane's fascination with the Rocca/Morrison story broke big on 27 June 1993 in a feature titled "I Van To Hold Your Hand". "Michelle Rocca is having an intensely platonic relationship with Van Morrison," she revealed. "She and Van looked a cosy item the other night in the Shelbourne before they headed off, chastely holding hands to Bad Bob's with their pals Shane MacGowan and Fiachna Ó Braonáin, head strummer with the Hothouse Flowers . . . Michelle insists that there is no romance. Van, she says, thinks she has a nice personality and that she understands him and she looks after him when he's in Dublin. Sounds like the basis of a very good non-platonic relationship to me." Keane monitored the pair's movements the following night when they were seen at the Break For The Border where a bottom-judging competition was in full swing. "There they held hands in the most platonic way. They rounded off the evening – if you'll pardon the expression – in their favourite night-spot, Lillie's Bordello."

The body language between the pair convinced most onlookers that they were an amorous item, but the extended tease continued. Morrison even met the Rocca family when he was invited to the wedding of Michelle's brother Patrick to Annette O'Brien. What Keane desperately needed was a photo opportunity. The following month, the perfect snap fell on her desk. After a night out, Morrison was leaving an establishment bustling with people when he stumbled forward amid the throng. Rocca grabbed his left arm to stop him falling and his head landed almost directly in front of her chest, so that his eyes were inches from her covered breasts. A photographer captured the moment in all its embarrassing glory. Keane responded with one of her finest and funniest pieces. Mixing her metaphors, mistaking her Shakespearean characters and throwing in some popular song lyrics and Irish colloquialisms, the columnist declared: "When it comes to protesting too much, Michelle Rocca leaves Lady Macbeth in the ha'penny place! But despite denials of any romance as mere rumour, Van the Man and Michelle the Model continue to Rocca 'n' roll their way around nightclubs . . . Michelle says that their relationship is platonic (though in his case it looks more like gin 'n' platonic, he certainly looks a few horsepower short of a Van!) Clearly Michelle gives him a place to rest his weary head – a head which, I must say, makes a coot look positively hirsute! A picture paints a thousand words – and 'platonic' just doesn't make it to the list. It could be that Michelle is 'in-denial' over this whole romance business – once bitten etc. Perhaps she should simply say 'I Van to be alone'."

Far from fleeing the media, Morrison seemed content to play along. At another fund-raising outing, he smiled for the cameras while Michelle and the stunning socialite Aisling Evans simultaneously planted a peck on each of his cheeks. He resembled nothing less than a grinning frog being kissed by two beautiful princesses. The summer season ended with Morrison appearing at social functions for the wealthy Guinness and Lawlor families, with Rocca in attendance. Amid the merrymaking there were lots of jokes about marriage, with Michelle jesting "my next boyfriend will be my husband" and Morrison supposedly retorting, "Could I be that man?" Keane provided her own end of term report: "So what is the state of play? Yes, Van is keen. No, they are not getting married because Michelle is holding out for love. The truly, madly, deeply stuff. Will that girl ever learn?"

Three weeks later, they were back in the news. "The lust-free liaison between Van Morrison and his escort Michelle Rocca continues to boggle the minds of close friends and confidants alike, not to mention my readers," Keane gushed. "A post-Curragh do at Rathsallagh was last week's setting for passionate peccadilloes . . . Confusing signals continue to emanate from this compelling couple. While protesting their platonicism to all who would listen, Van got a sharp slap on the wrist when he had the temerity to lift his shades to look at another pretty woman." The Keane spies even eavesdropped on some tongue-in-cheek banter with Morrison joking about buying a horse for "my fiancée" and Rocca replying, "Let's see how the horse pans out first and then we'll see about the fiancée." Always ready with a sprinkling of sexual innuendo, Keane added, "She's a cool customer and no mistake. Still, her birthday was in the offing and there's nothing a Virgo likes better than a ticket to ride."

Belfast media hounds were heartily sick of being scooped in the search for Morrison gossip by the irrepressible Keane and her Dublin crew. One week later, the *Sunday Life* managed to corner Rocca for a quick interview, which merely reiterated the platonic platitudes. "I would be very flattered if I thought he was wooing me, but we are just good friends and I think it will stay that way." In a revealing aside, though, she commented on his shyness and troubled public image, claiming: "I have been working on that part of him, trying to persuade him to relax more. He is pretty introverted except when he is in the company of good friends."

Morrison was in sore need of Rocca's behavioural counselling two weeks later when he travelled to Newport, Wales, to play at the King's Hotel. The unfortunate patrons were subjected to some of the most explicit examples of bad language ever heard on a British stage by a world-renowned musician. Ostensibly the shows had been booked to allow Morrison to unveil a new revue-style ensemble, featuring Brian Kennedy. The former Energy Orchard vocalist was young, Catholic, falsetto-voiced and gay – in short, the complete antithesis of Morrison. It was intended that his contribution would complement the performance, adding a pleasant sweetness to Morrison's darker vocal. Surprisingly, he even sang lead on numbers such as 'Crazy Love', 'Tupelo Honey', 'Into The Mystic', 'Queen Of The Slipstream' and 'Have I Told You Lately'. It was not Kennedy's singing that caused offence, but Morrison's incessant swearing and ranting at the audience. It was an unprovoked and disgraceful display of obscenities that largely confirmed Phil Solomon's old prediction about his unruly protégé: "He's not a professional. He never was and he never will be."

The scandalous utterances at Newport did not bode well for the revue but a live album was completed that December in San Francisco. It included vocal contributions from his daughter, now professionally known as Shana Morrison. During her time in Morrison's band she began dating drummer Dave Early, much to her father's chagrin. The percussionist was subsequently hauled over the coals in a fierce encounter after which he ceased working in the band. On 15 October 1996 he died, aged 40, following a car crash.

On his return from America, Morrison was greeted by further speculation in the *Sunday World* that he and Rocca intended to marry. The fact that the ever vigilant Terry Keane had yet to run this story confirmed the extent to which it was nothing more than wild rumour. Rocca had recently been to England and on the flight back told a stewardess, "I've bought some new clothes for my boyfriend". Soon after, Van the Boy found himself kitted in an outfit that was a cross between the *sub fusc* of the Blues Brothers and the tailored neatness of a Mafia boss. These were clothes designed to disguise. A hat covered his unfashionable comb-over hairstyle; dark glasses hid his porcine eyes; a black frockcoat suit drew attention from his frighteningly large girth. It was undoubtedly his most amusing sartorial statement since the Zorro chic of the early Eighties and would remain his stage uniform for the foreseeable future.

On St Valentine's Day, the new outfit was on display at the 1994 Brit Awards where Morrison received a special award for his Outstanding Contribution to British Music. The presentation was made by former Beirut hostage John McCarthy who testified to the importance of 'Wonderful Remark', "a song that he wrote more than 20 years ago [which] was very important to us". A series of televised tributes followed from Sting ("musical mentor and spiritual mentor"), Bob Geldof ("long may you teach all of us what we're meant to be doing"), Elvis Costello ("looking forward to listening when I'm a happy old man"), Bono ("you're the man!"), Peter Gabriel ("you've shown every artiste what it means *not* to compromise"), John Lee Hooker ("such a great person") and Bob Dylan ("congratulations on this prestigious award. No one's more deserving of it than you for writing all those fine songs and giving us all that inspiration over the years. Thanks a lot. God bless you, Van. Blah, blah, blah, blah blah!"). The evening concluded with Morrison duetting with his daughter, after which he was joined by Brian Kennedy and Shane MacGowan for the most startling version of 'Gloria' ever heard. MacGowan's affiliation with the nationalist community in Ireland was already well known. He had been photographed with Gerry Adams and had recently ended one of his shows with the Republican warrior cry "Tiocfaidh ár lá" ("Our day will come"). On stage at the Brits, he sang out a new chorus of defiance: 'G-L-O – *IRA*'. It was the ultimate subversive musical ploy to hijack Morrison's most famous song and transform it into a Republican anthem. What viewers on the Shankill felt after witnessing MacGowan's display of IRA solidarity can only be imagined. Certainly, the paramilitary UDA leading light Johnny 'Mad Dog' Adair, the scourge of Catholics in Belfast and a keen Van Morrison fan, would not have been amused. Remarkably, nobody in the press mentioned

MacGowan's sedition and neither he nor Morrison ever spoke of the matter in print.

Amid the recent accolades foisted upon Morrison was a less welcome High Court writ issued by his former tour manager Alan Morris seeking £32,000 in unpaid earnings. Morris, who had been hired in the spring of 1992, claimed Morrison had agreed to pay him five per cent of concert receipts from a number of European and American shows. Morrison vigorously contested the case which, despite its news-worthiness, was buried beneath a sheaf of press cuttings dominated by the new woman in his life.

Michelle Rocca's prominence in the Morrison story was increasing by the month. Having reconfigured his image and public persona, she next decided to break her media silence and conduct a major interview with a colleague of Terry Keane's at the *Sunday Independent*. Rocca's motives were twofold: firstly, to clarify personal matters, and secondly, to promote her new television venture, Michelle Rocca Productions. She had already secured Morrison's agreement to be filmed for an exclusive interview which she hoped would serve as her showreel. Journalist Patricia Deevy was invited to Rocca's home and found her open and engaging. During the interview Morrison rang twice and expressed astonishment that his girlfriend had allowed a journalist into her house. Rather than the politics of evasion preferred by the singer, Rocca specialized in information overkill, garrulously filling seven hours of taped interview. She even provided a dozen pages of hand-written points for good measure. The subsequent profile confirmed that Rocca was well equipped to teach Morrison lessons in media relations as well as dress sense. Still insisting that the couple were just good friends, she threw in a tantalizing "but watch this space" to add to the intrigue. Challenging the beauty and the beast caricatures and Marilyn Monroe/Arthur Miller analogies propagated by columnists, Rocca made the insightful point that the relationship was quite complex and evenly balanced. Indeed, there was good reason for considering her the dominant partner. "He listens to me more than I listen to him," she pointed out, "although I'm starting to listen to him now because his best advice in life to me has been 'Hold still and listen!'" A couple of weeks after the Deevy encounter, Rocca agreed to speak to Cork-based writer Reiseal Ní Cheilleachair who, coincidentally or otherwise, was interviewing myself around the same time. Once again, Rocca was happy to allow a visit to her home and greeted her interviewer while still in her dressing gown and woolly socks. At various moments, the children Danielle and Natasha would appear. Rocca was keen to break down the stereotypical image of the bimbo beauty queen, expressing her ambition to return to university and study psychology and philosophy. "You get compartmentalized," she complained. "Being a former Miss Ireland is something you live with and that is extended to Eurovision and then people get all confused and think you won Miss World. And if people relate you to any type of beauty queen or modelling, they assume you don't have a brain and then as what happens with all single women, you walk into a room and other women become very insecure."

The endless fascination of Irish columnists with the Rocca/Morrison relationship begged the question: Why? "You tell me," Rocca retorted. "I don't know. And the poor man doesn't understand it either. He hasn't had publicity for 27 years. He hates it but I say, 'Well, you sure picked the wrong girl to be friends with!' But he has a very good sense of humour too. I have a very black sense of humour that I got from my father. I like playing games with life. I don't like comedians. I like funny situations. I often do things in front of the camera for fun and people don't realize it." Given Morrison's shyness, it was intriguing to consider how he related to the Rocca brood. "Our relationship is not at that level," Rocca insisted. "He has a daughter of his own and I don't involve my children. I don't want to involve my children. I don't ask him about my children or anything because we are not at that level, but he is brilliant with his own daughter." What emerged most forcibly was Rocca's firm independence. Unlike Morrison she could charm her guests with pleasant conversation and had sufficient media savvy to provide revealing copy while always holding something back. The combination of self-confidence, self-effacement and self-knowledge – traits that Morrison seemingly found impossible to convey to strangers – came easily to Rocca. Her views on men in general were equally enlightening, particularly if applied to her current playmate. "I think Irish men have problems that have a lot to do with their mothers. A lot of men are incapable of showing their feelings and it is not the women's fault because we are all victims of victims. I'm not anti-men by any means. I just think it is harder for men to show their feelings. We can scream it or talk it out but they have to keep it all in. That's why we live longer, I think. But we can't drink as much! I don't need to be hopeful about any man. I'm not waiting to get my hands on anyone. They should be queuing up the road but they're not because it just isn't like that. It is the myth of the beautiful woman. Women who are beautiful are not stupid. Some are, but they don't all have to be . . . This glamour thing is all an illusion, I swear. I've got my mother's cheekbones. I haven't been to the gym for six weeks but I do try. If I don't get my sleep, I'm like a zombie. And I know alcohol poisons the system but that doesn't mean that I don't still love champagne. But what can you do?"

Nor was the animated Rocca content to play the part of Morrison's passive muse. "A muse to me is a house," she quipped, enigmatically. Instead, at his suggestion, she took on a Linda McCartney role as the singer's onstage adjunct. "I can't sing and I can't dance, so I'll just recite some poetry," she explained, clutching a copy of Paul Durcan's collection *Give Me Your Hand*. In addition to serving as Morrison's fashion consultant, reciter in residence, public relations guru and social companion, she became involved in planning an all-star tribute album, which brought together such Dublin habitués as Sinéad O'Connor, Phil Coulter, Elvis Costello, Marianne Faithfull and actor Liam Neeson. British fashion photographer Andrew MacPhearson was specially flown in to photograph the cover queen Rocca who was styled by Ian Galvin of Brown Thomas and Michael J. Doyle of Peter Mark wearing clothes from the latest Rifat Ozbek collection. When the album appeared later that summer under the title *No Prima Donnas – The Songs Of Van Morrison*, it was Rocca's face alone that graced the front sleeve.

The Morrison visage was also missing from the jacket of his latest release *A Night In San Francisco*, an epic two-and-a-half hour live set that served as a sprawling souvenir from his new Rhythm & Blues & Soul Revue, which included guest appearances from venerable bluesmen John Lee Hooker, Junior Wells and Jimmy Witherspoon. Oddly, Morrison singled out one of the new tunes, 'Soldier Of Fortune', as one of the most moving of his career and a perfect summation of his present state of mind.

A week after the album's release, a revealing interview with Morrison was published in the *Sunday Independent*. His interviewer was Michelle Rocca whose ubiquitous talents now seemingly covered everything bar producing and writing his songs. Like an all-devouring virago she was pictured caressing Morrison's face, eyes seductively closed and mouth open. It was indicative of Morrison's immersion in Dublin society that he was not only interviewed exclusively in the *Sunday Independent* but appeared as a lead item in the letters pages of the same issue alongside a controversy over Brendan Behan. Headed "I'm not a rock star says Van Morrison", the singer wrote: "Sir – There has been a lot in the papers lately in relation to myself being referred to as a 'rock star'. I'd just like to set the record straight if I may." What followed were six paragraphs in which Morrison detailed, largely unconvincingly, precisely why he was not a "rock star" and how he had spent "most of my life living the role of an anti-hero". His sensitivity spoke volumes. Several months later, Morrison continued his epistolary relationship with the *Sunday Independent* by composing a piece titled "How Not To Get Screwed" in which he offered six paragraphs of advice to young musicians on the pitfalls of the music business.

Despite protesting a loathing for the cult of celebrity, he was now centre stage in a drama set in Dublin with Michelle Rocca as the female lead. The photographs, the gossip column cameos and the open letters to the press all testified to an underlying and increasing ambivalence towards Dublin. While Jerry Lee Lewis found the city liberating, Morrison's feelings were becoming more complicated. Nowhere else in the world had he ever been regarded as such a celebrity and man about town. Yet, he played that part to perfection. He was a regular at late-night drinking haunts like Bad Bobs and Lillie's Bordello, along with a retinue of buddies. Not only was he still hanging around with MacGowan and Victoria Clarke, but had recently appointed Shane's sister Siobhan as his personal assistant. "We used to go down to Lillie's quite a lot," recalls journalist Marion McKeone. "I'd shared a flat with Siobhan and we used to knock around together. We all got on quite well and I found him good fun. A decent bloke. Like everybody he can be not always pleasant at times if he's hassled, but I genuinely liked him . . . He's stereotyped as this narky little Belfast man whereas in fact he has a great sense of humour and really enjoys a joke. His humour is very black and he likes a bit of repartee. He's someone you'd see for a couple of drinks occasionally and if you'd bump into each other you'd go to a club . . . I wouldn't say we talked of high art – it was more smutty jokes at five in the morning to be quite honest. I'll give you an example. We were down in Lillie's one night, sitting having a laugh in a bunch. Some American guy was there and he was basically full of shit – it was all this crap about 'what inspired these wonderful streams of consciousness?' Van just turned around and said: 'Arse and tit, like everybody else.' And that was it. The guy nearly fell off his chair. He thought he was going to get this great inspirational response. Van turned around, went back to his drink and everybody laughed. So he can take the piss out of himself. I don't think he takes himself as seriously as everybody would have us believe. But this is purely from a social point of view."

Significantly, Morrison's drinking was evidently no longer producing the worrying mood swings characteristic of earlier times. The sullenness and anger, all too familiar from his Belfast days, seemed neutralized by the social bonhomie of Nineties Dublin. Here was Morrison imbibing in public places and even fraternizing with journalists. His openness came as quite a shock to Sam Smyth, who was equally amazed by his choice of friends, which now included the columnist Stan Gebler-Davis. "He's quite a nice guy, full of Tory affectation and the least rock 'n' roll person in the world," Smyth confided at the time. "I'd meet him occasionally and we'd talk about upper-class gossip. He told me: 'Morrison's not a bad fellow at all. But, Jesus, when he gets stuck into the brandy . . .' Stan would have known he was a famous singer, but he's not easily impressed by rock 'n' rollers or anybody. I was surprised having always put Van's relationship with drink down to Indians and firewater. But Stan spent an evening with him at Lillie's Bordello and he left tickets for him for the next concert."

Morrison's accessibility in Dublin was quite remarkable. Often you would see him in the street or drinking at the Horseshoe Bar in the Shelbourne Hotel, a brisk walk away from his Ballsbridge townhouse. On 15 April 1994, he came into the hotel lounge and sat in the seat which I had just vacated and ordered a bowl of soup, a vegetarian salad and a coffee. He was dressed in a stylish shirt, presumably chosen by Michelle Rocca, and heel-heightened shoes. As we sat inches from each other, he stared, then made an urgent call on his mobile. His countenance was very grim indeed. Even that non-incident was picked up by the Dublin press for a "Morrison scowls at Rogan" story. In another report, he was spotted one morning with Bob Geldof at the Shelbourne allegedly breakfasting on porridge and red wine after a late-night session. They were animatedly debating the existence of aliens, with Morrison still insisting that UFOs existed, just as he had told Corvin all those years ago.

As summer beckoned, Dublin audiences were given the opportunity to sample Morrison's Rhythm & Blues & Soul Revue extravaganza. Many were unprepared for such a radical reworking of the familiar Morrison live experience. In an audacious attempt to simulate a black revue-style concert, he was more than willing to vacate the stage at key points, leaving the spotlight on the accomplished Brian Kennedy, whose sweet versions of several Morrison classics divided audiences. It was certainly a brave move on Morrison's part to challenge everyone's expectations, but there were surprisingly few champions for this innovative reappraisal of his stagecraft. Some understood the need for a younger singer to tackle his early recorded material, particularly in a carefully structured revue setting, while others preferred to hear Morrison singing all the songs himself. Perhaps such reservations accounted for the relatively poor turnout. "He did two nights at the Point," Éamon Carr remembers, "but it was a bit optimistic. It wasn't nearly sold out. The first-night crowd was the horsey, Shelbourne Hotel set. There were people around us who I'm sure didn't have a clue. They were there because of the social columns. Van had asked the record company what they were doing afterwards and they said, 'Michelle has something planned.' He said, 'Fuck that!' meaning it would basically be her socialites. They asked him 'What are you up for?' and he said, 'We'll go for a few pints.' It showed at the gig. He looked like a man who wanted to go for a pint." Carr sat patiently as the Revue was unveiled with contributions by Brian Kennedy and Shana Morrison. "Basically, Van fecked off at this stage," Carr complained. "The night went on like this with him only singing half the set. It was like he was conducting. A lot of the fans were really pissed off. Towards the end this punky-looking kid came out front and went bananas doing a Cossack dance while soloing on guitar. It was like a showband, cabaret job. It finished and Morrison went offstage, then came back in a white Panama hat singing Louis Prima. This cued the diva herself [Rocca] who was dressed in white, lurking like Cruella De Vil. She sauntered on stage holding a piece of paper. Then she goes to the mike and says, 'Paul Durcan says Van Morrison is a poet, and Van Morrison says Paul Durcan's a poet.' Then she reads a Paul Durcan poem. A lot of the punters were bored out of their minds and really disgruntled. I even got letters from as far away as Galway. I wrote a piece and said, 'His brilliance confused his fans' – this sort of nonsense, tongue in cheek. Those who had eyes and ears knew what was going on. I got a real chuckle out of it."

The concerts were only part of the story. Personality clashes added to the melodrama. Already there was evidence of a growing chasm within Morrison's circle. On the one hand, there was Michelle Rocca and her glamorous friends and on the other the nocturnal acolytes of Shane MacGowan. "I don't know Michelle but I don't rate her particularly highly from what I've seen of her in public," observed Morrison's journalist acquaintance Marion McKeone. Conversely, Rocca felt she had good reason to feel resentful towards Victoria Clarke who was in for a surprise after showtime at the Point. "I ran into Victoria on the night of the second gig," recalls diarist Katie Hannon, "and there was a note from Siobhan MacGowan saying 'Sorry about this, but Michelle says you can't come in under any circumstances.'" The tenacious Clarke did not have to wait long in the back bar before a member of Morrison's crew invited her into the inner sanctum. "He obviously didn't know anything about it," Hannon remarks, "and she decided to take him up on it. When she went backstage Siobhan said 'Get out! I'll be killed if you're here!' Later on, I met Michelle and she told me she'd said to Van before, 'Either she goes, or I go.' She told me, 'Victoria Clarke is a bad egg' and 'I'm wising Van up to her'. I think Michelle thought he had a thing about Victoria, that there was something going on between them. Shane seemed convinced that she'd run off with Van in that song 'Victoria'. "

The saga did not end with the Rocca/Clarke rivalry. In the background was daughter Shana who was evidently annoyed about the comic portrayals of her father in the Dublin gossip columns. "There was a huge row that night," Hannon reveals. "Someone went over to Shana and said, 'You really should be nice to Michelle' because they felt she'd been cutting her off dead. And Shana just flipped and screamed at the top of her voice that she was sick of Michelle, that she thought she was a bitch who was ruining her father's career. Everyone was in shock because all of Michelle's family were there. Van went over and took Michelle by the arm and walked out with her."

Adding another unintended stir to the cauldron was showbiz columnist Eddie McIlwaine, adrift in Belfast. Over the weekend, he had run a speculative piece suggesting that the romance between Morrison and Rocca was over. The article could hardly have arrived at a more sensitive time. A couple of days later, Katie Hannon had more news. "I was at a function last night," she told me, "and Michelle was there. I asked her about it because it was a front-page story in the *Belfast Telegraph*. She said, 'I don't know, all I can say is that I spent the weekend in Belfast.' So it was a manufactured story according to Michelle, but I'd say they're having their difficulties."

On top of all this were reports of Morrison grappling with the green-eyed monster in the form of Richard Gere. The actor had invited Morrison to appear at a benefit show for the Tibetan Aid Charity at London's Grosvenor House Hotel which led to Gere joining the singer onstage. Gere reappeared at several concerts that summer, but an after-show get-together in Brighton ended sourly. Morrison supposedly suspected Gere might have romantic designs on Rocca and allegedly called him "a Hollywood cunt". Whatever flare-up may have happened was soon forgiven and forgotten and Michelle insisted that both parties were very good friends, a view publicly confirmed when they again shared a stage the following year. In the meantime, the Rocca/Morrison relationship continued to attract attention, not least when they were spotted together at the Irish Derby. Across the paddock were the Taoiseach Albert Reynolds and the American Ambassador to Dublin Jean Kennedy Smith. Seven months before, in December 1993, Reynolds and John Major had signed the Downing Street Declaration which included a commitment to allow the "people of the island of Ireland" the "right of self-determination on the basis of consent, freely and concurrently given, North and South". Paisley had responded by telling Major "You have sold Ulster to buy off the fiendish Republican scum." The country 'n' Irish loving 'Rhinestone Taoiseach' was still dreaming of Irish unity and an end to hostilities in the North while Morrison was standing a few yards away betting on a likely Derby winner. Kennedy Smith, sister of the late JFK, was about to bring Reynolds' dream a step closer having persuaded Bill Clinton to allow former IRA Chief of Staff Joe Cahill a visa to visit the States. Cahill's meet-and-greet with IRA sympathizers and activists in America, just before an Army Council meeting back home, proved deeply significant. An eventful summer was about to end on an unexpected high.

TWENTY-FOUR

Sex Shame

When it happened it took almost everyone by surprise. The notion of the IRA ending its campaign in 1994 sounded fantastical. During the previous year John Hume and Gerry Adams had issued a groundbreaking statement initiating "an overall strategy for lasting peace". Few were convinced, including Republican Sinn Féin President Ruairí Ó Brádaigh who described the initiative as "proposed surrender". Yet there were some odd exchanges which, in retrospect, proved revealing. Colin McClelland, the editor of the *Sunday World* in Dublin, told me excitedly that he had received an unexpected call which raised sceptical eyebrows. He had last seen Gerry Adams in 1968 when the young Republican was working at the Duke of York pub in Belfast. Now, suddenly he was on the phone. "We had this bizarre conversation," McClelland confided. "We talked about characters from the Duke of York bar. After this chit-chat, he said, 'We have a few Sinn Féin candidates standing in the election, could I get Rita O'Hare to send you a press release?' I told him, 'Gerry you know the politics of this paper, it's so anti-IRA and anti-Sinn Féin it's not true.' He knew this, but he asked me if I could get a couple of paragraphs in. I went to the chairman of the company and he nearly fell off his chair. He said, 'No way', but I told him, 'Gerry Adams hasn't phoned me since 1968. Why is he going out of his way to ring me? There's something afoot.' Indeed there was. It was the start of the politicization of Sinn Féin/IRA. It must have taken something for Gerry to lift that phone after all those years and ask for a favour. He was obviously taking it *very* seriously."

Adams had good reason for pushing Sinn Féin into the limelight. As he well knew from his clandestine dealings with the Westminster establishment, his party was far from the pariah portrayed in the British media and routinely condemned in the House of Commons. This perspective became public currency after the announcement in the Belfast press that there had long been secret talks between the IRA and the British government. In the immediate aftermath of the Downing Street Declaration, Gerry Adams had been granted a US visa by President Clinton, much to John Major's chagrin. During a lightning visit to New York, Adams attended a peace conference addressed by SDLP leader John Hume and was greeted like a hero by the Irish community in televised scenes that caused consternation and jubilation in Downing Street and the Maze Prison, respectively. Yet, in the background of all these protestations of imminent peace was the physical reality of daily carnage in the North. Former Monarch Roy Kane drove me to the Shankill around this time where memories were still raw of an IRA attack on the UDA. A bomb had been placed in a fish shop beneath an office of the Loyalist Prisoners' Association, where various Ulster Freedom Fighters, including Van Morrison fan and West Belfast Commander Johnny 'Mad Dog' Adair, were meant to be gathered. The bomb detonated prematurely killing one of the perpetrators, Thomas Begley, along with nine innocent Protestants, including two children. The charred building told its own gruesome story. Over the next few days, the UVF and the UFF indiscriminately killed three Catholic men. During Halloween, loyalist gunmen took further vengeance for the Shankill fish shop bombing. Searching for an easy target, they journeyed to the small village of Greysteel, near Derry. In a grim reference to Halloween, one of the gunmen cried "Trick or treat?" as they entered a Catholic bar, the Rising Sun. Before anyone could answer they sprayed bullets into the 200-strong crowd, killing eight. Some felt there had never been a more dangerous time to be living in Northern Ireland, particularly Belfast. It was like 1972 all over again.

In June 1994, UVF paramilitaries singled out another obscure target, this time a Catholic bar in Loughinisland, Co. Down. Six more Catholics were killed, including 87-year-old Barney Green, who became the oldest murdered victim of the Troubles. Thereafter, loyalist and IRA killings continued remorselessly. Certain Sinn Féin members were insisting that there would be no ceasefire. But events in Northern Ireland have always been unpredictable and paradoxical, and so it was that, against the odds, this crescendo of violence was swiftly followed by a dramatic and unexpected ceasefire. At 11am on 31 August 1994, the leadership of Oglaigh na hÉireann (the IRA) announced a complete cessation of its campaign. There was unrestrained joy among the nationalist communities of Northern Ireland and celebrations in Dublin. London responded with cautious optimism while Unionists fretted over a possible sell-out and studied the wording suspiciously. A few weeks later, Albert Reynolds, John Hume and Gerry Adams were pictured on the steps of the Dáil in Dublin, smiling and shaking hands. History had been made. Six weeks into the ceasefire, loyalist paramilitaries followed suit, with former UVF prisoner Gusty Spence expressing "abject and true remorse" to "the loved ones of all innocent victims over the past 25 years", adding that "no words of ours will compensate for the intolerable suffering they have undergone during the conflict". Amid this tone of reconciliation, Paisley was again out on a limb. He urged all his followers to resist the "demand that we should become slaves in a country fit only for nuns' men and monks' women", adding, "We cannot bow the knee to these traitors in Whitehall, or to those offspring of the Vatican who walk the corrupted corridors of power." On remand at the Maze and soon to be sentenced to 16 years' imprisonment, the Shankill's director of terrorism Johnny 'Mad Dog' Adair maintained his vigilance and played his Van Morrison albums. Meanwhile, the loyalist paramilitary UVF was replaced at centre stage in the peace process by their political wing the Progressive Unionist Party (PUP), whose leading light was David Ervine, the former bomber and alumnus of Morrison's secondary school Orangefield.

Amid this drama, the wee man returned to Belfast to supervise improvement work on his mother's bungalow while news filtered through that he had just achieved his highest US chart placing courtesy of a belated cover of 'Wild Night' by John Mellencamp. Relations with Rocca were also close and the pair attended a BMI Awards ceremony at London's Dorchester Hotel. Chris O'Donnell, who had been reappointed as manager the previous year, was on the phone to me the next day enthusing about the evening. He had persuaded Morrison to take part in a brief photo shoot with Rocca and the singer was pleasantly surprised to discover that the paparazzi left him alone there-after. Between them, Rocca and O'Donnell were gently re-educating Morrison in the art of media relations.

Maintaining her influence, Michelle was once again cast in the role of interviewer for the latest Morrison promotional effort. Readers were no doubt amused to learn that he had never heard of the Pet Shop Boys, Nirvana or Kurt Cobain. Most of his answers were curt and dismissive, but there were also nuggets of revelation. It was clear from his responses that major changes had occurred in his life and world view over the past year or so. Asked what he was currently reading, he answered: "Nothing. I don't have time to read." This, from a man who not so long ago was putting himself forward as a putative philosophy tutor. He admitted that he felt more comfortable these days, but as for happiness and serenity, "I didn't get there, no." The past tense suggested that it was a search he now considered over. On his once favourite topic, the blood sacrifice of Christ, he was evasive. "That's another taboo subject because people read this stuff and you get them coming after you wanting to find out more. No matter how much they get, they always want more." But the most jaw-dropping response was to the question "Do you believe in the afterlife?" As a self-professed Christian, mystic and spiritual seeker, the obvious answer was "yes", but Morrison said, "No! No! No!" The treble denial was so emphatic that it threw up a thousand conundrums. Having spent most of his life searching for spiritual enlightenment, had Morrison's long journey finally ended in atheistic disillusionment? It was a question that would be more fully answered later in the year.

On 31 March 1995, Morrison appeared at the IRMA Awards in Dublin where he dedicated 'Have I Told You Lately' to Michelle Rocca. Two days later, Terry Keane broke the news: "It's official. Van Morrison and Michelle Rocca are engaged. She has accepted his proposal and has agreed to marry him." Oddly, there were no direct quotes from the couple, but Keane, like a seasoned detective, noted that "the radiant Michelle in stunning blue had swapped her old diamond solitaire for Van's Celtic-designed gold band (which Van had secretly made for Michelle – the beautiful diamond earrings Michelle wore were also an engagement present from Van)." Summing up, Keane said: "Although the Rocca/Morrison romance has been high profile the couple have actually taken the relationship slowly. They have been friends and business partners for over three years. No wedding date is set, but a long engagement is not envisaged. I've already put my call into Gianni for the gold dress." Keane was characteristically spot-on with the news of the engagement as Rocca herself later admitted under oath.

Further signs that Morrison had shaken off his demons and found love and good *craic* were evident during a television appearance on *Late Night With Letterman*. Towards the close of a duet with Sinéad O'Connor on 'Have I Told You Lately', he flailed his arms wildly, then trundled over and bumped into her microphone while crooning "you, you, you" with a large smile on his face. It was endearing to see Morrison making a buffoon of himself on television, seemingly without a care. Afterwards, he was heard joking to Rocca about David Letterman's resemblance to Bugs Bunny and quipping, "there's more *craic* in a morgue". That he was so easily critical of someone else's physical shortcomings and apparent lack of fun said much about his own confidence and avoidance of self-criticism.

The ubiquitous Rocca accompanied Morrison on his summer 1995 US tour, prompting more speculation. During a show at New York's Paramount she strolled onstage during 'Buona Sera Senorita' and presented her beau with a bouquet of roses and even sang along. They left the stage hand in hand.

Rocca's supremacy was enshrined on the cover of Morrison's concurrent new album *Days Like This*, where she was pictured at her glamorous best. Significantly, it was the first time he had shared a record cover with a woman since his marriage to Janet Planet. Up until this point, Morrison had always maintained his privacy and his personal relationships were undocumented in the media. No known pictures of him with either Carol Guida, Ulla Munch or Mira Radkovitch were logged at any photo agency in the world. In an age obsessed with celebrity, this might seem surprising, but Morrison was never regarded as a promising candidate for a spread in any lifestyle magazine. Instead, he occupied that rarefied space, just below the radar of the average millionaire rock luminary. Nor was he entirely alone in achieving such a degree of invisibility in a goldfish bowl. The enigmatic Bob Dylan, whose fame and influence eclipsed Morrison at every conceivable level, enjoyed an iconographical reputation largely unencumbered by intrusions into his private world. His life and work had inspired a publishing industry, including several doorstep-size biographies, but for all the efforts of investigative reporters and expert commentators, confusion still reigns over such basic data as family births and marriages. For more than a decade, Dylan miraculously managed to keep his second marriage out of the press and by the time the story broke, he was already divorced again. Even the precise number of children in his extended household seemed uncertain, or was at least disputed by different biographers. In a lengthy and hilarious dissection of these confusing discrepancies, critic Peter Doggett concluded his count-up with the caveat, "All of which leaves one marriage and one or two children unaccounted for . . ." Paraphrasing a Dylan song, he ended: "Never mind the groom: the biographers are still waiting at the altar." If Dylan could baffle biographers, journalists, scholars and gossip columnists with such bewildering aplomb, then Morrison's task was infinitely easier. All he had to do was avoid star-studded gatherings and persuade Rocca to keep a lower profile. Evidently, neither favoured this policy. Morrison seemed to be enjoying his nights out on the town and journalists knew that Rocca was always good for a quick quote. Indeed, she said more about Morrison in a single interview than Janet Planet had uttered during an entire marriage. On one level, Rocca was an enormous PR asset, but that situation would soon change.

Days Like This confirmed Morrison's new commercial standing since meeting Rocca. The album sold extremely well and was even nominated for the prestigious Mercury Music Award. Probably his most sustained and impressive recording of the Nineties, it offered a variety of moods and stylistic contrasts, guaranteed to appeal to all his followers. Fittingly, it began with 'Perfect Fit', a transparent paean to Rocca in which he complimented her looks and oddly praised his own "language" while questioning why the media "take the piss", then wondering what is so wrong with saying they're just good friends. Among the more upbeat tracks were a couple of desultory duets with his daughter, a song of personal resilience ('Raincheck') and a lengthy meditation ('Ancient Highway') which conjured fond memories of *Veedon Fleece*. Splendidly diverse, the album also emphasized the extent to which Morrison was refashioning his life. Although hardly cathartic, a couple of the songs thematically echoed the classic *John Lennon/Plastic*

Ono Band and *Imagine* in miniature. After undertaking Primal Scream therapy with psychologist Arthur Janov, Lennon had re-evaluated his life dismissing the myths imposed by media and fans and committing the ultimate heresy when he exclaimed at the end of 'God' – "I don't believe in Beatles". With other songs like 'I Found Out' he tore through every belief system from his childhood onwards.

On *Days Like This*, Morrison reveals, if not a similar epiphany, then at least a willingness to peel away some layers of illusion. He shuffles off the mental chains of various belief systems, starting with religion. 'No Religion' came about, he explained, when was he thinking: "Wouldn't it be great just to be born and nobody told you there was such a thing as religion? Say it didn't exist and you were just told that all you've got is this life and that's it . . . And there's no heaven, no hell." This was quite literally a thematic reiteration of Lennon's 'Imagine'. 'Melancholia' and 'Underlying Depression' similarly hinted at a troubled journey on the rocky road to self-discovery. 'Songwriter' focused specifically on the practical application of composing and served as a pointed rejoinder to the more fanciful comments he had once made about the unconscious process of creation. Ten years before, he had described his songs as transcendental and saw the purpose of his work "ideally to induce states of meditation and ecstasy as well as to make people think". When Michelle Rocca asked him whether his songs still retained a mystical aspect, he responded, "Well, I think they used to, but I'm not sure about it now because I've run out of steam on that." It was nothing new when he dismissed the illusory aspects of the music business, but now, possibly for the first time, he was seeing through his own mythologies. Having once referred to himself as a mystical poet, he was now more prosaic in his evaluation, admitting, "I'm a poet, but in the strictest sense, I'm not." The critically revered *Astral Weeks* was another disposable myth redolent of a "bygone era that doesn't exist anymore". It must have been difficult, if not impossible, to glorify the mystical when you ceased to believe in any form of afterlife as Morrison had already admitted. By mid-1995, he sounded suspiciously like a man whose spiritual search had reached a sudden and dramatic dead end.

The new atheistic Morrison appeared to have little in common with the spiritual seekers, cult religion followers, New Age enthusiasts, left-field weirdos and UFO believers that had once been such a vital part of his extended social circle. Figures like Cecil McCartney, Derek Bell and Clive Culbertson were still experiencing beautiful visions or flying through their own cosmic planes, but Morrison seemed permanently grounded. By this point, he was evidently more at home hanging out at the Shelbourne Hotel and swanning around Dublin society hot spots with Michelle Rocca. For those still forlornly dreaming of *Astral Weeks Part II, Common One Revisited* or *Beautiful Vision – The Sequel* this was bad news.

Of course, for Morrison the maturing human being, life had seldom been better. His relationship with Rocca, played out in the full glare of the media spotlight, seemed to be bringing him out of his shell. He looked and sounded like a man who had gladly rid himself of a number of unwanted and potentially crippling burdens. There was even news that he had bought a £600,000 house in Dalkey, presumably intended as a future marital home. Dublin suited him. In the new forward-thinking Ireland, the past – that perennial obsession – no longer gnawed at the heels of progress and revitalization. As one cultural observer of the period noted: "Lately the most curmudgeonly man in music appears to have got his own personal peace process underway."

Morrison promoted *Days Like This* with several summer festival appearances. Unfortunately, some of the reviews were brutal. His showing at the Fleadh in London's Finsbury Park prompted the once loyal *NME* to rail, "A rancid smog of blind reverence has cloaked Morrison for decades now, with nobody daring to peek beneath it . . . During his flaccid Fleadh set, the stench is overbearing. In fact, let's not hide behind metaphors here: Van Morrison is an overrated old donkey who has churned out endless variations on the same limp pseudo-soul formula for far too long. His influence on music, as the Fleadh proves, has been to inspire Mafia-style respect and lame imitation in equal measure, crippling generation after generation of potentially interesting Irish musicians." On the main stage at the Phoenix Festival, his performance was faulted for its "preternaturally bland consistency". His critic complained: "No wildness, no mystery remains – explained perhaps by him saying in a recent interview that he merely wants to entertain rather than purge his soul – leaving behind a pied-up Radio 2-style belter hanging around with cheesy goons . . . an annoyingly enthusiastic horn section, and a prancing gimp boy – the hopeless Brian Kennedy – to sing the high notes he can't reach any more. Excitement briefly intrudes when Morrison introduces a 'tribute to James Brown', but instead of the hoped-for and highly apt 'Sex Machine' he cheerfully murders 'It's A Man's Man's Man's World'. The muse has buggered off. For now, at least, the spirit of chicken-in-a basket, two-sets-and-no-shit supper clubs rules."

The muse, in fact, was alive and well when presented in a more appropriate setting than a festival. Freed from his spiritual encumbrances, Morrison felt less self-conscious about revisiting old material. Later that year, he would incorporate several songs from *Astral Weeks* into his set at smaller venues in Swansea, Waterford and Dublin. There was even a 'Madame George' interspersed with lyrics from 'Who Drove The Red Sports Car?' and 'T.B. Sheets', plus the rarely heard 'Listen To The Lion'.

Having established himself in Dublin society, Morrison was about to return triumphantly to Belfast. The Northern Ireland Office had successively adopted 'Brown Eyed Girl' and 'Days Like This' to back a £1.2 million television advertising campaign promoting the ceasefire. Suddenly, the apolitical Morrison found himself representing the official soundtrack of the peace process. On 30 November 1995, he appeared in front of an estimated 60–80,000 people outside Belfast City Hall. Tellingly, his opening song was not 'Days Like This' but 'No Religion'. The excited crowd was awaiting Bill Clinton who had arrived on a goodwill mission to persuade Ireland's political leaders to grasp the laurel of peace. After visiting Ulster's key trouble spots, Clinton descended upon Dublin, where he met the new Fine Gael Taoiseach John Bruton, who had replaced the engaging Albert Reynolds a year before. "My tour was absolutely overwhelming," Clinton enthused a week later. "I don't know if in my life I'll ever have a couple of days like that again. That vast crowd in the street in Belfast, the hill full of people in Derry, the intensity in the Shankill and the Falls Road . . . The people are saying these are our emotions, these are our desires, these are our hopes, these are our dreams. We don't know what the final political settlement ought to be. But the leaders owe the people a future that responds to the energy in the street. My judgement is this is a moment in history for the Irish."

As a fellow saxophonist, Clinton was pleased to see Morrison perform. On several occasions, he had voiced his appreciation of the artiste. The President also had the chance to meet the alluring Michelle

Rocca, whose presence caused mild consternation to the hovering Hillary Clinton. In the past, Rocca had admitted that other women were sometimes intimidated by her beauty-queen looks, but she could hardly have expected any reaction from one so powerful. Newspaper reports mentioned that "Michelle draped herself over the smiling President", prompting the First Lady to enquire frostily, "And what is it exactly that you do?" "Brain surgery," Rocca shot back. It was a slight that ensured she was removed from the troupe of celebrity guests that later met Irish President Mary Robinson. Victoria Clarke would probably have called this karma.

Irish newspapers, drooling over Michelle Rocca's "£60,000 engagement ring", had wrongly predicted a marriage by Christmas. Instead, Morrison continued working and touring. There was further evidence of his intention to transcend the rock pigeonhole with December 1995's *How Long Has This Been Going On?*, a jazz-influenced album with Georgie Fame that included a surprise updating of 'Moondance'. That same month, Morrison appeared at the UK Year of Literature and Writing festival in Swansea, alongside poet and Orangefield alumnus Gerald Dawe. If Morrison retained any lingering delusions about his abilities as a teacher or public speaker then they were all but extinguished by this disappointing display. "The idea of him engaging in a little chit-chat about his motives and methods just about beggared belief," quipped one critic. Poet Don Paterson reckoned that "Van Morrison in conversation" was about as appetizing as "Ian Paisley on ice" and lamented the "soul sapping pointlessness" of the discourse, adding, "even spoon-fed the answers, Van was still capable of getting them wrong and answering a totally different question instead; dead end followed conversational dead end." It was only the succeeding concert that made some sense of the affair.

If proof was needed of Morrison's stature as a performing artiste, then it came in the spring of 1996. First there was an impressive new recording of 'Saint Dominic's Preview' with Donal Lunny, Mary Black and a host of other Irish musicians for inclusion on the Gaelic television programme *Sult* ('fun' in Irish). This was followed by a short US tour, which included a series of concerts at New York's Supper Club, most notable for Morrison's exceptional animation. The shows were a revelation, although some of those who paid the $75 entrance fee must have bridled at Morrison's frequently scathing onstage putdowns. While never quite reaching the sorry depths of his King's Hotel, Newport, diatribes back in 1993, he nevertheless challenged audiences' perceptions with lacerating asides and several appalling obscenities. Responding to song requests, he sneered: "Fuck you. That's ancient history . . . We don't do that anymore. Listen, that's only lip service . . . Let me explain myself here, let's get this down. Supposed to be New York, right? Think so? How many people actually know what we're doing tonight? . . . I haven't done those songs . . . when I did them I didn't do them . . . 'Moondance' was put in as lip service for a start. Afraid so. This is the real me. 'Into The Mystic'? That's ancient history, a lot of water under the bridge . . . What are you talking about, bitch . . . You love me. You don't even know me!" Combative in the extreme, occasionally surreal, Morrison sounded like a cross between a preacher and a crazed therapist. "How many people are here to see the former artiste known as Van Morrison?" he announced. "Well, I've got news for you, you're in the wrong room. If you want to hear 'Brown Eyed Girl', you're not going to hear that . . . you're not going to hear 'Gloria', you're not going to hear 'Crazy Love', you're not going to hear 'Domino'. See the promoter! I used to be a person that had a fucking name called Van. I'm not. I've been Van Morrison for about 20 years. It's a publicity stunt . . . If you've got anything to say, this is the time to say it . . . This is the soul-cleansing part of the programme. Anybody got anything to say? You want to believe in something? Might be Jesus, might be Buddha, might be your Aunt Fanny. But anyway, if anybody's got anything to say, I think they should say it now, otherwise we're going to close this down." Beneath the dark sarcasm and acerbity was the arrogant self-belief of a performer ready to challenge his audience. The feelings of liberation that Michelle Rocca had brought to his life were there for all to see. He pointedly dedicated 'Who Can I Turn To?' to his muse and later kissed her onstage during the sentimental 'Have I Told You Lately'.

Despite his onstage utterances, Morrison was arguably more in charge of his life than at any time since first leaving Belfast. The type of business problems that had dogged his time in America seemed long past and there was none of the grim austerity of the Scientology period of the early Eighties when his self-control betrayed a distinctly puritan air.

Thanks to Rocca and Dublin, he was enjoying life without the need for flatline abstinence or painful privacy. These were the best of times.

June 1996 proved one of the most eventful months of Morrison's life. It should have represented a crowning achievement of sorts, but rapidly turned into a sordid melodrama. Morrison was touring with his hero Ray Charles, enjoying another of those collaborations that characterized his recent ebullience and news had just filtered through that he was about to be awarded an OBE by the Queen at Buckingham Palace. For a child of the Harland & Wolff shipyard there was no greater honour. All that changed on 7 June with the lead story on the front page of the *Daily Mirror*, headlined "Van's Girl Cheats With Racing Romeo". Inside was a detailed two-page spread, amusingly titled "Have I Told You Lately I'm Having An Affair?" Only days before, the paper had learned that Rocca had stayed the night of 30 May at Dublin's Berkeley Court Hotel with racing trainer Angus Gold. They had also discovered that the pair had previously spent nearly 12 hours together at the same establishment, where they ordered several bottles of champagne. In a remarkably detailed breakdown of events, the paper tracked Rocca's movements on the second night. After two-and-a-half hours having her hair styled and nails manicured, Rocca drove her Mercedes to the hotel at 8.45pm and met Gold and jockey Willie Carson, along with a couple of friends. After drinking a bottle of champagne the party took a taxi to the fashionable Fitzer's restaurant. While there, Rocca happily showed off the expensive diamond and ruby engagement ring that Morrison had bought for her, and one of her friends playfully sang 'Have I Told You Lately'. At 2am, the party left the restaurant and went clubbing until the early hours. With dawn approaching, Rocca and Gold entered the Berkeley Court Hotel and shared a double room. She left at 9.46am and drove home. The astonishing detail sounded like a testament to the newspaper's tenacity, but why would they treat Rocca with a degree of scrutiny usually reserved for a president's wife?

Irish journalist Sam Smyth subsequently unearthed a far more incredible story revealing that Rocca had been under intense investigation by a Dublin-based private detective agency paid to keep her under round-the-clock surveillance. A team of eight private detectives monitored her phone calls, bugged hotel rooms and made secret tape recordings and videos of her assignation with Gold. In a scene reminiscent of a spy movie they booked themselves into the hotel room next to Gold's and recorded Rocca's arrival with a hidden video camera. Electronic equipment was also used to monitor her conversation at Fitzer's restaurant and the team later followed Rocca, Gold and Carson when they drove to Weston aerodrome and booked a private plane for a weekend trip to England. The detectives successfully bugged Rocca's phone calls for eight weeks. At one point, it transpired, she had confided in a friend that she believed somebody was following her and pointed at some suspicious vehicles parked outside her home. "She noticed things but thought it might be coincidental," the friend confided. But Rocca was not paranoid and her instincts were sound. "Everywhere she went, they went," an investigator told Sam Smyth. "They went all over the country, tapped her phone and bugged the hotel room. They listened in on what was going on in the hotel room with electronic equipment and put their ear to the door. They even put a video camera below a towel in the hotel corridor." All these intimate details, including photographs, tapes and a lengthy written report were passed on to their client who paid a £30,000 fee. Amazingly, in order to maximize Rocca's embarrassment, the person who had allegedly hired the detectives allowed this provocative material to end up in the hands of the *Daily Mirror*.

Some months later, when the scoop about Rocca and the investigators belatedly appeared in Ireland's *Sunday Tribune*, Sam Smyth wrote a column to accompany the feature. He was characteristically forthright about what had allegedly occurred. "Poor Michelle had no idea!" he wrote, adding: "It was the detailed reporting of the assignation, the minutiae of conversations and the precise timing of trivia that drew suspicions on the *Daily Mirror*'s sources . . . The *Daily Mirror* declined to comment on any sources of information but stood by the accuracy of their story . . . But digging through newspaper cuttings, another story published in the *Sun* newspaper . . . came to light. Under an exclusive tag, the *Sun* reported: 'Jealous rock star Van Morrison hired a private detective to find out whether his stunning fiancée Michelle Rocca was cheating on him!' " Smyth went on to claim in the piece that, when contacted, "the *Sun* said they stood by their story and confirmed that Van Morrison had never questioned its accuracy."

Once the *Mirror* had such painstaking evidence in their hands, they duly contacted other unnamed sources who claimed that Rocca had been having long phone conversations with Gold and might even have fallen in love with the 'racing Romeo'. Armed with this explosive information, two *Mirror* journalists intercepted Rocca at Dublin's Heuston railway station and confronted her with the evidence. Michelle was on her way home with five-year-old daughter Claudia by her side and was clearly unprepared for an interrogation. "That's not true," she said at first. "Print that and I'll sue your balls off." Obviously angry, she allowed her Latin temperament to overrule her and fumed: "I'm Irish and you're English and let me tell you, the Irish hate the English. I'm going to make sure someone puts a bomb under your car, so you'd better be very careful." After calming herself, she apologized, explaining, "I'm quarter Italian and I get angry sometimes." Recovering her poise, she agreed to share a coffee with the journalists and provide her side of the story. Looking in a wall mirror while preparing to be photographed, she suddenly appeared very vulnerable. "I was a Miss Ireland once, you know," she said. "I was a beautiful woman. Do you think I'm beautiful now? Do you? I wish I'd brought some lipstick with me. Do you think I would look better with lipstick? What about my hair? It's the first time I've had it cut short since I was a kid and I'm not sure I like it." Responding to the allegations, she admitted: "OK, I spent a couple of nights with him. We were in the room together, but we were just talking. We didn't have sex. Nothing happened. I dare you to print the story. I'd love you to – because I'd be a rich woman." Impressively defiant, she insisted, "Van will never leave me", then teased the journalists by flashing her ring "Do you think I'm wearing this for fun? Van and I will get married." She then remembered that she had to return home promptly to attend her pregnant King Charles spaniel. "She's expecting nine puppies and Van isn't at all happy about it. He's a bit grumpy." Taking her leave, Rocca could not resist a provocative parting shot: "By the way, do you know how much Van is worth? £500 million – that means he can afford the best lawyers in town to sue your arse." The crushing irony was that Rocca had no idea of the involvement of the detective agency, nor who had hired them and tacitly co-operated in breaking the story.

Undeterred by Rocca's emotional outburst, the *Daily Mirror* ran the piece in fulsome detail. The following day, they ensnared Morrison who said: "I am disgusted by the behaviour of all the parties involved. Michelle and I are finished." It seemed that this story was over, but worse was to follow.

On 16 June, two days after Morrison received his OBE, the *Sunday Mirror* carried the mind-boggling headline "Sex Shame Of Van The 3-In-A-Bed Man!" The trailer read: "It's the OBE – Old Bonker Exposed!" In a salivating piece of investigative journalism, the crusading *Mirror* discovered that Morrison had become involved in a tryst with two middle-aged divorcees. After drinking heavily during the day, he had asked them to book a room at the unassuming Granada Lodge Hotel near Warminster, Wiltshire. There, in Room 213, he reportedly enjoyed "two hours of sex" with the women. It would be fascinating to learn more about Morrison's sexual performance, the extent to which he was able to satisfy both women and what methods or positions may have been employed to achieve this feat, but the complete details of his erotic adventures remain unpublished.

What we did learn was nevertheless engrossing and hugely entertaining. Just before he was due to appear on stage at Wembley, the singer was cornered by the irrepressible *Mirror*. His comments were laced with some hilarious, unintended innuendo. "I just felt lonely and rejected and wanted something to hold on to," he began, adding "It all happened so fast and things got out of hand. Everything got on top of me." Even better was a priceless quote from one of the women, who pleaded, "But there was no kinky stuff. It was straight sex." What a wonderful video it would have made. Forget Hyndford Street; someone should have erected a plaque outside Room 213 to mark the event.

As remarkable as this sexual encounter may have been, it was arguably surpassed by the revelation of Morrison in contrite mode. "I am so ashamed," he reportedly said. "I was devastated about the break-up of my engagement to Michelle – who I loved – and I just went over the top. I have let my fans and myself down but there's no excuse." Indeed there was not, but it was still gratifying to witness Morrison finally displaying some humility and shame for his actions. Assuming the quote was accurately transcribed, it served as an act of contrition from a figure whose apologies to the world were long overdue. He even brought some unexpected pathos to the occasion with the melodramatic explanation: "I went to a friend's house for dinner to try to escape from this nightmare and it was there that what she had done suddenly hit me like a bolt from the blue. I didn't know who to turn to. I feel bad about what I did. It's not the sort of thing I would normally do but I could not cope with Michelle's betrayal. I just wanted to go off with the first woman I met. We all make mistakes. This was one of mine. But I have been to hell and back. Nobody knows the torment I have been through."

Morrison's words had a distinctly tabloid ring and sounded totally out of character. Arguably, a more accurate barometer of his feelings was given to some fans outside Wembley who were told: "I was framed. Two people thought they could con me but they couldn't. I am no sucker, but I can't tell you the whole story tonight." From his comments, it seemed likely that further revelations and counter-accusations would follow but at this crucial juncture Morrison and Rocca appeared to reach a new understanding and the saucy disclosures ceased. This reconciliation was fancifully translated into a *Mirror* prediction that they would marry in early 1997.

Alas, it was not a wedding reception but a courtroom that awaited Michelle Rocca on St Valentine's Day. In one of the most publicized cases in recent Irish history, Rocca accused her former lover Cathal Ryan of assaulting her and breaking her nose after she found him in bed with another woman during a party back in March 1992. The trial dominated the broadsheet and tabloid press day after day with the *Irish Times* even introducing a new section to the paper titled "The Rocca Damages Case". Rocca told the court that she felt like a "Belsen victim" after being punched, kicked and dragged around a bedroom at a house in Co. Kildare. The incident had occurred at the 30th birthday party of June Moloney, a friend of Rocca and Ryan. According to Rocca she had spent an evening with Ryan a few days before at the Tulfarris House Hotel when he had again asked her to marry him. "We made love that night," she revealed in court. Ryan countered that no sexual intercourse had taken place, nor was there a marriage proposal. "I didn't invite her to stay nor did I object," he insisted, adding that they had merely lain on a bed and talked till 7am. At the time Ryan was still living with his father in Nenagh, while Rocca resided at a leased house in Booterstown, Co. Dublin. They arrived separately at

Moloney's residence at Blackhall Stud, Co. Kildare. While searching for Ryan, Rocca walked into an upstairs bedroom and found him lying on a single bed. As she approached, a girl with long blonde hair (later identified as Sarah Linton) emerged from inside the bed. Under cross examination, Linton put her hand to her head and provided a detailed account of being pulled by the hair around the bedroom. Rocca admitted that she was upset and had screamed, but maintained she did not assault Linton or drag her from the bed by the hair. "I don't think I'd have had the strength to pull a woman over a man on to the floor," she insisted. Amid this scene, Ryan pushed Rocca away, knocking her to the floor, then administered a 'haymaker' punch which broke her nose. She next alleged that he had dragged her across the room, battering her "again and again" in the face and chest and kicking her in the back, chest, arms and legs. "At one point he went AWOL completely and I thought I was going to die," she stated. According to her counsel, "This sustained pummelling lasted five minutes." Throughout the hearing, Rocca maintained that she was unaware that Ryan had another girlfriend and would not have entered the room or spent the night with him in Tulfarris in such circumstances. After the assault, she was given a bath while fretting over the sad condition of her face. She was shivering and her mouth was still bloody from the attack. Her friend June Moloney was, she felt, not particularly supportive in the wake of the incident and would have preferred that she was not there. Moloney's husband was allegedly upset because the house was owned by Arabs who would take a dim view of the proceedings. Two days after the alleged assault, Norah Griffin, who worked as a nanny for Rocca, took photographs of her injuries, which were also confirmed by a doctor's examination.

Cathal Ryan denied the claims, adding that if he had committed the acts complained of, then there was provocation. "Sarah was lying pretty much defenceless and being slapped and kicked," he said. "I slapped Michelle at that stage." Ryan's counsel, Mr Garrett Cooney, alleged that Rocca was in a violent mood in the bedroom and that Ryan had attempted to restrain her. She denied this, retorting that her face had been "thumped and smashed". Her relationship with Ryan was scrutinized remorselessly. When asked if their relationship had been "stormy", she objected to the adjective but claimed that she had once scratched his face when he tried to drag her upstairs and practically pulled off her red suit while in drink. "There were many occasions like that," she testified. Ryan denied any such bursts of violence, in drink, or otherwise. At one point, she was accused of assaulting his son but insisted that she had merely reprimanded the boy for being naughty and had asked him to leave the bathroom while she was having a shower. Ryan's counsel suggested that this incident was the "straw that broke the camel's back" in their relationship and that after driving his son to school he did not return, leaving the house just before Christmas 1990. Rocca agreed that from the time he left until the alleged assault at the stud farm in March 1992, they had not lived together. However, she still felt there was a relationship and that she was his fiancée and mentioned making love to Ryan four days before the alleged assault. She claimed that after the incident at Blackhall Stud she had suffered "four years of hell because of Cathal Ryan" and had been a patient at Dublin's Rutland Centre for four days in 1996 for stress and depression. She denied that she had ever received treatment at the centre for a drink-related problem but recalled what Ryan was like in drink and claimed he had often collapsed and she'd had to take him home. It was suggested that Rocca had seen Ryan and Sarah Linton drinking in the Berkeley Court Hotel, but she had no recollection of this and insisted that she was unaware that they were romantically involved.

Mr Cooney pointed out that Ms Moloney's account differed markedly from the evidence provided by Rocca. Moloney insisted that she had invited Ryan and Sarah Linton as a couple knowing that they had been going out for some months and had warned Rocca not to cause any trouble at the party. Rocca had no memory of this and remarked: "I don't know why she would want to say that to me." It next emerged that there had been another man in the room at the time of the alleged assault. David Marshall, a prominent figure in the hairdressing business, was asleep on a single bed in the room when Rocca appeared. She initially described him as having passed out drunk on the bed but later retracted this allegation, adding under cross examination that it was strange that he had not attempted to defend her or seek help. Mr Cooney reminded her that Marshall's version of events contradicted her own. He alleged that she burst into the room in a terrible rage, mouthing obscenities and calling Sarah Linton "a fucking bitch". Marshall also insisted that Rocca had attacked Linton and dragged her by the hair from the bed on to the floor.

On the second day of the trial, Rocca was questioned about her relationship with Van Morrison and she asked Mr Justice Moriarty if she could avoid answering the question. Thankfully, he insisted she reply and full confirmation was at last forthcoming that she had been engaged to the singer for the past two years, just as columnist Terry Keane had asserted. Although Rocca's counsel objected to further questions about the relationship, Ryan's counsel Mr Garrett Cooney persevered. It emerged that Rocca and Morrison had indeed begun seeing each other as friends for the best part of two years before their engagement. Asked whether they lived in adjacent houses in Clyde Road, Ballsbridge, Dublin, Rocca confirmed that she had leased the mews next to him and he had allowed her to have the house where she stayed with her three children and a nanny, whose wages were paid by Ryan. While she gave evidence, Morrison himself was present in the courtroom and listened stone-faced throughout, squeezed into the benches occupied by the media and several members of the Rocca family.

The case took another twist during the crucial evidence provided by Rocca's physician Dr Stephen Murphy. He had examined Rocca the day after the alleged assault and provided a visceral account of her injuries. These included numerous bruises, one measuring 8cm on the left side of her chest and others on her knee, ankle, bottom and thumb. He described a 6cm blood clot on her upper temple, a 5cm blood clot on her right eye, a nasal fracture, a black eye, a 1cm cut on her upper lip which was still bloody, a 5cm abrasion on her right elbow, a cut on her tongue and three bruises at the back of the neck caused by substantial finger pressure. Rocca had told him that she had been held by the neck and he tested the area with his own fingers. He concluded that substantial pressure must have been applied and felt the injuries were consistent with somebody who had been kicked and punched violently.

After hearing many conflicting accounts over several days, Judge Moriarty addressed the jury, reminding them that the trauma "occasioned to an attractive young lady" (Rocca) could not be viewed as "horrendous" as there had been no brain damage or amputation of limbs. The jury, therefore, was not entitled to award punitive damages "solely as a warning to Ryan or other males that they must not engage in violence against women". He added that they might wish to consider whether "Rocca's conduct by way of provocation should justify some lowering of the damages". As one journalist later quipped: "He did not give the going rate for a broken nose." Ryan's barrister went further, arguing that the accused had done "what any man worthy of the name of man would have done". Evidently, Ryan had not merely a right but "a duty" to defend his "wholesome girlfriend" against Rocca. Michelle's barrister countered that "no man was entitled to do that to a woman" and pushed for aggravated damages for the outrage. The jury retired, then returned with a verdict which many considered a pyrrhic victory for Rocca who was awarded a relatively derisory £7,500. Her family expressed jubilation, insisting that "This was never about the money, it was about truth and justice." The tabloids speculated inaccurately that Rocca might end up paying Ryan's costs, but he had failed to lodge money into the court to cover that eventuality. Even after the judgement, the case was retried in the media. The *Sunday World* contacted Ryan's ex-wife Tess De Cretze who accused Rocca of washing her dirty linen in public, adding "It's unfair to the children. She should just have got on with her life . . . Michelle should be really happy with Van Morrison. He'd given her everything. Cathal came out fairly unscathed in the court case. I am glad for him."

Rocca found a more sympathetic hearing in the broadsheets. The *Sunday Independent*'s Ellis O'Hanlon commented wryly on the jury's verdict, noting: "They concluded that, yes, she told the truth; yes, she was the victim of a vicious assault by a 15-and-a-half stone man; but, hey, what the heck? She was 'the authoress of her own misfortune', anyway, and he was only doing, to quote his own defence counsel, 'what any man, calling himself a man, would do'. So, here, take a few thousand quid, stop whining, and we'll send you the bill later. Come back, feminism, all is forgiven." A more sober analysis was provided by writer Stephen Dodd who saw the event as an important landmark in Ireland, both legally and culturally: "This was a civil case with none of the black or white distinctions that a criminal verdict offers." After considering the sociological aspects of the celebrity case and its endless fascination for the media and the Irish public, Dodd signed off with a forthright conclusion: "Had Cathal and Michelle been cast as boxers instead of lovers, no Board of Control would ever have allowed them in the same ring together. It would be a mismatch, a grossly prejudicial physical encounter . . . Those not present in the court will not have seen the photographs showing the extent of Michelle's injuries. They were not, it should be stated, a pretty sight. Bruises had coloured right up to her face to either side of her nose. She had the signs of a black eye . . . In short, Michelle had taken a hiding . . . For all the provocation and the insults, all the hair-pulling and alleged thumping between Michelle and Sarah, surely the sad affray in the bedroom at Blackhall Stud never warranted such a pathetic, unchivalrous finale. The last word on the fracas is this. To hit somebody in the face, to hit *anybody* in the face, is a dangerous attack on a hugely vulnerable part of the body. For a man to hit a woman in the face is, because of the difference in size, an altogether more serious action and can only be justified by dire circumstances. To commit such an assault, not in self defence but as a means of restraint, when a woman is already held to the floor, is, it seems to me, wholly reprehensible."

Writing in the *Sunday Tribune*, Anne Marie Hourihane offered this laconic coda: "Our love affair with glamour could never have lasted. As a nation we're much happier tearing idols down than slobbering at their feet. This country is too small to sustain the illusion of a golden élite, partying away behind closed doors. We burned our Bridesheads long ago and there is no point in attempting to reconstruct them in a borrowed stud farm."

Morrison had allowed himself to be photographed with Rocca on the steps of the Four Courts, but that was the end of their romance with the Irish media. Tellingly, there was no more talk of expensive engagement rings, showbiz weddings, intimate photo shoots or glamorous album cover portraits. Rocca no longer conducted interviews with Morrison on behalf of the music press nor was she seen cuddling him in public. Indeed, they all but disappeared from the gossip columns they had once dominated. Rocca's palatial Dublin home was later sold for £1.05 million punts just as the Irish property boom reached boiling point. She expressed her desire to move to England and continue studying philosophy, but made no mention of her relationship with Morrison, nor her intention to set up home with him in Bath. Discretion was her new watchword.

TWENTY-FIVE

The Collaborator

During the Nineties, Morrison devoted half of his time to collaborative projects, earnestly working on tribute albums to Mose Allison and Jimmie Rodgers, recording with Carl Perkins and contributing to John Lee Hooker's *Don't Look Back*. Meanwhile, his own canon continued to expand with the release of *The Healing Game* in March 1997. Although the musicianship was strong, the material appeared tired and dull with recycled platitudinous lyrics. Critic Nick Kent concluded that it was "probably Morrison's worst album to date", which was very harsh, but indicative of the jaundice felt by many reviewers towards the singer's output in the closing years of the century. In *Mojo*, David Hepworth was even fiercer, insisting that, "Since basing himself in the UK with *Common One*, he's made 11 albums . . . which have, whatever their other characteristics, exhibited a lack of ambition unparalleled among his contemporaries . . . Morrison has eased himself into the role of grand old actor-manager at the head of a company specializing in a standard repertoire and impervious to the changing textures of music elsewhere." For Hepworth, "the last five Van Morrison albums have lain back on the slab" while this latest effort revealed "all the shades of delight and wonder of his younger music now dispersed in a peevish fog of injured innocence". Certainly there was no escaping the cynical tone. On 'It Once Was My Life' Morrison's bitterness poured forth, while the apocalyptic 'Rough God Goes Riding' referred to his feelings upon reading newspaper headlines, an evident allusion to the 'Sex Shame' saga. The title track crudely described by Morrison on stage as "a song about East Belfast, back in the days before everything got fucked up" was one of the few memorable songs on the record. Only on 'Piper At The Gates Of Dawn' were there some glimpses of his former sense of wonder.

The Healing Game might have served as an alternative title for the ongoing situation in Ireland. Since the original announcement of the ceasefire in the summer of 1994, the peace process had been dogged by political intransigence. Although the Northern Ireland Office had confirmed that weapons decommissioning was not a precondition for Sinn Féin to enter all party talks, Unionist pressure coupled with resistance from John Major made the matter a key issue. The IRA, crucially sensitive to accusations of surrender, was quick to point out that it had not even been mentioned during discussions with Reynolds and Major, adding that in similar conflicts throughout the world weapons were not completely handed over until a final settlement had been achieved. An international body headed by Senator George Mitchell recommended that talks and decommissioning should run parallel but, even as the report was being published, Major was pushing for an elected forum that guaranteed Unionist dominance. This resurrected the age-old belief that the Irish question would never be solved while the Tory Party was in power. Fearing a sell-out, the IRA broke the ceasefire with one of their so-called "spectaculars" – a large bomb explosion at Canary Wharf in London's Docklands area. While the IRA were back on the offensive the talks began without Sinn Féin. More violence followed. The way forward was only reopened thanks to a change in government on both sides of the Channel.

In May 1997, Labour won a landslide General Election victory which saw Tony Blair appointed Prime Minister. The following month, Fianna Fáil (in coalition with the Progressive Democrats) removed Fine Gael from power, with Bertie Ahern emerging as the new Taoiseach. Sensing a new dawn, the IRA announced a second ceasefire in July, after which a decommissioning body was established led by General John de Chastelain. Sinn Féin at last joined the talks. After Blair met Gerry Adams and Martin McGuinness at Stormont, he was mobbed by furious loyalists in Morrison's hometown, East Belfast. Tensions mounted. In January 1998, Northern Ireland Secretary of State Marjorie 'Mo' Mowlam persuaded UDA prisoners in the Maze Prison to back the peace process. A tortuous period of negotiations, suspensions, expulsions and readmissions followed as Good Friday approached. On 7 April 1998, Blair arrived in Belfast proclaiming: "I feel the hands of history on my shoulders." Gusty Spence also spoke of "exorcizing the ghosts of history." Paisley countered: "There is not going to be peace, there is going to be war". The Big Man arrived at Stormont only to be greeted by UDP and PUP members catcalling, "Your days are over, dinosaur!" Finally on 10 April, agreement was reached. Twelve days later it was ratified in referenda on both sides of the Irish divide. Loyalists claimed they had secured the Union; Republicans felt they were a significant step closer to a united Ireland; the Irish government concluded that the British parliament was "effectively out of the equation"; both the Queen and the Pope sent separate congratulations and blessings. Paisley invoked the spirit of 'No Surrender' once again. The progress of the Assembly would be severely tested, not least by the carnage created by the Real IRA's bombing in Omagh that summer, which was the single worst massacre of the Troubles, killing 31, including two unborn children. But each setback hardened resolve. Dissident Republicans were seemingly left with nowhere to go after Omagh and the outrage was so intense that both the Real IRA and the INLA announced a ceasefire. After a period in the political wilderness both organizations declared that they had disbanded, although fragmented proved a more accurate description. Paramilitary operations, punishment beatings and organized criminal activities continued uninterrupted.

Morrison played at a tribute concert for the dead of Omagh at the Rose Of Tralee Festival that summer. It was an eventful year for live performances as he had earlier been included in one of the most mouth-watering bills of all time, opening for Joni Mitchell and Bob Dylan in the States. Minus Mitchell, the package reached British shores in June for several dates, including London's Wembley Arena. Morrison displayed either absurd arrogance, mad confidence or a love of hubris in agreeing to allow Dylan to play first. When Morrison appeared it was rather like witnessing Shakin' Stevens coming on after Elvis Presley or Freddie & The Dreamers attempting to follow the Beatles. The Dylan fans, out in force, vacated their seats as if an air raid had just been announced. Morrison played a reasonable set in the circumstances, taking pains between songs to remind his audience that it was not a nostalgia show and that he saw himself as a survivor living in the present.

That same month, the long-awaited archival album *The Philosopher's Stone* finally appeared. Originally rumoured for release in 1991 and issued as a promotional disc with a slightly different track listing in 1996, this 2-CD set of unreleased material was a welcome addition to the Morrison catalogue. Among the highlights were the post-*Moondance* outtake 'Really Don't Know', several sterling selections from the *Hard Nose The Highway* period and a sprightly finale of Irish material, including 'Crazy Jane On God', the absolutely extraordinary 'Song Of Being A Child' (written by German poet Peter Handke) and a closing Chieftains collaboration 'High Spirits'. It was regrettable that the legendary Peter Lloyd demos of Them and the post-*Astral Weeks* outtakes recorded with Lewis Merenstein were not featured, but perhaps those missing links may yet be unearthed for a future volume.

Despite a plethora of record releases in the Nineties, Morrison saw no reason to slow down. By 1999, he was licensing his latest material to Virgin Records which issued the optimistically titled *Back On Top* in March. It was another frustratingly uneven work, occasionally rescued by the beautiful string arrangements of Fiachra Trench. The forlorn 'Reminds Me Of You' spoke movingly of an addictive love, resisted by the head but demanded by the soul. Whether this was autobiographical remained a tantalizing question. Elsewhere, Morrison namechecked Lucifer on the revealing 'High Summer' while the closing 'Golden Autumn Day' included an odd lyric about a violent assault and imagined retribution. At best, the work was a low-key stop-gap record, much like its predecessor, *The Healing Game*. Reviews were wildly mixed, with detractors pouring scorn on the boastful title, *Back On Top*. "In your dreams Van!" quipped the *Irish Post*. "The album is full of the usual gormless dirges from the Belfast man. The only way the Curmudgeonly One will get back on top is the day he joins the Corrs." Dublin's *Irish Independent* reviewer George Byrne, a much respected music critic, was even tougher: "Somewhere in the mid-Eighties the poet/philosopher accolades seem to have seeped into his skull and he began churning out same-sounding albums on an almost annual basis. Musically, they were largely sub-Mantovani mush, while the lyrics resembled the work of chimpanzees cutting up extracts from Yeats, Hopkins, Blake and Donne, then pasting the resulting mess to the side of a bus shelter."

Dublin's denizens were equally as likely to honour Morrison as they were to ridicule his work. On 1 September 1999, he became the first inductee of the Hot Press Irish Music Hall of Fame, an institution masterminded by his former journalistic nemesis Niall Stokes who was effusive in describing Morrison as "Ireland's greatest living legend". Although he had once compared Stokes to Shylock ("Have you got your pound of flesh?"), Morrison attended the star-studded dinner and played a short set during which he was briefly joined on stage by Paddy Moloney. The highlight of the evening was a moving and passionate induction speech from Bob Geldof, who ably articulated Morrison's artistic achievements: "He is an extraordinary singer. No other person sounds like him. He is uniquely recognizable and he uses that beautiful thing to attempt to explore and examine areas and depths few have charted successfully. It is like some long journey for meaning. He is specific in location and mood but the themes are universal and nearly always have a profound and troubled spiritual dimension. It seems to be music from another place that takes you somewhere else. The range of his musical influences transcends any limited sense of what contemporary music is."

Geldof's tribute was timely. Critics of Morrison's recent solo work had invariably failed to appreciate the extent to which he was now pursuing a parallel career, working as a collaborator with a variety of minor luminaries, friends and musical legends. His love of roots music was underlined by a surprise collaboration with the Cardiff-based country/rockabilly outfit the Rimshots. Impressed by their album *A Tribute To Hank Williams*, Morrison hired them for a recording session and during a five-day spell completed 22 songs, including many of his all-time favourites. Hopes were high for an imminent release, but this was merely one of several outstanding extra-curricular projects.

The year 2000 began with the release of *The Skiffle Sessions*, credited to Van Morrison, Lonnie Donegan and Chris Barber. Originally recorded at Whitla Hall, Belfast, on 20–21 November 1998, it was a pleasant and occasionally invigorating outing culminating in a fine reading of Donegan's Fifties hit 'I Wanna Go Home'. The cantankerous Glaswegian was far from impressed with the recording, feeling that it was too rough for public consumption. Occasionally, he became exasperated with his singing partner and could be heard at the bar pointing out that

Morrison would never have had a career were it not for his pioneering work. Morrison remained respectful towards Donegan in interviews and was less critical of the album. It reminded him of his youth playing in a makeshift group in Hyndford Street. The work also fulfilled an age-old ambition to record a skiffle album, a project he had mentioned on several occasions, most notably at the time of his temporary 'retirement' from the music business in the mid-Seventies. In concert, he continued to perform with elder contemporaries, ranging from Chris Farlowe to Bobby Bland. Sometimes, there was evidence of a renewed intent to deconstruct the image of Van Morrison. At his first concert of the millennium, he told his audience: "The name Van Morrison is phoney. My real name is Ivan. I want to be known as Ivan. Welcome to the Ivan Morrison workshop."

During the spring Morrison went to dinner with the person who was to be his next major collaborator and legal opponent. He had first met Linda Gail Lewis in Newport in 1993 where he was attending a convention for her brother, Jerry Lee Lewis. A woman of the world, her romantic exploits rivalled those of her legendary brother. Married nine times (with three husbands before the age of 16), she had worked with Jerry Lee, most notably on the late-Sixties album of duets *Together*. Later she found a receptive audience in Europe and relocated to South Wales.

When her agent phoned to tell her of Morrison's dinner invitation she almost declined, but a musician friend encouraged her to attend, pointing out the possibility of a lucrative recording session or tour. "Well that got my attention because I'd never had any money so I said, 'OK'." Ominously, the meal was booked at the King's Hotel, the same Newport establishment at which she had previously met Morrison and dismissed him as offensive. Fortunately, on this occasion, she encountered a more polite and relaxed character. "It was a big surprise because we had a lot in common when it came to Jerry Lee Lewis. Van's a huge Jerry Lee Lewis fan. At dinner we talked about my brother so much and the tracks that we liked . . . When you sit down and talk to him under different circumstances you get a whole different idea about the person because he can be really nice." Convinced that she had misjudged Morrison, Lewis happily agreed to check out his next gig at the Coal Exchange, Cardiff, and was thrilled when the amenable King's proprietor Gordon 'Mac' McIlroy offered her a hotel room gratis. "I came back to the King's Hotel and they picked me up and took me to Van's gig and me, Mac and Van were sitting there drinking Dom Perignon. We stood backstage and there was this guy with cold champagne and every time my glass was empty he would come along and pour more of that Dom Perignon in my glass." By the end of the show, Lewis had happily emerged as a Van Morrison convert. The party then retired to Jury's Hotel until the early hours when Lewis got up to leave. At that moment, Mac turned to Morrison and casually said "Did you ask Linda Gail if she wanted to get together with you and do some songs?" Morrison repeated the question to her, and the following week she returned to the King's Hotel and teamed up with the house band, the Red Hot Pokers. The rehearsal began when Morrison asked her to transcribe the words of Otis Blackwell's 'Let's Talk About Us', one of their favourite Jerry Lee Lewis covers. "I wrote down the lyrics and he wanted me to sing the whole song with him," she marvels. "He kept motioning me to sing." It says much about Morrison's vague sense of communication that his new singing partner was still under the impression that she had been hired primarily as a backing vocalist. Perplexed, she kept asking whether he wanted her to contribute harmony on every line, prompting the impatient reply, "Well, how are we going to rehearse these *duets* any other way?" At that point, the penny dropped, but she was still surprised when Morrison phoned his engineer Walter Samuel at the Wool Hall, Bath, to book a recording session with herself and the Red Hot Pokers.

"It was loose and relaxed," she recalls. "When I got there Walter Samuel sat me down and said 'I want to warn you and prepare you. You're going to have to play the piano, sing with Van and we're going to cut everything live on the floor.' I said 'What?' At that moment, I made the decision that I wasn't going to let it bother me. I thought, 'This is so screwed up, nothing will ever come of it, so I'm just going to relax and have a good time.'" Towards the end of the session, Morrison introduced a tune titled 'No Way Pedro', which his partner failed to recognize. "I know you don't know it," Morrison told her, "I just wrote it!" She asked "Well, how the hell am I going to play it?" Morrison assured her it would be fine. "We cut it," she confirms. "I'm reading the lyrics off a sheet, turning to look at Van and playing piano on a song I'd never heard in my life. It's a miracle, isn't it? I think that's what he wanted – he wants [the recording] to be like it was in the olden days."

After the first session, Lewis departed for Tennessee convinced that the experiment was at an end. Her scepticism seemed well-founded. Lewis was well aware that Morrison had recorded a similarly spontaneous session with the Rimshots the previous year, and that was still in the vault. Cover artwork for the Rimshots' collaboration had already been commissioned and completed, but no firm release date had been announced. It therefore came as a surprise when she received a transatlantic phone call from Mac telling her, "It's in your best interests to get back over here as soon as possible." On her return, she was whisked across to Morrison's studio near Bath. When she and Mac walked into his office, he picked up a tape of their work and announced "I'm thinking of releasing this as my next album instead of the Rimshots' album." They still needed additional material to flesh out the set and agreed to return to the studio for further recordings soon after. Morrison then added one more caveat: "We'll have to do a live gig to see if we can work together before I decide to release the album."

There was obviously a musical and personal chemistry between Morrison and Lewis. Her insatiable *joie de vivre*, effervescent humour and down-home Southern politeness were an irresistible combination and welcome tonic for Morrison, who was keen to break free from the rigidity of recent live performances in search of freshness, spontaneity and fun. While she remained sceptical of his interest in touring or recording, he had evidently already made up his mind. During a showcase concert in Poole, Dorset, where they premiered the new material, Morrison informed the audience that he and Lewis would be releasing an album together later that year. His new partner almost fainted when she heard the announcement.

News of Morrison's latest collaboration was partly eclipsed by some bizarre bulletins from Belfast. As summer approached and preparations for the marching season commenced, Morrison's most prominent paramilitary fan, Johnny 'Mad Dog' Adair, commissioned some murals to commemorate his favourite sectarian atrocities against the Catholic community. One of the murderous murals was adorned in honour of Morrison with the words "Wouldn't it be great if it was like this all the time?" The singer was also bringing some understated Unionist humour to his shows by recruiting political impressionist John McBlain as the warm-up act. "I was doing a skit on Van meeting Ian Paisley in Cyprus Avenue," McBlain recalls. "Van used to clean windows there and Big Ian lives there. Van was charmed by it."

In September 2000, the country/blues-tinged Morrison/Lewis collaboration *You Win Again* was released. It was a sometimes stimulating collaboration, revealing a facet of Morrison's musical personality seldom seen. His sole compositional credit was the rollicking 'No Way Pedro', but by far the best track was an exuberant cover of Smiley Lewis's 'Real Gone Lover' which demonstrated the true potential of this unlikely partnership. "If the entire album was that strong, then it would have been a landmark in Morrison's career," critic Peter Doggett observed astutely. "For those who reckon Morrison has an artistic requirement to stretch himself at every opportunity, it will necessarily seem like a dead end. More generous souls can file it alongside *The Skiffle Sessions* as repayment of another kind of debt, to the music which liberated and created Van Morrison in the Fifties and Sixties."

Perhaps prompted by recent musical rediscoveries of his past, Morrison decided that the time was right to document his life story on film. Typically, he had total control of the project ensuring that its development remained a mystery. Only one piece of footage is known to exist. Dining at the Crawfordsburn Inn, he reunited with several of his skiffle pals, including key members of the Monarchs. The results remain unseen. Roy Kane remembers valiantly carrying on the festivities till 5am during which he introduced Morrison to a local brand of strong rum.

Retrospection was further evident in Morrison's genre-hopping exploits as he moved from jazz, blues and skiffle to country. Having repeatedly insisted that he was not a rock star or a pop performer, he was finally proving the point through the Nineties with a series of key collaborations that partly vindicated his argument. Ironically, many of the supporters who had naively called the man a genius and insisted his work had nothing to do with rock music now sounded impatient and frustrated. Even fanzine readers and internet contributors wondered when the next 'proper' Morrison album was scheduled, as if the Donegan and Lewis efforts were vanity projects rather than genuine artistic statements. The doubters were even less impressed by his live shows with Lewis. Most of the criticisms were directed against backing group the Red Hot Pokers whose rudimentary style contrasted with the precision jazz of former Morrison musicians. Of course, this was what Morrison wanted, an inchoate rock 'n' roll purity that recalled more innocent times. When Lewis implored him to recruit his regular pianist Geraint Watkins to bolster the line-up and assist with the more complex, jazzier arrangements, he refused. "He would not do it," she insists. "He would not have anybody from his old band. I was the only keyboard player and I ended up having to learn all those songs because I thought 'How stupid am I going to look on stage with Van Morrison when he's singing his hits and a lot of stuff from his albums and I'm just sitting there and can't play?' His fans were really critical of the Red Hot Pokers, but I got good reviews . . . It was a gig that I loved. I loved it so much because Van gave me more responsibility than my brother ever gave me and he really shared his stage and his album with me. It was our show. We talked about the material he was going to do and he would consult me about his own songs."

Within a month of the release of *You Win Again*, Morrison was back in the studio recording his next solo album. Tellingly Lewis was invited to participate on virtually all of the tracks at this early session. Optimistically, she still hoped that Morrison might record with both herself and Jerry Lee Lewis, but those illusions were soon dashed. "It was a doomed working relationship," she now admits. "My brother would tell you that I can't be controlled, and Van wants to control everything. Musically, I just had to tell him what I thought in a tactful way. I'm very tactful. But I can't just be a yes person and agree with everything somebody says just because it's what they said." Increasingly, she felt that Morrison was grooming her into a Brian Kennedy role and began to wonder whether she would ever have the time or energy to pursue a parallel solo career.

The New Year began with a short American tour which augured well. Lewis had persuaded Morrison to incorporate a horn section that enabled the Red Hot Pokers to deal more effectively with his jazz-influenced material. At first, everything went smoothly. Lewis was enthusiastic about the West Coast shows and thrilled by several positive reviews. There was a suggestion that Morrison felt she was show-boating at one concert, but most critics focused on her pleasing contribution and evident ability to enliven her partner's performance. Unfortunately, the working relationship soured during a show in Chicago and remained frosty for the remainder of their American sojourn. "It went from being the best it could possibly be to the worst," she notes with sadness. Fans and critics observed the friction onstage and expressed concern at Morrison's visible irascibility and pointed unwillingness to face his singing partner whom he cold-shouldered throughout. "I could never do that," Lewis says. "To be embarrassed in front of so many people when you don't deserve it . . . The other thing that worried me was that my daughter, Annie, was on stage with us, and she's very protective of her mother. It was all she could do to keep from just walking over there and knocking him out. And if Annie was mad at you, she probably could knock you out."

After the show, Lewis was reduced to tears by the oppressive atmosphere. Morrison was sullen and stone-faced and the Pokers seemed subdued. "The only person that looked really happy was Van's girlfriend, Michelle," Lewis recalls. "I think she enjoyed that show more than any gig we've ever done. She looked like a Cheshire cat. I didn't know that she hated me until that night. How could she have been smiling when Van was miserable and I was in tears?" On the flight from Chicago, Lewis confided in Colin Griffin of the Pokers. Still distraught, she told him: "I'm ready to put my rock 'n' roll shoes back on and do *my* gig. I have to get out of this now. I will not and cannot live like this. I would rather just live under a tree and eat bananas thrown at me by a monkey."

By the time the party returned to the UK, Lewis was calmer, but still determined to give in her notice. "I knew I would eventually have to leave the tour because my solo career is very important to me. I wanted to do the gigs I was advertised on because it was very important for me to live up to my word." At first, she proceeded subtly, seeking advice from David Conroy, the head of Morrison's road crew. Initially, she claims, there were attempts to dissuade and mollify her. The burden of performing Morrison's older work might have been lifted by the induction of an additional keyboard player, but that was merely one objection. "I wanted to do some writing and I didn't want to spend six to seven hours a day becoming a jazz player . . . I learned one Mose Allison song and it took a lot of time. That's not what I grew up with, that's not what I do best." She was also concerned about restrictions placed on her family life. "Working was interfering with my relationship with my son. Van Morrison demands so much from you. You have to be available even when you're not touring or rehearsing. So I missed every one of my son's football games. In America that's an important thing. I said, 'I'm going home for my son's graduation' and Van said, 'You're going home for your son's graduation if you don't have a gig or rehearsal.' I told his manager, 'There's no way I can continue because I am a mother.' Van even said, 'Oh, you're all so silly in America to act that way when somebody's graduating from high school – you need to leave your son alone and let him become a man, let him grow up . . .' We just didn't agree."

With their working relationship under threat, Morrison decided to re-record his solo album and studiously deleted all of Lewis' contributions. The project was completely reconfigured and some decent tracks were lost in the purge, including the jazz-tinged 'Just Like Greta'. "I think he left it off the album just because I liked it," she adds. Relations reached a new nadir when Morrison took exception to some personal criticisms. They were allegedly reduced to a slanging match on the phone, during which she claimed he gallantly called her "a bitch" and "a fucking cunt". Her attempt to leave quietly had totally backfired. "When I gave my notice in, it would have been nice if he'd understood, but he didn't understand, so I wasn't able to work out my notice." Indeed, Morrison evidently had no intention of ever working with her again. The once promising collaboration had ended in controversy, soon to be followed by bitter legal ramifications.

By the spring of 2001, Linda Gail Lewis had been frozen out of Morrison's performing and personal life. Perplexed concert-goers attended shows supposedly promoting *You Win Again* only to discover that the leading lady was nowhere to be seen. There was no explanation or apology from Morrison and no comment from theatre managers. Given the extent of her despondency, and considering some of the contentious and unprintable personal allegations she made which were later touched on in a court tribunal, it seems incredible that she remained in Morrison's orbit for so long. "Well, nothing's ever perfect, is it?" she offers. "It wasn't 100 per cent, nothing ever is. Ninety-nine per cent of the time it was wonderful and exciting but it had its moments where it was screwed up. I've been on the road all my life and I would never talk about anything that happened on the road unless somebody really pissed me off. We have a musicians' code and we don't talk about things on the road because people are under the influence of alcohol or the influence of exhaustion. You just overlook it. Then, when you get hurt or angry about something else, everything becomes big in your mind. It's like when you're mad at somebody you think about every little thing they said."

Lewis was evidently still "hurt, angry and mad" in the aftermath of the Morrison disagreement, although her feelings were couched in a characteristically courteous and sanguine Southern detachment. Clearly, she was not about to be silenced on the matter of Morrison and poured out her troubles to the tabloid press in often humorous and mischievous fashion. In a more serious moment, she portrayed the singer as fundamentally unhappy and at odds with the world. "Millions of people worship Van, but the real man seems convinced his fans leech off him. He said his biggest fear was that they were making money off him on the internet. This is a guy with millions but he hates the idea of someone making a few pounds from autographs. Van once said he hates his fans and they were pathetic losers and much worse . . . Van and I used to have enormous rows. I'd tell him he needed the fans and the media, but he never agreed . . . I don't hate Van, I pity him. He has all that money and is the most miserable man I know. He is not happy, the only thing he has ever created is his music and that brings happiness to other people, not him."

While Lewis was revealing Morrison's darker side, his achievements were being celebrated in Belfast at the 'Vantastic Day', a commemoration organized by journalist Stuart Bailie and promoted by the Cathedral Quarter Arts Festival. Among the highlights were a bus tour of Morrison's haunts, a seminar analysing his music and a musical evening featuring local performers. Some months later there was a celebration of a more personal nature when Violet Morrison reached her 80th birthday. Still in good health and remarkably fit for her age, she had recently joined a karate club and could be seen performing high-kicks at her granddaughter Shana's shows, a feat which her son would have surely struggled to achieve.

As autumn faded, the irrepressible Linda Gail Lewis continued to haunt Morrison with more public revelations. In October 2001, she appeared on Ulster Television's high ratings *Kelly* show entertaining viewers with stories which were sufficiently salacious to warrant repetition in several Irish and British newspapers. It proved enough to provoke a series of libel actions from Morrison. He immediately issued the following public statement: "Over the last week, Linda Gail Lewis has made claims on more than one occasion that she and I had an affair and sexual relationship. These outrageous allegations are a complete and utter fabrication. Ms Lewis makes these allegations knowing that I am intensely private about my personal life, and in the apparent belief that I would not engage in a public row and that her allegations would gain credence as a result. For a number of reasons I genuinely hoped that I could maintain a dignified silence in this matter, but I now feel compelled to issue this statement. The matter is now in the hands of my solicitors and I do not intend to say anything further in public on the subject."

Within a month, a number of newspapers meekly settled, including the *Sunday Independent* which read out a fulsome apology in the Belfast High Court acknowledging "We fully accept that the allegations contained in our article were defamatory of Mr Morrison and we are happy to clarify that there was absolutely no truth in these reported allegations. We wish to unreservedly apologize to Mr Morrison and to his long-term partner Michelle Rocca for the publication of these statements."

Ulster Television and at least one other national newspaper continued to defend the suit and, meanwhile, Lewis re-entered the fray by taking Morrison to an employment tribunal in Cardiff, alleging unfair dismissal and sexual misconduct. That action dragged on for the best part of two years. Early in the hearing, there was a reporting order specifically banning the identification of Van Morrison, although it was blatantly obvious to anyone with a remote interest in the singer who the "world famous millionaire rock star" was who stood accused of "wrongfully sacking" and "traumatizing" Lewis. It was only at the conclusion of the case in 2003 that the reporting ban was lifted and newspapers were free to tell the whole story.

By any standards, it was an extraordinary tale. During the preliminary tribunal hearing, Lewis alleged that she had suffered humiliation and was the subject of numerous unwanted sexual advances from Morrison who was accused of pressurizing her not to sleep with her husband. At one point, she had claimed that Morrison ordered her to guarantee that her husband, Eddie Braddock, would not shoot him in the event of her seeking a divorce. Many of the other allegations were even more bizarre. It was alleged that at a hotel party in May 2000, Morrison had supposedly told Ms Lewis to find a beautiful woman so that he could have sex with both of them and that, at a later date, he requested oral sex from Ms Lewis. She added that he had screamed at her on the telephone, humiliated her on stage and then sacked her when she announced she was intending to leave after the tour. As a result, she argued that she had lost work and was owed up to £20,000 in damages for earnings she never received. "He is a legend and very popular with a great reputation as a songwriter and singer," she told the tribunal. "Performing with him should have raised my profile but it didn't. What I didn't realize was that he was trying to ruin my career and life. He exploits other musicians all the time. He's a rock 'n' roll legend but he has a reputation for doing what he wants to do without regard for anyone's feelings . . . I went a lot further for him than I ever should have and I do regret some of it. I really thought he was my friend. I thought we had a great working relationship. I thought it was wonderful."

Morrison denied the allegations, insisting that members of his band were self-employed and therefore could not be fired. "I had previous experience where unscrupulous people used me," he noted. "They were involved to seek publicity, and some would leave me in the lurch . . . I stopped touring years ago in the real sense of the word. I like to do different projects and work with different musicians. There is no need for me to have full-time employees."

Although the claims for unfair dismissal were not upheld, the tribunal concluded that five of 13 allegations of sexual discrimination were to be investigated at a full hearing. This meant that, despite his denials, intimate details of Morrison's personal life would be placed under scrutiny and regurgitated by the tabloid press in regular bulletins. It was not a welcome proposition, but there was an alternative. On the eve of the hearing, a settlement was finally reached after six hours of legal wrangling. Newspapers reported that a financial deal had been struck in which Lewis agreed to accept £9,000 compensation for lost earnings and at least £5,000 in royalties from the sales of *You Win Again*. In return, she withdrew her claims and proffered an apology, the text of which was not made public, for reasons undisclosed. Solicitor Paul Tweed merely stated: "Mr Morrison remains very disappointed that the legal process has taken nearly two years to reach this stage. But he's pleased that these claims have finally been withdrawn. He has now accepted a full apology and comprehensive retraction which represents a complete vindication of his stance from the outset. Ms Lewis has given a full and categorical apology and retraction to Mr Morrison." Lewis's legal representative Christine Thompson said curtly: "Both parties have agreed to the terms of a settlement. They are happy to move on with their lives." A source close to Lewis added: "She sees it as closure of a difficult chapter in her life."

The source evidently spoke too soon. Within 48 hours, the *Daily Express* was running an interview with Lewis, which included more spicy revelations under the provocative and long-winded headline "Van Morrison broke my heart but I would not have missed our affair for all the world." Whether Morrison had the stomach for another libel action against a national newspaper remained an open question. Lewis later confirmed that the interview had taken place before the tribunal settlement and subsequently drew a veil over the sexual allegations that had provoked Morrison's litigious wrath. They would not be mentioned again.

With all the legal proceedings, there seemed little space in Morrison's life for the spiritual pursuits that had once dominated his leisure time. Since the mid-Nineties, it had been a subject dismissed in interviews and scarcely evident in his music. Perhaps the sole clue could be found in the odd composition 'High Summer', which focused on the fall of Lucifer. Rumours that the song may have been inspired by a discussion about Anton LaVey's Church of Satan raised many an eyebrow. Whatever else, it was certainly a long way from Cliff Richard and 'Whenever God Shines His Light'.

The publicity-loving, self-confessed controversialist LaVey had first come to prominence in the mid-Sixties when he boasted several celebrity followers, including Jayne Mansfield. A former lion tamer, carnival huckster and police photographer, LaVey was like a black magic version of L. Ron Hubbard, complete with his own take on psychiatry and philosophy, all of which was contained in his infamous and occasionally comic *Satanic Bible*. "The Satanic Age started in 1966," he claimed. "That's when God was proclaimed dead, the Sexual Freedom League came into prominence, and the hippies developed as a free sex culture. You could see this trend developing . . . Satanism preaches indulgence in man's natural animalistic desires instead of abstinence and guilt feelings encouraged by other religions. Indulging yourself is the only way to eliminate harmful frustrations and guilt feelings. We encourage our members to indulge in every one of the Seven Deadly Sins of Christianity – anger, envy, gluttony, greed, lust, pride and sloth – because they all lead to physical, mental or emotional gratification."

LaVey's services were notable for their sensationalist perversion and blasphemy. A naked woman acting as an altar would spread her legs and urinate in a "holy water" chamber-pot and a host would be inserted in her vagina then removed and placed on the tongues of those participating in the ceremony. Hexes against enemies and sexual gratification seemed high on the list of many of LaVey's followers. "He's the guy who made Satanism acceptable," quips Clive Culbertson. "It's almost like he became the Presbyterian Church of Satanism! If you read the Church of Satan stuff what they tell you is 'We'll give you control over people around you, control over your business affairs, control over your love life.' Control. Control. Control."

Although Morrison has often shown a passing interest in cult religions of every description, the Church of Satan sounded an unlikely avenue of interest. If 'High Summer' betrayed a touch of Milton in its focus on Lucifer, was this evidence that Morrison was now looking into darker areas for inspiration? If so, what could it possibly offer him? "It all depends what you want to get out of it," Culbertson says. "There may be beasties out there who will help you. It doesn't really need any more than that you do the ritual . . . There's words you can give people even if they don't know what they're doing, they can still do serious damage . . . So if other stuff hasn't worked for you and you haven't found God or reached the point where you don't believe there is a God, then you may as well try and manipulate the physical to your advantage as much as possible. I'll bet that's where he's at." Those accustomed to Morrison's insatiable interest in matters spiritual would no doubt regard any reference to Lucifer or indeed LaVey as nothing more than a small footnote in his personal encyclopaedia of comparative religion. For Clive Culbertson, however, all this brought back memories of the German Rosicrucian master and his famous theory of the Angelic Knot. "The knot's still there and if anything it's tightening, and the darker side is coming through even stronger than it ever has in his life. That's my personal opinion."

Apart from Culbertson's cautious asides from a distance and the lyrical reference in 'High Summer', there was nothing in Morrison's life or work to warrant the melodrama of black magic or any other dominating belief system. 2002 saw the release of another album, *Down The Road*, which betrayed an unusually resigned, elegiac air. 'Choppin' Wood' looked back with stoical affection at his father's early struggles in post-war Belfast, 'Whatever Happened To P.J. Proby?' spoke of lost dreams and old heroes, 'The Beauty Of The Days Gone By' lamented the passing of the passions of youth and 'What Makes The Irish Heart Beat' dealt with the familiar theme of Emerald exile. Musically, Morrison sounded steeped in the blues, as if the road he was taking was drawing him ever closer to the music of his youth. This was a record attempting to come to terms with old age and changing fashions with an obdurate dignity that was impressive and commendable, but seldom riveting. Inevitably, the album garnered mixed reviews, yet won surprisingly few accolades from seasoned Morrison watchers. Among the wearier responses was a scathing and uncharitable commentary from critic Tom Cox, who concluded: "Van Morrison is tired of making records. Now that his voice can't swoop like it did on *Astral Weeks*, he'd rather just sit in a big rocking chair listening to Sam Cooke. As he mutters wistfully about the days gone by, he betrays all the zest of someone rolled reluctantly into the studio by a team of hired labourers. The atmosphere is so stuffy, so staid, that when you see a song called 'Hey Mr DJ', you're half hoping for head-thumping techno. What you get instead is a man attempting to make a career out of clearing his throat."

In concert, Morrison appeared alongside Paul Brady and turned back the clock to the golden age of the Irish showband élite by introducing the legendary Brendan Bowyer. Once Ireland's chunkier answer to Elvis Presley, Bowyer was the main singer in the Royal, the most celebrated showband in Irish history. At a time when the Monarchs were starving unknowns, Bowyer was already a national celebrity, soon to leave Waterford and relocate to Las Vegas. As with Lonnie Donegan and many others, Morrison seemed to enjoy rewriting history by placing himself alongside the key figures of his lost youth.

If the new century brought anything home to Morrison, it was an awareness of his own mortality. Time was marching on and even Michelle Rocca was now a grandmother – 19-year-old Danielle having given birth to a daughter Alanah. But it was the roll call of death that proved most alarming. Every other month, it seemed that one of Morrison's former acolytes passed away – Connie Kay, John Lee Hooker, Peter Bardens, Kenny Craddock, Bob Schwaid, Derek Bell, Lonnie Donegan . . . RIP. Morrison was listed alongside the Chieftains as one of the tributees at Bell's funeral, which took place at St Anne's Cathedral, Belfast, on All Saints' Day 2002: "He told Derek's wife that he was coming to the funeral and wanted to speak," Clive Culbertson recalls. "I knew we were going to be sitting in the same pew. I was dreading it. Then he did what he normally did, sent his apologies and said that due to pressure of work he couldn't come. I thought 'That guy has probably been one of your best friends.' I'm glad he didn't come for my sake, but I think for Derek's memory he should have made the effort, even if all he did was sit outside and wait till he was called." The singer subsequently made amends by appearing at a Derek Bell tribute concert. It will be revealing to see how many people turn up for Morrison's funeral and what awaits him when the obituaries are finally written.

TWENTY-SIX

Poetic Champions Decompose

Van Morrison has inspired many provocative comments over the years. Along with a small band of contemporaries, he is one of the few to have negotiated the glamour of the Sixties and emerged more fully formed with each passing decade. Whenever he has been written off as yesterday's man, he has usually confounded expectations and prevailing fashions to restamp his authority with a work of quality. His longevity is impressive. Although it has now been some years since he produced an album that has garnered universal praise or lavish column inches, his collaborative work and concert appearances continue to attract attention. The world's music press and institutions like the Rock 'n' Roll Hall of Fame have recognized and celebrated his importance, and rock icons from Bruce Springsteen to Bono testify to his influence.

Classifying Morrison within the vanguard of rock music is nevertheless complicated by his frequently-voiced denial of the genre's very existence. "I think 'rock' has become a meaningless word," he has asserted. "I think you have to find a better one. Or, better still, categorize within that one word – make up categories, sub-words. Because it's gotten to the point where people think that the current trends are rock when they're not rock at all. I think some other word has to be invented because I personally don't have anything to do with rock, in any shape or form. For me, there's a couple of people still playing rock 'n' roll: Jerry Lee Lewis is one of them. Certainly there hasn't been any rock to come out in a long time. I wish I could find another category." Morrison often appears to regard rock and rock 'n' roll as virtually synonymous. When asked to classify himself, the closest he has come to a definition are the words "Rhythm & Blues singer".

This seems one-dimensional and wholly inadequate for a vocalist whose work has embraced gospel, soul, jazz, blues, folk and pop. At least the bastardized 'rock' is an embracing epithet that takes in elements of all these genres. Indeed, for such an eclectic performer as Morrison, you could argue that rock is the most representative catch-all term to define his work. But Morrison is dogmatic about this issue and speaks with the solipsistic certainty of Ian Paisley berating detractors with the truth of scripture or insisting that the Pope is by definition the Anti-christ.

Morrison has railed consistently against those who have dared place *Astral Weeks* and its successors in the rock category, but such is his fate. Walk into almost any record shop and you will find his albums under the label 'rock'. In music encyclopaedias Morrison can be found under rock or pop, while his name is conspicuously absent from the jazz, folk or blues volumes. Such categorization is understandable. Folk music followers regard him as too commercial or insufficiently authentic; jazz publications realize that his playing ability and technique are rudimentary compared to the greats; finally, the rude person who derided him at Montreux with the suggestion "only black men" can sing or play the blues summed up a prejudicial but still commonly held viewpoint. Morrison may not like the term rock musician but for most of the world that is what he is and is likely to remain. It is only in recent years that he has mounted a serious and convincing challenge to this classification, largely thanks to a number of collaborations with Georgie Fame, John Lee Hooker, Mose Allison, Lonnie Donegan and Linda Gail Lewis. Impressive as some of these efforts have been, most critics have regarded them as side projects distinct from his main body of work. Even in the fanzine network, where blind acceptance of Morrison's claim that he is not a rock musician is commonplace, his groundbreaking collaborations have been greeted coolly. It is ironic that some of his most ardent supporters often betray the 'rockist' tendency by denying these records their rightful place in his canon while secretly hoping for a 'proper' Van Morrison album next time around. Indomitable to the end, Morrison continues to argue his corner and will probably extend his collaborative work, in reverent imitation of the jazz and blues singers of his youth. In the meantime, as if to underscore the argument, he has arranged a licensing deal with the jazz label Blue Note commencing with the solo album *What's Wrong With This Picture?* "I want to be on an adult label that deals with music, not pop stuff for kids," he announced. "It doesn't make sense for me to be on a pop label anymore." Morrison's tenacity in bridging musical genres has worked to his artistic advantage in the past, but one of the ironies of his current stance is that the further he distances himself from the rock stereotype the less impact his work achieves, both critically and commercially. Perhaps in the fullness of time, his later work will be seen in a more favourable light as evidence of a rounded genre-crossing musical personality who has chosen demythology as an artistic weapon.

Surveying Morrison's long career, it has been his voice that has garnered the greatest plaudits. In his book *From A Whisper To A Scream* (subtitled *The Great Voices Of Popular Music*), Barney Hoskyns pays tribute to Morrison's early work, pinpointing the "regurgitive violence" in his phrasing and the way he made "the ugly, the uncouth, sound beautiful". He even claims that the "beautiful snarl" heard on Them's recordings "must rate as the most exciting punk-R&B voice of all time". Surprisingly, that view is echoed in the words of Morrison's old adversary Billy Harrison who dares to place the singer on a higher level than such sterling contemporaries as Eric Burdon, Mick Jagger and Chris Farlowe. "If Van's in the right form, there's nobody better. There isn't another white man can phrase blues like him. His phrasing's phenomenal. His diction is not the greatest but his phrasing is."

In *Astral Weeks*, there was evidence of a new Morrison, less aggressive but even more insistent in his vocal word play and improvisation. Hoskyns falls into uncharacteristic hyperbole when discussing this album, saying "Van Morrison gets closer to exposing the naked cry at the heart of human singing than anyone has ever done. In these performances, 'meaning' becomes irrelevant as the voice wrings all sense out of words, scrapes out their innards and tears out their lining." For Hoskyns, at least, Morrison never again sang with such a sense of abandonment and although he praises much of his mid-period work, he senses diminishment over the decades.

By the early Nineties that once unassailable reputation as a vocalist was under serious threat. The jazz publication the *Wire* noted: "The most registered complaint about Morrison's later music concerns his singing: the unchained wildness throttled by age into a congested, slobbish instrument." This was criticism that could not be easily ignored and had already been made by Hoskyns, who concluded: "the voice has steadily deteriorated over the years to the point where it now sounds irreparably clogged and congested. As though giving himself up to his self-loathing, even while singing of redemption, he has become ever more sloppy and grouchy . . . Since switching from Warner Brothers to Phonogram in 1979, he has tended to sing as though his mouth is full of molasses, and his short-winded, grumpily lazy delivery makes one think of Gertrude's description of Hamlet: 'he's fat and scant of breath'." Two years later, Hoskyns was more convinced than ever that Morrison was "nothing more than a grotesque travesty of his former glorious selves." The criticism was amplified by journalist David Sinclair in a telling review of the Morrison/Fame collaboration *How Long Has This Been Going On?* "The weak link, unfortunately, is Morrison . . ." Sinclair argued, adding "his ragged diction, approximate phrasing and often wildly suspect pitch fail to meet the exacting technical standards required in the world of straight jazz."

Even Seán O'Hagan, another firm believer in the *Astral Weeks* myth and a self-confessed connoisseur of Morrison's vocal strengths, admits "I'm not a fan of the late voice. On the record there's something going on with his voice. It's been reduced and not just by age either." Similar doubts have been levelled at Dylan in the past but with Morrison the criticism is all the more wounding as his entire career has been largely based on the power and resonance of that once-distinctive voice.

While fault-finding about the state of Morrison's voice has been a relatively recent debate, the same cannot be said of his standing as a lyricist or poet. This remains a contentious issue, not least with the man himself. Morrison has always bridled when faced with any questions about the meaning of his lyrics. Pathologically wary of academic or critical analysis, he has sometimes played the idiot savant to unconvincing effect. "I'm sure there are people at universities sitting around trying to figure out what James Joyce meant on the twenty-third page of whatever," he has noted wearily, "but I'm not interested in that . . . You've only got to read my lyrics to see for yourself that they're pretty straightforward. They are precisely what they state and nothing more than that. That's all there is." It was dogmatic and disingenuous however for him to suggest that songs such as 'Madame

George', 'Listen To The Lion', 'You Don't Pull No Punches, But You Don't Push The River' or 'Dweller On The Threshold' were in any sense "straightforward". Even some of his album titles – notably *Astral Weeks* and *Veedon Fleece* – are perplexing and allusive. Morrison himself has usually stumbled into exasperation or incoherence when asked to elucidate matters. Critical interpretations of his work have invariably left him incredulous, which is not entirely surprising. Some unsophisticated commentators and biographers have succumbed embarrassingly to the intentional fallacy, assuming that Morrison's lyrics are predominantly autobiographical rather than a confluence of unrelated thoughts and experiences. "There's very few of my songs that are biographical and even then it's fragments. Some part of your experiences you'll write into your songs and the rest you make up, but they're not generally about me . . . a lot of them are from various fragments of ideas, and then it's a case of putting the ingredients together."

The fragments that Morrison assembled from his imagination and experience helped him assemble *Astral Weeks* and its successors. With pop and rock culture in the ascendancy, Morrison established his reputation in America just before the mass advent of the singer-songwriter. This was a time when professional songsmiths were replaced by sensitive 'poets' whose confessional outpourings saw them elevated to godly status in the new pantheon of rock. Morrison was thus deified and served as LA's mad Irish poet in residence. It was an unfortunate stereotype based partly on ignorance and wishful thinking. Morrison was called a "Gael", a Celtic bard or one of "the children of the rainbow". Lazy critics later self-consciously mentioned W.B. Yeats, concluding that Morrison was obviously his successor on the spurious grounds that the former was an Irish poet with an interest in mysticism. Presumably, had Yeats been born 50 years later, he would have been a rock star writing about sailing to Byzantium. It reveals much about this simplistic media shorthand that nobody ever chose to mention Morrison in connection with any of the Northern Ireland poets of his own time. In such company, his lyrics would certainly have looked embarrassingly like trite poetry, but at least this would have been a saner comparison than any attempt to place him alongside one of the greatest poets of the twentieth century. What was frustrating and infuriating about the myth of Morrison the poet was that all the impressionistic nonsense written about the "genius" and the "child of the rainbow" was unsupported by any detailed lyrical analysis or serious appreciation of his work. Even more alarming was the obvious caveat that, in strictly lyrical terms, Morrison's work was inferior to that of many other songwriters of the period. The words of Bob Dylan, Leonard Cohen, Paul Simon or Joni Mitchell – to name but four – could all be analysed and appreciated to some degree on the printed page. Applying the same rigour to Morrison merely exposed his limitations. Many of his mid-Seventies lyrical flourishes were unspeakably banal and unworthy of even cursory critical comment. Even his most celebrated or contentious works – *Astral Weeks, Veedon Fleece* and *Common One* – appear wanting when the lyrics are inspected in isolation from the music. Meaningless repetition, poorly thought-out imagery, cloying sentimentality, cosmic buffoonery, faux and gratuitous literary name-dropping, heavy-handed symbolism or decorative words employed purely for their poetic associations are all there in embarrassing abundance. At worst, such work resembles portentous adolescent scribbling or what one critic called the "bloated equivalent of a breathless sixth-form blue stocking". It was galling that some of the worst aspects of his songwriting actually encouraged his deification.

Sadly, treating Morrison predominantly as a poet of the page not only did him a disservice, but distracted attention from his true strengths. Clearly, he was not one of those songwriters whose lyrics you could read and mull over with pleasure in complete silence without a record on the turntable. It was his music and vocal strengths working in conjunction with those words that transformed monstrous banalities into something of substance. In 'Astral Weeks', for example, it was the fine combination of flute and acoustic guitar, the subtle, unexpected introduction of strings and the unusual phrasing and accentuation with Morrison reducing his voice to a whisper in the final lines that provided the song's magic. Similarly, many of Morrison's greatest songs (the epics from 'Cyprus Avenue' to 'Listen To The Lion') looked embarrassingly poor on paper, but were a different proposition when appreciated orally with emphasis on the phrasing and performance.

There was a sea change in the Eighties when more sophisticated commentators decided to move the goal posts by championing Morrison, not as a poet *per se* but specifically as an 'oral poet'. This was a much needed and long overdue admission that, unlike Dylan, Morrison did not survive serious scrutiny as a writer whose lyrics alone could be savoured and enhanced by critical exposition. It was a sensible conclusion. Morrison's power always lay in the unique combination of voice, music and words working interdependently. Studied apart, the words were always by far the weakest of those three components.

During the autumn of his career, Morrison found fresh champions for his 'poetry', this time from renegade members of the Irish literati. Chief amongst them was poet Paul Durcan who wrote a charming appraisal of Morrison, provocatively comparing him with Patrick Kavanagh. The article occasionally read more like a fan letter than a rigorous appraisal and at one point Durcan found himself conceding that Morrison was "not really a poet at all". However, he did make the convincing point that "poetry is of its very essence part of an age-old oral and placename tradition (known in Irish as the *dindsenchas*) and Morrison is a modern Irish exemplar of that ancient tradition". Northern Ireland poet Tom Paulin also applauded Morrison's "sense of place" in discussion on BBC Television's *Late Review*. He subsequently offered a characteristically original comparison. "I always associate him with the great American action painter Jackson Pollock who came from the same Scotch-Irish roots. It is the sense that this is an imagination that owes a lot to Calvinism. Jackson Pollock said 'I don't paint nature, I am nature'. And I feel with listening to Van, you're inside a natural process. So it's something that's not composed from the outside, not formed and shaped, but it shapes itself from the inside. But it's endlessly in process. Like Blake, he comes out of the working class. He comes out of – not traditional Protestantism – but *evangelical* Protestantism. That's the foundation of his imagination. He's testifying." Which, of course, takes us back to the roots of Ian Paisley once more.

Not that everyone was convinced. While Durcan was rewarded with an invitation to collaborate with Morrison and Paulin's name was mentioned in concert, fellow poet Don Paterson was busy ridiculing the Belfast man's pretensions. The Whitbread award-winner and talented jazz guitarist stated emphatically that Morrison was certainly not a poet, adding that it would take more than sumptuous mentions of barmbracks and pasties to win that particular laurel.

The debate continues to this day. Meanwhile, Paterson's publishers, the renowned Faber & Faber, had long been ready to publish a book of Morrison's verse and song lyrics, having first mooted the idea in the late Eighties. Presumably, there is some vain hope that Morrison might emulate the sales of that other great laureate Paul McCartney. At the time of writing, the project, remains in abeyance. "Tom Paulin was asked to write the foreword," reveals Morrison's former English teacher and folklorist David Hammond. "I talked about a lot of this stuff with Tom. He's terrific but he's not musical at all. He's very diligent though. He listened to all the records and CDs sent to him, but the book wasn't going to include music, which I thought was a bad mistake. If you issued a CD with it, you might have been able to make *some* sense of it. People who aren't musical don't understand how much the melody inflames the work. When you see those bloody words on the page, they're so *banal*. Morrison, of course, is generally pleased and flattered by it, but he's genuinely mystified [and says] 'I don't know where I get the words from'."

It is revealing to consider how Morrison's view of his poetic standing has shifted over the years. During the Seventies, he accepted the hyperbolic accolades of poetic genius from excited rock critics without much comment. "I'm just a stand-up singer . . . I'm a poet and a musician," he said laconically in 1974, as if hedging his bets. He later admitted that there was a good reason to stay silent on the issue. Morrison's early reading list consisted mainly of adolescent beat poetry. Having attended a Protestant school in East Belfast, he had never been introduced to Irish literature. Rock critics, however, particularly in America, were ignorant of such cultural differences and sloppily placed his work in a hazy, mythical Celtic tradition of their own creation, loosely based on some Hollywood concept of Irishness. "I was just writing these songs instinctively," Morrison recalled, "and then I read other things where people were making references saying, 'This is sort of Yeatsian' and I would go, 'Really?' because I didn't know. I'd never read him. So I would go out and get Yeats and see, but I hadn't read him until I saw this article. Or some would say it was Joycean so I would think, 'Oh well, I must check Joyce out.'"

At least the much reviled critics were expanding Morrison's reading list. Meanwhile, his familiar reserve actively enhanced his mystique. By the late Seventies, he was alluding to a selection of Irish literary figures and English Romantics in song, most notably in the overwrought lyrics of *Common One*. The new decade saw Morrison in denial as a songwriter, for he was now more convinced than ever that he was the unconscious repository of poetic inspiration. Where it came from he did not know. When asked, he would mutter, "It's the unknown". Any suggestion of craft was firmly denied. "I don't see myself as a songwriter. I know songwriters and I'm not one. A songwriter's a guy who can come in at 9.30 in the morning and write a song on demand and I've never been able to do that. I'm an inspirational writer. I write when I'm inspired. If I'm not inspired I can't write. It's impossible for me. I'm not like a craftsman, which is what a songwriter is."

In 1987, Morrison portrayed himself as a Madame Blavatsky figure, plucking unfathomable truths from the ether. "I'm just channelling . . . that's what I prefer to call it. I'm channelling these ideas that are coming through me from wherever they are . . . I myself am not actually saying anything new either way. I just get ideas coming through. It might be a line. A bit of melody. I develop these things that come through that subconscious mind and put shapes on them and they become songs . . . I'm just putting down what I get and recording it."

Four years later, Morrison was a little more expressive and articulate and had even found some fancy genre classifications to explain his gift. "I've always had some idea of trying to explore the relationship between poetry and mysticism, poetry-religion, poetry and nature, and nature and healing. In the beginning with me it was unconscious. I started to write songs at a very early age. I didn't have a clue about what I was doing. Later on, I was trying to find a way to connect what I was doing with my contemporaries. I discovered, however, I was writing what some people call 'transcendental poetry'. Other people call it mysticism in poetry; other people call it nature poetry. Why was I writing this kind of poetry when my contemporaries weren't? I wanted to find out where I stood and what tradition I came from. Well, eventually I found out the tradition I belong to is actually my own tradition. It was like getting hit over the head with a baseball bat."

During the Nineties, Morrison was still pushing the 'stream of consciousness' line, pondering that "Jung's theory of the collective unconscious is the closest expression I can find for my work. Writing songs comes from the collective unconsciousness or my own unconsciousness, or both." However, in recent years, Morrison has evidently changed his mind again. When asked in 1997 whether he regarded himself as a poet or a songwriter, he replied emphatically: "A songwriter." This was a complete reversal of his stand a decade before. Now he was ready to abandon the mantle of poet. Indeed, he gave the impression that he was rising above it all. "The academics wanted the monopoly on it," he complained. "And you get these anthologies of poetry and they don't put any songs into them. They want to keep it safe, so they draw a line. I am a poet, but in the strictest sense I'm not because they've put a wall between poetry and lyrics. There's no advantage to being a poet nowadays. The worst thing you can be is a poet."

This was the new, super-cynical Morrison, the debunker of all myths, including his own. He spoke of the creative process with all the passion of a car mechanic and his album output as being little more than product. Previously, his best songs had been both conceived and appreciated as spiritual quests, but Morrison now wondered whether this was just another illusion, a magical trick conjured by the songwriter in search of inspiration or subject matter. "When you become a songwriter, then you write songs. Then after the second or third album you realize 'Yes, I'm doing what I want to do' . . . By the fourth or fifth album you're writing more songs but you write from the point of view that you are searching – but you're actually not. But in order to be able to write something you have to pretend you are. Otherwise there's nothing to write about . . . It seems like searching but in actual fact you're just telling little stories. But you have to do that to write the damn song, otherwise you couldn't write it . . . It comes with the job."

From the evidence of his recent albums, Morrison's lyrical power has not so much eroded as been extinguished. Old lines have been recycled lazily and there has been an alarming rise in the number of stale clichés and trite similes with Morrison at times reduced to throwing in 'moon and June' couplets to fill up lines. The transparent banality of the lyrics may simply reflect Morrison's expedient attempt to avoid the onset of writer's block. Alternatively, it may indicate a new determination to strip his work to a skeletal form, thereby revealing as little about himself as possible and scuppering the earnest efforts of internet enthusiasts, academic analysts and autobiography-fixated rock critics.

While any tightly focused examination of Morrison's lyrics proves spectacularly unrewarding, a wider lens offers some surprisingly positive results. Two aspects that give some strength and unity to his work are his strong sense of place and that strange conflict between the physical and imaginary within his lyrical landscapes. His long-standing affinity for his home city is such that supporters even initiated a local tour, taking in such Morrison landmarks as Cyprus Avenue, Sandy Row, Fitzroy Avenue and Hyndford Street. Of course, it is not just Belfast or Northern Ireland that has captured his imagination. Wherever Morrison has laid his hat has provided a possible place name for a song. In the Them days, there was Queensway and the Tottenham Court Road and, significantly, when he moved to America it was increasingly the New World panorama that drew his attention with songs celebrating Woodstock, San Anselmo, Venice (USA) and Kansas City. When he stayed with Corvin in the Irish Republic in 1973, the visit inspired the Celtic-tinged *Veedon Fleece*, which included his paean to the streets of Arklow. The circle seemed complete when Belfast re-emerged as the inspiration for so much of his work in the Eighties.

Apart from these physical places there are alternative metaphysical vistas that inhabit Morrison's imagination. These are the mythical worlds of Caledonia or Avalon, places detached from time and corporeal experience: it is within these landscapes that we might find Blake and the Eternals in search of the mysterious Veedon Fleece, or a narrator treading the haunts of ancient peace. There were always strong elements of quest literature – usually a celebration of the quest for its own sake – in Morrison's better epics: 'Listen To The Lion' and 'You Don't Pull No Punches, But You Don't Push The River'.

Equally intriguing are those moments when Morrison's different dimensions collide, and we see a juxtaposition of the concrete and the imaginary. On 'Astral Weeks' there is a shift from a distinctly urban setting to an intense contemplation of another place, almost another dimension. In 'Cyprus Avenue', external description suddenly turns inward as he becomes 'caught' and enters a trance. The appropriately named 'A Sense Of Wonder' emphasizes this technique, lovingly fusing the transcendent and the evanescent with the prosaic and the parochial. In the song, Morrison reflects on local places – from the Castle Picture House to Davy's Chipper – but they are all fuel to the indefinable sense of wonder that he experiences. The longing for transcendence emerges from an intense concentration on fond memories of mundane, everyday experience. Nor is this just nostalgia for a lost innocence or Edenic bliss – although it surely is that too – but an attempt to articulate a deep intensity of feeling that is so evanescent that it escapes even in the very moment of articulation, like a waking dream. Some of Morrison's more accomplished songs in this manner are also his most understated and underrated. 'Coney Island' is a meditation on a journey with abundant geographical references and pedestrian details including the unintentionally humorous food-fixated reference to picking up some potted herring. But it also aspires to the transcendent in the childlike enthusiasm of that memorable last line : "Wouldn't it be great if it was like this all the time?" The more prosaic 'Cleaning Windows', which is closer to genuine nostalgia, similarly conveys a deep satisfaction for a time when Morrison was happily employed and spent his leisure hours reading books or eating Paris buns. Again it is the Belfast vernacular that adds appeal here, particularly in the closing words omitted on lyric sheets and usually missed by commentators where he mentions the local tradition of leaving the 'three d bit' (three pence) on the window sill.

Morrison sings of the spirit and the flesh (sometimes in the same song) and can mentally commute from Ulster to America (sometimes in the same song). If there is a strong sense of belonging in his work, then there is an equally intense desire to escape. That tension is manifested in songs such as 'Cyprus Avenue' and 'Madame George'. Morrison has spoken of lost and found dreams of America as well as the common Irish experience of being too long in exile. Within his work, he seems dramatically torn between the longing for experience and an encroaching sense of elegy. Significantly, the Belfast he has always celebrated was never contemporary, but rather a past terrain that lives only in recovered memory and therefore, with each passing year, becomes more distant and increasingly aligned with his evocations of Caledonia and Avalon.

There is a fascinating Janus quality about Van Morrison, both in his music and life. Within the space of an album, he can seek ultimate transcendence, then dirty his hands by broadcasting petty grievances in minute detail. His spiritual quest has always been countered by a bitter immersion in music business and media politics. There is a skewed sensibility at work here. At times he emerges as sensitive, sentimental, impressionable, ameliorating and romantic, but he can be practical, cynical, cold, wary, calculating, aggressive and vengeful. In life, he is intensely private, but his work is full of place name references that serve to attract the curious. Fatally dour, stern and forbidding, he is also blessed with a dark, laconic, mordant Belfast humour. Morrison became famous as a rock star whose favourite mantra was the emphatic denial that he was anything of the kind. His life and work have always been characterized by these contradictions. The schoolboy dreamer, whose airy notions eventually led him through every esoteric belief system imaginable, never lost the self-questioning pragmatism and strong Protestant work ethic inculcated by his Belfast upbringing. He has often called himself, with pride, a working musician. At other times, he has referred to himself as a mystic and a poet who writes stream of consciousness lyrics. Now he prefers to call himself a song-writer and insists his songs are simply "entertainment". He has, intentionally or not, both mythologized and demythologized himself for public consumption. Sometimes he has come across as the ultimate New Age pundit, full of ethereal notions and spiritual tales, but he has also been blunt, earthy and awkward. Even during the Seventies when he was portrayed as a pastoral singer-songwriter, he could confound expectations with impatient ripostes like "What am I going to do, sit on a hill somewhere in Ireland and open a grocery shop? I'm in the music business." Ever since his apprenticeship with Phil Solomon and Them, he has been brutally aware of the painful collision of music business realpolitik and artistic creativity.

These tensions in Morrison's lyrics and music, along with the coarseness of his interview comments, are mirrored in his unresolved ambition. If he had chosen to become a poet his impact and reputation would no doubt have proven insignificant. Ever the pragmatist and the dreamer, he was not content to stay in Belfast and succeed as a local hero, even if his lyrical landscape suggested otherwise. Morrison, then and now, was aiming at a global market, from Germany to London, New York to Hollywood, and back. This, in itself, exposed many contradictions. Artistic ambition was, at least in Morrison's mind, not necessarily concomitant with a burning desire for fame. "The only thing that bothers me is that I don't really know why I became famous, because I wasn't one of those people that wanted it," he has claimed. "It was something that happened to me and I couldn't get back to where I was before that. It isn't something that I set out to be and I don't quite understand that. There's a lot of people who do want to be famous and can't be, and I never wanted to be. So it's ironic, isn't it?" Perhaps it is closer to the truth to state that Morrison once desired success – personal, artistic and financial – but found the taste of fame unpalatable. Whenever the god of celebrity tempted Morrison – the UK pop star success of Them; the American chart breakthrough with 'Brown Eyed Girl'; the international achievements of the Caledonia Soul Orchestra – his instinctive reaction was to retreat. "I just can't handle it and I've never been able to handle it, and I never will," he admitted. "There were times when I thought I needed to do this, that and the other thing . . . but it didn't go anywhere. I don't really want to be a celebrity. I just want to do the music. And celebrity is such a loaded word. It isn't what it appears to be . . . It's meaningless."

If there is a dichotomy between Morrison's music and ambition, and an inner conflict within his soul in which the rational and the ethereal battle for supremacy, then it is hardly surprising that his personality and character have provoked a variety of responses from those whose paths he has crossed. Those who spent time with him in those darker moments when he was struggling in Belfast still paint a bleak picture. "Everyone Van meets, he leaves an impression on them, whether it's good, bad or indifferent," Gwen Carson (McIlroy) reflects. "I always thought he'd commit suicide because he always seemed so unhappy."

Others see him as the inveterate, frustrated seeker. "Van's a lost soul really," Bobby Tench concludes. "He's got houses all over the place: San Francisco, Ireland, Holland Park . . . I think he's just looking for something that's not there."

"I think he is actually very shy," says his paramour Michelle Rocca. "He worked very hard from a young age and I don't think he got the chance to get to know real ordinary people."

Former collaborator Linda Gail Lewis remains nonplussed by his enigmatic personality. "Well, he's a mystery to me, quite honestly," she ponders. "He will tell you himself, 'I am a very complicated man.'"

Guitarist Eric Bell senses a continued ambivalence towards Belfast. "I don't know where his head's at. He writes a lot about his past but I think the guy's very bitter. And I'm very bitter myself, in a way. He's his own man. He's a mood person – like all the great artistes."

"Van is not a genius," stresses his ex-wife Janet. "He is just completely hooked on what he does. He doesn't have hobbies. He doesn't do anything else but music. It's his entire existence . . . that's all he does. That's all he knows about – and he knows a lot about it . . . He's really got a love-hate relationship with fame and success and pleasing people. I'm not really sure he wants to please people most of the time."

Herbie Armstrong, who has seen someone almost reduced to tears by Morrison's tough exterior, still retains fond memories of their working relationship and long-term friendship. "I'll never forget when I joined Van and went to play with him. I'd always wanted to play with him because I love his music. I like him as a person. I think he's very together. People think whatever they think about him because he's a very closed shop to the outside world. But inside I think he's a good guy. I've known him from way back so I know why he says what he says. When he cuts people off, I know why. He's been through it all and he gets fed up with it. He doesn't toe the line – he's not a 'yes' man. A lot of these artistes would probably like to be like him but they can't. He's himself – and that's what's great about him."

Morrison's old mentor Geordie Sproule is also generally positive. "I've got respect for him. He went for it. He did what I could have done. But I'd have to get things down in black and white whereas Van could take a chance, which he did do, and it paid off for him. What a lot of people don't realize is that Van paid his dues. He worked his dues. It saw him through. He'd listen and use his memory bank. He's got a good brain and he was always reading. A good kid."

Chieftain Paddy Moloney saw similar traits. "Some people, like myself, may go out there smiling all the time but behind it they're in agony. If Van is feeling that way, or angry, he doesn't hide it. And he also tends to shun intimacy. You could be talking to him for ages and feel that this conversation has to go on but at one point he'll have to get away from it. He feels if you've said what you have to say there's no point in coming back to that person the next day and saying the same thing all over again. And some people misinterpret that."

A lack of empathy with strangers has often led to accusations of coldness, moodiness or artistic aloofness. "I still feel it's a big problem with him in interviews," his old friend Gil Irvine reflects. "He's basically a shy person. The old story that he's rude – well, if you speak about what *he* wants to speak about, he could talk to you for hours. But it has to be something *he* wants to talk about. His concentration span is short. He gets bored very quickly. That's my feelings on him."

Others have been considerably less charitable and understandably found no valid excuse for Morrison's supposed "shyness", lack of social grace or other basic human failings. "He was always a little shit and he still is," says Ann Denvir, evidently without fear of contradiction. "I suppose some people never change. My friend Gwen and me went to see him in Belfast, nearly front row seats. If you knew a friend you'd go around and see them but there's no way we'd go to see him because he might say 'Fuck off' or something. Either he'd throw his arms around you or he'd say that. And you just don't take the chance with Van."

Asked to characterize Morrison, writer Steve Turner could not help recalling a familiar but revealing tale. "Remember the story of the neighbour [Mrs Nancy McCarter] asking him to pop over the garden wall and open the door to let her out? And he just says 'No.' If I was to take one theme from his life which summed him up, I'd take that one. Someone is asking for help and it's just . . . nothing! He only wants to do what he wants to do in the way he wants to do it. Cliff [Richard] is completely the opposite. In rehearsal he knows exactly what he wants and can be quite sharp about it, but you see him on television and he'll join in the spirit of things and give interviews without giving much away. But he'll give the interview whereas Van will just be rude and insulting. It's almost like he doesn't want to get on with people. He doesn't bend in people's directions in any way except when he wants to . . . That's what I find remarkable. As an artiste and writer he obviously does have perception and he's been into all these religions and psychologies. At the end of all that you should have some realistic estimation of what you're like. Some people might say 'I've got a bad temper' or 'I've got a bad temper and I'm trying to overcome it'. But Van Morrison will say 'I've *not* got a bad temper' and probably shout it at you. That's what I find funny. Why can't he admit that he does have these anti-social tendencies and is dealing with them? But it's like everybody else is wrong."

There is some evidence, however, that Morrison has indeed become aware of those inadequacies. "I'm not a nice person," he recently admitted. "I don't expect anyone to say I'm a nice guy. If somebody says I'm grumpy, I'm a cunt, or whatever, that's OK because I don't profess to be an angel . . . I think I'm a loner. I'm an outsider not because I want to be but I found I had to be. I was in a situation that if I didn't play along with the music business bullshit then I became an outsider."

For Morrison to concede that he was never an angel clearly seems to him an adequate excuse for his behaviour. There will always be defenders ready to argue that his truculence was a reasonable price to pay for the music he has given the world. Some may be shocked or indignant that certain associates consider him a "cunt" or worse, but that should not detract from his artistic worth or importance. It merely underlines the gap between the man and the work. Over the decades, he has spoken and sung about spiritual healing, beautiful visions, enlightenment and all the other virtues of New Age consciousness, but there is little if any positive evidence of their efficacy in turning him into a more virtuous, open-hearted human being. "Metaphysician, heal thyself" might be an appropriate response to all his religious and philosophical dabblings. His prickly personality and curt manner, once ludicrously excused as artistic temperament, are now seen in starker tones as a kind of misanthropic grumpiness. Refreshingly, there is a comic, or more accurately, tragi-comic element to the man's character which the majority of the public now accepts as no mere caricature. Even those misguided commentators who once promoted him as a shy, sensitive singer-songwriter now realize that he was always as hard as Ulster granite and as verbally vehement as his former near neighbour Ian Paisley.

EPILOGUE

Magic Time

Ian Paisley had ended 2004 on a knife edge with the DUP coming within a whisker of agreeing to go into government with Sinn Féin. What some saw as Paisley's petty obstinacy in demanding photographic evidence of IRA decommissioning and 'sackcloth and ashes' penitence probably saved his party from political embarrassment. For, less than a week before Christmas, Ireland was shocked by news of the Northern Bank robbery, which was widely reported as the work of the IRA. Worse followed with the killing of Robert McCartney in January 2005 and media attacks on Sinn Féin over alleged money laundering and punishment beatings (analyses of all these important issues is provided in the Endnotes to Chapter 25). As a result, Sinn Féin was frozen out of meetings in Downing Street and the Dáil, and ostracized in America where George Bush declined to offer the traditional invitation to celebrate St Patrick's Day at the White House. At home, the Justice Minister Michael McDowell made further damaging allegations against Gerry Adams and Martin McGuinness, prompting headlines predicting that Sinn Féin was now in political meltdown. It could hardly have happened at a worse time as this was *An Céad*, the 100th anniversary of the founding of the party and the year when many commentators believed that Sinn Féin might infiltrate the political mainstream. With elections beckoning in the spring, opinion polls suggested that Sinn Féin's popularity in the Republic had dropped by 25 per cent and, although the party's standing remained solid in the North, it was possible that Gerry Adams might face a serious backlash from moderate voters. For his old nemesis Ian Paisley, who remained uncharacteristically quiet while everyone around him was berating Adams, this must have seemed like a magic time.

Election month coincided with the publication of this book in hardback and the long-awaited release of a new Morrison CD, *Magic Time*. The combined publicity focused attention on the album, attracting particular interest from reviewers keen to evaluate Morrison's artistic standing in the year of his sixtieth birthday. It had been 19 months since his last CD, the disappointing *What's Wrong With This Picture?* That work had been licensed to the legendary jazz label Blue Note, but its contents had proven unworthy of such an illustrious home. It was an album of light jazz lounge music, devoid of passion, half-heartedly executed and lacking in empathy or inspiration. There was scarce evidence of Morrison's songwriting skill and, coming at the end of a series of sometimes critically derided collaborations, it suggested an almost wilful nadir. Morrison ignored the brickbats, concentrating instead on the label's lack of promotional clout in the rock marketplace. In response, he relicensed his work to Polydor and presented them with a more marketable album. *Magic Time* proved a sprightly collection and arguably Morrison's best record for a decade. Decent musicianship had always been a hallmark of Morrison's recordings but much of his recent material had been executed with a deadening studio efficiency which merely highlighted the paucity of the songwriting. What *Magic Time* provided were five or six songs of sufficiently high calibre to remind listeners of the Morrison of old. His vocal phrasing sounded more beguiling, largely because the songs warranted an emotional response patently absence from *What's Wrong With This Picture?* Whether Morrison saw this new material as a significant advance on his previous efforts is doubtful, but its strengths were evident from a single listening.

The title track reiterated the familiar theme of neurotically looking back in search of something transcendent. With unexpected magnanimity, Morrison tells his critics that he does not mind if they label the song nostalgic, but 'nostalgia' is a word that scarcely does justice to the type of soul-searching that characterizes his music at its best. In common with songs like 'And It Stoned Me', 'Cleaning Windows', 'Coney Island', 'In The Days Before Rock 'n' Roll' and 'Take Me Back', 'Magic Time' is another attempt to capture a moment now past and almost lost to memory. The knowledge of its lingering, fleeting aspect creates a tension and poignancy that Morrison attempts to translate through vocal incantation. It is as if he believes that a sound, a verbal tic, or an unknown combination of words and music might somehow unlock this mystery. Of course, he has done this far more effectively on superior songs like 'Listen To The Lion', but even though the compositions on *Magic Time* are more orthodox, and far less challenging, there is at least some evidence that the old quest has not been entirely forgotten. Coincidentally, the lion symbol, last used on *Saint Dominic's Preview*, returns here in one of the stronger songs, 'The Lion This Time'. Like its unsurpassable predecessor, it is a mysterious composition with a nursery-rhyme quality, enhanced by a delicate classical string arrangement and Morrison singing in a suitably low register. It's worth noting that 'Gypsy In My Soul', complete with Morrison's trademark scat singing, also harks back in title to the *Saint Dominic's* era. Whether this is Morrison spiritually attempting to reconnect with his former self or simply an arbitrary repetition of former song titles is debatable. But there is little doubt that he had been looking back during the creation of *Magic Time*. 'Just Like Greta', that lost composition from the Linda Gail Lewis era, is revived and transformed into a powerful testament of solipsistic certainty. Its theme is reiterated in the album's fine opening track 'Stranded', a confused lamentation of modern times from which the narrator sounds frighteningly dislocated. The memory of a lost Indian summer, another allusion to a song from his collaboration with Linda Gail Lewis, is present in the impressive 'Celtic New Year', which simultaneously recalls his work with the Chieftains. Evidently no new Morrison album would be complete without at least one assault on his detractors, real or imagined. Earlier in his career, these acerbic asides were less evident. The atypical 'The Great Deception', included on 1973's *Hard Nose The Highway*, was an astringent attack on the Seventies rock world with a spiteful undertone, seemingly directed at his hipper contemporaries. 'Drumshanbo Hustle', another composition from that era, was even more explicit and remained locked in the vaults for 25 years. The same fate befell a series of infantile comic diatribes directed at Bert Berns during the Bang Records era, which the public did not hear until the early Nineties. All these compositions sounded strangely jarring, particularly when placed beside Morrison's Eighties' work whose music and lyrics concentrated largely on promoting healing and reconciliation with the past.

But from the Nineties onwards there is a detectable shift towards a need for personal retribution. Songs like 'Professional Jealousy', 'Why Must I Always Explain?', 'Big Time Operators', 'New Biography' and 'Goldfish Bowl' are caustic, self-righteous complaints about the plight of the artiste in a celebrity-fixated culture governed by media moguls, soulless corporations, gangsters, begrudgers and dirt diggers. Morrison justified these sometimes bilious broadcasts as the most effective way of communicating his disillusionment. He was correct, inasmuch as no critic or record company executive should dictate a songwriter's subject matter. If social protest, introspective navel gazing and bitter naked love songs are perfectly acceptable in the pop marketplace, why shouldn't personal attacks or petty complaints also be allowed?

Unfortunately, Morrison's sour remonstrations often irked commentators and fans who dismissed the lyrics as trivial or self-pitying. Despite his frequently voiced aversion to celebrity, it still seemed ungracious to complain so vociferously about a media and music industry whose major crime had been colluding in a process that ultimately helped transform Morrison from a singing window cleaner into a critically-acclaimed multi-millionaire. There is little evidence that Morrison has ever understood the listening public's lack of sympathy towards rich people complaining about fame. While it is easy to empathize with grief, unrequited love, pain, suffering and death, it is much harder to appreciate an internationally successful songwriter's complaints about professional jealousy or money lost in deals executed decades before. None of this would pose a problem if Morrison had been able to transform these acrid reproaches into songs of merit. A powerful melody, a brilliant arrangement, a dramatic construction, clever phrasing, a snatch of verbal wit or a passionate vocal might easily suspend the disbelief of the listener and allow an engagement with the song, irrespective of its subject matter. With the exception of 'Drumshanbo Hustle', in which Morrison's angry vocal and equally strong melody take us forcibly into the murkier areas of the Sixties music business and demand we empathize, most of his other compositions on the same theme are grounded in a wearying petulance. The tiresome complaints tend to alienate the listener because the compositions are not strong enough to transcend their limiting theme. Unlike Dylan, whose righteous anger from 'Masters Of War' through 'Like A Rolling Stone', 'Positively 4th Street', 'Idiot Wind' and beyond are never less than riveting, Morrison usually descends into a bathetic pique. He has seldom been able to transform wrath into art. The chasm between the spiritually uplifting 'She Gives Me Religion' and the prosaic irritation of 'Goldfish Bowl' seems irreconcilable in both point of view and songwriting quality. By contrast Dylan could cleverly fuse female apotheosis with religious imagery, as Morrison had done during the *Beautiful Vision* period, but also throw in a terrifying vision of hell-fire damnation, in which screaming souls are tortured for eternity. This was achieved in 'Precious Angel', a composition commercial enough to be issued as a single yet seldom even considered among Dylan's 100 best songs. It is a wonderful example of the way love, anger and salvation can be combined in a single song and how the listener is forced to fathom its inherent incongruities, echoing Dylan's troubled juggling of New Testament celebration with Old Testament retribution.

On *Magic Time*, Morrison faced these same old problems in a song whose title testified to an over-familiar siege mentality. 'They Sold Me Out' took personal disappointment and bitterness to supremely arrogant levels with the singer implicitly comparing his setbacks to the betrayal of Christ. This was extreme even by Morrison standards. Identifying the persecutors who sell out the narrator for a handful of shekels, Morrison points the finger at "my own people". Here, he draws comparison to the complaint he made to Donall Corvin in 1973, "Everything I tried to do in Belfast, they put the screws on it . . . That's just the way the people are brought up there". Of course the song is not limited to Belfast, but could be applied to his entire career. Despite its title, the composition ultimately escapes any singular auto-biographical interpretation. There is no simile to connect the sentiments directly to Morrison's plight and although most commentators will assume, probably correctly, that he is singing about his own situation, the lyrics can also be appreciated without this subtext. Indeed, if it was added to a production of *Jesus Christ Superstar*, the song would work well as a powerful and moving lamentation from the Saviour about the duplicity of his own people. More importantly, the words can be applied to any situation in which a betrayal of trust has occurred. By resisting any temptation to step outside the Biblical imagery and name his usual targets, Morrison succeeds in creating a far more interesting, poignant and ambiguous composition with an everyman appeal. The song's cynicism also provides a much-needed edge to the album and complements the wistful, self-satisfied solipsism evident elsewhere.

Although *Magic Time* contained some quality work it was compromised by several weaker compositions. The hubristic titled 'Keep Mediocrity At Bay' served largely to provide detractors with the acerbic punchline, 'if only'. 'Carry On Regardless', a singing list of *Carry On* films, provoked laughter from Morrison at the close of the track but did little to further his claim as a stand-up comedian. The 12-bar 'Evening Train' sounded like easy-going filler. Finally, a questionable selection of cover versions, presumably intended to add variety, merely emphasized the need for stronger original compositions.

Reviews of *Magic Time* were unerringly consistent for a latter-day Morrison album. The general consensus was three stars out of five, which roughly translated meant 'good, but not exceptional, let alone great'. Not that anybody was expecting a *great* album from Morrison anymore. It had been many years since that adjective had been applied to his work. Nevertheless, the CD provided considerable cheer to long-time Morrison listeners and suggested a stronger engagement on his part. Statistically, the CD's number 4 position in the UK album charts equalled Morrison's best ever showing, although the sales peaked in the first week of entry.

While *Magic Time* was awaiting release, Ian Paisley had been having fun on the campaign trail, charming elderly voters by reciting the old Orange ballad about Edward Carson's cat who 'sat upon a fender' and whenever the feline saw a rat, it cried out 'No Surrender!' Paisley could afford to be in good cheer. Only a few years before he had been dismissed by fellow unionists as a dinosaur but now he bestrode the streets of Northern Ireland like a political colossus. He looked healthier and more ebullient than ever. In a political world dominated by sex scandals, financial irregularities, spin-doctoring and U-turns, Paisley stood out for his granite consistency and unwillingness to bend his beliefs to popular opinion. There was something refreshing about his moral absolutism and seeming inability to employ the traditional ambiguities of political language. In an Ulster weary of false promises, Paisley was still the intransigent giant who offered his followers the security of a 'No Surrender' policy. He had always seemed a man out of time, but now his time had come.

The election results confirmed that the DUP was now the most powerful political party in Northern Ireland with more seats than all the other parties put together. In Banbridge, the deafening sound of lambeg drums accompanied the downfall of Paisley's old rival David Trimble who was vanquished from the political landscape. The Ulster Unionists had once boasted 10 parliamentary seats, but after election night they found themselves reduced to one. The magnitude of their defeat suggested that there was nowhere else to go for a party that had been fatally compromised in its dealings with the Republican machine.

Sinn Féin's progress reflected that of the DUP, confirming a polarization in Northern politics of Balkans proportions. It seemed that the dreadful publicity Sinn Féin had received after the Northern Bank robbery and the Robert McCartney killing had done nothing to stem their appeal to nationalist voters. There was, however, one great shock. In Derry's Foyle constituency, SDLP leader Mark Durcan upset the odds by defeating the leading Republican Mitchel McLaughlin. It was a remarkable result, not least because McLaughlin had already boasted of winning the seat on local television. On polling day, several SDLP workers had conceded defeat by lunchtime and some were visibly reduced to tears. Evidently they had not counted on late tactical voting by DUP supporters, which helped provide Durcan with a 6,000 majority. The Socialist Environmental Alliance candidate Éamonn McCann, who stood against Durcan and McLaughlin, was amazed by the outcome. "Sinn Féin was absolutely certain the seat had been won. Cars had horns blaring and there were victory celebrations on the night *before* the election." Gerry Adams gave the performance of a lifetime when the result was announced on RTÉ, insisting with shocked innocence that Sinn Féin had never dreamed of winning the great John Hume's former seat. Adams' fellow panellists were so taken aback by his conviction and mock indignation that they could barely muster a reply.

If Adams' rise to political godhead was to be enshrined, he required further concessions from the IRA. At 4pm on 28 July 2005, the Provisionals provided precisely that when they announced the end of their armed campaign and ordered their members to dump arms and "assist the development of purely political and democratic programmes through exclusively peaceful means." Signalling an end to the criminal activities that had blighted political progress, their statement added: "Volunteers must not engage in any other activities whatsoever." These words were widely welcomed even by the loyalist PUP, whose leader David Ervine said: "If this is real then it's seismic and significant beyond belief."

Gerry Adams sounded like a man with historical greatness at his fingertips. He even spoke like a Taoiseach as he announced: "Today's decision by the IRA to move into a new peaceful mode is historic and represents a courageous and confident initiative. It is a truly momentous and defining point in the search for a lasting peace with justice. I commend the commitment of those who have taken this decision and I appeal for unity and solidarity among all Irish Republicans on the island of Ireland and beyond, and for the struggle to be carried forward with new energy and enthusiasm. The IRA decision presents an unparalleled challenge and opportunity for every nationalist and Republican." Inevitably, he soon turned his attention to the man who, 41 years ago, had ignited his political consciousness by attempting to remove a tricolour flag from the Sinn Féin office in Divis Street. "I would like Ian Paisley to reflect on what has happened today . . . But this is not a day for the hard word. We have to give Ian Paisley time to absorb today. But, whatever happens, the days of second-class citizenship are over. We are moving forward . . . Let's talk, let's engage, let's exchange ideas." Challenging the DUP's commitment to the peace process, he added, "They represent what they say is new, confident Unionism. Well, let's see it. We are quite prepared to talk to them tomorrow morning."

The Big Man was in no mood to accept an olive branch so quickly and stated, rather ominously, that he would judge the IRA's bona fides "over the next few months and years". Never a man to play the diplomat, he could not resist attacking the IRA's rhetoric and barked, "We treat with contempt their attempt to glorify and justify their murder campaign." Other political leaders were uniformly optimistic. British PM Tony Blair described the statement as a "step of unparalleled magnitude" and concluded, "this may be the day when finally, after all the false dawns, peace replaced war". The Taoiseach Bertie Ahern was less equivocal and stated categorically, "The war is over, the IRA's armed campaign is over, paramilitarism is over and I believe that we can look to the future of peace and prosperity based on mutual trust and reconciliation and a final end to violence."

Adams was cautious enough to remind the world that not all Republicans would be happy with the outcome. "I think it will take weeks and longer for people to absorb what happened today. Some people may never come to terms with it. Maybe it's a step too far for some Republicans." Judging from the immediate reaction in the Falls and elsewhere, Adams was not far wrong. Although many welcomed the announcement, others recalled the pogroms of 1969 and feared that a still armed loyalist faction might take advantage of a defenceless IRA which, in turn, might provoke a reaction from newly-formed dissident groups outside the control of the Provisionals and immune to Adams' political persuasion. One man, who pointedly refused to give his name for fear of being shot, complained: "It's a total disgrace. We are handing over the whole show, and that shite across the road [the loyalists] still have theirs . . . I never thought I'd see the day." Another added: "A lot of good men who died would be turning in their graves, just like my stomach is turning over listening to this."

Two months later – an instant in Northern Ireland's snail-like time scheme – the IRA completed its final act of decommissioning under the watchful eye of General John de Chastelain and two churchmen from each side of the community. Paisley did not get his much prized photograph, but no one was complaining. For Sinn Féin, the speedy decommissioning must have come as blessed relief after their disastrous start to the year. Beyond the grand gestures and propagandist language lay the realization that the IRA had executed a near perfect PR coup and robbed the Unionists of their greatest excuse for never surrendering. In reality, the IRA's cache of arms had long been a liability rather than an asset, particularly after 9/11. It was difficult to imagine how this huge arsenal could ever have been used effectively against the security forces, short of a suicidal offensive, which largely explains why so much of it remained underground for so long.

Between the announcement of the IRA decommissioning and its final execution, Van Morrison reached his sixtieth birthday on 31 August.

There were radio tributes in Ulster and a two-page appreciation in the *Irish News*. Unusually for such a celebration, there was little attempt to disguise his imperfections. Words like 'cantankerousness', 'irritability' and 'unsociability' opened the *Irish News* piece and, as its reporter noted, "We seem to enjoy the monster we have made and it seems are keen to make and remake it over and over." Even while this was being written, the rock magazine *Q* had already decided to feature Morrison among their list of the '30 Worst Front Men' in popular music, an odd proposition given his past reputation as a performer. The accompanying caption said it all: "Even his fans concede he has the emollient personality of the Reverend Ian Paisley during the Pope's funeral." If Morrison's personality was unlikely to win popularity contests, there was nevertheless a feeling among some supporters that his negative traits were inextricably linked to his artistic strengths. In their tribute, the *Irish News*. called him an 'anti-hero'. One could go further and argue that his best work might have been neutered in some way had he been more accommodating towards managers, producers, journalists or music business executives. Many others would retort that his suspicion and intransigence have prevented him from reaching far greater heights, commercially and artistically. There is no answer to this question except to stress that Morrison has always been his own person, often to his detriment, but sometimes to his advantage. Bitter experiences of music business *realpolitik* have hardened his resolve and placed him in a powerful position, ensuring considerable control over the way his work is exploited. Although some detractors insist that he is "one of rock's most overrated artistes", his standing in popular music is most likely assured.

While the 60-year-old Morrison was entering the closing years of a lifetime in music, two political giants of the North were preparing for the likelihood of an uneasy union that would establish their ultimate place in the annals of Irish history. Gerry Adams, already a serial autobiographer, was now the leader of the largest nationalist party in Northern Ireland with a realistic chance of ultimately assuming power in the Republic. The removal of the IRA from the political equation means that Sinn Féin are now free to follow a democratic path that may yet lead to a coalition with Fianna Fáil and a further step towards the Republican dream of Irish unity. When the centenary of the Easter Rising occurs in 2016, it will be fascinating to see where Adams has ended up on the political landscape. In the meantime he faces the daunting challenge of working with Ian Paisley. For the Big Man, accommodating the hated Sinn Féin must be anathema, but a coalition of Sinn Féin and the DUP, with the appointment of Martin McGuinness as Paisley's deputy, appears the most likely outcome. After half a century in politics during which he has outlasted everybody, Paisley is now only a step away from taking office as First Minister. Given his turbulent history this achievement would be all the more remarkable. He may even fulfil the ambitions that frustrated his political idol Sir Edward Carson and finally secure a place in history as the greatest Orange hero of the last 100 years.

As 2005 closed, the prognosis for Van Morrison's career as a sexagenarian was healthier than expected. *Magic Time* was not a great album and sounded patently inferior to such Eighties predecessors as *Beautiful Vision* and *No Guru, No Method, No Teacher*, but it provided optimism for die-hard fans who still believed in Morrison's ability to write something substantial. Those other great Sixties survivors Bob Dylan and Neil Young had consistently confounded critics by magically reconnecting with the moment, latterly with albums that confronted encroaching old age, mortality and death in a powerful, understated fashion reinforced by musical arrangements that were at once familiar and strikingly effective. One of the strengths of Dylan's brilliant *Love And Theft* was its remarkable musical palette which referenced styles stretching back to the minstrel era without any sign of bland pastiche. Completely outside the strictures of contemporary rock music, it nevertheless sounded startlingly fresh and original. In its way it was as important as any record in the Dylan canon and an object lesson in artistic maturity. One of the frustrations of listening to Morrison's work over the past few years is the feeling that he is either unable or unwilling to reinvigorate his tired oeuvre with something approaching passion or musical invention. Like Dylan, Morrison has always been a student of pre-rock 'n' roll music with a wealth of influences at his command. It is all the more vexing therefore that his current output fails to utilize that knowledge into something more powerful or engaging. Some followers maintain that it is his stubborn refusal to enlist an outside producer which has prevented his work from escaping a suffocating sonic homogeneity. Certainly, the idea of a

Daniel Lanois or Jack Frost adding a Technicolor depth and vision to Morrison's compositions, as they did with Dylan's work, is a salivating proposition. Equally important though is Morrison's desire to stretch himself as a songwriter, ignoring the fear of intrusive personal interpretations of his work and surrendering himself to whatever muse sparks his imagination. Too few artistes working in the popular music medium have learned the wisdom of age in producing great work. In terms of escaping the deadening cycle of stylistic repetition Morrison, who successfully reinvented himself as a songwriter and performer in the Sixties, Seventies and Eighties, stands a better chance than many of his lesser contemporaries. The hope of something greater than *Magic Time* in terms of passion, songwriting skill, melodic invention and, crucially, that indefinable feel that has always characterized Morrison's finest work, seems a not unreasonable expectation. Indeed, it is a thrilling challenge that should add a welcome tension and drama to the final stage of his life.

Morrison has given no indication of any desire to retire from the stage or the recording studio. Although his album output has decreased marginally in recent years, the touring continues relentlessly. Like Dylan, Morrison appears to regard live performance as the most natural way of expressing his artistry, even though certain shows have sounded like futile exercises in communication. The die-hards who document his every appearance have had a lot to complain about of late, but there is always the thrill of the unexpected. His performances are not subservient to his studio work, but few would argue that the shows could be enlivened or transformed by an attendant album of undisputed depth and quality. Whether Morrison will ever produce an album to rival the best work from his glory days is the stuff of crystal ball speculation, but surely it is not beyond him to provide something radical and totally unexpected even at this late stage of his career. He may yet confound us all. Searching for the ultimately bizarre but brilliant collaboration, the *Sunday Times* columnist Liam Fay recently suggested with his tongue burning in his cheek: "A duet with Ian Paisley has never seemed more likely."

Glossary

An Phoblacht: Provisional IRA newspaper meaning 'The Republic'.

Anglo-Irish Agreement: 1985 document signed by the Irish and British governments in the search for a solution to the Troubles.

Ard Fheis: High Conference.

Armalite: A semi-automatic/automatic rifle favoured by the IRA.

Army Council: The ruling body of the Provisional IRA.

B-Specials: The most prominent armed wing of the Ulster Special Constabulary with an almost exclusively Protestant membership. The Specials were originally a vigilante group evolving from the Ulster Volunteer Force with a remit to combat the IRA.

Blanket: 'On the blanket' was a phrase used to describe the detainees who refused to wear prison uniform.

Bloody Friday: Named after the events of 21 July 1972 when IRA car bombs detonated in Belfast injuring 130 people, including an estimated 11 fatalities.

Bloody Sunday: Named after the events of 30 January 1972 when British soldiers of the First Parachute Regiment shot dead civil rights marchers in Derry. The fatalities eventually numbered 14.

Bogside: A Catholic ghetto of Derry.

Clonard: A nationalist section of the mid-Falls Road, West Belfast.

Craic: Fun, a laugh, often associated with a get-together.

Cumann na mBan: The women's wing of the IRA, originally formed as an auxiliary force to the Irish Volunteers in April 1914.

Cumann na nGaedheal: Political party precursor of Fine Gael representing the pro-Treaty wing of the original Sinn Féin.

Dáil Éireann: The Irish Parliament in Dublin.

DUP: Democratic Unionist Party, founded by Revd Ian Paisley and Desmond Boal in September 1971.

Falls/Falls Road: The predominantly Catholic area of West Belfast.

Fenian: A name used, with intended disrespect, by Protestants of Catholics. It is derived from the nineteenth-century Fenian Brotherhood, an organization in Britain and North America that actively fought British rule in Ireland.

Fianna Fáil: 'Warriors Of Destiny' or 'Soldiers Of Destiny'. Ireland's major political party founded by Éamon de Valera in 1926 as a breakaway group from the original Sinn Féin, following opposition to the Anglo-Irish Treaty of 1921.

Fianna Éireann: Nationalist youth movement founded by Countess Constance Markievicz and Bulmer Hobson in 1909. It became the youth wing of the Provisional IRA.

Fine Gael: Major Irish political party, founded in 1933 from the embers of Cumann na nGaedheal.

Gaeltacht: Irish-speaking area.

Garda: Garda Síochána. Police Guards force in the Republic of Ireland, whose officers are known as gardaí.

Good Friday Agreement: Political agreement (April 1998) reached by the parties involved in the peace process.

Government of Ireland Act: British legislation of 1920 which partitioned Ireland – North and South.

H-Blocks: The H-shaped cell blocks in the Maze Prison.

Home Rule: Demand for self-government and self-determination made by Irish nationalists before the 1916 Easter Rising.

INLA: Irish National Liberation Army. An offshoot armed group of Republicans from the Official IRA, founded in 1974.

Internment: Internment without trial was introduced by the Northern Ireland government on 9 August 1971.

IRA: Irish Republican Army. Armed group formed to fight the British after the proclamation of the Irish Republic in Easter 1916. At the end of 1969, there was a split in the ranks which led to the formation of the Provisional IRA (sometimes called PIRA but more usually referred to simply as the IRA, in acknowledgement of their connection with the original rebels of 1916). See also: Sinn Féin.

Long Kesh: Prison camp near Lisburn, Co. Armagh, where internees were held.

Loyalist: Hard-line Unionist.

Lundy: Abusive term for a weak-willed Unionist. Named after Lieutenant Colonel Robert Lundy, who intended to surrender Londonderry to King James II's troops in 1688. He was later forced to flee the city.

Maze: Alternative title for Long Kesh. The name was changed by the British during the mid-Seventies. Provisionals still tend to favour the name Long Kesh.

Nationalist: A supporter of the unification of Ireland's 32 counties.

NICRA: Northern Ireland Civil Rights Association. Established in January 1967 as part of the civil cights campaign.

Official IRA: Section of IRA led by Cathal Goulding after the 1969 split in the organization. After declaring a ceasefire in 1972, this Marxist-influenced wing largely disappeared from the political map.

Official Sinn Féin: In January 1970, Sinn Féin split into two groups: Provisional Sinn Féin and Official Sinn Féin. The former later took the name Sinn Féin while the Officials evolved into the Workers' Party.

Oglaigh na hÉireann: Irish Republican Army.

Orange: A sectarian Unionist or, more specifically, a member of the Orange Order. The name is derived from the Protestant William of Orange whose victory over the Catholic King James II is celebrated during the marching season in Northern Ireland amid a triumphalist display of ritual pageantry.

People's Democracy: Radical left-wing political group formed in October 1968.

Provisional IRA: see IRA.

Provisional Sinn Féin: see Sinn Féin.

PUP: Progressive Unionist Party. Formed in the Shankill in 1978 as the Independent Unionist Group, it re-emerged as PUP the following year. The party was often linked to the paramilitary Ulster Volunteer Force. One of PUP's leading lights is Morrison's fellow Orangefield alumnus, David Ervine.

Real IRA: Breakaway dissident Republican group opposed to the peace process, formed in October 1997. Popularly known as the Real IRA, although officially calling itself Oglaigh na hÉireann.

RTÉ: Radio Telifís Éireann, the television and radio network of the Irish Republic.

RUC: Royal Ulster Constabulary, the police force of Northern Ireland which, until recent years, boasted an almost exclusively Protestant membership.

Sandy Row: The heartland of hard-line Unionism in central Belfast.

Scaldy: Ulster slang. A 'scaldy' refers to the method of placing a recently born chicken in boiling water, after which its feathers would fall off.

SDLP: Social Democratic and Labour Party. Formed in Northern Ireland, 21 August 1970, with a predominant Catholic/nationalist support, the party pursued a unified Ireland through non-violence.

Shankill/Shankill Road: Unionist/Protestant-dominated area of Belfast and stronghold of loyalism.

Sinn Féin: Translated as 'Ourselves Alone', 'We Ourselves' or 'Ourselves'. Republican party founded by Arthur Griffith in 1905. See also: Official Sinn Féin.

Six Counties: The term favoured by Catholic nationalists for the counties comprising Northern Ireland. Protestant Unionists more usually refer to the same area as the Province.

Stickies: The Official IRA. They were nicknamed the Stickies because their Easter Lily commemoration badge was attached to the lapel by a gum adhesive, while the Provos used a pin.

Stormont: The seat of government in Northern Ireland, situated near Belfast. Its buildings include Stormont Castle and the Parliament Buildings. The term Stormont usually alludes to the Unionist government which held sway over Ulster in the 50-year period 1921–72.

Sunningdale: The Conference between the British and Irish governments held at Sunningdale, Berkshire, from 6–9 December 1973, which was intended to form a political framework of co-operation. The Executive was scuppered by a loyalist strike.

Taoiseach: Irish Prime Minister. Literally translated as 'Chief'.

Third Force: Vigilante organization sponsored by the DUP.

Thirty-Two Counties: The entire island of Ireland sans partition, and the ultimate Republican dream.

Tit for Tat: A favourite term for revenge killings by paramilitary organizations. Significantly, or not, the phrase was used frequently in Morrison's song 'Fair Play' from *Veedon Fleece*.

Twelfth: Twelfth of July. The key date in the Unionist marching season calendar celebrating William of Orange's victory at the 1690 Battle Of The Boyne.

Twenty-Six Counties: The Republic of Ireland aka the South.

UDA: Ulster Defence Association. Loyalist paramilitary wing, founded in September 1971.

UFF: Ulster Freedom Fighters. Protestant paramilitary group, formed in mid-1973.

UVF: Ulster Volunteer Force. Originally founded in 1912 as a military force in opposition to Home Rule, the name was later revived by loyalist paramilitaries in 1966.

Notes

Chapter One: Ulster Says No!

page 5: ". . . Belfast has, until relatively recently, seemed undervalued . . ." The point was aptly made by Ulster poet John Hewitt back in 1951, when Morrison was six years old. Hewitt felt that Northern poets still had to "endure a climate of antagonistic opinion and endeavour to establish a precarious foothold in a community, at worst self-righteous in its arrogant disavowal of the arts, at best ostentatiously indifferent to them" [John Hewitt, *Rann* 13: 1951]. It was in later years, particularly amid the Troubles, that Northern poets found a voice to rival their Southern counterparts. Along the way, the emergence of John Montague, Roy McFadden, Seamus Heaney, Michael Longley, Derek Mahon *et al* tilted the balance. Although it would be presumptuous, to say the least, to mention Morrison in the context of those poets, he can claim to have introduced Belfast place names to a mass culture via the medium of popular music.

page 7: ". . . in a Machiavellian attempt to colonize the island . . ." The process was outlined in Chapter Three of Machiavelli's *The Prince*: "When states are acquired in a province differing in language, in customs and in institutions, then difficulties arise: and to hold them one must be very fortunate and very assiduous. One of the best, most effective expedients would be for the conqueror to go to live there in person . . . The other and better expedient is to establish settlements in one or two places; these will, as it were, fetter the state to you. Settlements do not cost much, and the prince can found them and maintain them at little or no expense." For a fuller appreciation of this issue, the reader should consult the chapter 'Machiavelli in Ulster' in Conor Cruise O'Brien, *States Of Ireland*, London, Hutchinson: 1972. Therein, O'Brien makes the revealing observation: "Curiously, the conquerors carried Machiavelli's advice both too far and not far enough. If the whole island had been settled as North-Eastern Ulster was settled, there would be no 'religious' or native-and-settler problem today. Alternatively, if Eastern Ulster had been settled, and native proprietors elsewhere left undisturbed, this might conceivably have had the effects which Machiavelli predicts. But in fact the result of the long and tortuous seventeenth-century conflicts was that real settlement, of farmers working the land, took root in Ulster only, while in the rest of the country, the native proprietors were dislodged and replaced by English proprietors, but the land continued to be worked by the natives. Thus, those who were injured, although poor and often scattered, were not a 'tiny minority'. In the event the policy of the British rulers of Ireland failed by Machiavelli's basic test, since the injuries inflicted by the various princes proved not to be 'of such a kind that there is no fear of revenge'."

page 8: "Under the leadership of Sir Edward Carson . . ." Born in Dublin in 1854, Carson became a Conservative Minister and was appointed Solicitor General for Ireland, and later England. He successfully defended the Marquess of Queensbury in his celebrated libel defence against Oscar Wilde which concluded with the poet's incarceration for gross indecency. In 1910 Carson replaced Walter Long as head of the Ulster Unionist Council and became the ultimate Orange hero. Yet, he was described in one book as "a man who did not care for the Northern Orangemen . . . their speeches, he said, reminded him of 'the unrolling of a mummy – all old bones and rotten rags'." (See Paul Arthur, *Government And Politics Of Northern Ireland*, London, Longman, 1980;1984, page 14; which, in turn, cites Brian Inglis, *Roger Casement*, London, Hodder & Stoughton: 1973, page 232.) Arthur makes the provocative proposition that Carson "was decidedly not an Ulster Unionist". But he was certainly a passionate supporter of the Union. Carson was drawn to Ulster by James Craig, a stockbroker and Presbyterian MP for East Down who would later become the first Prime Minister of Northern Ireland. Craig was convinced that Carson's leadership would assist the Unionist cause. Carson was initially cautious, informing Craig in 1911, "I am not for a mere game of bluff, and unless men are prepared to make great sacrifices which they clearly understand, the talk of resistance is no use." Carson received the public mandate he required when a crowd of over 50,000 turned out to cheer him. He told his supporters, "I know the responsibility you are putting on me today; in your presence I cheerfully accept it, grave as it is, and I now enter into a compact with you . . . we will yet defeat the most nefarious conspiracy that has ever been hatched against a free people." Carson made the point that "If Ulster succeeds Home Rule is dead; Home Rule is impossible for Ireland without Belfast." In order to defeat the Home Rule nationalists Carson was ultimately forced to accept a six-county Northern Ireland. It might have been worse. As late as 1919, Lloyd George's Cabinet had drawn up the Partition Act, intending to exclude the whole of nine-county Ulster. It was largely due to James Craig's persuasion, backed by Carson, that the Unionists pushed through the six-county bloc. The Anglo-Irish Treaty of 1921 left Carson thoroughly disillusioned with British politics. He saw the break-up of the Union as a defining moment. Despite his successes in resisting the nationalists, he had been unable to save the Union and felt let down by his contemporaries. His bitterness poured out in an extraordinarily vitriolic speech before the House of Lords in December 1921: "I did not know, as I know now, that I was a mere puppet in a political game. I was in earnest, I was not playing politics. I believed all this. I thought of the last 30 years, during which I was fighting with others whose friendship and comradeship I hope I will lose from tonight, because I do not value any friendship that is not founded upon confidence and trust. I was in earnest. What a fool I was! I was only a puppet, and so was Ulster, and so was Ireland, in the political game that was to get the Conservative Party into power."

page 8: "Some 471,414 citizens signed the Ulster Solemn League & Covenant . . ." On the eve of the ceremony, there was a large gathering in the Ulster Hall. Joining Carson on the platform was Reverend William McKean, a former moderator of the General Assembly of the Presbyterian Church in Ireland, whose words summed up the religious siege mentality of the congregation: "The Irish question is at bottom a war against Protestantism; it is an attempt to establish a Roman Catholic ascendancy in Ireland, to begin the disintegration of the Empire by securing a second parliament in Dublin."

page 8: "There are things stronger than parliamentary majorities . . ." Conservative leader Andrew Bonar Law, addressing a Unionist meeting at Blenheim Palace in 1913.

page 8: "Ireland cannot shift her frontiers . . ." Griffith's words were echoed by other nationalists, most notably Pádraig Pearse, who admonished: "The man who, in the name of Ireland, accepts a final settlement anything less by one fraction of one iota than separation from England . . . is guilty of so immense an infidelity, so immense a crime against the Irish nation . . . that it were better for that man that he had not been born."

page 9: "Belfast is bad enough as it is . . ." James Connolly, *Forward*: 21 March 1914. The previous week, Connolly had written in the *Irish Worker*: "Let us remember that the Orange aristocracy now fighting for its supremacy in Ireland has at all times been based upon a denial of the common human rights of the Irish people; that the Orange Order was founded not to safeguard religious freedom, but to deny religious freedom, and that it raised this religious question not for the sake of any religion, but in order to use religious zeal in the interests of oppressive property rights of rackrenting landlords and sweated capitalists. That the Irish people might be kept under and robbed whilst so sundered and divided, the Orange aristocracy went down to the lowest depths and out of the lowest pits of hell brought up the abominations of sectarian feuds to stir the passions of the ignorant mob. No crime was too brutal or cowardly; no lie too base; no slander too ghastly as long as they served to keep the democracy asunder."

page 9: "The Home Rule Bill entered the Statute Book on 15 September 1914 . . ." This represented both a defeat for Unionism and an empty victory for Redmond, who was about to be overtaken by events and worsening health. The British government's decision to attach an Amendment Bill to the Home Rule Bill in order to solve the 'Ulster problem' became a key issue. If the Unionists could not retain direct rule from Westminster, they were willing to accept Home Rule within an excluded Ulster as a preference to the dreaded alternative – Home Rule from Dublin. Redmond's followers supported Britain in the Great War in the hope that they would be given Home Rule for the entire island. This was to prove a political miscalculation and a personal tragedy for Redmond. If the War had been short, as many anticipated, then Redmond's commitment of Irish Volunteers to the cause would have worked to his advantage, strengthening the nationalist argument – morally and politically – in favour of Home Rule for the entire island or, alternatively, limiting the exclusion zone to a maximum four counties. The nationalist aspirations towards Home Rule were ultimately altered by the 1916 Easter Rising into a battle for a wholly independent Republic. It was widely accepted among hard-core nationalists that Britain would never grant Ireland freedom unless forced to by violent action. The 'Anglo-Irish War' that followed demonstrated the success of this militant philosophy.

page 10: "Sinn Féiners have seized the Post Office . . ." Although the Rising has always been linked with Sinn Féin, the party was not involved in any military activity. At this point, the political programme of independence for Ireland that Sinn Féin was pursuing did not necessarily demand a total break with the British Empire. Griffith was supposedly considering the Austria-Hungary monarchy as a possible model for Anglo-Irish relations. Crucially, Sinn Féin always held the conviction that elected Irish representatives should not take their seats in the House of Commons but rather establish an Irish government in which to serve. Griffith was never convinced by Redmond's pursuit of Home Rule, the fruits of which would have been a subsidiary parliament in Dublin whose powers were severely limited. As Griffith noted contemptuously: "If this is liberty, the lexicographers have deceived us."

page 10: ". . . signatories of the Republican proclamation . . ." The seven signatories comprised: Pádraig Pearse, Thomas J. Clarke, James Connolly, Thomas MacDonagh, Seán MacDiarmada, Éamonn Ceannt and Joseph Plunkett.

page 10: "Partition of a six-county Ulster . . ." Rhetoric against Partition continued to be passionately voiced after 1920. Éamon de Valera, who had once cried "Ulster cut from Ireland would leave her without her head – her heart" espoused the same arguments throughout his long political career. During speeches in Sligo and Kilkenny in June 1937, he dismissed the partitioned Ulster as "an imitation country" and Unionist concerns about unification as mere "hallucinations". Many political commentators followed his lead. Writing in 1946, David O'Neill pronounced: "What is this 'Partition' which draws all parties in free Ireland into a unity against it, which transcends all party-differences and binds into one every section of the Irish people in four-fifths of Ireland? Partition is the dismemberment of one of the most ancient nations in Europe. For all the years of recorded history and for many a century before history was written, Ireland was one nation, with indisputable boundaries set in the sea. Before the Christian era, it recognized itself as a unit; a High King of Ireland acknowledged by lesser kingdoms was the symbol of that unity. This unity survived all the changes that 2,000 years of history can bring. It was not broken by invasion. It was not broken by internal revolt. Under it, Ireland passed from paganism to Christianity, from a pastoral civilization to one in which she led Europe in many of the arts. Under it, Ireland as a single nation had her great victories and her great defeats. In the days of her power she sent armies overseas, in the days of her subjugation her sons could arm only in secret, but in both periods there was only one meaning to 'Ireland' – that is the whole island" [David O'Neill, *The Partition of Ireland – How And Why It Was Accomplished*, Dublin, M.H. Gill & Son: 1949].

In the public's mind de Valera remained the embodiment of opposition to Partition. The truth was more complex. It was only 50 years after Partition, when parliamentary papers were made available for public inspection, that a more complete understanding of de Valera's position could be appreciated. There is little doubt among modern historians that de Valera was moving towards an acceptance of Partition as an inevitable temporary measure and recognized that the outcome of the Treaty negotiations would fall short of the 32-county ideal. In the private sessions of Dáil Éireann he concluded that he would be "in favour of giving each county power to vote itself out of the Republic if it so wished". Both there and in his Document No. 2, he revealed a pragmatic approach to the Ulster question. Pertinently, the leaked, unamended Document No. 2 included *all* the Ulster clauses contained in the Treaty. At the time, the media and public were aware only of the amended version of Document No. 2 with the contentious Ulster clauses deleted. In public debate, de Valera never hinted at his earlier compromises on the Partition question and always maintained the moral highground. However, he was quick to conclude that the Boundary Commission attached to the Treaty was a sham designed to cajole the signatories and would do nothing to reverse the perfidious Partition of Ireland.

page 11: "Under immense pressure from Lloyd George . . ." The Oath was actually a far more contentious issue to the Treatyites than Partition. In the end, the Irish delegation accepted an Oath of 'Fidelity' to the Crown and an Oath of 'Allegiance' to the Irish Free State. This compromise was not enough to prevent civil war.

page 11: "I may have signed my actual death-warrant . . ." These words, occasionally misquoted, were used in conversation with Lord Birkenhead. I have followed the ever reliable Tim Pat Coogan (see *Michael Collins: A Biography*. London, Hutchinson: 1990; London, Arrow: 1991).

page 11: "Anti-Treatyites, led by Éamon de Valera . . ." De Valera had been the last of the Irish Volunteer commanders to surrender after the 1916 Rising. Sentenced to death, he was later reprieved and assumed the presidency of Sinn Féin and the Irish Volunteers from 1917. Imprisoned the following year, he escaped and became a leading figure in the Anglo-Irish War of 1919–21. Conspicuously absent from the Treaty negotiations, he later sided with the "irreconcilables" and voted against the London agreement at a Cabinet meeting in Dublin only days before the Treaty was signed. The Irish Civil War that followed ended with imprisonment for de Valera, who escaped a soldier's death for the second time in six years. A master strategist, he rose from the political wilderness and, in 1926, announced that he was forming a new party: Fianna Fáil. Within six years, the party won a narrow victory in the 1932 General Election, with an increased majority the following year. Meanwhile, de Valera was appointed President of the United Nations, and later of its Assembly. De Valera would dominate Irish politics for over half a century, serving as Taoiseach for a total of 21 years and as President for a further 14 years. Fulfilling many of the dreams of 1921, he hastened the break with imperialist Britain and set about establishing a genuine Republic. By 1937, the Oath of Fidelity to the King had been removed from the Constitution, the role of Governor General rendered irrelevant, and the draconian Land Annuities paid to the British Exchequer suspended. Saorstát Éireann (the Irish Free State) had also passed away and the country was renamed Éire. The new Constitution claimed sovereignty over the entire island, including the whole of Ulster, in what was a highly symbolic and platonic realization of the ultimate Republican goal. De Valera's essential Irishness was demonstrated in his constant championing of the Gaelicization process and his conviction that the language revival was an even more important issue than Partition. He was such a complex person and politican that it is easy to misinterpret many of his pronouncements, couched as they often were in symbolism, allegory and myth. His idyll of a rural utopia, memorably described in his famous 1943 St Patrick's Day broadcast, was later ridiculed by cultural commentators but made political sense in its time and proved an effective propagandist address directed towards an impressionable American audience as well as ordinary Irish citizens. In perhaps his finest political coup, he secured the return of the Irish ports retained by Britain under the terms of the 1921 Treaty. This ensured that Éire remained neutral for the duration of the Second World War and fulfilled the Taoiseach's promise that "small states must not become the puppets of the larger powers". As a statesman, de Valera secured his greatest rhetorical victory in his 'radio reply' to Winston Churchill. The British Prime Minister was severely critical of Ireland's neutrality and accused the Taoiseach of frolicking with the Germans and Japanese and, in a remarkable display of imperialist brinkmanship, suggested that it would have been quite acceptable to violate Éire's neutrality with force. Evidently Churchill had no sympathy with the theory that Irish neutrality may have been a political advantage, since the protection of Éire might have stretched the Allies' resources too far. In replying to Churchill, de Valera resisted any temptation towards aggression, instead preferring restraint and cunning magnanimity. "I know the kind of answer I am expected to make," he began, before conjuring another myth and projecting himself as the living embodiment of Erin. With cordial humility he said of Churchill: "Could he not find in his heart the generosity to acknowledge that there is a small nation that stood alone, not for one year or two, but for several hundred years against aggression: that endured spoilations, famines, massacres in endless succession; that was clubbed many times into insensibility, but that each time, on returning consciousness, took up the fight anew; a small nation that could never be got to accept defeat and has never surrendered her soul." The public responded to this speech in the same manner as if Ireland had beaten England in a football match. De Valera never quite managed to pull off anything as spectacular during his later years in office. He was frequently criticized for his economic policies and was held largely responsible for the mass haemorrhage of emigration in the 1950s. Many critics felt his intransigence had perpetuated the Irish Civil War that had crippled the country during the Twenties, and believed that his passionate opposition to Partition was, in reality, subservient to his political ambition. His major political and cultural ideals – the ending of Partition and the restoration of the Irish language – were not achieved. The extent to which he believed these to be realizable and the degree of myth involved remain matters for further debate. What cannot be denied is de Valera's astounding longevity as a political leader and chief arbiter of Ireland's cultural and moral identity. A shrewd politician by any standards, Dev combined the cold logic of a mathematician with the idyllic dreams of a romantic poet to create an enduring version of Ireland in his own image.

page 11: "For loyalists . . ." Alvin Jackson, 'Irish Unionism, 1905–21', included in *Nationalism And Unionism Conflict In Ireland, 1885–1921*, ed. Peter Collins, The Institute of Irish Studies, Queen's University of Belfast: 1994.

page 12: "In the year of George Morrison's birth there were 97 reported cases of murder . . ." Source: *Belfast City Commission*, 1922.

page 12: "When Orangemen and Catholics . . ." J.J. Kelly, 'A Journalist's Diary', published in *Capuchin Annual*, Dublin: 1944.

page 13: "Catholic and Orangemen united . . ."*Daily Worker*: 8 October 1932.

page 13: ". . . used as a cloak by the communist Sinn Féin . . ." *Belfast Newsletter*: 15 October 1932.

page 14: "I am an Orangeman first . . ." Lord Craigavon, Prime Minister of Northern Ireland, speaking in Stormont, 1934. Fully quoted in *The Troubles*, edited by Taylor Downing, London, Thames Television/Macdonald Futura: 1980. Craigavon's words clearly carried weight, as evidenced by the events of summer 1935. However, Craigavon could justifiably refer to similar sectarian statements from de Valera, who had asserted, "we are a Catholic nation," and reflected that ideal in the 1937 Constitution's reference to the "special position of the Catholic Church". In aligning Church and State in this manner, de Valera could argue that he was necessarily expressing the wishes of the nation. In the parliamentary debates in Dáil Éireann, he pointed out: "There are 93 per cent of the people in this part of Ireland and 75 per cent of the people of Ireland as a whole who belong to the Catholic Church, who believe in its teachings and whose whole philosophy of life is the philosophy that comes from its teachings." He added, "If we are going to have a democratic State . . . it is clear their whole philosophy of life is going to affect that, and that has to be borne in mind and the recognition of it is important."

page 14: "I recommend those people who are loyalists . . ." Basil Brooke, quoted in *Londonderry Sentinel*: March 1934. Brooke added, "If you don't act properly now, before we know where we are, we will find ourselves in the minority instead of the majority." As for Catholics in his employ, he stressed, "I have not one about the place."

page 14: "Even in racialist South Africa . . ." Paul Foot, *Ireland: Why Britain Must Get Out*, London, Chatto & Windus: 1989.

page 15: "I have one prayer for this young man . . ." W.P. Nicolson, *Tornado Of The Pulpit*, Belfast Martyrs' Memorial Publications: 1982.

page 17: "It was a real leather holster . . ." Gil Irvine, interviewed by the author. Belfast: 18 September 1994.

page 17: "We'd get up to all sorts of adventures . . ." ibid.

page 18: "Van could have been a good sportsman . . ." ibid.

page 18: "Most of us went to the hall . . ." ibid.

page 18: "There was Sunday School . . ." ibid.

page 20: "My mother [Alice Stitt] used to come up . . ." Violet Morrison taped interview. Belfast: 1969.

page 20: Leadbelly. Real name: Huddie Ledbetter, also known as Lead Belly. Morrison later described Leadbelly as "my guru". He also recalled some other less well known musical influences: "The first person I ever saw perform was Elton Hayes. He was singing 'Mr Froggy' and then I never saw him again. He was in the *Robin Hood* film – and he sang in that . . . Then there was Rory McEwan and he really made me take notice. My father had the records but then here was this guy on the TV singing the Leadbelly songs and what they called 'topical calypsos'."

page 20: "My father took me . . ." Van Morrison, interviewed by David Wild. *Rolling Stone*: 9 August 1990.

page 20: "It was a natural thing . . ." Van Morrison, interviewed by Edna Gundersen. *USA Today*: 12 June 1997.

page 20: "The father was a quiet, hard-working man . . ." Irvine/Rogan. Belfast: 18 September 1994.

page 21: "The mother was always a trouper . . ." ibid.

page 21: "My mother used to play bagpipes . . ." Transcribed late October 1973 interview with Van Morrison, from the surviving papers of Donall Corvin.

page 21: ". . . a rousing rendition of Leadbelly's 'Goodnight Irene' . . ." Writer Pete Frame, in conversation with the author, offered a revealing footnote: "The song had been plucked from obscurity and turned into a singalong favourite by the Weavers, who transformed it into a million seller in 1950. The Morrison household would also no doubt have sung 'So Long It's Been Good To See You' – a Woody Guthrie song, which the Weavers also popularized."

page 24: "He was lucky he didn't get typhoid . . ." Van Morrison, interviewed by John Kelly. *Irish Times*: 11 April 1998.

page 24: "The line-up was completed . . ." Gil Irvine notes: "A John McLean lived in the street and played bass guitar, but he never played in the skiffle group."

page 24: "There used to be the B-picture . . ." ibid.

Chapter Two: Orangefield

page 25: "The development of the Orangefield school site . . ." *Belfast Newsletter*: 2 September 1957.

page 26: "He was an unusual man . . ." David Hammond, interviewed by the author. Belfast: 21 May 2001.

page 26: "I think the concept was . . ." ibid.

page 27: "It was all based on classics like *Peter And The Wolf* . . ." Irvine/Rogan. Belfast: 18 September 1994.

page 27: "The way they taught music was enough to put you off . . ." Eric Bell, interviewed by the author. London: 5 August 1994.

page 28: "Nobody is in entire agreement about the precise evolution of the ensemble . . ." Weighing up the various comments and recollections, the order seems to be Javelins, Deanie Sands & The Javelins, Thunderbolts, card game names and, finally, the Monarchs/International Monarchs. Author Steve Turner, while admitting that his chronology was conjectural, placed the 'card game names' first, but this was based on interpreting information provided by Roy Kane. Morrison later contested this order of events. Since Kane (in an interview with this author) pointed out that he was in the Jokers (card names) and the Thunderbolts, but *previously* joined Deanie Sands & The Javelins *after* McAllen and Jones and *before* Morrison, it seems that the above order is the most likely. Morrison mentions membership of all of the above groups (although in one interview he refers to the Thunderbolts erroneously as the Thunderbirds), while the others agree that he joined whichever was the first aggregation after McAllen, Jones and Kane. Roy Kane guessed Morrison had arrived just after Deanie Sands & The Javelins had parted, but Jones, McAllen and Morrison all disagree. In a rare interview published in October 1966, Kane claimed that the Thunderbolts preceded 'Die Sieben Monarchs', but no other groups are mentioned. The arrival of Wesley Black (Blackie) requires a similarly subtle interpretation. McAllen and Kane claim Blackie was definitely part of the Thunderbolts. Indeed, McAllen reckons he was there even earlier. It may be that Black goes back much further to the Deanie Sands days, flitting in and out of the group depending upon the availability of a piano.

page 28: "They were only cheap . . ." Billy McAllen, interviewed by the author. Belfast: 30 October 1994.

page 28: "I'd known Evelyn for years . . ." Billy Harrison, interviewed by the author. Bangor, Co. Down: 18 August 1994.

page 29: "I didn't even know where Evelyn came from . . ." Roy Kane, interviewed by the author. Belfast: 27 October 1994.

page 29: "It was a plastic drumkit . . ." ibid.

page 29: ". . . the building of character you will obtain . . ." Mayor's speech reported in *Belfast Newsletter*: 5 May 1958.

page 29: "I think I did have delusions . . ." Van Morrison, interviewed by Chris Welch. *Melody Maker:* 3 February 1979.

page 29: "A lot of people didn't understand Van . . ." George Jones, interviewed by the author. Holywood, Co. Down: 6 March 1982.

page 30: "Preternaturally shy . . ." information gleaned from author's conversation with Nancy McCarter. Belfast: 14 January 1995.

page 30: "He was very huffy . . ." McAllen/Rogan. Belfast: 30 October 1994.

page 30: "They gave him everything . . ." ibid.

page 30: "I'd have guests at home . . ." Violet Morrison, taped interview. Belfast: 1969.

page 31: "We mostly went to mental hospitals . . ." Kane/Rogan. Belfast: 27 October 1994.

page 31: "The reason we were an instrumental group . . ." McAllen/Rogan. Belfast: 30 October 1994.

page 32: "It was Mrs Jones who really kept us all together . . ." McAllen/Rogan. Belfast: 30 October 1994.

page 32: "The school was enormously dynamic . . ." Hammond/Rogan. Belfast: 21 May 2001.

page 33: "This guy was a beatnik and bohemian to us . . ." Eric Bell/Rogan. London: 5 August 1994. In addition to his teaching, Hammond was already establishing himself as a folklorist and later became a BBC producer. During the Fifties he produced *As I Roved Out*, an important series centred on the Irish music revival. It included a recording of Frank McPeake's 'Will Ye Go Lassie Go', which was the probable inspiration for Morrison's version retitled 'Purple Heather'. Later, after his spell at Orangefield, Hammond produced the film *The Boho Singers*, about musicians, dancers and singers in Fermanagh. Hammond also produced various recordings and was a featured singer on his own albums including *I Am The Wee Falorie Man, Belfast Street Songs, The Singer's House, Irish Songs Of Freedom* and *Songs Of Belfast*.

page 33: "David Hammond was a big influence on him . . ." Irvine/Rogan. Belfast: 18 September 1994.

page 33: "It was about a bird . . ." Morrison/Kelly, op cit.

page 33: "I don't think they knew . . ." ibid.

page 34: "I don't think Orangefield engaged him . . ." Hammond/Rogan. Belfast: 21 May 2001.

page 34: "In the divided community here . . ." ibid.

page 35: "I didn't study poetry . . ." Van Morrison, interviewed by Victoria Clarke. *Irish Post:* 5 October 1991.

page 35: "It was *Orange*field . . ." Eric Bell/Rogan. London: 5 August 1994.

page 35: "If you live in a divided society, you're lulled by it . . ." Hammond/Rogan. Belfast: 21 May 2001.

page 36: ". . . an uncouth mixture of ignorance . . ." Dervla Murphy, *A Place Apart*, London, John Murray: 1978; Penguin: 1979. The notion of Northern Ireland as "a place apart" was keenly felt by citizens of the Republic. Wexford writer and novelist John Banville, who was born in the same year as Van Morrison, admits: "No-one of my acquaintance actually cared about Northern Ireland, or even knew about it. It was another country."

page 36: "They had what they call juveniles . . ." Irvine/Rogan. Belfast: 18 September 1994.

page 36: "When I was growing up in Belfast . . ." Morrison/Corvin, op cit.

page 36: "We'd go and collect wood for bonfires . . ." Irvine/Rogan. Belfast: 18 September 1994.

page 36: "The whole of our lives . . ." Brian Keenan, interviewed by Joe Oliver. *Sunday People*: 18 July 1999.

page 37: "The atmosphere moved swiftly . . ." ibid.

page 37: "It was East Belfast . . ." Billy Harrison, interviewed by the author. Bangor, Co. Down: 21 August 1994.

page 37: "All my uncles were in the Orange lodge . . ." Eric Bell/Rogan: London: 5 August 1994.

page 37: "They did that further down the Beersbridge Road . . ." Irvine/Rogan. Belfast: 18 September 1994.

page 38: "There were only a few Catholics in the street . . ." Nancy McCarter, interviewed by the author. Belfast: 14 January 1995.

page 38: "We got on very well . . ." Irvine/Rogan. Belfast: 18 September 1994.

page 38: "I lived in Hyndford Street. I know what it was like . . ." Gwen Carson (McIlroy), interviewed by the author. Fife: 28 August 1993. Interestingly, Gwen Carson's harsh appraisal was echoed in the unwittingly patronizing post-resignation speech of Prime Minister Terence O'Neill: "The basic fear of the Protestants in Northern Ireland is that they will be outbred by the Roman Catholics. It is as simple as that. It is frightfully hard to explain to a Protestant that if you give Roman Catholics a good job and a good house they will live like Protestants, because they will see neighbours with cars and television sets. They will refuse to have 18 children, but if the Roman Catholic is jobless and lives in a most ghastly hovel, he will rear 18 children on national assistance. It is impossible to explain this to a militant Protestant because he is so keen to deny civil rights to his Roman Catholic neighbours. He cannot understand, in fact, that if you treat Roman Catholics with due consideration and kindness they will live like Protestants in spite of the authoritative nature of their church."

page 38: "I brought him up to think for himself . . ." Violet Morrison. Belfast: 1969.

page 38: ". . . was never shoved down my throat . . ." Morrison/Gundersen, op cit.

page 39: ". . . indulged in doorstep evangelism . . ." See Steve Turner, *It's Too Late To Stop Now*. London, Bloomsbury: 1993. When challenged on whether Violet Morrison conducted "doorstep evangelism", Turner told me: "I checked back again with people in Belfast who belonged to the Jehovah's Witnesses and they said she did. I have a letter back from them saying, 'Yes she did.' That was from someone in the Jehovah's Witnesses. This was my original source and it's now confirmed in writing."

page 39: "If my mother . . .", Van Morrison, interviewed by Hugo Cassavetti. *Télérama*: 2 April 1997.

page 39: "Protestantism takes in everything . . ." Sam Smyth, interviewed by the author. Dublin: July/August 1993. Additional information from author's later interviews on 17 October 1993 and 19 January 2003.

page 39: "If I didn't have my bike I'd have to do a detour . . ." Eric Bell/Rogan: London: 5 August 1994.

page 39: "I saw so many . . ." Morrison/Cassavetti, op cit. "I wasn't even aware . . ." Van Morrison, interviewed by John Grissim Jr. *Rolling Stone*: 22 June 1972.

page 40: "Catholics all went to schools named after saints . . ." Gerry O'Hare, interviewed by the author. Dublin: 12 February 2004.

page 40: "My local fleapit was the Winkie in Woodstock Road . . ." Eric Bell/Rogan: London: 5 August 1994.

page 40 "Morrison never accepted this description . . ." Morrison has made the case for his ordinariness in legal correspondence and personal representation over the years. Further details are confidential.

Chapter Three: The Monarchs

page 42: "They were OK . . ." Eric Wrixon, interviewed by the author. Belfast: 21 June 1994.

page 42: "I can't ever remember playing in the South . . ." Kane/Rogan. Belfast: 27 October 1994.

page 42: "A lot of people thought he was simply mad . . ." Irvine/Rogan. Belfast: 18 September 1994.

page 42: "We used to buy this very cheap wine called Mundie's . . ." Eric Bell/Rogan: London: 5 August 1994.

page 43: "George Jones didn't like drinking . . ." McAllen/Rogan. Belfast: 30 October 1994.

page 43: ". . . the wee bit of controversy . . ." Kane/Rogan. Belfast: 27 October 1994.

page 43: ". . . a lot of us weren't that fussy about having him . . ." ibid.

page 43: "Maybe he needed that to loosen up . . ." ibid.

page 44: "I would honestly say that Geordie Sproule . . ." Wrixon/Rogan. Belfast: 21 June 1994.

page 44: "We'd go out, sing, have a nosh-up and a fight . . ." Geordie Sproule, interviewed by the author. Belfast: 29 October 1994.

page 45: "I took on two of the worst jobs you could do . . ." ibid.

page 45: "We were singing blues in the Fifties . . ." ibid.

page 45: "We went down a bomb . . ." ibid.

page 45: "It was then that I met the wee man . . ." ibid.

page 46: "Nobody knew it at the time . . ." ibid.

page 46: "We used to have a race to the next town . . ." ibid.

page 47: "The music was so earthy, it depressed me . . ." Eric Bell/Rogan. London: 5 August 1994.

page 47: "I learned more in those eight months than at any time in my life . . ." ibid.

page 48: "He couldn't do the top windows, so I did those . . ." Sproule/Rogan. Belfast: 29 October 1994.

page 48: "I set it up . . ." ibid.

page 48: "I'd had a late night . . ." ibid.

page 48: "There was always a bottle of hooch in the saxophone case . . ." ibid.

page 49: "That was the hard man look . . ." ibid.

page 49: "Geordie was a character . . ." Rod Demick, interviewed by the author. London: 5 October 1994.

page 49: "Me and Van were the ugly ones . . ." Sproule/Rogan. Belfast: 29 October 1994.

page 49: "I didn't trust enough . . ." ibid.

page 50: "Oh, a nasty piece of work . . ." ibid.

page 50: "The Olympics were a semi-pro band . . ." The Olympics evolved from the Cyclones with an original line-up of Jim Armstrong (lead guitar), Desi McBride (rhythm guitar), Harry Baird (bass) and Billy Roberts (drums). During the early Sixties, Jim Armstrong quit for the security of a spot in the Melotones, the resident band at Romano's ballroom. He had already left by the time of Morrison's temporary appointment in the Olympics, but would work with him later in Them. After an objection from Derry showband the Olympic All Stars, the Olympic Showband changed their name to the Regency Showband and played regularly on the Northern Ireland circuit until the end of the Sixties. Personnel fluctuated over the years, along with the name change, but some of the key players included Harry Baird (bass), Stuart Smith (drums), Jim Green (rhythm guitar), Desi McBride (lead guitar), Alfie Walsh (vocals), Al Berry (trombone), John Surplus (trumpet), Phil Denver (tenor saxophone) Dennis Wilson (tenor saxophone) and Bernie McAvoy (tenor saxophone).

page 51: "I was serving my time as a spark . . ." Harry Baird, interviewed by the author. Belfast: 31 October 1994.

page 51: "The showbands in the South knew what they were doing . . ." ibid.

page 51: "It was very difficult for a Belfast band to break into the South . . ." ibid.

page 51: "One of the funniest things . . ." O'Hare/Rogan. Dublin: 12 February 2004.

page 51: "It was a five-hour show in the wilds . . ." Baird/Rogan. Belfast: 31 October 1994. Baird was speaking metaphorically here. Dance halls, even in the rural areas, enforced a strict dress code, encompassing clean shoes, and the clientele, including farmers, would have been dressed immaculately.

page 52: "The whole hall came to a standstill . . ." ibid.

page 52: "We did the gig at Borderland . . ." ibid.

page 53: "carcinoma of jejunum due to ulcerative colitis." These details were taken from Gloria Gordon's death certificate.

page 53: ". . . a brain haemorrhage due to auricular fibrillation . . ." These details were taken from Alice Stitt's death certificate.

page 53: "Totally out of the blue he came to my house . . ." Jones/Rogan. Holywood, Co. Down: 6 March 1982.

page 54: "We were never going to get big gigs . . ." Kane/Rogan. Belfast: 27 October 1994.

page 54: "Van liked a good laugh . . ." Jones/Rogan. Holywood, Co. Down: 6 March 1982.

page 54: "He used to get into a frenzy which we encouraged for a laugh . . ." Kane/Rogan. Belfast: 27 October 1994.

page 55: "The mother and father were at work all day . . ." McAllen/Rogan. Belfast: 30 October 1994.

page 55: "The punters here didn't want anything else . . ." ibid.

page 55: "I'd call for him to hurry . . ." Kane/Rogan. Belfast: 27 October 1994.

Chapter Four: Germany Calling

page 58: "I tried to tell him that it was a very hard life . . ." Violet Morrison. Belfast: 1969.

page 58: "We all had great ideas about being big time . . ." McAllen/Rogan. Belfast: 30 October 1994.

page 59: "I remember driving through the Highlands . . ." ibid.

page 59: "At 4am, Van and I were playing . . ." Jones/Rogan. Holywood, Co. Down: 6 March 1982.

page 60: "We booked them into a few Irish dance halls . . ." Ruby Bard, interviewed by the author. London: 9 March 1982.

page 60: "I dealt with a German promoter who booked a few of my jazz bands . . ." ibid.

page 61: "He said he wanted to go to Germany . . ." Violet Morrison. Belfast: 1969.

page 62: "We had a friend in the police . . ." ibid.

page 62: "I was the guy with the single room . . ." McAllen/Rogan. Belfast: 30 October 1994.

page 62: "The Germans didn't like the Americans much . . ." Jones/Rogan. Holywood, Co. Down: 6 March 1982.

page 62: "I don't like talking . . ." Morrison/Kelly, op. cit.

page 62: "That was where Van became the basis of what he is today . . ." Jones/Rogan. Holywood, Co. Down: 6 March 1982.

page 64: "I'd had a row with my boss at the Co-op . . ." Kane/Rogan. Belfast: 27 October 1994.

page 64: "The boys scared the devil out of me . . ." ibid.

page 64: "It was only after the gig that I learned all the hassles . . ." ibid.

page 65: "We sat on top of our amplifiers . . ." McAllen/Rogan. Belfast: 30 October 1994.

page 65: "It was the wrong place . . ." ibid.

page 65: "We had dancing girls in the next room . . ." ibid.

page 66: "We lit the fuse then ran across the road . . ." ibid.

page 67: "We had money . . ." Kane/Rogan. Belfast: 27 October 1994.

page 67: "I didn't know until two years later . . ." Violet Morrison. Belfast: 1969.

page 67: "They hadn't enough to live on . . ." ibid.

page 67: "After the Scotch boys left, we all lived in each other's dirt . . ." Kane/Rogan. Belfast: 27 October 1994.

page 67: "Harry was a funny guy . . ." ibid.

page 67: "Van would start off and from the centre solo until the end . . ." Jones/Rogan. Holywood, Co. Down: 6 March 1982.

page 68: "Throughout it all Van was his own master . . ." ibid.

page 68: "He was just a bit strange compared to the rest of them . . ." McAllen/Rogan. Belfast: 30 October 1994.

page 68: "Van was always a weird wee fellow . . ." Kane/Rogan. Belfast: 27 October 1994.

page 68: "In Cologne, I started taking Dexedrine . . ." McAllen/Rogan. Belfast: 30 October 1994.

page 69: "We got a real fright . . ." Jones/Rogan. Holywood, Co. Down: 6 March 1982.

page 69: "I think it really frustrated Van a lot . . ." ibid.

page 70: "In the big band scene sax players also played clarinet . . ." Kane/Rogan. Belfast: 27 October 1994.

Chapter Five: The Sectarian Divide

page 71: "The bigotry was dying . . ." Harrison/Rogan. Bangor, Co. Down: 21 August 1994.

page 72: "Sectarianism wasn't an issue for us . . ." Wrixon/Rogan. Belfast: 21 June 1994.

page 73: ". . . causing a sensation in Belfast . . ." Jones/Rogan. Holywood, Co. Down: 6 March 1982.

page 73: "He had artificial feet and his hand was a metal claw . . ." McAllen/Rogan. Belfast: 30 October 1994.

page 73: "We went down well . . ." Sproule/Rogan. Belfast: 29 October 1994. The Manhattan Showband had many members during its existence including a female guitarist who was still in the band when McAllen first arrived. The line-up by early 1964 featured Billy McAllen, Van Morrison, Geordie Sproule, Ken Armstrong, Harry Smith (aka Junior), Bill Cavanagh, Herbie Armstrong and Gerry O'Neill.

page 74: "We nearly got thrown out of Clery's . . ." ibid.

page 74: "I was singing 'The Irish Rover' . . ." ibid.

page 74: "We did a wee tape one time . . ." ibid.

page 75: "That guy was as mad as a hatter . . ." Herbie Armstrong interviewed by the author. Sheffield: 23 November 1994.

page 75: "We finished our set but no-one left . . ." ibid.

page 75: "Van played it on sax and we all stood to attention . . ." ibid.

page 75: "It went down well . . ." Sproule/Rogan. Belfast: 29 October 1994.

page 76: "We were bouncing on these iron-sprung beds . . ." Herbie Armstrong/ Rogan. Sheffield: 23 November 1994.

page 76: "Van was smitten by them . . ." Sproule/Rogan. Belfast: 29 October 1994.

page 76: "We said, 'Great – girl guitarists!' . . ." Herbie Armstrong/Rogan. Sheffield: 23 November 1994.

page 76: "Van was really enthusiastic . . ." ibid.

page 77: "They had a hospital show on a Sunday night then . . ." Sproule/Rogan. Belfast: 29 October 1994. In an interview with Donall Corvin, Morrison was asked about the Maritime R&B nights and said they were opened by "the 3Js and G.D.", which confirms the veracity of Sproule's claims here.

page 78: "I told Van, 'you might not have much hope here' . . ." Herbie Armstrong/ Rogan. Sheffield: 23 November 1994.

page 78: "We were still teenagers . . ." ibid.

page 78: "By lucky coincidence, the overwhelming favourite Frankie Connolly . . ." Frankie Connolly was prominent on the Belfast scene and led Frankie & The Echoes before moving on to the Fugitives and Styx.

page 78: "The singers were paid half the rate . . ." Herbie Armstrong/Rogan. Sheffield: 23 November 1994.

page 79: "It was quite a step to be a vocalist in the Golden Eagles . . ." ibid.

page 79: "He kept saying to me, 'Blues is the thing and groups are going to happen,' . . ." ibid.

page 80: "After giving notice to the Golden Eagles . . ." According to Morrison: "There were two [sic] guys called Jerry who put an ad in the Belfast paper at one time. They were going to open a Rhythm & Blues club. So I went over to see them and they wanted me to put a band together. I was 17 [sic]. I lined up Them; the original Them. That was Herbie Armstrong and Billy McAllen. Gerry McIlroy was going to play drums. I forget who was playing bass but I think Eric Wrixon was going to be on piano. Something like that. Then Herbie and all those guys backed out. They didn't want to do it because it wasn't really steady bread." Morrison was a bit presumptuous here when referring to this desired prototype as "the original Them" as the name had yet to be coined. The momentarily forgotten bassist was most likely George Jones who recalls being asked by Morrison to join a Stones-like group and grow his hair long. Herbie Armstrong has indicated elsewhere that the unnamed bassist might have been his colleague Tito Tinsley, although that is conjectural and unlikely. Armstrong acknowledges that Tinsley did not even join the Golden Eagles until after Van Morrison's departure: "Van left and I brought in Tito Tinsley as bass player and Kit Carson as lead guitarist. When I got them in, the band turned around." The order of events leading up to the formation of Them has been challenged by some of its members who maintain that Morrison first joined the Gamblers *then* booked the Maritime. It is possible, of course, that Morrison was already casually rehearsing with the Gamblers and simultaneously attempting to form his ideal Them line-up for the Maritime. A more likely scenario is that Morrison kept his own counsel and the Gamblers were unaware of his previous attempts or plans to form an R&B group with McAllen, Armstrong *et al*. What is certain from the testimonies of George Jones, Roy Kane and others is that Morrison had already shown a keen interest in forming an R&B group having contacted various members of the Monarchs and the Manhattan since the beginning of 1964.

page 80: "Van said, 'I've got some great ideas,' . . ." Herbie Armstrong/Rogan. Sheffield: 23 November 1994.

page 80: "The Gamblers had originally formed in East Belfast . . ." Interestingly, Eric Wrixon speaks of another member who briefly appeared in the Gamblers. "They had a guitarist/singer called Phil who was run of the mill and a bit of an all-rounder. Billy will tell you his name." When I duly confronted Harrison on this, he dismissed Wrixon's recollection with the aside: "There were only three of us. Eric's full of crap! He wasn't even in the Gamblers really." However, I think it's likely that Wrixon was correct and the missing member was tenor saxophonist Phil Denver, whose CV also included stints in the Great Eight and the Olympics (later the Regency Showband), both of which, coincidentally, had brief links with Morrison. Despite his recent recruitment to the Gamblers, Wrixon was in the group long enough to play some dates just prior to Morrison's arrival, "We played as the Gamblers for about three months with me," he calculates roughly. "It'd become an R&B band by then. We were one of the few playing R&B. When Van joined we revamped the whole thing. He was playing in a band with my cousin, so he knew what we were trying to do. There were a couple of music shops in Belfast where people met at the time."

page 81: "My mind was still working on what I called rock 'n' roll . . ." Billy Harrison, interviewed by the author. Bangor, Co. Down: 9 July 1994.

page 81: "About the time I arrived they'd just gone R&B . . ." Wrixon/Rogan. Belfast: 21 June 1994.

page 82: "A lot of songs that later became R&B standards . . ." Harrison/Rogan. Bangor, Co. Down: 9 July 1994.

page 82: "We disappeared off the scene, unintentionally really . . ." ibid.

Chapter Six: Maritime Blues

page 84: "On Friday 10 April 1964, Them played their first date at the Maritime . . ." Eric Wrixon recalled to me: "The first night we played there we had someone else topping the bill [the College Boys]." In an interview printed in Belfast's *City Week* on 22 September 1966, Morrison confirmed that he'd missed "the first night of Them" on which "they played the break" for "the College Boys". Impressively, he recalled the exact date of 10 April, which was correct as advertisements confirm that the College Boys appeared at the Maritime that evening and, of course, Them's first *headlining* performance took place the following week on 17 April. That same week, despite suggestions that it was now passé, the Jazz Club continued to use the Maritime for its traditional Tuesday evening get-togethers. On 14 April the Swing College Band appeared as usual. Any suggestions that Them might have appeared this same night are erroneous – the support act were the Kentuckians.

page 84: ". . . supporting the in-demand College Boys . . ." The College Boys had recently been headlining at the Fiesta, the Cavern Club and Betty Staff Dance Studios. They soon became one of the leading showbands in the North. Interestingly, their emergence came via one of Morrison's former working bands, the Olympic Showband (later the Regency Showband). Their leader Harry Baird recalls the tradition whereby showbands would employ young groups to provide support as part of the package. Often, such meetings were fortuitous. "We were driving to pick up our drummer on the Old Park Road," he recalls. "It was a lovely day with the bus windows open. We heard a band playing. They were pretty good. We asked them what they were called and they didn't have a name. They'd just started and weren't playing anywhere. We took them under our wings and named them the College Boys. They were all still at school, thus the name. We'd thought about calling them the Graduates or the Students, but there were already bands called that. They travelled with us for six to nine months playing the first hour. After about two years they ended up being a bigger band than we were. They were taken under management by Trevor Kane who ran some halls in Co. Down. Sammy Smyth, who was a mate of our manager Tommy Bodel, then got involved and became their manager."

page 84: "The ads created a mystery from the very start . . ." Irvine/Rogan. Belfast: 18 September 1994.

page 84: "The Maritime was probably the first time that a band . . ." Wrixon/Rogan. Belfast: 21 June 1994.

page 85: "I'd never heard anything like it . . ." Demick/Rogan. London: 5 October 1994.

page 85: "Van was wild, Van was the best . . ." Carson/Rogan. Fife: 28 August 1993.

page 85: "We used to sit on the wooden chairs with our feet up on the stage . . ." Ann Denvir, interviewed by the author. London: 12 September 1993.

page 85: "We were playing for a certain bunch of people . . ." Van Morrison, interviewed by Roy Carr. *New Musical Express*: 4 August 1973.

page 86: "There's a great difference of opinion between Belfast and the rest of the world . . ." Wrixon/Rogan. Belfast: 21 June 1994.

page 86: "It was about 50/50 . . ." Harrison/Rogan. Bangor, Co. Down: 9 July 1994. Harrison adds, "Even after we went over to the mainland to record, I was still doing the chanting when we were touring. I would have come in with half-a-dozen Chuck Berry numbers. When the popularity came with the records it wasn't really needed. By that stage, Van was doing the chanting and it would only be an odd time when I did any singing except for the backing on songs like 'Gloria' or later 'Here Comes The Night'."

page 86: "This was my big night . . ." Janet Martin, interviewed by the author. Belfast: 1 October 1993. Teddie Palmer was involved in a number of Belfast bands of the era, including the Tribunes, the Spectres and the Exiles. He then formed Teddie & The Tigers with Tiger Taylor, who were managed by David Parkinson. As Palmer noted: "I sang with a croaky voice then because Belfast people thought all blues songs should be sung with a Van Morrison voice." Coincidentally, Palmer ended up as a member of the College Boys in 1967.

page 87: "It was an end of term concert for the school . . ." Joan McClelland, interviewed by the author. Belfast: 2 October 1994.

page 87: "We were there every Friday . . ." ibid.

page 87: "It was a classic period . . ." Billy Moore, interviewed by the author. Belfast: 6 August 1994.

page 88: "They'd only just started and there was this buzz around Belfast . . ." Eric Bell/Rogan. London: 5 August 1994.

page 88: "He had his head down . . ." ibid.

page 88: "Half the time, the wee man would have done these things pretending . . ." Harrison/Rogan. Bangor, Co. Down: 21 August 1994.

page 89: "When I saw him at the Maritime my memories of Van are that he used to perform better . . ." Terry Davis, interviewed by the author. Shropshire: 21 October 1994.

page 89: "Sam was a showbander . . ." Janet Martin/Rogan. Belfast: 1 October 1993.

page 89: "I was enthralled . . ." Eddie Kennedy, interviewed by the author. London: 12 March 1982.

page 90: "Van hung around with a seedy crowd of failed art college students . . ."

Wrixon/Rogan. Belfast: 21 June 1994.

page 90: "There were a few chicks . . . " Eric Bell/Rogan. London: 5 August 1994.

page 90: "She was tall, slim, had a very pale complexion and red hair . . ." Wrixon/
Rogan. Belfast: 21 June 1994.

page 91: "She was a beautiful looking girl . . ." Harrison/Rogan. Bangor, Co. Down:
9 July 1994.

page 91: "The first time I ever met Van was at the Plaza . . ." Denvir/Rogan. London:
12 September 1993.

page 91: "Jane was a bit like Jane Asher . . ." Sam Smyth, interviewed by the author.
Dublin: 19 January 2003. Additional material taken from our earlier interviews:
July/August 1993 and 17 October 1993.

page 92: "With Lloyd at the controls . . ." I have unearthed a Morrison interview in
September 1966 where he mentions 'Stormy Monday', 'I Got My Mojo Working'
and 'Don't Start Crying Now'. Back in February 1982, Mervyn Solomon told me:
"The tape was never issued because of its recording quality but it had a great
atmosphere. Peter [Lloyd] still has that tape. I heard it a couple of years back and it
still had all the magic." Mervyn Solomon also cites 'Turn On Your Lovelight' as
being recorded during this period. Another of my interviewees, Rod Demick, also
made reference to the tape, this time with a surprise addition, possibly from another
session at the studio: "I heard 'Gloria' from the Peter Lloyd date. It's much better
than the single. It's around the same length but it's just got more energy. It's
probably less commercial than the released version." Others recall an attempt at
'One Two Brown Eyes'. Perhaps in the fullness of time all this material might
emerge on some box set.

page 92: "I arrived there and Van was absolutely tearing them apart . . ." Mervyn
Solomon, interviewed by the author. Belfast: 25 February 1982.

page 93: "Philip first came in my direction originally through his father's connections
with Decca . . ." Dick Rowe, interviewed by the author. London: 5 May 1983.
Additional information stems from the author's earlier interview with Rowe.
London: 1 December 1981.

page 93: "The most powerful and influential managers of the era . . . spoke of
Rowe . . ." Two important managers in particular provided me with glowing testimonials – Larry Parnes (24 July 1984) and Andrew Oldham (8–10 September 1995).

page 94: "Other managers were critical of Epstein's display of spite but Rowe reacted
with a saturnine shrug of the shoulders . . ." When I was researching the book
Starmakers & Svengalis: The History Of British Pop Management, the Rowe story came
up again and again during interviews with Sixties managers, all of whom expressed
their unsolicited opinions about the lack of justice in the public's perception of
Rowe as a result of Epstein's biased account. As well as Parnes and Oldham (see
above), there was Peter Walsh (17 October 1983), Harvey Lisberg (10 November
1983) and Don Arden (29 July 1997). Rowe's A&R peers must have breathed a
collective sigh of relief when their names escaped inspection as fellow scapegoats.

page 94: "Mervyn appeared in his Sunday best and Phil patronized him dreadfully . . ."
Sam Smyth/Rogan. Dublin: 17 October 1993. Sam Smyth could not recall the

names of the other bands lined up at the audition with Them and the College Boys. He strongly suspects that Tony & The Telstars may have been present but Rod Demick, who calculates that he was a member of that showband at this point, refutes the suggestion. "Tony & The Telstars didn't do the Dick Rowe audition," he insists, "but we did do an audition for *Opportunity Knocks*. We didn't win that but we did get on *Ready Steady Win!* That was a competition run by *Ready Steady Go!* We won the heat in Northern Ireland and they brought us over to London. We were among the finalists, but the Bo Street Runners won."

page 94: "I didn't want Them without Philip . . ." Rowe/Rogan. London: 1 December 1981. Additional information, author's interview: 5 May 1983.

page 95: "You can have another night to think about it . . ." ibid. The signing proved a blow to the 3Js who, since Solomon's arrival, effectively found themselves out of the picture. Apparently, they had made a tentative approach to Philips Records hoping to attract the attention of Dick Rowe's great rival, Jack Baverstock. Like Rowe, he preferred experienced managers and would presumably have advised the 3Js to try and cut a deal with a London impresario. By then, of course, Solomon was already preparing to sign the group.

page 95: "I wouldn't have socialized with Van . . ." Wrixon/Rogan. Belfast: 21 June 1994.

page 96: "There was a problem with Them's drummer . . ." Mervyn Solomon/Rogan. Belfast: 25 February 1982. The suggestion that Morrison was never entirely happy with the first Them line-up has been frequently made. Herbie Armstrong, at one moment during our interview, vaguely recalled Morrison asking him and bassist Tito Tinsley to join Them at this point. "He said 'We're going to make a record, why don't you join?' That was at the Scrumpy Rooms in Belfast. We'd have replaced Harrison and Henderson . . ." This explanation was unlikely for any number of reasons, not least because Billy Harrison was a key player and, in any case, he and Henderson had just signed the Solomon/Decca deal. Armstrong is probably remembering the moment three months before when Morrison was very eager for him to form what he called "the original Them" with Billy McAllen *et al* before settling on the Gamblers.

page 96: "The session produced seven songs . . ." The listing was first documented by Steve Turner – hats off to him for the research. Oddly, Harrison referred to this as a "test recording" in our interview – as if there was another "proper" attempt later resulting in the released recordings. I assume this was a slip of the tongue and the "test" he had in mind was the aforementioned Peter Lloyd demo. In his book, Turner makes a parenthetical allusion, courtesy of Alan Henderson, suggesting that Them were "the first group to use two drummers". While others have taken this to imply a double drum set-up (like Adam & The Ants or the Glitter Band), I think Henderson actually meant using different drummers on the same session. Wrixon reckons: "There's a weird report about using two drummers. It's nonsense. We used Bobby Graham as a second drummer over the top of Ronnie Millings." Morrison confirms this, adding: "They brought in a session drummer as well as the drummer in the group." Whether any of Millings' work, prior to Graham's recruitment, appeared on vinyl is unknown. Incidentally, the group were flown over by Phil Solomon for this session at a time when air travel was incredibly expensive.

page 97: "I was enjoying myself too much . . ." Eric Bell/Rogan. London: 5 August 1994.

page 97: "Our curiosity led dozens of us to gather and peer into the window . . ." Gerry Adams, *Falls Memories*, Brandon, Kerry: 1993.

page 98: "We were beginning to get a sense of our essential Irishness . . ." ibid.

page 98: "He later founded the Yaks . . ." The Yaks featured Patsy McAuley (drums), Billy Hollywood (guitar) and John Hoy (bass). When Patsy left he was replaced by his younger brother Jackie, who also fronted the band as vocalist. "There were seven of us in the family," Jackie McAuley adds, "and everyone could play something. I was born on the road between Derry and Coleraine. My mother was a singer and played the piano and my dad played accordion and violin. Patsy started off on piano. I joined the Blue Angels on organ but only for a couple of months. I really wanted to get into playing R&B and I'd got a harmonica. When my brother joined Them he took my organ and I was left with the harmonica! I think we then brought in Dino Martin as the Yaks' drummer."

page 98: "Patsy was my musical mentor and the mainman in the Yaks . . ." Hollywood/Rogan. Belfast: 18 September 1994.

page 99: "He was enthralled by the group and bowled over . . ." ibid.

page 99: "There was an Irish club . . ." Harrison/Rogan. Bangor, Co. Down: 9 July 1994.

page 99: "The Bachelors never missed a date in their lives . . ." Philip Solomon, interviewed by the author. Dublin: 15 April 1982.

page 100: "Van Morrison and Them would *never* have made it without Phil Solomon . . ." Larry Page, interviewed by the author. London: 12 July 1994. Plus additional information from author's interviews with Page in London on 7 August 1982 and 24 June 1983.

page 100: "I was in a hotel with him up north and the phone rang at one in the morning . . ." Rowe/Rogan. London: 5 May 1983. Additional information from author's interview: 1 December 1981.

page 100: "Bronx-born Berns . . ." Bertrand Russell Berns, born on 8 November 1929, was christened in honour of the eminent philosopher and pacifist Bertrand Russell. A visit to pre-Castro Cuba in 1958 inspired a deep love of Latin music, a style that influenced many of his famous pop productions. As well as his work as a songwriter and producer, he briefly attempted to make his mark as a recording artiste, appearing as part of the Beatniks, and as the soloist Russell Byrd under which name he appeared on the television show *American Bandstand*.

page 101: "I told Philip what I had in mind, but it was going to cost a lot of money . . ." ibid.

page 101: "I remember labouring over them for hours . . ." Phil Coulter, interviewed by the author. London: 28 January 1982.

page 101: "That's when the Them situation turned around . . ." Rowe/Rogan. London: 5 May 1983. 'Baby Please Don't Go' was originally recorded in 1941 by Big Joe Williams and later covered by Hooker and Muddy Waters (1953). All these versions owe much to 'Don't You Leave Me Here', recorded by Papa Hervey and Long Cleve Reed as early as 1927. Oddly, there was a peculiar discrepancy in some publications during the 1990s over when precisely Bert Berns arrived in the story. Originally, when I first wrote about Them back in 1982, I confirmed that he arrived in time to record 'Baby Please Don't Go'. However, Turner (without a source quote) incorrectly assumed Dick Rowe produced that record and Pete Frame (who no doubt followed Turner here) noted the same in his highly informative Them family tree. During my exclusive interviews with Rowe back in 1981 and 1983 he made no claim whatsoever to have produced 'Baby Please Don't Go', indicating it was Berns. Billy Harrison also insisted in an interview with me that it was definitely Berns who produced the song and Van Morrison (see *Select*, October 1990) argues the same. Since Berns' recording of Lulu's 'Here Comes The Night' was issued as early as the beginning of November, this confirms that the producer was in the UK in late 1964 and not January 1965 as wrongly suggested in the aforementioned.

page 102: "It was about my cousin Gloria . . ." Morrison/Corvin: op cit. Corvin's rare interview was, to my knowledge, the only time that Morrison admitted that the song 'Gloria' was in any way connected with his cousin. Without access to this interview, Steve Turner correctly deduced that the song was "a disguised tribute to Van's cousin Gloria Gordon who died of cancer *while the Monarchs were away in Germany*". The italicized assertion appears to have been based on speculation from "neighbours in Hyndford Street", notably Walter Blakely. In a more recent biography, writer Clinton Heylin goes much further describing Gloria Gordon as the probable real life figure behind a number of compositions (including 'Little Girl', which mentions a 14-year-old girl) about "a deepening friendship with a girl *he had known since they were children*". He also asserts "the *fact* that Gloria had died . . . *whilst the Monarchs were in Germany*", repeating Turner's previous assumption. All of the italicized statements highlighted here are incorrect. As her death certificate confirms, Gloria Gordon did not die while the Monarchs were in Germany. More importantly, she and Morrison did not share a childhood together and nor did Morrison have any memory of her when she was 14 years old. Gloria was born in 1932 and was already 13 years old in the year of Morrison's birth. By the time Morrison was six, she was already married; Morrison was still only 16 when she died, aged 29. The above points underline the obvious danger of the intentional fallacy when approaching Morrison's lyrics. Recklessly assuming that Gloria or anyone else may have been a literal template for a series of Morrison songs like 'Little Girl' and its successors is self-evidently erroneous and, as it turns out in this instance, irresponsibly speculative.

page 102: "Solomon even suggested, perhaps ironically, that Morrison should wear pink tights . . ." This claim was made by Morrison to Corvin. I have not named the television show as I have conflicting accounts. Sam Smyth told me it was *Thank Your Lucky Stars* while Mervyn Solomon thought it was *Ready Steady Go!*

page 102: "I met them afterwards and they were delighted with themselves . . ." Sam Smyth/Rogan. Dublin: 17 October 1993.

page 102: "They bitched to me about it a lot . . ." Coulter/Rogan. London: 28 January 1982.

page 103: "Everybody was pointing their fingers and saying, 'You didn't make it!' . . ." Harrison/Rogan. Bangor, Co. Down: 9 July 1994.

page 103: "He opted to leave and get a job . . ." ibid.

page 103: "We weren't even fledglings, we were scaldies . . ." Harrison is using Northern Ireland vernacular here. A "scaldy" refers to the method of placing a newly-born chicken in boiling water, after which its feathers would fall off.

page 103: "You just had to take Van as he came . . ." Alan Henderson, interviewed by the author. Minnesota: 19 August 1994.

page 103: "Van wasn't that friendly with the rest of the group . . ." Davis/Rogan. Shropshire: 21 October 1994.

page 103: "It was more drink than we'd have had in a night . . ." Hollywood/Rogan. Belfast: 18 September 1994.

page 104: "I sat there for an hour and nobody spoke . . ." Jackie McAuley, interviewed by the author. London: 1 March 1995.

page 104: "Morrison's old friends Brian Rossi and Herbie Armstrong had been sacked from the Plaza . . ." The Plaza band that was fired for playing R&B at the 'Over 21s night' included Rossi, Armstrong, plus lead guitarist Kit Carson and drummer Victor Catling (a former member of the Banshees and the Sinners Showband). While forming the Wheels they contacted Rod Demick (ex-Telstars, then in the People). "I'd left school and got a job as an apprentice wholesale draper," Demick recalls. "I'd only been there three weeks when somebody came up to me in the Plaza and said, 'Big Herbie's looking for you!' When somebody says something like that in Belfast you think, 'Oh my God! What have I done?' I knew Herbie from seeing him at Crymbles, Betty Staff's and Sammy Houston's. He asked me if I wanted to join the Wheels. I'd seen them earlier so I said, 'Yes'. Kit Carson was already there and I was taken in as lead guitarist/vocalist but I ended up just playing a bit of guitar, harmonica and doing some vocals. But on records I did the vocals. At the first gig I played with the Wheels, Rossi said: 'I've got a new guitarist here and he's only 14 years old'. I was 17! All the girls loved that and went, 'Ah!' Rossi used to say to me, 'Right kid, get out there and *sweat*. Then people will know you're working.' He taught me how to work a crowd and how to jump around the place, run across the stage and throw mike stands so that it was an exciting show. Rossi was a legend since the late Fifties; the only star in Belfast except for Ruby Murray and Ronnie Carroll. Rossi would have been an influence on Van, both in terms of showmanship and respect. Whenever I bumped into Van over the years he would always say, 'What's happened to Brian Rossi?' The last time I saw him I had to tell him he was dead. God rest his soul. He died in 1984 from pneumonia, water on the lungs. He'd been on the cabaret scene for years after he'd left the Wheels."

page 104: "Eddie Kennedy was amazed to find himself this fashionable figure . . ." Sam Smyth/Rogan. Dublin: July/August 1993. Geordie Sproule's blues display was eagerly recounted to me by its creator: "I went into the Maritime and did 60 numbers! All the guys from Belfast will tell you that they were doing copies. I never copied records from anybody. When a guy asked, 'Do you sing the blues?', I'd say, 'Ay, no problem.' I didn't know one blues song. I just knew the usual run of the mill stuff like 'Walkin' The Dog' and 'Baby Please Don't Go'. I didn't want to do any of them so I just went in and made up 60 out of my head along with a fellow called Taig from the Falls Road. There was also someone called Freddie and another, P.J. Plus guitarist Terry Flynn – a brilliant player. We had different people in the band every night. When I was playing with Taig we called ourselves the Dirt Birds. If I was doing pop, rock and ballads, we were the Tokens."

page 105: "That was a biggie . . ." Harrison/Rogan. Bangor, Co. Down: 9 July 1994.

page 105: "We were the last thing they needed . . ." ibid.

page 106: "Goodnight pigs!" McAuley/Rogan. London: 1 March 1995.

page 106: "Van took control and was his own man . . ." ibid.

page 106: "When the chairs came flying we dived into the dressing room . . ." ibid.

page 106: "One thing is certain . . ." Jackie Middleton, press cutting: December 1965. In several listings and music press columns of the time, the Stratotones (a name presumably inspired by the Fender Stratocaster guitar) were referred to as the Stratatones. The correct spelling is conjectural.

page 106: "A lot of people then booked the band just for the controversy . . ." ibid.

page 106: "They had to hire a car and turn up in the middle-class suburb of Stillorgan . . ." Sam Smyth/Rogan. Dublin: July/August 1993. Smyth's impressions were echoed by Rod Demick, who observed in our interview: "Them were raw and different and captured that old feeling – Chicago R&B. I know that Van was never really happy with the original guys in Them. He never thought they were musically good enough. But at the time they were all that he could get because he was doing something new. To get work playing R&B was impossible."

page 107: "You can put us down as preferring girls to pennies . . ." Billy Harrison, interviewed by Ian Dove. New Musical Express: 22 January 1965. In this same interview Harrison confirmed the date of the Cookstown gig: "There was a Boxing Day dance and everybody was, well, merry, and some of the crowd started throwing pennies at us."

Chapter Seven: No Mass, No Lemass

page 108: "Every boy who asked me to dance . . ." Aisling Foster in My Generation, Lilliput Press, Dublin: 1996.

page 108: "They may not exactly represent the 'New Image of Ulster' . . ." John Trew in City Week. Belfast: 15 January 1965.

page 109: "The Spectres' manager . . . had even formed the first Them fan club . . ." David Parkinson, interviewed by the author. Belfast: 12 October 1994.

page 109: "Peter used to pull the birds . . ." Davis/Rogan. Shropshire: 21 October 1994.

page 110: "We used to hang out with him quite a lot . . ." McAuley/Rogan. London: 1 March 1995.

page 110: "We all got on well with Jimmy . . ." Harrison/Rogan. Bangor, Co. Down: 9 July 1994.

page 110: "Decca's Head of Publicity . . ." Information from author's interview with Tony Hall. London: 2 December 1981.

page 110: "A lot of the interviews were surly . . ." Harrison/Rogan. Bangor, Co. Down: 9 July 1994.

page 111: "They were the most boorish bunch of youngsters . . ." Des Hickey, recounted to the author: Dublin: August 1984.

page 111: "It was the most painful 15 minutes I have ever spent . . ." Coulter/Rogan. London: 28 January 1982.

page 111: "Eventually, she said, 'Well, who actually formed you?' . . ." Tommy Scott, interviewed by the author. London: 18 February 1982.

page 111: "He played rhythm guitar on one thing . . ." Morrison/Corvin, op cit.

page 112: ". . . Andy White . . . Perry Ford . . ." Information on backing musicians provided during author's interview with Tommy Scott. London: 18 February 1982.

page 112: "One of my abiding recollections of that or any other period . . ." Rogan/Coulter. London: 28 January 1982.

page 112: "Them were never meant to be on *Top Of The Pops* . . ." Morrison/Corvin, op cit.

page 112: "It was very clinical . . ." Harrison/Rogan. Bangor, Co. Down: 9 July 1994.

page 112: "We were shredded . . ." McAuley/Rogan. London: 1 March 1995.

page 113: "We all started arguing and fighting about everything . . ." ibid.

page 113: "We were at each other's throats . . ." Jackie McAuley, interviewed by Pete Frame in Queen's Park, London, tape box dated 2 October 1981. Full quotes previously unpublished. Used by permission.

page 113: "I was in the basement of our hotel and I crashed out . . ." McAuley/Rogan. London: 1 March 1995.

page 114: "The guy who used to give me the pills said, 'Try a bit of this – heroin' . . ." ibid.

page 114: "There may have been the odd grass blown . . ." Harrison/Rogan. Bangor, Co. Down: 9 July 1994.

page 114: "We weren't too pleased and he told us to piss off . . ." ibid.

page 114: "How long can you keep accepting this nonsense? . . ." Philip Solomon/Rogan. Dublin: 15 April 1982.

page 144: "Pot may not be harmful . . ." ibid.

page 115: "I reckoned Solomon was on the fiddle . . ." Harrison/Rogan. Bangor, Co. Down: 9 July 1994.

page 115: "It was a disgusting experience dealing with those people . . ." McAuley/Rogan. London: 1 March 1995.

page 115: "When I dealt with Philip he was straight with me . . ." Henderson/Rogan. Minnesota: 19 August 1994.

page 115: "The Solomon business got sorted out . . ." Harrison/Rogan. Bangor, Co. Down: 9 July 1994. Warming to his theme, Harrison went on to suggest that Them could easily have challenged Solomon. "I remember when he was having a rant and a rave. My attitude was 'Who needs a manager? We're number 2 in the charts'. Somebody else would've handled us, even if we had to fight. There was too much money to be made. They would have said, 'Piss of, Phil'. To hell with signed contracts. If you've got a commodity that's capable of making a few million quid you don't mind fighting. You'll pay for the right lawyers." Harrison's words are actually retrospective bravado. It is doubtful whether any manager of the period would have crossed Solomon, particularly over a group with only two hits. At that point there was little or no precedent for taking legal action along the lines casually suggested by Harrison. When the Kinks – then the third most successful group in Britain – attempted to break free from their manager Larry Page in the summer of 1965, it prompted a groundbreaking court action which made case law. The case dragged on for three years, including appeals, a point which underlines how difficult such a course of action would have been for Them. Not only were the Kinks a more lucrative commodity but they actually had three managers and it was the other two – Robert Wace and Grenville Collins – who helped negotiate the group through this tough period. Them had no such backing and even if they had, what manager would have bankrolled a group, especially on such a flimsy premise? The rapid demise of Them over the next year, and the constant personnel changes, emphasize how unwise and unprofitable any legal action would have been.

page 116: ". . . loveable rogue and a con merchant . . ." Mary King, quoted in *Scott Walker: A Deep Shade Of Blue*, Mike Watkinson & Pete Anderson, London, Virgin:1994.

page 116: "If we came back to London we usually ended up there . . ." Harrison/Rogan. Bangor, Co. Down: 18 August 1994.

page 116: "Someone was mouthing at Alan Henderson . . ." Harrison/Rogan. Bangor, Co. Down: 9 July 1994.

page 117: "Let there be no doubt about their popularity . . ." Reviewed by Derek Johnson, *New Musical Express*: 16 April 1965.

page 117: "That same week, the Beatles released their new single 'Ticket To Ride' which entered the charts at number 1, displacing Cliff Richard's 'The Minute You're Gone' . . ." The UK chart statistics used in this book covering the Sixties period are taken from the biggest-selling chart weekly the *New Musical Express* rather than the disturbingly ubiquitous *Guinness Book Of Hit Singles* or *The Complete Book Of The British Charts*. The tendency of book, radio and television researchers to use these easily available volumes has led to a serious warping of pop history. The charts featured in these volumes do not reflect what happened every week on *Top Of The Pops* or BBC radio, or in the big chart weeklies *NME* and *Melody Maker*. Over the years, the truth of the Sixties charts has been sacrificed on the altar of marketing, expediency and easy reference. The decision to change the chart source in these books from the *New Musical Express* Top 30 to that of *Record Retailer* from 10 March 1960 onwards has proven disastrous for any serious student of pop history. Anyone who lived through that era now has to suffer chart statistics that are an insult to the collective memory. The *RR* chart had little or no credibility in the Sixties before the advent of independent compilers such as BMRB (13 February 1969) and Gallup (8 January 1983). Back then *RR* was a dullard chart which specialized in abnormally low entries, something which BMRB thankfully reversed, finally bringing the charts closer in line to the *New Musical Express*. Worse, the *Record Retailer* chart was compiled from a shockingly low number of sampled shops (initially an absurdly low 30 for its March 1960 listing!). According to fellow chart enthusiast Alan Smith, "the *Retailer*'s points system for allocating chart positions was based on the placings that singles achieved in *RR*'s designated shops, rather than actual total sales figures . . ." Today, the so-called 'official chart' is universally recognized and those involved like to boast that it is the one used by the BBC and *Top Of The Pops*. This disguises the historical fact that the Sixties charts printed in *Record Retailer* and reproduced in these books were used by neither BBC radio nor *Top Of The Pops*. Indeed, the *RR* chart (which was inaugerated well after *NME*, *Melody Maker* or even *Disc*) was considered a joke by most of us, a point underlined in that its main outlet was the low-selling glossy *Record Mirror*. Readers of the weekly music press (primarily the big-selling *New Musical Express* and *Melody Maker*, but also *Disc & Music Echo*) saw things differently and so did the general public. The broadsheet and tabloid newspapers of the time used these charts: the *Daily Mail,* the *Daily Sketch,* the *People et al.* Listeners to Radio Luxembourg's Sunday night Top 20 were given the *NME* chart. Who bothered with *RR*? Certainly not the BBC. When *Top Of The Pops* valiantly searched for accuracy by compiling their own hybrid chart from the others available, they initially did not even consider *RR* as a worthwhile candidate. Complicating matters for the worst, the *RR* chart came out before the weekly sales receipts were calculated. This led to some peculiar and perverse statistics that continue to infuriate. Everyone, including the Beatles, their manager and producer always assumed that 'Please Please Me' was the group's first number 1. Not any more. Even their record label foolishly followed the gospel according to *British Hit Singles*, thereby pandering to the least adventurous and *only* chart to suggest that the single did not hit the top. As a result the best-selling Beatles *1* omitted their first chart topper and millions of record buyers were cheated. 'Please Please Me' *was* the first Beatles number 1 and all their singles from 'I Want To Hold Your Hand' through to 'We Can Work It Out'/'Day Tripper' entered the charts at number 1. That much was always obvious, except if you subscribe to the chart books, of course. They claim that no Beatles single entered at number 1 until 'Get Back' (the latter was in the 1969 BMRB era *after* the *RR* chart had at last been reformed). If you subscribe to the new chart statistics then you believe several significant untruths: the first Merseybeat group to reach number 1 becomes not the Beatles but Gerry & The Pacemakers; the Beatles have 17 number 1s instead of 18; the Rolling Stones '19th Nervous Breakdown' (*three* weeks at the top in *NME*) peaks at number 2; Slade, rather than the Beatles, become the first group to enter the charts at number 1 on a regular basis with successive entries. If the aforementioned books had followed logic and used the *NME* chart until 1969 and the dawn of the BMRB overhaul, then all of the above could have been avoided. Alternatively, they could at least have used the BBC charts (radio's *Pick Of The Pops* joining with television's *Top Of The Pops* from 1964 onwards). So, do not be fooled by talk of *Top Of The Pops* and official charts when discussing this period. Collective memory speaks considerably louder.

page 117: "When he said, 'we don't want you in the band anymore' . . ." McAuley/ Rogan. London: 1 March 1995. Pete Frame, in his impressive family tree of Them, reckons McAuley's last day in the group was on 23 April "when Them were dumped off *Ready Steady Go!* for being two hours late for rehearsal". However, an interview in *City Week*, coincidentally published on 23 April 1965 and conducted somewhat earlier on Billy Harrison's wedding day, revealed that McAuley had "left last week". The same publication had previously noted that Them were scheduled to appear on *RSG* on 19 March which I assume was the date in question. It may be that Them missed the *RSG* performance in March and were rescheduled the following month – or simply missed the April show. Either way, it seems McAuley was gone at least a week or more before 23 April.

page 118: "If I went to the shops . . ." Violet Morrison. Belfast: 1969.

page 118: "Did you know that Van Morrison's *one of them* . . ." Irvine/Rogan. Belfast: 18 September 1994.

page 118: "I had a wee spot singing R&B, rock 'n' roll, 'Summertime' . . ." Sproule/Rogan. Belfast: 29 October 1994. Since G.D. claims that Morrison was "still in the charts with 'Here Comes The Night'," I have included his testimony at this point. However, I think it is equally, or possibly more, likely that the incident took place during a later appearance at Queen's University in November 1966 when students were throwing paint against a wall to create a psychedelic mural.

page 119: "The long hair was frowned on then . . ." Sam Mahood, interviewed by the author. Belfast: 28 October 1994. Back in the mid-Sixties Sam was sometimes billed in the press as Sam Mahoud. I have stuck with Mahood as this was the name on the tape he sent me after our interview. The line-up of the Just Five comprised: Sam Mahood (vocals); Harry Curry (bass), Mervyn Crawford (lead guitar), Billy McCoy (rhythm guitar) and Roy Irvine (drums). Mahood's early life offered some interesting parallels with that of Morrison's Jehovah's Witness childhood: "In Banbridge I had a church upbringing and we had a quartet, my father, sister and her husband and me. We went round the missions and did street corners on Sunday afternoons and evenings. We used to do all the gospel songs. Even when I was going to church three times a week, I had a light blue suit that was made for me, with a gold thread in it. That was accepted. When I got older, I worked in a shoe shop after school and when the winkle pickers came in I got first choice. Then I started wearing my mother's imitation fur coat. Then the hair got longer. Just before I came to Belfast I started to grow a beard and my father said: 'No! You can keep your hair long, but you're not growing a beard!' At a chip shop in Banbridge, me and another school friend played 'I Don't Want To Go On Without You' by the Drifters on the jukebox. It had strings in the background and people would just look at us and think, 'Why are they playing that music?' That was how I got from gospel music into black soul music. I was a drop-out in limbo looking for something to be involved in. I never listened to Them, although we eventually did do 'Baby Please Don't Go' and one or two other numbers because of their popularity. We played mainly R&B, the latest Rolling Stones hits and a couple of Dylan songs. We had a couple of regular gigs, one of which was the school in Annadale. Later our circuit was the Jazz Club, the Maritime, the Elizabethan and the Ricky Tik. Sometimes we'd set up in the Jazz Club, play there for an hour, go to Betty Staff's for an hour, then back to the Jazz Club. That was three hours a night for maybe a fiver."

page 119: "Is the Belfast scene dying? . . ." columnist Johnny Robb, *City Week*. Belfast: 18 June 1965.

page 119: "It was because they were all Irishmen . . ." Peter Bardens, *Disc*: 20 August 1965.

page 120: "Harrison spent most of the interview cleaning his nails . . ." Keith Altham, interviewed by the author. London: 30 November 1981. The attendant, interspersed quotes are taken from the actual interview, published in the *NME*, 17 May 1965. In defending and elaborating on Them's poor performance in the media, Billy Harrison told me in 1994: "I remember Keith Altham saying to you that I picked my nails with a knife. I'm sure that's grown greatly. He was probably threatened with a knife by now! Phil Solomon did phone the *NME*, a severe case of overkill . . . I suppose we were classed as lunatics in a way. I think where the surly idea came from was that people came in with a very preconceived Angry Young Them idea and we'd been very hard to get for interviews. We were just working so hard that we didn't have the time. When they did start, they asked stupid questions like 'What's your favourite colour? What's your favourite food?' That was a load of crap as far as anybody with half an intelligence is concerned. OK, it might be what a lot of people want to know but they're stupid. What relevance is it what my favourite colour is?" Apart from showing a snobbish disregard for the pop press and the glossy teen magazines aimed at a younger readership, Harrison's claims are ultimately unconvincing. Them's press profile was very broad and impressive for the era, including confrontations with well-known Fleet Street journalists in broadsheet newspapers and several of the leading music writers of the time. Altham's questioning, for example, was forthright and relevant, focusing on their image, the non-appearance on *Ready Steady Go!* and the departure of McAuley. The group may have been over-sensitive to such enquiries but the approach was far removed from the 'favourite colour' style of inquisition mentioned by Harrison.

page 120: "I came away very disenchanted with Them . . ." Altham/Rogan. London: 30 November 1981.

Chapter Eight: The Angry Young Them

page 123: "I was just being a street cat from Belfast . . ." Van Morrison, interviewed by Jonathan Cott. *Rolling Stone*: 30 November 1978.

page 123: "He'd done a super job recording 'Baby Please Don't Go' . . ." Harrison/Rogan. Bangor, Co. Down: 9 July 1994.

page 123: "That was like giving a kid candy for a fortnight . . ." Coulter/Rogan. London: 28 January 1982.

page 123: "Except for Bert Berns . . ." Van Morrison, interviewed by Roy Carr, *New Musical Express*: 4 August 1973. Additional information provided in author's interview with Roy Carr. London: 28 October 1998.

page 124: "It was a very loose thing that the band was into . . ." Morrison/Corvin, op cit. In the same interview, Morrison went on to criticize his producer, insisting "And Scott kept pushing his own material. We didn't need his material. He just kept pushing it in. And the management company was pushing it. Phew! It was a whole number. We were in it for the music and just the general feeling of turning people on. That's how it started. And then all these people come in and try to put angles on it. It just dilutes everything that you're saying and doing. We would arrive at a session and Scott would have these lyrics on a piece of paper and Billy and I were supposed to take it from there and do one of Scott's songs. We were too nice about the whole thing. We should have put the clamps on right there. It was out of this world. And they didn't care whether the group broke up or whatever." These harsh words were considered unworthy of the main text mainly because the criticisms ultimately fail to convince. The complaint about Scott pushing songs at this point and how Harrison and Morrison "should have put the clamps on" is unsupported by the evidence of the album. Only half of one of its 14 songs is written by Scott – 'I'm Gonna Dress In Black' is co-credited to his pseudonym M. Gillon. By contrast, Morrison dominates the writing credits and Bert Berns offers three of his own songs. The much maligned Scott had an absolutely minimal role in the writing credits. It was the second Them album where he had a more noticeable presence.

page 124: "Half the stuff was ad-libbed . . ." Harrison/Rogan. Bangor, Co. Down: 9 July 1994.

page 124: "I appreciated their efforts and didn't at the same time . . ." ibid.

page 125: "We are getting £300 each . . ." ibid. Them's chart contemporaries the Kinks were earning £300 a show this same month. It therefore seems likely that Them at their peak would have pulled in approximately £300 a date before deductions.

page 125: "When you're on the road, money doesn't last long . . ." Henderson/Rogan. Minnesota: 19 August 1994.

page 125: "It's very slow indeed . . ." reviewer Penny Valentine in *Disc*: 12 June 1965.

page 126: "I remember going into the studio and cutting it . . ." Morrison/Corvin, op cit.

page 127: "We didn't plan a note . . ." Morrison quoted in Belfast's *City Week*: 21 October 1965.

page 128: "Van and Billy had vehement fights . . ." Peter Bardens, interviewed by Pete Frame. London: 1970. Reprinted in *The Beatles And Some Other Guys – Rock Family Trees Of The Early Sixties*, London, Omnibus: 1997.

page 128: "I play the father confessor . . ." Billy Harrison, interviewed by Penny Valentine, *Disc*: 10 April 1965.

page 128: "He worries a lot . . ." ibid.

page 128: "When things started to go to hell he had this girl Dee . . ." Harrison/Rogan. Bangor, Co. Down: 9 July 1994.

page 130: "I don't know what triggered me off . . ." ibid.

page 130: "After that they didn't want me . . ." ibid.

page 130: "We've no intention of breaking up . . ." Billy Harrison, statement to Johnny Robb in Belfast's *City Week*: 9 July 1965.

page 130: "These boys take their own decisions . . ." Solomon's press release, June 1965.

page 130: "My brother wouldn't have voted anybody out . . ." McAuley/Rogan. London: 1 March 1995.

page 131: "Things were OK for a while . . ." Billy Harrison, quoted in Belfast's *City Week*: 8 September 1966.

page 131: "Everything just got out of proportion . . ." Van Morrison, quoted in *The Beat*: 2 December 1967.

page 132: "Phil Solomon screwed that up royally . . ." Henderson/Rogan. Minnesota: 19 August 1994.

page 132: "I don't think he was ever happy with Billy Harrison . . ." McAllen/Rogan. Belfast: 30 October 1994.

page 132: "Phil Solomon was paying people a living wage . . ." Wrixon/Rogan. Belfast: 21 June 1994.

page 133: "We weren't in competition . . ." Herbie Armstrong/Rogan. Sheffield: 23 November 1994.

page 133: "We tore the place apart . . ." ibid. Rod Demick maintains the slap-up meal was a £5 round of sandwiches.

page 134: "The exuberant Kenny Lynch found Them . . ." Kenny Lynch, interviewed by the author, Nettlebed, Oxon: 10 January 1999.

page 134: "I always had a great belief in him . . ." Mervyn Solomon/Rogan. Belfast: 25 February 1982.

page 135: The Melotones, who were even older than the celebrated Clipper Carlton, played three nights a week at Romano's ballroom. Armstrong was still at school when he joined the band but practised with them all day during his summer holidays in order to develop his sight skills. The band did various sessions for UTV and BBC, playing a combination of Dixieland, jazz and pop. In 1963, Armstrong backed Melotones' bassist/vocalist Billy Candless on a Jim Reeves tribute single, which attracted the attention of Decca Records. The company's interest waned upon discovering that most of the Melotones were in their mid-fifties. In addition to his work with the Melotones, Armstrong was also involved in session work and backed singer Kenny McDowell on Moses K & The Prophets' single 'I Went Out With My Baby Tonight' which was arranged and produced by Tommy Scott and featured Phil Coulter on piano. Former Mad Lad McDowell would later front a version of Them which also included Armstrong.

page 135: "Van was a strange person . . ." Billy Kennedy, interviewed by the author. London: 12 March 1982.

page 135: "George Jones and Billy McAllen were in the Silhouettes . . ." Roy Kane, who later joined Jones and McAllen in the Silhouettes, remembers his comrades creating a sensation with their dark clothes and hooded masks. "Everyone thought they were an all-male band, but they had a woman on keyboards at one point. They were playing in the Fiesta and she went into the girls' toilet so there was this screaming and yelling match. They were trying to get this mystique and build a following. They bought the Plattermen's bus and drove into town with their masks on. It was good publicity."

page 135: "I have heard the Other Ones twice at the Harland & Wolff Social Club . . ." Violet Morrison, letter to Belfast's *City Week*: 3 September 1965.

page 136: "The sight of Van Morrison . . ." reviewed in *City Week*: 1 October 1965.

page 136: "It was a really hot show . . ." Henderson/Rogan. Minnesota: 19 August 1994.

page 136: "The clothes over there are a ridiculous price . . ." Jim Armstrong, interviewed by Jacqueline Rothstein. *City Week*: 4 November 1965.

page 137: "In those days the producer ruled the studio . . ." Demick/Rogan. London: 5 October 1994. At this point, Scott was working with other Solomon acts including the Capitol, the Wheels and Mad Lads' offshoot, Moses K & The Prophets.

page 137: "Van went dry for a while . . ." Scott/Rogan. London: 18 February 1982.

page 138: "The number wasn't going down . . ." ibid.

page 138: "I don't think anyone with half an ear . . ." Coulter/Rogan. London: 28 January 1982.

page 138: "I think I recorded everything Van wrote during that period . . ." Scott/Rogan. London: 18 February 1982.

page 138: "The second album was not thought of as an album . . ." Philip Solomon/Rogan. Dublin: 15 April 1982.

page 139: "Goodness, the surprises I get . . ." reviewed by Penny Valentine, *Disc*: 11 November 1965.

page 139: "I got a few phone calls where people hung up . . ." Harrison/Rogan. Bangor, Co. Down: 18 August 1994.

page 139: "We went there for a laugh . . ." Harrison/Rogan: Bangor, Co. Down: 9 July 1994. The ubiquitous Viv Prince actually guested onstage with Them during a filmed show at Tiles in London's Oxford Street, *circa* March 1966. The footage was included in a Belgium television documentary *Contrastes,* transmitted on 18 May 1966.

page 140: "He had a glass of wine in one hand . . ." Jim Armstrong, interviewed by the author. Antrim: 17 July 1994.

page 140: 'When he took up that run he was sliding to grab the mike . . ." Henderson/Rogan. Minnesota: 19 August 1994.

page 140: "It was laughable . . ." Harrison/Rogan. Bangor, Co. Down: 21 August 1994.

page 140: "Wilfie (John Wilson) was totally embarrassed by the whole affair . . ." Jim Armstrong/Rogan. Antrim: 17 July 1994.

page 141: "He was mad . . ." John Wilson, interviewed by Paul Charles. *City Week*: 17 November 1972.

page 141: "Two weeks before Christmas . . ." Back in Belfast, local scribe Johnny Robb was already penning the group's obituary having no doubt observed Morrison's abject failure to register among the list of the Top 25 British male vocalists. "The sad history of Them is the most distressing thing that happened to pop music. For a multiplicity of reasons Them were fated to have personnel changes from the very start through personality conflicts. Instead of putting them in the background like the Kinks, the Who and half-a-dozen other top groups have done, Them chose to have their disagreements in public. Undoubtedly, the confusion that arose is primarily responsible for the group's current failure to get back on its feet."(*City Week*, 30 December 1965).

page 141: "We went to Paris, then Stockholm . . ." Harrison/Rogan. Bangor, Co. Down: 21 August 1994. Harrison also has vivid memories of returning to Them for a gig in Paris during which Bobby Hamilton was road manager. I have assumed this accompanied the trip to Sweden in the chronology. I doubt that it refers to the show at the Olympia, Paris, in October as Them would not have required two lead guitarists and Armstrong was definitely there. Oddly, Alan Henderson could recall only one visit to Paris, but I believe his memory was faulty on this matter. Armstrong later confirmed to me that there were at least two appearances in Paris.

page 141: "It is quite ridiculous . . ." Maurice King, press statement on behalf of Capable Management, 27 January 1966.

Chapter Nine: Hollywood

page 143: "*Them Again* . . ." The US version of *Them Again* regrettably omitted 'Hey Girl' and three of the cover versions: 'Hello Josephine', 'I Put A Spell On You' and 'I Got A Woman'.

page 144: ". . . had signed with Reg Calvert and Terry King . . ." Terry King, interviewed by the author. London: 14 November 1983.

page 145: "Our group Them have lost work all over the world . . ." Philip Solomon's statement was published in the *New Musical Express*: 4 February 1966. For further details on the strange life and bizarre death of Reg Calvert, see J. Rogan, *Starmakers & Svengalis: The History Of British Pop Management*, London, Queen Anne Press: 1988.

page 145: "She was just right for him . . ." Bobby Hamilton, interviewed by the author. Worcester: 16 October 1994.

page 145: "Van was contrary . . ." Jim Armstrong/Rogan. Antrim: 17 July 1994.

page 145: "He'd drink a bottle of vodka . . ." Hamilton /Rogan. Worcester: 16 October 1994. Oddly, nobody else mentioned that Morrison may have had some missing teeth. At first I assumed this might have been a slip of the memory on Hamilton's part, although it was such an unusually visual detail that this also appeared strange. Morrison seemed very young to have lost teeth, that is until I found a contemporaneous feature in a Belfast newspaper with the hilarious headline: "Ulster Says No To Fluoride!"

page 145: "It was a shame . . ." Demick/Rogan. London: 5 October 1994.

page 146: "We sat up half the night . . ." ibid.

page 146: "He used to ring in the middle of the night . . ." Jim Armstrong/Rogan. Antrim: 17 July 1994.

page 146: "Later, it transpired that she had subsequently died, reportedly from a brain tumour . . ." The circumstances of Dee's death have prompted various theories, not least because Morrison has never spoken about her in any interview. Indeed, the absence of her surname from anyone's memory has meant that it has been impossible to locate a death certificate to confirm the date and cause of her demise. Inevitably, songs like 'T.B. Sheets' and 'Slim Slow Slider' have been connected with her in Morrison mythology but to assume that they are literal evocations of the details of her life or death would be mistaken. Bobby Hamilton's wife assured me that Dee's mother had told her that she had died from a brain tumour. Until Morrison provides us with her surname and her death certificate is consulted, the matter is unlikely to be resolved to anyone's satisfaction.

page 146: "The irrepressible Geordie Sproule and fellow Federals Ricky Maitland and Eddie Campbell had teamed up with Billy McAllen and George Jones of the Silhouettes, plus Keith Donald of the Greenbeats, to form a one-off showband supergroup mischievously named the Half Cuts . . ." George Jones has consistently and erroneously referred to this show with the Half Cuts as a get-together between the Federals and the *Monarchs* (rather than the Silhouettes), thus confusing the chronology. Newspaper reports (see *City Week*, 17 March 1966) confirm his error. His slip is explained by the fact that he and Billy McAllen were both members of the Monarchs before they moved on to the Silhouettes. "I let Alexis Korner use my guitar to do the gig," McAllen recalls. "There were a lot of musicians there and we decided to go on with Geordie Sproule and the others. We were in the dressing room with Alexis Korner and we said, 'What'll we call ourselves?' I said, 'The Half Cuts'. It was just a one-off. The guitarist Eddie Campbell [who was later involved with Morrison in a late 1966 version of Them] is now dead and buried. He went to Canada with a Dublin band, married a Canadian girl, then came home. He was walking around the supermarket with her and went just like that – a brain haemorrhage. He died in his early thirties." Keith Donald, the sole Greenbeat in the group, was a former member of the Federals. "Keith was blowing an exceptional sax," G.D. adds. "We went on before Alexis Korner. We were one of the few groups there that was asked back on stage twice."

page 148: "Philip wasn't too keen on their discipline . . ." Scott/Rogan. London: 18 February 1982.

page 148: "The relationship had been deteriorating . . ." Coulter/Rogan. London: 28 January 1982.

page 148: "Ray Elliott and Van Morrison went completely senseless . . ." Wrixon/Rogan. Belfast: 21 June 1994. Speculating on Them's troubled history, Wrixon added, "They put their money on Van. Van just wanted to be famous. Billy Harrison actually wanted to see money because he was married. He was also sensible. He always asked awkward questions. Van was some sort of mildly arty poet who wandered around the place and wasn't too much trouble at all. He was ripe for exploitation."

page 148: "The thing was falling apart . . ." Jim Armstrong/Rogan. Antrim: 17 July 1994.

page 148: "The man is as thick skinned as a crocodile . . ." Philip Solomon/Rogan. Dublin: 15 April 1982.

page 149: "We did a slow version of the song with harmonica . . ." Jim Armstrong/Rogan. Antrim: 17 July 1994.

page 149: "We arranged the meeting with Philip . . ." ibid.

page 149: "I was finished with that game . . ." ibid.

page 149: "It became a trial . . ." *The Beat*: 2 December 1967.

page 150: "They wanted me to go to the States . . ." Morrison/Corvin, op cit.

page 150: "I felt it could all be regenerated . . ." Scott/Rogan. London: 18 February 1982.

page 151: "Do you think it's too disrespectful? . . ." ibid. 'Walkin' In The Queen's Garden' was later recorded by Them without Van Morrison. On the album on which it appears, Morrison's name is not included in the writing credits. "It was an ad-lib," Alan Henderson explained. "It started on stage and when we recorded it, there were no words to it. I recorded it. It had been done on stage in the USA – it was never done in England. I more or less wrote my own words."

page 151: "If he'd said 'I'll take 35%' . . ." Jim Armstrong/Rogan. Antrim: 17 July 1994.

page 151: "The truth is 101 per cent as follows . . ." Philip Solomon/Rogan. Dublin: 15 April 1982.

page 152: "On our first night at the Whisky A Go-Go . . ." Ray Elliott, interviewed by Donall Corvin, *Spotlight*: 18 December 1971. Them's drinks bill has been variously estimated over recent years, but this figure is the earliest mentioned. Armstrong recalls that it totalled $5,200 (very close to Elliott's figure), with a 50 per cent discount, making $2,600. The meeting with Frank Zappa led to a lasting friendship and he subsequently performed with Elliott and Armstrong when they returned to the USA with a later version of Them, without Morrison. "He came down and played blues with us on his Les Paul," Armstrong recalls. "That was on the tour with Kenny McDowell. We played Chicago as well."

page 153: "We didn't see much of her . . ." Jim Armstrong/Rogan. Antrim: 17 July 1994. Writer Steve Turner claimed that Morrison "almost certainly" wrote the song 'Ballerina' in honour of Janet, while Armstrong confirms that the composition was premiered on the 1966 American tour. Turner quotes Morrison from an interview in which he says, "I had a flash about an actress in an opera house appearing in a ballet and I think that's where the song came from." The writer then adds teasingly: "Janet Planet was an actress." His assertion although very plausible, is hardly "almost certain" and underlines the need for caution in assuming any biographical intent. Was she a practising actress at the time? Nobody has ever associated her with ballet or opera. Moreover, none of Morrison's colleagues recall him visiting a theatre or hearing anything about ballerinas. The "flash" about an actress sounds as if Morrison is merely picturing a ballerina at work. It could have been inspired by almost anything or more likely, as he suggests, it was simply an image plucked from his imagination. Significantly, Turner does not complete the aforementioned quote in which Morrison adds, "The song may possibly be about a hooker. Part of it anyway may be about a hooker . . ." which, mischief aside, again suggests that the composition is not transparently biographical but part fictional or at the very least based on several different images or incidents.

page 153: "This was the sort of guy you'd see in a film . . ." Jim Armstrong/Rogan. Antrim: 17 July 1994.

page 153: "We did gigs with the Mafia, sure . . ." ibid.

page 154: "Well, for a certain sum . . ." ibid.

page 154: "I was emotionally intimidated by him myself . . ." Coulter/Rogan. London: 28 January 1982.

page 154: "I'm not a violent man . . . He was a very honest solicitor . . ." Philip Solomon/Rogan. Dublin: 15 April 1982. One year after our interview, Walter Hofer died from a heart attack. His reputation as an "honest solicitor" was later questioned. According to Fredric Dannen in *The Hit Men* (London, Muller: 1990): "By the early Eighties, Hofer's practice was in a shambles. Furious clients accused him of embezzling large sums from their accounts, and he was unable to pay them back."

page 155: "Van jumped and fell into the drums . . ." Jim Armstrong/Rogan. Antrim: 17 July 1994.

page 155: "It was Them and the Ramsey Lewis Trio . . ." Henderson/Rogan. Minnesota: 19 August 1994.

page 155: ". . . . 'The Sash' . . ." Also known as 'The Sash My Father Wore', this Orange anthem was the most well-known of loyalist songs.

page 155: "It's etched for ever . . ." Jim Armstrong/Rogan. Antrim: 17 July 1994.

page 156: "He didn't talk to anybody at this time . . ." Elliott/Corvin, op cit.

page 156: "He was singing away, then he lifted his mike stand . . ." Jim Armstrong/Rogan. Antrim: 17 July 1994. After this show, Armstrong was presented with a birthday cake and drummer David Harvey, who missed the awaiting limousine, was escorted back to his hotel in a police car.

page 157: "We were hitting a brick wall . . ." Henderson/Rogan. Minnesota: 19 August 1994.

page 157: "Thereafter, he diversified his interests . . ." Over the summer Solomon had signed Spanish hitmakers Los Bravos whose 'Black Is Black' offered chart action without the administrative horrors provided by Them. Solomon added a legion of Spanish groups to his books but sensibly delegated his responsibilities. With Radio Caroline he was co-ordinating an ambitious European broadcasting operation involving France, England, Spain and Ireland. In addition, he was about to launch his own record label Major Minor, signing acts like the Brian Brothers and Odin's People.

page 157: "There comes a time when you have to say, 'Is it worth it?' . . ." Philip Solomon/Rogan. Dublin: 15 April 1982.

page 157: "I regret that we couldn't have controlled Morrison better . . ." ibid.

page 157: "He was an Irish Jew . . ." quoted in Ritchie Yorke, *Van Morrison: Into The Music*, London, Charisma/Futura: 1975.

page 157: "Phil Coulter attempted to console Morrison . . ." Coulter remembers this period as possibly the lowest point in Morrison's career. The singer stayed at his London home for a brief spell, but nothing seemed to be happening for him. Lemmy Kilminster, later of Motorhead, told journalist Gavin Martin that Morrison was rooming in a cheap, sparsely-furnished hotel room around this time. When approached, he offered the forlorn lament: "Times are bad, Lemmy."

Chapter Ten: Belfast Before The Troubles

page 159: ". . . Battle of the Somme . . ." This anniversary was a highly emotive time for Unionists as thousands of UVF members had given their lives at Somme in 1916, many marching to the chant of 'No Surrender'.

page 159: "The Republicans' Easter parades . . ." On 8 March 1966, in the run-up to the Easter celebrations, Republican sympathizers blew up Nelson's Pillar in Dublin. This was regarded as an isolated incident and greeted lightheartedly in the South. New picture postcards of Dublin city centre had to be printed. A novelty song, 'Up Went Nelson' was played frequently on the radio, and the Dubliners reached the Irish Top 10 with their tribute single, 'Nelson's Farewell'. Coincidentally, in the same week as the explosion the Johnny Flynn Showband were number 1 in the Irish charts with the rebel song 'Black And Tan Gun'.

page 160: "There had always been a heavy nationalism within me . . ." Gerry O'Hare, interviewed by the author. Dublin: 12 February 2004.

page 161: "To those of us who remember the Thirties, the pattern is horribly familiar . . ." Prime Minister, Captain Terence O'Neill, Stormont, Hansard, House of Commons: 15 June 1966.

page 162: "There is a part of Britain . . ." Insight, the *Sunday Times,* June 1966.

page 162: ". . . past the lavatory-wall patriotism . . ." *Observer,* June 1966.

page 162: "They are a touchy people . . ." ibid.

page 163: "That was always going on . . ." Van Morrison, interviewed by Niall Stokes. *Hot Press*: 28 October 2003.

page 164: "the permissive manners and morals . . ." Donald S. Connery, *The Irish*, London, Eyre & Spottiswoode: 1968.

page 164: "Belfast? The town has had it . . ." Peter Docherty, quoted in *City Week*: 12 May 1966. The Doc had an up-and-down summer of 1966. A sensation at the Plaza, he ended the season washing up in a pub. By late autumn, he had secured a job as resident disc jockey at Blackpool's Beat City club under the alias Jason Peters.

page 165: "It doesn't have much to do with the Irish scene . . ." Van Morrison, interviewed by Happy Traum. *Rolling Stone*: 9 July 1970.

page 165: "Roy Kane had recently joined Billy McAllen in the Silhouettes . . .": The classic Silhouettes line-up was completed with the arrival of Kane. It comprised Bernie McAvoy (saxophone), Bob Steele (trombone), Stan Lynn (trumpet), Billy Davie (rhythm guitar), Billy McAllen (lead guitar), George Jones (bass) and Roy Kane (drums). Previously there had been a female keyboardist. "There was always a lead singer – several lead singers," Kane remembers. "Ron Masters was one. The Silhouettes were originally the Stan Lynn Showband. They were known in the Belfast ballrooms as an old-time band who got a younger element in and became a showband. My introduction to playing in the South was with Stan Lynn. We played Donegal on Sunday. They used to give out the Gaelic football results while you were playing. It was great. With the Silhouettes, we had one of the finest bands that anyone could wish to hear playing up-to-date stuff from the pop charts. We were the resident band at Romano's where the main attraction would be a Southern showband. They pulled in the crowds. A lot of the bands used to sit around and listen to us while we played the first half because we were so good. Many of them said we should have been doing big work on the Southern circuit. I don't think we ever wanted to work in the South. Nobody seemed to want to know. Maybe we didn't have a good enough image. The Silhouettes broke up and Billy and I joined the Tara showband, with George Jones. The other members were Bob Steele (trombone), Mickey Fox (trumpet) and Seán Fox (saxophone). They'd brought in Deke Arlon who played Benny in *Crossroads* – not the woolly-hatted character but the heart-throb. I don't know why they launched him as a showband singer in Ireland. The Tara proved a short-term thing. I then went with Wesley Black (Blackie) who formed the Wes Black Combo with myself and guitarist Davy Chappell. It was possibly the first band that went into cabaret playing the Trocadero in Cromac Street. We were the forerunners of the cabaret scene in Belfast."

page 165: "Meanwhile, the indefatigable Georgie Sproule (G.D.) was enjoying unprecedented success . . ." The Federals line-up prior to the arrival of Armstrong and Elliott comprised founding member John Wallace (rhythm guitar), G.D. (lead vocalist/tenor saxophonist), Vaughan Byrne (bass), John Alexander (saxophone) and Gerry McEldruff (drums). During the late autumn of 1966, Sproule was involved in a bewildering number of part-time groups in addition to his regular stint in the Federals. They included the G.D. All Stars and the Untouchables, plus a makeshift unit featuring Vaughan Byrne and some members of the Misfits. "There were many people who never got the chance to show their talent on stage," G. D. says. "I got to show mine a wee bit. Ray Elliott went to America with another version of Them and later played with Duane Eddy."

page 165: "He was a great musician . . ." Sproule/Rogan. Belfast: 29 October 1994.

page 166: "We want to play our original music now . . ." Van Morrison, interviewed by Donall Corvin. *City Week*: 22 September 1966.

page 166: "Them are the most mucked-about group . . ." Corvin, ibid.

page 166: "He never spoke English until he was seven . . ." Sam Smyth/Rogan. Dublin: July/August 1993.

page 167: "It was very important at that time . . ." ibid.

page 167: "I had a lot of time for Corvin . . ." Kane/Rogan Belfast: 27 October 1994.

page 167: "There was a dark side . . ." Colin McClelland, interviewed by the author. Belfast: 16 September 2002.

page 167: ". . . a fascinating character . . ." Wrixon/Rogan. Belfast: 21 June 1994.

page 167: "It'll be good to play in a Belfast club again . . ." Van Morrison, interviewed by Donall Corvin: September 1966. Part published, *City Week*: 6 October 1966.

page 168: "I had to pay his 30 shillings fare back . . ." Dino Martin, interviewed by the author. Antrim: 24 November 1994. Journalist B.P. Fallon also recalls one of Morrison's visits to Dublin during this period. He appeared on stage briefly with the End at a coffee bar, the Coffee Kitchen. Like Dino Martin, Fallon remembers offering some small financial assistance to the singer.

page 168: "When I went back to Belfast . . ." Morrison/Corvin, 1973, op cit.

page 169: "Some of them acted very strange . . ." ibid.

page 169: "I wouldn't let him on . . ." Brian Russell, interviewed by the author. Belfast: 20 October 1994.

page 169: "You're talking to somebody from Northern Ireland . . ." Cynthia MacHenry (Russell), interviewed by the author. Belfast: 16 June 2002. Although I have no reason to question Cynthia's detailed memory of this incident, it should be added that her husband's use of a swear word was evidently out of character. On the two occasions when I spoke to him at length, he did not utter a single profanity or vulgarity of any description, not even in jest, and he was also very polite and well-mannered. Additionally, he was one of the few people from that era who still actively followed Morrison's career, regularly bought his records, paid to see him in concert and spoke authoritatively about numerous live shows. In short, he was a Morrison fan.

page 169: "I asked him why he didn't get the boys together . . ." Russell/Rogan. Belfast: 20 October 1994.

page 169: "I never rubbed him up the wrong way . . ." Janet Martin/Rogan. Belfast: 1 October 1993.

page 170: "Even if you were in a bar drinking . . ." Dino Martin/Rogan. Antrim: 24 November 1994.

page 170: "Obviously, Corvin was looking for a way to sell Van . . ." ibid.

page 170: "Van and Donall went drinking together . . ." Sam Smyth/Rogan. Dublin: July/August 1993.

page 171: "I went home and told my folks . . ." Eric Bell/Rogan. London: 5 August 1994.

page 171: "It was like nothing I'd ever seen . . ." ibid.

page 171: "People were giving out nuts and raisins . . ." ibid.

page 172: "I was one of the first intellectual, thinking people that he met . . ." Cecil McCartney, interviewed by the author. Bangor, Co. Down: 30 October 1994.

page 172: "I'm one of the most advanced people . . ." ibid.

page 173: "It was a painting . . ." ibid.

page 173: "Van had a blue velvet suit or cloak . . ." ibid.

page 173: "Van came panting up . . ." ibid.

page 174: "I thought it was really weird . . ." ibid.

page 174: "He would just sit there . . ." ibid.

page 174: "He was trying to explain to me how Hitler got his name . . ." ibid.

page 175: "The Cavalier was in the Markets area . . ." MacHenry/Rogan. Belfast: 16 June 2002.

page 175: "he was not a good-looking boy" Deborah Thompson, interviewed by the author. Brighton, East Sussex: 26 May 2002.

page 175: "Och, he tried that with everyone . . ." MacHenry/Rogan. Belfast: 16 June 2002.

page 175: "I was great friends with Sammy and Corvin . . ." Ursula Graham-White, interviewed by the author. East Grinstead: 17 November 1993.

page 175: "I used to dress unusually . . ." ibid.

page 176: "We also used to hang out at the Jazz Club . . ." ibid.

page 176: "He was a total bore . . ." MacHenry/Rogan. Belfast: 16 June 2002.

page 176: "If you were walking along University Road . . ." ibid.

page 176: "He used to do dreadful things . . ." ibid.

page 177: "He was a loner, definitely . . ." ibid.

page 177: "Van was always very much the same . . ." Graham-White/Rogan. East Grinstead: 17 November 1993.

page 177: "We'd been painting the club . . ." ibid.

page 177: "Van not getting into places . . ." MacHenry/Rogan. Belfast: 16 June 2002.

page 178: "It was really strange . . ." Eric Bell/Rogan. London: 5 August 1994.

page 178: "I had a list of all the songs . . ." ibid.

page 179: "I'd simply run back and forth between them . . ." McCartney/Rogan. Bangor, Co. Down: 30 October 1994.

page 179: "It was very weird . . ." Russell/Rogan. Belfast: 20 October 1994.

page 179: "I don't think Belfast will ever produce a 'show' to equal the opening night . . ." Reviewer, Donall Corvin, City Week: 3 November 1966.

page 179: "it wasn't real hot" Henderson/Rogan. Minnesota: 19 August 1994.

page 179: "It looked pretty deserted . . ." Eric Bell/Rogan. London: 5 August 1994.

page 180: "A flustered McCartney . . ." The projectionist confirmed the ugly incident: "The Teddy Boys at the back of the crowd were really offended. I saw the reaction. They threw coins at him and the gig closed early." McCartney/Rogan. Bangor, Co. Down: 30 October 1994.

page 180: "Morrison was in the front . . ." Eric Bell/Rogan. London: 5 August 1994.

page 180: "I think Morrison was a bit jealous of Eric . . ." Moore/Rogan. Belfast: 6 August 1994.

page 181: "They'd booked Van to do the gig, but they wanted to expand it . . ." O'Hare/Rogan. Dublin: 12 February 2004.

page 181: "I was so drunk that I turned up my guitar . . ." Eric Bell/Rogan. London: 5 August 1994.

page 181: "That was all he said . . ." ibid.

page 182: "A three and sixpenny peak at Blackpool illuminations gone wrong . . ." Reviewer, Donall Corvin. City Week: 24 November 1966.

page 182: "They wanted showband material at Newry . . ." McAllen/Rogan. Belfast: 30 October 1994.

page 182: "I just used my snare drum with my drumkit . . ." Kane/Rogan. Belfast: 27 October 1994. Beyond the dates mentioned here, it is possible that this late 1966 'Them' line-up may have played a few other scattered performances. Cecil

McCartney confirms that he was co-opted to provide another light show for Morrison and the group at a date in Enniskillen. The Federals' Eddie Campbell who was auditioned at Morrison's house may have played at one date but, if so, that secret now lies in the grave. Roy Kane could only recall the Newry gig as an example of the Silhouettes/Them line-up in action. Billy McAllen adds: "When Van came home, I actually did *the odd gig* with him as Them." However, after recalling the Newry performance in some detail, he qualified his statement with the conclusion, "It was a one-off." Guitarist Mick Cox also recalls playing with Morrison during this period in a line-up which included his brother John Cox, Mike Brown and Joe Hanratty.

Chapter Eleven: Fitzroy To Manhattan

page 185: "When we played the Plaza ballroom in Chichester Street . . ." Baird/ Rogan. Belfast: 31 October 1994. Baird's 'fight and unite' anecdote is a stark reminder that all is far from black and white in Green and Orange politics. Irish history and religion is full of ironies and paradoxes. The simplistic alignment of Catholicism and Irish nationalism has often betrayed some decidedly grey hues. An effigy of the Pope is ritually burned at Orange parades celebrating the Battle of the Boyne. It's worth recalling that the Pope supported William Of Orange in 1609, not his adversary the Catholic King James II. Conversely, the devout Éamon de Valera, one of the modern fathers of Irish Republicanism, faced excommunication by the Catholic Church after the 1916 Easter Rising. Many Northern Presbyterians, facing discrimination from the Church of Ireland, were heavily involved in the 1798 rebellion, pursuing, of all things, a united Ireland. And, of course, many of Ireland's most famous patriots, nationalists, rebels and reformers were part of the Protestant ascendancy. Such anomalies always provide a pleasing pause for thought.

page 185: "I was a pacifist . . ." McCartney/Rogan. Bangor, Co. Down: 30 October 1994.

page 185: "The Troubles were smouldering long before 1969 . . ." Baird/Rogan. Belfast: 31 October 1994.

page 186: "We did this medley of 'kick the Pope' stuff . . ." ibid.

page 186: "Jimmy Green, who was a good Catholic sang the whole lot . . ." ibid.

page 186: "The Protestants danced in the Orange Hall . . ." ibid.

page 186: "He didn't want to play . . ." ibid. Ignatius Hughes, named after the founder of the Jesuit order Ignatius Loyola, was encouraged to take the stage name Mike Hughes to draw attention away from his Catholicism when playing the Orange circuit.

page 187: "He'd usually start off by playing and just humming . . ." Violet Morrison. Belfast: 1969.

page 187: "He was on a downer . . ." Coulter/Rogan. London: 28 January 1982.

page 188: "I'd been wanting to go to the States for a while . . ." Morrison/Corvin, 1973, op cit. In a much later interview Morrison referred to the record company casually as "European", which may mean it was not even Philips in London, but a continental branch of the label. Either way, it underlines the point made by Coulter that there was no longer any easy outlet for his work in the UK. The advance Morrison received from Berns ($2,500) may seem parsimonious but it should be noted that the astute Neil Diamond – who negotiated a $50,000-per-album deal with MCA's Uni Records in 1967 and, four years later, a reported $4 million ($400,000 per album) arrangement with CBS Records – also accepted $2,500 from Berns.

page 188: "The one-year contract . . ." By modern standards, Bang's recording contract – which demanded the artiste record 12 songs a year, plus a further 50 at the company's discretion – sounds slavish. However, Berns was a figure from the Brill Building era when songwriters working in cubicles would think nothing of knocking off an album's worth of songs in a matter of days. Even after the emergence of the album as an art form, major record companies continued to demand product, at least contractually. The giant CBS, for example, in a renegotiation of the Byrds contract in early 1968, required the group to record two albums a year and a third "at our election". By mutual consent, the artistes themselves could apply to record a fourth album within a calendar year. In practice, of course, these tough terms were not rigidly applied. The Byrds, who were committed to a seven-year contract after this point, continued to release only one album a year between 1968-72 (excepting a double live/studio album in 1970). This should underline the main point that Bang's terms, especially for a small company, were not so outlandish or unfair as some might assume.

page 188: "Indeed, an addendum to his Bang contract . . ." The seven-clause 'Amendment And Addendum' to the Bang contract provides an insight into Morrison's wishes at the time. Clause 1 ensured that Bang would not be permitted to apply "the excess of the minimum number of record sides required to be recorded during any year period of the Agreement against the record sides required in any subsequent year . . ." Clause 2 insisted that Bang actually record the minimum number of sides [12] required. Clause 3 betrayed Morrison's fears about the possibility of Bang exploiting his connection with his former group. "Artiste had recorded certain musical selections as part of the group 'Them' . . . Company agrees that: Company will not make any reference to the name 'Them' on phonograph records, or in advertising copy in connection with the recordings of the Artiste. Company may, however, issue publicity material stating the connection between Artiste and 'Them' as a portion of Artiste's history in the music industry." Morrison's former wife Janet reminds us, "He was dying to get out of Them, absolutely dying to go solo. I think it was growing pains for him because he had been in a group since he was 15." Clause 4 prevented Bang from including Morrison on a recording with any of their other artistes without his written consent. Clause 5 stated: "Company's recoupment from Artiste's royalties of payments to unions shall be in respect to those payments made in connection with wages only. Company shall not be able to recoup from Artiste's royalties any payments made by Company to any union, guild or federation in respect of any trust fund, or its equivalent, based on sales of records made by Company." Clause

6 confirmed: "Company shall pay Artiste's transportation from England to the United States as a non-returnable advance to Artiste, shall charge said costs against Artiste's royalties and deduct them from royalty payments to Artiste if and when earned." Clause 7 increased Morrison's advances in the event of Bang taking up their renewal option. For the second year, they would be required to pay a non-returnable advance against royalties of $3,500 and for the third, fourth and fifth years a sum of $5,000.

page 188: "Cox had recently established himself . . ." Billy Hollywood recalls Cox's stay in the Alleykatz: "Mick Cox was a fabulous player. I was playing guitar in the Alleykatz and was ready to leave. The line-up was Joe Hanratty, Mike Brown, Jim Ross, me and vocalist Brian Godfrey who was a good singer with the hair and a thin face like a skull. Mick Cox turned up at a show that we did at the Square One in Royal Avenue. He liked the band and knew I was leaving. He said he had a Telecaster and could play good blues and would they be interested in giving him a job. He'd played with Jeff Beck. He hadn't got an amplifier so he took over the payments on my VOX AC 30. He was in. I saw him play with the band a few times and he was very good, but he wasn't very easy to get along with. He may have had an ego. The original keyboard player Jim Ross and he left shortly afterwards." Cox, in an interview with the magazine *Wavelength*, reckoned the End was formed after he left the Alleykatz, but contemporary reviews and notices in the local *City Week* confuse the issue.

page 189: "You might come home and find 20 people around . . ." Joan McClelland/Rogan. Belfast: 2 October 1994.

page 189: "We were all girls because mixed flats weren't the thing . . ." Carson /Rogan. Fife: 28 August 1993.

page 189: "Van was very keen on Ursula . . ." Joan McClelland/Rogan. Belfast: 2 October 1994.

page 189: "Ursula was great fun . . ." ibid.

page 189: "Ursula in her day was drop dead gorgeous . . ." MacHenry/Rogan. Belfast: 16 June 2002.

page 190: "Van was madly in love with her . . ." Carson/Rogan. Fife: 28 August 1993.

page 190: "It was a one-off time . . ." Graham-White/Rogan. East Grinstead: 17 November 1993.

page 190: "Van and Mick Cox teamed up as a kind of songwriting team . . ." Carson/Rogan. Fife: 28 August 1993.

page 190: "Offstage he had very little going for him . . ." Joan McClelland/Rogan. Belfast: 2 October 1994.

page 190: "Because he was so ugly he was always infatuated with beautiful women . . ." Denvir/Rogan. London: 12 September 1993.

page 190: "He would fall in love with somebody different every single week . . ." Carson/Rogan. Fife: 28 August 1993.

page 191: "At Fitzroy . . ." Janet Martin/Rogan. Belfast: 1 October 1993.

page 191: "We had a 1920s fancy dress party and he wore a boater hat . . ." Joan McClelland/Rogan. Belfast: 2 October 1994.

page 191: "There was a sunken pool there . . ." Janet Martin/Rogan. Belfast: 1 October 1993.

page 191: "He had this thing about graveyards . . ." Carson/Rogan. Fife: 28 August 1993.

page 192: "Everyone we knew was drinking and we were often very drunk . . ." Joan McClelland/Rogan. Belfast: 2 October 1994.

page 192: "Van was a mess . . ." Sam Smyth/Rogan. Dublin: July/August 1993.

page 192: "You could never get close to him . . ." Davis/Rogan. Shropshire: 21 October 1994.

page 192: "Everybody drank, and he did . . ." Carson/Rogan. Fife: 28 August 1993.

page 192: "He always reminded me of a soul in torment . . ." Denvir/Rogan. London: 12 September 1993.

page 192: "drinking anything that came to hand" Janet Martin/Rogan. Belfast: 1 October 1993.

page 193: "We spent a lot of time there . . ." Dino Martin/Rogan. Antrim: 24 November 1994.

page 193: "Sam was a one-off with wild red hair and staring eyes . . ." Denvir/Rogan. London: 12 September 1993.

page 193: "We were the main band . . ." Sam Mahood, interviewed by the author. Belfast: 28 October 1994.

page 193: "The audience started booing . . ." Thompson/Rogan. Brighton: 26 May 2002. Mick Cox was temporarily back in London when the Annadale debacle occurred. He recalls his brother John contacting him with the news that Morrison was seeking a guitarist to play some local shows. Other contemporaries point out that Morrison and the Cox brothers were already friends by this point and had been hanging out together. However, Mick reckons it was after this gig that he first teamed up with Morrison in a group setting, along with his brother, plus Mike Brown and Joe Hanratty of the Alleykatz. His chronology may be slightly awry as Brown and Hanratty had been playing with Morrison several months before, along with Eric Bell. When remembering this period, Mick Cox seemed unaware that Brown and Hanratty had worked with Morrison and spoke as if he had first introduced them to the singer. There are no known notices or reviews in the Belfast or surrounding press that I have found to confirm the exact date when Mick Cox was gigging with Morrison, but it was, according to the guitarist, either early 1967 or summer 1967, just before one of the trips to New York. There remains the remote possibility that it might have been earlier, closer to the time period when Brown and Hanratty and Eric Bell played together.

page 194: "He walked in, slipped down the wall and sat on the floor . . ." Rusty, interviewed by the author. Belfast: 28 October 1994.

page 194: "a cryptic person . . ." undated profile by Donall Corvin in *City Week*.

page 194: "He was a victim of his looks more than anything . . ." Carson/Rogan. Fife: 28 August 1993. This emphasis on the increasing importance of looks in the youth-obsessed Sixties should not be underestimated. In his book *The Sixties* (Oxford University Press, 1998), Professor of History and cultural commentator Arthur

Marwick pinpoints 1964, the year of Them's formation, as a pivotal moment in society's re-evaluation of the definition of beauty. As he argues, "One important product of the interacting changes, and challenges to previous conventions, becomes apparent in the late Fifties and accelerating from around 1964 onwards was the triumph of the 'modern' view of beauty, of physical beauty, detached altogether from moral judgements, wealth and class . . . This 'modern' conception of beauty, of beauty as 'an autonomous status characteristic', did not of course fill the hearts and minds of every single individual (traditional evaluations and confusions continue to this day), but as never before it dominated society at large, in its public mores, its newspapers, its advertisements, its television programmes, its social, cultural, and political behaviour. More and more people behaved as if they recognized that 'mere' physical beauty had a particular value of its own. Male beauty was increasingly recognized as having something of the same significance that had always (despite the conventions and confusions) attached to female beauty. In the middle and later 1960s beauty was universally praised and sought after; it had achieved a kind of parity with wealth and status, and certainly was no enemy to either."

page 194: "He'd given me a black eye! . . ." Denvir/Rogan. London: 12 September 1993.

page 195: "Isabeal's was a fabulous place . . ." ibid.

page 195: "Matthew was the queer boy" Russell/Rogan. Belfast: 20 October 1994.

page 195: "the queer there, Matthew . . ." Moore/Rogan. Belfast: 6 August 1994.

page 195: "the life and soul of the party . . ." ibid.

page 195: "Van got on very well with him . . ." Ann Denvir, interviewed by the author. Belfast: 9 December 2002.

page 196: "Although he and Corvin got on well . . ." Sam Smyth/Rogan. Dublin: July/August 1993.

page 196: "He's a very troubled person and always was . . ." Denvir/Rogan. Belfast: 9 December 2002.

page 196: "I think they were joined at that time . . ." Janet Martin/Rogan. Belfast: 1 October 1993.

page 196: "A nicer or more human guy you could not have met . . ." MacHenry/ Rogan. Belfast: 16 June 2002.

page 197: "Corvin was always good fun . . ." Thompson/Rogan. Brighton: 26 May 2002.

page 197: "When we used to go to Isabeal's with Donall Corvin . . ." Carson/Rogan. Fife: 28 August 1993.

page 197: "If you said black, he'd said white . . ." Denvir/Rogan. London: 12 September 1993.

page 197: "Oh Matthew really fancied Van . . ." Demick/Rogan. London: 5 October 1994.

page 197: "We used to call it the Scrumpy Rooms . . ." Thompson/Rogan. Brighton: 26 May 2002.

page 198: "It was just to get away . . ." Violet Morrison. Belfast: 1969.

page 198: "He was in the kitchen talking to all the boys . . ." Janet Martin/Rogan.

Belfast: 1 October 1993. Morrison's melodramatic departure from the party at Fitzroy clearly had an impact on the participants involved. It may also have influenced Morrison during the later writing of one of his most famous songs, 'Madame George'. In his liner notes to the Legacy CD *Bang Masters*, writer Bill Flanagan describes the composition in a way that brings to mind the events described here for the first time by Janet Martin and Gwen Carson: "'Madame George' is a song about saying goodbye to one's youthful friends and the old scene – it's a song about outgrowing a place and moving on. The lyric describes a party full of laughing, rowdy people. The singer, who finds himself no longer feeling like one of the gang, looks around for the last time and then slips out into the night to catch a train that will take him away. As he moves towards the station, he hears the sound of the party growing softer behind him."

page 198: "And I'll just say, 'Fuck you!' . . ." Carson/Rogan. Fife: 28 August 1993.

page 198: "That gives you a good insight into his character . . ." ibid.

page 198: "But he was such a nasty character . . ." ibid.

page 199: "It never happened . . ." Morrison/Corvin, 1973, op cit.

page 200: "I play harmonica and I used to play guitar . . ." Violet Morrison. Belfast: 1969.

page 200: "He'd come over to our house . . ." McCartney/Rogan. Bangor, Co. Down: 30 October 1994.

page 201: "He was really pleased with it . . ." Mick Cox, interviewed by Simon Gee, *Wavelength* 11. The gigs that Cox played with Morrison featured his brother John, bassist Mike Brown and drummer Joe Hanratty. Although Cox assumed they were undertaken after the Bang recordings, the line-up with Hanratty and Brown suggests that the more likely date may have been late 1966.

page 202: "We stood outside a fish and chip shop in Belfast . . ." Herbie Armstrong/Rogan. Sheffield: 23 November 1994.

page 202: "I'm into a completely different thing now . . ." Van Morrison, interviewed by Richard Robinson. *GO*: 4 August 1967.

page 202: "He asked me to go over with him . . ." Irvine/Rogan. Belfast: 18 September 1994.

page 203: "We were hippies and she was rooming in a place where I ended up staying . . ." Michael Maggid, interviewed by the author. Northern California: 5 June 2002.

page 204: "I wasn't really happy with it . . ." Morrison/Corvin, 1973. op cit.

page 204: "I give [Berns] . . ." Janet 'Planet' Morrison, interviewed by Joel Selvin, California: 1998.

page 205: "That's a dream he had . . ." Violet Morrison. Belfast: 1969. Morrison's 'death songs' seem to have inspired more fanciful theories and accounts than anything else in his canon. Apart from those who connect the song with the death of 'Dee', we have Violet Morrison's testimony that the song was based on a nightmare and Janet Planet's sleeve notes that vaguely suggest it was based on a real life experience. Even Tom Kielbania, who worked as bass player with Morrison in 1968–69, provides his own fanciful off-the-cuff interpretation. "We did 'T.B.

Sheets' a lot," he told me. "It was about a girl he knew in high school. From what I understand there was this girl he knew who had tuberculosis and he really liked her. They were pretty close and she was in hospital dying. He went to see her and all she wanted to do was listen to the radio and it really bummed him out. She wasn't interested in spiritual things but was more interested in listening to the radio. She died – I think. He used to do the song a lot." Kielbania's speculative account, which I have deliberately omitted from the main text, has various flaws, not least the fact that Morrison attended an all boys' school and therefore did not know any girl in high school. Also, Kielbania was not privy to Morrison's Belfast past and words like "from what I understand" imply a second-hand feel to his story. A more convincing contention might be that part of the song, consciously or unconsciously, refers back to the death of Morrison's cousin Gloria Gordon who also spent time in hospital and was extremely debilitated. Although any autobiographical interpretation of the song is, of course, at best dubious, its history continues to fascinate students of Morrison's late Sixties career. For his part, Morrison has attempted to close any such debate by claiming that the song was "complete and utter fiction", a view that does not contradict his mother's account of its origins as a dream. More recently, Morrison elaborated: "Somebody said it was about a girlfriend of mine who died. People sit around, have a few drinks and talk bullshit. That's all it was. Somebody [his ex-wife] picked it up and wrote about it on one of the sleeves of my records. It's a completely fictitious song. It's not about anybody I knew." Beyond the autobiographical argument must be the importance of tuberculosis as a theme relevant to the history of Belfast. As detailed in Chapter One, the disease killed off a massive proportion of Belfast's population in the nineteenth century. By 1938, 46 per cent of the Northern Ireland population in the 15–25 age group died from TB. Improvements in public health and the introduction of new medicines meant that Van Morrison's generation largely escaped TB, although the fear of the disease was still common during his childhood and adolescence. Indeed, as late as 1963, just before the formation of Them and Morrison's last year in Belfast, a Special Tuberculosis Authority was set up in the city. It is unsurprising, therefore, that Morrison should compose such a vividly moving depiction of the disease in song.

page 205: "It was done with me in Denmark Street in early 1965 . . ." Harrison/Rogan. Bangor, Co. Down: 21 August 1994.

page 206: "It was just a boat full . . ." Planet/Selvin, op cit.

page 206: "Sometimes I feel I may be just an underground thing . . ." *The Beat*: 2 December 1967

page 206: "He hired these three Bronx girls . . ." Jake Holmes interviewed in 2001 by Will Shade on the internet magazine *Perfect Sound Forever*.

page 207: "When somebody pays to see you . . ." Philip Solomon/Rogan. Dublin: 15 April 1982. Solomon did not provide details of precisely where or when the alleged and unprintable incident took place. His allegation was unsupported by testimony from Harrison (during his period with Them) and denied by Morrison. Oddly, the substance of his allegation was the same as that provided by Ilene Berns.

Perhaps Solomon and Berns were alluding to the same story, but that seems unlikely. Of course, Morrison's actions during this period, and even in the Them era, were seldom reported in the press or elsewhere. The more provocative allegation by Ilene Berns was featured in a review in *Vox* magazine, having been originally included in a review copy of Turner's biography.

page 208: "If Philip had done to Morrison what he did to McWilliams . . ." Eddie Kennedy/Rogan. London: 12 March 1982.

page 208: "When I informed Bang . . ." Neil Diamond, counter affidavit to *Web IV Music* v. *Tallyrand Music and Neil Diamond*. New York State Supreme Court: 18 January 1968.

page 209: "I did another session with him . . ." Morrison/Corvin, 1973, op cit.

page 209: "Van dug being in New York and the whole Greenwich Village scene . . ." Coulter/Rogan. London: 28 January 1982.

page 209: "I'd write a song . . ." Morrison/Traum, op cit.

page 210: "We were just mortified . . ." Planet/Selvin, op cit.

page 210: "Van felt really bad . . ." ibid.

page 210: "I really respected him . . ." Morrison/Corvin, 1973, op cit.

page 210: "He's deeply conflicted . . ." Joel Selvin, interviewed by the author. San Francisco: 6 October 2004.

Chapter Twelve: The Recording Of Astral Weeks

page 212: "He was a piece of work..." Planet/Selvin, op cit.

page 212: "One guy pulled a knife . . ." Carmine 'Wassel' Denoia, interviewed by Nick Tosches. *Vanity Fair*: December 2000.

page 213: "Everybody was trying . . ." ibid.

page 213: "I was the only Italian guy . . ." ibid.

page 213: "The record business . . ." Selvin/Rogan. San Francisco: 6 October 2004.

page 213: "Carmine's a wonderful guy . . ." Selvin/Rogan. San Francisco: 6 October 2004. Carmine Denoia acquired his nickname as a boy when someone noticed he misprounounced the word "rascal" as "wassel". Even in his mid-seventies, Denoia could make his presence felt in a New York restaurant. "We'd go to restaurants in Greenwich Village," Selvin recalls, "and [the staff] would surround our table and everyone would be nodding, 'Mr Wassel, how are you tonight? . . .' Some guy waved to him from across the bar and Wassel gave a scowl and looked away. Then he said to me: 'That guy's a scumbag.' About two minutes later I looked over there and the guy wasn't there any more. They'd taken him out of the restaurant."

page 213: "One of the memories . . ." Planet/Selvin, op cit.

page 214: "Bert was eclectic . . ." Jerry Wexler & David Ritz: *Rhythm And The Blues: A Life In American Music,* New York, Alfred A. Knopf: 1993.

page 214: "He sued us . . ." ibid.

page 215: "Later, when the Ardens . . ." David Arden was subsequently sentenced to two years' imprisonment for the offences. In a separate trial, his father Don was found not guilty.

page 215: "Bang was a horrible experience for him . . ." John Platania, interviewed by the author. New York: 20 June 2002.

page 217: "He had no skills . . ." Planet/Selvin op cit..

page 218: "There were immigration problems . . ." Joe Smith, interviewed by Timothy White. Original typed transcript: undated. Used by permission.

page 218: "There was speculation about Morrison's contract . . ." Smith/White, op cit.

page 219: "He was murdered in Boston by his room-mate who flipped out on acid . . ." Tom Kielbania, interviewed by the author: Chicopee, Massachusetts: 4 October 1993.

page 219: "Van tried to move into my house . . ." John Sheldon, interviewed by Alex Beam. *Boston Globe*: 18 September 2003.

page 219: "There were people coming and going all the time . . ." Kielbania/Rogan. Chicopee, Massachusetts: 4 October 1993. Kielbania elaborates on the "friend who came to their rescue": "The manager/agent's name was Frank – an Italian. He just got us a few places to play in the summer of 1968, mainly amusement parks. He had a guitar player who was only in high school. He was so good; his father was a professor at MIT. This guy was fabulous – his name was John. But he was too young and couldn't play with us." I assume this was the aforementioned John Sheldon.

page 219: "I'm tired of this rock 'n' roll . . ." Kielbania/Rogan. Chicopee, Massachusetts: 4 October 1993.

page 220: "It was a weekday night . . ." John Payne, interviewed by the author. Providence, Rhode Island: 19 September 1993.

page 220: "I have a way with singers . . ." ibid.

page 220: "I'd heard the song before . . ." ibid.

page 220: "He offered to pay me . . ." ibid.

page 220: "I figured I'd finally made it . . ." ibid.

page 221: "He was very confused . . ." Kielbania/Rogan. Chicopee, Massachusetts: 4 October 1993.

page 221: "They lived in one room . . ." Peter Wolf, interviewed by Vin Scelsa, Radio WNEW, Boston: 24 January 1999.

page 222: "It was some present to give to a grieving widow . . ." Reviewer Peter Doggett, *Record Collector* and in conversation with the author. See also *Record Collector* 178 (June 1994) in which Doggett wrote: ". . . . they're some present for a woman whose husband had just died".

page 222: "You couldn't even copyright them . . ." Ilene Berns, interviewed by Steve Turner. *c.* 1992. Full quote used herein, previously unpublished.

page 223: "We started playing at the Cafe Au Go Go . . ." Payne/Rogan. Providence, Rhode Island: 19 September 1993.

page 223: "Live, we were more folkie . . ." Kielbania/Rogan. Chicopee, Massachusetts: 4 October 1993. Morrison had already premiered much of *Astral Weeks* at the Catacombs in Boston, just after John Payne was recruited. Peter Wolf taped an entire performance of this material which he offered to air during a radio interview in Boston in 1999. As yet, the tapes have evidently not been broadcast.

page 224: "What does 'Tutti Frutti' mean? . . ." Van Morrison, interviewed by Ritchie Yorke, *Stage Life*: July 1977. The discovery of meaning through vocal expression rather than cold lyrical analysis has attracted considerable critical attention in recent years, particularly in studies of Bob Dylan whose playfulness with pitch, timbre and melody consistently adds endless footnotes to interpretations of his work. Of course, it is possible to cite many examples of juvenile rock 'n' roll where accentuation or vocal dexterity provides fresh meaning to the most banal of utterances. A literal reading of Buddy Holly's 'Peggy Sue', for example, in no way inclines us to regard the character as special or multi-dimensional. Yet, listening to the record, we are convinced of her innumerable qualities as a result of Holly's ingenious and seemingly infinite capacity to recite her name in a different fashion in almost every line. Much the same can be said of Little Richard's 'Tutti Frutti' in which "AwopBopaLooBop ALopBamBoom" serves not as incoherent gibberish but a process Morrison himself might call the inarticulate speech of the heart. Morrison heard the same multiplicity of emotional responses in listening to blues, jazz and early rock 'n' roll and incorporated those experiences into his own repertoire and vocal styling.

page 224: "I just wanted to get back . . ." Van Morrison, interviewed by Niall Stokes, *Hot Press*: 15 March 2000.

page 224: "They were business-type people there to make a killing . . ." Kielbania/ Rogan. Chicopee, Massachusetts: 4 October 1993.

page 225: "Schwaid and Merenstein were definitely into Morrison . . ." Payne/Rogan. Providence, Rhode Island: 19 September 1993.

page 225: "Van knew I'd be upset . . ." Kielbania/Rogan. Chicopee, Massachusetts: 4 October 1993.

page 225: "I idolized him . . ." ibid.

page 225: "It was an amazing session . . ." ibid.

page 226: "I can't remember him having a conversation . . ." Payne/Rogan. Providence, Rhode Island: 19 September 1993.

page 226: "He never had a thing to say to us . . ." Richard Davis, interviewed by Barney Hoskyns. *Mojo* 97: December 2001.

page 226: "All the other guys were seasoned studio players and read music . . ." Payne/Rogan. Providence, Rhode Island: 19 September 1993.

page 226: "I hadn't even brought my flute . . ." ibid.

page 226: "It was done in the morning . . ." ibid. In *Zig Zag* 36 Morrison told the interviewer John Tobler that the outtakes supposedly included a 45-minute stream-of-consciousness exposition recorded on two-track prior to the sessions which was ignored because of its length. Apparently, there was also some "uptown blues jazz", "a long saga about trains" and a song "about Jesse James". In a previous study, I pondered whether the Jesse James composition might be an early version of 'Crazy Face', which later featured on *His Band And The Street Choir*. Other commentators have casually adopted that information, but now it seems more likely that the composition in question was 'The Ballad Of Jesse James', the Chris Barber-arranged tune that Morrison later played with Lonnie Donegan. Alternatively, the song may well have been a lost Morrison original. Presumably, it will appear on bootleg CD or some archive release in the fullness of time.

page 227: "They put the chart in front of me . . ." Payne/Rogan. Providence, Rhode Island: 19 September 1993.

page 227: "That was the tape on the floor . . ." ibid.

page 227: "It was five to 10 minutes of instrumental jamming . . ." ibid.

page 227: "Larry did a great job with great sensitivity . . ." ibid.

page 228: "I'll never forget that as long as I live . . ." Kielbania/Rogan. Chicopee, Massachusetts: 4 October 1993.

page 228: "We weren't headlining there . . ." Payne/Rogan. Providence, Rhode Island: 19 September 1993.

page 228: "We did Channel 11 . . ." ibid.

page 228: "They'd always get into politics . . ." Kielbania/Rogan. Chicopee, Massachusetts: 4 October 1993.

page 230: "a direct command from the neo-god of love . . ." King Om (Cecil McCartney), quoted in *City Week*: 24 December 1968.

page 230: "Partly inspired by Martin Luther King's . . ." Writer Steve Bruce provides a provocative counter-argument: "To see the Ulster civil rights movement as parallel to the black civil rights campaign in America misses the crucial difference between Ulster and America. American blacks were always assimilationist because they had nowhere else to go. There was never a time when any more than a handful of eccentrics advocated the establishment of a separate black nation-state. The issue in America was, and still is, the relationship between two populations *within* a nation-state . . . The Ulster situation has always been quite different. Perhaps some parts of the civil rights movement were genuinely, rather than tactically, assimilationist. Presumably the small number of liberal Unionists who became involved believed that to be the case. However, the speed with which many of its leaders shifted to more traditionalist nationalist and Republican positions suggests that a large part of the movement was always ultimately interested in dismantling Northern Ireland." [Steve Bruce, *God Save Ulster!*, Oxford, Clarendon Press: 1986]

page 231: "Rather than joining the Civil Rights, I joined the People's Democracy . . ." O'Hare/Rogan. Dublin: 12 February 2004.

page 231: "Every time you met . . ." Éamonn McCann, interviewed by the author. Derry: 11 June 2005. Additional information was obtained during our meeting at Derry Visual Arts Centre, 18 May 2005. McCann, born 10 March 1943, came from a staunch trade unionist family and had attended Queen's University as a psychology student. Along with Éamonn Melaugh he was involved in protest activities with the Derry Housing Action Committee and was famously active in the civil rights march of 5 October 1968 that had been banned by William Craig, Minister of Home Affairs for Northern Ireland. Elaborating on the membership of the People's Democracy, McCann reveals: "It was very chaotic as so many things were at that time. In one sense I was never a member of the PD and in another sense I was a founding member. The reason for that is that it was impossible to work out who were members of the PD and who were not. There was never anything as bourgeoisie and respectable as a membership list. There was no way of telling who could vote in a meeting. The PD was any group of people gathered anywhere defining themselves as the PD. And this was taken to extremes. There were similar groups at the time like the Revolutionary Socialist Students' Federation in England, who operated in the same way. This was an expression of Jerry Rubin's 'Just Do It!' . . . I was a member of the Derry Labour Party at the time and the Derry Party Young Socialists and was very committed to both. We would go as a contingent from the Derry Labour Party to take part in PD events. Many may say, 'Well you were part of the PD then, weren't you?' and there's no answer to that. I never actually joined the PD but then there was no formal mechanism for joining."

page 232: "Strangely enough . . ." ibid. One of the legacies of the march was the famous slogan "You Are Now Entering Free Derry" painted in black letters on the wall adjacent to the Bogside on the morning of 5 January 1969. "It was the only sentence I ever come up with in my life that has lasted," says McCann. "And I didn't really come up with it. The originator of that phrase was Lennie Glaser who was a big counter cultural hero in the 1960s. He was associated with the Berkeley Free Speech Movement. I'd seen a photograph of Berkeley College where they'd written 'You Are Now Entering Free Berkeley' and that's where the slogan came from. It became a nationalist expression meaning freedom from British rule but at the time it was an expression of internationalism. It's a good example of the way a slogan or a political intention can be set down in one context or one historical period, and over time it can change meaning. And I don't complain about that. Now it means something quite different because the situation and the area around that wall is now very different –particularly after Internment, Bloody Sunday and the IRA."

page 232: "One female resident . . ." The woman, identified as Mrs Donnelly, telephoned the police to complain about the abuse, only to discover that it *was* the police who were rampaging up and down the street, smashing windows and causing havoc.

Chapter Thirteen: The Politics Of Astral Weeks

page 233: "We did 'Domino' in the same studio as *Astral Weeks* . . ." Kielbania/Rogan. Chicopee, Massachusetts: 4 October 1993.

page 234: "The government is satisfied . . ." Minister of Health Kenneth Robinson, addressing the House of Commons: 25 July 1968.

page 234: "I think you're more psyched about this . . ." Payne/Rogan. Providence, Rhode Island: 19 September 1993.

page 234: "Van was never open with anybody . . ." Bob Schwaid, interviewed by Barney Hoskyns. *Mojo* 97: December 2001.

page 235: "Janet was very centred . . ." Payne/Rogan. Providence, Rhode Island: 19 September 1993.

page 235: "It wasn't the kind of music they really wanted to hear . . ." Kielbania/Rogan. Chicopee, Massachusetts: 4 October 1993.

page 235: "Poor Van Morrison . . ." Reviewer Judy Sims. *Disc & Music Echo*: 22 February 1969.

page 235: "Janet was always concerned about his health . . ." Kielbania/Rogan. Chicopee, Massachusetts: 4 October 1993.

page 236: "There were always people smoking grass . . ." ibid.

page 236: "Samuel Devenny, subsequently died . . ." Oddly, for such a prominent figure in the history of the Troubles, Sam Devenny's surname has been consistently spelt Devenney in virtually all the major accounts of the incident. These include books by the impressively meticulous Peter Taylor (*Provos, The IRA & Sinn Féin* and *Loyalists*) not to mention a wealth of other histories, biographies and autobiographies, including those of Gerry Adams (see *Before The Dawn: An Autobiography*). Even Derry-born writer Susan McKay in her *Northern Protestants: An Unsettled People* refers to him as Devenney and she appears to have spoken to a family member. Derry legend Paddy 'Bogside' Doherty, who interviewed Phylis Devenny for his autobiography, proves a notable exception with "Devenny". That is the name also found on the death certificate lodged at the Belfast Registrars' Office, which is my major source.

page 237: "We weren't getting too good a response . . ." Kielbania/Rogan. Chicopee, Massachusetts: 4 October 1993.

page 237: "I just jammed and then Van scribbled my name . . ." Platania/Rogan. New York: 20 June 2002.

page 237: "We did one television show in New York . . ." Kielbania/Rogan. Chicopee, Massachusetts: 4 October 1993.

page 237: "After we went to Woodstock . . ." ibid.

page 238: "The reason I left is that I'd just got married . . ." ibid.

page 238: "We did this gig together in Woodstock . . ." Morrison/Corvin, 1973, op cit.

page 238: "That's how we first met . . ." Jon Gershen, internet posting.

page 238: "They weren't into commercial things . . ." Morrison/Corvin, 1973, op cit. Although Morrison insists that Jeff Labes was a member of the Woodstock-based Colwell-Winfield Blues Band, he was not part of the 1968 line-up that recorded their sole studio album for Verve Forecast, *Cold Wind Blues*. That line-up comprised Bill Colwell (guitar), Mike Winfield (bass), Jack Schroer (alto, tenor and soprano saxophone), Colin Tilton (flute/tenor saxophone), Charles 'Moose' Sorrento (vocals/piano) and Chuck Purro (drums). Tilton was subsequently recruited for the *Moondance* sessions.

page 239: "The town of Woodstock did not like hippies . . ." ibid.

page 239: "Minnowburn was Corvin and Sammy's idea . . ." Dino Martin/Rogan. Antrim: 24 November 1994.

page 240: "Bernadette Devlin, seemingly immune to CS gas . . ." Gerry Adams, *Before The Dawn: An Autobiography*, Brandon, Ireland: 1996; 2001.

page 240: "The Irish government can no longer stand by and see innocent people injured . . ." speech by Taoiseach Jack Lynch. In some commentaries, the words "stand *idly* by" have been used, but Lynch did not use the word "idly".

page 241: "You're giving them tea . . ." Bernadette Devlin. Speech at Bogside, Derry: August 1969.

page 241: "This was unheard of . . ." McClelland/Rogan. Belfast: 16 September 2002.

page 242: "The songs came out of some inner expression . . ." Van Morrison, interviewed by Seán O'Hagan. *Select*: October 1990.

page 242: "The album's full of sketches . . ." Morrison/Corvin, 1973, op cit.

page 244: "The song is actually 'Madame Joy' . . ." ibid.

page 245: "Well, I think the concept was suggested to me . . ." Van Morrison, interviewed by Al Jones. Copenhagen: March 1985. Although several songs on *Astral Weeks* are linked by theme or imagery, they fail to form a complementary pattern. 'Sweet Thing' and 'The Way Young Lovers Do' both allude to walking in fields and gardens in the rain, but there is no 'Beginning' or 'Afterwards' concept there. Similarly 'Madame George' and 'Cyprus Avenue' are less antithetical than similar, both reflecting aspects of lost innocence. Other pairings prove equally tenuous and unconvincing. The sequencing of *Astral Weeks* was probably largely determined by the timing of the sessions and the length of two of the tracks. The epic 'Madame George', too long to be included on the same side as 'Cyprus Avenue', was switched to side 2 ('Afterwards') in exchange for 'Sweet Thing'. Apart from that, both sides correspond with the session dates – 'In The Beginning' (25 September) and 'Afterwards' (15 October). The ordering seems less conceptual than convenient.

page 245: "She had a lot on her mind . . ." Foster, op cit.

page 245: "Bernadette's a fierce Republican . . ." O'Hare/Rogan. Dublin: 12 February 2004.

page 246: "When I was a teenager . . ." Éamonn McCann, interviewed by the author. Derry: 11 June 2004.

page 246: "The album is as far removed from Them as possible . . ." Reviewer Nick Logan, *New Musical Express*: 27 September 1969. Logan's criticisms were echoed in *Beat Instrumental* whose reviewer complained that the songs on *Astral Weeks* were "lacking in originality, and there is a great deal of monotony about it".

page 247: "I would change the arrangements . . ." Morrison/Traum, op cit.

page 247: "Like the Beach Boys' *Pet Sounds* . . ." As time passes, it seems unlikely that either *Pet Sounds* or *Astral Weeks* will ever be rivalled in reputation by other work in the catalogue of either artiste. Strong albums like *Moondance, Saint Dominic's Preview* and, most tellingly, *Veedon Fleece*, have performed poorly in such polls, partly perhaps because of spread voting and received opinion down the years. Champions of Morrison's other work may take heart from the example of the Beatles' *Sgt Pepper's Lonely Hearts Club Band*, which triumphed in countless such listings for decades only to be supplanted in recent years by *Revolver*.

Chapter Fourteen: Internment

page 248: "I make albums primarily to sell them . . ." Van Morrison, interviewed by Danny Holloway, *New Musical Express*: 17 August 1972.

page 248: "I had to forget about the artistic thing . . ." Van Morrison, promotional interview with Mick Brown: 1986.

page 248: "Chief amongst them was 'Lorna' . . ." The tradition of siren schoolgirls in blues/pop can be traced at least as far back as Sonny Boy Williamson's 'Good Morning Little Schoolgirl'. Other examples include Wynonie Harris' 1950 R&B hit 'Good Morning Judge' which discusses a relationship with a 15-year-old girl, and Andre Williams' self-explanatory Fifties recording 'Jail Bait'. Rod Stewart later inverted the theme by dramatizing the relationship between a schoolboy and an older female in 'Maggie May'. During 1969 Morrison also recorded such titles as 'If I Had A Rainbow', 'I Can't Get Straight', 'At The Station' and 'The Sky Is Full Of Pipers'.

page 248: "He did a few songs . . ." Platania/Rogan. New York: 20 June 2002.

page 249: "He rattled around with all those good guys in the Band . . ." Mary Martin, interviewed by the author. Nashville: 10 July 1994.

page 249: "I manage you – you manage the band! . . ." ibid.

page 249: "He said, 'If you make sure Van Morrison re-signs' . . ." ibid.

page 249: "We did our jaunts into the city . . ." Platania/Rogan. New York: 20 June 2002.

page 250: "For five minutes everything was really quiet . . ." Van Morrison, interviewed by Steve Turner, *Too Late To Stop Now*, London, Bloomsbury: 1993.

page 251: "He wails as the jazz musician speaks of wailing . . ." Ralph J. Gleason, *San Francisco Chronicle*: c. 1970.

page 252: "Just weeks before the release of *Moondance*, there had been an historic break in Republican ranks . . ." Space precludes a full analysis of this complex issue. Much has been made of the differences between the Marxist-style Official IRA and the more militant Provisional IRA. Some naive commentators interpreted the 1970 split as a clash between Right and Left opponents, but it was never that simple. The Provisionals also became a movement of the Left and stated their desire to establish a 'Democrat Socialist Republic' following the complete overthrow of British rule in the North. In *Where Sinn Féin Stands*, a four-page pamphlet circulated soon after the split in January 1970, the Caretaker Executive of the organization provided this revealing footnote: "Ours is a Socialism based on the native Irish tradition of *Comhar na gComharsan*, which is founded on the right of worker-ownership and on our Irish and Christian values. It is hoped to expand and explain this in the near future." For the present, Sinn Féin was ready to offer the following: "Our Socialism envisages the nationalization of the monetary system, commercial banks and insurance companies, key industries, mines, building land and fishing rights: the division of large ranches; an upper limit on the amount of land to be owned by any one individual; the setting up of worker-owner co-operatives on a wide scale in industry, agriculture, fishing and distribution, but still leaving ample room for private initiative under state supervision. The extension and development of Credit Unions is also included." In explaining why half the delegates walked out of the Ard Fheis in January 1970, the Caretaker Executive provided the following five major reasons: 1. "The Sinn Féin organization since its foundation in 1905, has consistently denied the right of the British Parliament to rule in Ireland. Similarly, Sinn Féin has refused to recognize the two partition parliaments at Stormont and Leinster House, forced on the Irish people under the British Government of Ireland Act, 1920, and the Treaty of Surrender of 1921." 2. "Sinn Féin's alternative to these British institutions of government was the All-Ireland Republican Dáil which it assembled in January 1919. It remains the task of Sinn Féin today to lead the Irish people away from British, Six-County and 26-County parliaments and towards the re-assembly of the 32-County Dáil which will then legislate for and rule all Ireland." 3. "Those who remained in the Intercontinental Hotel on Sunday 11 January 1970, sought to reverse this basic principle of the Sinn Féin organization down the years and to participate in all three existing parliaments. That sitting and participating in the affairs of these assemblies constitutes 'recognition' of them, all reasonable people will agree without hesitation." 4. "Those who walked out stand by the Constitution and Rules of the Sinn Féin organization and claim the historic name of Sinn Féin while those who remained sought, without success to alter that Constitution and change a National Movement into yet another political party seeking votes at all costs." 5. "Having failed to secure the necessary two-thirds majority to effect these changes they then pressed on the Ard Fheis a resolution requiring a simple majority only, viz: 'expressing allegiance to an IRA leadership' which had prior to the Ard Fheis adopted recognition of Westminster, Stormont and Leinster House as policy. This the delegates loyal to a 32-County Parliament could not tolerate and since the resolution in question seemed likely to be carried, they took the only action open to them if they were not to be compromised – they walked out and resumed the Ard Fheis elsewhere."

page 253: "There wasn't much ideology involved . . ." O'Hare/Rogan. Dublin: 12 February 2004.

page 253: "Seán was shot dead . . ." Kane/Rogan. Belfast: 27 October 1994. The Tara Showband of this era featured Roy Kane (drums), Bob Steele (trombone), Mickey Fox (trumpet), Seán Fox (saxophone) and Billy McAllen (guitar).

page 253: ". . . There were the Officials (the Stickies) . . ." ibid. The Official IRA were nicknamed the Stickies because their Easter Lily commemoration badge was attached to the lapel by a gum adhesive, while the Provos used a pin.

page 253: "There was no patriotism involved . . ." Sam Smyth/Rogan. Dublin: 19 January 2003.

page 254: "Things were getting off the ground in the late Sixties . . ." Sproule/Rogan. Belfast: 29 October 1994.

page 254: "Those ballrooms were barracks, cold and wet . . ." Baird/Rogan. Belfast: 31 October 1994.

page 254: "Given that it took a mile . . ." Janet Morrison Minto (formerly Janet Planet) interviewed by Louis Sahagun. Los Angeles Times: 17 November 1998.

page 254: "David and I sat up with Van . . ." Jon Gershen, internet posting.

page 255: "Melody Maker's senior critic Richard Williams provided a glowing review . . ." An early advocate of Morrison in the Seventies rock press, Williams noted: "Just how much Brinsley Schwartz lacked was emphasized most cruelly when

Van Morrison took the stage in front of his orchestra. Morrison, sometimes strumming an absurdly loud jumbo, has it all down. He has obviously tuned himself and the band to the highest possible peak of empathy so that he can rely completely on them. Morrison uses the backing like a trampoline, bouncing his voice off the sympathetic, yielding surface with startling rhythmic agility. He's not afraid to improvise or use repetition to build intensity."

page 255: "I don't ever remember playing to empty halls . . ." Platania/Rogan. New York: 20 June 2002.

page 255: "He was holding his own in concert . . ." Mary Martin/Rogan. Nashville: 10 July 1994. Mary Martin maintains that Morrison was most comfortable working at the Fillmore. "Bill Graham was one of the most important people in Van Morrison's life," she told me. "If Bill Graham put you on concerts he believed in you. When it came time for the Fillmore staff to vote who they liked best of all and who they wanted to return either on the West or East Coast, the first was obviously the Grateful Dead and the second Van Morrison . . . The most significant thing I remember was when we were doing a PBS TV Special [23 September 1970] at the Fillmore East. That had a great deal to do with how you marry the goals of the cameras versus the needs of the audience. And, God, Bill Graham was very pernickety about that. As I remember that was one of the more glorious Van Morrison concerts."

page 256: "In America when I went solo . . ." Van Morrison, interviewed by Larry Blumenfeld. *Jazziz*: April 2004.

page 256: "The record company was asking me for singles . . ." Mary Martin notes that "there was always the cry to make commercial records and while Van Morrison made records that we knew could stand out in the time capsule, the record company had a difficult time getting any of those singles played on the radio."

page 257: "I had a group of people in mind . . ." Morrison/Corvin, 1973, op cit.

page 257: The Street Choir line-up comprised Janet Planet, Ellen Schroer, Martha Valez, Larry Goldsmith and Andy Robinson. Morrison then recruited Dahaud Elias Shaar/Dauod Shaw (bass clarinet and drums), Alan Hand (keyboards) and Keith Johnson (trumpet and organ) to add to the familiar nucleus of John Platania, Jack Schroer and John Klingberg.

page 257: "I was never a hippie . . ." Morrison/Corvin, 1973, op cit.

page 258: "I think he'd gone through a serious amount . . ." Mary Martin/Rogan. Nashville: 10 July 1994.

page 258: "He's Irish! . . ." ibid.

page 260: "I took the heat on that one . . ." ibid.

page 260: "I didn't want to go out there . . ." Platania/Rogan. New York: 20 June 2002.

page 260: "He decided it would be best . . ." Mary Martin, press release.

page 260: "We got him such a substantial record deal . . ." Mary Martin/Rogan. Nashville: 10 July 1994.

page 261: "I'm not the type of person . . ." Morrison/Grissim, op cit.

page 261: "I thought at the time that it was a most shocking sentiment . . ." Janet Planet internet posting: 2 April 1999.

page 262: "There was a riot . . ." Kane/Rogan. Belfast: 27 October 1994. Internment was heavily supported by Unionists and thousands of workers from Harland & Wolff had marched demanding its implementation. In July 1971, Ian Paisley's *Protestant Telegraph* denounced the Provisional IRA with the words: "The vermin must be suppressed either by internment or effective action by our security forces." However, Paisley himself was firmly against internment. A constitutionalist and defender of working-class people, he realized that the process of imprisonment without trial could not only be used against Republicans, but also turned on hard-line loyalists. His reservations ultimately proved sound. Over the succeeding months, a number of Protestants were detained under the Special Powers Act.

page 263: "In Sandy Row and the Shankill, a pamphlet was distributed . . ." Its message read: "Being convinced that the enemies of the Faith and Freedom are determined to destroy the state of Northern Ireland and thereby enslave the people of God, we call on all members of our loyalist institutions, and other responsible citizens, to organize themselves immediately into Platoons of 20 under the command of someone capable of acting as Sergeant. Every effort must be made to arm these Platoons with whatever weapons are available." Over the years, the pamphlet's words have been reprinted in various books, including *The Troubles, Political Murder In Northern Ireland, Beyond Orange & Green, et al.*

page 265: "It was a radio station that moved around the place . . ." O'Hare/Rogan. Dublin: 12 February 2004.

page 265: "I was held for 48 hours and got the shit kicked out of me . . ." ibid.

page 265: "I was the only man in the world ever to sing or play guitar at the bottom of the North Sea . . ." Sproule/Rogan. Belfast: 29 October 1994.

page 265: "You'd play light pop, country and ballads . . ." Irvine/Rogan. Belfast: 18 September 1994.

page 266: "The Troubles killed the music scene . . ." Kane/Rogan. Belfast: 27 October 1994.

page 267: "The funniest thing was when he wanted me to vouch for him to join a country club . . ." Smith/White, op cit.

page 267: "Morrison had again reshuffled his studio group . . ." The new recruits for *Tupelo Honey* included Clover's John McFee (steel guitar), Ronnie Montrose (guitar), Mark Jordan (keyboards), Bill Church (bass), Rick Schlosser (drums), Luis Gasca (trumpet) and the flute players Boots Stuart Houston and Bruce Royston.

page 268: "They were very much in love . . ." Maggid/Rogan. Northern California: 5 June 2002.

Chapter Fifteen: Marin And Dublin

page 271: "Every now and then I'll be lying down . . ." Morrison/Grissim, op cit. Morrison later complained about this interview in a number of oblique comments. "He taped the interview – and he gave me his word that he was going to print it exactly word for word off the tape," he told *Zig Zag*'s John Tobler in 1973. "When it came out it was all changed around. It was like his book or something, and didn't have much to do with me or the interview." Clearly referring to the astral projection story, he complained: "I once told someone in a joke that I fly around the room and again it was made into something. Needless to say, I don't fly around the room." The most damning comment concerned a quote about the song 'Saint Dominic's Preview'. According to Morrison, the journalist fabricated a story about a prophetic dream that was supposed to have inspired the composition. "The guy was using his imagination rather heavily," he told Tobler. "He said that I had a dream about a mass in a church. I didn't have a dream – the only thing that happened was I mentioned to him that I'd seen in the paper that there was a service in St Dominic's in San Francisco. That was all I said, and he did the rest. That was after I wrote the song. I just mentioned I saw the name in a paper and he made up the rest." Morrison's criticisms seemed an unreasonable attack on what was undoubtedly one of the more sympathetic profiles of his career during the Seventies. A close look at the offending article indicates that the maligned journalist was totally innocent of the fabrication purported by Morrison. Contrary to Morrison's assertion, the printed interview never even mentioned a dream. The quote attributed to Morrison read: "I'd been working on this song about the scene in Belfast. And I wasn't sure what I was writing about but anyway the central image seemed to be this church called St Dominic's where people were gathering to pray or hear a mass for peace in Northern Ireland. Anyway, a few weeks ago I was in Reno for a gig at the University of Nevada. And while we were having dinner I picked up the newspaper and opened it at a page and there in front of me was an announcement about a mass for peace in Belfast to be said the next day at St Dominic's church in San Francisco. Totally blew me out. Like I'd never even heard of St Dominic's church." This account tallies remarkably well with Morrison's later version of the 'true' story. Precisely what misdemeanours the journalist was meant to have committed in the transcription remains a mystery. The facts tend to place Morrison's perspective of the media in a more critical light. For years, he has complained about journalists or editors misrepresenting him in an attempt to impress their readership. It is a great irony then that Morrison should be proven guilty of the very crime that he accuses the media of perpetrating. In analysing his relationship with them, it seems that ultimately they may be more sinned against than sinning.

page 271: "That was certainly his idea of a clever joke . . ." Maggid/Rogan. Northern California: 5 June 2002.

page 272: "The mood of the crowd was a happy one . . ." John Lennon, interviewed in *Red Mole*, 1972.

page 272: "I went because I was one of the first internees . . ." O'Hare/Rogan. Dublin: 12 February 2004.

page 272: "Lennon was taken *very* seriously . . ." ibid.

page 273: "Resisting Unionist protests, he suspended the Northern Ireland government at Stormont . . ." The 'abolition' of Stormont resulted from the efforts of the Civil

Rights Association and the reactive oppression by the loyalist sympathizers in government. In the background, of course, was the ubiquitous Ian Paisley whose lecturing fuelled the flames of loyalist aggression. However, it would be an exaggeration to state that his agitations caused the introduction of direct rule. As Steve Bruce observed: "There has always been a liberal wing of Unionism which blames Paisley for the proroguing of Stormont and which supposes that his real ambition throughout has been to lead an independent Ulster. My response to this view is the same as my response to the claim that Paisley and his Ulster Protestant Volunteers prevented the peaceful evolution of Northern Ireland into a genuine democracy. Although Paisley's leadership certainly played a part in exposing the contradictions in liberal Unionism, he did not bring down Stormont. Stormont collapsed because successive Stormont and Westminster governments have mistakenly assumed that a moderate 'centre' could be created in Northern Ireland. The correct judgement must be that Paisley has risen to political prominence because he has steadfastly expressed most clearly the core of Unionist ideology and the heart of what it means to be a Protestant."

page 273: "I'm definitely Irish . . ." Van Morrison, interviewed by Shay Healy, *Spotlight*: 25 June 1972.

page 273: "He is incredibly Irish to live with . . ." Janet Planet, interviewed by Shay Healy, *Spotlight*: 25 June 1972.

page 273: "And he's different too . . ." ibid.

page 273: "He doesn't like a lot of people around . . ." ibid.

page 273: "Janet wanted to get into acting . . ." John Platania, interviewed by Steve Turner, *Van Morrison: Too Late To Stop Now*, London, Bloomsbury: 1993.

page 274: "I wanted more than anything to make him happy . . ." Janet Morrison Minto/Sahagun, op cit.

page 274: "I don't know what 'Saint Dominic's Preview' means . . ." Morrison/Corvin, 1973, op cit.

page 274: "We found a beautiful little church in San Anselmo . . ." Maggid/Rogan. Northern California: 5 June 2002.

page 274: "Oh my goodness . . ." ibid.

page 274: "I got the feeling that he and Janet may have split up . . ." ibid.

page 275: "I know to a certain extent . . ." Press release for the group Fake I.D. by Janet Morrison Minto & Lauren Wakefield, 1998. Printed in *Wavelength* 18.

page 277: "One of the reasons he moved his mother and father . . ." Platania/Rogan. New York: 20 June 2002.

page 277: "I think about going back . . ." Morrison/Healy, op cit.

page 277: "His back was hurting . . ." Platania/Rogan. New York: 20 June 2002.

page 277: "By then our life together was very traumatic . . ." Minto/Sahagun, op cit.

page 277: "Janet Planet was never . . ." Planet/Selvin, op cit.

page 277: "When the US label Parrot decided to release a compilation album . . ." Morrison had already turned to Warner Brothers for help and their legal department duly consulted the Federal Trade Commission's Phonograph Industries Guideline on repackaged material. Section 5 of the FTC code, an agreement made between the leading record companies, stated that all repackaged material must indicate so on the cover. In his letter to the Assistant Attorney General of the United States, Morrison claimed: "I never signed a contract with Parrot or with London or any of their licensers as a featured artiste. The public is about to be defrauded by this 'new' London two-record package. Not only are they getting performances seven or eight years old which are totally unreflective of my style and writing as it is presently known, but they are re-buying the same old stuff contained in *Them* and *Them Again* which are still on the marketplace. Please help me and the record buying public by using your good office to compel London Records to tell the truth on their products . . . No member of the public should be able to pick this product up and think that they're getting anything other than what it really is."

page 278: "There were points when he seemed certifiable . . ." Smith/White, op cit.

page 278: "It's ridiculous . . ." Morrison/Grissim, op cit.

page 278: "They arrived late . . ." Smith/White, op cit. Joe Smith later reckoned this cantankerous meeting was possibly around 1975, but judging from his prior list of the "petty grievances" the Christmas of 1972 seems the more likely date. According to Smith, one of the complaints ("bullshit list of crimes") was a recent interview published in *Rolling Stone* which was meant to have been conducted by Jon Landau. Another journalist (presumably John Grissim Jr) had been sent instead. Smith also pointed out that he had just been to England to begin secret negotiations with a major singer in the lead-up to Christmas, details of which also point to this earlier dating.

page 279: "I don't want to deal with Van Morrison anymore . . ." ibid.

page 279: "He was as difficult as anyone I ever dealt with . . ." Mo Ostin, interviewed by Robert Hilburn, *Los Angeles Times*: 6 June 1996.

page 281: "I'm going to have to start doing double albums . . ." Morrison/Corvin, 1973, op cit. At least, Morrison, for once, seemed happy about the sleeve artwork. Its futurist, pastoral imagery depicted the moon, an oriental peasant and elements of Americana. In describing the cover, Morrison was surprisingly complimentary towards the artist Rob Springett. "He asked me what was in my head," Morrison explained, "and we just went for a drive. I dropped him off somewhere and between the time he left and I dropped him off we just rapped about what was in my head. He just based the picture on what I told him. You know, my psyche. That's what came out, and it was right on. I mean I saw it and said, 'That's exactly what I'm thinking!' The cat's incredible."

page 281: "That's about things that I know about . . ." ibid.

page 282: "A brass and string section . . .": The complete line-up of the Caledonia Soul Orchestra during this period comprised: John Platania (guitar), Jeff Labes (keyboards), Jack Schroer (saxophone), David Hayes (bass), Dahaud Shaar/Dauod Shaw (drums), Nathan Rubin (violin), Tom Halpin (violin), Terry Adams (cello), Nancy Ellis (viola) and Bill Atwood (trumpet). "They were great people," Platania adds. "Nathan Rubin was fantastic. I roomed with him. He turned me on to Charles Bukowski."

page 283: "I'm an artiste, a musician . . ." Amsterdam press conference: July 1973.

page 283: "He had a funeral for a lot of his old songs . . ." Platania/Rogan. New York: 20 June 2002.

page 283: Morrison's signed statement read: "The reason I never appeared in Ireland last summer was because I never agreed to appear. I want to straighten a few people out now. These are the events that led to the conclusion as I know them. While preparing for *The Old Grey Whistle Test* the host, Bob Harris, asked me if I planned on appearing in Ireland. I told him I wasn't sure because a personal matter might require me to return to California by the end of the month. So, I would prefer if he just didn't bring the subject up. He agreed and nothing was said about it while I was in the studio. Prior to this, I'd a meeting in London with the promoter Mr Jim Aiken; a representative of the Agency Chrysalis named Richard; and Mick Cole of Warner Brothers Records in London. I told Aiken the same thing, that I was waiting for a call from the States and if I could I would be happy to play Dublin. But not to plan on anything until he got a call from me personally. After I left the TV station, Mick Cole, who heard me say I could not commit to the gig, told Bob Harris it was definitely on. Harris, believing what he heard, added a late flash to the video tape that I was going to Ireland. Jim Aiken claims that he didn't advertise 'til after he saw the show. I, by the way, never saw the show on the air. So, Mr Aiken was advertising while I was receiving word from the States that I was due back in California before I could play the proposed date in Ireland. These are the facts. Please draw your own conclusions." Morrison added that he hoped to appear in Ireland the following March, which indeed he did.

page 283: "One has only to look at the Shankill Road . . ." Gusty Spence had been sprung from captivity by UVF members while attending his daughter's wedding. During his four months of freedom he helped reorganize the UVF and gave this interview to Granada's *World In Action*. Both Spence and his supporters insisted that he did not kill anybody in the infamous 1966 Malvern Street shootings in the Shankill. "His only crime was loyalty," they claimed. At one point, towels were manufactured bearing his image and, in a typical example of arch Unionist humour, counterfeit £5 notes were distributed featuring his face in place of the Queen's.

page 284: "At that time he wasn't planning any touring . . ." Stephen Pillster, interviewed by the author. Hollywood, California: 12 September 1993.

page 284: The title *Reliable Sources* was a private joke. A supposedly misleading item had once appeared in *Rolling Stone* and upon enquiring the source of the story Warner Brothers were told it had been provided by "reliable sources".

page 284: "He and Janet were separated . . ." Pillster/Rogan. Hollywood, California: 12 September 1993.

page 285: "It preoccupied him . . ." ibid.

page 285: "Part of it was the Troubles . . ." ibid.

page 285: "I relaxed and toured . . ." Van Morrison, quoted in *New Spotlight*: 22 November 1973. Two weeks before, the same magazine revealed that Morrison was visiting Belfast to film a 90-minute television special. In the *NME* (3 November) Colin McClelland noted that "initial sequences will be filmed in Belfast and Dublin next week . . . one of the locations being talked about is Cypress [*sic*] Avenue and the film will include interviews with Belfast people that Morrison knew when he was resident in the city."

page 285: "We were delighted . . ." Bill Keating, press statement printed in *New Spotlight*. 13 December 1973.

page 286: "What you saw was one of the worst shows in the series . . ." ibid.

page 286: "She was a one-woman metaphor for California . . ." Smyth/Rogan. Dublin: July/August 1993.

page 286: "He'd given up drink . . ." ibid.

page 286: "He said Morrison was with Corvin in town and they didn't want anyone to know . . ." Colin McClelland/Rogan. Belfast: 16 September 2002.

page 287: "I think a musician who gets involved in politics . . ." Morrison/Corvin, 1973, op cit.

page 288: "What I'm not part of is the hatred thing . . ." ibid.

page 288: "No compromise is possible in the North any longer . . ." Michael Farrell, *Northern Ireland: The Orange State*, London, Pluto Press: 1976.

page 289: "I felt the antagonism . . ." Morrison/Corvin, 1973, op cit.

Chapter Sixteen: Veedon Fleece

page 291: "The reason he gave was that they couldn't guarantee Van's security . . ." Pillster/Rogan. Hollywood, California: 12 September 1993.

page 292: "He makes life very difficult for himself . . ." Coulter/Rogan. London: 28 January 1982.

page 292: "It's common practice to go back and fix things . . ." Interviewer uncredited, *Mojo* 21: August 1995.

page 292: "I went to the soundcheck . . ." Payne/Rogan. Providence, Rhode Island: 19 September 1993.

page 293: "I swear he was looking straight at me . . ." ibid.

page 293: "It confirmed that Morrison . . ." The doctor's certificate read: "This is to certify that I was called to see Mr Morrison, on the 21st March 1974, when he had collapsed and retired to bed with a high fever. The man had had a previous bout of fever when he was in Hawaii, three weeks previously. He had probably returned to full activity before he was properly cured at that time, and has now had a severe relapse with the same virus. His condition was the same today with high fever and a respiratory disease. In my opinion he will not be able to resume his occupation for several days. Signed, Dr F.J. Hughes, MRCS, IRCP."

page 293: "People regarded him as a traitor . . ." Colin McClelland/Rogan. Belfast: 16 September 2002.

page 293: "Music and political reporter . . ." Violet Morrison's letter to Chris Moore stated: "Having read your article on Van Morrison and knowing he won't defend himself, I felt I ought to enlighten you as to the reason he did not visit Belfast. His father and I pleaded with him not to, as we did not want him to go home (yes *home*, Mr Moore, he still thinks of Belfast as home). He isn't worrying about his own safety, we are. We love him."

page 294: "They just put me on stage while I was sick . . ." Van Morrison, interviewed by Rob Mackie. *Sounds*: 3 August 1974.

page 294: "There was a huge crowd down from Belfast . . ." Smyth/Rogan. Dublin: July/August 1993.

page 294: "I didn't come here to enjoy Van Morrison . . ." As related to *Melody Maker*'s Geoff Brown and also quoted in Ritchie Yorke's book.

page 294: "The last train to Belfast had already gone . . ." Pillster/Rogan. Hollywood, California: 12 September 1993.

page 294: "Eddie was off the stage . . ." ibid.

page 295: "It was quite an evening, . . ." ibid.

page 295: "There was a full moon . . ." ibid. The song listing for the Falconcenteret, Copenhagen concert (6 April 1974) included: 'Ain't Nothing You Can Do'; 'Warm Love'; 'Listen To The Lion'; 'I Believe To My Soul'; 'Try For Sleep'; I've Been Working'; 'Take Your Hand Out Of My Pocket'; 'Pure' (instrumental); 'I Like It Like That/Kansas City'; 'Night And Day'; 'Caldonia (What Makes Your Big Head Hard?)'; 'Help Me'; 'Moondance'; 'Bring It On Home To Me'; 'I Just Want To Make Love To You'; 'Come Running'; 'Street Theory'; 'Don't Look Back'; 'Since I Fell For You'; 'Gloria'; 'Buona Sera Senorita'; 'My Babe'.

page 295: "I think you could call her a fiancée . . ." ibid.

page 296: "The bombers were never apprehended . . ." Coincidentally, the day after the UVF atrocities, the British authorities ceased force-feeding IRA prisoners. Thereafter, the Price sisters continued their hunger strike, along with Frank Stagg and Michael Gaughan. On 3 June, 24-year-old Gaughan died on the 65th day of his fast, officially of pneumonia. Stagg was subsequently ordered to end his fast. The Price Sisters, close to death, spent a total of 206 days on hunger strike before calling a halt.

page 296: "Who do these people think they are? . . ." Prime Minster Harold Wilson, political broadcast: 25 May 1974. In his speech, Wilson observed: "British parents, British taxpayers have seen their sons vilified and spat upon and murdered. They have seen the taxes they poured out almost without regard to cost − over £300 million this year − going into Northern Ireland. They see property destroyed by evil violence and are asked to pick up the bill for rebuilding it. Yet people who benefit from this now viciously defy Westminster, purporting to act as though they were an elected government, spending their lives sponging on Westminster and British democracy and then systematically assault democratic methods. Who do these people think they are?" The extent of Wilson's pessimism about Ulster was recently revealed in a top secret memo addressed to his principal private secretary Robert Armstrong released by the National Archives. Therein, Wilson indicated his plans for a 'Doomsday scenario' following the collapse of the May 1974 power-sharing Executive. He suggested the possibility of establishing Northern Ireland as a Dominion State similar to the birth of the Irish Free State in 1922. "This would mean that the Ulstermen were subjects of the Queen. It would mean the transfer of sovereignty from Westminster. Dominion status would not, of course, carry with it automatic entry into the Commonwealth. I would think this would be most unlikely, and so would membership of the UN." The success of the workers' strike persuaded Wilson that loyalists might use the same tactic again to scupper interference from Westminster. "As soon as the constitutionalists have got over the effects of the recent strike, we are at their mercy again." Wilson was acutely aware of the possible consequences of British withdrawal from Northern Ireland, including "outbreaks of violence and bloodshed, possible unacceptability to moderate Catholics, ditto the Republic, the UN and the possible spread of trouble across the water, to name but a few." The Doomsday plan would clearly depend on a number of favourable factors. "If we can in some way remain in control of the situation we can perhaps work out a more coherent scheme, with a built-in time scale and possibly some guarantees – or at least sanctions protective to ourselves. Negotiations would have to ensure that Dominion status would not be granted without the provision for protection of the minority in terms of civil rights, human rights and constitutional rights." In addition to Wilson's memo, there was a surprise intervention from abroad. The unlikely figure of General Idi Amin had previously offered to solve the Ulster problem as a mediator, even inviting Catholic and Protestant leaders and members of the British government to a summit in Uganda to "discuss with and make suggestions . . . as to how to end the fighting in Northern Ireland". A humorous Foreign Office memo noted: "As the General's messages go, this is one of his more lucid . . ."

page 297: "I'm really happy with this one . . ." Morrison/Mackie, op cit.

page 297: "They put up with a lot . . ." Pete Wingfield interview, *Beat Instrumental*: undated clipping. The band went the way of all flesh after their tour with Morrison. During September, the Belfast singer made some sporadic appearances with several San Franciscan musicians who played under the name Sound Hole.

page 298: "It all became completely unreal . . ." Van Morrison, interviewed by Seán O'Hagan. *New Musical Express*: 3 June 1989.

page 298: "It was the most penetrating distillation . . .": Of course *Veedon Fleece* was far more evidently a conceptual work, focusing on a fictional landscape that was nevertheless predominantly Irish. Morrison stated more than once that the album was completed immediately after his late 1973 visit to Ireland. This was a time when he was assimilating every aspect of Irish culture. Even the strings and acoustic instruments used on the album seemed carefully adapted to provide lingering echoes of traditional Irish music as well as maintaining a sense of drama. Morrison once spoke of producing *Astral Weeks* as a film, but of all his albums only *Veedon Fleece* might provide a cinematographic narrative combining both mythological and naturalistic events. Over the years, Morrison has rarely been asked about the origins of *Veedon Fleece*, but in an interview in *Sounds* (1 July 1978), conducted by Davitt Sigerson, he observed: "*Veedon Fleece* was a bunch of songs that I wrote and then I just recorded it about four weeks after I wrote it. When you make an album you write some songs; you might have four songs and maybe you write two more, suddenly you've got enough songs for an album, so you go in and you do it. The way I work, which is basically spontaneous, in the moment, in the non-moment, I really don't think about it. I just do it. And afterwards, I really don't think about it either. It isn't that complicated for me. You have a certain set of musicians, you block out the time period, and you just go for it. And it comes out the way it comes out."

Chapter Seventeen: Linden Arden And The Shankill Butchers

page 303: ". . . more easily in organizations which lack the cultural traditions and historical respectability of the IRA . . ." Ken Heskin, *Northern Ireland: A Psychological Analysis*, Cambridge University Press: 1980.

page 303: "Whenever I used to see him he'd scream . . ." Kane/Rogan. Belfast: 27 October 1994.

page 303: "He had his daughter out for the day . . ." ibid.

page 304: "I was very fond of Wesley . . ." ibid.

page 304: Morrison's rare show took place at the Keystone, Berkeley. Although given short notice, a reasonable-sized audience turned up for the performance. Morrison had put together a line-up consisting of old friends and established players. Former Caledonian bassist David Hayes was on loan from Terry And The Pirates, Marin sessioner Mark Jordan was brought in on keyboards and Stoneground's former guitarist John Blakely was added, along with drummer Tony Dey. Morrison spent much time playing saxophone. Press reports reveal that the set began strangely with two successive versions of 'Wild Night', one funky, the other rocking. Probably the biggest surprise was a cover of the Drifters' 'Under The Boardwalk' with Morrison offering a dynamic vocal, backed by the harmonies of Hayes and Blakely. The night ended with an encore of 'Saint Dominic's Preview', after which Morrison dismissed the group and effectively retired from public appearances.

page 304: "I got to the point where music just wasn't doing it for me . . ." Van Morrison, interviewed by Robin Denselow. *Guardian*: 21 June 1977.

page 304: ". . . an extended jamming session . . ." Elaborating on this to Ian Birch of *Melody Maker*, Morrison recalled: "We got a few tracks out of it, but it was more or less kind of a blow and we ran the tape. Really the whole thing was just getting out of the hotel because we had this gig in Amsterdam that was supposed to happen on a certain day and then went wrong. You go nuts if you're in a hotel all the time." The missing tracks remained in the vaults for years, although the hilarious 'Mechanical Bliss' did appear as the B-side of 'Joyous Sound' in 1977. Several other selections were featured on the archive album *The Philosopher's Stone* in 1998.

page 305: "Donall never had any money . . ." Sam Smyth/Rogan. Dublin: July/August 1993.

page 305: "Clearly, there was no advisorial role to play in Morrison's life . . ." Even the vague book project that Corvin had once planned came to nothing. He liked to joke to friends about the seemingly irreconcilable perspectives offered by the singer. Éamon Carr, the drummer in Horslips, saw some of the papers and suggested, in half-seriousness, that it would be a wonderful idea just to print Morrison's contradictory comments on recto and verso pages. Corvin was amused by the suggestion but remained wary, fearing that the singer would be insulted or annoyed.

page 306: "Showbands faced extinction . . ." Vincent Power, *Send 'Em Home Sweating: The Showband Story*, Dublin, Kildanore: 1990. Additional information comes from a combined lecture/discussion between Power and Rogan titled 'The Showband Phenomenon' at the Irish Centre, Camden, London: 18 April 1998.

page 306: "I just had to stop . . ." Van Morrison, interviewed by Paul Vincent, KMEL Radio: November 1981.

page 307: "As far as the past year was concerned . . ." WEA Records press handout dated May 1976.

page 307: "I want to get back to the roots . . ." ibid.

page 307: "I've thought about it . . ." Harvey Goldsmith, interviewed by the author. London: 5 January 1982.

page 307: "Everybody told me I was nuts! . . ." ibid.

page 307: "After two days . . ." ibid. Following lengthy auditions, Morrison and Dr John settled on a musical line-up comprising Marlow Henderson (guitar), Jerry Jumenville (saxophone), Reggie McBride (bass) and Ollie Brown (drums). Interviewed by Ian Birch in *Melody Maker* (25 June 1977), Morrison revealed: "I don't like working in the studio . . . normally I get too keyed up about it . . . But Mac slowed me down. It was really good for my head and we had a lot of fun. It came off the way I wanted it to . . . no real concept. Just the same players on every track. That way it's a clean album."

page 308: "Van is more of an expressive person . . ." Dr John, interviewed by Elliot Cohen, *Circus*: 1977.

page 308: "He was really up for it . . ." Goldsmith/Rogan. London: 5 January 1982.

page 308: "It was one of the most magical performances . . ." ibid.

page 309: ". . . *A Period Of Transition* . . .was roundly pilloried . . ." Arguably the most lacerating and provocative criticism came from the *NME*'s Nick Kent who wrote: "One could have hoped that *Transition* would have at least spotlighted the man's pre-eminence . . . to have borne proof once and for all that this is where all the *Heat Treatment*s have stolen their thunder. Unfortunately, the album's failure in that area is one dilemma for which there are no answers. And the questions themselves look right now to be so uncomfortably close to the bone that I, for one, don't even want to ask them." Morrison did not respond to the negative criticism at the time but later stated: "I don't know why the hell I put that out because there's a lot of better stuff that I'd recorded." With the benefit of 26 years' hindsight, he interpreted the *Transition* project as his first attempt as a collaborator. In short, it would probably have made more sense if the work had been billed as 'Van Morrison & Dr John' with Rebannack being allowed more creative input during the writing and recording process. If the album had been distanced from the main body of Morrison's solo work – in a similar way to his collaborations with Georgie Fame, Lonnie Donegan and Linda Gail Lewis – critical expectations might have been lowered and the reviews correspondingly more charitable.

page 309: ". . . his most ill-timed . . ." Morrison agreed to promote the work and, according to Goldsmith, made some in-store appearances at US record stores. Considerable critical attention was given to the title of the album and the cover artwork. At first, Morrison suggested that the title referred to the sleeve concept and had no connection with either his words, music or career. Apparently, he went to Ken McGowan's photo shoot in pensive mood, a state reflected in the first 14 shots on the cover. Along the way his mood lightened and the final caption captured his relief in a half-smile. There was further critical speculation as to whether the 'period of transition' was past, present or yet to come. Morrison concluded that the title represented all of these. He added that the period of transition was also a comment on his current situation, including the acquisition of a new manager. While *A Period Of Transition* was receiving a critical mauling in the UK, Morrison appeared on NBC's *Midnight Special* jamming alongside host George Benson and guests, including Carlos Santana, Tom Scott, Etta James, Dr John and Stanley Banks. The ensemble played a seven-minute 'Moondance' and a surprise 'Bring It On Home To Me' with Morrison and Rebennack trading verses. At rehearsals, Morrison stayed onstage for an unscheduled duet with guitarist Benson on 'Misty'. As a finale, Morrison brought out his own musicians, John Platania, Jeff Labes, Dr John and Ollie Brown for a four-song set featuring 'Heavy Connection', 'Cold Wind In August', 'The Eternal Kansas City' and 'Joyous Sound'.

page 309: ". . . one of the weirdest and most excruciating interviews ever heard . . ." Prior to the Capital Radio appearance, Morrison attended a press reception at Maunkberry's, a swanky club near London's Piccadilly. With Granada Television on hand to film the shebang, Morrison played a short set. A line-up comprising Dr John (keyboards), Mick Ronson (guitar), Mo Foster (bass) and Peter Van Hooke (drums) warmed up until Morrison, dressed in black silk shirt and white trousers, took the stage. The hastily assembled and under-rehearsed unit played a series of blues standards, several cuts from *A Period Of Transition* and a new number, 'Venice USA'. Following a short break, the musicians were augmented by Ray Russell, Brian Auger, Alan Spencer, Roger Chapman and former Them member Peter Bardens.

page 309: "Who are you? . . ." Nicky Horne, interviewed by the author. London: 12 January 1982.

page 310: "Well, I was going along the freeway . . ." Van Morrison, interviewed by Nicky Horne, Capital Radio. London: June 1977.

page 310: "There's no mystique about me . . ." ibid.

page 310: "The whole interview was perpetuating the mystique . . ." Horne/Rogan. London: 12 January 1982.

page 310: "The interview went on . . ." ibid.

page 310: "I was born with a natural gift . . ." Morrison/Horne, op cit.

page 311: "I have never done an interview that bad . . ." Horne/Rogan. London: 12 January 1982.

page 311: "It's good to see the Queen . . ." Van Morrison, interviewed by Vivien Goldman. *Sounds*: 25 June 1977.

page 311: "Can't tell you . . ." ibid.

page 311: "This is nothing new . . ." ibid.

page 312: "That was a big disappointment . . ." Morrison/Vincent, op cit.

page 312: "He had a very strict diet . . ." Goldsmith/Rogan. London: 5 January 1982.

page 312: "One day the switchboard lit up . . ." Van Morrison, interviewed by Ritchie Yorke. *Stage Life*: June/July 1977.

page 312: "Suddenly, one day . . ." Goldsmith/Rogan. London: 5 January 1982.

page 312: "He got to the point where he got crazy . . ." ibid.

page 313: "When I can earn as much money out of you . . ." ibid.

page 313: "In some respects I'm surprised our thing lasted . . ." ibid.

page 313: "All warring factions . . ." Gusty Spence, interviewed in Long Kesh: 11 November 1977.

page 313: "Within four months of that plea . . ." In Roy Garland's authorized biography *Gusty Spence* (Belfast, Blackstaff Press: 2001), Spence's retirement as C.O. is simply dated as 1978. However, Spence previously claimed that this occurred on Armistice Day (11 November 1977). I have taken the latter as the more likely date.

page 314: "I was a bad example . . ." O'Hare/Rogan. Dublin: 12 February 2004.

page 314: "He's the first person I know to leave the IRA . . ." Sam Smyth/Rogan. Dublin: 19 January 2003.

page 314: "It was a smokescreen . . ." O'Hare/Rogan. Dublin: 12 February 2004.

page 314: "Adams was the man of the moment . . ." ibid. Gerry O'Hare never joined Sinn Féin during his IRA years, but his ex-wife Rita became one of the leading lights within the party and one of Gerry Adams' most valued associates.

page 315: "We stayed at the Manor . . ." Bobby Tench, interviewed by the author. London: 14 September 1994.

page 315: "He'd just got the songs on acoustic . . ." ibid.

page 316: "Every time you deliver an album . . ." Van Morrison, interviewed by Chris Welch. *Melody Maker*: 2 February 1979.

page 316: "The only real reference to America . . ." Van Morrison, interviewed by Tony Stewart. *New Musical Express*: 10 March 1979.

page 317: "It was like going from the frying pan to the fire . . ." Goldsmith/Rogan. London: 5 January 1982.

page 317: "Loads of people came to see that one . . ." Tench/Rogan. London: 14 September 1994.

page 317: "If we were doing 'Help Me', he used to go off . . ." Herbie Armstrong/Rogan. Sheffield: 23 November 1994.

page 317: "I kept looking in the wings . . ." Tench/Rogan. London: 14 September 1994.

page 317: "While we were onstage . . ." ibid.

page 318: "I know Van and I know what he's like . . ." Herbie Armstrong/Rogan. Sheffield: 23 November 1994.

page 318: "You know what freaked me out? . . ." ibid.

page 318: "He was more comfortable in smaller venues . . ." Tench/Rogan. London: 14 September 1994.

page 319: "Maybe it's a good thing he's been walking out . . ." Reviewer, Sylvie Simmons. *Sounds*: 16 December 1978.

page 319: "Corvin told me stories . . ." Russell/Rogan. Belfast: 20 October 1994.

Chapter Eighteen: Belfast Revisited

page 320: "Two months before . . ." The offending item originally appeared in *Melody Maker*: 18 November 1978 under the title "Morrison In Stage Rumpus". The story was reprised in the same publication on 27 January 1979.

page 321: "I walked into the restaurant . . ." Altham/Rogan. London: 30 November 1981.

page 321: "You're just stroking me . . ." Morrison/Welch, op cit.

page 321: "He turned up and staggered up the stairs . . ." Altham/Rogan. London: 30 November 1981.

page 322: "You should get a parrot . . ." ibid.

page 322: "It was as near to an apology . . ." ibid.

page 322: "Many of the murders you have pleaded guilty to . . ." Mr Justice O'Donnell sentencing the Shankill Butchers: 20 February 1979.

page 323: "It's very hard for me to relate . . ." Morrison/Stewart, op cit.

page 324: "They're not coming to see Van Morrison . . ." ibid.

page 324: "How the hell can I live in Ireland? . . ." ibid.

page 324: "I wouldn't even dare answer that question . . ." ibid.

page 325: "He came on, saw the stage and shoved Peter Bardens . . ." Tench/Rogan. London: 14 September 1994.

page 325: "He freaked out . . ." Herbie Armstrong/Rogan. Sheffield: 23 November 1994.

page 325: "Morrison doesn't emerge as a character of much conviction . . ." columnist Simon Frith, *Melody Maker*: 24 March 1979.

page 325: "It's a pity that he is so lacking in his ability to handle the media . . ." Altham/Rogan. London: 30 November 1981.

page 326: "Television crews appeared in Roscommon . . ." Sam Smyth/Rogan. Dublin: 19 January 2003. Further details of Corvin's exploits during this period were provided by ex-girlfriends, former colleagues and journalists, including Colin McClelland (16 September 2002) and Seán Boyne (24 January 2003).

page 326: "I think it was the first time anybody noticed that Garret FitzGerald wore odd socks . . ." ibid.

page 328: ". . . a young boy whose looks are a combination of Georgie Best and the Giotto painting of St John the Baptist . . ." Edna O'Brien, *Mother Ireland*, London, Penguin: 1978; first published by Weidenfeld & Nicolson, London: 1976.

page 328: "There's no doubt that he was prone to terrible depressions . . ." Smyth/Rogan. Dublin: 19 January 2003.

page 328: "He spoke to a lot of his friends about it . . ." ibid.

page 329: "I went to the funeral . . ." Colin McClelland/Rogan. Belfast: 16 September 2002.

page 329: "It had been a monastery . . ." Cox/Gee, *Wavelength*, op cit.

page 332: "I ripped off a lump of the mattress . . ." Gerard Hodgkins, quoted in Peter Taylor, *Provos, The IRA and Sinn Féin,* London, Bloomsbury: 1997.

page 332: "One could hardly allow an animal to remain in such conditions . . ." Cardinal Tomas O'Fiaich, Roman Catholic Primate of All Ireland, press statement after visiting the H-Blocks on 31 July 1978.

page 333: "This is a small token of men . . ." Paisley's speech reported in *Belfast Telegraph*: 6 February 1981.

page 333: "the most nefarious conspiracy . . ." ibid. Paisley's words were borrowed from Sir Edward Carson's address to 50,000 men at Craigavon on 25 September 1911 at an anti-Home Rule rally.

page 334: "Bobby Sands was close to death . . ." Jim Gibney, quoted in Peter Taylor, *Provos, The IRA and Sinn Féin,* London, Bloomsbury: 1997.

page 335: "Who here really believes we can win the war through the ballot box? . . ." Danny Morrison, addressing the Sinn Féin Ard Fheis at the Mansion House, Dublin: 31 October 1981. The following year the Republican paper *An Phoblacht*, noted: "The essence of Republican struggle must be in armed resistance coupled with popular opposition to the British presence. So, while not everyone can plant a bomb, everyone can plant a vote."

page 336: "He's not angry any more . . ." Coulter/Rogan. London: 28 January 1982.

page 336: "One of the nights I was there . . ." ibid.

page 336: "Religion has been an ongoing awareness in his life . . ." ibid.

page 337: "There was a management dispute . . ." Herbie Armstrong/Rogan. Sheffield: 23 November 1994.

page 337: "They're trying to turn me into Rod Stewart! . . ." ibid. When re-recording the album, Morrison settled on a line-up featuring Robert Wasserman (bass), David Hayes (bass), Gary Malabar (drums), Chris Michie (lead guitar), John Allair (organ), plus guest guitarist Mark Knopfler. Herbie Armstrong believes that the dispute with Bill Graham led to the cancellation of the original album. "I'd done nearly all the album," he told me. "He decided to break up with Bill Graham . . . We'd already put loads of tracks down, including 'Scandinavia'. Then Van scrapped the whole thing and got rid of the tapes. I think the reason he kept 'Scandinavia' was because me and Mark Isham did this weird tuning with the guitar and keyboard and I don't think anybody knew how to do it again. I don't know if that's the reason he kept it. Mark played the keyboard synths and I played rhythm guitar. Tom Dowd was supposed to produce the album but it didn't work out. What happened was he [Morrison] kept 'Scandinavia' and destroyed all the other tracks like 'Cleaning Windows', then redid it all. You're going into another studio with a whole set of tapes and putting something that's been done somewhere else into something else. That's why the track 'Scandinavia' could have sounded 'out' with the rest of what was happening."

page 338: "It's important for people . . ." Van Morrison, interviewed by Dermot Stokes, *Hot Press*: April 1982.

page 339: Not long after his return to England, a couple from Taunton, Somerset, wrote to Morrison's record company asking permission to use the artiste's music during their wedding ceremony. Permission was granted and, on the day of the wedding, the couple was astonished to receive a call asking if it would be possible for Morrison and a friend to attend the reception. The day went well, and the couple remained in brief written contact with Morrison. Years later, when their local church was attempting to raise money to restore a wall painting, they sheepishly asked him if he would consider doing a benefit concert. Morrison agreed and over 200 tickets were sold and approximately £2,000 raised. The contrast between the small and the gargantuan was never better exemplified than Morrison's switch from church hall to stadium rock. On 4 April he appeared at Grugahalle, Essen, West Germany, for a concert with Rick James that was televised throughout Europe as part of the *Rockapalast* series. Morrison's group featured Mark Isham, Pee Wee Ellis, Peter Van Hooke, plus drummer Tom Dollinger, guitarist Chris Michie and pianist John Allair, with backing vocals provided by Pauline Lozano, Bianca Thornton and Annie South. Morrison clearly was not enjoying the show, despite a positive response from the audience and, in sulky fashion, announced: "And if you're wondering what I'm doing here at a rock 'n' roll event, well, I'm wondering the same thing myself." The audience continued to show their appreciation by letting off firecrackers while Morrison left the stage, having completed an interesting version of 'Summertime In England' in which the Blake references had been replaced by some flattering references to Bob Dylan. He went on to quote several lines from Dylan's acerbic 'Idiot Wind', arguably the key song on the superb *Blood On The Tracks*. Morrison clearly regarded Dylan as one of his few kindred spirits in the music business and admitted that he had been an inspiration during the early Eighties. "Dylan's not pop," he told Bill Flanagan. "No way. We're definitely connected on various levels. It was interesting because I'd stopped thinking about the whole music business, making albums. I was quite fed up with it. Then I saw him and I thought, 'Well, here's somebody who's still doing it and he's good.' It sort of gave me a kick in the arse."

page 339: "He always wanted to retain his home ties . . ." Jones/Rogan. Holywood, Co. Down: 6 March 1982.

page 339: "If I went out and tried comedy . . ." Morrison/Vincent, op cit.

Chapter Nineteen: Rave On, Ian Paisley

page 342: "I first met Ulla during the *Wavelength* tour . . ." Pillster/Rogan. Hollywood, California: 12 September 1993.

page 342: "I'm not particularly fond of Las Vegas . . ." Morrison/Stokes, op cit.

page 343: "He'd only just come back from America . . ." Peter Hayden, interviewed by the author. London: February 1994.

page 343: "I found him friendly . . ." ibid.

page 343: "I've just done some research . . ." Morrison/Stokes, op cit.

page 344: "Van was deeply searching for an answer . . ." Derek Bell, quoted in John Glatt, *The Chieftains*, London, Century: 1997.

page 344: "He'd been ringing me at one and two in the morning from California . . ." Martin Lynch, in conference with the author. Belfast: 5 May 2001.

page 344: "I'm trying to create forms . . ." Van Morrison, interviewed by David Thomas, *The Times*: 4 June 1984.

page 345: "If God gave me the due reward for my deeds . . ." I.R.K. Paisley, *Paisley, The Man, The Myth And His Message*, Belfast, Martyrs Memorial Publications: 1976.

page 345: "I actually think he's a very Protestant artiste . . ." Seán O'Hagan, in conference with the author. Belfast: 5 May 2001.

page 347: "He wrote tens of thousands of pages . . ." *Report of the Board Of Inquiry Into Scientology*, Kevin A. Anderson, QC. Victoria, Australia: 28 September 1965.

page 347: "The Herculean task . . ." ibid.

page 348: "Scientology is evil . . ." ibid.

page 348: "Expert psychiatric opinion . . ." ibid.

page 348: "Hubbard continually distorts and misrepresents . . ." ibid.

page 348: "Scientology students are specifically taught . . ." ibid.

page 348: "Many active Scientologists believe they have obtained benefit . . ." ibid.

page 349: "robs people of their initiative . . ." ibid.

page 349: "If there should be detected in this Report a note of unrelieved denunciation . . ." ibid.

page 351: "To become 'clear' of all engrams was the goal devoutly to be pursued . . ." Russell Miller, *Bare-Faced Messiah: The True Story Of L. Ron Hubbard*, London, Michael Joseph: 1987.

page 351: "The organization clearly is schizophrenic and paranoid . . ." Judge Paul G. Breckenridge, Los Angeles Superior Court: May 1984.

page 352: "immoral, socially obnoxious, corrupt, sinister and dangerous . . ." Mr Justice Latey, High Courts of Justice, London: June 1984.

page 352: "I bumped into him at the Festival of Mind, Body and Spirit at Olympia . . ." Demick/Rogan. London: 5 October 1994.

Chapter Twenty: Spiritual Friends

page 353: "He's not a natural get-out-there-and-do-it guy . . ." Hayden/Rogan. London: February 1994.

page 354: "No, I transcended all that . . ." Van Morrison, interviewed by Gavin Martin. *New Musical Express*: 28 May 1983.

page 354: "I did a lot of investigation . . ." McAuley/Rogan. London: 1 March 1995.

page 354: "I phoned to tell him . . ." Demick/Rogan. London: 5 October 1994.

page 355: "She was reviled . . ." Danny Morrison, interviewed by Peter Taylor. *The Brighton Bomb*, broadcast BBC 1: 14 September 2004.

page 355: "Today we were unlucky . . ." IRA statement: 12 October 1984.

page 355: "The sorrow of the Brighton bombing . . ." Morrissey, interviewed by Ian Pye. *Melody Maker*: 3 November 1984.

page 355: "there's a big part of me . . ." Van Morrison, interviewed by Bill Flanagan, *Written In My Soul*, Chicago, Contemporary: 1986; London, Omnibus: 1990.

page 356: "As far as contemporary Belfast is concerned . . ." Gillian Russell, *Belfast Review*: Winter 1984.

page 356: ". . . my songs are better than Yeats's . . ." This boast was related to several journalists, including Stephen Davis. Some promotional copies of *A Sense Of Wonder* did include 'Crazy Jane On God' and are much prized by Morrison collectors. Despite his rebuff from the Yeats estate, Morrison subsequently recorded another of the poet's works, 'A Woman Young And Old', which remains in the vaults. There was also a recording of 'Before The World Was Made' and, apparently, several other tracks recorded at Colin Martin's studio in Comber, Co. Down. According to Clive Culbertson, who played on this session with June Boyce and Rod McVey, "Colin Martin still has the only remaining tapes of that session. There are none out there that I'm aware of. There was some Yeats poetry done to music and it was beautiful. It was some of the best stuff he'd ever written. When Van had done it he sent off some rough copies to the Yeats estate and they said, 'No way. You're not using it. We'll sue you.' He said, 'But I've paid all this money.' It was good stuff and he was on good form."

page 356: "It took a long time to finish . . ." Van Morrison, 1989.

page 357: "Alcoholics Anonymous wasn't anonymous . . ." Van Morrison, interviewed by Michelle Rocca. *Sunday Independent*: 8 May 1994.

page 357: "I have to thank Ulla for getting me back . . ." Pillster/Rogan. Hollywood, California: 12 September 1993.

page 358: "To me, he was still the same Van Morrison . . ." Platania/Rogan. New York: 20 June 2002. Among the artistes who turned up at the sessions was Pretenders vocalist Chrissie Hynde, whom Morrison invited along to provide a contrast to the soul-styled backing singers featured on the tracks. Unfortunately, Hynde's contribution failed to work out in the way Morrison expected so she did not appear on the final album. Another unsuccessful candidate was the renowned musician Ry Cooder. Apparently, Morrison was impressed by the title of Cooder's album *Jazz*, but failed to listen to its contents. When Cooder arrived at the sessions he went through a series of songs, while Morrison remained impassively silent. After listening to an entire album's worth of songs, Morrison finally turned to the guitarist, thanked him and said good-bye. After Cooder took his leave, a rather puzzled Morrison supposedly turned to his producer Mick Glossop and enquired innocently: "I thought he played jazz."

page 359: "I actually take you through . . ." Morrison/Brown, op cit.

page 359: "You can also call this a press release . . ." ibid.

page 360: "I took courses in Scientology . . ." Van Morrison, interviewed by B.P. Fallon. *Guardian Weekend*: 15 June 1996.

page 360: "This is my job . . ." Van Morrison, interviewed by Robin Denselow. *Observer*: 3 August 1986.

page 361: "It was a loyalist pub . . ." Richie Buckley, interviewed by Barry Egan, *Sunday Independent*: 18 February 2001.

page 361: "What do you think of the blood of Christ? . . ." Turner/Rogan. London: c. February 1994.

page 362: "It's the case nowadays . . ." Clive Culbertson, interviewed by the author. Coleraine: 11 December 2002.

page 362: "Sitting in my bedroom . . ." ibid.

page 363: "I think Scientology did free him . . ." ibid.

page 363: "The only way you can find out . . ." ibid.

page 363: "Probably the stuff I gave him was too simple . . ." ibid.

page 363: "The answer to the mystery of being . . ." ibid.

page 364: "She was a great woman . . ." ibid.

page 364: "He was funny . . ." ibid.

page 365: "When he came over to Crawfordsburn, he would drink . . ." ibid.

page 365: "I know there were times when he was a fucker . . ." ibid.

page 365: "He grabbed me by the shoulders . . ." ibid.

page 366: "Have you ever thought of being a teacher? . . ." Morrison/Flanagan, op cit.

page 366: "I've had no offers . . ." ibid.

page 366: "There's something inside of me . . ." Steve Turner, *Hungry For Heaven*. London, Virgin: 1985.

page 366: "I never had anything to do with rock culture . . ." Van Morrison, interviewed by Bill Graham. *Hot Press*: 6 November 1986.

page 366: "I certainly don't want to do this album-tour bit . . ." Morrison/Brown, op cit.

page 367: "Psychologists will tell you . . ." Van Morrison, interviewed by Chris Salewicz. *Q* issue 4: January 1987.

page 368: "Since the beginning of human culture . . ." brochure for the seminar *The Secret Heart Of Music: An Exploration Into The Power Of Music To Change Consciousness*. Loughborough University: 18–20 September 1987.

page 368: "This unique gathering . . ." ibid.

page 369: "His passion for music . . ." ibid.

page 369: "Few dared go near him . . ." John Etherington, interviewed by the author. London: 22 September 1987; events were mulled over again in 1994 and 1997.

page 370: "She singled out Van in the poem . . ." ibid.

page 370: "I don't suffer fools gladly . . ." Van Morrison, interviewed by Desmond Hogan. *Hot Press*: 5 November 1987.

Chapter Twenty-One: Are You A Proddy?

page 373: "Van's not a great one . . ." Paddy Moloney interview. *Q*: August 1991.

page 373: "When we were doing *Irish Heartbeat* . . ." ibid.

page 374: "It wasn't a joke . . ." Derek Bell, undated interview by Nancy Lyon.

page 374: "Morrison was going to come and talk about his work . . ." Martin Lynch, in conference with the author. Belfast: 5 May 2001.

page 374: "He went through each LP . . ." ibid.

page 375: "On 22 April . . ." Details taken from George Morrison's death certificate. Although newspaper articles and other Morrison biographies claim he was 68 at the time of his death, he was still only 65. The error may be linked to the false information he gave on his marriage certificate discussed earlier.

page 375: "I think when we did that tour . . ." Moloney, op cit.

page 375: "There were nights when you were on stage and you'd see the robed guys, the angelic beings . . ." Culbertson/Rogan. Coleraine: 11 December 2002.

page 376: "They're all Irish songs . . ." Van Morrison, interviewed by Seán O'Hagan. *The Times*: 9 March 1991.

page 376: "From the purist's point of view it's grotesque . . ." Derek Bell/Glatt, op cit.

page 377: "For a long time . . ." Morrison/Salewicz, op cit.

page 377: "Is it OK if I go to sleep? . . ." Van Morrison, interviewed by Liam Mackey, *Hot Press*: 1988.

page 377: "Hello, you've got your pound of flesh . . ." ibid.

page 377: "These questions, God, they're unanswerable . . ." ibid.

page 378: "Well, if you have all the answers . . ." Van Morrison, interviewed by Gavin Martin. *New Musical Express*: 15 October 1988.

page 378: "It's basically a cross section . . ." ibid.

page 378: "He was stuffing his face with buns . . ." Gavin Martin, interviewed by the author. London: 15 March 1994.

page 378: "Rule number one, you don't sit anywhere . . ." Culbertson/Rogan. Coleraine: 11 December 2002.

page 378: "He would arrive . . ." Culbertson/Rogan. Coleraine: 11 December 2002.

page 379: "Considering they were so good for him . . ." ibid.

page 379: "If Derek Bell hadn't been on that tour . . ." ibid.

page 379: "Derek knew something else . . ." ibid.

page 380: "probably the most powerful human being I've ever met in my life . . ." ibid.

page 380: "What do you want from me? . . ." ibid.

page 380: "Of course, he went through Derek and they wrote the Violet Flames Symphony . . ." ibid.

page 380: "I want to know how to get hold of you . . ." ibid.

page 380: "Visualize this in violet . . ." ibid.

page 380: "Ah, I'm Van Morrison . . ." ibid.

page 380: "I would like to know that there's some part of me . . ." ibid.

page 380: "He gave me a visualization to do . . ." ibid.

page 381: "I was told that from a past life . . ." ibid.

page 381: "He's got Whitehouse over the edge . . ." ibid.

page 382: "They were about to go at it . . ." ibid.

page 382: "There were times . . ." Kevin Conneff/Glatt, op cit.

page 382: "She was great, she was a joy . . ." Culbertson/Rogan. Coleraine: 11 December 2002.

page 382: "she was totally unimpressed by him . . ." Hayden/Rogan. London: February 1994.

page 383: "I went away for quite some time . . ." ibid.

page 383: "He rang up . . ." ibid.

page 383: "He hated coming to the States . . ." Pillster/Rogan. Hollywood, California: 12 September 1993.

page 384: "I never saw him take a drink . . ." ibid.

page 384: "Cliff Richard? You're joking . . ." Van Morrison, interviewed by Seán O'Hagan. *New Musical Express*: 3 June 1989.

page 385: "He's a professional . . ." ibid.

page 386: "You get a great rush of satisfaction . . ." Reviewer Stuart Bailie. *New Musical Express*: 3 June 1989.

page 387: "You have a very strange charisma . . ." Van Morrison, interviewed by Spike Milligan. *Q*: 1989.

page 387: "Are you a Proddy? . . ." ibid.

page 387: "I'm not into talking about myself . . ." ibid.

page 387: "The man was a pig . . ." Spike Milligan's recollections. *Q* 117: 1996.

page 387: "The timing had to be spot on . . ." Sheelagh Allen, interviewed in *Glastonbury Festival Tales*, Crispin Aubrey and John Sherlaw, London, Ebury: 2004.

page 388: "Van's a man that makes your average King Edward spud look svelte . . ." reviewer David Thomas. *Punch*: 12 May 1989.

page 388: "They're the difficult ones . . ." Morrison/O'Hagan, *New Musical Express*: 3 June 1989, op cit.

Chapter Twenty-Two: Don't Call Me Jack!

page 390: "Dylan didn't want to sing . . ." Anthony Wall. Even while the *Arena* Morrison special was being completed, the Ulster man was featured in another *Arena* tribute to Slim Gaillard, which was broadcast on 29 October 1989. Morrison greatly respected the veteran jazz player who had also inspired another of his childhood heroes – the beat poet Jack Kerouac. Appropriately, Morrison read extracts from Kerouac's *On The Road* in which a meeting with Gaillard was described. Following the reading, Morrison questioned Gaillard about the Kerouac meeting, while the jazzer played piano and discussed his musical technique. Within weeks of the Gaillard broadcast, Morrison met another of his early influences when he joined Jerry Lee Lewis on stage at the Hammersmith Odeon. The audience was taken aback as Morrison joined in the vocals on Ray Charles' 'What'd I Say', a song that he had performed frequently during the early Sixties in his showband phase with the Monarchs.

page 391: "Chris O'Donnell was experienced . . ." Pillster/Rogan. Hollywood, California: 12 September 1993.

page 391: "I was lying flat on a rock . . ." McCartney/Rogan. Bangor, Co. Down: 30 October 1994.

page 392: "He sat in this front room . . ." ibid.

page 392: "As we were going through the door of the Crawfordsburn Inn . . ." ibid.

page 392: "It's really beneficial for the mind . . ." ibid.

page 393: "They wouldn't believe this . . ." ibid.

page 393: "Several times in the conversation . . ." ibid.

page 393: "I'd read all the books . . ." ibid.

page 393: "I've always wanted Van to go on a vegetarian diet . . ." ibid.

page 394: "Van was saying how marvellous it was . . ." ibid.

page 394: "I said 'That woman's a monster' . . ." ibid.

page 394: "He got angry . . ." ibid.

page 394: "He got very annoyed by that . . ." ibid.

page 395: "I said, 'Look, Van, when you were drinking . . ." ibid.

page 395: "Poor Cecil . . ." Culbertson/Rogan. Coleraine: 11 December 2002.

page 395: "The rehearsals had been much nicer than the recordings . . ." Culbertson/ Rogan. Coleraine: 11 December 2002.

page 395: "When I was in the band, he phoned my house . . ." ibid.

page 396: "The master had written out some musical meditations . . ." ibid.

page 396: "We had a row . . ." Derek Bell/Glatt, op cit.

page 397: "Here was a guy that Van idolized . . ." Pillster/Rogan. Hollywood, California: 12 September 1993.

page 397: "He'd gotten more reliable in doing a whole set . . ." ibid. The US tour had many highlights. Following a well-received show at the Spectrum, Philadelphia, Morrison celebrated his 45th birthday the following evening with a memorable show at Lake Compounce Park, Bristol. One of the best moments of the evening was Georgie Fame's warm-up set, which included the memorable chart topper 'Yeh Yeh'. The fact that the latter was dominating the charts just prior to Morrison's finest pop moment with 'Here Comes The Night' seemed strangely apposite. Following the Fame set, the birthday boy walked on stage in a plain grey suit for the emphatic 'Did Ye Get Healed?'. A string of Morrison favourites followed including 'Jackie Wilson Said', 'Domino' and 'Cleaning Windows'. After covering Dylan's 'Just Like A Woman' and offering a harmonica solo on 'Help Me', Morrison again left the stage to Fame, who once more proved himself a consummate performer. More importantly, he was also a formidable musical director and the perfect foil for Morrison, who was clearly relaxed by his commanding presence. Even old friend Phil Coulter was quick to credit Fame for bringing Morrison out of himself: "Georgie, apart from being a great musician, is a very personable guy who transmits so well to audiences. He's somebody who can direct a band and keep a nice tight but easy rein on musicians. I think it's an inspired choice." With Fame in the ascendant, Morrison returned to the stage for a rousing 'Raglan Road' and 'Star Of County Down'. The perennial 'Summertime In England' closed the set, while the encores included 'Full Force Gale', 'Whenever God Shines His Light', 'Bright Side Of The Road' and the unreleased 'Buona Sera Senorita'. The group played 'Happy Birthday' aided by a singalong from the crowd and Morrison closed his 45th birthday with his most famous flip side, 'Gloria'.

page 397: "Chris O'Donnell was involved briefly . . ." Pillster/Rogan. Hollywood, California: 12 September 1993.

page 398: "I like Morrison because I know that his work comes from the same level . . ." Paul Durcan. *Magill*: May 1988.

page 399: "I didn't know what to play on that . . ." Georgie Fame, interviewed by Michael Walsh. *Into The Music: The Van Morrison Fanzine*.

page 400: "I don't think he would have been if the cameras had been there . . ." Anthony Wall, interviewed by Gillian Reynolds. *Daily Telegraph*: 16 March 1991.

page 400: "The songs don't measure your life . . ." from the programme *One Irish Rover*, broadcast BBC 2: 16 March 1991.

page 401: "Van loved Jerry Lee Lewis . . ." Tom Jones, interviewed by Joe Jackson. *Hot Press*: 13 June 1991.

page 402: "Van is always trying to find something . . ." ibid.

page 402: "It's got nothing to do with enlightenment . . ." Morrison/Clarke, op cit.

page 402: "You do the album, you do the music . . ." ibid.

page 403: "They think you're having a great time . . ." ibid.

page 404: ". . . solicitors Cleaver, Fulton and Rankin . . ." The letter read: "We act on behalf of Ivan Morrison ('Van Morrison') and we are instructed to write to you in regard to the news reports in the *Belfast Telegraph* on November 11 and 27, 1991, in regard to the erection of a plaque bearing our client's name at premises in Hyndford Street, Belfast. The following points arise: Firstly, our client was not consulted nor asked for permission for the use of his name in this matter. Secondly, our client is not a member of nor is he associated with any group known as 'the Belfast Blues Appreciation Society'. Finally, the statement in the report on November 11 that our client was intending to inspect the plaque is incorrect. Our client appreciates public support but equally values his privacy and does not desire that his name be used in or in connection with promotional activities whether for commercial gain or otherwise without express permission."

page 404: "First there was George Best . . ." *Sunday Life*: 1 December 1991.

Chapter Twenty-Three: Dublin

page 406: "A sneak peak . . ." Financial source for Exile Productions' cash in hand, courtesy of Companies House.

page 406: "Towards the end of the year, he attended a fund-raising dinner party . . ." Morrison's first meeting with Rocca has previously been wrongly dated as 'summer 1992' based on an interview she gave which casually referred to the dinner as "a few months ago". However, the charity dinner took place in November 1992. It was there that Marina Guinness introduced Morrison to Francis Pakenham (Lord Longford) who upon hearing that this man was "in the music business" insisted that he perform in a forthcoming protest concert at Tullynally Castle to prevent the felling of Coolattin Oaks, a 250-year-old forest. Remarkably, Morrison agreed and played the date the following February, backed by Arty McGlynn, Nollaig Casey and Nicky Scott.

page 407: "He came back from lunch and sat shaking his head . . ." Colin McClelland/Rogan. Belfast: 16 September 2002.

page 408: "I'm anything but a bohemian . . ." Michelle Rocca, interviewed by Reiseal Ní Cheilleachair. Dublin: March 1994. Additional information was obtained during the author's meeting and interview with Reiseal Ní Cheilleachair. Cork: 14 April 1994.

page 408: "What do you do? . . ." Michelle Rocca, interviewed by Patricia Deevy, *Sunday Independent:* 27 February 1994.

page 409: "Forget the *Hello!* interview . . ." Arts correspondent for *The Times* Susannah Herbert in May 1995.

page 411: "I went to see him because Dylan was in town . . ." Éamon Carr, interviewed by the author. Dublin: July/August 1993.

page 411: "When I rambled backstage . . ." ibid. Some reports have extended the list of stage guests to include, *inter alia*, Larry Mullen, Steve Earle, Jerry Lee Lewis and even Johnny Cash.

page 412: "It was such a great atmosphere . . ." Tadgh Coughlan, interviewed by the author. Dublin: June 1994.

page 412: "He turned up to meet his idol . . ." ibid.

page 412: "He was rude to me . . ." Linda Gail Lewis, interviewed by the author. Cardiff: 25 April 2004.

page 412: "He started fussing at Eddie . . ." ibid.

page 413: "I've been abused, sued, jailed, ridiculed . . ." Jerry Lee Lewis, interviewed by Julian Lloyd. *Independent Magazine*: 22 January 1994.

page 413: "They not only took the freezer . . ." Kerrie Lee Lewis, ibid.

page 413: "I've always been Irish . . ." Jerry Lee Lewis, interviewed by Éamon Carr. *Dublin Evening Herald*: 11 June 1993.

page 413: "They talked about 'Bright Side Of The Road' . . ." Coughlan/Rogan. Dublin: June 1994.

page 415: "Van depressed me . . ." Shane MacGowan in *A Drink With Shane MacGowan*, Victoria Mary Clarke & Shane MacGowan, London, Sidgwick & Jackson: 2001; Pan: 2002.

page 415: "It is surely the most unlikely coupling in human history . . ." Sam Smyth/Rogan. Dublin: July/August 1993.

page 416: "Michelle Rocca is having an intensely platonic relationship . . ." Columnist Terry Keane. *Sunday Independent*: 27 June 1993.

page 416: "When it comes to protesting too much . . ." Columnist Terry Keane. *Sunday Independent*: 25 July 1993.

page 417: "So what is the state of play? . . ." Columnist Terry Keane. *Sunday Independent*: 29 August 1993.

page 417: "The lust-free liaison . . ." Columnist Terry Keane. *Sunday Independent*: 19 September 1993.

page 418: "I would be very flattered . . ." Michelle Rocca, interviewed by Stephanie Bell. *Sunday Life*: 26 September 1993.

page 418: "He's not a professional . . ." Philip Solomon/Rogan. Dublin: 15 April 1982.

page 419: "I've bought some new clothes for my boyfriend . . ." related by Éamon Carr to the author. Dublin: June 1994. The emphasis on Morrison's appearance reached a peak during this period, unsurprisingly given his ubiquity in the gossip columns. The unflattering description that follows is included to underline that point and show how even in the Nineties Morrison agreed to a sartorial makeover that became an onstage uniform for many years.

page 420: "He listens to me more than I listen to him . . ." Rocca/Patricia Deevy, op cit.

page 421: "You get compartmentalized . . ." Rocca/Reiseal Ní Cheilleachair. op cit.

page 421: "You tell me . . ." ibid.

page 422: "I think Irish men have problems . . ." ibid.

page 423: "I'm not a rock star . . ." The full letter in the *Sunday Independent*, 8 May 1994 read: "Sir – There has been a lot in the papers lately in relation to myself being referred to as a 'rock star'. I'd just like to set the record straight if I may. To call me a rock star is absurd as anyone who has listened to my music will observe. For the benefit of the unenlightened it is not my nature to be a rock star. What I am is a singer and songwriter who does blues, soul, jazz, etc, etc, etc. If anyone is really interested they would find I made my reputation as a blues singer in Belfast on the R&B scene, which I started in that city. To suddenly be called a rock star at this stage is not only amusing but ridiculous. I was not even called that 30 years ago before anyone knew what I was capable of. With all due respect don't you think it's time that they called a spade a spade? I am flattered by all the attention, but this time last year did the same people think I was a rock star? In fact, I have never claimed, in any shape or form, to be the above and if anyone would care to do a bit of groundwork they would very easily discover what I have been saying for the last 30 years that I am not that, and do not believe in it and never have. On the one hand I am flattered by the sudden attention of the rock star mythology, but on the other hand I do not need, or want the attention, having spend [*sic*] most of my life living the role of an anti-hero and getting on with my job, so I tip my hat to the gods and goddesses of the media and say thanks, but no thanks – Van Morrison, Chiswick, London, W4."

page 423: "How Not To Get Screwed . . ." The 'How Not To Get Screwed' article featured in the 9 April 1995 edition of the *Sunday Independent* and contained some of the following advice: "1. Get a lawyer. If you can't afford one, then borrow the money. You must have good legal representation. 2. Play every hole in the wall – even if it's just for experience. You are going to need the discipline if you become successful. 3. Don't believe your own publicity – it's not worth it. And remember, the media worships youth and glamour. But that doesn't last. 4. Test your lifestyle. Find out if your personality fits show business because if it doesn't, don't bother in the first place. 5. If you're in a position to, try to get a proper education first. 6. Decide whether you want to be a gifted amateur or a dedicated pro. Work out what level you want to operate at." It was interesting and instructive to observe the extent to which the younger Morrison had succeeded or failed to live up to the advice offered by his older self.

page 423: "We used to go down to Lillie's quite a lot . . ." Marion McKeone, interviewed by the author. Dublin: 14 June 1994.

page 424: "He's quite a nice guy, full of Tory affectation . . ." Sam Smyth/Rogan. Dublin: July/August 1993.

page 425: ". . . Bob Geldof at the Shelbourne . . ." The incident with Geldof was reported by Adrian Deevoy in the *Independent Magazine*: 9 April 1994.

page 425: "He did two nights at the Point . . ." Éamon Carr, interviewed by the author. Dublin: June 1994.

page 425: "Basically, Van fecked off at this stage . . ." ibid.

page 426: "I don't know Michelle . . ." McKeone/Rogan. Dublin: 14 June 1994.

page 426: "I ran into Victoria on the night of the second gig . . ." Katie Hannon, interviewed by the author. Dublin: June 1994.

page 426: "He obviously didn't know anything about it . . ." ibid.

page 427: "There was a huge row that night . . ." ibid.

page 427: "I was at a function last night . . ." Katie Hannon, phone call. Dublin: June 1994.

page 427: "You have sold Ulster to buy off the fiendish Republican scum . . ." Ian Paisley's tirade, reported in the *Belfast Newsletter*: 16 December 1993.

Chapter Twenty-Four: Sex Shame

page 429: "We had this bizarre conversation . . ." Colin McClelland/Rogan. Belfast: 16 September 2002.

page 431: "We cannot bow the knee to these traitors in Whitehall . . ." Paisley's speech reported in David Kitterick & David McVea, *Making Sense Of The Troubles*, but the original source is unstated.

page 432: "Nothing. I don't have time to read . . ." Van Morrison, interviewed by Michelle Rocca. *Vox*: January 1995.

page 432: "That's another taboo subject . . ." ibid.

page 432: "No! No! No! . . ." ibid.

page 432: "It's official . . ." Columnist Terry Keane. *Sunday Independent*: 2 April 1995.

page 434: "All of which leaves . . ." "Coda: Bob Dylan's Happy Families", Peter Doggett, in the *Journal*, issue 1: Summer 2001.

page 435: "Well, I think they used to . . ." Morrison/Rocca, *Vox*, op cit.

page 435: "I'm a poet, but in the strictest sense, I'm not . . ." ibid.

page 436: "A rancid smog of blind reverence . . ." Reviewer Stephen Dalton. *New Musical Express*: 24 June 1995.

page 436: "No wildness, no mystery remains . . ." Reviewer John Mulvey. *New Musical Express*: 22 July 1995.

page 437: "My tour was absolutely overwhelming . . ." President Clinton in a White House press conference with interviewers from the *Times*, the *Irish Times* and several American newspapers: 8 December 1995. The Derry appearance was notable for a rendition of 'The Town I Loved So Well' by Phil Coulter.

page 438: "Michelle draped herself over the smiling President . . ." Reported in *Sunday Mirror*: 16 June 1996.

page 439: ". . . . That's ancient history . . ." For a fuller account of Morrison's Supper Club raps, the reader should consult the transcripts by Joe Hauldren printed in *Wavelength* 9.

page 441: "She noticed things . . ." Columnist Sam Smyth, *Sunday Tribune*: 16 February 1997.

page 441: "Everywhere she went, they went . . ." ibid.

page 441: "Poor Michelle . . ." ibid.

page 442: "That's not true . . . I'm Irish . . . I'm quarter Italian . . ." Michelle Rocca, interviewed by John Kierans and Nic North. *Daily Mirror*: 7 June 1996.

page 442: "I was a Miss Ireland once . . ." ibid.

page 442: "OK, I spent a couple of nights . . ." ibid.

page 442: "Van will never leave me . . ." ibid.

page 442: "She's expecting nine puppies . . ." ibid.

page 442: "I am disgusted . . ." Van Morrison, interviewed by John Kierans and Nic North. *Daily Mirror*: 8 June 1996.

page 442: "It's the OBE – Old Bonker Exposed! . . ." *Sunday Mirror*: 16 June 1996. The *Sunday Mirror* was not alone in making fun of Morrison's OBE. Even before the tabloid exposé, the august *Financial Times* (18 June 1996) noted: "Van Morrison OBE – no, not Obese Balding Eccentric – Ulster's greatest gift to world music has been honoured by the Queen with the Order of the British Empire. Significantly, she was not acting on personal whim. Van Morrison will collect his gong because he is the people's choice – his fans petitioned in his favour by the sackload."

page 443: "I just felt lonely and rejected . . ." Van Morrison, interviewed by Andrew Golden. *Sunday Mirror*: 16 June 1996.

page 443: "I am so ashamed . . ." ibid.

page 444: "I went to a friend's house . . ." ibid.

page 444: "I was framed . . ." reported in a profile of Michelle Rocca by Helen Callanan. *Sunday Independent*: 30 June 1996.

page 444: "The trial dominated . . ." The succeeding quotes were made under oath by the various participants who appeared in the witness box. Oddly, in several of the newspaper accounts Sarah Linton was referred to as Sarah Lindon. I have assumed the former is correct.

page 448: "It's unfair to the children . . ." Tess De Cretze, interviewed by Joanne McElgunn and Mike McNiffe. *Sunday World*: 16 February 1987.

page 448: "They concluded that, yes, she told the truth . . ." Ellis O'Hanlon. *Sunday Independent*: 16 February 1997.

page 448: "This was a civil case . . ." Stephen Dodd. *Sunday Independent*: 16 February 1997.

page 449: "Our love affair with glamour . . ." Anne Marie Hourihane. *Sunday Tribune*: 16 February 1997.

Chapter Twenty-Five: The Collaborator

page 450: "Since basing himself in the UK . . ." Reviewer David Hepworth. *Mojo* 40: March 1997.

page 452: "Paramilitary operations, punishment beatings and organized criminal activities . . ." The peace process was bedevilled by problems over the next few years, amid accusations of criminal behaviour, vigilante reprisals and gangland intimidation on both sides of the community. Meanwhile, political progress was interrupted by a frustrating series of stops and starts. In February 2000, N.I.

Secretary Peter Mandelson suspended the assembly over the issue of IRA decommissioning. Three months later, the IRA promised to place their weapons "completely and verifiably" beyond use. An impasse followed, culminating in David Trimble's resignation as First Minister in the summer of 2001. The ever patient General John de Chastelain re-entered the fray and by September reported that there had been "a significant disposal" of arms. During April 2002, another arsenal was dumped. Unfortunately, there was a further setback towards the end of that year following accusations of IRA espionage and intelligence gathering from offices in Stormont. Over the next year both Sinn Féin and the DUP increased their electoral majorities and it seemed a new deal beckoned. By October 2004, Paisley had fully re-emerged as the unionists' leading light, eclipsing the more moderate UUP's David Trimble. After Paisley attended a key meeting with the Taoiseach Bertie Ahern, political commentators predicted a definitive breakthrough within a matter of weeks. Repeating the earlier intervention of Bill Clinton, President George W. Bush contacted the individual parties and urged Paisley and Adams to reach a final settlement. It later emerged that a detailed timetable had been set for 8 December 2004. It was to begin at 10 am with confirmation from the IRA of a total disarmament before the close of the year. An hour after that announcement de Chastelain would reveal that he, along with two observers from both sides of the religious divide, were to witness the destruction of the IRA's stockpile of weapons. By midday the DUP were to issue a statement agreeing to sit in government with Sinn Féin. Adams would then recommend that Sinn Féin end their boycott of the PSNI (Police Service of Northern Ireland). And by lunchtime, Tony Blair and Bertie Ahern would take their place in history amid jubilant celebrations at a world press conference.

Nothing is ever so straightforward in Irish politics and the entire timetable was abandoned at the eleventh hour after Paisley demanded photographic proof and publication of the acts of disarmament. Blair was quick to point out that the IRA had made no such commitment but, not wishing to offend loyalists, suggested it might have been a "reasonable compromise". Characteristically, Paisley felt no need to play the diplomat and, speaking of "sackcloth and ashes", emphasized a need to humiliate the IRA. "The situation is this: that the IRA are dead set on keeping their arms and going on with IRA/Sinn Féin's twofold policy of democracy and terrorism. They have brought murder and mayhem to this country and I, for one, and my party, aren't going to be ruled or dictated to by IRA gunmen."

Adams replied with cool assurance that the IRA would not be shamed and humiliated. This latest stalemate prompted some simplistic and misleading headlines in the British press implying that the peace process had been irrevocably lost on the bartering of a single photograph. In fact, Sinn Féin's refusal to sign a document renouncing violence had proven a more serious stumbling block. The Taoiseach hoped that the peace deal might be back on before Christmas, but few shared his optimism. Tony Blair was cautious and predicted that this latest impasse was ultimately nothing more than a temporary setback. Like many others, he still believed that the remaining obstacles – full decommissioning, a cessation of IRA militarism, and unionist acceptance of power-sharing – could be overcome before long. "I look back and see the vast expanse of territory we have covered and I know that the extra bit we have got to go, that would have looked unattainable a few months back, is attainable." In a key part of his speech, he added: "As a traveller I may be weary, but not downhearted. I cannot see the process going backwards, but I do know it is going to require extra effort to finish the journey."

Blair's words were tinged with hubris. Within weeks the peace process was plunged into rapid reverse. On 19 December, there was an audacious raid on the Northern Bank in Belfast resulting in a cash loss of £26 million. It was widely suspected that the culprits were the IRA, although both Gerry Adams and Martin McGuinness insisted that they had absolute assurances from the Provisionals that they were not guilty of the crime. Political commentators were largely unconvinced and speculated whether the heist was sanctioned by Sinn Féin or, alternatively, represented a last opportunity to secure a pension for redundant IRA militants. There was soon a discernible shift away from moderate unionist opinion in the North and a growing conviction that the Big Man's complaints were nearer the mark than many had assumed. Could it be that Paisley had been right all along?

Gerry Adams remained bullish in January 2005 when he appeared before Sinn Féin representatives at Dublin's Mansion House. This was *An Céad* – the 100th anniversary of the founding of the party by Arthur Griffith. It was a time of celebration, consolidation and the vanquishing of enemies, real or imagined. Responding to media attacks, Adams defiantly proclaimed: "The political establishment was at it 100 years ago. If those who founded Sinn Féin were alive today and watching recent events they would conclude that the more things change, the more some things remain the same . . . Those who vilified and excluded us need look no further than tonight as evidence of the failure of their strategy. We are back in the Mansion House bigger and stronger and better than ever."

Sinn Féin's strength in the Republic soon ebbed as they were all but overtaken by a series of cataclysmic events. On Sunday 30 January, a number of hard-core Provisionals were drinking in Magennis's Bar near the High Court in Belfast. They had just returned from the annual Bloody Sunday commemorations in Derry. Later that evening, they became involved in an argument with two men – Brendan Devine and Robert McCartney. Amid the exchange of words was an imputation that the Provos were little more than gangsters, more interested in buying houses in Donegal than defending the Catholic community. At one point, the leader of the gang drew a finger across his windpipe prompting one of his colleagues to take a knife from the pub's kitchen which was used to cut the throat of Brendan Devine. The mêlée then spilt into the street and the Provos began whipping their two victims with sewer rods. Devine was stabbed twice more and a bottle smashed over his head. McCartney, while attempting to help his friend, was also stabbed near the heart and several of the assailants jumped on his head. Leaving the men bleeding in the street, the perpetrators returned to the bar and systematically removed all evidence, wiping away their fingerprints and removing videotape from the CCTV camera. They also intimidated 72 witnesses present, ordering them to say nothing to the police. Finally, they left the premises by the back door, disappearing into the night and making their way home through the Markets area.

Devine miraculously survived his brutal assault, but McCartney died the following morning. The slaying sent shockwaves through the nationalist community and prompted McCartney's sisters and his fiancée to take on the IRA and demand justice. McCartney's aunt Margaret Quinn wrote an impassioned letter to the *Irish News*, congratulating her nieces on their courageous stand and denouncing the murderers as "the scum in the IRA who, by association, disgrace that entire organization". In a telling comparison, she wrote of "Shankill Butcher-types and psychopathic cowards, disguised as our so-called protectors," concluding: "If Sinn Féin's leaders fail to publicly and unambiguously call on every person with information regarding this crime to give that information to the police – everything, from the seemingly insignificant to the perpetrators' names – then I see, in the not too distant future, Sinn Féin's headstone etched with the words, 'Death By Suicide'."

In parallel with the McCartney murder, Sinn Féin faced further attacks over alleged money laundering in the wake of the National Bank raid. A report from the Independent Monitoring Commission stated that the IRA carried out the robbery and that it was sanctioned by leading members of Sinn Féin. Justice Minister Michael McDowell dismissed denials by Adams and the IRA, and condemned the Provos as a "colossal crime machine". There were already rumours that the £26 million taken in the raid had overloaded the IRA's money laundering operation to such an extent that it was unable to function without detection. The PSNI and the Garda were targeting solicitors, accountants and other professionals in the Republic and claimed to have uncovered a money laundering operation in Cork. Some of the reports bordered on the bizarre and comical. Two men from Derry were detained at Heuston Station, Dublin after £54,000 in cash was discovered wrapped in cling film and concealed in a box of Daz washing powder. If nothing else it put a new slant on the term "clean money". In Passage, West Cork, a man was found burning sterling notes in his back garden and a search of his property produced 150 bullets (initially reported as 30) said to be compatible with a Kalashnikov AK 47 rifle. Another person was required to explain money in excess of £1.5 million held in his bungalow. A businessman, who had recently received a dividend in cash, walked into Anglesea Street Garda Station in Cork and handed in £175,000, fearing that he had been the victim of a money laundering scam. The stories were becoming weirder by the week.

"I don't want to be tainted by criminality. I don't want anybody near me who is involved in criminality," Adams pleaded, but the pressure on Sinn Féin was increasing with each new revelation. After a decade successfully winning over political rivals, Irish voters and the heads of government in Britain, the Republic and the USA, Sinn Féin were frozen out of both Downing Street and the Dáil and treated like a pariah by George W. Bush who declined to proffer the traditional invitation to the White House for the St Patrick's Day celebrations. At home, the Taoiseach was demanding that Sinn Féin accept democracy and his entreaties were repeated by other party leaders. Labour's Pat Rabbitte said: "The reality is that whatever little credibility they had, it is now in tatters. The goodwill extended by other parties has been shamelessly abused by them." Fine Gael MEP Gay Mitchell added: "They have corrupted democracy, and they have corrupted businesses." Ian Paisley could hardly have put it more forcibly and, for once, could afford to sit back and allow Sinn Féin's opponents in the South to provide the righteous indignation.

By the third week of February 2005, the heat on Sinn Féin was scorching. Justice Minister Michael McDowell hit the headlines after revealing that Adams, McGuinness and Kerry North TD Martin Ferris were members of the IRA's Army Council, an accusation emphatically denied by all three. Pressed on the issue, the Taoiseach claimed that he had no idea who was on the Army Council and awaited further developments. McGuinness accused the Justice Minister of trying to "criminalize our party in the best tradition of Margaret Thatcher", adding that "given he is probably recognized as one of the most right-wing ministers in the history of the southern State, none of this can come as any surprise to Republicans . . . Neither Gerry Adams nor I would have anyone near us who was in any way involved in criminality of any description." Few seemed convinced. Foreign Affairs Minister Dermot Ahern was "absolutely satisfied" that there were links between the Sinn Féin leadership and the IRA. "It is quite obvious to us from all of our intelligence that there is an interweaving . . . The Irish had exercised self-determination North and South in 1998 when they voted for the Good Friday Agreement. Those people did not vote for robbery or money laundering or punishment beatings. They voted for an end to criminality and paramilitary activity. We need honesty in this and we haven't got it. We need an end to what I would call Red Diesel Republicanism. Sinn Féin need to move on the policing agenda. We have heard of the type of intimidation that goes on, and we are talking about Sinn Féin and the people associated with them . . . It is inconceivable now for anyone to argue other than that there was Provisional IRA involvement in this money laundering. It gives me no pleasure to say that."

The Minister's sentiments were recapitulated in the barbed comments of other prominent politicians, many of whom expressed their disillusionment and total loss of faith in Sinn Féin. Fine Gael leader Enda Kenny concluded: "This process has now foundered on the rocks of criminality and both governments must go back to the drawing board." Labour leader Pat Rabbitte called on Republicans to end two years of political prevarication and manoeuvring by laying down their arms permanently. "Failure to make such a declaration, in the face of the mounting sense of betrayal, will force all of us to believe that for Sinn Féin, the peace process was never more than a tactical weapon . . . long after the final weapon should have been decommissioned, we learn beyond any reasonable doubt that the movement is up to its neck in the sort of criminality that would shame any true Republican."

The anger felt by those who had once supported or tolerated Sinn Féin during the troubled times of the peace process was translated into increasingly cynical column inches. One paper even went as far as to compare Sinn Féin to Germany's Nationalist Socialists. The *Irish Independent*'s security editor Tom Brady conjured a horrifying vision of Sinn Féin and the IRA creating a parallel state with their own police force controlling and intimidating communities, their own hand-picked ministers of finance and justice and a unique welfare system "providing weekly payments to volunteers – either those who continue to busy themselves with robberies, cleaning up murder scenes, laundering cash and wholesale smuggling, or those whose chosen career is in community work and spreading the word according to Sinn Féin." Looking back at recent events, he lamented: "They duped the two governments and the UUP leader David Trimble into believing that they would eventually play a key part in the newly reformed policing system in the North, and in later months the DUP also bought into that concept." Brady ended on an salutary note, predicting a new era of policing in which "the big losers" would be "the Provisionals, and the major crime gangs, whose movements in border counties are inextricably linked with the terrorists."

Adams resisted the innumerable broadsides. Speaking in Strabane at a 20th anniversary commemoration for three IRA members killed by British soldiers, he condemned slurs by his political and media opponents. Rounding on detractors, he accused, "At all costs they want to stop the growth of Sinn Féin and halt the radical political alternative to the forces of conservatism in Ireland and in order to achieve this, and to distract attention from all other matters, they are trying once again to smear Republicans . . . People across Ireland are concerned that the peace process appears to be in freefall and that 10 years of work and progress is now being cast aside. No Republican worthy of the name can be involved in criminality of any kind. If any are, they should be expelled from our ranks. We are not involved in criminality and we will not tolerate such behaviour. Our opponents know that, but some of them can barely disguise their glee at the recent turn of events. There has been trial by media. A Sinn Féin member is arrested and released without charge and the entire Sinn Féin party is condemned as criminal. Money from the Northern Bank robbery is found in the RUC Athletic Association Club in Belfast and this is reported as being an effort to embarrass British forces. All of this is stated as fact, and let there be no doubt that this campaign of vilification is going to continue for some time."

Adams' words pre-empted a deeper crisis, forcing both Sinn Féin and the IRA to take unprecedented protective measures. The McCartney sisters were invited to the party's Ard Fheis and the IRA, in a rare public broadcast of their inner workings, announced that three men had been expelled from the organization over the McCartney killing. Sinn Féin also suspended seven of its members. Pickets for the sisters gathered outside the Ard Fheis and were joined by supporters of Ann McCabe, whose husband Jerry, a policeman, had been murdered by an IRA unit in 1996. Inside, Martin McGuinness admitted publicly that IRA members had killed Robert McCartney. His *mea culpa* was accompanied by a promise to save the peace process. "Painful as it is, we have to face the reality that there is a crisis of confidence that could destroy the Good Friday Agreement. I am not prepared to let our struggle be demonized, or to be caught in a downward spiral that leads inexorably to a return to violence. Instead, Republicans are determined to find a way, however difficult and challenging, to put all conflict and violence behind us for good. We want to see the weapons put beyond use, to prevent criminality, to participate in policing on the right terms and to pursue a purely political, peaceful and democratic path to the Irish

unification that every one of us wants to see . . . We cannot allow Republicanism
to be diminished in this way. To do so would be a betrayal of our struggle, of our
own personal commitment, of the hunger strikers and of those brave Republicans
who selflessly gave their lives and liberty for a noble and worthy cause."

The McCartney sisters promised to continue their campaign until all those
involved in their brother's murder, including the gang leader who evidently still
remained an active presence in the IRA, were brought to justice and convicted.
Meanwhile, other families of murdered victims, previously intimidated into silence,
were coming forward and speaking to the press in defiance of the IRA. Even
representatives of families who had lost relatives in the Omagh bombing – an
atrocity committed by the Real IRA – were calling on Gerry Adams to encourage
all Republicans to cooperate with the authorities. Opinion polls revealed that Sinn
Féin's standing in the North had been largely unaffected in the aftermath of the
Northern Bank robbery, but the McCartney murder had dented the party's
popularity among moderate voters. In the Republic, reaction was more critical
with polls indicating a drop in party support of over 25 per cent in less than five
months. At the time of writing, the IRA have just released an extraordinary
statement admitting that they had met with Robert McCartney's sisters and his
fiancée Bridgeen Hagans for a five-hour meeting during which they offered to
shoot the people directly involved in his killing. Part of their statement read: "We
have urged any witnesses who can assist in any way to come forward. That remains
our position. The only interest the IRA has in this case is to see the truth and justice
achieved . . . We are doing our best to work with the family and to respect their
wishes." This vision of a new, caring IRA found little support outside of senior
Sinn Féin circles. The IRA's offer of violent, summary justice, which the
McCartney family predictably rejected, prompted Ian Paisley to remind the world
that "terrorism is the only stock and trade of Sinn Féin/IRA". Alex Attwood of the
SDLP concluded: "The message that goes out across the North today is that the
IRA reserve unto themselves the right to visit murder where they deem it
appropriate." Newspaper leader columns continued to implore or demand that
Sinn Féin sever their links with the IRA and make the tough political choice to
embrace democracy unconditionally. Although the prospect of Sinn Féin
denouncing the IRA seems unlikely, it is not entirely inconceivable at some future
point of crisis. In different circumstances, some of Ireland's greatest patriots,
including Michael Collins and Éamon deValera, had been forced to turn on former
colleagues and, after achieving political office, had outlawed the IRA. For students
of Irish history, Sinn Féin's present troubles and ideological dilemmas have an all
too familiar ring.

page 453: ". . . the long-awaited archival album *The Philosopher's Stone* . . ." One
amusing rumour surrounding the release concerns a record company executive
who supposedly complimented Morrison on the track selection, mentioning a
handful of songs. When the CD was finally issued, those songs were conspicuously
absent from the set. The 1996 promo version included 'When I Deliver', 'John
Brown's Body' and 'I'm Ready', which were replaced by 'The Street Only Knew

Your Name', 'Western Plain' and 'Joyous Sound'. Fans no doubt welcomed the much discussed *Naked In The Jungle* sessions from the "missing years" in the mid-Seventies, even if they demonstrated that the material was, as Morrison had once suggested, "just a jam". One of the great songs on *The Philosopher's Stone* was Peter Handke's 'Song Of Being A Child', a poem that appeared in longer form in the Wim Wenders' film *Wings Of Desire*.

page 453: "In your dreams Van! . . ." *Irish Post*: 20 March 1999.

page 453: "Somewhere in the mid-Eighties . . ." Reviewer George Byrne. *Irish Independent*: 3 April 1999.

page 454: "On 1 September 1999 . . ." Bob Geldof's speech at the Hot Press Irish Music Hall of Fame began provocatively with the extravagant assertion: "Van Morrison is the most important musical artiste Ireland has ever produced and one of its greatest artistes in any field in the last 50 years." Thereafter, Geldof thankfully dispensed with the hyperbole for a more realistic but still flattering appraisal, noting: "His great achievement has been to produce a body of work that is so seamlessly pure a recent review could only say 'same old magnificent thing'. It's true not one of us other Irish players have come even vaguely close to this artistic achievement. It is difficult to sum up or analyse exactly what that achievement is. Van certainly cannot – nor does he want to. Nor typically, does he want anybody else to. But as *Rolling Stone* has written: 'His influence among other singer-songwriters is unrivalled by any living artiste besides that other prickly legend Bob Dylan.' His [Morrison's] musical influences were common enough for his time and they had a resonance for thousands of his contemporaries. But it was uniquely Van who, although giving hints of the musical distillation that was occurring somewhere in his soul, produced within one 48-hour period one of the true and rare seminal works of contemporary music in *Astral Weeks*. Somehow he had blended, instinctively and seamlessly, everything he knew musically and, in experience with an Irish romantic mysticism, into a meandering and exquisitely impressionistic piece of music that, like so much of what he has written, endures to this moment. He is an extraordinary singer. No other person sounds like him. He is uniquely recognizable and he uses that beautiful thing to attempt to explore and examine areas and depths few have charted successfully. It is like some long journey for meaning. He is specific in location and mood but the themes are universal and nearly always have a profound and troubled spiritual dimension. It seems to be music from another place that takes you somewhere else. The range of his musical influences transcends any limited sense of what contemporary music is. It's not just R&B or jazz or soul or rock 'n' roll or Celtic, or whatever, but a blend of those borders into a unique notion of what is true. He becomes famously irritated by those lesser mortals who can't understand how this happens. 'Its something I do.' But once, I pushed him about this aching sense of loss, confusion, mystery and in exasperation, and in order to shut me up, he blurted, 'Look, it's in the blood.' And he's the only one with that blood. He has written remarkable songs; ones that seem, the first time you hear them, to have always existed. They still play 'Gloria'. It's kind of song number 1, isn't it? Every start-up band has to learn it. How many murdered 'Moondances' have you heard in how many late-night lounges? Was 'Have I Told

You Lately' really not just some reworked love song? But it is a body of work in that utterly recognizable voice that has had such a huge impact on our consciousness outside of the enormous influence on other musicians. From an Irish perspective, the impact of Morrison is inspirational. To hear a work so epic, so expansive, so unclassifiable, so out of place and time as *Astral Weeks* and recognize in it Belfast – that dour, grim city of the Sixties – was a shock to us. To hear Irish place names turned into rhymes of magic like 'Route 66' and all those Delta towns was truly weird. Philip Lynott was electrified. This sense of location, but being dislocated – of being here but not belonging – sent him off on his own quest. I simply try to rip him [Morrison] off. How do you write a street epic about the place you live and those around you? I imitated the sound and tried to copy the style. I got a hit or two but the master was in another area of operation altogether, high art. Bono, Sinéad, Shane *et al* keep looking, so does Van. It has become the *sine qua non* of Irish music, but there is only one who has taken us on such a brilliantly beautiful journey. For his peace of soul, you hope he'll get there but, for our sakes, I hope the ride never ends. He genuinely is great. It is apt that he should be the first inductee into the Irish Music Hall of Fame."

page 454: ". . . Cardiff-based country/rockabilly outfit, the Rimshots . . ." The Rimshots' line-up comprised John Lewis (vocals/rhythm guitar), Rob Nedin (lead guitar), Mark Kembo (drums) and Tony Biggs (upright bass).

page 454: "2000 began with the release of *The Skiffle Sessions* . . ." In addition to *The Skiffle Sessions*, Morrison had also made a guest appearance on the title track of Lonnie Donegan's 1999 album, *Muleskinner Blues*.

page 455: "The name Van Morrison is phoney . . ." Van Morrison, onstage at Oxford: 9 February 2000.

page 455: "Married nine times . . ." Albeit to eight husbands, one of whom she married twice.

page 455: "Well that got my attention . . ." Linda Gail Lewis/Rogan. Cardiff: 25 April 2004.

page 455: "It was a big surprise . . ." ibid.

page 455: "I came back to the King's Hotel . . ." ibid.

page 456: "Did you ask Linda Gail . . ." ibid.

page 456: "I wrote down the lyrics . . ." ibid.

page 456: "Well, how are we going to rehearse these *duets* . . ." ibid.

page 456: "It was loose and relaxed . . ." ibid.

page 456: "I know you don't know it . . ." ibid.

page 456: "We cut it . . ." ibid.

page 457: "It's in your best interests . . ." ibid.

page 457: "I'm thinking of releasing this . . ." ibid.

page 457: "We'll have to do a live gig . . ." ibid.

page 457: "I was doing a skit on Van meeting Ian Paisley . . ." John McBlain. Reported in *Wavelength* 25.

page 458: "If the entire album was that strong . . ." Reviewer Peter Doggett. *Wavelength*, 25.

page 459: "He would not do it . . ." Linda Gail Lewis/Rogan. Cardiff: 25 April 2004.

page 459: "It was a doomed working relationship . . ." ibid.

page 460: "It went from being the best it could . . ." ibid.

page 460: "I'm amazed by the people . . ." ibid.

page 460: "The only person that looked really happy . . ." ibid.

page 460: "I'm ready to put my rock 'n' roll shoes back on . . ." ibid.

page 460: "I knew I would eventually have to leave . . ." ibid.

page 460: "I wanted to do some writing . . ." ibid.

page 461: "Working was interfering with my relationship with my son . . ." ibid.

page 461: "With their working relationship under threat, Morrison decided to re-record his solo album . . ." According to Linda Gail Lewis in our interview: "I did all those recordings before he got mad at me. He, of course, didn't go with those versions of those songs. In fact he nearly ruined 'Indian Summer'. He put 'Indian Summer' on his album, a horrible version. It was the most awful thing. I can't even stand to listen to it. But he was so desperate to make that album a success that he then released 'Indian Summer' – the old original version, without me on it. But it was the original version that we had done together. All that he did was take my voice off of it. But then we did another version with me on piano with the Red Hot Pokers. There were, let's see . . . about four versions. There was the version we did with the Pokers when he first wrote it, which was a really great version and I played piano on that. Then there was the version he did without the Red Hot Pokers and I didn't play piano on it – but I did on some of the tracks; so the next version of 'Indian Summer', that was before we went to America and he had me come back to the studio and said, 'Listen don't tell the guys that I don't want to use them on this song' and he recorded it with [members of] his old band. He'd flown them in from America and everywhere to get them there to do it. Then he overdubbed me on all the vocals. But he left my favourite song 'Just Like Greta' off the album."

page 461: "I think he left it off the album . . ." Linda Gail Lewis/Rogan. Cardiff: 25 April 2004.

page 461: "When I gave my notice in . . ." ibid.

page 461: "Well, nothing's ever perfect . . ." ibid.

page 462: "Millions of people worship Van . . ." Linda Gail Lewis, interviewed by Roisin Gorman. Sunday World: 6 May 2001.

page 463: "Over the last week . . ." Van Morrison, press statement, reported in Sunday Independent: 28 October 2001.

page 464: "He is a legend . . ." Linda Gail Lewis, speaking at the Cardiff Tribunal.

page 464: "I had previous experience . . ." Van Morrison, speaking at the Cardiff Tribunal.

page 466: "The Satanic Age started in 1966 . . ." Anton LaVey, interviewed by Burton H. Wolfe. Knight, Volume 6, number 8: September 1968.

page 466: "He's the guy who made Satanism acceptable . . ." Culbertson/Rogan. Coleraine: 11 December 2002.

page 466: "It all depends what you want to get out of it . . ." ibid.

page 467: "The knot's still there . . ." ibid.

page 467: "Van Morrison is tired . . ." Reviewer Tom Cox. *Daily Telegraph*: 18 May 2002.

page 468: "He told Derek's wife that he was coming . . ." Culbertson/Rogan. Coleraine: 11 December 2002.

Chapter Twenty-Six: Poetic Champions Decompose

page 469: "I think 'rock' has become a meaningless word . . ." Morrison/Flanagan, op cit.

page 471: "regurgitive violence" Barney Hoskyns, *From A Whisper To A Scream*, London, Fontana: 1991.

page 471: "I want to be on an adult label . . ." Van Morrison, promotional interview for *What's Wrong With This Picture?*: October 2003.

page 471: "If Van's in the right form . . ." Harrison/Rogan. Bangor, Co. Down: 9 July 1994. Harrison went on to note: "He doesn't enjoy Dylan's charisma, which is unfortunate. It stops him being a total star. He's a singer but he's not an entertainer. Neil Diamond's an entertainer. If he has a bad night you'd never know. Van doesn't have that."

page 471: "Van Morrison gets closer to exposing the naked cry . . ." Barney Hoskyns, op cit. Hoskyns was less impressed by Morrison as a lyricist, adding: "As Johnny Rogan rightly makes clear . . . the myth of Van the Man as mystical seer is so much Celtic baloney, serving only to obscure what makes this landmark LP so extraordinary."

page 471: "The most registered complaint . . ." Reviewed by Mike Fish. *The Wire* 92: October 1991.

page 472: ". . . the voice has steadily deteriorated . . ." Hoskyns, op cit.

page 472: "nothing more than a grotesque travesty of his former glorious selves" Barney Hoskyns, *Mojo* 1: November 1993.

page 472: "The weak link, unfortunately, is Morrison . . ." Reviewed by David Sinclair. *The Times*: 2 December 1995.

page 472: "I'm not a fan of the late voice . . ." Seán O'Hagan, in conference with the author. Belfast: 5 May 2001.

page 472: "I'm sure there are people at universities . . ." Van Morrison, interviewed by Vivien Goldman. *Sounds*: 30 March 1974.

page 473: "There's very few of my songs . . ." Morrison/O'Hagan, *Select*: October 1990.

page 474: ". . . bloated equivalent of a breathless sixth-form blue stocking . . ." Barney Hoskyns, *Mojo* 1: November 1993. Such criticism was hardly new. Back in the early Eighties, I argued the case against Morrison as a poet of the page and pointed out some of his shortcomings as a lyricist as well as challenging the lazy sanctification of the artiste as some sort of 'poetic genius'. This was a time when Morrison was still the subject of hagiography, not least by Canadian-based writer/journalist Ritchie Yorke, who worked as his publicist for a spell. Later biographers and commentators, perhaps coloured by my earlier criticisms, treated the Morrison poetic myth with caution. In his study, Barney Hoskyns concurred with my earlier view of Morrison and agreed that the myth of Morrison as "mystical seer" actually detracted from the worth of *Astral Weeks*. He was equally cynical about other aspects of Morrison's work, observing that his "set text on old Albion is so gauche and jejeune it makes me wince". Steve Turner, himself a published poet, amplified my original negative reading of *Common One*'s lyrics, dismissing the work as Morrison's "most self-indulgent album to date" and seeing 'Summertime In England' as tipping the balance "from inspired improvisation to embarrassing ramble", adding, "instead of walking in the steps of Blake and Eliot in order to see what insights their approach to art would provide today, he merely mentioned them by name, as though it would be enough to impress his audience that he read serious literature". At the time I wrote about Morrison, he was re-establishing his critical reputation and actually produced a solid body of work in the mid-Eighties which, when compared and ranked alongside his earlier recordings, provided surprisingly new insights into his artistic worth. Although analysis of individual songs still highlighted lyrical lapses, a wider approach looking at themes, the sense of place and different landscapes within his work produced, for me at least, some unexpected rewards.

page 475: ". . . not really a poet at all . . ." Durcan, op cit.

page 475: "poetry is of its very essence . . ." ibid.

page 475: "I always associate him with the great American action painter Jackson Pollock . . ." Tom Paulin, interviewed for BBC Radio 2's *Van The Man*, broadcast: 2 September 1997.

page 476: "I talked about a lot of this stuff with Tom . . ." Hammond/Rogan. Belfast: 21 May 2001.

page 476: "I'm just a stand-up singer . . ." Morrison/Goldman, 1974, op cit.

page 476: "I was just writing these songs . . ." Morrison/Clarke, op cit.

page 477: "I don't see myself as a songwriter . . ." Morrison/Vincent, op cit.

page 477: "I'm just channelling . . ." Morrison/Hogan, op cit.

page 477: "I've always had some idea . . ." Van Morrison, interviewed on Channel 4 television's *Coney Island Of The Mind*: March 1991. The programme's title was borrowed from Lawrence Ferlinghetti's *A Coney Island Of The Mind* (1958), one of the most popular poetry collections of the period, boasting US sales in excess of 500,000 copies.

page 477: "Jung's theory of the collective unconscious . . ." Van Morrison, interviewed by Seán O'Hagan. *The Times*: 9 March 1991.

page 478: "The academics wanted the monopoly . . ." Van Morrison, interviewed by Michelle Rocca. *Mojo*: August 1995.

page 478: "When you become a songwriter . . ." Polygram promotional interview conducted by Bill Morrison: 12 August 1997.

page 478: "The transparent banality of the lyrics . . ." Even in the partisan pages of the unofficial Van Morrison magazine *Wavelength*, Morrison's recent work has been under fire for its lyrical shortcomings. In issue 12, reader Jeremy Sharp listed a number of lyrical lapses when discussing *The Healing Game* and concluded: "many of the lyrics seem to be little more than meaningless retreads, as if Van had consulted a secret copy of the Van Morrison Phrase Finder Book." In issue 20, *Back On Top* received an even rougher ride. One fan, Holly Wright, complained with regret: "I could barely stomach it. The lyrics are trite and self-absorbed; the melodies completely forgettable . . . if this album were released under someone else's name, none of us would have paid it the least bit of attention." Another fan, Mark Watt, went further and lamented – "The songs are mostly retreads . . . As a self-anointed poet, he'd get laughed out of any self-respecting 'Creative Writing 101' class for the lyrics on this latest one . . . If you want to count clichés, we've got 'baby blue', 'feet on the ground', 'white with snow', 'silver lining in the clouds'. Van even reuses his own clichés: 'the red sportscar'; 'golden autumn day'; 'backstreet jelly roll'." The above reactions are reasonable and well argued but perhaps ignore the wider point that many of Morrison's lyrics, even during his peak period in the Seventies, were quite often banal or bathetic, especially when read in isolation from the music.

page 481: "The only thing that bothers me . . ." Van Morrison, interviewed by Paul Du Noyer. Q 127: April 1997.

page 482: "I just can't handle it . . ." ibid.

page 482: "Everyone Van meets, he leaves an impression . . ." Carson/Rogan. Fife: 28 August 1993.

page 482: "Van's a lost soul really . . ." Tench/Rogan. London: 14 September 1994.

page 482: "I think he is actually very shy . . ." Rocca/Reiseal Ní Cheilleachair. Dublin: March 1994.

page 482: "Well, he's a mystery to me . . ." Linda Gail Lewis/Rogan. Cardiff: 25 April 2004.

page 482: "I don't know where his head's at . . ." Eric Bell/Rogan. London: 5 August 1994.

page 483: "Van is not a genius . . ." Planet/Selvin, op cit.

page 483: "I'll never forget when I joined Van . . ." Herbie Armstrong/Rogan. Sheffield: 23 November 1994.

page 483: "I've got respect for him . . ." Sproule/Rogan. Belfast: 29 October 1994.

page 483: "Some people, like myself, may go out there smiling . . ." Paddy Moloney, Hot Press, Christmas: 1991.

page 483: "I still feels it's a big problem with him . . ." Irvine/Rogan. Belfast: 18 September 1994.

page 484: "He was always a little shit . . ." Denvir/Rogan. Belfast: 9 December 2002.

page 484: "Remember the story of the neighbour . . ." Steve Turner, interviewed by the author. London: February 1994. Part of this quote was previously published with my permission in The Van Morrison Newsletter (Spring 1994)

page 484: "I'm not a nice person . . ." Van Morrison, interviewed by B.P. Fallon. Guardian Weekend: 15 June 1996.

Epilogue: Magic Time

page 491: "Everything I tried to do . . ." Morrison/Corvin, 1973, op cit.

page 493: "Sinn Féin was absolutely certain . . ." McCann/Rogan. Derry: 11 June 2005. Additional information collated during election night in Dublin.

page 493: "At 4 pm on 28 July 2005, the Provisionals . . ." The full text of the IRA's statement on decommissioning read: "The leadership of *Oglaigh na hÉireann* has formally ordered an end to the armed campaign. This will take effect from 4 pm this afternoon. All IRA units have been ordered to dump arms. All volunteers have been instructed to assist the development of purely political and democratic programmes through exclusively peaceful means. Volunteers must not engage in any other activities whatsoever. The IRA leadership has also authorized our representative to engage with the IICD [Independent International Commission On Decommissioning] to complete the process to verifiably put its arms beyond use in a way which will further enhance public confidence and to conclude this as quickly as possible. We have invited two independent witnesses from the Protestant and Catholic churches to testify to this. The Army Council took these decisions following an unprecedented internal discussion and consultation process with IRA units and volunteers. We appreciate the honest and forthright way in which the consultation process was carried out and the depth and content of our submissions. We are proud of the comradely way in which this truly historic discussion was conducted. The outcome of our consultations show very strong support among IRA volunteers for the Sinn Féin peace strategy. There is also widespread concern about the failure of the two governments and the Unionists to fully engage in the peace process. This has created real difficulties. The overwhelming majority of people in Ireland fully support this process. They and friends of Irish unity throughout the world want to see the full implementation of the Good Friday Agreement. Notwithstanding these difficulties, our decisions have been taken to advance our Republican and democratic objectives, including our goal of a united Ireland. We believe there is now an alternative way to achieve this and to end British rule in our country. It is the responsibility of all volunteers to show leadership, determination and courage. We are very mindful of the sacrifices of our patriot dead, those who went to jail, volunteers, their families and the wider Republican base. We reiterate our view that the armed struggle was entirely legitimate. We are conscious that many people suffered in the conflict. There is a compelling imperative on all sides to build a lasting peace. The issue of the defence of nationalist and Republican communities has been raised with us. There is a responsibility on society to ensure that there is no reoccurrence of the pogroms of 1969 and the early 1970s. There is also a universal responsibility to tackle sectarianism in all its forms. The IRA is fully committed to the goals of Irish unity and independence and to building the Republic outlined in the 1916 Proclamation. We call for maximum unity and effort by Irish Republicans everywhere. We are confident that by working together Irish Republicans can achieve our objectives. Every volunteer is aware of the import of the decisions we have taken and all *oglaigh* are compelled to fully comply with these orders. There is now an unprecedented opportunity to utilize the considerable energy and goodwill which there is for the peace process. This comprehensive series of unparalleled initiatives is our contribution to this and to the continued endeavours to bring about independence and unity for the people of Ireland."

page 494: ". . . . assist the development . . . " ibid.

page 494: "Volunteers must not engage . . . " ibid.

page 494: "If this is real . . ." David Ervine, press conference. Belfast: 28 July 2005.

page 494: "Today's decision by the IRA . . ." Gerry Adams, speaking at the Sinn Féin press conference. Dublin: 28 July 2005.

page 494: "I would like Ian Paisley . . ." ibid.

page 494: "They represent . . . " ibid.

page 494: " . . . over the next few months . . . " Ian Paisley, press conference. Belfast: 28 July 2005.

page 494: "We treat with contempt . . . " ibid.

page 494: " . . . a step of unparalleled magnitude . . ." Prime Minister Tony Blair, press conference. London: 28 July 2005.

page 494: " . . . this may be the day . . . " ibid.

page 495: "The war is over . . ." Bertie Ahern, press conference. Dublin: 28 July 2005.

page 495: "I think it will take weeks . . ." Adams, op cit.

page 495: "It's a total disgrace . . ." Anonymous, reported by Alan Erwin. *Irish Independent*: 29 July 2005. Television reporters and representatives of the leading Irish newspapers favoured Danny Molloy's bar in the Ardoyne, north Belfast as a gauge for Republican reactions to the IRA's statement.

page 495: "A lot of good men . . ." ibid.

page 496: " 'cantankerous', 'irritability' and 'unsociability' . . ." Noel McLaughin. *Irish News*: 30 August 2005.

page 496: "Even his fans concede . . ." Q : October 2005.

page 496: " . . . one of rock's most over-rated . . ." Tony Clayton-Lea. *Irish Times*: 6 May 2005. Other writers I spoke to offered similar opinions.

page 498: "A duet with Ian Paisley . . . " Liam Fay column titled 'Morrison Sings Paisley's Tune' in Irish edition of *Sunday Times*: 8 May 2005.

Select Discography

This select discography is divided into three main sections – Singles, EPs and Albums (incorporating CDs). All record numbers are UK originals unless stated. For the US market, significant changes of release date or serial number are noted in parentheses. Compilations, unofficial greatest hits packages, reissues, foreign releases (outside UK/US territory), cassette singles, promotional releases, singles exclusively distributed to radio stations, sampler albums, various artistes collections, spoken word recordings, interview discs, specific guest appearances and bootlegs are not included. For details of videos, DVDS, radio, television and film appearances, all of which are beyond the scope of this discography, the reader should consult the booklet *The Wavelength Videography: 1962–1999* available from PO Box 80, Winsford, Cheshire, CW7 4ES. *Wavelength* also provides a thrice-yearly magazine devoted to Morrison's activities with particular emphasis on his live performances, plus additional discographical information, features and articles. The Van Morrison Website is also recommended.

SINGLES

Georgie & The Monarchs
'Boo-zooh'/'O Twingy Baby'. CBS 1307 (Germany/Holland).
Released: November 1963. Unissued anywhere else in the world.

Them
'Don't Start Crying Now'/'One Two Brown Eyes'. Decca F 11973 (UK)/ Parrot 97042 (US).
Released: September 1964.

'Baby Please Don't Go'/'Gloria'. Decca F 12018 (UK)/Parrot 9727 (US).
Released: November 1964. Sides later reversed in US.
'Here Comes The Night'/'All By Myself'. Decca F 12094 (UK)/Parrot 9749

(US).
Released: March 1965.

'One More Time'/'How Long Baby?'. Decca F 12175 (UK).
Released: June 1965.

'(It Won't Hurt) Half As Much'/'I'm Gonna Dress In Black'. Decca F 12215 (UK)/Parrot 9784 (US).
Released: August 1965. Sides reversed in US.

'Mystic Eyes'/'If You And I Could Be As Two'. Decca F 12281 (UK)/Parrot 9796 (US).
Released: November 1965.

'Call My Name'/'Bring 'Em On In'. Decca F 12355 (UK)/Parrot 9819 (US).
Released: March 1966. Both sides alternate takes to album versions.

'Richard Cory'/'Don't You Know'. Decca F 12403 (UK)/Parrot 3003 (US).
Released: May 1966.

'Gloria'/'Friday's Child'. Major Minor MM 509 (UK).
Released: July 1967.

'The Story Of Them (Part 1)'/'The Story Of Them (Part 2)'. Major Minor MM 513 (UK).
Released: September 1967.

Van Morrison

'Brown Eyed Girl'/'Goodbye Baby (Baby Goodbye)'. London HLZ 10150 (UK)/Bang 545 (US).
Released: June 1967 (US)/July 1967 (UK).

'Ro Ro Rosey'/'Chick-A-Boom'. Bang 552 (US).
Released: September 1967. A-side alternate take.

'Spanish Rose'/'Midnight Special'. Bang 585 (US).
Released: November 1967.

'Come Running'/'Crazy Love'. Warner Bros WB 7383 (UK/US).
Released: April 1970 (US)/May 1970 (UK).

'Domino'/'Sweet Jannie' WB 7434 (UK/US).

Released: November 1970 (US)/December 1970 (UK).

'Blue Money'/'Call Me Up In Dreamland'. Warner Bros WB 7462 (UK/US).
Released: June 1971 (UK). B-side in US was 'Sweet Thing', released February
1971.

'Call Me Up In Dreamland'/'Street Choir'. Warner Bros WB 7488 (US).
Released: April 1971 (US).

'Wild Night'/'When The Evening Sun Goes Down'. Warner Bros K 16120
(UK)/WB 7518 (US).
Released: September 1971 (US)/October 1971 (UK).

'Tupelo Honey'/'Starting A New Life'. Warner Bros WB 7543 (US).
Released: January 1972 (US).

'(Straight To Your Heart) Like A Cannonball'/'Old Old Woodstock'. Warner
Bros WB 7573 (US).
Released: March 1972.

'Jackie Wilson Said'/'You've Got The Power'. Warner Bros K 16210 (UK)/WB
7616 (US).
Released: July 1972 (US)/August 1972 (UK).

'Redwood Tree'/'Saint Dominic's Preview'. Warner Bros WB 7638 (US).
Released: October 1972.

'Gypsy'/'Saint Dominic's Preview'. Warner Bros WB 7665 (US).
Released: January 1973.

'Warm Love'/'I Will Be There'. Warner Bros K16299 (UK)/WB 7706 (US).
Released: June 1973 (US)/July 1973 (UK).

'Bein' Green'/'Wild Children'. Warner Bros WB 7744 (US).
Released: September 1973.

'Ain't Nothing You Can Do'/'Wild Children'. Warner Bros WB 7797 (US).
Released: February 1974.

'Caldonia'/'What's Up Crazy Pup?' Warner Bros K 16392 (UK).
Released: May 1974.

'Bulbs'/'Who Was That Masked Man?' Warner Bros K 16486 (UK)/Warner Bros

WB 8029 (US).
Released: November 1974. US B-side is 'Cul De Sac', released July 1974.

'The Eternal Kansas City'/'Joyous Sound'. Warner Bros K 16939 (UK).
Released: April 1977.

'Joyous Sound'/'Mechanical Bliss'. Warner Bros K 16986 (UK)/Warner Bros WB 8411 (US).
Released: July 1977.

'Moondance'/'Cold Wind In August'. Warner Bros WB 8450 (US).
Released: November 1977.

'Wavelength'/'Checkin' It Out'. Warner Bros K 17254 (UK)/Warner Bros WB 8661 (US).
Released: September 1978.

'Natalia'/'Lifetimes'. Warner Bros K 17322 (UK)/Warner Bros WB 8743 (US).
Released: February 1979.

'Kingdom Hall'/'Checkin' It Out'. Warner Bros WB 8805 (US).
Released: April 1979.

'Bright Side Of The Road'/'Rolling Hills'. Mercury 6001 121 (UK)/Warner Bros WB 49086 (US).
Released: September 1979.

'Full Force Gale'/'You Make Me Feel So Free'. Warner Bros WB 49162 (US).
Released: December 1979.

'Cleaning Windows'/'It's All In The Game'. Mercury MER 99 (UK)/Warner Bros WB 50031 (US).
Released: March 1982. US B-side is 'Scandinavia'.

'Dweller On The Threshold'/'Scandinavia'. Mercury MER 110 (UK).
Released: June 1982.

'Cry For Home'/'Summertime In England'. Mercury MER 132 (UK).
Released: February 1983. B-side, live version. 12-inch version (MERX 132) adds 'All Saints Day'.

'Celtic Swing'/'Mr. Thomas'. Mercury MER 141 (UK).
Released May 1983. 12-inch version (MERX 141) adds 'Rave On, John Donne'.

'Dweller On The Threshold'/'Northern Muse (Solid Ground)'. Mercury MER 159.
Released: April 1984. A-side, live version.

'A Sense Of Wonder'/'Haunts Of Ancient Peace'. Mercury MER 178/MERX 178.
Released: October 1984. B-side, live version.

'Tore Down A La Rimbaud'/'Haunts Of Ancient Peace'. Mercury [unconfirmed]
Released: [Unconfirmed release] 1985. B-side, live version.

'Ivory Tower'/'New Kind Of Man'. Mercury MER 223.
Released: June 1986. 12-inch version (MERX 223) adds 'A Sense Of Wonder' and 'Cleaning Windows'.

'Got To Go Back'/'In The Garden'. Mercury MER 231.
Released: August 1986.

'Did Ye Get Healed?'/'Allow'. Mercury MER 254.
Released: August 1987.

'Someone Like You'/'Celtic Excavation'. Mercury MER 258.
Released: November 1987.

'Queen Of The Slipstream'/'Spanish Steps'. Mercury MER 261.
Released: April 1988.

'I'll Tell Me Ma'/'Tà Mo Chleamhnas Déanta'. Mercury MER 262.
Released: June 1988. With the Chieftains. 12-inch version (MERX 262) and CD (CD 262) add 'Carrickfergus'.

'Have I Told You Lately'/'Contacting My Angel'/'Listen To The Lion'/'Irish Heartbeat'. Polydor VANS 1.
Released: June 1989. 12-inch (VANX 1) adds 'Listen To The Lion'. CD (VAN CD 1) adds 'Listen To The Lion' and 'Irish Heartbeat'.

'Whenever God Shines His Light'/'I'd Love To Write Another Love Song'. Polydor VANS 2. A-side with Cliff Richard.
Released: November 1989. 12-inch (VANX 2) adds 'Cry For Love'. CD (VAN CD 2) adds 'Cry For Love' and 'Whenever God Shines His Light'.

'Orangefield'/'These Are The Days'. Polydor VANS 3.
Released: December 1989. 12-inch version (VANX 3) adds 'And The Healing

Has Begun'. CD (VAN CD 3) adds 'And The Healing Has Begun' and 'Coney Island'.

'Coney Island'/'Have I Told You Lately'. Polydor VANS 4.
Released: January 1990. 12-inch version (VANX 4) adds 'A Sense Of Wonder'. CD (VAN CD 4) adds 'A Sense Of Wonder' and 'Spirit'.

'Gloria'/'Rave On, John Donne'. Polydor VANS 5.
Released: July 1990. Track 1 is Them recording. 12-inch version (VANX 5) adds 'Vanlose Stairway'. CD (VAN CD 5) adds 'Vanlose Stairway' and 'Bright Side Of The Road'.

'Real Real Gone'/'Start All Over Again'. Polydor VANS 6.
Released: September 1990. 12-inch version (VANX 6) and CD (VAN CD 6) add 'Cleaning Windows'.

'In The Days Before Rock 'n' Roll'/'I'd Love To Write Another Love Song'. Polydor VANS 7.
Released: November 1990. 12-inch version (VANX 7) and CD (VAN CD 7) add 'Coney Island'.

'Enlightenment'/'Avalon Of The Heart'. Polydor VANS 8.
Released: January 1991. 12-inch version (VANX 8) and CD (VAN CD 8) add 'Jackie Wilson Said'.

'I Can't Stop Loving You'/'All Saints Day'. Polydor VANS 9.
Released: May 1991. With the Chieftains. 12-inch (VANX 9) and CD (VAN CD 9) add 'Carrying A Torch'.

'Why Must I Always Explain?'/'So Complicated'. Polydor VANS 10.
Released: September 1991. 12-inch version (VANX 10) and CD (VAN CD 10) add 'Enlightenment'.

'Gloria'/'It Must Be You'. Polydor VANS 11.
Released: May 1993. A-side with John Lee Hooker. B-side live version. CD (VAN CD 11) adds live versions of 'And The Healing Has Begun' and 'See Me Through'. CD (VAN DR 11) excludes 'It Must Be You', but adds live versions of 'Whenever God Shines His Light', 'It Fills You Up' and 'Star Of County Down'.

'Have I Told You Lately'/'Love Is A Teasin''/'Fenny Hill (Instrumental)'. Polydor 74321271702.
Released: March 1995. Morrison features on Track 1 only, with the Chieftains.

'Days Like This'/'I Don't Want To Go On Without You'/'That Old Black Magic'/'Yo'. Polydor VAN CD 12/CDX 12.
Released: May 1995.

'Perfect Fit'/'Raincheck'/'Cleaning Windows'. Polydor 577 015–2.
Released: September 1995. Track 3, live version.

'No Religion'/'Whenever God Shines His Light'/'Have I Told You Lately'/'Gloria'. Polydor 5774892.
Released: November 1995. Digipak version omits tracks 2–4, substituting 'Raincheck'.

'That's Life'/'Moondance'/'That's Life'. Verve/Exile 576 205–2.
Released: February 1996. With 'Georgie Fame & Friends'. Track 1, live.

'The Healing Game'/'Have I Told You Lately'/'Whenever God Shines His Light'/'Gloria'. Polydor/Exile 573–391–2.
Released: January 1997. Alternate CD (573–393–2) omits track 2 but adds 'Full Force Gale 96', 'Look What The Good People Done' and 'Celtic Spring'.

'Rough God Goes Riding'/'At The End Of The Day'/'The Healing Game'. Exile/Verve 573 9334.
Released: May 1997. Track 3, alternate take.

'Precious Time'/'Jackie Wilson Said'/'Call Me Up In Dreamland'. Exile/Pointblank POBD 14.
Released: February 1999. CD POBDX 14 adds live versions of 'Naked In The Jungle' and 'Give Me A Kiss'.

'Back On Top'/'John Brown's Body'/'I'm Ready'. Exile/Pointblank POBD 15.
Released: May 1999. CD POBDX 15 adds 'Tell Me' and 'Sax Instrumental No. 1'.

'Philosopher's Stone'/'These Dreams Of You'/'Raincheck'. Exile/Pointblank POBD 16.
Released: August 1999.

'I Wanna Go Home'/'New Burying Ground'/'Midnight Special'. Virgin 64972.
Released: January 2000. Track 3, alternate take. With Lonnie Donegan & Chris Barber.

'Let's Talk About Us'/'Singing The Blues'/'The Ballad Of Jesse James'. Polydor 7243754–7–4/POBD 18. With Linda Gail Lewis.
Released: September 2000.

'Hey Mr DJ'/'Someone Like You'/'Bright Side Of The Road'. Polydor
570596–2.
Released: May 2002.

'Meet Me In The Indian Summer'/'In The Afternoon'/'Raincheck'/'In The
Midnight'. Polydor 570902–2. Track 1, orchestrated. Remaining tracks, live
versions.
Released: August 2002.

'Once In A Blue Moon'/'Walkin' My Baby Back Home'/'When You're
Smiling'. Blue Note CDR 6628.
Released: December 2003 [Withdrawn prior to release].

A number of Morrison singles, primarily in the US, have been produced as radio
station promotional items only and are therefore not included here.

EPs

Them Decca DFE 8612.
'Don't Start Crying Now'; 'Philosophy'; 'Baby Please Don't Go'; 'One Two
Brown Eyes'.
Released: February 1965.
Two other EPs were released on the continent, *Them* (France Decca 457 073) and
Friday's Child (Holland Decca 700–500).

ALBUMS

Them

Them Decca LK 4700.
'Mystic Eyes'; 'If You And I Could Be As Two'; 'Little Girl'; 'Just A Little Bit';
'I Gave My Love A Diamond'; 'Gloria'; 'You Just Can't Win'; 'Go On Home';
'Don't Look Back'; 'I Like It Like That'; 'I'm Gonna Dress In Black'; 'Bright
Lights Big City'; 'My Little Baby'; '(Get Your Kicks On) Route 66'.
Released: June 1965. The US issue of the album released in August 1965 (Parrot
61005), in common with other LP releases of the time, was a truncated and
resequenced version, omitting 'Just A Little Bit', 'I Gave My Love A Diamond',
'You Just Can't Win', 'Bright Lights Big City' and 'My Little Baby', but including
three songs previously available on single, 'Here Comes The Night', 'One Two
Brown Eyes' and 'One More Time'.

Them Again Decca LK 4751.
'Could You Would You'; 'Something You Got'; 'Call My Name'; 'Turn On
Your Love Light'; 'I Put A Spell On You'; 'I Can Only Give You Everything';
'My Lonely Sad Eyes'; 'I Got A Woman'; 'Out Of Sight'; 'It's All Over Now,

Baby Blue'; 'Bad Or Good'; 'How Long Baby'; 'Hello Josephine'; 'Don't You Know'; 'Hey Girl'; 'Bring 'Em On In'.
Released: January 1966. Again, the US version (Parrot PAS 71008), released April 1966, was truncated and resequenced with the removal of 'I Put A Spell On You', 'I Got A Woman', 'Hello Josephine' and 'Hey Girl', and included no additions.

Since their break-up Them have been the subject of many compilations. Among the most notable UK vinyl releases are *The World Of Them*, *Them Featuring Van Morrison* and *Them: Rock Roots*. The last is particularly recommended as it was the first British released Them LP to feature the single version of 'Call My Name', the complete 7.15 minute version of 'The Story Of Them Parts 1 & 2', and the rare 'Mighty Like A Rose', which is still unavailable on CD. It also featured several tracks which were then rarities: 'Times Getting Tougher Than Tough', 'Stormy Monday', 'Baby, What You Want Me To Do' and 'Friday's Child'. Vinyl collectors are also directed to *14* (Decca LK 4695), the charity album released in May 1965 in aid of the 'Lord Taverners' Playing Fields Association' which featured various Decca artistes. On the original pressing, Them recorded a version of 'Little Girl' which included an obscene word during the fade-out. A re-recorded version appeared on later issues. At the time, Morrison dismissed this controversy as "just a publicity stunt". Them compilations have continued to appear since the dawn of the CD age, with value for money collections such as *Them Featuring Van Morrison* (a title used for several different albums), *The Story Of Them* (which features an alternate take of 'I Gave My Love A Diamond', 'Bring 'Em On In' and 'Richard Cory') and *The Collection*.

Van Morrison

Blowin' Your Mind! Bang BLPS 218 (US)/London HAZ 8346 (UK).
'Brown Eyed Girl'; 'He Ain't Give You None'; 'T.B. Sheets'; 'Spanish Rose'; 'Goodbye Baby (Baby Goodbye)'; 'Ro Ro Rosey'; 'Who Drove The Red Sports Car?'; 'Midnight Special'.
Released: September 1967 (US)/February 1968 (UK).

Astral Weeks Warner Bros WB 1768 (UK)/WS 1768 (US).
'Astral Weeks'; 'Beside You'; 'Sweet Thing'; 'Cyprus Avenue'; 'Young Lovers Do'; 'Madame George'; 'Ballerina'; 'Slim Slow Slider'.
Released: November 1968 (US)/September 1969 (UK). 'Young Lovers Do' has since been retitled 'The Way Young Lovers Do'.

Moondance Warner Bros WB 1835 (UK)/WS 1835 (US).
'And It Stoned Me'; 'Moondance'; 'Crazy Love'; 'Caravan'; 'Into The Mystic'; 'Come Running'; 'These Dreams Of You'; 'Brand New Day'; 'Everyone'; 'Glad Tidings'.
Released: February 1970 (US)/March 1970 (UK). Sleeve artwork mistakenly

prints 'Stoned Me' instead of 'And It Stoned Me'.

His Band And The Street Choir Warner Bros WS 1884 (UK)/WS 1884 (US).
'Domino'; 'Crazy Face'; 'Give Me A Kiss'; 'I've Been Working'; 'Call Me Up In Dreamland'; 'I'll Be Your Lover Too'; 'Blue Money'; 'Virgo Clowns'; 'Gypsy Queen'; 'Sweet Jannie'; 'If I Ever Needed Someone'; 'Street Choir'.
Released: November 1970 (US)/January 1971 (UK).

Tupelo Honey Warner Bros K 46114 (UK)/WS 1950 (US).
'Wild Night'; '(Straight To Your Heart) Like A Cannonball'; 'Old Old Woodstock'; 'Starting A New Life'; 'You're My Woman'; 'Tupelo Honey'; 'I Wanna Roo You (Scottish Derivative)'; 'When The Evening Sun Goes Down'; 'Moonshine Whiskey'.
Released: November 1971.

Saint Dominic's Preview Warner Bros K 46172 (UK)/WS 2663 (US).
'Jackie Wilson Said (I'm In Heaven When You Smile)'; 'Gypsy'; 'I Will Be There'; 'Listen To The Lion'; 'Saint Dominic's Preview'; 'Redwood Tree'; 'Almost Independence Day'.
Released: August 1972.

Hard Nose The Highway Warner Bros K 46242/WS 2712 (US).
'Snow In San Anselmo'; 'Warm Love'; 'Hard Nose The Highway'; 'Wild Children'; 'The Great Deception'; 'Bein' Green'; 'Autumn Song'; 'Purple Heather'.
Released: July 1973. Early acetates reveal that 'Feedback Out On Highway 101' was originally considered in place of 'The Great Deception'.

It's Too Late To Stop Now Warner Bros K 86007/WS 2760 (2) (US).
'Ain't Nothing You Can Do'; 'Warm Love'; 'Into The Mystic'; 'These Dreams Of You'; 'I Believe To My Soul'; 'I've Been Working'; 'Help Me'; 'Wild Children'; 'Domino'; 'I Just Wanna Make Love To You'; 'Bring It On Home To Me'; 'Saint Dominic's Preview'; 'Take Your Hand Out Of My Pocket'; 'Listen To The Lion'; 'Here Comes The Night'; 'Gloria'; 'Caravan'; 'Cyprus Avenue'.
Released: February 1974. Although spelt correctly on the actual record, 'Cyprus Avenue' was mistitled 'Cypress Avenue' on the sleeve artwork.

Veedon Fleece Warner Bros K 56068/WS 2805 (US).
'Fair Play'; 'Linden Arden Stole The Highlights'; 'Who Was That Masked Man?'; 'Streets Of Arklow'; 'You Don't Pull No Punches, But You Don't Push The River'; 'Bulbs'; 'Cul De Sac'; 'Comfort You'; 'Come Here My Love'; 'Country Fair'.
Released: October 1974.

A Period Of Transition Warner Bros K56322 (UK)/WS 2987 (US).
'You Gotta Make It Through The World'; 'It Fills You Up'; 'The Eternal Kansas City'; 'Joyous Sound'; 'Flamingos Fly'; 'Heavy Connection'; 'Cold Wind In August'.
Released: April 1977.

Wavelength Warner Bros K 56526 (UK)/WS 3212 (US).
'Kingdom Hall'; 'Checkin' It Out'; 'Natalia'; 'Venice USA'; 'Lifetimes'; 'Wavelength'; 'Santa Fé'; 'Beautiful Obsession'; 'Hungry For Your Love'; 'Take It Where You Find It'.
Released: October 1978.

Into The Music Mercury 9102 852 (UK)/Warner Bros WS 3390 (US).
'Bright Side Of The Road'; 'Full Force Gale'; 'Stepping Out Queen'; 'Troubadours'; 'Rolling Hills'; 'You Make Me Feel So Free'; 'Angeliou'; 'And The Healing Has Begun'; 'It's All In The Game'; 'You Know What They're Writing About'.
Released: August 1979.

Common One Mercury 6302 021 (UK)/Warner Bros WS 3462 (US).
'Haunts Of Ancient Peace'; 'Summertime In England'; 'Satisfied'; Wild Honey'; 'Spirit'; 'When Heart Is Open'.
Released: September 1980.

Beautiful Vision Mercury 6302 122 (UK)/Warner Bros WS 3652 (US).
'Celtic Vision'; 'Northern Muse (Solid Ground)'; 'Dweller On The Threshold'; 'Beautiful Vision'; 'She Gives Me Religion'; 'Cleaning Windows'; 'Vanlose Stairway'; 'Aryan Mist'; 'Across The Bridge Where Angels Dwell'; 'Scandinavia'.
Released: February 1982.

Inarticulate Speech Of The Heart Mercury MERL 16 (UK)/Warner Bros 2 3802–1 (US).
'Higher Than The World'; 'Connswater'; 'River Of Time'; 'Celtic Swing'; 'Rave On, John Donne'; 'Inarticulate Speech Of The Heart No. 1'; 'Irish Heartbeat'; 'The Street Only Knew Your Name'; 'Cry For Home'; 'Inarticulate Speech Of The Heart No. 2'; 'September Night'.
Released: March 1983.

Live At The Grand Opera House Belfast Mercury MERK 36 (UK)/Mercury 8183361 (US).
'Introduction: Into The Mystic (Instrumental)'/'Inarticulate Speech Of The Heart'; 'Dweller On The Threshold'; 'It's All In The Game'/'You Know What They're Writing About'; 'She Gives Me Religion'; 'Haunts Of Ancient Peace'; 'Full Force

Gale'; 'Beautiful Vision'; 'Vanlose Stairway'; 'Rave On, John Donne/
Rave On Part Two'; 'Northern Muse (Solid Ground)'; 'Cleaning Windows'.
Released: February 1984.

A Sense Of Wonder Mercury MERH 54 (UK)/Mercury 822895 (US).
'Tore Down A La Rimbaud'; 'Ancient Of Days'; 'Evening Meditation'; 'The
Master's Eyes'; 'What Would I Do?'; 'A Sense Of Wonder'; 'Boffyflow And
Spike'; 'If You Only Knew'; 'Let The Slave'; 'A New Kind Of Man'.
Released: January 1985.

No Guru, No Method, No Teacher Mercury MERH 94 (UK)/Mercury 830077
(US).
'Got To Go Back'; 'Oh The Warm Feeling'; 'Foreign Window'; 'A Town Called
Paradise'; 'In The Garden'; 'Tir Na Nog'; 'Here Comes The Knight'; 'Thanks For
The Information'; 'One Irish Rover'; 'Ivory Tower'.
Released: July 1986.

Poetic Champions Compose Mercury MERH 110 (UK)/Mercury 832585 (US).
'Spanish Steps'; 'The Mystery'; 'Queen Of The Slipstream'; 'I Forgot That Love
Existed'; 'Sometimes I Feel Like A Motherless Child'; 'Celtic Excavation';
'Someone Like You'; 'Alan Watts Blues'; 'Give Me My Rapture'; 'Did Ye Get
Healed?'; 'Allow Me'.
Released: September 1987.

Irish Heartbeat Mercury MERH 124 (UK)/Mercury 834496 (US).
'Star Of The County Down'; 'Irish Heartbeat'; 'Tà Mo Chleamhnas Déanta';
'Raglan Road'; 'She Moved Through The Fair'; 'I'll Tell Me Ma';
'Carrickfergus'; 'Celtic Ray'; 'My Lagan Love'; 'Marie's Wedding'.
Released: June 1988. Credited to Van Morrison & The Chieftains.

Avalon Sunset Polydor 839262 (UK/US).
'Whenever God Shines His Light'; 'Contacting My Angel'; 'I'd Love To Write
Another Love Song'; 'Have I Told You Lately'; 'Coney Island'; 'I'm Tired Joey
Boy'; 'When Will I Ever Learn To Live In God'; 'Orangefield'; 'Daring Night';
'These Are The Days'.
Released: June 1989.

Enlightenment Polydor 847100 (UK/US).
'Real Real Gone'; 'Enlightenment'; 'So Quiet In Here'; 'Avalon Of The Heart';
'See Me Through'; 'Youth Of 1,000 Summers'; 'In The Days Before Rock 'n'
Roll'; 'Start All Over Again'; 'She's My Baby'; 'Memories'.
Released: October 1990.

Hymns To The Silence Polydor 849026 (2) (UK/US).
'Professional Jealousy'; 'I'm Not Feeling It Anymore'; 'Ordinary Life'; 'Some Peace Of Mind'; 'So Complicated'; 'I Can't Stop Loving You'; 'Why Must I Always Explain?'; 'Village Idiot'; 'See Me Through Part II (Just A Closer Walk With Thee)'; 'Take Me Back'; 'By His Grace'; 'All Saints Day'; 'Hymns To The Silence'; 'On Hyndford Street'; 'Be Thou My Vision'; 'Carrying A Torch'; 'Green Mansions'; 'Pagan Streams'; 'Quality Street'; 'It Must Be You'; 'I Need Your Kind Of Loving'.
Released: September 1991.

Too Long In Exile Polydor 519219 (UK/US).
'Too Long In Exile'; 'Big Time Operators'; 'Lonely Avenue'; 'Ball And Chain'; 'In The Forest'; 'Till We Get The Healing Done'; 'Gloria'; 'Good Morning Little Schoolgirl'; 'Wasted Years'; 'Lonesome Road'; 'Moody's Mood For Love'; 'Close Enough For Jazz'; 'Before The World Was Made'; 'I'll Take Care Of You'; 'Instrumental'; 'Tell Me What You Want'.
Released: June 1993.

A Night In San Francisco Polydor 521290–2 (UK/US).
'Did Ye Get Healed?'; 'It's All In The Game'; 'Make It Real One More Time'; 'I've Been Working'; 'I Forgot That Love Existed'; 'Vanlose Stairway'; 'Trans-Euro Train'; 'Fool For You'; 'You Make Me Feel So Free'; 'Beautiful Vision'; 'See Me Through'; 'Soldier Of Fortune'; 'Thank You Falettinme Be Mice Elf Again'; 'Ain't That Loving You Baby?'; 'Stormy Monday'; 'Have You Ever Loved A Woman?'; 'No Rollin' Blues'; 'Help Me'; 'Good Morning Little Schoolgirl'; 'Tupelo Honey'; 'Moondance'; 'My Funny Valentine'; 'Jumpin' With Symphony Sid'; 'It Fills You Up'; 'I'll Take Care Of You'; 'It's A Man's Man's Man's World'; 'Lonely Avenue'; '4 O'clock In The Morning'; 'So Quiet In Here'; 'That's Where It's At'; 'In The Garden'; 'You Send Me'; 'Allegheny'; 'Have I Told You Lately That I Love You?'; 'Shakin' All Over'; 'Gloria'.
Released: April 1994.

Days Like This Exile/Polydor 527307 (UK/US).
'Perfect Fit'; 'Russian Roulette'; 'Raincheck'; 'You Don't Know Me'; 'No Religion'; 'Underlying Depression'; 'Songwriter'; 'Days Like This'; 'I'll Never Be Free'; 'Melancholia'; 'Ancient Highway'; 'In The Afternoon'.
Released: June 1995.

How Long Has This Been Going On? Polygram/Exile 529136 (UK)/Verve/Exile 529136 (US).
'I Will Be There'; 'The New Symphony Sid'; 'Early In The Morning'; 'Who Can I Turn To?'; 'Sack Of Woe'; 'Moondance'; 'Centrepiece'; 'How Long Has This Been Goin' On?'; 'Your Mind Is On Vacation'; 'All Saints Day'; 'Blues In The

Night'; 'Don't Worry About A Thing'; 'That's Life'; 'Heathrow Shuffle'.
Released: December 1995 (UK)/January 1996 (US). With Georgie Fame &
Friends.

The Healing Game Exile/Polydor 537101 (UK/US).
'Rough God Goes Riding'; 'Fire In The Belly'; 'This Weight'; 'Waiting Game';
'Piper At The Gates Of Dawn'; 'Burning Ground'; 'It Once Was My Life';
'Sometimes We Cry'; 'If You Love Me'; 'The Healing Game'.
Released: February 1997.

Back On Top Exile/Pointblank/Virgin VPB CD50 7243 847148 2 6 (UK/US).
'Goin' Down Geneva'; 'Philosophers Stone'; 'In The Midnight'; 'Back On Top';
'When The Leaves Come Falling Down'; 'High Summer'; 'Reminds Me Of
You'; 'New Biography'; 'Precious Time'; 'Golden Autumn Day'.
Released: March 1999.

The Skiffle Sessions Live In Belfast Exile/Virgin 7243 848307 2 (UK/US).
'It Takes A Worried Man'; 'Lost John'; 'Goin' Home'; 'Good Morning Blues';
'Outskirts Of Town'; 'Don't You Rock Me Daddio'; 'Alabamy Bound';
'Midnight Special'; 'Dead Or Alive'; 'Frankie And Johnny'; 'Goodnight Irene';
'Railroad Bill'; 'Muleskinner Blues'; 'The Ballad Of Jesse James'; 'I Wanna Go
Home'.
Released: January 2000. Credited to Van Morrison, Lonnie Donegan, Chris
Barber.

You Win Again Exile/Pointblank/Virgin VPB CD54 7243 850258 22 (UK/US).
'Let's Talk About Us'; 'You Win Again'; 'Jambalaya'; 'Crazy Arms'; 'Old Black
Joe'; 'Think Twice Before You Go'; 'No Way Pedro'; 'A Shot Of Rhythm &
Blues'; 'Real Gone Lover'; 'Why Don't You Love Me'; 'Cadillac'; 'Baby (You
Got What It Takes)'; 'Boogie Chillen'.
Released: September 2000 (UK)/October 2000 (US). Credited to Van Morrison
& Linda Gail Lewis.

Down The Road Exile/Polydor 589177 (UK/US).
'Down The Road'; 'Meet Me In The Indian Summer'; 'Steal My Heart Away';
'Hey Mr. DJ'; 'Talk Is Cheap'; 'Choppin' Wood'; 'What Makes The Irish Heart
Beat'; 'All Work And No Play'; 'Whatever Happened To P.J. Proby?'; 'The
Beauty Of The Days Gone By'; 'Georgia On My Mind'; 'Only A Dream'; 'Man
Has To Struggle'; 'Evening Shadows'; 'Fast Train'.
Released: May 2002.

What's Wrong With This Picture? Blue Note 590167 2 (UK/US).
'What's Wrong With This Picture?'; 'Whinin' Boy Moan'; 'Evening In June';

'Too Many Myths'; 'Somerset'; 'Meaning Of Loneliness'; 'Stop Drinking'; 'Goldfish Bowl'; 'Once In A Blue Moon'; 'Saint James Infirmary'; 'Little Village'; 'Fame'; 'Get On With The Show'.
Released: October 2003.

Magic Time Exile/Polydor 9871528 (UK/US)
'Stranded'; 'Celtic New Year'; 'Keep Mediocrity At Bay'; 'Evening Train'; 'This Love Of Mine'; 'I'm Confessin''; 'Just Like Greta'; 'Gypsy In My Soul'; 'Lonely And Blue'; 'The Lion This Time'; 'They Sold Me Out'; 'Carry On Regardless'.
Released: May 2005

In recent years, CD serial numbers throughout the world have been uniform, as can be seen from the latter entries above.

ARCHIVAL ALBUMS

Apart from the rarities in the Them canon, mentioned earlier, Morrison's recording career has not produced many archival releases. The exceptions, of course, are the sessions he undertook for Bang Records, which have been released in many configurations over the years. After he left the company and signed to Warner Bros, the presumptuously titled *The Best Of Van Morrison* (Bang BLPS 222) appeared in 1970, and was belatedly issued in the UK in May 1971 on President (PTLS 1045). Despite its title, it actually featured a number of previously unreleased songs, 'It's All Right', 'Send Your Mind', 'The Smile You Smile', 'The Back Room' and 'Joe Harper Saturday Morning'. Bang returned to the vaults to unearth two previously unreleased and radically different versions of 'Beside You' and 'Madame George', which were included on *T.B. Sheets* (BPLS 400), released in the US in January 1974, and in the UK two months later on London (HSM 5008). Other compilations of previously released material followed, notably *This Is Where I Came In* (Bang 6467 625) and 1991's *Bang Masters* (Columbia/Legacy 4683092), the latter taken direct from the original master tapes and featuring extended versions of 'Spanish Rose' and 'Joe Harper Saturday Morning', an alternate take of 'Brown Eyed Girl' and an early version of 'The Smile You Smile' under the provisional title 'I Love You'. In 1993, an album titled *The Lost Tapes* appeared in Portugal (Movieplay Gold 74012/13) and the following year its dubious contents appeared in the UK on Charly Records' double CD *Payin' Dues* (CP CD 8035). The first CD of the double package featured 18 previously heard songs, but the second CD consisted entirely of the notorious 'gibberish' recordings that Morrison had given to Bang as part of his contract release. For the discographical record, the new titles comprised: 'Twist And Shake', 'Shake And Roll', 'Stomp And Scream', 'Scream And Holler', 'Jump And Thump', Drivin' Wheel', 'Just Ball', 'Shake It Mable', 'Hold On George', 'The Big Royalty

Check', 'Ring Worm', 'Savoy Hollywood', 'Freaky If You Got This Far', 'Up Your Mind', 'Thirty Two', 'All The Bits', 'You Say France And I Whistle', 'Blow In Your Nose', 'Nose In Your Blow', 'La Mambo', 'Go For Yourself', 'Want A Danish', 'Here Comes Dumb George', 'Chickee Coo', 'Do It', 'Hang On Groovy', 'Goodbye George', 'Dum Dum George', 'Walk And Talk', 'The Wobble' and 'Wobble And Ball'. One odd anomaly: in all the legal documentation relating to Morrison, Web IV and Bang, it is consistently stated that he delivered 32 songs "devoid of any substance or originality or artistic merit", but there are only 31 such songs on the CD.

Although a Van Morrison box set has yet to appear, a long-awaited archival double CD set was issued:

The Philosopher's Stone Polydor 531 789-2 (UK/US).
'Really Don't Know'; 'Ordinary People'; 'Wonderful Remark'; 'Not Supposed To Break Down'; 'Laughing In The Wind'; 'Madame Joy'; 'Contemplation Rose'; 'Don't Worry About Tomorrow'; 'Try For Sleep'; 'Lover's Prayer'; 'Drumshanbo Hustle'; 'Twilight Zone'; 'Foggy Mountain Top'; 'Naked In The Jungle'; 'There There Child'; 'The Street Only Knew Your Name'; 'John Henry'; 'Western Plains'; 'Joyous Sound'; 'I Have Finally Come To Realise'; 'Flamingos Fly'; 'Stepping Out Queen Part 2'; 'Bright Side Of The Road'; 'Street Theory'; 'Real Real Gone'; 'Showbusiness'; 'For Mr Thomas'; 'Crazy Jane On God'; 'Song Of Being A Child'; 'High Spirits'.
Released: June 1998. This release was delayed by several months during which three songs – 'When I Deliver', 'John Brown's Body' and 'I'm Ready' were replaced on the album by 'The Street Only Knew Your Name', 'Western Plains' and 'Joyous Sound'.

Apart from the Decca- and Bang-era material, Morrison has not suffered from repackaging of his post-1967 era material in the US or UK. In October 1975, there was the unnecessary *Two Originals Of Van Morrison* (Warner Bros K 86009), which combined *His Band And The Street Choir* and *Tupelo Honey*, as a double album. Since then, Morrison has sanctioned the release of two greatest hits packages:

The Best Of Van Morrison Polydor 841970-2 (UK/US).
'Bright Side Of The Road'; 'Gloria'; 'Moondance'; 'Baby, Please Don't Go'; 'Have I Told You Lately'; 'Brown Eyed Girl'; 'Sweet Thing'; 'Warm Love'; 'Wonderful Remark'; 'Jackie Wilson Said (I'm In Heaven When You Smile)'; 'Full Force Gale'; 'And It Stoned Me'; 'Here Comes The Night'; 'Domino'; 'Did Ye Get Healed?'; 'Wild Night'; 'Cleaning Windows'; 'Whenever God Shines His Light'; 'Queen Of The Slipstream'; 'Dweller On The Threshold'.
Released: March 1990. Vinyl version (841970–1) omits 'Wonderful Remark', 'Full Force Gale', 'Queen Of The Slipstream' and 'Dweller On The Threshold'.

The Best Of Van Morrison: Volume Two Polydor 517760 (UK/US).
'Real Real Gone'; 'When Will I Ever Learn To Live In God?'; 'Sometimes I Feel Like A Motherless Child'; 'In The Garden'; 'A Sense Of Wonder'; 'I'll Tell Me Ma'; 'Coney Island'; 'Enlightenment'; 'Rave On, John Donne'; 'Rave On Part Two (Live)'; 'Don't Look Back'; 'It's All Over Now, Baby Blue'; 'One Irish Rover'; 'The Mystery'; 'Hymns To The Silence'; 'Evening Meditation'.
Released: January 1993.

TRIBUTE ALBUMS/GUEST APPEARANCES

Morrison has also featured on various 'tribute recordings'. Radio and television tribute appearances are not dealt with in this discography, but his major contribution on record was the following:

Tell Me Something: The Songs Of Mose Allison Polygram/Exile 533203 (UK)/Verve 533203.
'One Of These Days'; 'You Can Count On Me (To Do My Part)'; 'If You Live'; 'Was'; 'Look Here'; 'City Home'; 'No Trouble Livin''; 'Benediction'; 'Back On The Corner'; 'Tell Me Something'; 'I Don't Want Much'; 'News Nightclub'; 'Perfect Moment'.
Released: September 1996 (UK)/October 1996 (US). Credits read: "With Van Morrison, Georgie Fame, Mose Allison, Ben Sidran".

In addition, Morrison has recorded a spoken word recording *Cuchulainn* on cassette (Sulis Music BCM 3721; reissued Mole MRILC 012). He has performed 'Saint Dominic's Preview' with Donal Lunny, Mary Black and others on *Sult: Spirit Of The Music* (Hummingbird HBCD 09), contributed 'Muleskinner Blues' to *The Songs Of Jimmie Rodgers: A Tribute* (1997), and included 'Boffyflow And Spike' on the Chieftains' silver anniversary collection *A Chieftains Celebration* (RCA RL 87858). Morrison has also guested on albums by a number of artistes, including The Band, John Lee Hooker, Jackie De Shannon, Bill Wyman, Jim Capaldi, Chet Baker, Georgie Fame, Roger Waters, Mick Cox, the Chieftains, James Hunter, Tom Jones, Lonnie Donegan, Shana Morrison, Pee Wee Ellis, B.B. King, Solomon Burke, Mark Knopfler, Chris Farlowe and Ray Charles.

Index

Singles releases are in roman type and albums in italics.

www.randomhouse.co.uk/vintage